THE DANCE PROGRAM

A Series of Publications in Dance and Related Arts

Volumes in Preparation

The Bournonville School (in four parts), including music and notation, by Kirsten Ralov, *foreword by Walter Terry*

The Bennington Years: 1934-1942, a chronology and source book, by Sali Ann Kriegsman

The Art and Practice of Ballet Accompanying (in two volumes), by Elizabeth Sawyer

The Ballet Russe (in four volumes), edited by George Jackson

Imperial Dancer, a biography of Felia Doubrovska, by Victoria Huckenpahler

Antony Tudor, a biography, by Fernau Hall

Dancer's Diary, by Dennis Wayne, *introduction by Joanne Woodward*

Marius Petipa: Materials, Reminiscences, Articles, edited by A. Nekhendzi, *translated from the Russian by Tamara Bering Sunguroff*

Handbook of Television Dance, by Richard Lorber and Peter Grossman

Jean Cocteau and the Ballet, by Frank W. D. Ries

Manhattan Dance School Directory, by Barbi O'Reilly

Memoires d'un Bourgeois de Paris, by Dr. Louis Veron (originally published in 1856), *translated from the French by Victoria Huckenpahler*

Les Petits Mystères de l'Opéra, by Albéric Second (originally published in 1844), *translated from the French by Victoria Huckenpahler*

I WAS THERE

SELECTED DANCE REVIEWS AND ARTICLES—1936–1976

by WALTER TERRY

COMPILED AND EDITED BY ANDREW MARK WENTINK
FOREWORD BY ANNA KISSELGOFF

AUDIENCE ARTS

a division of

MARCEL DEKKER, INC.   NEW YORK and BASEL

Library of Congress Cataloging in Publication Data

Terry, Walter.
  I was there.

  (The Dance Program ; v. 10)
  Includes index.
  1. Dancing--United States--Collected works. I. Title.
II. Series.
GV1623.T42   793.3'1973   78-9650
ISBN 0-8247-6524-9

191834

Marcel Dekker, Inc.
270 Madison Avenue, New York, New York 10016

ISBN: 0-8247-6524-9

Current printing (last digit)
10 9 8 7 6 5 4 3 2 1

PRINTED IN THE UNITED STATES OF AMERICA

For
DONALD SADDLER
Artist, colleague-in-dance and longtime friend,
with
Admiration, respect, and affection

Foreword

For those of us who grew up reading Walter Terry, this book is a welcome old friend. Terry began his professional career as a dance critic and dance editor in 1936 with the Boston Herald. But it was on the New York Herald Tribune, between 1939 and the better part of the 1960s, that he made his international reputation.

The Trib was a wonderful newspaper—its loss is a major tragedy in the history of American journalism—and Walter Terry was very much a Herald Tribune writer. This fact is important to remember. By this I mean that the formality of style in some of these reviews should be recognized as part of the well-bred tone of the paper as a whole. At the same time, the Trib style allowed for personal flavor. Like other Trib writers, Terry was asked to be himself.

This individual coloring explains why there is a genuine continuity to the reviews, interviews, and other pieces in this volume. You can find the essential Terry peering out behind the novice critic in 1936 on the Boston Herald and you will find the same Terry in the magazine-writing format to which he turned increasingly in the 1960s and 1970s. Terry worked for the Herald Tribune as a dance critic and editor in 1939–42 and 1945–66. (In 1942–45, he served with the United States Armed Forces in Africa and the Middle East.) In 1966–67, he was dance critic and editor for the World Journal Tribune, the merger in which the Tribune breathed its last gasp. Since 1967, he has been dance critic for Saturday Review.

What is that essential Terry? It is the reporter-analyst rolled into one, with a great deal of irrepressible Connecticut Yankee.

The great value of his writings is the overview of American dance that they afford us. No aspect is overlooked. Terry's interviews as well as his reviews here chronicle the growth of the American ballet and modern dance movements since the pioneering 1930s. One need not agree with Terry's opinions to find them interesting. It is striking, however, how often history has proved him "right."

In addition to ballet (professional and regional), modern dance and ethnic dance, Terry covered dance on Broadway, in vaudeville, in films. Even on ice. The Jack Cole reviews remind us that a leading choreographer could find a hospitable setting in the supper clubs.

iv

Terry has always paid attention to his duties as a reporter—a function vital to all criticism. It was he who first helped bring the glad tidings about an unknown company called the Royal Danish Ballet. He was also our man in Brooklyn—as the only major daily critic to write up Rudolf Nureyev's New York debut there in 1962. Rereading that review today, I am astounded at the accuracy with which Terry defined the route that Nureyev's career has taken.

A reader might wonder about the inclusion of a "Dance Notes" column. To Terry, however, these expanded concert listings on Sunday were an integral part of his job to disseminate information about dance to the public. Such columns sum up a past era in both journalism and dance. For the dance audience, they were required reading.

One of the most important sections of this book comes in the early years. Mary Wigman has written of the loneliness of the creative artist who is inventing new forms and new techniques. A critic like Walter Terry who started out in the 1930s must have had a similar sensation of exploring the unexplored. Terry was faced with the absence of an accepted literary vocabulary to explain the new modern dance just as the same new modern dance was still evolving its own movement vocabulary. Critics today do not have that problem, even when they are confronted with the most experimental forms.

Even in ballet, with its 300-year-old technique, there was some explaining to do. It was the new purposes to which this technique was being applied that had to be defined. Very often, Terry was obliged to reiterate first principles for each dance esthetic.

For example, in his revealing interview with Martha Graham in August, 1936, Terry noted that the dancer "has turned her attention to the emotional and intellectual reasons for human movement."

In the same piece, he continued: "Martha Graham tries to be as abstract in her dancing as possible. The reason is simple. Miss Graham believes that for an art to be truly great, the audience must do as much as the artist. On seeing Miss Graham's abstract movement, the audience must evolve its own interpretation of her dance, it must think and it must feel."

It is, of course, easy to forget that Graham was "abstract"—that she searched for essence of emotion prior to creating theater pieces after 1938. Here, Terry is describing the Graham of the early 1930s. At root, it is also the Graham one sees today. Who will dare to say that her *Dark Meadow,* revived again at this writing, does not invite the audience to bring its own emotions to the work of the art and "evolve its own interpretation?"

In the same period before World War II, Terry's reporting documented the common belief that ballet was a foreign import that had no place in American culture. The distance traveled since that time is self-evident. Terry

v

was one of the first to lend his support in print to the idea of an American classical ballet.

Looking at the first season of Lincoln Kirstein's Ballet Caravan in July 1936, the young critic wrote: "It is evident then, that American dancers are trying to make the traditional ballet of Europe an integral part of American culture as close to the inhabitants of America as the music of Bach, Mozart, and Beethoven."

Forty years ago, this statement was hardly acceptable to the modern dance world and to a public-at-large inured to "Russian" ballet.

Like all of us, Terry is a product of his times. In 1937, the nationalist current was still strong enough to have him declare that Catherine Littlefield's *Barn Dance* was a "truly American ballet" because it had an American subject. Yet it is important as well to point out that while Terry became a proponent of American ballet (see his nationalist campaign in favor of Ballet Theatre) and of modern dance as an American art form, he has never been a polemicist.

Critics of critics might find it hard to believe that it is possible to write without prejudice. Yet this is so. But it is not possible, deep down, to have no preference. Terry admits that this is his first-night review of *Agon* in 1957.

"Usually," he writes, "I lean toward those dance works which are born of the urgency of the human heart." Nonetheless, Terry is able immediately (under deadline pressure) to define *Agon* as the very different and enduring masterpiece it still is today.

"*Agon* does not pretend to mirror the frailties and the nobilities of man's character," Terry writes. "*Agon* has an almost nuclear-age brilliance about it. . . . One could not and should not compare it with ballets born of other premises. For in its own sphere of abstraction, it is, I believe, the finest ballet of our era and the greatest of the Balanchine-Stravinsky collaborations."

A similar openness is visible in the Sunday piece that sums up the distinctions between the Alicias in *Giselle*—Alicia Markova and Alicia Alonso. I would also pick out the pieces on Alexandra Danilova, on Nora Kaye, and certainly all the writing on Martha Graham and the brilliant first-night review in 1942 of Antony Tudor's *Pillar of Fire*, which exudes the excitement of a new psychological drama in ballet.

It is naive to say a review can bring back a performance. But as Walter Terry proves in this collection, it is possible to bring back the clear eye-witness account.

Anna Kisselgoff
The New York Times

Contents

Illustrations

I WAS THERE

1936

Some Beginnings at Bennington

The third session of the Bennington Summer School of the Dance opens • Ballet Caravan premieres at Bennington • Ted Shawn at work in the Berkshires • Martha Graham discusses her work • Humphrey-Weidman offer With My Red Fires at Bennington

All Aspects of the Dance Found at Bennington Summer School

July 21, 1936

Two hundred of them! And all of them students of the dance. Boys and girls from 28 of the states have journeyed to Vermont, where, during July and August, the Bennington School of the Dance is holding forth on the Bennington College campus.

Here is to be found an organization devoted entirely to the dance in all its aspects. Under the tutelage of a faculty consisting of 38 members, the students study many types of the modern dance both in technique and choreography; courses in dance history and criticism; staging; costuming; musical composition for the dance; the use of percussion instruments in the dance; and a study of the basis of dramatic movement.

The activities of the group are watched by the advisory board, whose members are Dr. Robert Leigh, president of Bennington College; John Martin, dance critic; Louis Horst, composer, and Martha Graham, Doris Humphrey, Charles Weidman and Hanya Holm, dancers.

Perhaps the most interesting group at the school is the Humphrey-Weidman Workshop, for its program takes the student from the fundamentals of dance technique through actual dance creation and concludes with a finished dance production at the end of the six weeks' course.

Doris Humphrey directs the girls' division of the Workshop in a schedule that makes muscle-ache a constant companion to the dancer. The 24 beginners augmented by 10 members from Miss Humphrey's New York concert group spend two hours each morning on dance technique, two hours in the afternoon on dance creation, and two hours in the evening rehearsing. Along with this busy program, the girls are required to attend the daily lectures on dance history and criticism presented by John Martin, dance critic for the New York Times, and a course in the use of percussion taught by Nancy McKnight.

During the periods devoted to the creation of a new dance composition, Miss Humphrey explains to the girls how a dance is formed, the changes that take place in the choreography during rehearsal and why they are necessary. At the end of the season this new dance will be given a production, and the girls will appear as dancers in the work they watched and studied in the process of creation.

Miss Humphrey's new composition has not yet been named, nor has it been completed. The theme, however, is the tragedy of romance, and Miss Humphrey feels that it will complete a cycle in her work. Two of her dances which have already been presented in concert, offered comments on other aspects of life: *New Dance,* which depicted Miss Humphrey's beliefs in the ideal life; and *Theatre Piece,* which attempted to show life as it is. In conjunction with Charles Weidman and his men's Workshop group, Doris Humphrey will offer these older compositions at the final concerts that end the Workshop season.

Charles Weidman has definite opinions about war, politics, and social troubles. And these opinions are to be danced! But because he is an artist and has the viewpoint of one, Weidman is going to comment on these problems only as they affect the artist in his life and in his work.

Aided by his now famous solo dancer, José Limón, and six boys from his New York concert group, Charles Weidman is already creating the dance which will embody these strong opinions on contemporary life. His new students are able to watch the important aspects of modern existence take shape in dance movement. They see how deftly Weidman uses satire and humor when he comments on the slightly annoying elements that hamper the artist in his work. And when this new dance is produced at the end of the course, they should be an important part of a forceful social comment.

The boys work eight hours each day while nursing "shin-splints," aching muscles, bruised knees, cut feet; and they plan on that for the rest of their lives. These boys believe in the dance and its ever-growing importance; and so they have chosen the eldest of the arts as a medium for the exposition of their thoughts, their hopes, and their contributions to this modern world. [*Boston Herald*]

2

Ballet Caravan Aspires to Build
a Genuine American Ballet Soon

July 23, 1936

"We are going to adhere closely to the traditions of the European ballet, but the emphasis of our work will be on new choreography." In this statement by Lincoln Kirstein, youthful director of the Ballet Caravan, one finds the unusual combination of loyalty to the past coupled with the search for something new. A glance at the history of the Ballet Caravan will, perhaps, explain this strange phenomenon.

At the close of the Metropolitan Opera season, 12 members of the American ballet decided that stretching at the bar and working on technique in their studies was not a particularly inspiring way to spend the long months before the reopening of the Metropolitan Opera. Thus the idea of a summer caravan ballet took shape.

Under the able direction of Mr. Kirstein, author of the recent book called *Dance,* the Ballet Caravan put its plans into being. The traditional ballets received a courteous bow, and were told that they wouldn't be needed. These youthful dancers had new ideas that they wanted to work out; but they believed, however, that the traditional ballet technique was fundamentally sound and the only basis on which to test their plans.

Several ballets were created by these young dance enthusiasts, still in their early twenties, and a summer tour was arranged by the well-known concert manager, Frances Hawkins. The modest "world premiere" of the Ballet Caravan took place in the little studio-theater at Bennington College as a presentation of the Bennington School of the Dance.

The program consisted of *Encounter,* a classic ballet created by Lew Christensen; *Harlequin for President,* with choreography by Eugene Loring; and a group of divertissements. The audience kindly overlooked the flaws in technique, and heartily applauded a talented group of young men and women for their promising efforts and sincerity of purpose. The emphasis here was on dance and performance; not on elaborate lighting effects and multi-colored settings. This seemed to suggest rather plainly that these young artists had discovered the real meaning of the word "theater."

"Later," said Lincoln Kirstein, "we hope to find material for a ballet based on an American theme, and particularly one of contemporary interest." It is evident, then, that these American dancers are trying to make the traditional ballet of Europe an integral part of American culture as close to the inhabitants of America as the music of Bach, Mozart, and Beethoven.

This summer tour offers "a proving ground, a time for rehearsal, a chance for the evolution of new ideas," as Mr. Kirstein described it, and if all

3

goes well, some of the new ballets will be presented at the Metropolitan Opera House this winter. The American ballet organization is in accord with the plan of the Ballet Caravan, and the traveling dancers will return to the mother institution in the fall with no idea of secession in mind. [*Boston Herald*]

Ted Shawn Teaches and Dances at His Studio in the Berkshires
July 28, 1936

"That which cannot be spoken, can be sung; that which cannot be sung, can be danced." At his Friday afternoon lectures and demonstrations in his Berkshire studio, Ted Shawn is attempting to explain to his audiences the meaning of this old French proverb: just what things need to be danced, and how they can be danced.

Approximately 300 persons regularly attend these dance lectures. They come from all over New England to learn about the dance from Shawn, America's dance pioneer. They hear lectures about the history of dancing; the work of Delsarte, France's scientist of movement; the ballet and its great traditions; the dances of foreign nations, ancient and modern; the differences between masculine and feminine movement; and the development of the dance in America.

The dance of the orient was the subject of the lecture-demonstration at Shawn's farm last Friday. In the theater art of the orient one finds the old French proverb in actual use, for as Shawn pointed out, when the Chinese or Japanese actor reaches the intensely emotional scenes of the drama, he ceases to speak; instead, he dances.

In his lecture, Shawn described how the Japanese actor uses his fan with such consummate artistry that it ceases to be the symbol of a falling leaf, a dagger, or a warrior's visor, and becomes the actual object itself. This purely oriental dance development was demonstrated later in the afternoon in two numbers that were a part of the dance program.

The demonstration opened with a dance by Mary Long Hanion. This dance was built around the character of Golden Bells, the little heroine of Donn Byrn's legend-novel, *Messer Marco Polo*. The costume, the movement, and the use of the fans presented a motion-painting of the Chinese dancer's art.

One of the highlights of the afternoon was the appearance of the famous American dancer, Miriam Winslow. Miss Winslow offered a dance suggested by

4

the bas-reliefs on the ancient temple of Angkor Vat in that land of mystery, Cambodia. Here were displayed the use of the difficult oriental arm ripple and the intricate designs of the fingers. With this exacting technique as a basis, Miss Winslow created a mood that, within the duration of the dance, seemed to push aside the veil that hid the mysteries of Cambodia and its forgotten people.

Next in the program came the *Japanese Rickshaw Coolies*, a light, humorous dance performed by Barton Mumaw, Dennis Landers and Wilbur McCormack. Created by Shawn, this dance depicted the lighter and fun-loving side of the rickshaw coolie's existence.

The program closed with Ted Shawn as soloist in his famous *Japanese Spear Dance.* As a warrior of old Japan, Shawn demonstrated the use of the actor's mime coupled with the robust movement of the dancer. In this instance, the fan lost all of its feminine quality, and seemed to be a natural and logical article in the dancer-warrior's equipment.

From an old French proverb to the oriental dance seems, on the surface, to be a long step, and the explanation of just such a thought is the reason for Shawn's lectures. In his present series, Shawn is endeavoring to show the dance in all its forms, and in this manner point out the common focus of dances of the world, the universal need of all races for the dance as a means of expression, and the art of the dance as a bond between nations. [*Boston Herald*]

Martha Graham, Dancer, Discusses the Basic Theories of Her Work

August 4, 1936

"In the early days of the dance renaissance in America," said Martha Graham, "a slowly rising arm signified growing corn or flowers; a downward fluttering of fingers perhaps suggested rain. Why should a hand try to be corn; why should an arm try to be rain? Think of what a wonderful thing the hand is, and what vast possibilities of movement it has as a human hand and not as a poor imitation of something else."

In those words of Martha Graham one finds her basic dance tenet; movement coming from the body itself; not the movement of the body trying to adapt itself to foreign elements. Miss Graham has left the realm of murmuring zephyrs and waving corn stalks, and has turned her attention to the emotional and intellectual reasons for human movement.

5

Martha Graham tries to be as abstract in her dancing as possible. The reason is simple. Miss Graham believes that for an art to be truly great the audience must do as much as the artist. On seeing Miss Graham's abstract movement, the audience must evolve its own interpretation of her dance, it must think, and it must feel. In this way a means of communication is effected between audience and artist, and the art reaches its fullness in an emphatic understanding and appreciation.

"I do not make social or political comments in my dances," continued Miss Graham. "If I had something of great social importance to say, I would say it from a lecture platform." According to Martha Graham many people believe that her dance, *Imperial Gesture*, contains within it a political comment. Such is not the case. The dance was created to demonstrate the movement of the body influenced by an imperial feeling. It may suggest to one the imperial attitude of a duchess, an English butler, or a police sergeant. As a dance its sole purpose lies in presenting imperial movement in the abstract.

Last Friday and Saturday evenings at the Bennington School of the Dance, Martha Graham presented a solo recital which clearly demonstrated her dance beliefs. An audience of several hundred people applauded and cheered Martha Graham the dancer, and Martha Graham, the creator.

In the dance *Lamentation,* one did not see a specific character undergoing sorrow and remorse. Instead one saw a human body, the dancer's only instrument, moving as man would under the stress of sadness and lamentation. Again in *Frontier* no character from American history was in evidence, only the body moving under the emotional and intellectual experiences of the pioneer.

Although most of the program was of serious content, humor had its place. Miss Graham clad in a black and white striped jersey costume that did harrowing things to the figure, danced her *Satyric Festival Song* in the abstract manner of the ageless Satyr motif.

A generous program closed with *Pessimist* and *Optimist* and from the approval of the audience, one gathered that Martha Graham's success in the abstract dance was not limited to the serious.

Miss Graham does not object to the bitter controversy that surrounds her work. "I want people to think. I welcome the arguments that follow my concerts, for if people don't discuss my dance-work, why then I shall have failed in what I set out to do." [*Boston Herald*]

Humphrey-Weidman Workshop Group
Offers New Dances at Bennington

August 18, 1936

Six weeks of constant dance training—six weeks in which to teach a group the beginnings of a dance technique, and to wind up the course with four concerts. That, in brief, is the story of the Humphrey-Weidman Workshop at the Bennington School of the Dance.

For two concerts, Miss Humphrey and Mr. Weidman presented two dance creations which had been produced in New York last season. The remaining concerts saw the premieres of two dances created during the Workshop's short course.

Last Thursday evening at Bennington, the dance program opened with Doris Humphrey's newest work, *With My Red Fires*. Miss Humphrey described it as the Tragedy of Romance, and found her title in the lines of William Blake: "For the divine appearance is Brotherhood, but I am Love elevate into the regions of Brotherhood with my red fires." In this number, Miss Humphrey was aided by Mr. Weidman, their New York concert groups, the Workshop students, the entire stage, and half the floor of the auditorium.

It was difficult to judge just how much dance knowledge was absorbed by the Workshop students, for *With My Red Fires* focused the attention on Doris Humphrey, Charles Weidman, and their concert groups. However, the young students performed their lesser roles adequately, and what they learned in watching this dance in the process of creation only they themselves could say.

As for the dance itself, *With My Red Fires* is not yet a worthy successor to Miss Humphrey's *New Dance* and *Theater Piece*. The movement was somewhat scattered, and the focal point was tossed back and forth between Miss Humphrey, Mr. Weidman and Miss Katherine Litz. This focal point, we believe, should have been on the relationship of the three, and not on three distinct individuals.

Miss Humphrey, calling herself the Matriarch, danced the role of the Destroyer of Love, and using mime as a basis, created a forceful and theatrically effective character. Had she relied on her excellent pantomimic movement and less on facial contortions, Miss Humphrey's work, in this particular case, would have come closer to the artistic demands of this dance.

With My Red Fires needs revision before it can hope to attain its utmost value. Part of it needs cutting, sections demand pointing up, other sections should be toned down, and the various movements must be assembled into a unified whole with a focus that is ever present and clear.

7

The music sounded like a broken down organ attached, in some mysterious way, to a cement mixer. We feel that either percussion alone should have been used, or else music with melody and quality on an equal plane with the theme and movements of the dance.

"The artist, in his endeavor to find or create conditions under which he may achieve full and free expression, encounters many obstacles, in many lands. Today he struggles alone, with nothing but his inner strength to aid him. Perhaps tomorrow he will unite his forces with those of his fellows, and reach his goal." In these words, Charles Weidman has described the theme and reason for his new dance, *Quest*.

When it comes to satire, Charles Weidman is at his best. In the sections of *Quest* devoted to the satirical, Weidman's dance comments were particularly forceful. In the part called Trivia (sub-titled Patronage), several girls entered with the unmistakable movements of portly, overbearing dowagers, and in spite of the warnings of Allegory (Miss Humphrey), the artist (Mr. Weidman) carried his art to them for financial support. Again in the second Trivia (sub-titled Anthropometry), Weidman's biting comments were in evidence.

Although the production of *Quest* was not as smooth as *With My Red Fires,* the focus was always clear, and the theme was developed logically to its climax in the final section called Affirmation.

In this dance, as in the first one, much needs to be cut; and repetition of movement should be removed. The music for *Quest* has already been covered in the comments on the music for *With My Red Fires.*

Without discussing the merits of the Humphrey–Weidman technique, it can be said that their summer season was a success, and that their final concerts were of admirable quality considering the short time allotted to them. [*Boston Herald*]

1937

Boston and New York

The Jooss Ballet premieres at Jordan Hall, Boston • Michel Fokine discusses the creation of his ballet, Coq d'Or • Dance International opens its celebration of world dance at Rockefeller Center

Jooss Ballet Combines Modern Dance with Classic Forms

October 17, 1937

Sneers, leers and cutting remarks have almost become the traditional property of the balletomanes and their adamant opponents, the devotees of the modern dance. As yet no blood has been shed, each group giving the impression that they thought the other would probably die of its own accord before very long. While this terpsichorean banter has been going on, Kurt Jooss has welded together the warring technique of the ballet and the modern dance, and has proved to himself and to his audience that the pair can be not only amicable but also quite devoted.

Instead of everything being smoothed out, Jooss has opened another field for argument and has made himself the target for both ballet and modern. The ballet-minded critics find his dancing awkward and reprimand him for not using toe slippers on his girl dancers. The moderns accuse him of forgetting that his background and training were modern just because he uses, at times, ballet entrechats, leaps and turns.

The dance technique of the Jooss school grew out of the need for a dance form which would employ the valuable contributions of the modern dance and the technique of the theatrically experienced ballet. To accomplish this task, Kurt Jooss combined the "labile" and the "stabile." These terrifying words are quite simple to understand: "labile" means "readily changing" or "fluency of movement" and is the basic system of the German school of modern dancing; "stabile" means "not giving" or "stationary" and belongs to the school of the classic ballet. The stabile system gives us the beautiful static poses of the ballet, while the labile system gives us movement of great sweep and constant fluidity.

Jooss has fused these two systems together by creating exercise sequences which employ movements from each system, and in turn these movements fall into two groups; "central" movements, which come from the torso, and were contributed by the modern school; and "peripheral" movements, which originate in the arms and legs, and were contributed by the ballet. By combining these two types of movement, Jooss has added richly to the vocabulary of the dance.

To the dancer and to the dance lover this is an exciting story of discovery, experimentation and dance development. But what do audiences think? Does Jooss work interest them? Kurt Jooss is not merely a dance scientist and scholar, he belongs to the theater, and he sees to it that his art entertains. Social comment, satire, humor are to be found in his work. Colorful costumes and unusually fine lighting enhance or strengthen the story or idea he has to tell. It is a long jump from the pretty fairy tales of the old ballet to Jooss' *Green Table* and his other social comment ballets, which have such potent themes that some of the world powers have thought it wise to ban appearances of the Jooss Ballet in their countries.

No one is starred in the Jooss company, and the badly trained and distracting corps de ballet of many of the old classic ballets is pleasantly missing. Each member of the company can dance, and does so throughout the entire period he or she is on the stage.

The dancers are well trained, the technique is sound and the themes are vital; but the secret of Jooss' success may be found in his own words: "We desire to serve the dance of the theater. . . ." and again, "We find the basis of our work in the whole range of human feeling and all phases of its infinite expression, and by concentration on the essential we arrive at our form in the dance." With such a credo, Kurt Jooss and his ballets are certainly destined for even greater success than those they have already achieved.

Social comment was again the theme of last evening's most important ballet, *The Mirror,* a worthy sequel to the famous *Green Table,* depicted the tragic aftermath of a great war. Everything about this ballet was splendid: choreography, the dancing and the acting of the company members, the lighting, the costumes and the music—all these elements essential to the theater of the dance—were fused together with such skill and with such a sense of the dramatic that Jooss' ballet offered more than exciting entertainment; it offered a message and a warning to all thinking people.

The Mirror fostered no one group; it hit at the capitalists, the middle class and the laborers—all were blamed for the after-war chaos, the discontent, the jealousies and the seeking after new sensations. Aside from its excellence as a dramatic ballet, *The Mirror* is important as a commentary on man in his relationship to the social structure of his times.

As a decided contrast to *The Mirror* the Jooss Ballet offered *Johann Strauss, Tonight!* a quick and light-hearted ballet, sparkling with wit and colorful in Viennese costumes. Here the movements were rapid and precise, and the technique of the classic ballet was very much in evidence. Although this company uses the stronger and more sustained movements of the modern dance to a great extent, it seems to be equally at home in strict ballet. The leaps, the turns and the leg beats were executed with ease by Hans Zuellig, Noelle de Mosa and Rolf Alexander, while Atty van den Berg saw to it that the audience received a generous supply of comedy. The story and the dance movements were in perfect accord with the Strauss music, and the dancers seemed to enjoy themselves as thoroughly as the audience enjoyed watching them.

Pavane was interesting as a study in contrast. The story told us of a spirited young Spanish Infanta who finally broke down under the heavy and elaborate etiquette of the court. The stiff, severe movements of the lords and ladies made an imposing background to the lithe quick movements of the Infanta. The beautiful costumes added immeasurably to this theme of contrast; the courtiers and ladies dressed in stiff, deep-toned clothes; the Infanta clad in soft material, light in hue. *The Big City* was repeated last evening, and was again received with great enthusiasm by the audience. [*Boston Herald*]

Jooss Ballet (Jordan Hall)

October 22, 1937

The Jooss Ballet has achieved something noteworthy in the balletic theater—it brings forth laughter and it arouses thought. Another point in its favor is that it lacks the customary virtuosic exhibitionism of the ballet. Each member of the company is a dancer, and he dances whether he is in the spotlight or in the background of a group, and this is as it should be, for it keeps the performance moving with smoothness, vitality and exuberance.

Potent satire etched with bitterness, strong character dilineation and a theme foremost in the minds of all of us—that was *The Green Table*, a thought-stirring study of the stupid futility of war, those that start it, those that gain by it and those that suffer for it. The language of movement was in this case, more powerful, and more moving than any words could have been.

This fearless work alone should place Kurt Jooss among the very few great artist-thinkers.

Satire of a more personal type danced throughout *The Seven Heroes,* and the amusing foibles of this comic crew kept the action of the story at a breakneck pace. *The Big City* was another comment on human beings, this time on a more serious note. The dancers in this ballet were all excellent, but Hans Züellig deserves special praise for performing the most difficult movements with technical perfection and ease, and for his dramatic and deeply moving mime of the young workman whose sweetheart deserted him for the rich libertine.

The waltz as it should be done, with grace, fluency, lightness and brilliance was the only reason for *A Ball in Old Vienna*; but that was reason enough, for its light story, its beautiful costumes and its real waltzing were a distinct pleasure and privilege to see. But aside from the quality of the ballets, the company itself is remarkable. They are all accomplished dancers and actors, and each member has retained his individuality to such a degree that monotony is impossible. The Jooss Ballet is undoubtedly one of the most important organizations in the dance world, and this is due to the fact that it not only entertains generously, but it also has something vital to say, and says it well. [*Boston Herald*]

Coq d'Or Ballet Created in 16 Days, Says Michel Fokine on Boston Visit

November 4, 1937

"I created the present version of *Coq d'Or* in 16 days," said Michel Fokine. In answer to our look of incredulity, he added "And *Les Sylphides* took only three days to create—*Carnaval* the same." Explaining how these ballets were created in such a short space of time, Fokine continued, "When I am composing a ballet, I work from 18 to 20 hours a day—during my bath, at meals, between rehearsals, in bed at night, every moment is used." In spite of his long and active career, Fokine does not shy away from hard work.

More than 20 years ago, Fokine decided that the operatic version of *Coq d'Or* was not to his liking. He found that "the illusion was spoiled by the singers, "who often lacked the necessary physical and histrionic equipment." With this belief as a basis, he created his first version of *Coq d'Or* in which the singers were hidden while the dancers enacted the story. The present ballet does not make use of singers; the orchestra has complete charge

12

of the music, while the ballet dancers see to it that the fairy tale unfolds with all its fantasy, its color and its subtle shadings intact.

Fokine and his wife, Madame Fokina, came to America 20 years ago for a short concert tour, but America's interest in the ballet excited them so much that they decided to remain and open their own school. During his long years here, Fokine has noticed many things about the Americans. He has found that we are often in a great rush, and that we don't take time to learn properly. A girl may be in such haste to give a dance concert that "she will study from another girl who doesn't know anything; then give a performance." Fokine continued, "All singing teachers know how to sing, but many dance teachers don't know how to dance." At this point Madame Fokina murmured, "There is too much liberty in America."

Fokine finds that the modern dancer lacks training. "The young dancer of the modern school will get on the stage and make ugly movements, while her mother and small brother make noises off-stage—that is called percussion!" When asked if he did not believe that every school had something to contribute to the development of the dance, he said, "Everybody gives something, but often something terrible." He feels that every dancer is limited who does not know ballet and the technique which it has developed and perfected during hundreds of years of activity.

Fokine has joined the deBasil company for two reasons: To create new ballets for the organization, and to revive many of his older works. To date he has no plans for new productions, but when he joins the company permanently in February, he will set to work on new ballets. In discussing his choreographic approach, Fokine said, "I do not try for novelty. Newness comes naturally. When I compose I forget my audience, and I forget myself. My ideas come from a book, from music or from a dream—my themes are from no one period, for I love art from ancient Egypt up to the present."

During our talk with him, Fokine seemed filled with vitality and energy; his keen wit was very much in evidence; and even after 30 years of constant work, his interest in ballet was as fresh as ever. But when we asked if he would continue his teaching in New York, he said, "I think I shall rest a little while. I am very tired." [*Boston Herald*]

Dance International

December 12, 1937

We Americans should be envious of these folk dancers from other countries, for their dances are truly social and honestly joyous. In this country our folk dance is the ballroom dance, and because the same man and woman frequently dance together a whole evening, it hardly merits the descriptive word "social" —"intimate" would be more accurate. We too dance for enjoyment yet our facial expressions suggest acute bereavement.

The Norwegians, who opened the program, demonstrated these qualities which we so sadly lack. The dances were not at all complicated or spectacular, but the dancers performed with such gusto and joy that they transmitted these feelings to the audience. Floor patterns of squares and circles were the bases for almost all of these dances; a boy and a girl would dance a few steps together and then change partners by a relay movement of the "Paul Jones" type. Although these dances were done in a gay and carefree manner, the joy of the dancers was a refined joy and their movements were meticulously performed.

In direct contrast were the Bulgarians, who shouted their way onto the scene. Their costumes were a riot of color, and their actions matched. They stood in a little group, singing, swaying and playing their primitive instruments; then, as if by sudden impulse, the whole group would start to dance, shouting and singing all the while. Individuals darted out from the group, danced a little solo to the accompaniment of group yells of approval, and then rejoined the group. The dances had no beginning and no end, but they were exciting because of their suddenness, their wildness and their unfettered joy.

The delicate grace and perfection of Chinese art were shown to us in two dances performed by Miss King Lan Chew. Danced in the male manner, Miss Chew's "shadow boxing" was a study in brilliant, precise and stylized movement. The "double sword" dance was dramatically exciting because of the glittering swords, twirled into designs with lightning skill.

Relaxed pleasure coupled with courtly propriety might well describe the folk dances of England. Some of the dances were very stately and refined, and suggested that the dancers were cognizant of their noble heritage. The famous "sword dance" is really folk virtuosity, for the dancers, constantly united by holding each other's swords, perform intricate patterns and athletic movements without ending in a tangle of steel.

The Austrian dancers were disappointing, for their work suggested Broadway vaudeville rather than the Alps, and their crude humor was not the natural deviltry of the laughing peasant. But Spain won rounds of applause for her stamping, swaggering, finger-snapping dances. Antonita possessed the graceful elegance necessary for the exacting *Sevillanas* as well as the fiery passion that the Flamenco required. Señor Martinez practically made his feet talk with the intricate and rapid heel beats of the traditional *Zapateado*.
[*Boston Herald*]

14

The Dance International, which has been holding forth at Rockefeller Center with dance exhibits of movies, sculpture, painting, photographs and tri-weekly dance performances at the Rainbow room, climaxed its first two weeks of existence with this history-making ballet event.

Of the three ballet companies which appeared, Catherine Littlefield's group certainly walked off with first honors. Her ballet, *Barn Dance,* was the first truly American balletic composition that we have ever seen. The technique of the traditional ballet was present, but the theme, the humor and the execution were decidedly American. We saw typically American mothers tearing about in an attempt to discipline their mischievous children; we laughed at the young farmhands and their slightly gauche sweethearts; there was our own Nellie Bly adding her robust fallen-woman air to the proceedings; a city slicker received his just deserts at the hands of the country folk; and a somber deacon tried in vain to keep things on a refined level. Catherine Littlefield succeeded in creating a truly American ballet because she adapted the ballet technique to suit the *Barn Dance* rather than adapting the *Barn Dance* to suit the classic ballet, and that in itself was certainly a pioneering achievement.

In spite of the vivacity of its members, the Ballet Caravan failed to make *Show Piece* particularly interesting. The composition itself is merely a group of divertissements, and the dancers are not yet mature enough artists to carry off something that relies solely on technique. This organization attempts to be completely American, yet many of its compositions with American themes are superficial and are performed with the detached elegance that is in character with the foreign ballet companies.

The Sandor-Sorel ballet, *El Amor Brujo,* had moments of effective group design, but it seemed much too long, for the mood was constantly depressing and the movements of the principals, although executed with surety, were repetitive. Felicia Sorel and José Limón failed to project the shadings of their characterizations.

As soloist in *Russian Dance,* Paul Haakon demonstrated again that he is one of the few great dancers of our time. His every movement proves that there is such a thing as masculine grace, and as for his virtuosic technique, with its tremendous leaps and jumps and its rapid turns, it makes one feel that perfection actually exists.

Patricia Bowman danced charmingly and accurately in the trivial *Tennis,* and won bursts of applause for her pantomimic humor. Paul Draper dared to tap dance to the music of Scarlatti and Strauss, and proved that tap dancing can be an art. Unlike most tap dancers, whose arms look like those of apes and whose bodies are just something that appear above the feet, Draper uses arm and body movements that have form and meaning. Of course, the accent of the dancing is on the feet, but the rest of his body dances also. The same things are true of the Spanish flamenco dancer, and he appears on the concert stage. Paul Draper is experimenting with something that may turn out to be a truly native American dance form of artistic worth. [*Boston Herald*]

1938

Birthpangs of American Ballet

Dance International finishes its New York stay • Hanya Holm, pioneer choreographer and teacher, presents Trend • Ballet Caravan brings Yankee Clipper and Harlequin for President to Boston • Mordkin Ballet presents an unsuccessful Lucia Chase as Giselle and Lisette in La Fille Mal Gardée • The Hampton Dancers and Negro Dance • Massine's Choreartium, Cimarosiana and Le Beau Danube performed by the Ballet Russe de Monte Carlo at the Boston Opera House • An analysis of Massine's St. Francis

Dance International

January 4, 1938

For more than a month Dance International has been treating capacity crowds to dance lectures, art exhibits of the dance, movies of the dancers of the world, tri-weekly performances in the Rainbow Room at Rockefeller Center of folk dancers from 40 nations and an evening of ballet. It seemed appropriate that the greatest dance festival America has ever witnessed should close with a performance of the modern dance in which our own American dancers displayed dance forms and dance themes which they themselves have contributed to the ever-growing art of the dance.

It was fitting, also, that Ruth St. Denis should open this program, for without the brave pioneering and the great ideals of Miss St. Denis there might not have been a modern American dance of worth. The magic and beauty of Ruth St. Denis dancing has remained undiminished throughout the 34 years of her dance career, and once again we were privileged to behold the flawless artistry of this great lady whose every movement is beauty. The prolonged applause and the bravos could not have sprung from sentiment—they were given, we believe, as a tribute to a great pioneer and to an artist, still young and vital.

17

Martha Graham presented her familiar *Frontier* which grows more powerful and more exciting with every performance. Using movement in the abstract and movements of small dimensions, Miss Graham succeeds in suggesting the vast spaces of the plains in relationship to the small scope of the human body—in this case the American pioneer. Because it is not a literal interpretation of the frontiersman, it excites and arouses thoughts in the beholder, for it gives him the freedom of personal interpretation and makes him a part of the dance, not merely a relaxed onlooker.

Doris Humphrey and Charles Weidman presented their well known satiric comment on present day life, *Theater Piece,* which again displayed Miss Humphrey's command of effective group movement and Mr. Weidman's mastery of humorous movement alive with biting satire. *Theater Piece* is a comment on our life of conflict and competition, and although its satire is strong and to the point, it is never disagreeable nor belligerent; thus making its comments acceptable to an audience which is amused and interested and not antagonized.

Tamiris' *Momentum* contains some good group movements which suggest the plodding hopelessness of the unemployed and also the frantic movements of those whose needs have driven them past fear and past reason. Hanya Holm presented a portion of her new work *Trend,* which is one of the most forceful and worthwhile dances of social comment that we have ever seen. [*Boston Herald*]

Importance of Hanya Holm: A Great Teacher

January 9, 1938

There are many reasonably experienced dancers on our present day stages who don't know how to dance. They move, of course, and they frequently move in an interesting fashion; they don't stumble; they respect the timing of movement; and they follow religiously the choreographic demands. Yet they don't dance. This state of affairs is found particularly in the modern dance, and these people we are speaking of are the group dancers of well known leaders of the modern school.

The teachers apparently are to blame, for the members of their company show no individuality of movement and they project no personality of their own. In most instances they are unexciting mimics of their leaders—they are the shadows of their artist and teacher, and they lack life.

Hanya Holm must be a great teacher, for the members of her group

18

actually dance. They follow her choreography, they conform to the manner in which she wants an idea to be expressed; but each of them has an individual quality of movement. Their hands, for instance, aren't completely stylized, and each girl moves her hands as if they were an expressive part of her body, not lifeless marionette hands controlled by the manipulating wires of the "boss." In another way their knowledge of true dance projection is evident: at the end of a movement sequence, they don't hold a pose, they dance it. Such a thing is actually possible although it is rather intangible and is sensed by an audience rather than seen. One can lock the body in a pose and hold it until the time comes to move; or one can dance a pose by keeping the body alert, the rhythm of breathing steady and strong, and the muscles of the body still dynamic in their movement of pause. It can be done. Hans Züellig in Jooss' *Big City* stood perfectly still, at one point in the ballet, and yet he projected the feeling of hope, of love, of sorrow and of tragic searching.

Hanya Holm has contributed something else to the growth of the modern dance. In her composition of major dimensions, *Trend,* she has succeeded in making a social comment that is not limited to the present, nor has she attempted to present her own ideas for the betterment of our social, political and economic structure. *Trend* shows our struggle to earn our daily bread; it shows the satiety, the money-madness, the superficialities, the formalized religion which cause the decadence of civilizations; and it shows the toil, the brotherhood, the understanding and the faith that are necessary to restore civilization. *Trend* is not merely an American comment; it would have been understandable to civilization yet to come; for it is a comment on mankind.

Of course Hanya Holm and her work are not flawless. It is to be hoped that in time she will discard the so-called music used by the Moderns, which at its best is sound effects with various rhythms. The beauty and strength of her ideas call for music with themes, with phrasings and with melodic and harmonic development. In the field of movement, we noted that her shorter pieces are based almost entirely on percussive movement, short, quick and abrupt, and lacking the legato quality of movement flow, which every dancer should know how to use effectively. And there is one thing more that Hanya Holm may be allowed to boast. Ask most modern dancers to get up and dance for the sheer love of movement; they look a bit blank, and ask you to state a theme, or tell what kind of movement you want. But it is a safe bet to say that Hanya Holm's girls would be able to dance at a moment's notice, for their teacher has taught them more than the mechanics of movement, she has taught them the essence and the spirit of dancing. (Boston will have the opportunity to witness these dance contributions of Miss Holm when she appears, with her company, on Thursday evening at the Lee auditorium in the Boston Y. W. C. A.) [*Boston Herald*]

January 14, 1938

Hanya Holm and her company carried the spirit of dance with them throughout their demonstration program; thus making it a real dance presentation rather than the customary series of body exercises which mark most lecture demonstrations. The first part of Miss Holm's program covered types of fundamental dance movement; relaxation; with the accent on movements of swing; rhythm and its use in both solo and group forms; and elasticity, which presented a variety of skips and leaps. Even in this section of fundamental movements where no emotion and no dance theme were employed, Miss Holm's superb teaching was in evidence, for each girl had an individual quality of movement that made one feel that the movement sprang from her own impulse and was not just an exercise mechanically learned.

In the second part of her presentation, Miss Holm demonstrated the significance of space in the dance: direction, which was concerned with circles, angular paths, and curved paths; dimensions, showing the use of depth, width and height in dance terms. This difficult section could easily have been haphazard and confused, but Miss Holm carefully arranged it into a series of dance etudes with form, meaning and logical sequence, so that the audience could follow the progress of dance forms as easily as it could have followed the thematic development of a good musical study.

Elizabeth Waters, the most accomplished member of the company, has precision and strength of movement, but that strength occasionally takes the form of an attack and in such a case makes the movement a virtuosic bit rather than a strong segment of a progressing theme. However, in her dance rhythm of earthy quality, she moved with a joyous freedom that suggested a self-inspired folk dance. The entire company was good, but special mention should be made of the fine dancing and the beautiful leaps of Louise Kloepper, and the dramatically sustained movement of Carolyn Durand in her etude *Attraction Towards Depth*. When she discards the ear-offending music of the modern dance, and when she colors her work with the richness of American folk characteristics, the dance of Hanya Holm will be even more welcome than it now is. As it is, we are grateful for her sincerity and her constant experiments for honest progress. [*Boston Herald*]

Ballet Caravan

January 23, 1938

Yankee Clipper turned out to be first rate ballet entertainment, and again the Caravan company proved that Americans can dance American themes and still employ the great traditions of the classic ballet. The story concerns itself with a young farmer who leaves the girl he loves and seeks his fortune as a sailor on a clipper ship. This ballet voyage takes him to strange ports, it introduces him to the dances of exotic peoples, it subjects him to the bullying of experienced sailors, and finally it makes a man of him.

The foreign dances made no pretense at being authentic, and they were shown to us as the humorous eyes of fun-loving American sailors would see them. Particularly successful were the three Japanese dancers—two of them were as shy as we would expect Japanese girls to be, and the other was a veritable Gilbert and Sullivan Katisha with gnashing teeth and machinating gestures. The strange movements of the Indo-China dancers were broadly burlesqued by Jane Doering and Lorna London, whose head-wobblings, fingers and arms describing definitely weird designs and utterly blank expressions, made this section enjoyable to those of us who see things we don't understand as cartoons.

The dance of friendship was splendidly choreographed and excellently executed by the brusque self-conscious sailor who tried to make the young lad's life a happier one through friendship, understanding and protection. Lew Christensen displayed a fine sense of character movement as the rough but brotherly sailor, and Eugene Loring's mime as the frightened and bullied boy was finely delineated in form and subtly yet profoundly shaded in emotion. Eugene Loring, the choreographer, certainly succeeded in creating a ballet not only American in theme, character and movement, but also American in viewpoint. As danced by the Ballet Caravan it is one of the high-spots of American theatrical entertainment.

In not too flattering contrast, the company presented *Folk Dance* which sought to catch the spirit of the native dances of Spain and Italy. In this they failed, for they appeared as a group of Americans having a gay time in costumes that were alien to them. The members of the company danced with their customary vigor, enthusiasm and infectious good humor, so the proceedings were by no means dull; but we would rather see this company dancing American themes with their robustness and agreeable satire, or strictly classical ballets such as the vivacious *Encounter*.

Harlequin, Columbine, the Doctor and the Captain have been making successful appearances since the long past debut of the Commedia dell 'Arte, and their freshness, their romantic actions and their humorous complications have not diminished during the passage of centuries. *Harlequin For President* brings these lovable characters and their ridiculous actions back to us again. The program note tersely stated that "Harlequin loves Columbine who is not impressed"—with such a situation something had to happen, and it certainly did. The members of the company called on all their robust qualities, their deviltries and their speed, and made this ballet-pantomime a vital and hilarious bit of theater. Not content with first honors as dancer and choreographer of *Yankee Clipper,* Eugene Loring again stole the show in the role of Harlequin in this ballet of his own creating.

The costumes for *Yankee Clipper* were colorful and clever in their stylization. The satirized native dances were enhanced by costumes which were extravagantly burlesqued and which aided the dancers in making their movements appear even more ridiculous than they were intrinsically. [*Boston Herald*]

Mordkin Ballet

January 28, 1938

The role of Giselle was created almost 100 years ago by Carlotta Grisi, and later recreated by such great names in the ballet as Karsavina, Pavlowa and Spessivtzeva. Last evening Lucia Chase essayed the role—it was a mistake. The fragile, delicate and antique beauty of this old ballet was not aided any by Miss Chase's technique. Leon Varkas, as the noble lover of the peasant Giselle, displayed a smooth and precise technique that was a joy to watch; his turns and leaps were done with ease, assurance and dramatic effect. *Giselle* was dull in spots, but it was easy to see that a great artist in the title role could bring out the intrinsic shadings of emotion and mood and make the ballet an effective and moving bit of fantasy.

The Mordkin company seemed much happier and performed to better effect in *The Goldfish*. Mordkin was splendid as the old fisherman, and although he relied entirely on mime, he created such a rich and believable character that his performance outshone those of the more athletic members of the company. Lucia Chase was good as the wife, and her talents seemed more tilted to the broad humor of the shrew than to the fragile Giselle. This ballet offered within its story a series of divertissements: Nina Stroganova did a nice bit as the "Top" and displayed some well controlled (if not always neat) fouettes; and in this section, Leon Varkas again showed us precise ballet movements executed with ease. The costumes and decor for *The Goldfish* were richly colored and cleverly designed. And against this gaudy background and clad in glittering costumes, the entire company presented us with an entertaining ballet in welcome contrast to the unfortunate *Giselle* with its unhappy heroine and its corps de ballet aptly cast in the roles of the "Willys." [*Boston Herald*]

The life, death and after-death of *Giselle* having been attended to on the opening night, the Mordkin Ballet turned to gayer fields with the eighteenth century *La Fille Mal Gardée*. Although this ballet was quite long, it managed to be entertaining thanks to the vitality and good dancing of some of its principals. Mordkin was excellent as the ill-tempered and harassed mother; once again he demonstrated a command of mime which projected the humorous characteristics of his role. His make-up was good and his stuffed figure properly overpowering in its moments of storm and stress.

Once again we must report that Lucia Chase danced badly and mimed worse. She would do well to work with the corps de ballet until she achieved a technique that a ballerina should have. The ballets would be decidedly more effective and more entertaining if Karen Conrad, Nina Stroganova or Katherine Sergava were given the leading roles. However, we are most grateful for their work in lesser capacities. These three with the aid of Leon Varkas highlighted *La Fille Mal Gardée* with a beautifully executed pas de quatre in the Variations of this ballet. Dimitri Romanoff as the young lover of the "badly-guarded daughter" was enthusiastic and robust in the part. Although his balletic movements have not yet achieved precision and sureness, they are performed with such vitality and obvious enjoyment that the beholder is able to watch his work with pleasure.

The Mordkin Ballet actually presents mimo-dramas, and in spite of the fact that mime is a powerful medium for the projecting of story, character and mood, we would like to see more actual dancing, for constant miming on the part of comparatively inexperienced performers tends to become monotonous and repetitive. Action, on the other hand, keeps the audience aroused, and although the dancing may be inadequately performed, the active movements of the body at least keep one wondering what is going to happen next. With the exception of moments of broad humor, it might be wise if this company would leave the miming to Mordkin, and let the members of the company do more actual dancing—youthful action is easier to watch than immature miming. [*Boston Herald*]

The Hampton Dancers and the Problems of Negro Dance

March 27, 1938

In a conglomerate program, the Hampton Dancers diaplayed exciting and valuable work along with frankly boring creations. This is not particularly strange, for any experimental group is certain to err in its attempts to find the proper form for its expression of ideas. Negroes are certainly not aliens to the dance, for their African forebears have left them a rich heritage of rituals and their American fathers have certainly developed a varied and worthwhile folk dance; but the Negro is new to the field of the concert dance, and he is still searching for a dance form that will express his ideas in terms of theatrical art and at the same time retain his racial qualities and inheritances.

The African Dances on the Hampton program were decidedly exciting and colorful, but they were borrowed from an almost forgotten past and hence could not be considered as truly creative work. They have a definite place on the program for they are theatrically stimulating, but the problem under discussion is the contemporary dance of the contemporary Negro. Spirituals come to mind, but it must be admitted that the spirituals on the Hampton dance program were not only disappointing, they were irritating—stern stylization, plodding movement and a complete lack of emotional projection robbed them of the thrilling spiritual quality. It seems incredible that the spirituals of Tamiris and Ted Shawn should be more effective than those of the Negroes themselves.

In creating dances to the spirituals, one might suggest that the group improvise in the studio to the spiritual music, and from that improvisation a visually pleasing form might spring without the sacrifice of the freedom, the beauty and the emotional shadings of the songs themselves.

Choral, the opening number on the program was a study in design and in contrapuntal movement. Because it was pure dance movement without emotion and without message, it belonged to any group that could perform it with technical assurance. Such creations are the property of any competent dance ensemble, for they have little bearing on race, heritage or custom. In the *Characteristic Dance Rhythms,* the Hampton dancers came into their own. The Juba and the Cake Walk were their own vital fork dances, and as such had forms that were natural and easy. Because the form and the content were both familiar, the projection took care of itself.

The *Labor Rhythms* were of course, the most important section of the program, for here in terms of strong Negro movement, we were shown the work of the Negro and his opinion of that work. The influence of Ted Shawn's masculine dance form was much in evidence, and the heroic, dramatic movements were admirably suited to the rugged bodies of the men in the group—in time and with experience they will probably find a form that not only suits their physiques but is also even better suited to their tempers and ideas. As this labor section stands, we are given a brief glimpse of the Negro's joy and sorrow, his patience and his hope, and his innate artistry, for these dances show us the sufferings of the old slaves and their ability to stand these sufferings because they knew faith. They show us too, hard work and play,

24

docility and strength. And as the Negro dance grows, these qualities will be developed and accented until the Negro dance at last becomes an articulate form of contemporary theatrical expression.

Charles Williams, director of the group, deserves praise for his intelligent pioneering. Now that his company is definitely launched, it might be wise for him to forget the techniques of contemporary schools except in the case of body developing, and turn his attention to a dance form that will suit the requirements of his group. It seems logical that such a form will be freer in movement, somewhat improvisational, more generous in its use of pantomime, chant and song than the dance forms of the white race in America. It should be a stimulating experiment to watch, and it should certainly contribute generously to the exciting renascence of the dance in America. [*Boston Herald*]

Ballet Russe Makes First Appearance of Season at Opera House

November 13, 1938

All that remains to the public of Cimarosa's opera, Aztuzzle Feminili, is the ballet divertissement now called *Cimarosiana,* which the Ballet Russe presented to Boston for the first time last evening. Colorful costumes and a maximum of gay movement were its salient features, for *Cimarosiana* was, at best, as inoffensive and light-heartedly trivial as the music of its 18th century composer. As for the principals, they seemed to enjoy the frivolity of the work, and blessed the audience with nicely executed fouettes, entre-chats, and the other virtuosic offerings of the ballet.

In *Choreartium* came the really important and exciting event of the evening. Massine has carefully avoided the bad effect of interpretive dancing, and instead we find a parallel symphony, a symphony of movement. The themes of movement accurately parallel the musical themes, and the complete effect suggests an audible symphony with a visual symphony, neither one being pushed aside for the advancement of the other. The first two movements seemed to be finer, more carefully worked out, and perhaps more inspired than the last two movements. The second movement was truly a triumph in that the quality of movement, the choreographic pattern, and the development of mood were in perfect accord with the Brahms music.

The principals in this instance deserve almost as much acclaim as the choreographer. Toumanova never once displayed the fault that is to be found in so many dancers, that of trying to interpret the music through the force of personality; instead, she did what was correct, she reacted to the music, which is the only thing a human being can do. Much of the success of the second movement must be laid to the excellent dancing of Verchinina, whose power of movement, strength in the usually lyric ballet arms, and adeptness in the creating of space consciousness, made her part as potent as the symphonic theme that was the basis of her dancing.

Mention must also be made of the excellent work of the corps de ballet, who rarely displayed the solo tendencies, which in other seasons, were predominant in the group. In a minor part, Shabelevsky displayed his welcome ease of technique, and his own delightful use of the humorous.

The familiar *Spectre de la Rose* was the third presentation on the program, and there seems to be practically nothing else to say about it. We realize that it's delightfully old-fashioned, traditional, and beautiful; but we still don't like to see a man impersonating a rose, or the spirit of the rose, for that matter. We would like to call it a museum piece that should be seen only at rare intervals.

The enthusiastically received program of ballets closed with the everdelightful *Le Beau Danube*. Here is to be found a light, entertaining book, built on the gay music of Johann Strauss. Matching the joyousness of the score, the choreography busies itself with humor, drama, and even at times, slapstick fun. In it the principals have the opportunity to display their individual characteristics, and do so with pleasing effect. Massine, Danilova, and Riabouchinska walked off with the dancing and miming honors, and add the finishing touch to a ballet which deserves the American word of greatest praise, "swell." [*Boston Herald*]

Evaluating Massine's New Ballet, St. Francis

November 13, 1938

Massine has always been an innovator. He has experimented with movements alien to the ballet tradition; he has developed the theatrical value of dance abstractions; and he has built symphonies of movement upon symphonies of sound. But it is a far greater task to seek the depths of a man's spirit, to recreate the tenor of a period and to analyze in terms of movement the delicate processes of religious discovery. For an accomplished and profound artist in a form of the dance dedicated to serious and profound themes, the problem

26

might not have been as difficult, but Massine had to overpower the surface glitter, the purely visual beauty, the pyrotechnics and the spectacle which have come to mean "ballet" to us.

In most respects, *St. Francis* is a great work. The choreographer has marked his work with craftsmanship and with sincerity and these necessities helped one to overlook the occasional flaws in this study of a saint. To many of us, the first scene was somewhat startling, for Massine dispensed with the classic style and the flowing quality of the traditional ballet, and employed instead a flat, angular style vitalized by percussive, brittle movements. The scenery and costumes suggested that the period was the transitional one between decadent Rome and the medieval era of meaningless opulence. Amid this splendor moved the young Francis, marked by this environment but with his personal quality of quiet kindliness already prophesying his emergence as a great human spirit.

Massine danced this first scene with a fine sense of the many conflicting elements of his nature, and his subtle characterization was developed through actual dancing and not through the traditional miming. His company seemed no more vital than did the scenery, which was fitting, for the sensitive Francis must have felt that his shallow-spirited companions were at best additional embellishments for his father's establishment.

As the ballet progressed Massine encountered more difficulties. The first scene had been certain of successful projection due to the multi-colored decor and to the contrast in both movement and characterization between Francis and his friends. But with the glitter and the contrasting personalities gone, Massine had to project himself the shining beauty of his emotional discoveries and had to dilineate himself the contrasting moods of his transitional state. Certainly his sincerity was always present, but his St. Francis, although experienced the rich nourishment of isolated discoveries, he never quite achieved a union of these discoveries, a knowing, humble fulfillment of his deep emotional searchings.

But if the ballet of St. Francis didn't quite succeed in attaining its goal, it surely had moments of stimulation and of quiet beauty; and if Massine's personal performance as the Saint didn't quite sweep to an apotheosis, at least it let us experience the warm humanity, the unaffected humility of a rare spirit.

The Hindemith score was an integral part of the ballet, and was almost uncanny in its unbroken communion with the texture and the tempo of the dancing. It is a rare thing to find fine music and fine dancing so ideally mated. In most instances one or the other is destined to suffer, but with *St. Francis* the music and the dancing progressed with power and with beauty through the great range of sound and movement dynamics.

Perhaps the greatest achievement in this new work was the use of the theatrical. Massine, remembering that his dance is a part of the theater, couched this religious theme, this delicate characterization in theatrical terms. He gave us vivid colors, unusual costumes, a definite story sequence, a certain virtuosity of movement, but instead of crushing his quiet and reverent theme, they served as highlights to this theme, accenting its salient moments, tightening its structure, organizing its development. For this more than for anything else he deserves unending praise—in this *Saint Francis* Massine has added his proof to that of other dancers, that profundity and the theatrical dance can be mated and that this union fosters an unending wealth of stimulating experiences for beholder and creator alike. [*Boston Herald*]

1939

So Long, Boston! Hello, New York!

Argentinita performs • Passacaglia presented by the Humphrey–Weidman Company in Boston • Saltonstall and Lincoln Kirstein urge Blue Law Repeal • A preview of the Fall, 1939 Dance Season in New York initiates a new career on the New York Herald Tribune • The Ballet Russe opens at the Met • Angna Enters dances • Religious dance • Martha Graham presents Every Soul is a Circus • The birth of Ballet Theatre announced

Argentinita

January 7, 1939

Clappings, yellings. Almost every number encored. Laughter. Bravas. These were the things that greeted Argentinita on her first Boston appearance. For once advance publicity underestimated the artist, for the concert by Argentinita and her company was most surely a triumph, a triumph in performance and in friendship—before the program was even well under way, Argentinita and colleagues were close and ardent friends with the members of their audience. They understood each other and they had a swell time.

Time and space prevent a discussion of the complete program, and it is difficult to choose outstanding dances in a program of highlights. The *Anda Jaleo* presented the three dancers in a brilliant fusion of song, dance, romance and story with the gypsy source of the dance coming through in the abruptly changing rhythms and the fiery texture of the movement. Argentinita's *Mazurka* brought forth her subtly telling comedy in dance motion and in mime. Perhaps the most delicately appealing dance on the program was the Peruvian *Huayno* with the subdued monotony of the Indian movement, the peace, the awe and the faith of a quiet and noble people.

We must mention in passing the wild *Farruca* of Lopez and Triana; Argentinita's *Jota* of Aragon, depicting the strong and simple movements of

29

the peasant in high moments of gauche play. The *Jaleo Andaluz* of Triana with his incredibly exciting zapateados (heel beats) defies you to sit back and take it easy—its fire, speed and passion make you want to get up and yelp with excitement. The *Bulerias* could be called a Spanish jam session, for the dancers set a tempo upon which they each improvise—the results make the American version seem like a primary school picnic in contrast.

As we have said before, you don't need to know anything about dancing or about Spanish art to enjoy Argentinita and her group. They tell you all about it with their chattering castanets, the Morse code of their heel-beats and with every articulate gesture in their large repertory of motion. The dances are constantly fresh and exciting, for one of the charms about good Spanish dancing is that it never seems set and rehearsed—it seems to be extemporization, new and gay and friendly. We might as well admit here and now that words can't describe it. We advise you to see Argentinita and her group for yourself, for this company affords the most exciting event (dance, drama, motion picture, politics and hurricane included) that Boston has witnessed in many a season. [*Boston Herald*]

January 8, 1939

A good play can run for two weeks in Boston. A good movie can do the same thing. And we get Argentinita for only two performances. It's not fair, for this great Spanish lady and her brilliant ensemble put on a better show than almost any all-star movie or drama. We hope that Aaron Richmond will bring her back to Boston as frequently as she is available for concert engagements.

Yesterday's program disclosed these artists in dances that were dignified and comic, restrained and passionate, a program of song and dance and laughter. There was Argentinita's traditional and elegant *Valencia* and Triana's snorting, strutting *Polo*. *The Fire Dance* of de Falla presented Argentinita as a concert choreographer in movements of intricate rhythm projecting the quality of suspense. The exciting *Anda Jaleo* with the three love-making, story-telling dancers was repeated along with Argentinita's rich and human *Jota* of Aragon. But we could go on indefinitely, and wind up with the discovery that we liked everything on the program and recommended them all.

There is no need to discuss the intricacies of Spanish dance technique, for they can be seen and appreciated by the untutored eye: the magnificent posture of the dancers, their unerring sense of line, the fluidity of their movements. The wonderful rhythms projected by the clear heel-beats and the talkative castanets, the rhythm that is in their every gesture, their eyes and their smiles—all these are transmitted to the beholder, and he must be a sad

30

specimen of living matter if he cannot feel the blood coursing more rapidly in his own veins and his feet almost uncontrollable in their desire to stamp. The dance of Argentinita springs from the spirit and the life of a people; it has swept past the barriers of centuries from the times of the ancient Iberians to the present, and its mighty progress has been strengthened and enriched by Romans, Goths, the oriental Moors, the peasants, the bourgeois, the courtiers and by an ever-dancing race. And so Argentinita brings to use the treasures of an ageless, living dance, filled with rich blood and healthy romance.

For us who have no such heritage, Argentinita lends us hers, and urges us to cherish our own small dance beginnings that one day they may become as great and as human as the indestructible "Jotas" of Spain. [*Boston Herald*]

A Dancing Race Presents
The Great Argentinita

January 15, 1939

Why was Argentinita greeted with such unrestrained enthusiasm? The Spanish dance is not unknown to Boston. Several performers of Spanish dancing have offered interesting and enjoyable theatrical programs to the audiences of this city. Just what happened? Argentinita is not just a handy wielder of castanets; she is not possessed of a footlight hurtling personality; she is not breathtakingly beautiful. But Argentinita has two enviable things that mark her for greatness: Her native dance is rich with the blood of history, and she has the ability to project that ageless living quality of a people's dance.

The dances of Spain are far ahead of any other national dances of the Occident. We in America have numerous schools of dance, we have the contribution of the Negro, we possess the vital dances of the American Indian, we have the dances of the various races who populate this country. But as yet they are not fused into an American national dance, for they retain the flavor and the salient features of their home territory.

In Spain the fusing processes of history have welded similar dance contributions into a dance we know as Spanish. Naturally, one can observe Oriental influences, ballet influences, and the many others, but the completed dance is undeniably Spanish. Long before the time of Christ, Phoenicians brought the gestures and the dances of Egypt and the East to the peninsula. Rome came and added her dance to that of Spain. Then followed those lovers of beauty, the Moors, who cherished the dance they found, added to its scope and assured it a place in the active life of the people. But one could go on

31

indefinitely with the influences that came to Spain from her alien subjects of her great empire, the ballet that crossed the mountains to lose itself in the native dances.

Spain was conquered by Roman and Goth and Moor. Her empire has gone. Much of her art has been destroyed; but her people live, and with them, and inseparable from them, their dances. It is this history of human motion and human activity that Argentinita brings to us. She is not merely a performer and her dance is not just a show, for she gives us a dance that is rich with history, alive with humanity.

Of course, she puts on a good show. The technical brilliance of her castanets is in itself exciting, her heel-beats are virtuosic in their execution, her form and posture speak beauty. But it took more than those to make elderly and refined ladies yell "Olé" and "Bravo," and it took more than those to make self-conscious and restrained men stamp their feet and clap their hands off. Argentinita took us to the peasant's door and let us look at a healthy, fun-loving girl dancing on the hard-packed earth surrounding her home. She was the Peruvian Indian whose centuries of abuse called for the patient, monotonous motions of prayer to her god. She was the elegant lady of the court whose steps had touched only shining floors and whose body was prepared to move with elegant serenity through life. Argentinita was the fiery gypsy who told us of her passionate love, her hate, her fun, her coarseness, her pride.

She and her group gave us a "jam session" too—that was the ultimate proof of the point we stated when we said that her dance was alive. For here was something that was not set and rehearsed (or at least it didn't seem so, and that is the important thing), but was actually happening right before the eyes of her audience. And that same quality of extemporization was in all her dances and the dances of her company. Yes, the Iberian, the Moor and the courtier were there, but they were not brought to life as a museum exhibit, but they were shown as they actually exist, to the present moment in the daily dances of a living race.

It seems to us that the dance of Spain as brought to us by Argentinita might well serve as a model for the American dance and American dancers. That revolt from the past is stupid. That we should retain and develop our dance heritage, for the bad will disappear from its own intrinsic decay, is true of a few American dancers, notably Ted Shawn, who makes the richness of the past serve his present and point the way to his future. A dancing people made Argentinita possible. We are not a dancing people, but perhaps American dancers can make this work conversely—by relating their dances so closely to daily activity, perhaps they can urge us into becoming a dancing people. It certainly would be worth the try if it aided us to participate in an activity of dance that Argentinita shared with those of us who had the unforgettable privilege of seeing her, feeling her dance. [*Boston Herald*]

32

Humphrey–Weidman at Jordan Hall

February 11, 1939

A finer fusion of art and entertainment in the theater of dance would be difficult to find, for Doris Humphrey brought us the majesty of the Bach *Passacaglia,* Charles Weidman showed us habit, the vise which holds human life, in his *Traditions*, and together this noted couple danced for us the completely mad, the utterly beguiling *Race of Life,* a veritable theatrical belly-laugh.

There are many things about this Humphrey–Weidman program that make it the best the modern dance has yet produced. First of all, they have developed a vocabulary of movement that gives form and lucidity to their work. *To the Dance* consists of movements and movement combinations that are used by Miss Humphrey as technical studies in classroom periods, yet she has arranged them in such a way that one design flows beautifully into another, and into these strong and sure and proven molds she has poured the shadings, the moods and the spirit of dance. In this use of technical combinations, Miss Humphrey's work is like the ballet, which is almost invariably based upon arrangements and rearrangements of technical combinations. This, surely, is the mark of a fine artist, for almost any one can toss off a novelty movement, but only such a superb artist as Miss Humphrey can take familiar movements and can breathe freshness and new meaning into them by the richness of her dancing.

Mr. Weidman's popular *Traditions* again presented this artist in his best vein, for in it he comments on the problem of habit which afflicts all of us. He makes us look pretty silly, he makes habits look silly, and he certainly gives us an hilarious time.

We have discussed *New Dance* in these columns and have said that the Variations and Conclusion is one of the most exciting dance sections that you will ever find in the wordless wonder of movement that is dance. Miss Humphrey's *Passacaglia* is similar in that once again she displays her mastery of group motion. One can forget the ideas that underlie the movement, for the actual dancing, the postures, the moving designs and the weavings and interweavings of bodies in constant motion are almost peerless examples of the difficult craft of group choreography.

Race of Life brought the program to a close. Do you like Thurber's drawings? If you laughed when you saw them, you'll howl when you see them come to life with Doris Humphrey as a neurotic, slap-happy wife, José Limón as the man swathed in dumb masculine arrogance, Katherine Litz as the come-hither damsel, and Charles Weidman having the time of his career as the child. If we were asked to describe it from the technical angle, we would say "completely zany." For everyone who likes to laugh, *Race of Life* is a theatrical "must see." [*Boston Herald*]

A Temple in Ten Lessons;
Should Dance Be Fun?

February 17, 1939

The dance Forum received a long letter from Katherine Dickson, director of a Cambridge dance school, and in that letter Miss Dickson brought up again the problems of dance teaching. She says: "One of my own most acute personal problems—and I am sure that of any teacher whose interests go beyond the money which she makes from her business—is the education of parents. People just do not understand what they should expect when they spend money on dancing lessons. They want all the wrong things, and hardly seem to know that the right things even exist.

"Constant small compromises are required of the teacher, or she does not hold the pupil long enough to give either pupil or parent a conception of what dancing really is, what it can do. The teacher hates these concessions, but she knows perfectly well that if she does not make these concessions in the beginning she will lose her pupil, and that that pupil will run immediately to the teacher that talks the loudest, promises the most and does the least."

Miss Dickson's letter covered a great many other dance problems, but these two paragraphs afforded us the opportunity to say just a few words more on this business of the dance in the brutal hands of bad teachers and thoughtless students—if they take their five-year-olds to a tap dancer they want Shirley Temples in 10 easy lessons. Be it tap, ballet, modern or whatever, the paying parent wants the fond offspring to shine in that particular form of dance in a very short time. Mother wants little Euphemia to do a split, execute 30 fouettes, develop an extension like Martha Graham and improvise almost as well as does Ruth St. Denis. Most of these desires could be termed acrobatic and not dance. For your daughter to persecute 30 fouettes for the assembled guests is no more dancing than if she touched the floor with her palms 30 times.

The ability to accomplish technical feats of body mechanics is not dance—these feats become dance when they are filled with some quality, when they are used to project some meaning, when they relate to preceding and succeeding movements. Parents don't send their son or daughter to a piano teacher, and expect a smooth performance of several Beethoven sonatas to

34

emerge after the end of a few lessons. You can't play the piano well until you have trained your fingers to obey your mental commands, and you can't dance until your body is able to carry out the orders of the brain.

We suggest that parents visit frequently the schools their children attend. And parents, don't be fooled by the number of so-called dances your child can do or the prettiness of the costume. Do you notice her muscles becoming firm and smooth and long, does she move her body with greater ease, is her posture better, her shoulders more relaxed, does she respond more quickly to new exercises? These are some of the things to look for in the development of your dancing daughter. Look for slow, healthy, thorough progress, and be wary of spectacular feats.

But teachers, here is something for you to note. The dance may be the very breath of life to you, but to most of your students it is something to do for an hour or two every day, and that hour may be gay and exciting or it may be incredibly dull. If the dance is your way of living, if it symbolizes the higher plane of being and doing, remember that it must have joy as well as tragedy, repose as well as activity, play as well as work, imagination as well as reality. And these things hold true for all who teach a balanced healthy dance. Destroy balance and your dance becomes a warped and unhealthy activity of an esoteric cult. This law of balance is for the trainer of prospective dancers as well as for teachers of children.

The teacher or trainer must relate the dance to life. Some students want to find in the dance the physical pep of sports, others will relate it to drama and accent the pantomimic qualities, some will find it the best medium for expressing their personal feelings on current events both political and social, still others will find in the dance endless variations on a swell Viennese waltz, and so on indefinitely. The teacher should certainly try to bring his students a dance that is rich and varied, a dance that does not busy itself with grim probings of why students move in such and such a manner, but rather a dance that can be the physical expression of joy and with no hidden meaning other than the fun of moving. For teacher, parent and student, the dance should be a balance of all the guiding forces of life. And don't forget that without discipline and without the spirit of fun, the growing processes of the dance are likely to create a dance (and a dancer, perhaps) that is a formless mass of grim matter. [*Boston Herald*]

Saltonstall, Kirstein Urge
Blue Law Repeal

March 12, 1939

The Boston Dance Council has received the enthusiastic support of dancers and dance followers. The first work of this council was to urge for a repeal of the blue law which forbids dance concerts on Sunday. A bill to make this amendment possible has already been introduced in the State House. Members of the dance council have received the following comments from several noted Bostonians. Their letters appear in part:

From Hans Wiener, the dancer: "As a member of the newly formed dance council, I am interested to see it established on a basis that will bring the greatest good to the greatest number of those interested in the dance, professionally or as spectators. I feel that the immediate and important problem is to enlist public sympathy with the dance as an art and that the first step connected with that is to show the dance under the most favorable auspices. For that reason I have concentrated on the effort to bring about an amendment in the Sunday dance laws which will permit Sunday dance recitals . . . unlike a concert, the dance needs an adequate stage with lighting and elevation for the audience. It is only fair that both dancers and spectators should be in an environment favorable to the performance."

Lincoln Kirstein continues Mr. Wiener's plea for Sunday dance in theaters rather than in concert halls on week-days. "Due to the economic structure of the theatrical business, it is almost impossible for any dance artists to appear in Boston for more than a single performance, and theaters will not rent during the week. Sunday night is the ideal time for dance performances. It has become an institution in New York, Chicago and San Francisco to hold dance concerts on an evening when there is no other competition from the theater. A very loyal audience is built up by continuous attendances on these Sunday evenings. I feel sure that it would mean a great deal to the cultural growth of Boston to permit these performances."

Mr. Nathaniel Saltonstall, president of the Museum of Modern Art writes: "I am more than delighted to have my name associated with your committee which is working for the repeal of the Sunday dance law. The dance is an art which is just as important as music and if music is allowed in Boston on Sunday nights, I can see no reason for not having the dance." And from Frederick B. Robinson of the Fogg Museum, "The art of the dance (not, of course, in the ballroom or dance hall sense) can be as fine an art as any of the paintings, sculptures, prints, etc. shown in our museums and galleries. These institutions are open to the public for their enjoyment and education on Sundays. The great ballets are not infrequently combinations of the genius of outstanding painters for the scenery and costumes, eminent composers for the accompanying music, and great desire for the choreography. The dance is, and should be more generally recognized as such, a great artistic manifestation of a race or period."

Aaron Richmond, sponsor of many noteworthy dance concerts here in Boston writes, "In common with many of those who follow important events in the dance world, I am hoping that the time is not too far distant when the ordinances will be altered so as to give Boston the opportunity to witness dance recitals on Sunday."

Dr. Frederick Rand Rogers, director of physical education at Boston University, and organizer of B. U.'s impressive dance series of fifteen lecture-demonstrations, gives the following reasons for his desire to see the repeal of the Sunday Blue Law: "(1) Dance is the first art and should be treated so again. Because there are pornographic pictures in print we do not close the art museums on Sunday. Rather, we do the reverse. So also with dance. (2) Dance was once a means of worship and may become so again. Church rituals today are a form of dance. Let us be logical! (3) Dancing is a natural release of repressions. People who dance properly do not engage so often in vice. (4) Dance is one of the best developers of health known to physiologists. It is actually a heightening of the Sunday stroll into expressive as well as locomotor activity."

We might add that the entertainment seekers are permitted to watch Eleanor Powell perform a cinematic hula on the Sabbath, yet serious followers of the dance would not be allowed to see Ruth St. Denis perform an *Ave Maria* on the same day. Such lack of logic is not the crux of the matter. Our plea is simple. We simply urge all those who respect and enjoy the arts, all those who respect and enjoy healthy activity and all those who would like to respect and enjoy the cultural wealth that Boston could have—we urge these people to support the dance council in its attempt to bring a Sunday dance to Boston. [*Boston Herald*]

The Dance Season

September 24, 1939

Whirling, stamping savages danced before their gods. They danced to win their mates and they danced to show their strength. Their arms raised in supplication, the swaying bodies, arrogant postures or the stamping of feet disclosed their hopes, their fears, their fun and the very essence of their lives. Down

37

the centuries history has found that it needs the pageant of dance to tell the story of man, and dancers are still telling that great story with every muscle, sinew and bone of their bodies.

Primitive man and his dances have gone but his reasons for dancing still exist in our time and in our City of New York. They have merely moved from the communal dancing in the forest clearing to the highly trained dancing upon a stage. One might think at least the union of dance and religion has disappeared, but it hasn't. Ruth St. Denis who is perhaps America's greatest living dancer, has turned her back on the Oriental opulence of her long career, and is fighting for a reunion of the dance and religion. Aside from directing her large dance department at Adelphi College on Long Island, Miss St. Denis is scheduled to tour the country in a program of lectures and dances. She hopes to appear under the direction of Jack Cole in a major work employing dance, music and the spoken word. It is based on the New Testament and treats the life of Christ in the form of a primitive mystery.

Shawn Uses Religious Ritual   When Ted Shawn presents his three Carnegie Hall performances in February, audiences will see that he makes use of religious ritual, that he has some telling comments on war and dictatorship, that he and his men dancers display the movements of men at their labors and that humor plays no small part in his program. We may anticipate the appearance of Martha Graham with her flawless technique and her frequent use of vital current topics. We will see Charles Weidman again bounding about and having the time of his life in *Opus 51*, which permits him to prove that he is really a great satirist and a great dance clown. Sharing honors with him will be Doris Humphrey, and we hope she will again bring to life the drawings of James Thurber in her hilarious *Race of Life.*

Helen Tamiris plans to restage her *How Long Brethren* and *Adelante*, and Hanya Holm will again offer New York *Metropolitan Daily, Dance of Work and Play* and *Tragic Exodus.* Those two promising young dancers, Miriam Winslow and Foster Fitz-Simons, plan to wind up a long tour with a dance performance in New York.

Two Ballet Engagements   The Ballet Russe de Monte Carlo will open a two-weeks' engagement at the Metropolitan Opera House on Oct. 10. With its glitter, its virtuosity and its glamorous personalities the Ballet Russe rarely fails to please, for it offers old favorites as well as novelties. Some of its creations are great art, some of its works are pretty silly, but most of it is fine theater. For those who can dispense with the art aspect, it is wise to look at the Ballet Russe as a great circus; pick the ring and the performer you like best and you are certain to have a good time. Among the new works will be *Ghost Town,* a ballet based on the gold rush, *Bacchanale,* with decor by

Salvador Dali, and *Rouge et Noir,* Massine's fifth symphonic ballet, this time to the music of Shostakovitch.

Col. deBasil's Covent Garden Russian Ballet, which was formerly a part of the Ballet Russe, plans to make an American tour this season. Our own Ballet Caravan, composed of American dancers and dancing American themes, will offer two new ballets, *Coming Out Party* and *Under the L.* An important debut of the season will be that of Carmalita Maracci, who has been widely acclaimed in the West, and from all reports will excite New York with the brilliance of her dancing. Argentinita and her ensemble will return to be one of the highest spots in a full dance season. Kreutzberg, now in Salzburg, is scheduled to appear here if the war in Europe does not prevent his departure.

Dance series are becoming important in this vicinity, with four dance attractions booked for the Brooklyn Academy of Music series—Ted Shawn, Jooss Ballet, Bali and Java Dancers and the Von Grunow Negro Dancers. The Y. M. H. A. will present seven dance events and the Washington Irving Dance Series will soon launch another season.

Stage shows, night clubs and musicals will undoubtedly bring us such favorites as Jack Cole, Paul Draper, Paul Haakon, Patricia Bowman and Bill Robinson.

These are just a few of the events scheduled for New York's dance season. On the surface one will note the reappearance of old favorites and the debut of younger artists. But probing a bit deeper, one will find that beneath the glow of modern lighting and novel costuming, there is the dancer saying in movement all the things that man has ever said and felt. Somewhere within those dances of religion, of social comment, of romance, of satire, of strength and joy, the beholder is sure to find something for which he has been seeking. Perhaps it is faith. Perhaps it is fun. They are both there, for those qualities form a part of the rich pageant of dance. [*New York Herald Tribune*]

Dance Notes — 1939

September 24, 1939

Devi Dja and her group of thirty-five Javanese and Balinese dancers are en route from Holland to New York and will open here on Oct. 28 at a theater to be announced.

Yurek Shabalevsky, until recently one of the leading members of de Basil's Ballet Russe de Monte Carlo, will head his own company this season under the sponsorship of a new producing firm, Gordon Mendelssohn, Inc.

The company will begin a tour under the management of Mark Byron, Jr., at the end of October. Sonia Wcicikowska, who appeared here at the World's Fair with the Polish Ballet, and Anna Ricarda, an American, will be Mr. Shabalevsky's premieres danseuses. The orchestra will be conducted by Eugene Fuerst. The decor and costumes have been designed by Michel Baronoff.

The English Folk Dance and Song Society will open its season with an open country dance evening at the Russell Sage Foundation, 130 East Twenty-second Street, next Saturday. On Thursday evening, Oct. 5, a series of classes in country and Morris dancing will be opened at 9 East Fifty-ninth Street. Further information may be obtained from the society's offices at 15 East Fortieth Street.

The Hanya Holm Studio will open its regular season tomorrow with courses for professionals, teachers, laymen and children. Special classes for men will also be held.

The Barbara Mettler School of the Dance will commence its sixth season at 139 West Fifty-sixth Street. Courses in body-building, dance technique, improvisation, composition, percussion, music, theory and pedagogy are included in the curriculum. [*New York Herald Tribune*]

October 1, 1939

The Ballet Caravan is scheduled to start is annual trans-continental tour Oct. 16. Aside from the already established ballets of *Filling Station, Billy the Kid, Pocahontas* and *Air and Variations,* the tour will see the premieres of two new ballets. The first is *Charade,* with choreography by Lew Christensen and music arranged by Trude Rittman. The coming-out party of a 1900 debutante is the theme of the ballet. Eugene Loring, another leading dancer of the company, has created the second ballet, *City Portrait*, which deals with the struggle for existence in an American metropolis.

Under the auspices of the Brooklyn Y. W. C. A., Meta Rom will offer a fifteen-week course in the modern dance and in ballroom dancing beginning Oct. 4. The first of two free lectures offered with the course will be presented in November and will deal with the modern dancer in its relation to health and poise.

Argentinita, the distinguished Spanish dancer, and her ensemble have completed their South American tour and will shortly commence their nation-wide circuit of more than seventy engagements. New York will again see them in performance during the coming season.

The Dance Theater Series, centered at the Y. M. H. A., will present the following artists throughout the coming season: TAC Dance Group, Nov. 5;

Carma Lita Maracci, Jan. 14; Agnes de Mille, Jan. 21; Pauline Koner, Feb. 4; Esther Junger, March 10; Humphrey, Weidman and Group, March 31; Martha Graham and Group, with Louis Horst, April 14, and Hanya Holm, at a date to be announced. [*New York Herald Tribune*]

October 22, 1939

Ted Shawn announces that in May, 1940, at the close of his present tour, he will disband his group of men dancers, dissolve the corporation, Shawn Dancers, Inc., and place his 200-acre Berkshire estate and training quarters on sale. When the tour ends the Shawn Dancers will have played close to one thousand performances before more than a million persons during the seven-year period of their activity.

Mr. Shawn feels that he and his men have achieved what they set out to do; to prove to public, press and educators that dancing is a distinguished profession and a truly masculine activity for men. During the last years Mr. Shawn has seen more men dancers on the concert stage and an ever increasing number of male dance students in colleges and schools than ever before, and he is certain that the men of his company will carry on his work in whatever division of the dance field they may now choose to enter.

He has decided to take a year off in which to work out, clarify and create the next phase of his career, but he refuses to divulge just what he has in mind. In his twenty-six years before a world-wide public he has had a career with his wife, Ruth St. Denis, both in concert and in the development of their Denishawn School, and he has had a career with his company of men dancers. With such outstanding dance leadership behind him, one can be certain that the next period of his life will find him again in the role of dance pioneer with still another goal to be attained in the progress of the American dance.

Under the direction of Mary Binney Montgomery, Painters' Farm at Chester Springs, Pa., will offer classes in the dance for children from the ages of seven to fourteen. Miss Montgomery and her dancers are remembered for their appearances with the Philadelphia Orchestra at the Robin Hood Dell and at the Academy of Music. Both ballet and modern dance will be taught, and the course will culminate in a student dance recital in the Outdoor Theater at Painters' Farm.

The sixteenth season of the Students' Dance Recitals will be opened by Tashamira at the Washington Irving High School auditorium on Saturday evening, Oct. 28. This distinguished and worthy dance series will present several other notable dance attractions during the present season.

The Alvin Theater has been selected for the New York engagement of

Angna Enters, which will consist of four appearances: Sunday evenings, Dec. 10 and 16; Tuesday and Thursday afternoons, Dec. 26 and 28. Madeleine Marshall will again be Miss Enters's accompanist.

Eleanor King, who heads the modern dance division of the Westchester Workshop at White Plains County Center, is now offering courses in choreography and advanced movement techniques to her classes. Because of student enthusiasm and capacity for hard work, Miss King hopes soon to be able to present her students in dance programs with the Westchester Chamber Music Society.

After a record two-year engagement at the Rainbow Grill in Rockefeller Center, the young ballroom team of Marlynn and Michael have turned to teaching and will conduct a school in ballroom dancing at the Hotel Delmonico. Because they helped to popularize the polka and the minuet with modern American audiences, they will continue in their teaching to accent the smoother and simpler forms of social dancing.

Walton Biggerstaff and his partner, Ruth Vollmer, will give a dance recital at the Barbizon-Plaza Concert Hall next Sunday evening, Oct. 29. Among the dances to be presented will be *Mid-West Sketch Book* (a suite of four dances), *Funeral March to a Politician* and *Episodes From a Dude Ranch*.

Boris Novikoff's Russian-American Ballet Company will give an afternoon performance for young people at the Brooklyn Academy of Music on Saturday, Oct. 28. The following program will be offered: *Coppélia,* with music by Delibes; *Le Miracle,* with music by Rubenstein, and *Rumanian Fantasy,* to the music of Enesco. Mr. Novikoff will head the list of leading dancers.

Devi Dja and her Bali and Java Dancers will make their American debut Friday evening, Oct. 27, at the Guild Theater. The company of thirty, which toured Europe last spring, is accompanied by a native gamelan orchestra and by several artists who supervise the collection of jeweled headdresses, garments and authentic trappings used in performance. In addition to the Balinese dances the troupe will present a group of comic sport dances from Sumatra, war dances of Papua and one of Java's most elaborate court dances.

Nimura, the Japanese dancer, and his partner Lisan Kay are now appearing in a series of performances in Honolulu. Because the war has caused them to cancel their annual European tour, they will return to the United States for a New York concert, their first in two seasons.

The Ballet Theatre announces the engagement of Anton Dolin, one of the foremost classic dancers of the day, head of the Dolin-Markova Ballet and former associate of Diaghileff. He will dance all of the principal classic roles in the forthcoming productions of the Ballet Theatre, which opens in New York in January. Mr. Dolin is also scheduled to stage a ballet to music by Raymond Scott.

The first benefit performance of the Ballet Russe this season will be given the evening of Nov. 2 under the auspices of the women's committee of the Church of the Epiphany. Mrs. Charles Howland Russell jr. heads the executive committee which has taken over the entire Metropolitan Opera House for that performance. [*New York Herald Tribune*]

December 10, 1939

Harald Kreutzberg, who was scheduled to appear in Frances Hawkin's Holiday Dance Festival, has had to cancel his engagement because the German government refused him permission to travel. The final schedule for the Hawkins' Dance Festival at the St. James Theater is as follows: American Ballet Caravan, Tuesday evening, Dec. 26; Thursday matinee, Dec. 28; Saturday matinee, Dec. 30, and Sunday evening, Dec. 31. Martha Graham and Dance Group, Wednesday evening, Dec. 27; Friday evening, Dec. 29, and Saturday evening, Dec. 30. Sai Shoki, the Korean dancer, will offer one program on Thursday evening, Dec. 28.

The Stars for Spain program, sponsored by Dorothy Parker's Spanish Children's Milk Fund, will feature Martha Graham in *Deep Song,* Maria Gambarelli in *The Javanese Porcelain* and in *Rhapsody in Blue,* Helen Tamiris in *To a Tired Business Man* and Paul Draper in several of his own specialty numbers. The event will take place tonight at Mecca Temple.

Frank Roberts (Toniea Massaquoi), descendant of King Peter of the Vai tribe in Liberia, will offer a program and teach some of the ancient Liberian ritual and folk dances at the New School for Social Research on Tuesday evening. Mr. Roberts came to the United States several years ago and has since been an active member of the Hampton Institute Creative Dance Group. Presented on the Folk Festival Council series, Mr. Roberts will present *Mamah Parah, Pagan's Prayer* and *Bride and Groom's Dance.*

When Angna Enters opens her New York season tonight at the Alvin Theater, she will present five new works: *Hurry Up It's Time, Confirmation, Women Without Men, Crackpot Americana,* and *Wiener Blut—1939.* The remainder of the program will consist of *Odalisque, Boy Cardinal, Spain, Sixteenth Century, American Ballet 1914-'16, Vienna Provincial 1910, Balletomane-Conniseur, Oh, the Pain of It!, Mme. Pompadour Solitaire 1900, End of the World, Paris, August, 1914, Grand Inquisitor, Spain, Fifteenth Century, Aphrodisiac-Green House,* and *Artist's Life.*

Madeleine Marshall will be at the piano.

The Ballet Theater, scheduled to open its first season on Jan. 4, has completed its roster of twelve choreographers with the engagement of Bronislava Nijinska and Yurek Shabelevsky. Mme. Nijinska, sister of the great Vaslav

Nijinsky and distinguished dancer and choreographer in her own right, will re-stage the eighteenth-century classic ballet, *La Fille Mal Gardée*. Shabelevsky, former leading dancer of the De Basil Ballet Russe, will choreograph and dance the leading role in *Ode to Glory*, a Polish ballet with music by Chopin. Harold Byrnes, German-American conductor, has been engaged to replace Antal Dorati. Mr. Dorati resigned in order to conduct a series of concerts in Australia.

Hanya Holm and her company will present a dance concert in New York on Jan. 7 at a theater to be announced. The program will include *Three Primitive Rhythms, Dance of Introduction, Dance of Work and Play, Tragic Exodus, Metropolitan Daily* and a new major work now in rehearsal and as yet untitled. After the engagement the company will embark upon a transcontinental tour.

The American Waltz, danced to Peter de Rose's music of the same name, has been created by Arthur Murray and will be a feature of the Television Ballet to be held at the Waldorf on Dec. 15. In this new work Mr. Murray continues his interest in participation dancing, for the American Waltz is performed in a circle with couples changing partners at the end of every sixteen measures, making for a ballroom dance that is truly social.

Jack Cole's popular Ballet Intime with Fe Alf, Eleanor King, Katherine Litz, Marguerite Sane and George Bockman, will dance at Anita Walton's annual Christmas Cocktail-dansant in the Italian Room of the Ambassador Hotel on Dec. 15. The dances to be presented will include *The Conga, A Southern Prayer Meeting* and a ballet based on a Mexican street dance.

Doris Humphrey and Charles Weidman will present their concert company in repertory at their own studio at 151 West Eighteenth Street on Dec. 28, 29 and 30. There will be a change of program each performance. On the second evening, José Limón will offer his *Mexican Suite,* a work new to local audiences.

The December meeting of the New York Society of Teachers of Dancing, Inc., will be held this morning at the Hotel Astor. Thomas Riley will demonstrate ballroom steps, Marguerite O'Neil and Franklyn Oakley will exhibit a conga, Irene Lingo Tungate will have charge of ballet, Rosetta O'Neil will direct a quadrille and Carla Petersen will demonstrate tap routines.

Argentinita, the great Spanish dancer, will pause on her transcontinental tour for two performances at the Fifty-first Street Theater on Tuesday and Wednesday evenings, Jan. 2 and 3.

Grant Code, associate editor of *The Dance Observer,* will lecture on Tuesday afternoon at the Brooklyn Academy of Music. Mr. Code will speak on "Types of Dancing" and will survey the techniques employed by contemporary dancers. His lecture will be illustrated with lantern slides.

The American Folk Group announces its next monthly "Open House" on Saturday, Dec. 16, at Studio 61, Carnegie Hall. The evening will be spent in dancing square sets, reels, running sets and European folk dances.

The Students' Dance Series at Columbia University's Mc Millin Theatre will present a matinee recital on Dec. 12. Elizabeth Waters, Louise Kloepper and Henrietta Greenhood, soloists of the Hanya Holm Group, will be the performing artists.

Still another folk-dance party will be that of the English Folk Dance and Song Society of America to take place on Dec. 15 at the Beekman Tower ballroom. This Christmas masque will include a boar's-head dance, a bergomask dance, a horn dance and other folk dances from both England and the United States. [*New York Herald Tribune*]

Ballet Russe Opens Its Season in Spirit of Gaiety and Glitter

October 28, 1939

Glitter, virtuosity and good spirits marked the opening Thursday evening of the Ballet Russe de Monte Carlo. Old favorites, including ballets and performers, were back, and a new work danced its way into the fore of the repertory.

The evening was off to a nostalgic start with the old Petipa ballet, *Le Lac des Cygnes,* a ballet which concerns itself with enchanted swans and a romantic prince. Frankly speaking, it is little more than a museum piece, but it is good to see it revived and it affords the classic dancers of the company an excellent opportunity to display the line, the cold precision and the delicate designs of their art. In such a work Markova is superb, and she is complemented by Eglevsky, who brings breath-taking virtuosity and reasonably restrained miming to his role. The corps de ballet, it is nice to report, seems to have discarded some of the solo tendencies of its members, who at last are dancing in something approaching unison.

The highlight of the evening was, of course, the new ballet *Devil's Holiday.* Frederick Ashton, the choreographer, has devised many novel movements to enhance the familiar story of the devil who toys with the lives of a young girl, her fiance and her beggar-lover. It possesses humor, pep, engaging music, gorgeous costumes and fine scenery, and it also possesses Danilova and Franklin. Danilova can make a series of simple relevés more exciting than all the vertiginous viruosity of almost any other dancer. Her sure sense of characterization and her humor would make any ballet in which she participated worth seeing. The American [*sic*] Frederick Franklin is by no means

45

lacking in technical skill, and aside from that fact, he exerts a robustness and an healthy athleticism that are gratifying to behold in a male ballet dancer. If *Devil's Holiday* contained spots that were loosely knit and lacking in punch, they were amply atoned for by the sprightliness and laugh-provoking qualities of the ballet as a whole.

The evening was brought to a rousing close by the can-can girls of *Gaîté Parisienne*. The theme of this ballet is that everyone can have a good time no matter what his position in economic life. And everyone in the audience must certainly have a good time watching the antics of Massine as the provincial Peruvian set down amid a bevy of beautiful girls, madcap waiters and pleasure-seeking officers. Massine, Delarova, Slavenska and Franklin dance their stellar roles with zest, but the ballet is primarily designed for ensemble dancing and this results in the concerted efforts of the entire company to project the spirit of gay living, which they most certainly do.

It was a gala evening in the theater that the Ballet Russe accorded to its enthusiastic audience of capacity size. Brilliant decor, the pleasing music of Efrem Kurtz and his orchestra and the varied dramatic episodes of the ballets shared honors with the actual dancing, which was first rate. One could ask little more of a theatrical event, and minor bits of adverse criticism would most certainly be out of place on such a festive occasion. [*New York Herald Tribune*]

October 30, 1939

Massine's fifth effort in the symphonic ballet form discloses this great choreographer at his best. Although his previous symphonic ballets were meritorious, they nevertheless were somewhat experimental, and one found in them a sometimes awkward fusion of the classic ballet with the technique of the modern dance. Some of the episodes in these earlier works were representational and others were abstract. But in the Shostakovitch *Rouge et Noir* Massine has triumphantly overcome most of these difficulties. The technique is always that of the pure ballet, and the precision, the clarity of line and the crispness of this highly stylized technique is admirably suited to the parallel qualities of the music.

The theme of the ballet deals with the struggle of man to beat the brutal forces of life. This rather complex situation is treated quite abstractly, and the beholder is never subjected to realistic pictures of a man struggling against a symbol of Fascism, the personification of poverty or the wages of sin. In fact, the form of this symphonic ballet is so coldly abstract that it resolves itself into a study of design, a brilliant kaleidoscope that fascinates the eye with a progression of highly colored patterns. The decor of Matisse afforded a superb background for the dancers and aided immeasurably in projecting the clean-cut outlines of solo and ensemble designs.

The corps de ballet, it is gratifying to report, danced with accuracy and verve. In the solo parts, Markova, Platoff, Franklin and Guérard reflected in their dancing the briskness, the clarity and the rich texture of the music. *Rouge et Noir* is a work that one would like to see several times, for the scope of its movements is so broad and so varied that one would be certain to find something new and stimulating each time that it is on view. [*New York Herald Tribune*]

November 13, 1939

An applauding, cheering audience bestowed its audible approval upon Marc Platoff and Richard Rodgers last night at the Metropolitan Opera House. The occasion was the world premiere of *Ghost Town,* a new production by the Ballet Russe de Monte Carlo, which saw the debut of the American Marc Platoff as choreographer and the debut of Richard Rodgers as a composer for the ballet. As far as the audience as a whole was concerned, *Ghost Town* was a great success and quite understandably so. The Rodgers score found the composer at his melodic and rhythmic best, with at least two hit tunes just waiting for some one to write the words. The settings and costumes of Raoul Pène du Bois were smart and colorful, the dancing was lively and Slavenska was beautiful.

All of the aforementioned items are just dandy, but they don't necessarily constitute a ballet that is worthy of a place in the repertoire of the Ballet Russe. I would like to be able to praise a new American choreographer on his first valiant effort, but the best I can do is to say that *Ghost Town,* choreographically and musically, could be condensed into a good musical comedy number. The Platoff work fails to depict a great and lusty era out of the American past when men were tough and women tougher, when strength and sweat were necessary for survival and when humor and tragedy followed the path of the fabulous glitter of gold. *Ghost Town* should and could have been this instead of a hero and heroine, a hit tune and a vaudeville miners' dance.

There was little design to *Ghost Town* and the transitional passages were decidedly gusty. Although the dancers were lively, they were just ballet dancers in different costumes, and characterizations, either in movement or in pantomime, failed to materialize. *Ghost Town* will probably be a theatrical success, but it is to be hoped that Marc Platoff's next choreographic venture will find this young man offering us a work that captures the robust spirit of the America he is trying to portray. [*New York Herald Tribune*]

Angna Enters Dances

November 17, 1939

"Hoop Skirt-Crescent Moon-Interpretive-Abstract-Machine-Modern-Primitive-
American Indian-Muscular Thinking-Kinesthetic Dance in Empty Space. . . .
It seemed to me that this Pure Dance had been permitted to get away with
esthetic murder long enough." Although she makes this attack in her book,
First Person Plural, Angna Enters is by no means anti-dance. She is anti-fake
and pro-theater.

Is she a dancer? Is she an actress? There seems to be some confusion
about it all. Because she communicates her ideas to an audience in terms of
rhythmic, patterned, mimetic movements, I call her a dancer. The stumbling
block seems to be that she has no halo-ed technique; that, in many dance
quarters, is heresy, and the artist who makes use of more than one technique
is subsequently ostracized from the select company of the pure dancers.

Enters does not take a theatrical idea and drape it over a standard technique. She finds that each idea calls for its own technique, its own style, its
own manner of presentation. Imagine the decadent, restless *Boy Cardinal* and
the serene, compassionate *Queen of Heaven* couched in the same style and
projected with the same iron-bound technical facilities! This does not necessarily mean that Enters is right and other dancers are wrong. She draws her
themes from many characters and many periods. Other American dancers dispense with character and period and find that one technique is sufficient to
communicate to the audience their ideas on contemporary activities. There
are still other dancers who fall into neither category. Not any one of them
has a corner on the dance, but together they constitute the dance.

Although she indorses no specific technique nor employs a single style
Angna Enters frequently makes use of a distinctive form. It is rather like the
form of the Japanese Hokku, a poem that often holds within its brevity the
seed of an entire novel. The Hokku resembles a magic flashlight that illumin-
ates for an instant the heart of a man, the tip of a mountain, the dress of a
woman. From that flash we know the secret autobiography of the man; we
can visualize the slopes that lie below and the sky that is above the mountain
top; we know the nationality, the era and the social caste of the woman.

Enters is like the flash of the Hokku. Her *Boy Cardinal* is neither an
historical character nor a dance biography of a dissolute priest. The arrogant
walk, the brilliant red of the costume, the sideward glance of the eyes, the
insinuating chatter of the castanets suggest to the imagination the lavish guadi-
ness of the Renaissance, when lust and evil headed a culture of synthetic
grandeur. There is the *Grand Inquisitor,* whose sacerdotal torture of a heretic
reveals the wholesale sadism of the medieval Spanish Church. It is more than

an isolated episode. It is the trade mark of a horrible activity that saw the proud and free Aztec and Inca emperors murdered, thinking men mutilated and destroyed in the name of a Christian Church.

Enters is theater. She makes equal use of costuming, lighting, movement and drama united in exciting dance. The diversity of her dance characterizations make for popularity, but she doesn't give the audience a series of sure-fire hits. She gives her followers comedy for them to laugh at, romance to warm them, melodrama to excite them. But she also gives them unpleasant truths because they are an indivisible part of the life she so honestly reflects in her art.

When she takes the cudgel of satire in hand she uses it with telling effect. She left a goodly portion of the British Empire black and blue with her *London Bridge Is Falling Down,* she gave a pettish slap to the effiminate ballet hanger-on in *Balletomane-Connoisseur* and she literally (with angles) thumbed her nose at fake modern art in *Oh, the Pain of It!* In all these works she proves her point not through viciousness, but through ridicule. In *Totalitarian Hero* and in one or two other works it seems to me she loses her temper and the dances become ranting or sarcastic rather than critical or satirical. But Enters at her frequent best is a splendid dance artist and one of the great women in the American theater. [*New York Herald Tribune*]

November 11, 1939

When Angna Enters holds her theatrical mirror up to life, it reflects everything from a pipe-chewin' gun-totin' mountain woman to a leering Boy Cardinal of the Renaissance. Some of her reflections are not pretty sights to see, some of them will have you in gales of laughter and all of them will teach you something of the foibles of man.

Most of last night's program at the Alvin Theater was familiar. There was the provincial lady of 1910 Vienna, with her exactitude in dress and etiquette and fun. There was *Mme. Pompadour-Solitaire 1900,* which Miss Enters has spoken of as a "strip-tease in reverse." She showed us the decadence and the arrogant beauty of the Borgia era through the actions of one character—the sneering, sensual *Boy Cardinal* with his scarlet robes and provocative castanets. In *Balletomane-Connoisseur* (subtitled *Riviera Stay Way From My Door*) she brutally satirized the worst in ballet, that effeminate lad whose life is one prolonged ballet position and who will do *Prince Igor, Spectre de la Rose* or *Afternoon of a Faun* at the slightest urging.

Oh, the Pain of It! remains one of my favorites. It could be seen as a satire on the worst aspects of the modern dance, or one could view it as a ham actress with acute laryngitis, carrying on in noble fashion with gestures.

In any event, it satirizes fake modernity in any art. It is cruel, and it is hilariously funny.

In her new works, Miss Enters is pretty much concerned with the sad state of the world. The age-old story of persecution returns in new guise in *Wiener-Blut Vienna 1939*. It is a deeply touching episode in which the tragic, wistful qualities of the character are beautifully drawn by Miss Enters. *End of a World* is one of the most depressing things I have ever seen. It unfolds the story of a normal girl from the time of her confirmation, through adolescence and unthinking youth to a broken, neurotic war-widow with nothing but a shattered life left to her.

In *Crackpot Americana,* Miss Enters gives a resounding wallop to the fake sentiment of gray-haired mother at her work, at her prayers and nursing a geranium; she laughs at the hyper-folk character of the mountaineer lady with pipe, gun and poke-bonnet; she garbs herself as a Ku-Klux Klanner and salutes the flag with one hand while wielding a whip with the other. It was a good idea; but most of it lacked the Enters skill. It was too obvious, too formless and much too ill-humored.

The rest of Miss Enters's program consisted of *American Ballet 1914–'16, Grand Inquisitor, Spain Fifteenth Century, Aphrodisiac-Green Hour, Odalisque* and *Artist's Life.* Madeleine Marshall was at the piano. The next program in the Theater of Angna Enters will take place on Sunday evening, Dec. 17, at the same theater. [*New York Herald Tribune*]

The American Dance

November 19, 1939

This column has bandied about the term "American Dance" quite frequently of late. It's a nice sounding term that implies all sorts of patriotic and stirring things, but just what does it mean? What is the American dance? Why should any one care whether the dance that is prevalent in this country is American or Tasmanian? First of all, there is the matter of national pride. For years America was considered the stronghold of barbarism, a nation that could afford to buy art, but which could not produce art itself.

During this era the art of the dance was brought to us by Fanny Elssler and later by the Russian Ballets. These imported attractions convinced us that they were the dance and that home talent was negligible. If an American girl had dance ambitions, her biggest chance for success would be to assume the name of Olga Trebinskaya—a name like that could do anything and get away with it.

50

Two American girls, however, kicked over the Russian ballet conventions, and not only put America on the dance map but also changed the history of the dance. Although she made her success in Europe, Isadora Duncan was a real American, and in her we can see one of the characteristics that marks the American artist—the pioneering spirit. She gave the ogre of custom a resounding wallop and danced to the symphonies of the great masters, discarded the traditional apparel of dancers, stuck her tongue out at the accepted technique of the ballet and danced her individual way into the hearts and the esteem of the world's art lovers.

Sharing the seat of genius with Duncan was Ruth St. Denis, a New Jersey girl, who danced the great religious rituals of the Orient, shocked society with her bare feet and nude stomach, developed the possibilities of theatrical lighting and fought and is still fighting for the union of religion and dance. She and her distinguished husband, Ted Shawn, were not answerable to patrons; they earned their own way and they made their dance a worthy and necessary commodity that was decidedly worth buying. With the American leaning toward business-like organization, they formed and developed their great Denishawn School. With the American quality of freedom in mind, they offered not one technique of dance, but rather all the available forms of dance that their pupils could possibly desire.

Shawn became and remains a dancer who makes use of American themes, who has successfully pioneered for men's place in the dance and who can combine artistry and showmanship so cannily that his dances are understandable and stimulating to an audience of mine workers as well as to the highly sophisticated audience of New York.

Doris Humphrey, Martha Graham and Charles Weidman have carried on the pioneering spirit. They have probed into the possibilities of the abstract dance. They took a fling at social and political comment. They faced popular misunderstanding because of the starkness of their technique and because of the many highly unattractive audiences which their political choreographies drew, and they have won for themselves an esteemed position in the theater of dance.

It seems to me that only in America could there be found two such dissimilar young dancers as Anna Sokolow and Miriam Winslow. Miss Sokolow, armed with strength, irony and fire, dances the sorrows, the oppressions, the hates, of mankind, while Miss Winslow brings graciousness, reserve and refinement to her many and varied dances. They are both splendid young artists, and one is no more American than the other. It is their individual differences and the still further differences of their dancing colleagues that make for the rich and varied dance that is strictly American in character.

Our American dance is as eclectic as the activities of the American people. It is not limited to one technique, one form or one message. It is nourished by the contributions of the Negro, the American Indian, the Oriental, the ballet, the African savage, the European folk dancer. These constitute the rightful dance heritage of every dancer and they are to be used as he sees fit. In theory these dance aliments are foreign, but when they are spiced with pep, satire, athleticism, unrestrained humor, romance and robustness they can be served up as a theatrical dish that is as ever-different as our much maligned American hash. Such a comparison may appear insulting, but I think not. We don't want a creampuff sort of dance; we want a dance that has substance, nutriment and variety, as well as tastiness, and these are the attributes of the American dance. [*New York Herald Tribune*]

The Religious Dance

December 24, 1939

"America dancing will produce a dancing church." When Ruth St. Denis spoke these words, she gave the clue to her entire career. At the turn of the century when her interpretations were regarded by many as sensation, she was a religious dancer, but because her profound beliefs were shrouded in the mysticism of the Orient, they were lost to the general public or else marked "pagan."

For the last decade, St. Denis has worked to develop a Christian dance. This move lost her the position of the world's leading theatrical dancer, marked her as a has-been and suggested that she was slightly queer. In 1935 when she danced in a New York church, a member of the congregation who absented himself from the service wrote, "A distinct attack against the purity of the church." And St. Denis replied, "We do not abandon human speech, although songs are sung and speeches made that are obscene. In a word, the human voice is neither moral or immoral. It is a neutral instrument of expression, and I claim the same thing for the rhythm of the human body." The words of a person that was slightly queer? I think not.

Ruth St. Denis is not a revolutionary. She is a crusader for progress, progress based upon the firm foundation of the past. Not only did primitive people dance before their gods, but the highly cultured Hindu faith worships Shiva, the dancing god, whose movements represent the perfect rhythm, the perfect motion and the perfect pattern of all things. In our own Bible we read of David dancing before the Ark, and we find "Praise Him with timbrel and dances," "We have piped unto you and ye have not danced," and many other references to dancing. In a Gnostic hymn of the second century called the "Acts of John," Christ says, "Whosoever danceth not knoweth not the way of life."

When a religion is not aenemic intellectualizing, it employs the dance, for in dancing men unite in harmony, they praise their God not with word or song but with every fiber of their bodies, they experience beauty and ecstasy, and they participate in an activity that is on a higher plane than the activities of daily living.

Just what the future religious dance in America will be, Ruth St. Denis does not know. She recognizes the fact that the peoples of the West constitute a motor race, that they seek to control and subdue everything around them. She knows that the peoples of the East are a meditative race and that they seek to intuitively understand and harmonize with nature. Because America is between the Occident and the Orient, St. Denis feels that the American religious dance will contain some of the static beauty of the Orient and some of the activity of the Occident.

I am inclined to think that the religious dance in America will not be highly ritualized. Take an agricultural community, for example. Farmers would not be satisfied with an esoteric church service. They would expect to see in the dancers the same strength and freshness and spaciousness they see in their daily lives, for a religious dance should be a sublimation of our way of living, a spur to our personal progress.

When Ruth St. Denis presented her Masque of Mary at Calvary Church last week, she seemed to sweep away the obscuring dust of centuries. Mary was no longer a Biblical figure or a word spoken by a minister, she was a living, vibrant symbol of good and compassion and beauty. Through the magic of her artistry, St. Denis made the Christmas story not a fable but an actuality, not of the past but of the present. For when art and religion are united, the creative artist takes the eternal truths of religion and communicates them to the beholder in a dance that is as fresh and as alive as the body of the dancer himself.

I hope that one day every American will be able to dance his faith, whatever it may be. At the expense of being branded a mystic (which is inconceivable in a Connecticut Yankee), I would like to say that those who participate in the rhythm, the pattern, the movement and the beauty of the dance must certainly feel themselves a part of the unseen power that controls the stars in their courses, the endless surge of the waves, the wonder of birth and growth and death. This religious dance is not the superficial symbol of an archaic creed; it is the outward manifestation of man's faith in himself, in his fellows and in his progress. Because for more than thirty years she has fought to attain such a goal, I want to pay tribute to Ruth St. Denis, the world's greatest living dancer and one of America's truly great women. [*New York Herald Tribune*]

LORETTE WILMOT LIBRARY
NAZARETH COLLEGE

Martha Graham Dances
in New Satirical Work

December 28, 1939

Martha Graham ought to be reprimanded. Last night she turned out to be the Beatrice Lillie of the dance, and she's been hiding it from us all these years. The audience at the St. James Theater was quick to appreciate this heretofore dormant genius and rewarded her with bursts of laughter, much applause, bravos and curtain calls.

This second attraction on the Holiday Dance Festival highlighted the new Graham work, *Every Soul Is a Circus,* and it is safe to say that it is by far her greatest contribution to the theatrical dance. It is derived from Vachel Lindsey's "Every soul is a circus, every mind is a tent, every heart is a sawdust ring where the circling race is spent." It is a magnificently constructed work in the use of design, character-drawing movement, variety, rhythm, satire and broad humor. In it Miss Graham dances the Empress of the Arena, who has all sorts of ambitious plans in mind but who is thwarted in the midst of carrying them out by the ringmaster, who carries her out instead. She accomplishes the most active lolling on a couch that I have ever seen; she executes the terrific leg extension for which she is famous by using a bright-red rag as a sort of cloth crane, and her courting of a young man is broken up by the ringmaster, who carts her away from the scene of her nabbing.

Every Soul Is a Circus is a hilarious satire on the circus of life. The tritest gestures and actions of the stage, of the art world and of daily living come in for lusty lampooning, and Miss Graham's theatrical mirror reflects us as a pretty silly bunch of mortals, but she makes us like it. The entire cast of dancers was excellent, but it was Martha Graham who was Empress of the Arena and Empress of Hilarity.

The remainder of the program consisted of Miss Graham's great solo, *Frontier* and the major group work, *American Document.* The less said about *Columbiad,* the new solo, the better. To state that it is obscure in meaning, unhitched in construction, and accompanied by ear-torturing music is putting it politely, and I prefer to remember my great enjoyment of *Every Soul Is a Circus.* Louis Horst was the musical director of the evening and the composer of *Columbiad.* For *Every Soul Is a Circus,* Paul Nordoff composed the music, Edythe Gilfond designed the costumes and the setting was by Philip Stapp. [*New York Herald Tribune*]

54

The Ballet Theatre

December 31, 1939

"The organization is strictly American. What it offers is a perpetual and dynamically growing dance theater which is, in a sense, an 'art gallery' of all the great works of ballet, from the earliest extant to the newest and most modern." When the Ballet Theatre makes its world premiere at Radio City's Center Theater on Jan. 11, the public will discover what truth there is in this ambitious statement.

Before I become enmeshed in explanations of what qualities are strictly American, it would be a good idea to discuss the "art gallery" possibilities of the Ballet Theatre. It will be a gallery in every sense of the word, a gallery directed by the old choreographic masters Fokine, Bolm and Mordkin; the younger element will be headed by de Mille, Shabelevski, Loring, Dolin, Howard and Tudor; add Gavrilov, Nijinska and Fernandez to the roster and you have quite a board of directors.

Scenery and costumes will cross the periods from Bakst to Soudeikine, Simonson, Sakhnoffsky and Tack, and Chopin and Schubert will share musical honors with Raymond Scott and Henry Brant. As for the ballets themselves, they will start with the antique *La Fille Mal Gardée*, the oldest ballet in any repertory, and wind up with William Saroyan's *Great American Goof*, which will employ the spoken word as well as music and dance.

I especially anticipate the production of Fokine's *Les Sylphides* and *Carnaval* under the master's personal direction; Agnes de Mille's all-Negro ballet, *The Creation of the World* and Nijinska's version of *La Fille Mal Gardée*.

But of all the works in the repertory of the Ballet Theatre, I am most curious about *The Great American Goof* and *Ode to Glory*. In the former work, Eugene Loring is doing his best to fuse dialogue, movement and music into a dramatic theater piece, a rich synthesis of three great arts. *Ode to Glory* will introduce Yurek Shabelevski as a choreographer, and his ballet will deal with a man, a woman and their fight to protect their homeland. Although the theme of the work derives from Shabelevski's personal sorrow for the cruel fate of his native Poland, *Ode to Glory* is universal in its treatment, for it represents no one nation but rather any oppressed race that fights for its freedom. Shabelevski is one of the most brilliant dancers I have ever had the good fortune to see. His technique is clean and sure, his movements are virile and dramatic, his character delineations are supreme in the field of ballet. If these personal qualities emerge in his choreography, *Ode to Glory* should be one of the smash hits of the dance season.

Now for the "strictly American" aspects of the Ballet Theatre. A release states: "It is the ballet stepping out from the red plush, gilt and palm, and making its bow in a new dress." To my way of thinking, it had better step out of a few other things, too. Simply calling an organization "American" does not necessarily make it so, and some bad habits of the European ballet system must be discarded before an American ballet can exist. Perhaps the Ballet Theatre has anticipated all the warnings I am about to make and has corrected them. I hope so, but I'm going to issue them anyhow.

The custom which demands that male dancers toss themselves with a flick of the wrist into the wings may have been extremely alluring in the days of the French court, but it doesn't go in America. Jump off, walk off, stamp off, stumble off, but don't try to look like the queen of the fairies in pursuit of a naughty moonbeam! Grace and masculinity may easily be combined. Look at the basketball players, the athletes at a track meet and learn from them. The first step in the Americanization of the ballet is to leave effeminate affectation behind, and to match the virility of the American athlete.

An American ballet organization must necessarily project those characteristics that seem to be identified with the people of this land. They would consist of good healthy athleticism, pep, broad humor and smart satire. If it hasn't already done so this mammoth Ballet Theatre would do well to take a cue from the American Ballet Caravan, for the Caravan possesses these qualities to an enviable degree and has achieved a truly American ballet.

The Ballet Theatre is out to do a big job. Its members have engaged the great Center Theater and they are going to stay in it as long as possible. After that a tour is planned. Then will come the foundation of a ballet school, rehearsals, further productions, until they have proved that the dance knows a great deal about the art of entertainment, and, along with other far-sighted dance groups, convince the public that the dance has the right to share honors with the best in theater. [*New York Herald Tribune*]

56

First radio interview. With David Lichine, star of the Ballet Russe de Monte Carlo, on New York City's own station, WNYC, 1939.

Publicity portrait for first book, *Invitation to Dance,* 1941.

Donald Saddler, Miriam Golden, Maria Karnilova, Virginia Wilcox (all of Ballet Theatre), Walter Terry at Jacob's Pillow, 1941.

Walter Terry with ballet-Broadway musicals-movie star, Vera Zorina, and Ballet Theatre's premier danseur, Anton Dolin, at a "Bundles for Britain" World War II fund-raising exhibit, 1942.

With Charles Tate (of Irving Berlin's *This is the Army*). Walter Terry (right), Helwan, Egypt, 1944.

M/Sgt. Terry as principal dancer in a British production of the American operetta *Rose Marie*. Photo taken during performance, Royal Opera House, Cairo, Egypt, 1944.

Walter Terry rehearses for American Indian dance in English production of *Rose Marie* (American operetta). Royal Opera House, Cairo, Egypt, 1944.

Alicia Markova, in costume for *La Sylphide,* with Walter Terry, 1941. Photo: Dwight Godwin.

Great Ballet, Glorious Ballerinas, Grand Graham

Ballet Theatre's premiere season • Florence Rogge's creations at Radio City Music Hall • The Negro dances • Dance at the World's Fair • A survey of dance in American colleges • El Penitente and Letter to the World created by Martha Graham at Bennington • Catherine Littlefield creates ballet on ice • An appreciation of the great Alexandra Danilova • Alicia Markova in Giselle with the Ballet Russe de Monte Carlo • de Basil's Original Ballet Russe presents Aurora's Wedding, Coq d'Or, Petrouchka, Firebird, Carnaval, Spectre de la Rose, Paganini, Protée, Les Cent Baisers, and the premiere of Lichine's Graduation Ball • Jack Cole at the Rainbow Room • The dances in Disney's Fantasia • A look at America's "moderns"

Ballet Theatre in Premiere at Center Theater

January 12, 1940

The Ballet Theatre is a new theater baby, and a lusty one. The world premiere of this organization last night at the Center Theater disclosed a large ensemble of excellent dancers, several brilliant soloists, an enthusiastic symphony orchestra and a ballet play. Not the least of the Ballet Theatre's virtues was the fact that it broke all dance recital traditions and began on time and permitted only brief intermissions between the ballets.

The evening was off to a great start with the finest performance of Fokine's *Les Sylphides* that New York has seen in many a season. With the master himself in charge of directing it, *Les Sylphides* emerged the beautiful, breath-taking work that it has not been away from his guiding hand. The Corps de Ballet danced with verve and with such unity that the constantly shifting patterns never once lost focus. Karen Conrad walked off with first honors as one of the soloists and won a round of cheers and applause for her amazing elevation, the clarity of her entrechats and the brilliance she brought to every one of her moments on the stage. William Dollar was the single flaw in an otherwise notable performance. His dancing was just plain messy, to put it technically.

The most exciting event of the occasion was William Saroyan's bow as a writer of ballet. *The Great American Goof* told the story of a young man who wanted to change the world. He tried love. He tried poetry. He tried facts and statistics, and still the world seemed a rather sorry place. His only friend in the passing stream of humanity was an unsmiling girl. When he finally said, "I give up," she smiled. Her name was destiny. And so the Goof came to the conclusion that very little about humanity could be altered, and so he decided to start with breathing, just plain breathing, and work up from there.

The Great American Goof had choreography by Eugene Loring, music by Henry Brant, the Saroyan dialogue spoken aloud, and projected scenery by Boris Aronson. Much of this work was extremely touching, for the Goof was a likable, bewildered youth, earnest in his desire to bring facts and statistics to the half-fantastic world about him. Loring dances the title role well, and as choreographer he is responsible for many striking and stimulating moments. Heavy cutting is in order, however, for each of the episodes is too long, dissipating its dramatic force in repetitive movements. But as a whole *The Great American Goof* is an important innovation in the dance theater and should certainly open up a new field of dance composition.

The program closed with Mordkin's gay *Voices of Spring,* in which Karen Conrad again outshone her colleagues by the virtuosity and the sparkle of her dancing. Yurek Shabelvski had no opportunity to display the dance prowess for which he is famous, but the role of the Flower Girl gave Patricia Bowman a chance to show us her technical ability and her skill at amusing characterization. The ballet has the now familiar Mordkin fault of too much pantomimic mouthing, but it is a gay ballet of flirtations in Vienna and every one can have a good time watching the budding and bristling stage romances.

The Ballet Theatre may certainly look back on its premiere with glee, for a cheering audience gave every sign of thoroughly enjoying a top-notch performance of lively, exciting and technically assured dancing, with Karen Conrad as the brightest star of the evening and with William Saroyan as a new ballet pioneer. Tonight will see the premiere of Anton Dolin's version of *Giselle* and a repeat performance of Mordkin's *Voices of Spring.* [*New York Herald Tribune*]

The time is ripe to turn a critical eye upon the activities of the Ballet Thea-tre—to commend it for its contributions to the development of the ballet and to offer suggestions for the betterment of future productions. As a producing organization it merits unqualified praise, for the Ballet Theater is, in every sense of the word, a collaboration. What goes on behind the scenes may be peaceful or it may be murderous. It doesn't matter, but what does matter is that when the theater curtains part, one is faced with a smooth collaboration of solo dancing, group dancing, choreographic designs, decor, lighting and music. Collaboration goes even further. Those mysterious forces that dim the house lights and pull the curtains collaborate with the printed announce-ments, and everything commences according to schedule. The only blatant lack of collaboration has come from certain members of the audience who wait until the ballet is well under way, and then under the cover of darkness launch a vicious attack upon the already seated audience members, cowardly trampling them when they are down.

Everything about the Ballet Theatre is fresh and new. Even *Swan Lake* has lost its air of fatigue, and emerges a work of great beauty and liveliness. This is due to the splendid work of the corps de ballet, a real dance unit whose members respect the intentions of the choreographer and who dance as if they enjoyed it. But it is in this very ballet, with its lovely decor and its spirited ensemble work, that one finds a lack in the Ballet Theatre. Patricia Bowman is a splendid technician and a very gracious dancer, but she is not yet ready to bring forth the many qualities inherent in the role of the Swan Queen. It needs a Danilova, or at least a Markova, to light the role with bril-liant majesty and to make one believe, for the duration of the ballet, that the Swan Queen is really an enchanted princess. The Ballet Theatre needs a great classic ballerina to perform the great roles.

In the matter of revivals, the Ballet Theatre has been most intelligent. The aforementioned *Swan Lake, Sylphides, Carnaval, Giselle* and *La Fille Mal Gardée* are in the repertory not as museum pieces for the octogenarians in the audience, but as living masterpieces of balletic art. New settings and costumes have added surface freshness to them, and the performances of spritely and vital young dancers have brought out the intrinsic beauties of the works themselves.

New productions have highlighted the Ballet Theatre's season, and world premieres pop up every time you turn your head. Every new work cannot be a sure-fire success, and the Ballet Theatre gave us several disappointments, but even these errors were lusty and promised better things "next time." Antony Tudor's haunting and dramatic *Jardin aux Lilas,* the same choreographer's hilarious and bawdy *Judgment of Paris,* Andrée Howard's simple and beautiful

Death and the Maiden are three new works that may be recommended without qualification. *The Great American Goof* of William Saroyan and Eugene Loring proved to be a poor ballet but an exciting experiment, another attempt to synthesize dance, music and the spoken word. Agnes de Mille did her best to make *Black Ritual* a worthy vehicle for the talents of the Negro. She failed, but her attempt was honest and workmanlike. Those of us who have admired the dancing of Yurek Shabelevski were sorely disappointed in the young artist's first choreographic venture. But as poor as *Ode to Glory* was, it nevertheless showed that hard work and further experimentation with different types of movement will enable Shabelevski to create a ballet that is worthy of his essential artistry.

Andrée Howard's *Lady Into Fox* was so very good that its one big flaw almost spoiled the rest of the work. Based on the novel of David Garnett, the Howard work was a magnificently constructed dramatic ballet, with splendid ensemble dancing and exciting solo performances by Leon Danielian as the huntsman and by William Dollar as the tragic husband. The flaw was in Miss Howard's personal performance, for rarely did she give one the impression that she had assumed the characteristics of a fox. I am convinced that this could be quickly remedied if Miss Howard would discard some of the obvious balletic movements and try mimetic movements which would enable her to draw the vixen with more clarity and dramatic force.

I hope that future appearances will find the Ballet Theatre still fresh and youthful, still willing to experiment with new ballets and still giving us smart and lively versions of the beloved classics. And there must be further productions, for this organization has made a place for itself in the American theater, and with that place has come a certain responsibility. It is the duty of the Ballet Theatre to contribute constantly to the American dance renaissance and to bring to its audiences the finest that ballet has to offer. It must be organized on a lasting basis and managed in such a way that it has a working capital for new productions and booked in such a way that it is self-supporting as far as actual performances are concerned. In other words, the Ballet Theatre is much too important to fade away. It must be made enduring for the sake of the dance and for those of us who love the dance. [*New York Herald Tribune*]

Radio City Dances

March 3, 1940

Under the leadership of two tireless directors, Florence Rogge and Russell Markert, the Radio City Music Hall is in truth a dance center, giving work to a great many dancers, boasting the only permanent and resident corps de ballet in America and housing the greatest precision group in the world. The ballet purist may sneer at some of the ballet presentations. Where is the Danilova, the Markova, the Dolin? Who ever heard of creating new choreography for the familiar music of *Les Sylphides*? Nevertheless, Florence Rogge has given the public the classic ballet and she has made them love it. Old works have had to be adapted to the hugeness of the great stage and spectacle has been created to delight a "movie"-going audience, but the ballet dancers display an enviable mastery of classic technique and when it comes to precision and unity of action, they can shame any corps de ballet that I have ever seen.

The lovely, poised director of this corps de ballet was once the terror of her family. As a youngster she tried to put Theda Bara to shame with the zest of her acting, and neighbors must have been used to the sight of a young tragedienne issuing expiring gasps for an imaginary audience. No one will ever know whether Miss Rogge's early melodramatics in the living room could have led her to dramatic eminence on the stage. She displays no curiosity along that line of thought, and seems content with her non-acting fame as associate producer of stage shows at the Music Hall and director of its corps de ballet.

Forty million film fans have seen Florence Rogge's dancing girls. Perhaps these millions couldn't call off the names at the right moment, but they have thrilled to "renverses," "tour jetes," "fouettes" and the rest; they have been introduced to the brilliance, the classic line, the grace and the beautiful designs of the ballet; and those who saw the recent *Chopiniana* and the current *Harlequinade* have watched one of the most brilliant guest stars that any organization could have, Paul Haakon.

In order to retain the excellence of the corps de ballet, the youthful Florence Rogge requires stiff admission try-outs, daily rehearsals and frequent periods when the girls go back to the old ballet barre to remind themselves of the fundamental technique of their work. Thirty-two girls are constantly dancing, and a unit of ten is constantly on vacation, so that a theatrical relay race is the result. In rehearsal, Miss Rogge and her assistants tighten the ballet, clear up musical problems and see that Phyllis's face is facing the audience. Since the inception of the Music Hall seven years ago, the ballet girls have worn out ten thousand pairs of ballet slippers in order to keep fine ballet before the eyes of the public. Miss Rogge, who works harder than all her girls, has worn well, and looks as if she were still in her teens.

The ballet girls are very feminine of build and even in moments of relaxation, they seem conscious of a sense of line. But the Rockettes let their boyish builds slouch about, and they look very much like picked stars from American girls' basketball teams. To call them chorus girls is to invite physical disaster of the bloodier sort; they are Rockettes and extremely proud of it. Their benevolent boss, Russell Markert grins from ear to ear when he recalls their triumphant appearances in Paris where they won first prize at the Paris Exposition in the *Gala de la Danse*. The Rockettes themselves can grin like their boss, and although they are a precision team, their dancing possesses the same good spirits and infectious humor that one finds in Markert.

Markert is possessed of humor-filled modesty. He assures you that he was no child prodigy in dancing or in anything else. His present career is due, he will tell you, to two aspects of his anatomy which needed correction: The overweight problem and the fact that he was muscle bound. In an aura of aches he tap-danced the pounds away and he unbound his muscular system with a few well chosen acrobatic exercises. So well did he perform his health-restoring exercises, that he danced his way into professional dance jobs, and although he no longer dances in public, he is known to a great public as producer of Music Hall stage shows. It is probable that this same public envies him and his co-director, Gene Snyder, for these two young men spend every day with thirty-six engaging Rockettes.

Russell Markert requires much of his girls. They have to be able to tap, to rumba, to perform a few ballet steps, to execute military routines, to hula and in fact to do almost any kind of theatrical dancing that their ingenious director may conceive. One thing you can count on is that somewhere in their number they will form a single line and kick together. Markert told me that once, for the sake of variety, he left that important moment out of a show and was well night annihilated by Music Hall staff and the general public. Now the precision kick is to be found in all performances as a sort of trademark of the Rockettes.

Naturally, not all the Music Hall shows are good, but for the most part, Russell Markert, Florence Rogge and their colleagues see to it that their activities in the American dance are on a high plane of variety, good taste and healthy spectacle. And if you see a person in the audience who does not applaud the precision kick of the thirty-six Rockettes, you know that he is a "dratted furriner" who needs to be introduced to a fine and steadfast American tradition. [*New York Herald Tribune*]

The Negro Dances

April 28, 1940

If the elevator had dropped from the fiftieth floor of the Chanin Building to the basement you'd hardly have noticed it after a visit to *Zunguru,* for this

62

savage bit of Africa on a New York skyscraper was exciting stuff. With the help of magnificent bodies, pounding drums, demoniacal shrieks and bursts of lighting effects, *Zunguru* told a story of love and life and politics in the jungles of Africa. My Nigerian is rather shaky, so I can't vouch for the authenticity of the native dialogue, but the forceful manner in which the speeches were delivered left no doubt about their meaning. As a matter of fact, *Zunguru* was a drama of action in which every muscle seemed to play a role.

Asadata Dafora, the fifty-year-old director and leading dancer of this African wing of the world's dance, turned to his own story for the plot of his recent production, and many of the melodramatic events which occurred on the Chanin stage actually happened to Dafora. There is the youth whose mother, educated by an American missionary, wishes him to go to the land of plenty for his studies. When the yelling and storming of the tribal senate is of no avail, the witch doctor enters and finds that the omens are good for such a venture. On his return, his people are wary of his Harlem finery, but his king-father finally succumbs to the charms of a popping opera topper, and the youth is welcomed home. Then comes romance, and of course he picks a princess from another tribe, taboos are broken, rice fields are fired, the hero is almost killed, but finally peace is made and the lovers united. Then politics rears its ugly head, and the young man struggles to unite the tribes in a functional confederation.

Jungle Jitterbugs   The preceding is merely a summary of the plot, for it is the way the plot unfolds which counts. Solo, duo and chorus singing, dangerously active pantomime and the wildest dancing you ever saw were inextricably involved in the progress of the story. Dancing is an essential activity in the life of the African, and in *Zunguru* the characters danced at the slightest provocation, and such dance! I am sure the American jitterbug must have evolved from Asadata Dafora's teaching of the African dance in Europe and in this country, for the dancing of the village girls, the whirling and leaping of the warriors, the magnificent performing of Kruba the spear dancer, could show the local rhythm boys and girls what the human body can actually do. The leading dancer seemed to be able to move any of the muscles of her body at top speed and in a variety of rhythms and why she didn't throw all her bones out of joint was a mystery to me. *Zunguru* was dance and drama untouched by the softening hands of civilization. At least it seemed untouched to me, and I think its blood-tingling qualities would have convinced you that it was quite savage enough.

The American Negro Dance   But while Africa possessed a rich store of native dances and ceremonies, the Africans in America were not content to perform the dances of their remote ancestors nor did they have a dance which was both Negro and American at the same time. In past seasons we have seen the Negro dancers fettered by the technique and the stark style of the contemporary dance, so that they were neither good exponents of a modern dance nor were they good Negro dancers. In the field of entertainment the great Bill Robinson and his dancing colleagues upheld the dance genius of the race, but the art expression of the Negro dance was still stumbling.

This spring a new company of Negro dancers showed New York the beginnings of a really splendid racial dance, for Katherine Dunham turned not to the techniques and the styles of the white race, but to the folk dances, the music and the legends of her own people. As a Rockefeller and Rosenwald fellow she studies in the West Indies and in Brazil, places where the folk expressions of the transplanted Negro have been tinged with the characteristics of the Indian, French and Spanish inhabitants. As an American girl, she knew that her native dance ranged from the shuffling steps performed on the hard-packed earth surrounding the Southern cabin to the wild and slick dances of Harlem.

Tropics and Le Jazz Hot   Under the provocative title, *Tropics and Le Jazz Hot,* Katherine Dunham has offered her programs at the Windsor Theater. Boleros, rumbas, drum beats and song are all focused upon the activities of the Latin-American Negro, and we see the rich humor, the physical strength, the romanticism and the rare simplicity which mark his life. The juba, the cake-walk, the shimmy and the Harlem hoofing represent the folk expression of the North American Negro.

Now this does not sound like a dance that is profound of content, and it isn't profound, for Katherine Dunham is laying the groundwork for a great Negro dance. At present she has, through her craftsmanship, been able to transplant the social dances of her people to the stage and to make them theatrically effective. At the same time she has retained the freshness and that quality of improvisation which we find in Negro music and which we want in the Negro dance. There is a real sense of immediacy about the dancing of her company as if the performers were dancing because they felt an overpowering urge for rhythmic movement and not merely because they were scheduled to give a show. This thought is well borne out by Archie Savage, a leading dancer of the company, who has had no formal dance training, but whose improvised passages with drum accompaniment constitute some of the finest dancing that you are likely to see.

One day Katherine Dunham, or one of her colleagues, will dance the contemporary problems and the hopes of her race. She will not use exclusively the alien techniques and the styles of the white race to project these ideas, but she will use techniques and styles which have sprung from the street dancing of the Southern Negroes, the jitterbugging of the Harlemites, and which have been colored by the contributions of neighboring peoples. Lili Romero, Archie Savage, Talley Beatty and the group aid Miss Dunham in the presentation of an exciting evening of dance, but *Tropics and Le Jazz Hot,* as good as it is, is only a start, for Katherine Dunham is surely destined to develop a theater dance great enough to mirror the character and the real stature of her race. [*New York Herald Tribune*]

Fair Ballet

May 18, 1940

Popular belief to the contrary, the ballet's function is not limited to plain entertainment, for this august theater art can be brazen as well as versatile in its activities. Back in the sixteenth century that royal vixen, Catherine de Medici, produced the *Ballet Comique de la Reine,* the first ballet production on record. But rumor has it that the lavishness and glitter of this fabulous event were designed to keep the political powers amused while Catherine devoted her attention to those machinations of government which made her a notorious figure of history.

At present the ballet is serving still another function, a commercial one, for the Ford Motor Company is presenting a ballet production at its World's Fair exhibit. The Ford Ballet boasts three firsts: a full-length ballet has a commercial sponsor for the first time; a professional ballet is staged with recorded sound for the first time, and, for the first time, there is a ballet that will be performed twelve times a day for a period of six months. Although *A Thousand Times Neigh* will make its public bow today, preview performances disclosed a good show. After a long period of blatant advertising, the eighteen-minute ballet begins and a horse called Dobbin immediately wins your heart. The three scenes progress from 1903 to a farm a few years later and to a city of the present. Throughout them all Dobbin (whose prancing hooves give an engaging equine twist to ballet steps) vies with the motor car. In the ballet, at least, he comes off with first honors.

A Thousand Times Neigh is well danced by a group of young Americans who obviously know their ballet and how to execute it with zip and humor. William Dollar's choreography for the ensemble is simple and effective, and for Dobbin hilarious. Lincoln Kirstein, head of the American Ballet Caravan, directed the work; the story and lyrics are by Edward Mabley; the musical score by Tom Bennett; the costumes by Alvin Colt; the orchestra conducted by Norman Cloutier for the sound-track recording, and the entire production was designed by Walter Dorwin Teague. William Duncan built Dobbin (two male dancers are responsible for Dobbin's actions). Two and a half companies relay the twelve shows a day. *A Thousand Times Neigh* may be frankly commercial, but smart entertainment and superior ballet dancing will make you like it. [*New York Herald Tribune*]

May 26, 1940

With great gusto and sparkle, ballet has made its bow at the New York World's Fair, ballet that is easy to understand, alive with humor and marked by the movements of athletes, ballet that is truly American. The two people responsible for this are Catherine Littlefield and Lincoln Kirstein, who have already spent much time and energy on this thing we call American ballet. Miss Littlefield and her Philadelphia Ballet have long been famous for their native touch and native themes, but although Europe applauded them and dance followers in America cheered them, the paucity of local performances demonstrated the lack of popular support. Their *Barn Dance* was good ballet and good Americana, but the presence of exciting dance technique, the appearances of Nellie Bly and the city slicker were evidently not glamorous or exotic enough to enchant the general public.

Mr. Kirstein and his American Ballet Caravan evidently had the same trouble, for the valiant group produced such ballets as *Filling Station* and *Yankee Clipper* far superior in conception and execution to half the ballets of the foreign troupes, yet they failed to capture the public fancy. In theory, people wanted an American ballet, but when it came to box office a motheaten sylph with an unpronounceable name seemed to possess a mysterious allure far stronger than the robust and humorous appeal of the native product. It is taking the World's Fair to prove to the public that American ballet is different from but as fine in quality as the ballet of Europe.

Patriotic Spectacle *American Jubilee* is patriotic in theme and a spectacle in form. There could be no better way to boom the ballet than in such a production, for people at the Fair are in the mood for spectacle and the burst of patriotism is well attuned to the times. Albert Johnson has conceived this pageant on a panoramic scale, far from profound, but bright and good-natured. In charge of the dances, Catherine Littlefield has demonstrated both ingenuity and variety. The opening flag drill with her dancing girls and boys flashes the red, white and blue colors, while well trained legs flash in the movements of the ballet. Then to the music of the waltz, comes brilliant Paul Haakon to dance with clusters of girls, to soar over them in his famous leaps and to convince you (in case you had forgotten it) that the waltz is about the most beautiful dance that one can see.

With the Bicycle Routine, Miss Littlefield transplanted the problem of balance from the toe slipper to the wavering wheels. The girls cycled with the same precision found in their dancing and occasional looks of stark terror as curves were rounded only added to the charm of the occasion. The young men raced at faster speed and scrambled about their bicycles in the best Tom Mix and His Horse fashion. Standing on one pedal with the other leg raised high in the air in the famous ballet arabesque brought the proceedings away from the rodeo motif and back to dance.

Cakewalk with a Leap   Pirouettes, leaps and struts marked Haakon's second appearance with the ballet company in a cakewalk brightly costumed with Lucinda (Ballet Theatre) Ballard's smart work. This was the real American folk touch embellished for theatrical purposes and given style and precision by the technique of the ballet. The male members of the company dance like men should dance, which proves my oft-stated contention that the effeminate quality of the foreign danseur is only an affectation and not an essential part of ballet. This talented gang of young Americans put on a good show and perform excellent ballet under the leadership of Catherine Littlefield, a really important American figure.

At the Ford Exposition, the American Ballet Caravan is making history as the first ballet to have a commercial sponsor, first to be accompanied by a sound track and first to be presented twelve times a day for a period of six months. *A Thousand Times Neigh* is good stuff theatrically as well as commercially. William Dollar devised the movements for the work and his dancers unfold incidents in an American city of 1903, a farm a few years later and a city of the present.

Dobbin Does a Dégagé   The star of the ballet is Dobbin, a horse whose hooves are well acquainted with the intricacies of the entrechat, the dégagé and the glissade. As the years pass, the people change their styles and horseless carriages come and develop, but Dobbin goes merrily along. As a vehicle, he is supplanted by motors, but at Saratoga he is still supreme. This slight American episode is alive and zestful, humor is the keynote and Dobbin (animated by two pairs of masculine legs of human shape) is hilarious with his rolling eyes and balletic gait.

The World's Fair has given American ballet its chance, and Catherine Littlefield and Lincoln Kirstein are showing us what their ballet boys and girls can really do in the way of smart and swift entertainment. When the Fair closes in the fall, I hope the American ballet will not be left to hibernate in Flushing, but will have proved its theatrical worth so thoroughly that a long New York season and transcontinental tours will be the order of 1940-'41.
[*New York Herald Tribune*]

67

Collegiate Dance

June 9, 1940

You'll find the word "dance" in the catalogues of almost every major American college. And what does that word suggest to you? One person will summon memories of the exquisite and unreal Pavlowa, another will think of the strong and sometimes ferocious qualities of the modern dance, some will remember the exotic motions of an Oriental St. Denis or the unhampered sensuousness of a Duncan, others will find that the joyous physical gusto of the folk dance comes to mind. There are, also, a great many people who assume that "dance" means social dancing or, on a plane of great skill, tap.

This diversity of approach is reflected in the collegiate dance to such a degree that a plea for recognized standards of dance education would probably be tossed aside as the raving of a dance faddist. During the last few years I have frequently discussed the evils which mark the educational dance, pointing out that one college grudgingly offers the dance because of student demand, another because it is a good substitute for calisthenics and still another (and this rarely) because its directors recognize the power of the dance as a molder of character as well as a valid mode for artistic, physical and emotional expression.

Survey of the College Dance   A few months ago the Herald Tribune Dance Department sent letters to 120 American colleges and universities asking a few simple and direct questions about dance courses offered in each of the institutions. Here are the questions: (1) Is the dance a credit course in your institution? (2) What technique or techniques of dancing do you offer (ballet, Denishawn, modern, ballroom, folk, etc)? (3) Do you offer dance in the department of physical education, in the department of drama or do you accord it a department of its own? (4) Does your institution present courses in the dance because its directors believe that the dance is an essential part of good education, because students demand it or because of a combination of both? (5) What benefits do you believe your students derive from dance training? Is it aimed at preparing them for a dance career? For physical development? For better health? For cultural growth? Do you believe that the dance can be an actual influence upon the daily life of the individual, that it can help to mold his character? (6) Additional comments.

Lack of Dance Standards   Statistics may be dull, so I shall make mine as brief as possible. They should, however, tell quite a story. Only half the letters were answered, and it is natural to assume that silence meant the lack of any dance courses. However, of the sixty-six replies, only seven colleges stated that they offered no dance instruction. The remaining institutions disclosed the teaching of the following technique: Fifty-three colleges offered the modern dance, forty-seven colleges gave folk dancing, thirty-four colleges presented ballroom, thirty-two taught tap, three presented Denishawn, two offered ballet, two gave Dalcroze eurhythmics, five taught clog and several offered courses entitled "basic rhythms." All these courses overlapped, with some institutions presenting several techniques while others presented only one.

In fifty-seven of the colleges the dance came under the direction of the department of physical education, at Colorado College it was directed by the music department and at Adelphi College it boasted its own department. Benefits resulting from dance training were extremely varied. Physical development, health, cultural growth, recreation, dance appreciation and character molding all had their adherents. Some institutions stated that calisthenics could take care of physical development and health, and that cultural growth was the goal of the dance. Others snapped their professional fingers at culture and upheld the recreation aspect.

A Battle of Beliefs   Here are a few examples of diversities of opinion, not healthy variances, but completely opposed dance viewpoints. Mabel Lee, director of dance at the University of Nebraska, says: "I certainly would not say that the dance molds character. That is absurd! Just as absurd as to say that football molds character!" Lehigh University finds that the dance fosters "facility in the amenities of social intercourse." Only ballroom dancing is available there, of course. But at Connecticut College for Women Elizabeth Hartshorn, dance director, finds that the contemporary dance stimulates desire for activity, integrates the body and the mind, leads to appreciation and acquisition of beauty in human movement, increases sensitivity to environment, develops interest in the other arts as well as the dance, develops poise and self-assurance and accuracy.

It is quite true that some colleges make a specialty of dance courses, while other institutions present brief courses as electives. Mills College in California, Bennington College in Vermont and New York University are known for the breadth and scope of their dance courses, yet other distinguished universities ignore the dance completely or retire it to the recreation department. It must be confusing to the student and to the parent to know that one college president will consider the dance essential to good education and that another president will be completely indifferent to it.

This survey cannot change the face of the educational dance, but I hope in succeeding articles to arouse the interest of the college student to the point where he investigates the stature and quality of his college dance course as compared with those of other universities. I hope that dance educators and leaders will cooperate with college boards and parent organizations, explaining succinctly the potentialities of the educational dance to them and suggesting courses and teaching methods that will be of benefit to student, to the college and to the dance. [*New York Herald Tribune*]

Dance in Colleges

June 16, 1940

Many of you know and respect the dance as a great theater art and as a vehicle for healthy recreation, but I wonder how many of you actually believe that dance instruction is an essential part of good education? In this, my second article on the college dance, I want to quote from the letters received in answer to my survey of dancing in colleges. Thurston Davies, president of Colorado College, writes: "We present courses in the dance because we believe that the dance is an important field of education. We believe that a sound liberal arts curriculum should include emphasis on all fields of the liberal arts. We believe that as normal concomitants of this work, students develop physical skills and confidence in themselves. We have already seen instances in which the whole attitude and approach of the student toward living with other people has been improved."

Wellesley College, whose dance department frequently collaborates with the Theater Workshop, the art and music departments and the Dramatic Association, finds more than recreational benefits resulting from dance. Dance Director Charlotte MacEwan says, "We do believe modern dance to be one of the best means to physical development, and—by its nature as an expressive medium and its association with other arts, its encouraging of exploration of other fields, periods of history, customs, et cetera—to contribute to the cultural growth of the individual. Certainly dance may prove an excellent vehicle for character building. Specifically, it lends itself to developing initiative in exploring the possibilities of movement, in self-direction and self-criticism in the use of material, tenacity in perfecting performance, and broadening of understanding in group work."

Dance, Drama, Music and Design   At the University of Michigan, dance is not presented as an isolated activity, but is constantly in association with its sister arts. "I think the unique feature of dancing at Michigan," writes Ruth Bloomer, instructor in charge of dancing, "is our collaboration of departments in fostering the dance on this campus. The music school recommends dance

70

to its students and a special class is offered which considers their particular problems: i.e., rhythmic training, proper use of music for dance, elementary musical and percussion accompaniment and emphasis on dance composition to music. The play production department recommends dance to its students and a special course is offered them. This class contains men and women students and covers the problems of movement for the theater, dance material usable in plays, operettas and operas, experiments in dramatic movement forms and individual correction of poor co-ordination that leads to bad stage presence.

"A third department interested in the dance activities is the school of architecture and design. From time to time classes have been offered for these art students. These courses have attempted to correlate dance materials with the students' knowledge of other art forms, along with the development of dance technique as another medium of expression." At the University of North Carolina, the dance groups frequently work in collaboration with the Carolina Playmakers, and Drama Director Frederick Koch urges his young drama students to limber, co-ordinate and articulate their bodies through dance instruction.

Training of the Dance Educator   "A dance instructor must have thorough preparation in anatomy, physiology, psychology, kinesiology, education and the arts, as well as specifically in the techniques and theory of dance." So writes Violet Marshall, chairman of the department of physical education for women at the University of California at Berkeley. I wonder how many college dance instructors have such a background? Several of our leading American dancers have told me of the great harm done to dance and to education by those gymnasium instructors who, because of student demand for dance, have taken a few lessons in dance at the Bennington School of the Dance or from Ted Shawn, and have returned to their classes with a garbled mass of motor activity which tried to pass muster as educational dance. Such teaching is not fair to Bennington, to Shawn, to the dance, to students, to education or to calisthenics.

There is probably no greater dance educator and pioneer in America than Margaret H'Doubler, whose courses at the University of Wisconsin have turned forth splendid dance teachers as well as non-professional dance believers. Because she is a dance scientist as well as a teacher of an art, Miss H'Doubler has the respect of educators and the solid support of her university, which accords the dance a leading place in the curriculum. Quite simply she says: "We present courses in the dance because we believe dance is an essential part of good education and should be available to the students." This survey of the collegiate dance will continue with further articles on dancing for men, on dance courses available to students and on the creation and recognition of worthy standards in the educational dance. [*New York Herald Tribune*]

71

Dancing Athletes

June 2, 1940

The Herald Tribune's survey of the educational dance systems in colleges has disclosed a trend toward admirable dance progress. In previous articles I have had to point out the fact that there was no accepted standard of dance education, that one college president would consider dance training essential to good education and another educator would find it of negligible value. In spite of such divergencies of opinion, letters from college physical education departments have told of the growth and betterment of dance courses with college boards coming gradually to the point where they recognize the real potentialities of the educational dance.

A good proportion of the answers to the questionnaire sent out by the Herald Tribune stated that dance was considered to play a vital part in sound education. Dorothy Ainsworth, director of physical education at Smith College, writes: "It is very definitely believed that dance is an essential part of good education. In fact, were it possible in as large an institution as ours, every student would be required to take the dance. Quite aside from the obvious health and recreational value, the general social and aesthetic values are highly prized in an institution of liberal arts."

Dance and Sports   The survey has also made clear the recognition of dance in its relationship to sports and it has also showed a gratifying progress in dancing for men. From the president's office of Wheaton College, in Massachusetts, comes the following: "The college believes that modern dancing takes the place of much of the old prescribed courses in physical education and that it does their work in a much more effective and satisfying manner" . . . Dr. J. Anna Morris, director of physical education at the University of Minnesota, says: "At Minnesota we are trying to show our people how the fundamentals of rhythm apply to all movement: sports, golf, swimming, etc., walking down the street, lifting, carrying, etc. The point is, that by the proper timing and dynamics, all movement becomes more economical—therefore an approach toward greater harmony and style is made."

Dancing for Men   In the not very distant American past, dancing in schools was designed to add grace and litheness to the bodies of young ladies. This period saw the so-called "aesthetic dance" hold sway, and young girls dancing barefoot on the grass while gracefully manipulating draperies was the accepted thing. But the dance has changed from those days, and the great dance leaders of today in collaboration with doctors and physical educators have made the dance a veritable science of movement designed for the male body as well

72

as that of the female. Dance educators are still fighting the misconception that dance is feminine; slowly but surely they are seeing public approval turned upon the dance and its place in masculine education, as each season more schools and colleges offer their young men training in dance.

There is no shilly-shallying about the masculine dance at Berea College in Kentucky, and with the answers to the survey questions the department of physical education sent me an impressive illustrated program of the men's group in a "Dance Drama of Kentucky." Under the direction of Oscar Gunkler, the young men have been trained in the techniques of the contemporary dance and they have put that training to immediate use in this production of their state's history. Divided into six parts, this dance work demanded choreographic as well as performing versatility: *Dark and Bloody Ground* dealt with the era of the Red Man; *Boone and the Early Settlers* told a story of pioneering; *Slavery and the Negro, Agricultural Development, Present Situation* and *Future Development* make one think that these young dancing athletes can not only make a good dramatic production out of their traditions but that they can visualize through dance a way to meet their present and prepare for their future. How well they performed their dance drama I cannot say for I was not present, but certainly one can have nothing but admiration for the way in which these men of Berea strive to employ the power of dance.

The University of North Carolina has had dance classes for men as well as women, and so popular were these courses this last season that coaches complained to the dance instructor that he was keeping the young athletes from their track, football and other sports activities. I have talked to letter men in wrestling, track and boxing and they have told me that dance training has given them invaluable help in matters of speed, agility, balance and stamina. A short movie feature and newspaper articles have told in pictures and in words of Springfield College of Physical Education and its extensive use of dance in the training of athletes and physical educators. Next season Boston University will add to its already established courses in tap and folk dance, a course for men under the direction of Hans Wiener, teacher of modern dance techniques.

Now that America is learning that dance and sports are closely allied and that dancing is a worthy activity for men, we can be sure that the educational dance will win for itself a place of universal respect in all systems of education. If the dance becomes recognized as an exciting activity and not as a modern substitute for old-fashioned calisthenics, if its value to the athlete is stressed and if it has the participation of young male sportsmen, it cannot fail to become an indispensible part of collegiate activity. [*New York Herald Tribune*].

Academy of Dancing

July 7, 1940

Adeline Genée, one of the greatest stars in the long history of the ballet, slipped unnoticed into the country last May. Although Mme. Genée retired from active performing in 1916 at the height of her career, so great was her popularity in Europe, Australia and America that her name is still familiar to all ballet and theatergoers. Americans probably remember the Danish ballerina in such musical shows as *The Soul Kiss, The Silver Star, Bachelor Belles* and others which brought her frequently to New York from 1907 until her retirement.

Probably her greatest success was in her own program, *La Danse,* which she presented at the Metropolitan Opera House in 1912. On this occasion she re-created the styles and the characteristics of the great ballerinas who preceded her: Prevost, Camargo, Sallé, Taglioni, women who helped make ballet one of the world's most glamor-filled theater devices. Genée's retirement has consisted of hard work; from time to time she has danced for worthy causes and pioneered in television, she has studied and taught, encouraged young people to participate in dance and directed her inexhaustible energies into the building and development of a great academy of dancing.

Royal Academy of Dancing   In 1920 Mme. Genée founded the Association of Operatic Dancing of Great Britain, in 1928 Queen Mary became patroness of the organization, and in 1935 by the command of George V the title was changed to the Royal Academy of Dancing. The most interesting statistics of the academy tell of a total of 462 members in 1924 and more than 3,000 members in 1937, and the founding of branches throughout the entire British Empire.

Here is the creed of the Royal Academy of Dancing: "To improve the standards of operatic or ballet dancing and the elevation and the advancement of the art of dancing throughout Great Britain and the British Empire. (a) By accepting as members only those who are able to satisfy the committee that they have a knowledge of the correct technique of dancing. (b) By insuring that all members who are teachers continue to teach this technique correctly and in accordance with the rules laid down for this purpose. (c) By stressing the educational and physical value of dancing for young children by holding children's examinations in simple operatic and other approved forms of dancing which encourage poise, line and physical development. (d) By holding and organizing lectures and demonstrations and classes on all phases of dancing and the kindred arts, including choreography and production."

Due to the war, Adeline Genée has been unable to return to her English home. In spite of her sixty years, the great dancer is still unwilling to lead a life of leisure, and she plans to busy herself with a lecture tour of America. It seems to me that we Americans ought to learn from Genée while she is with us. If an American Academy of Dancing is a possibility (and there is a definite trend toward the creation of such an organization), I am sure that Mme. Genée would be glad to help us in the planning of such an academy. Her years of experience in the field would enable her to show us how to best employ the great talents of our St. Denis, our Shawn, our Graham, our La Meri, our Loring and their colleagues. Certainly, Genée would be of great assistance in the ballet wing of such an academy, and I know that her love of all forms of dance would enable her to make wise and fair suggestions for departments other than ballet.

I am not suggesting that Genée form and direct an American Academy of Dancing; we want Americans for that position. But I am sure that the president of Britain's Royal Academy of Dancing could give us invaluable advice, and she assured me that while she remains in America it is her one wish to contribute as much as she can to the growth of our American dance. I think we ought to accept this offer of one of the world's greatest dance artists.

An American Academy   England has worked hard to develop a native ballet. I wrote on May 9 about the Ballet Club which Marie Rambert directs and which affords student dancers and choreographers a chance to try their wings on a stage before an audience. The Royal Academy of Dancing, a non-profit-making organization, seeks to raise the educational and artistic standards of the dance. We Americans have let our lusty dance grow up without discipline, and our dancers, our audiences and our students are frequently subjected to bad direction, poor performing and inferior teaching. Perhaps some day we will have a national academy of the dance, but, until we do, I hope that those individuals who are so generous in their support of imported attractions will turn their attentions and part of their purses to the endowment of an American academy of dancing. [*New York Herald Tribune*]

Martha Graham at Bennington Festival of Arts

August 11, 1940

Bennington, Vt., Aug. 11.   The Bennington Festival of the Arts, which is to conclude Saturday evening, presented its first dance production tonight with

75

the appearance of Martha Graham and her company at the Bennington College Theater. Miss Graham offered two new dance works and also performed *Every Soul Is a Circus,* which met with great success in New York last winter.

Of the two premieres, *El Penitente* and *Letter to the World,* the former work was the one more successfully realized. Based upon the characteristics of the Penitentes, the members of that new Mexican sect who believe in purification through intense penance, *El Penitente* was conceived as a dramatic ritual in which the figures of the Penitente, Christ and Mary appeared as leading characters. The work was simple and naive, with great dramatic episodes from the Bible retold with childlike reverence by these folk performers. The flagellation of the Penitente, the seduction of the Penitente by Mary Magdalene, the Crucifixion and the other episodes were well performed by Miss Graham, Erick Hawkins and Merce Cunningham, who danced their roles with refreshing simplicity, quiet humor and sensitivity.

Letter to the World, the major offering of the evening, has a long way to travel before it becomes an important theater piece. Martha Graham has tried to fuse dance, music and spoken word into exciting drama, and in spite of the lovely lines from Emily Dickinson, the beautiful costumes and background by Arch Lauterer and many measures of effective music by Hunter Johnson, *Letter to the World* is an over-long and under-dramatic story of a moody woman. Margaret Meredith spoke the lines of the main character and Martha Graham danced the secret emotions of this character. This should have been dramatically exciting (but it wasn't), for the speaking lady possessed the demeanor and the reserve of a well bred lady of New England, while her hidden self was reflected by a dancing character who disclosed the secret yearnings, the heightened phobias and the deep passions which good breeding and inhibitions kept below the surface.

This business of drawing together the arts of music, dance and drama into a single theater piece is not an easy task, and although *Letter to the World* is not a good theater piece, I feel that very intensive revision might turn the trick. More variations in tempo, a closer contact between the character of the living lady and the character of her imagined self, emotions projected with greater force and clarity, and discarding of movements that have not a definite reason for being used would certainly improve the work tremendously.

It was a pleasure to see again *Every Soul Is a Circus.* This rich and meaty satire of the frustrated woman who wants to "do a star turn" once in her life is as hilarious as ever, with Miss Graham being thwarted in all her attempts at becoming the center of the stage. Since it was last presented in New York, the work has been improved. The group sequences are briefer and have a closer bearing to the actions of the main characters, Miss Graham has pointed up the innumerable humorous gestures which make her role so funny and she has also high-lighted those few moments which show us that this

76

ridiculous woman is really a tragic figure because of her inability to achieve anything from her life and her seemingly inability to know what things of life are worth achieving.

Louis Horst was responsible for the fine score of *El Penitente* and for the direction of the evening's music. Merce Cunningham and Nelle Fisher danced well in small roles. Erick Hawkins should learn that facial mobility is necessary to a dancer and that his set expression makes him look not quite bright. Martha Graham, of course, was brilliant of technique and vivid of person, and one could have wished that she had been more successful as choreographer—at least as far as *Letter to the World* was concerned. [*New York Herald Tribune*]

Ballet on Ice

October 6, 1940

Swan Lake is about to freeze over, and the swans themselves are getting ready for it. The old Tchaikovsky favorite has long given sanctuary to swan maidens and their queen, but Catherine Littlefield has taken away their toe slippers and put them on skates. If any one has a right to surprise swan lassies with a change of climate, that one is Catherine Littlefield, for Miss Littlefield is a classic ballerina in her own right, she has directed her own companies in successful appearances here and abroad, she put dancers on bicycles in *American Jubilee* and she is a choreographer of recognized ability. Now she is trying to unite spread eagles with arabesques in *It Happens on Ice,* the new extravaganza coming to the Center Theater on the tenth of this month.

Fairly quivering with ideas on the possibilities of ballet on skates, Miss Littlefield dashed into her first rehearsal and threw most of her young athletes on their faces with the intricacies of her skating steps. Soon she discovered that skates have a double edge and that an attractive arm movement could throw the skaters balance from one edge to the other so suddenly that disaster was the only possible result. A little study cleared up matters, and before long she had her skaters conscious of ballet line, group composition, able to adapt their spins into ballet turns, their jumps into long ballet leaps. Until he came under the Littlefield direction, one young man had supposed that music was only to keep the audience's ears busy, but he soon learned that ballet on skates meant that music and motion were destined to pay close attention to each other.

Littlefield Directs   At rehearsal the other day I saw some of the new works. Little, blonde Catherine Littlefield kept warm with coat, mittens, a blanket and coffee while she shouted directions to her skaters. There was *Swan Lake,* with its swan maidens, its queen, its prince, its hunters and the evil magician. Hedy Stenuf, the "prima skaterina" for the company, glided, soared and swirled in breathtaking fashion, while Gene Berg, as the magician, pursued her more fleetly than man ever pursued fair lady. These two dancing skaters, along with Skippy Baxter as the prince, are certain to win stellar positions for themselves in the great field of ballet.

Before anti-classicists get worried, I want to assure them that Littlefield has more tricks up her sleeve. A ballroom polonaise replete with elegance, etiquette and elan is on the schedule, and a Currier & Ives glimpse of a day on the old skating pond is in production. This latter work is a gentle but hilarious satire on the naughty boys who trip every one up, the bevies of girls being taught to skate by patient swains, the governess and her elite charges, the young lovers and the show-off skater who builds up to near-decipherable figure eight to the tune of ardent applause. A jazz number, *So What Goes,* splices its pep with all the appurtenances of love: a huge ring, a rose, angels, the lovers' knot and the necessary lovers. A swing ballet and an iced version of a Negro spiritual will complete the Littlefield contributions.

I have always maintained that the American dance should and must partake of athleticism, for the simple reason that a nation's dance should honestly reflect the character of its people, and Americans are decidedly sports minded. Great dancers have contributed richly to this union of sports with dance, but here at last is an actual fusion of the two, for ballet on ice possesses the rhythm, the patterns, the drama and the characterizations of dance while it partakes of the skill, the speed and the muscular prowess of the sport of skating.

American Style Rehearsal   The character of the rehearsal was typically American. No foreign yells, no posturing in front of mirrors marked the proceedings. Miss Littlefield issued terse, vernacular commands in a loud, firm voice. The skaters called her Catherine, the boys winked as they sailed by, but Miss Littlefield was boss, and the skaters snapped to attention when a reprimand was launched at them. The girls and boys have quickly learned the group spirit necessary to good sports of good dancing, and the men have managed to assume the grace of ballet without submitting to the effeminate gestures which curse so many males in the ballet.

It Happens on Ice should do several things for the American theater. It should help to carry those who profess disinterest in dance over the hurdle which separates athletics from dancing. It should influence American dancers who have failed to see the tie between dance and sports. It should, of course, open up a new field of entertainment, for the possibilities of ballets on skates are limitless. For the sake of upholding the supremacy of dance, I would like to mention in passing that skate dancing does possess certain limitations in the matter of movement: small gestures, subtle mime and slow movements are practically out, detracting somewhat from the range and diversity of expression. But take skating, dancing or theater entertainment in any form of motion as your criterion, and you will be convinced, I think, that Catherine Littlefield is becoming a theater figure of the first rank, a girl who is leaving her mark in the revue, in the ballet and on ice. [*New York Herald Tribune*]

Alexandra Danilova

October 13, 1940

Wit, technical skill and consummate artistry have united to make Alexandra Danilova one of the great ballerinas of all time. She is a dancer's dancer, for the fine points of her technical equipment never fail to evoke sighs of satisfaction from those who recognize the flawless line of her body, the brilliance of her batterie, the phrasing of her movement sequences and her perfect reflection in motion of the qualities inherent in the music to which she is dancing. But Danilova is also an audience favorite, for she boasts that intangible essence known as sparkle. I am not an authority on personality vibrations, yet I can assure you that Danilova's personality fairly bounds over the footlights so that you laugh as she bats her eyelashes in *Igrouchki,* you fall under the spell of romance as she dances the lovely waltz from *Gaîté Parisienne* and you find yourself believing in magic as she dances the role of the enchanted Queen of the Swans in *Swan Lake.*

Alexandra Danilova is not the highly bred result of a string of ballerina-premier danseur forebears. She was born in Russia of a military family and even at the age of five (when most geniuses are prepared for the launching), the word "ballet" held neither meaning nor interest for her. One Christmas, however, at a public school she was asked to be a butterfly for the annual party. As she puts it, "I jomp around successfully and I enjoy so much jomping that my aunt tell me to be a ballerina." Theatrical school followed, and with the end of the war, poverty. According to Danilova, she and her schoolmates owe their lives to Herbert Hoover and his organization, for starvation seemed inevitable until the American organization came to the rescue of the school children.

Danilova, Balanchine, Geva   Along with George Balanchine and Tamara Geva, the young dancer left Russia for Germany, where she spent much of her time eating huge meals and dancing frequently to pay for them. The trio gave successful summer concerts in Germany, made a quick trip to America in 1924 and returned to Europe in 1925 where Danilova joined the famed Russian company of Serge Diaghileff. Under the direction of this fabulous figure in the world of ballet, Danilova moved out of the corps and into solo roles where she remained until Diaghileff's death in 1929. The 1930's saw her intrenched in the affections of American audiences both with Col. de Basil and later with Massine's group.

This season New Yorkers will see Danilova in the leading role in *Vienna—1814,* as a milkmaid in *The New Yorker* and in *Poker Game,* as well as in the roles she has made famous. Watching her, one is never conscious of technique alone. Each of her characters is superbly drawn: in the story of *Baiser de la Fée* she greets you with the warmth and simplicity of young womanhood; in *Coppelia* she introduces you to a mischievous lass with a quick temper and a large store of devilty; she exudes come-hither technique in *Gaîté Parisienne,* and in *Swan Lake* you see her as the epitome of feminine beauty and elegance. Because this is the greatest season of ballet that New York has ever seen, I have taken this opportunity to salute Alexandra Danilova, whose great artistry has contributed immeasurably to the growing popularity of dance.

Danilova is aware of her position as one of the world's great dancers, yet she never says, as so many artists do: "I was a great success in this." Instead, she speaks with great humility about her successes, believing that she owes them to those audiences who bestowed their approval and their affection upon her. "I'm not a goddess, I like to improve," she says, and so you will find that the rigors of long rehearsals do not prevent her from studying under a master teacher, who will yell at her to pull in her hips and point her toes just as if she were a wide-eyed novice from Ponca City.

Offstage she is just as vivacious, albeit more refined, as she is in the role of the cancan dancer in *The Fantastic Toyshop.* She mimics people and activities with great effect and her imitation of an ice skater generating speed is so right that you would never believe her acquaintance with sports begins and ends with pingpong. She would probably let you criticize her dancing, but her pingpong game is a sacred thing and she will tell you with great glee that she was the towering champion on the ship which carried the Ballet Russe to South America last summer.

Alexandra Danilova busies herself with things other than dancing and pingpong. She is writing her autobiography, but it will deal with people she has met rather than with herself. If her literary talents match her vocal wit, her autobiography should be one of the few dance books in which the writer

can see the funny side of herself, her colleagues and her profession. Another problem is her nationality, for she is the widow of an Italian, a Russian by birth and an American at heart. She plans to become a citizen of the United States, but the process seems very complicated to her Russian, balletic mind.
[*New York Herald Tribune*]

Ballet Russe de Monte Carlo

October 25, 1940

Giselle, so often hailed as the "Hamlet of the dance," tests the histrionic and technical abilities of its principals and the precision of its corps. *Giselle* is close to one hundred years old, times have changed, and it takes a truly fine production to turn the melodramatics into tragedy, quaint make-believe into effective fantasy. The Ballet Russe de Monte Carlo, in its second week at the Fifty-first Street Theater, did well by *Giselle*. Alicia Markova brought her great skill to the role of the simple, peasant girl who loses her sanity when she discovers that her lover is betrothed to another. The first act is almost entirely mimed drama, and Markova, through this difficult medium of expression, created a character that was warm, human and hauntingly tragic. The mad scene was superbly done as Markova tremblingly and haltingly danced for the last time the measures she had stepped so gayly with her lover.

The last act, in which the young man comes to the tomb of his beloved and is swept into his dance of death by the spirits of maidens who died before their wedding day, is one that must be brilliantly done to appear credible. Again Markova, as the spirit of Giselle, danced with technical skill and great beauty of movement. Igor Youskevitch was flawless when it came to the business of executing pirouettes, tours en l'air and the bits of virtuosity which the role demanded, but he has yet to plumb the dramatic depths of the part. The first act was Giselle's tragedy and the second act should certainly focus the despair and the inevitable march to death of the lover. Alexandra Danilova was a regal queen of the ghost maidens, and the corps, aside from some trips into uncharted fields, danced smoothly and briskly as the nocturnal Wilis.

The rest of the program consisted of an extremely poor *Spectre de la Rose* with Mia Slavenska far from her best and with André Eglevsky completely unable to suggest a spirit of a rose. The evening closed with *Vienna 1814,* notable for its lovely costumes, a few good divertissements and the dancing of Alexandra Danilova. Efrem Kurtz was the conductor for all three ballets.
[*New York Herald Tribune*]

November 4, 1940

It was a gala farewell that the Ballet Russe de Monte Carlo gave last night at the Fifty-first Street Theater. Yells of delight, bravos, curtain calls and enthusiastic applause were bestowed upon the major ballet of the evening, *Giselle,* one of the greatest works in all dance and a ballet which this company performs brilliantly. Alicia Markova and Igor Youskevitch, repeating their earlier successes in the roles of Giselle and her lover, danced as few artists in this world can dance. Markova's dancing is as light as thistledown, technically flawless, and she draws her character with warmth and rare tenderness. Youskevitch performs his athletic feats with dash and grace, and at each succeeding performance seems to bring out more of his character's qualities. The remainder of the program consisted of *The New Yorker* and *Vienna— 1814.*

Last night's program was a good example of the Ballet Russe de Monte Carlos standards, and now that the season is over, it might be well to briefly examine its record. The current company should be the culmination of all the rich experiences and the vital traditions of Russian ballet, but some parts of the organization have failed to culminate into anything recognizable. On the credit side, we find the stars of the ensemble: Alexandra Danilova, who brings humor, zip and technical facility to every role she touches; Alicia Markova, the greatest Giselle and a superb dancer of the classic school; Igor Youskevitch, who translates virtuosity into great dancing; Mia Slavenska, beautiful to look at, technically facile and an engaging performer when she doesn't look the audience full in the face and practically demand applause; André Eglevsky, who improves steadily; Frederic Franklin, whose unfailing energy, ability and communicable humor constitute one of the ballet's greatest assets, and Efrem Kurtz, whose musicianship and thorough understanding of the function of music in ballet are always apparent in spite of the limitations of his orchestra.

On the debit side, one finds a lighting system which seems to be left entirely in the hands of pixies, and a corps de ballet which sends you streaking for the Music Hall Rockettes. There is no excuse for a company whose ensembles cannot move as a unit. If the current regisseur can't train them to follow a choreographic pattern, I suggest that Gene Snyder be called in from the Music Hall to teach them something of the art of dancing. Some of the ballets which miss fire are not choreographically unsound, but matters of production, direction and execution can be blamed.

One more debit goes to the men of the company. I insist that limp wrists and butterfly exits on the part of males may have been dandy at the court of Nicholas II, but they don't belong in America, they have nothing whatever to do with technique or style or anything else. *Spectre de la Rose* is a good example of this. Who says the spirit of a rose is a sissy? Yet you would think so by all the arm fluttering and fashion-show posturing which the male dancer employs. How about a rose spirit that is resilient and tough, romantic and graceful yet strong? If men are to be respected in dance, the current type of rose spirit had better do its famous leap out of the window and stay out.

Let us hope that next season will see first-rate production and direction, masculine movements from the men and a spirit of mutual interest from the corps. In the meantime all of us salute the great stars of the Monte Carlo for bringing us a theater season of beauty, excitement and superlative dancing. [*New York Herald Tribune*]

De Basil Ballet Russe Returns
After Absence of Three Years

November 7, 1940: Tamara Toumanova Stars in
Aurora's Wedding; Lichine Work Performed

With youth, vim and generous dashes of virtuosity to the fore, the Original Ballet Russe of Col. de Basil, absent from New York for almost three years, opened its long engagement at the Fifty-first Street Theater last night. Tamara Toumanova, Irina Baronova and Tatiana Riabouchinska, the baby ballerinas of other seasons, have come back to us again along with such familiar figures as David Lichine, Paul Petroff and Roman Jasinsky. Two of last evening's works were also familiar: *Aurora's Wedding* and *Coq d'Or*. David Lichine was responsible for the premiere: *Graduation Ball* to music by Johann Strauss.

Aurora's Wedding is the last act of the old Petipa-Tchaikovsky ballet, *The Sleeping Princess,* and because it is a plotless divertissement it can stand alone as an isolated work. The costumes of Alexandre Benois are dull of hue and unflattering of cut, and, in fact, some of the male get-ups resemble a tarnished gilt version of campfire-girl bloomers. The scenery of Leon Bakst is pallid, but with brightly colored costumes it might prove effective.

Toumanova and Petroff The brief dances are charming, and last night's young soloists danced them well, but the high point of the ballet was the dancing of Tamara Toumanova, more beautiful than ever and with a technique that was breath-taking. Beautifully partnered by Petroff in the pas de deux, Toumanova moved with striking effect, sustaining her arabesques with steellike strength and performing her multiple turns with virtuosic fire.

83

Riabouchinska and Jasinsky danced the famous *Bluebird* variation with great vigor and bravura, the ballerina faring better than Jasinsky, who is more of a character dancer than he is a classicist.

But if the decor of *Aurora's Wedding* lacked color, the original Ballet Russe made up for it with the eye-smacking hues of Gontcharova's sets for *Coq d'Or*. The story of the ballet deals with the machinations and counter-desires of an astrologer, a king, warriors, a fairytale queen and a golden cockerel with magical powers. If you like opulence à la Russe, *Coq d'Or* is for you; otherwise, you'll find it too long and much of its humor too childish. Buffoonery and fantastic props are jumbled together in the Fokine manner and the ballet has many of that choreographer's familiar mob-scene sequences. Baronova danced the role of the Queen exceedingly well, but no one person has a chance to star in a stage piece which is so gaudy of surface and so crowded in design. Riabouchinska managed nicely to attract attention to her dancing by the simple expedients of killing the king and dancing before the outer curtain in the prologue and epilogue.

Cadets and Schoolgirls *Graduation Ball*, the evening's premiere, turned out to be good fun as the shy pupils of a girl's school played hostesses to some neighboring cadets on graduation day. With legs and pigtails flying, the lassies lunged for the cadets, decorum was thrown aside, and after the first few minutes of male shyness, the boys and girls indulged in fine revel. Nicholas Orloff, as a drummer, danced an effective number, and Tatiana Leskova performed an impromptu with near-ballerina technique and appropriate school-girl expression. Just to get virtuosity over and done with, a fouetté contest was held, and two girls took turns whipping themselves into balletic spins that became increasingly difficult. Lichine danced one of the cadets, good-naturedly satirizing in his movements the postures and airs of the military student. *Graduation Ball* was fast of pace, ingenious of choreography and enabled Riabouchinska, Lichine and the members of the ensemble to exude vigor and talent to the delightful music of Strauss.

It's too early to discuss all the attributes of this company, but from last night's performance, one could discern the fresh and youthful charm of its ballerinas, weakness in the male wing, a fairly well trained ensemble, good lighting and plenty of exuberance. First-night honors certainly go to Toumanova for her exciting dancing, to Gontcharova for the sheer spectacle of her *Coq d'Or* sets and to David Lichine for his gay *Graduation Ball*. [*New York Herald Tribune*]

De Basil's Ballet Russe Offers
New Fokine and Lichine Works

November 9, 1940

A great work has come to enrich the treasury of ballet masterpieces, a work created by one of the few living geniuses of dance. After fifty years of conceiving and producing ballets which have altered the course of dance and which have already taken on the quality of enduring master works, Michel Fokine has given us a fresh and vital theater dance that literally glows with the undimmed fire of his genius. Last night at the Fifty-first Street Theater, the Original Ballet Russe premiered this work, *Paganini,* to the music of Rachmaninoff's "Rhapsody on a Theme by Paganini," with scenery and costumes by Serge Soudeikine.

Paganini reveals the personal tragedy born of genius, and in this dramatic fantasy we see the great violinist beset by the calumny, the hate and the jealousy of his rivals, his spirit torn by the revulsion of his fellow men at the sight of his physical ugliness. So great was his music that enemies convinced the superstitious that Satan wielded his bow for him.

Paganini Shown at Concert   As the ballet opens Paganini is shown on a stage within a stage playing his divine melodies, and as he plays to his audience the fantastic figures of popular superstition dance about him and the Devil himself leans over the artist's shoulders to touch the strings of the instrument. The second scene shows Paganini with his fellowmen, the terror they feel at his uncouth presence and the moment when a beautiful girl falls under the enchantment of his music and dances for him. The final scene is a nightmare wherein Paganini finds himself faced with diabolic hordes of his imitators, his critics and his enemies. But they fade away as the artist realizes that his gift is not from the Devil but from God.

The Fokine work is intensely dramatic, for the great choreographer has maintained the quality of fantasy throughout, building steadily to an exciting climax. There is great ingenuity and freshness of movement for the ensembles and for Tatiana Riabouchinska, who performs to perfection the brief role of the girl who dances for Paganini. Dmitri Rostoff drew the main character brilliantly through the difficult medium of mime-acting. There is much more to be said about this great work, but for the present I will simply say that it is profound and rich of content, and a magnificent show by standards of pure entertainment.

Lichine Work Performed   The evening's other new work fell into quite a different category. Choreographed by David Lichine to music of Debussy,

85

Protée turned out to be an episode about a Greek sea god and some neo-pseudo-Greek bathing beauties. From the bas-relief designs, you might guess that it was a wet version of *Afternoon of a Faun*. A poor soprano can bring down the house if she hits a high note at the end of her aria. Lichine, as Protée, took a high dive off a prop into a back-drop sea, and that just about sums up the current activities of that particular deity. Giorgio di Chirico's sets were fine.

The evening opened with Bronislava Nijinska's *The Hundred Kisses,* to music of d'Erlanger and with decor by Jean Hugo. Neither music nor choreography is earth-shaking in importance, but Irina Baronova dances with technical skill and beautiful style the role of a princess who doesn't know true love when she sees it. Paul Petroff plays the part of the true love. Fire and lustiness brought the evening to a close with Fokine's dances from *Prince Igor*. Antal Dorati led the orchestra through a superior performance, and salutes go to Yola Miller for her splendid lighting effects for all ballets.

This afternoon the Ballet Russe will offer *Aurora's Wedding, Coq d'Or* and *Graduation Ball*, and the evening performance will be the same. Sunday matinee will bring a repeat of last night's program, and for Sunday evening several changes in cast have been announced: Baronova will dance Princess Aurora in *Aurora's Wedding* and Genevieve Moulin will dance the Bluebird variation; Olga Morosova will replace Baronova as the Queen of Shemakhan in *Coq d'Or. Graduation Ball* will complete the bill. [*New York Herald Tribune*]

Jack Cole at the Rainbow Room

November 20, 1940

Great dancing is usually found in the theater, the concert hall or some hallowed spot devoted to art, but the Rainbow Room at Rockefeller Center can boast of a great dancer in the person of Jack Cole. Quite naturally, his dances are not profound of theme or philosophic of content, for they are designed to amuse dinner and supper audiences, but although these numbers are not great works of art his dancing of them is matchless. With one of the best physiques in the masculine dance, an unerring sense of rhythm and a technical equipment that enables him to execute the most difficult movements, Jack Cole can easily hold his own with the topnotch dancers of the day.

Flores de la Noche is the title of the show, and suggests the romantic lushness of Latin-American entertainment. The dances are peasant in character, marked by sudden changes in rhythm and mood, potent in their romantic fire. Florence Lessing danced exceedingly well in a duet with Cole, and in the trios Anna Austin displayed those facile movements and engaging grins which mark her style in concert or in floor show. The lovely voice of Elsie Houston and the show-stopping guitar playing of Vincente Gomez added beauty and excitement to the performance, both in their solo moments and in their joint appearances with the Cole dancers. Eddie Le Baron led the orchestra.

Last evening Karen Cooper began a singing engagement at the Rainbow Grill, her first appearance in New York. She joins the show which features Barry Winton and his orchestra with Jean Murray and Don Julian and Marjori, dancers. [New York Herald Tribune]

Ballet Stages Petrouchka, Work by Fokine

November 22, 1940

Petrouchka, one of Michel Fokine's greatest ballets, has been given some down-right insulting productions in the past. Until last night's presentation, in fact, I had never seen Petrouchka done the way Fokine and Stravinsky, its composer, must have conceived it. The Original Ballet Russe with its authoritative stage direction, its first-rate lighting and its lively corps de ballet, managed to turn the trick, and under Fokine's personal supervision the work emerged in all its brilliance and poignancy.

Against the boisterous celebrating of merry-makers at Russian carnival time there unfolds the story of three puppets: Petrouchka, the clown; the Blackamoor and the Dancer. Petrouchka's tragedy is that under the wooden joints and the cotton stuffing of his body there exists the soul of a man. His love spurned by the Dancer, who prefers the virile Blackamoor, Petrouchka suffers the pangs and despair of a human. Yura Lazovsky, in the title role, brought out all the pathos of the character. His pattering steps, the abrupt and futile flutterings of his hands made you laugh a little, but, although puppet-like, they were touched with such human warmth that Petrouchka's tragedy truly wrung the heart. Tamara Toumanova was cool and technically proficient as the Dancer and Alberto Alonso was amusing as the Blackamoor, but a little more viciousness in his fight with Petrouchka would have given greater dramatic impact to that scene of the ballet. The vivacious and extremely personable girls and boys of the ensemble imparted gayety and good dancing to the carnival scenes. The orchestra seemed to take some odd liberties with the Stravinsky score. [New York Herald Tribune]

Nemtchinova Makes Her Bow
in Swan Lake

November 24, 1940

Vera Nemtchinova, at one time leading ballerina of Serge Diaghileff's great
Russian ballet, made her New York debut with the Original Ballet Russe yesterday afternoon at the Fifty-first Street Theater. *Swan Lake,* in its first
seasonal presentation by this company, was the ballet chosen for Nemtchinova's
first appearance. A wise choice it was, for the role of the Swan Queen demands maturity of style as well as technical proficiency, and Nemtchinova
possesses both of these elements of superior dancing.

Classic dancing in the grand manner marked the ballerina's performance.
Each arabesque was clean and sure of line, the little running bouree steps were
neatly defined and the posture of her head and body was one of regal beauty.
Youthful ballerinas are sometimes inclined to shoot their individual personalities right over the footlights and into the audiences' laps; this is engaging and
permissible in an informal divertissement, but not in a classic ballet which is
refined, delicate of mood and aristocratic in style. Nemtchinova, with her
mature artistry, submerged her own personality in the role of the Swan Queen,
and you could believe her a queen, you could believe in the magic enchantment which held her in its spell and you could believe in her refined but
ardent love for a prince she could never have. There was nervousness present,
but the mature performance of a fine artist in a great role amply atoned for it.

The rest of the dancing did not match that of the star. Michael
Panaieff danced the role of the Prince with a fair amount of technical accuracy, no verve at all and much la-de-da fluttering of the wrists. The men of
the ensemble, clad as hunters, acted as if they had lost several rubbers of
bridge and were arguing about the scores instead of looking for game. The
same scene on skates in the "It Happens on Ice" show might give the ballet
men a clue or two about animation at the hunt. The pas de trois for two
swan lassies and the Prince's friend has disappeared again. Some companies
include it and some don't; this company also took the friend's big solo away
from him, which seemed too bad, for it is invariably an exciting bit. The
setting by Korovine seemed to be of the picture postcard school, its lines and
colors much too representational a background for the delicate and haunting
theme of *Swan Lake. Petrouchka, Protée* and *Prince Igor* complete the bill.
[*New York Herald Tribune*]

Fantasia's Dances

November 24, 1940

Mademoiselle Upanova is the perfect ballerina. She has long legs that give scope to her movements, she has a willowy neck and her little white ballet skirt is an inseparable part of her anatomy, for she was born wearing it. Of course, Mlle. Upanova is an ostrich, but she can execute an entrechat or an arabesque with the best of her dancing sisters. Currently appearing in *The Dance of the Hours* from *Fantasia,* this tripping ostrich exudes fake eye-lash glamour and displays the virtuosity of ballet technique in a performance which is a riotous, satiric reflection of the real thing.

Walt Disney is a great choreographer. Moments of beauty, human tenderness and humor are conceived in terms of dance, and the sequences of pure fantasy are projected through rhythm, pattern and motion. Donald Duck in his most thwarted and irate episodes would blow up and bust if he didn't dance out his frenzy; the pallid Snow White had real moments of loveliness when she danced in the cottage with the dwarfs; and who can ever forget the first Silly Symphony when the skeletons danced to the macabre accompaniment of their rattling bones. In *Fantasia* Walt Disney has assembled the richest qualities of his choreography: humans, animals and flowers dance in ballets which poke fun at dancing and in ballets which exalt it.

A Slam at Ballet During the production of *Dance of the Hours,* the Disney staff turned into balletomanes. Artists followed the Ballet Russe on its tour of California, making performance and back-stage sketches of Paul Petroff, Irina Baronova and others. A group of ballet dancers were taken to the Disney studio where they danced over and over again the traditional passages of *Dance of the Hours.* Repetition caused exaggeration to creep into their movements, and at this point the sketchers managed to capture on paper a suggestion of ballet to its silliest. The final result in *Fantasia* is an immortalization of ballet's pet foibles. You see the ostrich ballerina looking archly at the audience while her frenzied feet writhe through a complicated pattern; you see Ben Ali Gator, the premier danseur, giving his partner, Hyacinth Hippo, extra impetus in her pirouette by pulling her tail, and you see pretentious coyness in the attitude of every animal performer. These are kind-hearted and honest cracks at the worst aspects of ballet.

In the *Nutcracker Suite,* Disney turned to the sheer visual beauty of dancing. Flower petals falling upon water were swept into the gliding measures of a waltz, bits of milkweed-down were tossed by the breezes into the lightest of ballerinas, dewdrops slid down blades of grass and quivered from leaf to leaf in a fairy dance, frost designs spun an ice ballet and a cluster of mushrooms turned into a gamboling gang of midget mandarins.

89

Dances of Nature   The person who dares to express his belief in a system of nature which is rhythmic and patterned is branded a mystic, yet Disney has done just that in *Nutcracker Suite* and in *Rites of Spring*. He has succeeded, I think, because he has not relied upon the inadequacy of words to express this theme but has shown us through his great and visible art that such a system does exist. Both of these sequences are purely fantasy, yet a fantasy which gives significance and drama to reality. In *Rites of Spring* we are shown the surging, rhythmic and planned growth of microscopic life carried to its ultimate in the gigantic beasts of pre-historic days. Seeking food and water, the titanic animals make their final trek across the desert wastes, their weary movements resembling a great processional of death. *Nutcracker Suite* is based upon the nature of our own times, a slow-moving nature whose rhythms and patterns are lost to our eyes; but with the speed and clarity of Disney's discerning brand of fantasy, these rhythms and patterns become clear and credible for the first time. With man pretty impressed with his own importance, it's a good thing to show him that other forms of life are also possessed of beauty, growth and a valid place in the schemes of things.

Beethoven's *Pastoral Symphony* has many moments of beauty and humor, and they are due to the dancing and the capering of the animals rather than to any of the bloodless activities of the human characters. *Night on Bald Mountain* is an excellent ballet in the grotesque. The spirits of evil and of death race throughout as the lesser furies dance wildly on the brink of Hell and the unfortunate captives dance their last halting measures on the palm of Satan before he crushes them to death. Dance lovers will find much of *Fantasia* rewarding in its choreographic scope, stimulating in its brilliant use of a great art. Others, I think, will be led to an understanding of dance, an excitement in it, for Walt Disney, through the medium of motion pictures, is bringing great dance and simple dance to every one. [*New York Herald Tribune*]

Fokine Works are Presented by Ballet Russe

December 8, 1940

In tribute to the creative genius of Michel Fokine, the Original Ballet Russe presented Friday night at the Fifty-first Street Theater an all-Fokine program. *Paganini, Cinderella* and other recent works of the great Russian master were not on the bill, for the presentations consisted of such lasting favorites as *Carnaval, The Firebird, Spectre de la Rose* and *Prince Igor*.

With Irina Baronova in the title role, Stravinsky's *The Firebird* was given its first local performance in several seasons. It is a fairy-tale ballet about enchanted maidens, a princess and a prince, and it is the magic of the Firebird that breaks the spell and allows the prince and princess to be united. *The Firebird* is an intensely national ballet, for much of it is devoted to the display of opulent Russian costumes and Russian folk steps.

These aspects undoubtedly warm the heart of a Russian audience, but they are not dramatic enough to excite the average audience in this vicinity; folk dancing is fun to do, but too much of it is not particularly stimulating to watch. An American ballet with pioneer, Puritan or Pilgrim costumes would probably arouse our national fervor and at the same time bore a continental audience. However, it is rather late to find fault with such a traditional ballet as *The Firebird*, and it should be reported that the true balletic interludes are exciting. The adagio sequences and the passages that employ the skills and style of classic ballet represent Fokine at his most ingenious, and one can ask little more of theater dance.

Baronova was technically assured as the Firebird, regal and dynamic in her movements, but the Firebird, after all, is a bird, and one wished for more fleetness and alertness of motion than Baronova brought to the role. The scenery of Nathalie Gontcharova was rich of hue and the lighting of Yola Miller added immeasurably to the fantastic air of the ballet.

The evening opened with a lively version of *Carnaval* in which Tatiana Riabouchinska and Yura Lazovsky as Columbine and Harlequin turned in some of the best dancing that this company has ever disclosed. In the Original Ballet Russe's first presentation of *Spectre de la Rose,* Paul Petroff essayed the male part with generally poor results, for his technical equipments did not allow him the lightness and the agility which the role demanded. The costume is never much help, and I maintain that a healthy man who finds himself plastered with rose petals from head to foot is fighting a losing battle. The ballet is a great work of imaginative dance, and a more subtle and virile male costume would do wonders for its artistic stature.

The exciting dances from *Prince Igor* brought the evening to a close.
[*New York Herald Tribune*]

America's Moderns

December 15, 1940

"We must back our audiences," said Martha Graham. "We have alienated them through grimness of theme and a non-theatrical approach to our dancing. Now that we modern dancers have left our period of 'long woolens' behind us, we must prove to our audiences that our theater pieces have color, warmth and entertainment value. We must convince our audiences that we belong in the American theater."

What has happened to the modern dance? This is a great dance season so far as ballet is concerned, for ballet performances have been presented daily for more than six weeks, but modern dance has remained silent. Financial difficulties may account for this, but in earlier seasons the vital and resourceful modern dancers managed somehow to get into the theaters. Miss Graham feels that the current inactivity marks a period of re-energizing, a period that modern dancers will use for self-criticism and for concrete plans to win a permanent place in the theater.

Ill-Behaved Moderns   During the past decade modern dance had its ardent followers, an audience composed of cultists, dance enthusiasts and perceptive persons who saw in it the seed of great theater dance. The average ticket-buyer, however, was on the losing side. He paid his good money to find entertainment and emotional stimulation, and naturally expected to find these elements in an art which was housed in a theater. Instead, he was met with an array of figures in uninteresting and drab costumes, who never smiled, who moved in fierce angles and whose remote goings-on he couldn't possibly fathom. Perhaps he was kind-hearted and gave these dancers a try each year for several years, granting them a right to indulge in experiments.

Modern dancers battled valiantly for their way of dancing. They probed the psychological as well as the anatomical functions of movement and they fought for the right to interpret in dance the social, political and economic problems of the times. With few exceptions, they wound up as scientists and current events commentators, and not as artists of the theater. Their dance was a splendid skeleton with nice, strong bones, interesting to the student, but hardly capable of arousing warm response from a general audience. At last the modern dance is about to cover that skeleton with healthy, living flesh, transforming it into a real character with human features and a likable personality. In the matter of themes and their manner of presentation, Martha Graham feels that here, too, is a change. With the rest of the world in chaos, the great dancer knows that abstractions of great ideals are not particularly heartening to American audiences. These followers of theater want to focus their attention upon a definite personality, a stage figure who possesses an ideal or a problem. In other words, we don't want bloodless abstractions upon the stage, but we do want to see a fellow human who presents, through the theater art, the hopes and problems of man with such strength and understanding that he may guide us and give us courage.

92

A People's Dance   Modern dance will never become the rousing theater-spectacle that ballet is, for ballet, on its points and with its soaring leaps and whirls, flashes like a bird in air, while modern dance is an earthbound art, a potential folk expression of the joys and sorrows and hopes of humanity. Until the average person's dance experience is on a plane with his experiences in music, drama and painting, all dance forms must face this average person's suspicion of anything unfamiliar. Under ideal conditions, great works of modern dance should draw the same thinking audience that supports a Robert Sherwood play.

Martha Graham is the only modern dancer who is definitely scheduled to give a major New York performance this season. At that time she will offer three theater pieces: *Every Soul Is a Circus, El Penitente* and *Letter to the World.* These works constitute Miss Graham's bid for popular support, a bid for the recognition of the modern dance as an exciting, stimulating and entertaining people's art. I think Miss Graham will win her battle, for belligerence and dogmatism have left this vital revolutionary, and in their place is strength with tolerance. She says, "I know that modern dance is not the only way. I'm not even sure that my style of dancing can be passed on to any one else. There is ballet, there is fancy dancing and there are many styles of dance; modern dance happens to be my way of dancing, and my goal is to dance it well."

I am glad that New York can support several months of ballet, but I think many of us miss the other forms of dance. By scouting about you can find that Helen Tamiris is giving some studio performances that are definitely worth seeing, that Doris Humphrey and Charles Weidman have intimate recitals on their schedule. But Ted Shawn's first year of leave in almost thirty years is leaving a big gap in the current season, for that great artist's dynamic presence, his rich and exciting dance works are greatly needed in the theater of dance. As for the modern dance, I hope that those of us who have fought for and chastised it will see it emerge into theatrical adulthood, and if Martha Graham's words are words of prophecy, the modern dance should soon come back as a valid and popular theater art. [*New York Herald Tribune*]

1941

Spectacle, Fantasy, Faith, and the Emotional Structure of Man

Humphrey–Weidmans present On My Mother's Side, Lynchtown, Portraits of Great Dancers, and Decade premieres at Bennington • Balanchine and Graham — two giants discussed • Elizabeth Burchenal • Three Virgins and a Devil, Gala Performance, Billy the Kid, Jardin aux Lilas and Pas de Quatre premiered by Ballet Theatre, and Nana Gollner in Giselle • Louisiana Purchase, Crazy With the Heat, Pal Joey and Lady in the Dark on Broadway • Erick Hawkins, Valerie Bettis, and Sybil Shearer make their solo debuts • Graham's Punch and the Judy • The tap dance trend • An Indian Dance festival • Ballerinas and Dancing Gentlemen • The gesture language of La Meri

Humphrey–Weidman—1941

January 2, 1941: Dance Group Shows Aspects of Life in U.S.

Doris Humphrey, Charles Weidman and their company commenced the second week of their dance festival series at their new studio-theater, 108 West Sixteenth Street, last evening. *On My Mother's Side* was the only dance repeated from last week's performances, and the other three works were chosen from the established repertory of the company. High spots of the evening were *Bargain Counter* and *Lynch Town* from Weidman's suite called *Atavisms*, to music of Lehman Engel.

Bargain Counter calls to mind the recent hectic hysterics of the pre-Christmas rush, for in it we are shown the harried floorwalker literally attacked by hordes of stampeding females. They shove him all over the floor, they tear the goods on the counter, they yank each other's hair, and we see these erstwhile ladies revert to the savagery of their primitive ancestors who won and kept their goods and chattels through brute force. Every one who is

95

familiar with the clowning genius of Charles Weidman can surely imagine that he made the floorwalker a hilarious figure—elegant, dignified and gratifyingly bewildered in the midst of a vortex of howling feminity.

In direct contrast was *Lynch Town,* presenting another atavism of man—the desire to kill. The choreography for this work is superlative, as it shows the movements of men and women watching another being tortured and killed. Their bodies tremble with frenzy intermingled with fear and lust and the sense of immediate power over life and death. *Lynch Town* is a terrifying and intensely dramatic comment on one of the not-too-savory aspects of modern America.

The program opened with *To the Dance,* a brief work which is based upon the most familiar movements of the modern dance. It is without plot or definite mood, but it serves as an introduction to the dance style of the evening, the vocabulary which the artists will use to communicate their thoughts, their themes and their moods to the audience in the dances which follow. The program closed with the Variations and Conclusion from Doris Humphrey's suite entitled *New Dance.*

These two sections are almost a Humphrey trade-mark, for they are to be found on many of the company's programs, and if they are not there, some one is sure to ask for them. As isolated works they appear primarily as designs of pure dance, inventive and stimulating to see. The dancers move together in perfect harmony; suddenly one will emerge to set a variation of her own, marked by her own personality, and then she will return to the group, bringing to it the freshness of her solo flight.

This dancing can be viewed as a reflection of what life could be in its most ideal state: each individual possessed of talents and initiative but able to live in harmony with his fellow men, willing to adapt himself to the needs of the community but enriching the life of that community with his personal abilities. [*New York Herald Tribune*]

January 26, 1941: Weidman Gives His "Portraits of Famous Dancers"

Hilarity reigned during most of the evening at the Humphrey–Weidman little theater in last night's performance, which featured light, theatrical dances. Other week-end appearances have seen more serious works emerge from the distinguished repertory of Doris Humphrey and Charles Weidman, but last night, at 108 West Sixteenth Street, Mr. Weidman turned on his mimic abilities full blast and devoted half the evening to impersonating famous dancers. Aside from poking fun at his own buoyant self, he tore into Ruth St. Denis, and satirized the most characteristic gestures of that great lady: the constant arrangement and rearrangement of draperies, the low-slung nautch turns, the yelps to the electrician for a different lighting effect and, in fact, all of the most celebrated St. Denis mannerisms, including a reference to "dear Teddy" (Ted Shawn).

Weidman, preceded by a replica of Donald Duck, flew onto the scene as the Prince from *Swan Lake,* and as his ballerina he had a dressmaker's dummy on wheels. For Martha Graham, he put his leg in a noose and yanked the rope in order to simulate Miss Graham's favorite leg extension, and followed it with the peg-leg lope down to the front of the stage, just as Graham does in her solo *Frontier.* He brought to life Anna Duncan and her lullabies and military polonaises, executed with dripping coquetry; Doris Humphrey came in for her portrait as Mr. Weidman got himself thoroughly involved in all available stage properties. To wind up, Weidman appeared as Mary Wigman, flanked by drums and gongs, and he even had a tambourine tied to his posterior. Needless to say, all movements were consumated with expressions of deepest agony.

These *Portraits of Famous Dancers* were done with such deftness that you would have to see them to believe how hilarious they really were. Weidman also offered two new works, a beautifully constructed and visually pleasant *Rumba to the Moon* and another funny number in the prancing, preening, dinner-jacketed *Penguins.* Lee Sherman, a principal dancer in the company, turned choreographer for *Jazz Trio* and *Du Barry Was No Lady,* both of which had moments of ingenuity along with many passages that found him still wanting in style and authority.

The rest of the program offered the gay *Square Dances* and *The Shakers.* In these, Miss Humphrey danced brilliantly. The company, as is customary, was in good form, with especially good dancing by Katherine Litz, Beatrice Seckler, Lee Sherman and Charles Hamilton. The whole evening was a rewarding one, and the Humphrey–Weidman little theater has decidedly become one of the high-spots of the season's dance. [*New York Herald Tribune*]

August 17, 1941: Dance Document

A dance work of major significance was given its debut last week at the Bennington Festival of the Arts in Bennington, Vt. Doris Humphrey's *Decade*, a full evening's theater-piece, is functionally rich and rewarding, for it finds Miss Humphrey in a reflective mood, looking back over ten years of achievement, failure, hope and determination. Its autobiographical aspects make it intensely interesting, revealing honestly and ardently the artist, not as a behind-the-scenes stager of entertainment, but as a human being who pours her personal ideals, her passions into art-creation. The second function of *Decade* is to disclose to the layman the simplicity of modern dance. You are taken into the studio where new ideas are tested, and by watching what is discarded, what is retained and expanded and developed into a finished dance product, your own discernment gains in acuteness. The third function deals with a desperate situation: the plight of the American dancers who have fought their battles without financial help from any one and who face the future with no backing to aid them in the carrying out of their plans.

The fourth function of *Decade* includes the other aspects of the work, for *Decade* is exciting because of theatrical variety. Composers run from Bach to Aaron Copland, many variations on modern dance style are present, there is pure dance, pantomime and the spoken word, and the rich texture of autobiography gives both cohesion and scope to the work. The entire dance is given focus in the person of Miss Humphrey who turns in the most brilliant performance I have ever seen her give. Radiant, beautiful and strong in her characterization, she dances *Decade* in magical fashion.

A Story in Movement   This story, told in dance, opens with a vision of the future. Miss Humphrey and Mr. Weidman are shown as they come together in search of that same vision, and although the movements of this opening dance are pure and not mimetic, it is not difficult to perceive in the free yet ordered motion, in the dignity and warmth which touches them, a shining credo of living through dance. The next episode leaves the visionary theme and finds the dancers choosing a loft for the home of their dance ideals. There is the business of moving in, of starting the evolvement of new forms, and in this there is constant personal contact as each of the stars watches the other's work, helping with criticism and encouragement. The company, too, is on hand to learn and to work and to become a part of the new scheme.

The theme of business occurs again and again throughout the two acts of *Decade*. The dancers are wanted to serve as a background for a motion picture which is to advertise some commercial product. Mr. Business takes on another guise as a representative of an enterprising opera scheme, and he returns in other roles to lure them with plans of musical shows. Federal theaters and what not, but although the spoken words of Mr. Business always give hope to the dancers, making them believe that here at last is an outlet for their creative wealth, one scheme after another fades into nothingness. The business theme is projected with a bitterness so honest that you find yourself sharing the momentary hopes and the resultant despairs of these courageous dancers. This does not mean that there is no humor in *Decade*; there is plenty. Mr. Weidman has hilarious moments in his testing of new forms, in his conducting of rehearsals and in those completed dances which are built upon his own sublime inanities.

Behind the Scenes   The opera scenes, showing the dancers' brief fling in a grandiose scheme, is brightly and amusingly staged. You see first a dress

98

rehearsal of a work specifically designed for gilt and plush and then you are taken to the performance itself and watch the same dance as if you were sitting in the wings. If all theater presentations look as silly on a slant as did the Humphrey–Weidman number, then the stagehands must live a hilarious existence. Other dance numbers from the company's repertory were presented in fragmentary state as they fitted into the story's progression. Weidman's slap-happy *Kinetic Pantomime* was there in toto and also Miss Humphrey's brilliant study in pure dance motion, *Circular Descent*.

The weaknesses of *Decade* are apparent, but I believe that they are only transitory and that Miss Humphrey will see fit to revise and tighten the whole work. The last act has more fragments of the company's works than does the first act, making for occasional moments of jumble. These fragments are dangerous, for those of the audience who are not familiar with the repertory cannot, in every case, grasp either the theme or the quality of the original work. It seems to me that these fragments should have been less in number and more carefully chosen. The episode from *With My Red Fires* had little meaning removed from its context, for the glaring, evil matriarch in full pursuit gave the uninitiated no clue as to the reasons for glaring or pursuing. The bits from *Theater Piece* and *Opus 51* suffered from the same trouble, but although they weaken *Decade* they in no way shroud the intrinsic greatness of the work which should be fully revealed when revisions have been made. The very close is also in need of tightening. It is designed to bring the cycle of ten years to a close with a departure toward a new vision, but at present it is not as strong as the opening statement of faith. Perhaps Miss Humphrey intended it to be weaker because of the discouragements of the years. Whatever she does, the final statement should be potent: a determined renewal of faith; a cynical and embittered outline for the future; or complete bewilderment and resignation as if to say "Where do we go from here?" In its potentialities and even admitting to its present flaws, *Decade* is a great personal document and a great document of American dance. [*New York Herald Tribune*]

Balanchine and Graham

January 23, 1941: The Balanchine Touch

There is always an air of expectancy about a world premiere, and in the case of *Balustrade* that air is never dissipated, for you never cease to wonder which leg will go where next. That is the secret of the George Balanchine touch, and last night's performance by the Original Ballet Russe at the Fifty-first Street

Theater found Mr. Balanchine still taking delightful liberties with the traditional ballet. There are the familiar pirouettes, turns in air, arabesques and balletic sequences, but they are ever so slightly tinged with a touch of honky-
tonk, and a good classic line is certain to dissolve into a surrealist design.

Perhaps a description of some of the movements will give an idea of
what transpired in *Balustrade*. At one point Tamara Toumanova and Paul
Petroff are about to cast off into a romantic adagio, but Roman Jasinsky evidently decides that this moonlit garden idyll had better be nipped in the bud
and, hoisting himself over Mr. Petroff's head, he slithers down between the
Toumanova–Petroff anatomies, thus breaking up the embrace. Balanchine is
obviously interested in the movements of the human leg, and throughout the
duo, trio and ensemble sequences of *Balustrade* the dancers are called upon to
weave their limbs into one fantastic design after another. But Balanchine is a
real craftsman and never once does he lose clarity of pattern or misrepresent
the rhythm and quality of the Stravinsky music.

There is no story to *Balustrade*; it is only a scene pervaded by moods.
Perhaps it's a dream, a fantastic dream that is peopled with unpredictable figures which move as they will through moods of passion, acquiesence, gayety
and low humor. From the point of view of dance construction, *Balustrade*
boasts ingenious movements welded together without a hitch. Perhaps you
will find that it weaves a spell of fantasy, or perhaps you will find that its
odd movements are just plain zany, but however you look at it, *Balustrade* is
first-rate entertainment.

In the featured role, Tamara Toumanova was all that one could hope for
in a dream, fantastic or otherwise, for she was beautiful to look at and danced
with the sureness, ease and electric manner which have distinguished her dancing this season. Paul Petroff and Roman Jasinsky were fine and particularly
effective in the slow motion romance with Toumanova. Lesser principals and
the ensemble were unusually precise and coped with the difficult dancing
without many errors. Paul Tchelitcheff designed the costumes and setting for
Balustrade. A good-sized audience cheered the dancers, Mr. Balanchine, Mr.
Stravinsky, the conductor, and Samuel Dushkin, the evening's solo violinist.
[*New York Herald Tribune*]

January 26, 1941

Two new dance works made their debuts last week, each important in its own
way and one very different from the other. The first to be seen was Martha
Graham's *Letter to the World,* a courageous experimentation in the fusion of
poetry, music and dance, resulting in a work of great dramatic power and
generally sound in theatrical values. The second piece was George Balanchine's

Balustrade, produced with the glamorous stars of the Russian ballet, conducted by Igor Stravinsky, and emerging as a brilliant, superficial bit of pure entertainment. Which was more important? Which was more worthy of production? No one can ever decide which work deserves the laurel, for each served a different function.

There has been much discussion about the relative merits of ballet and modern dance, and in previous columns I have tried to point out the major differences; that ballet is primarily spectacle and fantasy; that modern dance deals with the problems, the faith and the emotional structure of man. Naturally, each form borrows from the other, but these are the essential differences. *Balustrade* is as different from *Letter to the World* as *Louisiana Purchase* is different from *The Corn Is Green.* One is smart entertainment, slick, ingenious, amusing and skillful; the other is warm and human; it touches the heart and stimulates the mind. The only point of contact is that both *Balustrade* and *Letter to the World* are designed for theater and both have to respect the requirements of any theater production.

The Skill of Mr. Balanchine   Mr. Balanchine's opus is the work of a craftsman, for it is composed of good dancing, interesting movements, clarity of design, contrasts in timing and in mood and a thorough understanding of the Stravinsky score. Plot? It has none at all. The scene is a garden and figures move about in attractive designs, suggesting passion, humor, fantasy and nonchalance. Tamara Toumanova is beautiful in the featured part and Balanchine has given her ample opportunity to display her brittle technique and her electrifying presence. The dancers get their legs and bodies almost inextricably entwined, but emerge from all clinches unruffled and without missing a beat. Roman Jasinsky hoists himself upon Paul Petroff's shoulders, goes over the top and slides down Petroff's body to the floor. Other odd movements are put to effective use and *Balustrade* adds up to good entertainment, worthy of the lavish production accorded to it by the Russian ballet system for the simple reason that it affords ticket-paying theatergoers a good time.

Miss Graham's modern ballet, on the other hand, is not lavish of production, backed by a symphony orchestra, nor conceived in terms of spectacular body technique. It has moments of rare humor, but you don't leave the theater saying, "Very amusing, wasn't it?" *Letter to the World* is an experiment in theater. Perhaps it will remain the only theater piece of its kind, or perhaps it will open up a whole new field of dance theater possibilities. The purpose of the work is to reveal, in dramatic form, the character of Emily Dickinson, and in that revealing introduce the audience to the thoughts, the love of beauty, the human warmth of a great figure in American literature.

Letter to the World   Although *Letter to the World* was too long, much of it was intensely potent. The group danced brief interludes which suggested the well-being and the reserve of Dickinson's New England background. Jean Erdman, regal and gracious of bearing, spoke the poetic lines of Emily Dickinson, while Miss Graham danced the hidden emotions, the wild passions, the moments of despair, the breaths of exaltation which surely must have generated those great lyric outbursts which the world now reads. Of course *Letter to the World* is not easy to take—no work of art is—but although it leaves you emotionally and even physically tired, I think you carry away with you some of the greatness, some of the beauty and some of the knowledge of Emily Dickinson.

It has been my hope that modern dance would learn to use the sound theatrical tricks of ballet, so that a brilliant and entertaining surface would be there for those who do not want to delve through it into the core of art; and that ballet would put its tremendous production facilities into the creation of a profound and adult theater piece. Even if that day should arrive, there will always, and rightly so, be works that are designed for lighthearted amusement and works that are designed to challenge the mind and the spirit. There is an audience for both and a need for both. [*New York Herald Tribune*]

Elizabeth Burchenal

February 9, 1941

A great career was started by an Irish maid named "Annie" and by a trip to West Virginia, for on festive occasions Annie used to dance for her employer's family, and one summer that family made first contact with American folk dancing in the Virginia hills. With this background, Elizabeth Burchenal started out to become one of the world's most distinguished authorities on folk dancing. Combining scholarliness with an irrepressible sense of fun, Miss Burchenal has covered Europe and America many times, bringing people into contact with the good spirits and frolic of folk dancing. She has twelve books to her credit, containing photographs, diagrams, music and descriptions of native dances. A chautauqua sprint was her meat, and at every performance she had the audience remove the chairs from the barns, tents or lecture halls, and join her in the measures of dance. Adding it all up, she finds that in America alone she has taught 50,000 persons many of whom carried on her work in their own communities.

Elizabeth Burchenal's first bit of pioneering took place here in New York in 1905, when she slipped in some folk dances between exercises in her physical education classes at Teachers' College. Luther Gulick, Director of Physical

Education for Greater New York, saw her work and liked it so much that he persuaded her to resign her college post and head the girls' branch of the Public Schools' Athletic League. She held that position for ten years and left when she felt certain that folk dancing was thoroughly intrenched in the recreational activities programs of New York schools.

Jubilee Season   The year 1941 is a jubilee year for Miss Burchenal, for it was just twenty-five years ago that she founded the American Folk Dance Society. The purpose of the organization was to promote the folk dance movement in America as it had been promoted in some of the Scandinavian countries several years before, and to train teachers and leaders for folk dance work in schools and communities. To do the job right, Elizabeth Burchenal couldn't rely on book information and so she traveled year after year to Europe, watching the folk dances of Europeans and returning to America to find out which of those dances had been transported to the New World. Through her work she has helped to keep alive the rich folk expressions which Americans inherited from their European forbears.

Because any folk expression is rarely crystallized and changes from generation to generation, Miss Burchenal has herself actually influenced folk dance by introducing a community to folk dances of another group. She introduced the old American dance, *John Brown,* to the people of a German town. On that occasion there was an extra man in the gathering and because he was wary of the American system of "cutting in" on a girl, he fled. The dancers, missing him, yelled, "Jacob, wo bist du?" and if you happened to go to that part of Germany a year later and saw the dance, you would have been told that it was called, "Jacob, wo bist du?" It is this very quality of improvisation, of communal high spirits that Miss Burchenal feels is so important to Americans. "You don't give up fresh air and fresh water just because most of your time is spent in offices and artificially lit rooms," she says, "and just because modern life is run on such a demanding schedule, you don't have to give up natural activities." That's why Miss Burchenal wants every one to get back to normal, healthy fun with folk dancing.

In the archives of the American Folk Dance Society you will find books and pamphlets and maps, motion pictures of authentic folk dances, native folk dance music and an abundance of data on the dance activities of a nation. Miss Burchenal herself is a walking archive, for she can tell you why the folk dances of New England are predominantly Scotch-Irish in origin, why the dances of many of the Southern states are surprisingly German in flavor and, in fact, she can actually give you an intimate and intensely human history of the United States through her knowledge of folk dancing.

An American Tradition   If Elizabeth Burchenal had her way every one would learn something of the simplicity and freshness of American pioneers through dancing such traditional dances as *Boston Fancy, The Green Mountain Volunteers, Jefferson and Liberty,* or such figures as *Alabama Tatervine* and *Twistification.* To her, American folk dancing is a dateless, fine and human material that can bring refreshment and a much-needed simplicity to a highly sophisticated scheme of living. It is not enough to see it or read about it, for folk dancing is designed for participation. Miss Burchenal believes so strongly in participation that she pulled me gently but firmly into one of her dancing groups. Was it fun? I'm going back for more. [*New York Herald Tribune*]

Ballet Theatre Speaks

February 12, 1941

Every one has been waiting to see whether the Ballet Theatre could possibly match its tremendous initial success of last season. Last night at the Majestic Theater most of us found that the Ballet Theatre had not only matched that challenging record but had also surpassed it. It proved itself worthy of the two names it bears, for it is first-rate ballet and it is certainly first-rate theater. Be it antique or modern, if a ballet is good theatrical material you can count on the Ballet Theatre's doing it, and so last night saw a production of the hundred-year-old *Giselle* and the premieres of Agnes de Mille's *Three Virgins and a Devil* and Antony Tudor's *Gala Performance.*

Giselle, when you come right down to it, is pretty silly in spots, what with the ghosts of lovelorn maidens flying about a graveyard, but it has some fine dramatic moments and it is filled with beautiful dancing. Anton Dolin, with better make-up and far more direct and strong miming than he showed last season, danced magnificently and proved beyond question that he is one of the very few great classic dancers of the day.

Nana Gollner is Giselle   Nana Gollner, making her New York debut, was a beautiful Giselle, fresh and free in her movements and touching in her mad scene when she discovers her lover's infidelity. She was not as good in the second act, for her healthy spirit did not lend itself easily to the projection of a ghost maiden, but further performances will undoubtedly see growing improvement in this splendid young dancer. The corps danced as only the Ballet Theatre corps can dance, and that is high praise.

Three Virgins and a Devil is a riotous medieval allegory done à la Harpo Marx, and the brilliant costumes and setting of motley make the near-slapstick

104

goings-on even more hilarious. Agnes de Mille, Lucia Chase and Annabelle Lyon try like all get-out to be properly pious, but the Devil lures them one by one into his den. Eugene Loring is the Devil, and his plan of campaign for capturing the three Virgins is nothing short of ingenious.

Ballerinas Fight It Out   The final ballet of the evening was, appropriately enough, *Gala Performance,* and it contained down to the tiniest item all of the most annoying aspects of ballet satirized to the hilt. Nora Kaye as the Russian ballerina, Nana Gollner as the Italian ballerina and Karen Conrad as the French ballerina fought it out with fouettés in a story of professional jealousy behind the footlights. Miss Kaye smoldered in the best Tartar fashion and whipped herself into a fine Russian frenzy.

With all the dignity of the Pantheon, Nana Gollner carved a regal progress through the ranks of her corps de ballet, and Karen Conrad, with a blond wig and ruffles, come-hithered the audience with her dancing coquetries. When the three ballerinas were on stage together, some not-so-gentle shoving was evident as each ballerina discharged her individual brand of glamour like an erupting volcano. *Gala Performance* had the audience in a state of shrieking. [*New York Herald Tribune*]

February 14, 1941: The Pioneer Spirit

Eugene Loring is a choreographer of great promise, but although there are many magnificent moments in his *Billy the Kid,* there is also a goodly number of sequences sadly lacking in theatrical craftsmanship. Ballet Theatre gave this American work a fine production at the Majestic Theater last evening, and the company danced it with characteristic vim and vigor. *Billy the Kid* reveals the pioneer spirit of the American people and as the ballet opens we see the cowboys, the wives, the dance hall girls suggesting by their movements the virility of a people. And from this background emerges the story of Billy, whose talents are directed towards killing.

There is blood and thunder, tenderness and courage in *Billy the Kid,* and they are clearly defined in some of the shooting sequences, in the gay bits of folk dancing and in Billy's moonlit dance with his sweetheart. But Loring has made each episode too long and there are movements that seem to have no valid place in the development of the ballet, for they have neither visual appeal nor thematic reasons for being.

Loring is splendid as Billy. He draws his character with great tenderness and understanding. Alicia Alonso dances beautifully the role of Billy's best girl, and there is no fault to find with the spirited dancing of the company. I'm afraid that all of *Billy the Kid*'s weak points may be laid to choreographer

Loring, and because he has brilliant choreographic ability and because *Billy* is in essence a fine and exciting ballet, I feel certain that Eugene Loring can make *Billy the Kid* a really great theater work. [*New York Herald Tribune*]

February 15, 1941

At this point I want to eat an uncomfortable amount of my words. In a previous review, I said that much of Eugene Loring's *Billy the Kid* suffered from unclearly defined choreography. On seeing it a second time I must take it all back, for the fault of the first performance was due to the dancing of the company and not to Mr. Loring. Last night the company danced it well and filled the really difficult movements with the meanings and the qualities which were there all the time, but which were hidden. Now I know that Loring's *Billy* captures the spirit and reveals the heart of American pioneers, and that it is a work of which the Ballet Theatre may be justly proud. [*New York Herald Tribune*]

February 16, 1941

A girl, about to marry a man she doesn't love, gives a farewell party in her garden and invites, for the final time, her lover. Unknown to her, the fiance has a mistress who also comes to this party, and these tragic four break their dearest ties amidst a scene of gayety. That is the story in dance which the Ballet Theatre told at the Majestic Theater last evening. But Antony Tudor's *Jardin aux Lilas* is more than a surface narration; it is an emotion-shaking experience in drama. His four characters are well bred and their schooling has trained them to behave with graciousness and respect for one another, but their passionate instincts, kept in check by the unwritten laws of school behavior, break loose for moments of breathless release, and as suddenly return to their bonds. It is this seething undercurrent of human desires that gives almost unbearable dramatic suspense to *Jardin aux Lilas,* and it is the courage, the almost hidden agonies and the tender moments when the lovers give each other fleeting caresses that literally tear your own emotions to shreds.

Unlike the fairy-tale romances of traditional ballets, *Jardin aux Lilas* deals with adult love and its accompanying complexities. Over and over again the lovers are alone for a minute in the garden, and just as the precious moment of farewell is at hand, the guests appear, and with a shuddering return to pretense, they turn away from each other. The tremendous dramatic force of *Jardin* is not easily defined, for the mechanics of the choreography are never obvious. Each movement, each gesture reveal the ceaseless struggle between outer control and inner revolt in this ageless story of human beings and their desires.

Antony Tudor appeared as the mature and emotionally balanced bridegroom-to-be, and Karen Conrad was splendid as the discarded mistress. Annabelle Lyon and Hugh Laing were the lovers, and they, too, were perfect in their roles. The musical background was by Ernest Chausson and the set and costumes were designed by Raymond Sovey. [*New York Herald Tribune*]

February 18, 1941

Nothing short of a royal command by the Queen-Empress Victoria herself could ever have brought the world's four greatest ballerinas together on the same stage. That is exactly what happened, for in 1845 Taglioni, Grisi, Cerrito and Grahn shed their bitter rivalries to dance for Victoria at Her Majesty's Theater, London. They never danced together again, but that single performance remains one of the great stories of ballet and is immortalized in A. E. Chalon's famous lithograph, the *Pas de Quatre*. Sunday night at the Majestic Theater Anton Dolin recreated the great event for the Ballet Theatre.

Nana Gollner was the Taglioni, and she danced the role to perfection. There was just a hint of arrogance in her gracious bearing, as if she knew she were "queen of the dance" and destined to be immortal in the minds of dance lovers. The speed and lightness of her movements evoked the Taglioni legends, and although no one living would possibly be able to compare the recreator with the original, Gollner most certainly created the atmosphere of great dancing. Danish Nina Stroganova portrayed her countryman, Grahn, and executed her demanding sequence of entrechats with the aplomb and skill befitting a great ballerina. Katharine Sergava was lovely in the simple lyric passages which were given Cerrito, and the most engaging dance of all was done by Alicia Alonso as Grisi, with the twinkling feet.

Anton Dolin did a masterful job of restoration, for he kept *Pas de Quatre* an elegant period piece both in spirit and in execution. He used only the vocabulary of movements known to that day, and each ballerina danced the variation which best displayed those qualities which history said she possessed. The manner of the piece was delightful, for each ballerina was haughtily gracious to the others, and although the celebrated ladies danced well together, a delicate aura of malice spiced the occasion. I imagine that Queen Victoria noticed that same aura at the first *Pas de Quatre,* and that is undoubtedly why Dolin has kept it in his restoration. The music was a transcription of the original score by Cesare Pugni. *Pas de Quatre* is certainly another Ballet Theatre "must." [*New York Herald Tribune*]

March 9, 1941

With tonight's final performance at the Majestic Theater, the Ballet Theatre will bring to a close the first phase of its short but brilliantly successful career. It can look with pride upon its past achievements, for the two New York seasons showed Ballet Theatre to be the most vital force in the American theater-dance. An unmatched corps de ballet, a democratic system that permitted minor members of the company to assume leading roles, a group of choreographers that recreated the great works of the past and produced new works of inestimable artistic value, a vigorous, native personnel that put the stamp of America on ballet, these were Ballet Theatre's contributions to the progress of dance. Ahead lies the difficult process of reorganization, for Ballet Theatre has proved its right to permanancy, and the initial plan of a few individual backers must give way to the more impersonal system of a managing guild or a board of businessmen.

In previous columns and reviews I have discussed the worth of Ballet Theatre and its productions. There is no need to compare it either favorably or unfavorably with imported ballet companies, for most of us want Ballet Theatre to succeed because it is our own theater-child and because it has shown us how fine and exciting American ballet can be. Today I want to tell you what Ballet Theatre has meant and continues to mean to the men and women who are Ballet Theatre. Perhaps you don't remember Mimi Gomber; she isn't famous yet, but her job in the corps of the Ballet Theatre "means more than earning money. I have had jobs in musical comedy and I know that I can get more, but all I ask is Ballet Theatre; it's home to me, it's where I want to be and it gives me a chance to dance the way I want to dance."

An Opportunity for All   Donald Saddler, one of the most promising members of the Ballet Theatre's ensemble, said: "In a foreign group you almost have to wait until some one dies before you get a solo chance, but here in Ballet Theatre I know that the minute my dancing becomes proficient I will be given my chance. During the company's lay-off I'm going home to study more ballet, but I'll come back as soon as the company needs me." Miriam Golden is sure, and I agree with her, that no other company would have used her talents as they have been used by Ballet Theatre. "I'm too tall to be a classic ballerina, but I can dance in the modern style. Mr. Tudor seemed to know what I could do and took me right out of the corps for a featured part in *Dark Elegies.*" Mr. Loring did the same for Miss Golden in *The Great American Goof,* in which she danced a main role.

Dwight Godwin is impressed with the democratic air of Ballet Theatre. "Why, even the ballerinas take stiff direction without a murmur, and we know that when new productions are cast we of the ensemble have as good an

108

opportunity of landing featured roles as do the company's already established soloists." David Nillo, with more training in modern dance than in classic ballet, finds that Ballet Theatre can use his particular style in the new works, and he, too, speaks of the democratic system: "A part calls for individual talent and not for a star, and with such a policy every one knows he has a fair chance." Leon Danielian and John Kriza seem more interested in their colleagues and in Ballet Theatre as a whole than they are in their personal successes, content to be members of a company that is "home" to them. This fellowship is a well known trait of Ballet Theatre, for I know of an instance (contrary to the traditional jealousy of theater) when a group of the dancers went to their director and asked him to give a certain girl in the company a try at a major role "because she has improved so much in class and is really a swell dancer."

Gollner Admits Flaws   Even Nana Gollner, who stars in the classic ballets, knows humility, for before the season opened she admitted before the entire company that her debut at the Lewisohn Stadium last summer was notable for its poor dancing, and she never tried to excuse it by mentioning her foot-accident and the subsequent lay-off from rehearsals. Right now she is going back to California to study further so that she will be a still finer ballerina for Ballet Theatre's next season.

Anton Dolin says, "Ballet Theatre means more to me than did the Markova-Dolin Ballet. In England Miss Markova and I carried on the tradition of the European ballet, but here I feel that I am taking part in a new idea, in the birth of an American ballet. Antony Tudor and I are English, but we are trying to be worthy foster-fathers of Ballet Theatre. Yes, we do the classics, but there are no cobwebs to be removed; the American boys and girls of the company have made these traditional works live again." During the company's process of reorganization, Dolin will be active in other quarters, but all new contracts will state that Ballet Theatre has first call on his services whenever they are again required. That is an Englishman's loyalty to an American idea. Mr. Tudor would like to have his whole future unfold within the scope of Ballet Theatre, for he feels that new forms in ballet will grow up under Ballet Theatre's dual policy of "ballet" and "theater." Native-born Eugene Loring says that he would lend his dance services to Ballet Theatre whether his own ballets were produced or not, for he believes that Ballet Theatre is destined to guide American dance and guide it well.

From an established artist right down to the least known dancer in the corps de ballet, the members of Ballet Theatre give their loyalty to the organization and the principles upon which it is founded, and so great is that loyalty that individual success means far less to them than the ultimate success of Ballet Theatre. I have set down this record of these dancers' faith in each other and in their directors, because I think it is significant. It is this very faith that will lead Ballet Theatre to permanency and that in turn will assure the permanency of ballet in America. [*New York Herald Tribune*]

November 16, 1941

Ballet Theatre's opening night answered several questions that had long been in the minds of many of us. Was the company's reorganization for better or worse? Was the Ballet Theatre just another Russian ballet? Was the corps de ballet still the best in the world? Had the initial zip of the company been retained? When the reorganization occurred last summer, I was resentful, for it meant that the strong American wing, headed by Eugene Loring, would be lost, and that the intrenched European aspects of ballet would predominate. Those of us who had hailed the original Ballet Theatre as the standard bearer for ballet American style announced that there were enough European countries and that Ballet Theatre would be wise to continue to foster the native dance. The new management, however, has given direction, new choreographies and stellar roles to the foreign born. The opening night performance proved that this reorganization produced first-rate ballet, and although a belief in the skill of our American dancers may have made us wish that Americans were at the helm, there was every reason to give credit to and cheer these imported ballet leaders for bringing us great ballet art.

The Ballet Theatre is not completely Russianized, for the presence of American dancers in the ensemble and in occasional featured roles is still to be felt. When Karen Conrad soared onto the stage in *Les Sylphides* the full-bodied strength and the clean-cut action of American dance held the spotlight. It may be the destiny of some other organization to foster pure American ballet, but there is enough native talent within the framework of the Ballet Theatre to serve as a healthy nucleus for an expanding native ballet. Take a look at Nora Kaye, for here is a girl that is going to be sharing ballerina status with Markova and Baronova before many seasons have passed. Maria Karniloff, Annabelle Lyon, Jerome Robbins and Donald Saddler are dancing splendidly and effectively no matter how minor the role, and they, too, as the seasons progress, are going to add more American spice to Ballet Theatre.

Ballet Theatre is quite obviously less American that it was before its reorganization, but it is a great dancing company and as such should be welcomed by all lovers of the dance art. As a matter of fact, the presence of Alicia Markova and Irina Baronova is cause for cheers, for these two great ballerinas bring authority, glamour and stellar strength to the company, and we Americans, as well as the Ballet Theatre, are fortunate in having them with us. With Markova comes great aristocracy of bearing and style, a way of dancing

110

that is so personal and so perfect that it erases the boundaries of nationality and emerges as pure and flawless art. Baronova, a technical wizard and a radiant woman, is a constantly appealing theater figure. Evidently she has found ideal co-operation with her Ballet Theatre colleagues, for she is dancing better than she ever did with any other group, and in a short rehearsal season has grown from a charming girl into an artist of distinction.

From the choreographic angle, the Europeans win out, for Eugene Loring and his American ballets are gone and Agnes de Mille is represented by one brief work. In this I disagree with the new Ballet Theatre policy, for I believe that the lustiness of a *Billy the Kid* and the straightforward, emotionally adult and fresh movement invention of American choreographers would give added power to the Ballet Theatre repertory. The only new work I have seen as this is being written, is Michel Fokine's *Bluebeard,* an opulent, hilarious ballet which finds the great Russian master in fine fettle. When several yards of it have been cut out, *Bluebeard* will surely be one of the most theatrically effective ballets in many a season, for its complicated plot of marital mayhem, clandestine romances, murder and associate actions is treated in buffoon style and the actual dance movements are fresh and pungent.

Yes, Ballet Theatre has changed. The loss of some American characteristics is to be deeply regretted, but the addition of Markova and Baronova brings added prestige and artistry to the company. The corps de ballet is still the best in the field, and with few exceptions, its members dance with the zip and sparkle which distinguished them in earlier seasons. The absence of *Billy the Kid* is a black mark, but the new Fokine ballet is all to the good. Summing it all up, on the strength of the opening performance, it can be said that the new Ballet Theatre is a keen and lively organization, the freshest and the most theatrically sound of all the international companies. [*New York Herald Tribune*]

Broadway Dance

March 23, 1941

Broadway is giving its musical comedy patrons quantities of dance art; it may be provocatively draped with an aura of physical allure or knocked into hilarious shapes for satiric purposes, but it is still good dancing. Vera Zorina surely heads the list of Broadway's dancing stars, for although her beautifully deadpan acting is half her charm in *Louisiana Purchase,* the other half can be claimed for dance. Zorina could not be called a great ballerina, but what she does do she does extremely well. Her husband's choreography is designed to show her ability at its best. Any one who has ever seen George Balanchine's choreography, either in ballet or musical, knows that intricate, slow-motion leg work is the trade mark of his romantic adagios. Zorina has just such an episode in her current work. If you insist upon being scholastic about dancing you'll find that it is well fashioned choreography beautifully danced by Zorina. To the trained or the untrained eye, Zorina and her dancing look swell.

Louisiana's Ensembles   The non-Zorina dance parts of *Louisiana Purchase* are shared by Balanchine and Carl Randall, and Mr. Randall's dances are far better than Balanchine's balletic bits. The dances are built on the established lines of girl-show formations, but Randall has tossed in enough free-style ballet twists to make everything fresh, lively and inventive. The ballet girls, given trite movements, perform with all the dash of marathon dancers on their last lap. Nick Long, Jr. has one good tap dance, and dark-hued Nicodemus does one of those fascinating Negro shuffles that makes you think his body is made of vitalized molasses.

For sheer loveliness of movement just trot over to *Crazy With the Heat* and see Mary Raye and Naldi, for their exhibition ballroom dancing is apparently flawless. Their dancing goes to prove that dignity and cool beauty of movement are as exciting and as sure-fire, theatrical material as are the more familiar bombastic elements of musical revues. Even the most difficult lifts are done with such easy smoothness that the dancers seem to float beyond the reach of gravity's laws. Raye and Naldi do three numbers, and that's not half enough.

And now we come to that premier danseur de luxe, Willie Howard. Watching Mr. Howard's Ivan Roushinska in *Crazy With the Heat,* I was not certain from which ballet tradition he sprang, but there was a fine Balkan frenzy about it all. He danced a solo called "Morning Mist," but my report of his virtuosity must be second-hand for it was danced behind a screen and Luella Gear's ecstatic description of it may have been slightly exaggerated. Diosa Costello was on hand for her own brand of muscle-wrenching as the Puerto Rican Heat Wave, and Tip, Tap and Toe turned in the best routines of the show with their two specialty numbers. Their actual tapping had a wide range of rhythms and the body movements were virtuosic to the hilt, for Negro artists seem to be able to indulge in movements that would leave a dancer of another race with splintered bones and mangled vertebra. The important thing is that Tip, Tap and Toe accomplish these physical feats as dance and not as acrobatics.

A hoofing cad is the role Gene Kelly plays in *Pal Joey,* and he really knows how to hoof. His performing is directed right at the audience with the hail-pals spirit of the old vaudeville days, but his tapping is nicely mated with the ballet touch of the contemporary style. There are leaps and spins and intricate rhythms which Mr. Kelly puts across in engaging fashion. The Robert Alton dances for ensemble are as fine as you could want, for Alton is the best musical comedy choreographer in the business. His girls can't get by with looking beautiful; they have to dance tap, ballet, acrobatic and whatever other styles may pop into the Alton head. Variety is the secret of the Alton successes, for he uses large groups, small units and solo bits in rapid, yet always well defined sequence. Swift of pace, ingenious and humorous, the *Pal Joey* dances are first-rate stuff, and responsible, I think, for much of the show's success. I'm not sure that the things that slap-happy June Havoc does could be called dancing, but her odd movements have certainly added something to the vocabulary of dance.

Miss Lawrence, Dancer   As you know, Gertrude Lawrence turns on the works in *Lady in the Dark* and as you also know she is star stuff no matter what she does. Her dancing, though far from complex, is tremendously effective and even in the straight dramatic episodes, the movements of her body are those of a dancer who knows how to reflect character and mood in terms of gesture and motion. In *The Saga of Jenny* Miss Lawrence struts and throws her hips to the breezes in a fine burlesque of the "hot" dancer and to prove her versatility further, she manages to look like and move like Ruth St. Denis in the first act finale called *This Woman at the Altar.*

Albertina Rasch devised the dances for the ensembles in *Lady in the Dark* and did a bang-up job of them. The choreography as such is not epochmaking, but Mme. Rasch had made the dance episodes an integral part of the whole scheme of production. *Dance of the Tumblers* in the circus scene provides a moment of real dancing that recalls, perhaps, a vivid sequence from some glittering Russian ballet. Several fine young dancers are in the ensemble: George Bockman from the Humphrey–Weidman group, Jerome Andrews, Fred Hearn and Bill Howell from the Shawn Dancers, Dorothy Bird from Martha Graham's company and others. They aren't given a chance to show their prowess in solos, but their joint efforts are splendid.

The season's dance on Broadway seems better than ever. The only thing it lacks is Beatrice Lillie in tutu and on points as the maddest of ballerinas.
[*New York Herald Tribune*]

Three Debuts—Hawkins, Shearer, Bettis

April 27, 1941: Erick Hawkins

With bright-eyed assurance every young dancer sets out to show that he has something new to contribute to the age-old art of dance. He probably has something new to say and a new way in which to say it, but sometimes he forgets, in his quest for fresh forms, that there are certain unalterable standards of art, craft and entertainment. It's not fair to criticize a young dancer by the tough standards set up by mature and experienced performers, but you have a right to find eagerness, agility, punch and other youthful qualities atoning for lack in profundity, authority and polish.

Last Sunday I spoke about the achievements of several young American dancers, and today I would like to mention some of the pitfalls that beset young artists of dance. An example of pitfalling is Erick Hawkins, who made his New York debut as a solo dancer last Sunday at the Y. M. H. A. Dance Theater. He has appeared as a ballet dancer and choreographer for Lincoln Kirstein's American Ballet Caravan and in recent seasons as leading male dancer in the productions of Martha Graham. In each of these brief dual careers he did good work, and under Miss Graham's direction developed a personal style that was well suited to such works as *El Penitente* and *Every Soul Is a Circus.* Because I believe that an exciting theater dance can spring from a fusion of ballet and modern dance, I was hoping to find that Mr. Hawkins, well trained in both schools, would do some worthwhile fusing. He didn't.

A Dancer on His Own   Erick Hawkins had demonstrated his dance ability when he was under direction, but once on his own, he gave a performance that to my mind had not one bit of actual dancing in it. There was movement and there were patterns, but the spirit of dance lay buried as Mr. Hawkins paced out the actions he had set for himself. His first solo was called *Pilgrim's Progress,* but it could have been called anything else under the sun, so obscure was the meaning of the dance. There were copious program notes that recalled the famous book, but I, with some experience at watching all kinds of dancing, couldn't see or sense any relationship between the notes and the stage actions. With a literary theme such as this, the work could be conceived as an allegorical ballet, or a single performer, using kinetic pantomime, could draw the character and his emotional experience as a kind of dance biography. In some cases the dancer employs the difficult process of dancing his reactions to a theme, an emotion or a mood, and his movements are distillations rather than representations of the motion at hand. This process is not always successful and distinctly discouraging to the untrained dance audience. I think Mr. Hawkins was employing these tactics (but I'm not certain), and although he may have been seething inside, he projected nothing in the way of character, emotion nor mood.

The whole Hawkins program followed a similar pattern. Everything was well staged, nicely costumed and the dancer did his stint with great assurance and complete command of his body, yet nothing seemed to happen. Hawkins is not a performer of warmth and his dances suggest that he leans toward a ritual form. That's all very well, but even a ritual can be rip-snorting and exciting, filled with subleties of mood and meaning. Whatever his goal may be, the young dancer should make clear his aims so that even if he stumbles you can say, "Well, he flunked that one, but I see where he is going."

The Simplicity of Dance I believe that Erick Hawkins and other young dancers must strive to remember that dancing is a very simple and a very human activity. When they dream up some terrific theme and some unique way of presenting it, they would do well to avoid the occult and the pretentious. At the Hawkins concert I was wishing that some one would swing into a Strauss waltz, and that this dancer would just get up and dance as if he loved it, for the audience would have loved it too. No one expects the young dancer to slip back into the "fancy dancing" of another day, but swing and rhythm and good spirits belong to every dance.

This has been intended as a constructive criticism of a young dancer whose sincerity and potential promise I thoroughly respect. Perhaps he will prove me wrong and at a later date show that he has really developed a valid style of dance, but at present writing he is unable to clearly project his ideas. As a tonic I suggest a combination of simplicity and the spirit of fun. Let him and his young colleagues show us and make us feel that dance is joyous, and for the serious and important things which they must express in dance, let them be expressed as simply as possible even if these dancers have to resort to a traditional dance style, for the style itself will become new and fresh through the touch of youth. [*New York Herald Tribune*]

October 22, 1941: Sybil Shearer

An exciting debut took place last evening at the Carnegie Chamber Music Hall when young Sybil Shearer danced her way into the top-notch rank of American dance artists. Miss Shearer has been seen in the Humphrey–Weidman programs and also with the Agnes de Mille company, but this marked her bow as a solo dancer, and the tremendous difficulties of varying a dance performance single-handed bothered her not at all. She has a style of movement unlike that of any other dancer, and this freshness of articulation makes her a constantly absorbing artist. Her technical equipment enables her to reach the heights of virtuosity, for her balance alone would make a Russian ballerina assoluta green with envy. This virtuosity, however, is not used to create applause-getting tricks, but is made to serve as a dramatic accent on the theme at hand.

The opening *Sarabande and Passepied* were presented in the traditional style, but flavored with a slight personal characterization and the *O Sleeper of the Land of Shadows, Wake! Expand!* was a beautiful exposition of the quality of reverence. Quick of motion and released in spirit was *In Thee Is Joy,* a dance which brought to the fore Miss Shearer's breadth and ease of movement. The quality of *Nocturne* is difficult to describe, for it is a dance of quiet exploration, of subdued self-appraisal. And *Prophesy* on the other hand, was stirringly dramatic. Miss Shearer's body was flooded with dynamic energy, to the point of explosion. Here again the wealth of newly designed movement and of unbelievable body control made for stimulating dance.

For her closing solos, the dancer offered *In the Cool of the Garden, In the Field* and *In a Vacuum. In the Field* was a dance of rare beauty, a stylization of the labor rhythms of sowing seed. In the center of the dance was an interlude which seemed to be an incantation for fruitfulness, an almost forgotten ceremony to celebrate the magic of growth. The closing dance *In the Vacuum* was one of the funniest things I have ever seen. The dancer's arms, legs and body flew about in split-second rhythm, running the gamut of impossible positions. This dance of intense aimlessness with no theme nor characterization, was an example of pure kinetic slap-stick, and there is nothing funnier in this world than a giggling musculature.

Sybil Shearer's choreography, as well as her dancing, was splendid. There were occasional flaws as far as dance structures were concerned and moments that could have done with more dramatic accent, but these are inconsequential in the face of Miss Shearer's dance achievements, for she is an exciting dancer and an artist who is surely destined to contribute richly to American dance. Mari Harding, pianist, shared the program with Miss Shearer and also played the dancer's accompaniments. The program will be repeated this evening. [*New York Herald Tribune*]

November 29, 1941: Valerie Bettis

Valerie Bettis, a former member of Hanya Holm's company, made her debut as a solo dancer Thursday evening at the Carnegie Chamber Music Hall. It must be said right off that Miss Bettis is not yet equipped to carry an evening of theater alone, but regarded in the light of a demonstration of capabilities, the performance revealed Miss Bettis as a dancer of promise. She boasts superb control of her body, and as far as physical action is concerned, nothing

116

seems too difficult for her. A sense of style is discernible, there is authority in her manner and her face possesses endless dramatic possibilities which so far she fails to employ. On the debit side of the Bettis dance one finds a tendency to accent percussive movements. There is dramatic power in the use of sudden halts following passages of whirling action, but Miss Bettis uses this device so often that it loses its potency as her dances progress. The dynamics are pretty much on the same plane, and this, too, makes for monotony.

Her choreographic virtues and faults are, of course, similar. In her final dance, *Country Lane,* she projected a sense of joy for the one and only time of the evening, but because of her sameness in dynamics the joy never got anywhere. Here was an opportunity for the dancer to cut loose and have some fun. All of the dances were episodic and, although they displayed her technical skill to good advantage, they were lacking in form and in integration. In the *City Streets* suite the Broadway character came off the best, and Miss Bettis suggested in amusing fashion the tawdry vapidity associated with some of Broadway's less attractive show girls.

Triptych, divided into three sections dealing with the past, present and future, had some wonderful isolated dance movements, but again the complete dances did not quite come off. Valerie Bettis has splendid dance material at hand, but she has yet to organize it for the theater. There is fine technical skill at her command, and the next step is for her to learn how to command it. [*New York Herald Tribune*]

Native Dance Art

August 3, 1941

It takes courage to be an American dancer. For him there is no security and no subsidy, only constant hardship. Artistic success and cultural achievement have been won by American dance artists, but as men and women they have failed to earn money through their jobs. Imported ballet companies are pretty thoroughly subsidized to the point where lavish productions and all-star casts are possible. Wealthy balletomanes come through with backing for a choreographer's new work, for there always seems to be some individual whose generosity can be counted on for carrying out the artist's pet scheme. This system of subsidy works well in many ways: it produces a large organization, it enables the choreographer to collaborate with the finest of theater artists, it keeps a repertory fresh and progressive through the production of new ballets. It is this subsidy that has made Russian ballet the most glittering attraction in the world of dance.

American artists have had to make their own way in the theater world, backed only by the applause of the American public. Ruth St. Denis, Ted Shawn and their Denishawn Dancers carved for themselves a fabulous theatrical career. There were lavish productions, large ensembles and coast-to-coast tours, and it was all done without one cent of backing. In 1930, at the end of fifteen years of Denishawn activity, the heads of the company found themselves without a profit. Members of the company had had high salaries through all these years, new theater dances had been shown before countless audiences, the American dance had proved its artistic and entertainment values, but the security that St. Denis and Shawn had earned was to be found in popular affection and not in dollar bills.

Dance Without Subsidy　For more than a decade Doris Humphrey, Charles Weidman and Martha Graham have followed the course of Denishawn, bringing great and important dance to the people of the country, but bringing it without subsidy. Today they and their colleagues face a desperate situation. New York performances are so expensive that one or two a season are all that are possible. The touring field is overcrowded, making it almost impossible for any one to finish a tour with a substantial profit. Somehow American dancers seem to scrape along season after season, giving us glimpses of great dance and then rushing back to teach classes in order to raise money for further appearances. This state of affairs should not continue for long or one day the American dance might die in a studio. With financial support our native dance art should reach new heights of achievement. If it is accused of being unglamorous, just stop and think what it could do with the money that a Russian ballet company has to work with.

This brings me to the Ballet Theatre. Two weeks ago I discussed the changes that seem to be taking place in that organization, and I wondered whether it was going to continue to represent the traditional ballet, the contemporary European styles and the American contributions in balanced fashion or whether it was going Russian with a bang. The response to that article convinces me that a good many persons think that American dancers and choreographers are really good and that they deserve a showing in such a company as Ballet Theatre. This is not pure nationalism, although I would like to see American artists earning good money, but it is an honest conviction that American dancers and American choreography can hold their own with any in the world.

American Style Ballet　Ballet is not a folk form, it is an international theatre art, and as such is open to the contributions of every race. The time is ripe for Americans to flavor this traditional theater dance. One Russian-born gentleman told me that he thought American dancers were swell but that the choreographies and styles of the natives would not fit into the ballet mould. How, may I ask, did the Russian trepak and its associates ever get into the classic ballet? How did Flamencos, can-cans and tarantellas find their way into the realm of white tutus? Some stubborn choreographer stuck to his guns and enriched the ballet with native dances, and aren't we glad he did? The French traditionalists were probably horrified with what the Italians did to ballet and the Italians infuriated with the Russian additions, and I'm sure the Russians are going to try (because they honestly believe they are right) to keep Indian dances, cowboy dances, Ted Shawn and Martha Graham movements out of ballet.

Ballet Theatre may turn back on its founding principle of fostering native dance and dancers as well as keeping alive the traditions from abroad, and turn its energies to the perpetuation of Russian ballet. In this latter capacity it would undoubtedly achieve a worthy success. But how much more exciting it would be and how invaluable to the dance art as a whole, if Ballet Theatre would be the first organization to help bring to fruition an American ballet idiom. American ballet is destined to come. American dance artists are due for the backing and support of which they are worthy. Ballet Theatre cannot, singlehanded, put American dance on its feet, but it can lead the way. If fate and the managers decree that Ballet Theatre is not the one for the task, then some other organization will come along to do the job. For American ballet is definitely on the way and nothing can stop it, thanks to the courage and the greatness of American dancers themselves. [*New York Herald Tribune*]

Punch and the Judy

August 12, 1941

Bennington, Vt., Aug. 11   Martha Graham and her company presented the second dance concert of the Bennington Festival of the Arts Sunday night at the college theater, and for the occasion offered a bill consisting of *El Penitente, Letter to the World* and a new theater piece, *Punch and the Judy*. According to the program note the dance "concerns man and woman." The text is squabble and scuffle. The fates are any three women who direct the lives of others. The three heroes are the idealists. Pegasus is the force which enables us to imagine or to escape or to realize.

Following the comic, satiric trend she set in her highly successful and thoroughly hilarious *Every Soul Is a Circus*, Miss Graham's *Punch and the Judy* finds her again making great play with the foibles of men. The three

119

fates, looking for all the world like three disagreeable and domineering great-aunts, create the situations of squabble and scuffle in which Punch and Judy battle it out with each other and passersby. A serene domestic bit between man and wife is interrupted by playful daughter who causes a sturdy row consisting of physical tussles and well-aimed kicks. In her fury, friend wife seeks solace from Pegasus, who flies in the window to bear her off to a world of pleasant dreams. There is trouble with a flossy soubrette, Punch momentarily forgets wife and family while Judy runs the gamut from rage through martyrdom to despair. In the final shambles the fates, the idealists, Pegasus, Punch and Judy create a scene of marital discord that is riotous, and in the end Punch is forgiven by a happy Judy as the fates turn to the audience and say, "Shall we begin our story again?"

Punch and the Judy is great comedy from any angle. All the ravings and sarcastic remarks of such a situation have been translated into dumb-show, and if you think that a lady cannot tell her spouse what she thinks of him through actions of arm, legs, body, and head through gesture and grimace, you should see Martha Graham. Domestic bliss and its antithesis come to vital and hilarious life, as Miss Graham and her cohorts hold their magic mirror up to life and show us how silly we all are.

Miss Graham was in rare form, giving forth with ridiculous bits of mime, indulging in snake-hips when the occasion demanded and disporting herself through many sequences of highly inventive dance movement. Erick Hawkins, as Punch, dispensed with the remote and highly stylized quality which usually marks his work, and let himself go. Pegasus was beautifully danced with lightness, ease and fleetness by Merce Cunningham, and Jean Erdman as one of the fates, delivered her remarks on the stupidity of human action with fine and expressive sarcasm. The production was splendidly staged, for the costumes of Charlotte Trowbridge and the set and lighting by Arch Lauterer made for the best theatrical presentation that modern dance has shown to date. The music of Robert McBride was admirably suited to the choreography and boasted a hit tune in the first measure of the score. Arch Lauterer also collaborated with Miss Graham on the plan of Punch and the Judy. A capacity audience was on hand to yell for many curtain calls. [New York Herald Tribune]

August 24, 1941

Balletomanes will tell you that modern dance is thoroughly mystifying or, if not that, too serious. Both of those aspects may have been true a few years ago, but no longer. Martha Graham's new work, which she presented two weeks ago at the Bennington Festival of the Arts, is not only understandable, it is riotous. Her theme is "squabble and scuffle" and her characters are man and woman, for *Punch and the Judy* is the eternal comedy of home life. Those who remember the stark days of modern dance staging will be glad to hear that the Charlotte Trowbridge costumes are richly colorful, the decor of Arch Lauterer smart and inventive, the Robert McBride score tuneful. In fact, *Punch and the Judy* is as thoroughly an entertaining theater piece as any you are likely to see.

The Three Fates, looking like female disciplinarians of a school for Victorian girls, set the stage in haughty fashion. Throughout the course of the dance they direct the channels of action, causing one squabble after another, after which the head Fate turns to the audience and makes some cutting comment on the general stupidity of man. The opening scene is one of peace, with Punch reclining comfortably on his couch and with the Judy contentedly mooning out of a French window. The Fates give a stir to this domestic scene and the next thing you know Punch and the Judy are battling fiercely over their child. Baby bawls, wife gets a good swift kick from her husband and the scene ends with Punch returning sullenly to his couch and the Judy, complete disgust embedded in her stride, going back to her window. But this is just the beginning, more marital scuffles are on the way.

Family Scrap   During the course of this theater-piece, Punch takes a fling at infidelity while the Judy takes turns at raging, despairing, being noble and forgetting the whole affair. When things get too thick, the Judy goes to her window, and Pegasus, who symbolizes the release to dreams, flies in and bears her off into the shimmering moonlight of joyous fantasy. This is the general outline of the plot, but it is not plot alone that makes *Punch and the Judy* such a masterful piece of theater-dance. The theme of squabble and scuffle is as old as theater itself, family characters give a warmth and familiarity to the occasion and Miss Graham's selection of incidents to project her theme and to develop her characters gives the piece a universal touch.

Punch and the Judy is a treasury of expressive movement. Miss Graham has given herself a broad range of dance action from the furious steps and steel-spined defiance of her squabble scenes to the lovely, lyric passages that wing her away with Pegasus. Erick Hawkins has his best dancing role to date in Punch, for Miss Graham has given him movements that thoroughly describe Punch's rampant masculinity, his head-of-the-family stance, his boyish bounce when he catches the eye of a pretty girl. Merce Cunningham is as light and as air-conscious as Pegasus should be, his movements as softly designed as the dream-world from which he comes. Jean Erdman, as the speaking Fate, delivers her lines to the audience with fine sarcasm, while her sister Fates listen approvingly. The final portion of *Punch and the Judy* was not yet as thoroughly realized as the earlier scenes when it was shown at Bennington. The judgment episode, in which the faithless Punch, the Judy, the Three Heroes (representing idealists) get into a frenzied scramble is just a bit too scrambled, and Miss Graham will have to define the scene more sharply if it is to match the clear, comic brilliance of the rest of the work.

Graham Changes Her Style   For many seasons Martha Graham has been one of the most vivid figures in the contemporary American dance. Earlier works found her dealing with abstractions of human experience rather than with characterization. She went through what she calls her "long woolen" period in which any kind of theatrical embellishment was taboo. Whatever she did, popular in style or requiring the eye of a trained dancer, Miss Graham not only broadened her own dance range, but she also contributed generously to the range of American dance. Now she has chosen to swing her talents into the realm of real theater, employing all of the facilities of stage production and adapting her own technique to the projection of dramatic theme and characterization. This trend came with the satiric *Every Soul Is a Circus* and continued with the beautiful and great *Letter to the World*. In her new *Punch and the Judy* Martha Graham has produced a theater dance that can be understood and enjoyed by any one, no matter how nebulous his dance education may be, for her movements are as articulate as the spoken word—at moments as lyric as poetry and at others as pungent as your favorite cuss word. [*New York Herald Tribune*]

Tap Dance Trend

August 31, 1941

Tap is certainly America's most popular form of theater-dance. Ballet, modern and its derivatives have their followers, but to many these forms of dance are unknown, while tap is understandable and entertaining to any one. Serious dance lovers rate tap pretty low in the dance scale, for although they may enjoy individual performers such as Bill Robinson or Fred Astaire, the actual technique of tap is generally considered superficial and limited in scope. An over-dose of slam-bang tapping, of posture that resembles that of an anthropoid ape and of accompanying music that is cheap in quality has set tap at a low level. Yet with the exception of Indian dance, tap is America's only ingenous dance form. Born of the Negro and enhanced by the clogs of Irish settlers, tap is the style of dance which Americans find most natural to do and most entertaining to watch.

It is true, however, that tap is far more limited in style, in thematic range and in emotional scope than the ballet or the dance systems of a St. Denis, Shawn, Graham or a Maracci. With few exceptions its musical background is limited to the popular and ephemeral tunes of the day, and about the only human quality it can project is good spirits. These two major aspects of tap account for its popularity as well as its limitations. Tunes are hummable and the simple projection of good fun is always pleasant to watch. A tap dance you will enjoy for the moment, or if it is danced by an Astaire the memory of it may remain in the mind indefinitely, but Martha Graham's *Letter to the World* can, through its dramatic potency, infuse you with the beauty, the passion and the rich living of its central character, Emily Dickinson.

Tap Possibilities With proper and knowing guidance, there is no reason why tap dance should not expand into a richer dance art than it is at present. The tapping of feet is a basic dance impulse, and with the Spanish Flamenco dancer it has developed into a lusty and varied dance style, but feet rhythms alone did not turn the trick, for the Flamenco artist used the movements of the body to broaden the range of his dance. There is a limited number of things that can be said with the feet, but by using the entire body in dance, the range of human expression is boundless. If tap is to grow from fine entertainment to fine art, it will have to add a vocabulary of body movement to the engaging prattle of its tapping feet.

Paul Draper, who recently appeared with great success on the International Dance Festival at Lee, Mass., has already raised the standard of tap. By dancing to the best in music, from Bach to American folk melodies, from Debussy to Latin American sambas, he has inevitably captured and translated into dance the rich qualities of the music. When he dances to Bach, his feet tap out a counterpoint to the score, while his body reflects the aristocratic quality of the music. At the festival he danced a medley of folk tunes, and in the true folk spirit he suggested that the audience members participate through singing whatever words they remembered. In *The Golliwog's Cakewalk* his feet played a tapping game with the laughing melody while his body movements suggested the grotesqueries of the title. *The Brazilian Samba* had the intensity of a primitive dance while a *Malaguena* boasted the fire, the intricate foot rhythms and the arrogant flavor of a Spanish dance.

Paul Draper, Pioneer Although he has done so much for tap dance and has achieved enviable success as a dancer, I am sure that Paul Draper is not yet through with experimentation. Intelligent, energetic and possessed of great dance skill, he is certain to add still more to the range of tap dance. He has explored the possibilities of music and he has touched upon the use of different styles in body movement to augment his taps. Under his guidance,

123

there is every reason to believe that tap dance will become a valid facet of the American dance art, that it will no longer be limited to the field of pure entertainment but that it will unite with ballet, modern dance and other forms of theater-dance in giving America an unrivaled native art. [*New York Herald Tribune*]

Indian Festival

September 14, 1941

Not at all wearied by two barn-storming tours with her self-booking, self-supporting *Dancers en Route,* Elizabeth Waters trotted out to the Southwest this summer to see more of America in dance. She was present for the last three days of the Hopi religious festival at Mishongovi, Arizona, and in the following letter tells us an American dancer's view of a truly American dance festival:

"Arriving in time to see the last three days of a sixteen-day religious festival, we spent the first day getting acquainted with the land and its people. The little Hopi villages are located on the very tops of six barren mesas. Looking out across the mesas and the lower lands, one can see miles and miles of nothingness, except for here and there a small orderly corn field, a few peach groves or the usual melon patch. The utter dryness of the summers is what makes for the 'Snake Dance' which culminates their festival, for the Hopis believe that the snakes are their little brothers who will aid them in making the fields fruitful. The Hopis themselves are very gentle and kind and are glad to have outsiders see their rituals. One evening I heard the singing of various groups and somewhere the sound of a drum. I followed the sound and came to a tent where young boys and girls were singing and dancing. I was invited in and found that here was the way the youngsters learned the traditional dances, for the older boys guided the children through the routines that time had long since set.

Ritual Races at Dawn "Dawn races are held two mornings at sunrise, the day before and the day of the 'Snake Dance.' The young men of the village run the sacred race through the cornfields, covering distances of four miles. Everything here is of absorbing interest, but the 'Snake Dance' is, of course, the most exciting event of all. Two clans, the Antelope and the Snake participate in it. Both clans wore similar costumes with short, knee-length, wrap-around skirts. The torso was bare except for a band of seashells carried over one shoulder and brought together at the left hip. Some wore real jewelry while others were painted up to look as if they wore it. The skirts were of burnt red-brown, bordered with a block design and bearing across the front a stylized design of lightning. Each dancer had a small feature securely tied on-to a wisp of hair at the top of the head. The Antelope Clan carried corn-meal rattles, while the Snake Clan had turtle shells tied just behind the right knee. Paint effects varied. The Antelope people were covered with a thin white paint which allowed the tone of the skin to come through, thus giving an odd blue tinge to their bodies. The Snake dancers painted their bodies a deep red, but their faces were almost entirely black with a diamond-shaped outline drawn from the bridge of the nose to the lower jaw at the ear. But to the dance . . .

"The Antelope Clan launches this final dance-prayer for rain. They walk into the plaza and form a large circle. Three times they move around, each time making smaller the circle's circumference. Then they stop in a straight line as the Snake Clan enters, following an identical formation and facing the Antelope people. During the circling movements, each group passes over a board that is level with the ground but covering a hollow. Each dancer stamps on this board once with every circle walk, making for a steady and even drum beat.

The Snake Dance   "The chant begins while the two clans are facing each other in straight lines, but as yet there is very little movement. Slowly the chant grows in intensity and with it the right foot stamps on the ground fol-lowed by a rebound in the knee. This builds to a semi-climax and then is abruptly cut off. So far as I could tell the same chant is started again, but here movement really begins. The snakes are being handed out from a tem-porary shelter made of green boughs with a blanket over the opening. Only the Snake Clan dance and handle the snakes, for the Antelope people stay in their line singing. The snake dancers dance in couples traveling in a circle. Each couple is composed of one old man with his arm over the shoulder of a young boy. The boys handle the snakes in their mouths with lips tightly pressed around the snake, near the head. Each snake is released to the ground when a certain point in the ritual has been reached. You can imagine this process going on until all the snakes are out. I would judge that about thirty were used. When on the ground, they are alarmingly active, but skillfully guarded. Some dancers carry five snakes at a time, yet the dance rhythm and the chanting remain unbroken.

"In time the snakes and dancers are sprinkled with sacred cornmeal by the women, who are dressed in full traditional costume and who calmly fuse their portion of the ritual with such daily domestic routines as baking. The end comes with the sprinkling of a cornmeal circle on the ground into which the snakes are tossed. Then the scramble begins with each dancer trying to

pick up as many snakes as possible. They run from the plaza in all four sacred directions, and about a mile from the starting point, release the snakes. The Antelope people finish the ceremony with the opening dance; but this time the three circles, instead of decreasing in size, expand until the dancers have swept out of the plaza itself and up to the entrances to their kivas. The beautiful and deeply religious dance of a gentle, gracious people is over."
[*New York Herald Tribune*]

Ballerinas

October 12, 1941

Probably each ballerina is convinced that she is the greatest dancer of her era, but balletomanes never cease to squabble and scrap over the respective merits of their favorites. The position of the little finger is brought into the argument, or how this or that ballerina moves her shoulder blades. Do away with quibbling, and I think you will find that a ballerina wins her place through three qualifications: personality, technical skill and that heightened beauty we call artistry. Each of the ballerinas now before the public is deserving of her position and each has won a personal following through one or more of these dance qualities.

Alexandra Danilova, first ballerina of the Ballet Russe de Monte Carlo, is unquestionably one of the great artists of dance. She is popular with the general public as witness the tremendous ovation which greeted her entrance in *Gaîté Parisienne* on the opening night at the Met. Danilova is not a virtuoso in the sense that a sheaf of pirouettes marks the high point of her dancing, for the high point is to be found in the way she moves her body, the exuberance that she brings to a coquettish role, the regal bearing that marks her classic characterizations. Her body invariably reflects to perfection the tonalities of the music to which she is dancing. Her really twinkling feet can make you chuckle along with a Strauss or Offenbach rhythm, and as the Swan Queen, her whole body is eloquent in its expression of a tragic, passionate woman. Her personality bounds across the footlights with no trouble at all, for when Alexandra Danilova makes her entrance, you know that you are seeing "ballerina." Technically she is never startling but in the pure art of dancing she is unfailingly magnificent.

Ballet Make-Believe That great English ballerina Alicia Markova brings to ballet a presence that is sheer magic. Tiny and wistful, light and delicate of

126

movement, Markova seems to be a figure from a dream world, for she touches ballet with the shadow of make-believe. In spite of a physically strong technique, there is little of the virtuoso performer about her; she moves so easily that one is conscious of no effort, but rather of light and beautiful dance. To see her *Giselle,* in which she makes credible a story of ghost maidens and their luring of men to their deaths, is to see dance fantasy at its best.

Irina Baronova, on the other hand, is very much of this world. Her particular quality is that of womanly radiance, and the beautiful Baronova, now that she has left her artistic adolescence behind her, brings to her roles a warmth that touches the heart, a glow that makes shining dance out of the choreographer's patterns. Baronova, although not a bravura artist, is technically skilled, and the business of virtuosity is in good hands when it is designed for her. As a comedian, she possesses sparkle and given an opportunity, I believe that she would be nothing short of riotous in near-slapstick roles.

Tamara Toumanova is the glitter-girl of ballet, both in physical qualifications and in dance. Breathtakingly beautiful, she is exciting to look at, but Toumanova is also a virtuoso star of the first order. The steely strength of her body enables her to toss off multiple pirouettes in electric fashion, and other feats of dance skill are achieved in bravura style. She is an exciting instrument of dance, closing each sentence of movement with the dance equivalent of an exclamation point. On occasion this technical brilliance pushes matters of characterization and style out of focus, but in a work like *Fantastic Symphony,* Toumanova is as brilliant dramatically as she is technically.

Texan Ballerina　　In Nana Gollner America finds its first top-notch ballerina. As last season's star of Ballet Theatre Gollner proved that she is potentially the most vivid ballerina of our times. Beautiful and thoroughly glamorous, she boasts an amazing technical equipment which culminates in an arabesque that she seems to be able to sustain for indefinite periods. Some of her Texan background is discernible, for Gollner's movements are space-creating. Her leaps are broad and free, and even in static poses there is the impression of movement flowing out through her fingertips. As a classic ballerina she is showing the traditionalists that a Texas Swan Queen or an Aurora can hold her own with her Russian sisters in the balletic art.

Which one of these five ballerinas is the greatest? I like them all and for the reasons that I have stated. Your choice depends on what you look for in a ballerina—technical skill, dramatic fire, lightness, glamour—on the personality most pleasing to you. No one of these dancing ladies is a perfect model of ballet art, but together they make ballet a rich and constantly changing theater experience. [*New York Herald Tribune*]

Dancing Gentlemen

November 2, 1941

A few weeks ago I wrote an article entitled "Ballerinas," and the response to that analysis of ballet ladies was so gratifying that I would like to discuss the performing qualities of the men dancers in the Ballet Russe de Monte Carlo. Heading the company is, of course, Léonide Massine, artistic director, choreographer and principal dancer. As a creator of certain character roles Massine has no peer in all ballet, and this generation of ballet-goers will not easily accept any other dancer as the google-eyed Peruvian masher of *Gaîté Parisienne,* as the diminutive yet heroic Hussar of *Le Beau Danube,* as the highly rhythmic cancan doll of *Fantastic Toyshop* or as the Miller in *The Three-Cornered Hat.* To these dance roles he brings a performing smoothness that is the special quality of the mature artist, the characterizations themselves are richly dramatic and the Massine style of movement fuses flawlessly with the rhythms of the music and with the patterns of stage action. He is not a classic dancer nor a virtuoso performer, but he is a great artist, and the force of his theater personality makes his presence on the stage as exciting as anything ballet has to offer.

Igor Youskevitch is the company's first classic dancer. To him falls the task of translating traditional virtuosity into real dance, of making the intricate adagios with the ballerina appear romantic and not acrobatic. Youskevitch fulfills these requirements with ease, for sequences of beats and turns and leaps resolve themselves into smooth and flowing dance action. Unlike many of his colleagues, he has an articulate torso, for his entire body weaves the patterns of dance, and it is a joy to sit and watch a magnificent human body move with physical skill and unstudied grace. As a partner to the ballerina he is noble of carriage and tender of action, bringing verity to the passages of dance romance.

The Franklin Zip   There is no stage grin in the world to match that of Frederic Franklin, for the Monte Carlo's young British star fairly grins with his whole body. There is zest and good nature in all of his actions as well as an enviable amount of technical skill. He literally pulled the miserably flopping *Saratoga* into the realm of entertainment, when he was on stage, with the boundless exuberance of his dancing. The hoofer in him gives zip and humor to his roles in *The New Yorker* and *Le Beau Danube,* and the artist comes to the fore in such beautiful characterizations as the boy in *Devil's Holiday.* He can easily cope with classic roles as far as technique is concerned, but his communicable high spirits and air of boyish good fun make him better suited to character parts. His virtuosity can bring down the house in the warrior's dance from *Prince Igor* or the trepak from *The Nutcracker,* but the simple and quiet dancing which finds him in the waltz from *Gaîté Parisienne* accounts for one of the most memorable moments at the ballet.

André Eglevsky is cast both in classic roles and in character parts. In either case his technical skill is apparent, particularly in matters of turns, for Mr. Eglevsky can go round and round and come out in a still vertical position. His most appealing role is that of the peasant boy in *Baiser de la Fée,* a character that he invests with youthful charm. His elevation and his neatness of movement account for his success as a classic dancer, but he has yet to become a realiable partner for the ballerina. The great flaw in his dancing lies in his personal mannerisms. He is a husky man, but he is inclined to move like one of delicate cast and winds up making himself appear heavier than he really is. With greater scope to his movements and a disclosure of the muscular power which is his, he would be far more effective as a creator of heroic roles and as a protagonist of pure dance movement.

Tomorrow's Stars   Of the company's supporting soloists, George Zoritch and Marc Platoff are far and away the most distinguished. In fact, Zoritch is intrinsically one of the great classic dancers of the day. More than any other male dancer in the balletic idiom, he has a natural flair for movement. It is impossible for him to make a bad line, to move unrhythmically, for there is a catlike smoothness about everything he does. A surer and broader technical base is all that he needs to make him worthy of leading classic roles, a less remote personal quality and a more vital approach to his dancing are all that are necessary to make him a star. Platoff, like Franklin, has the advantage of a winning stage presence, but more than that, Platoff is highly skilled in dance characterization. Not through stock miming gestures does he draw his part, but through full-bodied dance action. As the figure of evil in *Rouge et Noir,* as the girl-seeking officer in *Gaîté Parisienne* and as the Innocent in *Seventh Symphony,* Platoff brings to the fore the important dramatic qualities of ballet. Alexandra Danilova and Tamara Toumanova may be your reasons for going to the ballet (and I can think of no better ones), but once there the skill and artistry of the Monte Carlo's leading men dancers will make themselves felt through the magical power of theater dance. [*New York Herald Tribune*]

Gesture Language

December 21, 1941

La Meri has long been welcomed for her ability to bring the world to one's door. Through magnificent costumes, authentic folk music and the movements of dance, she has taken her audiences on visits to the nations of the earth. Flashes of India, Java, Spain, Hawaii, China and other countries are made possible by the world's No. 1 eclectic dancer. While her colleagues in America are busy with the work of creating an ever-progressing native dance art, this Texan dancer has done yeoman service in acquainting American audiences with the richly varied dance patterns of other peoples and bringing to her students a vast knowledge of human movement.

Although she is more of a recreative artist than a creative one, her theater performances are entertaining and stimulating, for her range of dance action keeps one wondering what is to come next, as she reveals the folk flavors of alien peoples. This is no mean public service, for the written word cannot describe the quality of a people as well as the age-old dances of that people can do. The Hindu, his religion, his behavior and his likes and dislikes are probably all very vague to most of us, yet after you have seen La Meri perform many of the traditional dances of India, the native himself begins to take shape. Through the costumes you learn something of his taste in colors and design, and through the dances themselves you learn of his powerful religious faith, of his personal dignity, of his serenity of spirit, of his love of quiet beauty. The themes of India's dances and the manners in which they are danced reduce a nation to human size, thus making it possible for an American audience to watch and to understand.

La Meri—Guide to India   Naturally, it is not possible to go to a single La Meri performance and say: "Ah! now I understand India." But frequent visits to her concerts, to her studio recitals at the Master Institute of Arts and to her lecture demonstrations guide an audience into an appreciation of foreign cultures. All of her performances are marked by authenticity of material, and many of them are scholarly. Some of the scholarly gatherings are slow of pace, and unless you are willing to forgo pure entertainment for learning, they are not fun, but if you are actively interested in finding out about other races (and also something about geography), the material is thoroughly stimulating. For her Broadway appearances, La Meri has wisely accented variety of subject matter, so that if the quietude of her Hindu solos should begin to pall upon an Occidental audience, she could rip into a snorting Spanish Flamenco or cast her body into the amorous insinuations of a Moroccan street dance. For her performance this evening at the Guild Theater she is changing her tactics: India is to be the sole scene, and the three ballets to be given, although executed with traditional movements and gestures upon traditional themes, are La Meri's own compositions. Through the pioneering performances of Uday Shankar and through the La Meri performances, American audiences seem to be ready for a full evening of Hindu dance, created and performed by an American and her company of American dancers who are thoroughly schooled in the dance craft of India.

The visual beauty of the Hindu dance is easily appreciated, and the hand gestures are invariably delightful, but the meanings of the gestures escape most of us. To help broaden an appreciation of the Hindu dance, La Meri has written a book which should prove of great value to the layman as well as to the student. Entitled *The Gesture Language of the Hindu Dance,* and published by the Columbia University Press, it makes a brief yet authoritative survey of the Hindu dance, its sources, its purposes and its qualities. Included in the book is a list of major differences between the Oriental and the Occidental dance, and this list should aid the prospective onlooker in his approach to a foreign form. Some of the differences are pretty arbitrary and not totally accurate, for American dancers have absorbed a goodly amount of Oriental dance action, but perhaps the fine distinctions were necessary for purposes of clarification.

Vocabulary of the Hands   Of major importance in the new book are the many illustrations of hand gestures and their meanings and of traditional body postures and their significances. The photographs are clear and beautiful, and the explanations equally lucid. In fact, the material of the book is so well presented that an apt student could almost create a dance through the study of the movement vocabulary recorded in the book. For any one who desires to completely understand and miss nothing of a Hindu gesture dance, the La Meri work is a "must," for the vocabulary of Hindu hand language is there to study, and having once studied it, the student will miss little or nothing of the Hindu artist's stories in dance. [*New York Herald Tribune*]

1942

From Pillar to Post

Doris Humphrey and Charles Weidman dance in Flickers and With My Red Fires • Ruth St. Denis and Edwin Strawbridge create children's ballets Marco Polo and Daniel Boone • Carmen Amaya's Spanish dancing burns up the stage • The Y.M.H.A. • Gaîté Parisienne and Capriccio Espagnol on the silver screen • Martha Graham, 1942 • Nora Kaye triumphs in the premiere of Tudor's Pillar of Fire • Jack Cole and Paul Draper keep alive the tradition of vaudeville dance • Ray Bolger in By Jupiter • A farewell to dance audience before active duty in the armed forces

Humphrey–Weidman, 1942

January 3, 1942: Weidman Gives Flickers, Dance Satire on Films

Rudolph Valentino, Theda Bara and their wild-eyed, passionate, evil and heroic colleagues of the silent screen lived once again last evening as Charles Weidman offered the premiere of his new theater dance, *Flickers,* at the Humphrey–Weidman studio-theater. Mr. Weidman could have chosen no better theme, for his comic genius enabled him to capture the hilarious distortions of action which marked the early efforts in motion pictures.

Reel 1 busied itself with *Hearts Aflame,* and here Mr. Weidman saved the heroine from marrying the mortgage-holding villain. The dancing actors moved in the scuttling fashion of the early screen and mugged their faces to exhaustion.

In *Wages of Sin,* Doris Humphrey was first shown squeezing her voluptuous shape through the bars that imprisoned a leper colony. From there the siren went to the big city where she lured a good man away from wife and child. The fade-out showed the fallen hero dead on the floor, while the evil vamp lolled on her couch and gorged herself on chocolates. The luring scene on the sofa would certainly have earned the envy of Theda Bara herself, for

133

Miss Humphrey writhed her way over the couch, over her victim and over everything else that could be writhed upon.

Flowers of the Desert In a dashing white burnoose and associate Arab impedimenta, Charles Weidman leered his way through *Flowers of the Desert*. Ladies swooned in droves at the flash of his smile and one timid miss actually worked her way up the side of a wall in her efforts to escape his passionate embraces. To his harem she was taken, but the hero arrived in the nick of time to save her from her desert fate. The final reel was a Western with pioneers, Indians, battles and Mr. Weidman.

  Flickers has been cleverly staged and brilliantly choreographed. A real motion-picture screen, upon which are flashed appropriate scenes, is used for a background and easily shifted props designate the changes in locale. The movements, as I have suggested, are slightly exaggerated versions of what actually took place on the screen of the past, and the best description of them is to be found in the title itself, *Flickers*. But the humor runs much deeper than that, for Mr. Weidman has laid his finger directly upon the acting style of the period, upon the choice of themes of that day, and the results are hilarious.

  Wages of Sin and *Flowers of the Desert* are the best of the four reels, and if any revisions are needed they should be directed toward the Western, which could do with a dash more of heroics. Lionel Nowak was responsible for the splendid musical background, William Martin staged the production and Alan Porter and Mr. Weidman devised the scenarios.

Weidman's Family Portrait The remainder of the program consisted of familiar works from the Humphrey–Weidman repertory. The stars danced well in Mr. Weidman's charming and slightly satirical *Alcina Suite,* and Mr. Weidman was truly magnificent in his solo *On My Mother's Side.* In this dance work, Mr. Weidman draws dance portraits of several of his ancestors, bringing the theme down to the present with "Sonny," who is, of course, Mr. Weidman himself. And in the final solo he wonders which of his ancestors was responsible for the dancer of today. Was it the pioneer grandfather, the builder, the sensitive and beautiful blind grandmother? Was it Aunt Jessie, the fancy dancer? And Mr. Weidman discovers that each forebear contributed his bit to this dancer of today. Some of the episodes are comic and some are tragic, but all are revealing and dramatically powerful. [*New York Herald Tribune*]

April 27, 1942: Miss Humphrey Presents With My Red Fires

With My Red Fires, a drama of love—romantic love versus possessive love— was presented Saturday evening at the Studio Theater, 108 West Sixteenth

Street, by Doris Humphrey, Charles Weidman and their company. This dance drama is one of Miss Humphrey's most compelling works, and that is praise indeed for a choreographer who has enriched the repertoire of American dance with so many great theater pieces. *With My Red Fires* is not new. It was created several seasons ago as the third part of a trilogy which included *Theater Piece* and *New Dance,* but the revival seems even more exciting than the earlier productions. Certainly Saturday evening's performance was beautifully staged and lighted, and danced to perfection by Miss Humphrey and her large company.

From the aspect of pure dance movement, *With My Red Fires* is a constantly rewarding work. It is no secret that Miss Humphrey has few rivals when it comes to group choreography, for she moves masses of dancers into majestic patterns of action that make one feel he is witnessing a symphony of movement. But Miss Humphrey is not content with visual grandeur, and each phrase of movement, pregnant with meaning, contributes to the dramatic sweep of the piece. *With My Red Fires* is in two parts. The first is subtitled *Ritual* and opens with a religious festival to the God of Fertility. There is the search for the mate, the betrothal and the departure of the young couple for a life of their own. The second part is subtitled *Drama,* and it is here that the Matriarch, the symbol of possessive love, enters the scene. A malevolent figure, she uses all her wiles, cajolings, rantings and mature powers to drag the girl from her mate and to place her again under the maternal hand. The Matriarch wins for the moment, but the girl manages to escape. There is the pursuit, the judgment and finally the power of romantic love triumphs over the selfish symbol of possessive love.

Miss Humphrey enacted the role of the Matriarch magnificently, making the character at once terrifying and tragic. Mr. Weidman and Katherine Litz were splendid as the young couple, and cheers are due to the members of the group for revealing so clearly the wonderful choreographic lines of the work and for filling their movements with the dramatic fervor necessary to its success. [*New York Herald Tribune*]

Children's Ballet

January 4, 1942

Fun and education were neatly fused in last week's two ballet productions for children. Both *The Adventures of Marco Polo* and *Daniel Boone* were historically informative, yet there was nothing of the textbook about them, for

135

the producers saw to it that the pageantry of the past was reproduced in terms of exciting theater. Extensive tours carry these ballets to the towns, cities and schools of America, and their importance cannot be exaggerated. The dancers of today are frequently faced with audience ignorance and indifference, and although they are steadily drawing more followers to the theater of dance, a great portion of the public, because it has had little contact with the dance art, shies away from an activity that it fancies is esoteric. Junior Programs with its *Marco Polo* and Edwin Strawbridge with his *Daniel Boone* are helping to build the intelligent, adult dance audiences of tomorrow by acquainting children with the excitement of ballet, with the expressive power of dance.

History, geography, legend and a dash or two of moral preaching are to be found in *The Adventures of Marco Polo*. The curtain for the show is a large map of Asia, and tiny, silhouetted figures move across its face as a narrator describes the travels of Marco Polo over mountains, across deserts, through great Oriental cities to his goal of Cathay. The first scene is laid in Venice, the second in China, and through the brightly-hued sets and costumes, a junior audience learns something about the architecture, the dress, the taste in design of the peoples of an earlier day. The dances themselves help to distinguish the traits of two nations, for the Italian dances are gay and bouncy and suggest spur-of-the-moment action, while the Oriental dances are softly delicate, stylized, refined.

In Quest of Adventure   The figure of Marco Polo steps out of a history book as an adventurous youth, who happened to make history because he had the initiative and the daring of a Tom Swift. Through the narrator, the dialogue, the songs and the dances a segment of history is given contemporary reality to a child audience. The dialogue of Saul Lancourt, the author and producer, is not always effective from a dramatic point of view, for the preachments on religious tolerance, filial devotion and other desirable aspects of human behaviour are presented in stilted fashion. The action, however, is swift of pace, and the dances devised by Ruth St. Denis are as colorful and as effective as one would expect from the hand of that great lady. The performing, too, is robust and assured and most of the dancing is first-rate. Charles Tate is particularly good as Marco's Chinese friend. His pure dance episodes are agile and virtuosic, and the characterization itself is achieved almost entirely through splendid comic dance action.

Edwin Strawbridge's *Daniel Boone* follows a similar pattern, although the stage characters do not speak as they do in *Marco Polo,* all dialogue being cared for by the narrator. Here again the producer has succeeded in bringing the past to life in terms of theater, and children find themselves faced with the dangerous living, the hardships, the Indian battles and the lusty good times

136

of an earlier American era. The narration offers the historical background, the sets and costumes give picture-book clarity to the pioneer West and the actions of the performers, to the delight of children, remove the dry dust of history from the figure of Daniel Boone. Mr. Strawbridge is not particularly adept nor agile when it comes to dancing, but he marches through his part with gusto and authority, making Daniel Boone the noble-souled and intrepid hero that he should be.

Indians and Melodrama   The Indians, of course, account for much of the excitement in the ballet of *Daniel Boone*. The war dances, war whoops and general savagery lend real American melodrama to the occasion, and in many cases steal the show from the more nobly inclined pioneers. Rex Cooper, as an Indian brave, accounts for the ballet's best dancing in a hoop solo, notable for its rhythmic power, its skill and its real beauty of movement. Albia Kavan, blonde and lovely to look at, is a perfect heroine of pioneer days, whether she is dancing gayly for her friends or displaying the heroic bravery of a frontierswoman.

These two organizations, the Strawbridge company and Junior Programs, deserve fostering on the part of the public, for their recreational and educational qualities are of undeniable value to children. In connection with local performances, school teachers frequently turn the attention of their classes to the geography, the history, the music and the literature associated with the ballet to be presented. By enhancing school subjects with the vigor and the virtuosity of a theater art, young pupils are certain to take a livelier interest in their studies. Beyond that, the children are brought into contact with theater dance, and this contact will pave the way for an adult understanding and appreciation of the greater dance artists and the greater dance works that lie ahead of them. [*New York Herald Tribune*]

Carmen Amaya

January 14, 1942: Dynamite

Carnegie Hall certainly had need of asbestos curtains and reinforced floorboards last evening, for Carmen Amaya let loose the elements in her first New York recital. Her black hair lashed her face as she spun through a tempest of movement, her heel-beats and hand-claps sounded like rhythmic thunder and her twisting body seemed to generate fire as it tore through the movements of her dances. The burning intensity of Amaya's dance makes for an indescribable impact. You find yourself stamping your own feet, twisting your muscles in accord with her stage actions and wishing you knew enough Spanish to yell your approval, for Amaya can weave a spell as potent as pagan magic. She belongs in a small theater where every one can see the expressions of her face, yet her power of projection is so terrific that even the expanses of Carnegie Hall seem to shrink to suit her personal dynamism.

Many of the Amaya clan took part in last night's proceedings both as dancers and musicians, and for a partner, Carmen Amaya was fortunate in having a first-rate flamenco dancer, Antonia Triana. For their first duet they offered *Sacro Monte,* a dance in which the gypsy woos his "gitana." Woo is hardly the word to describe the tactics of approaching an Amaya, for the girl herself was far from coquettish. Violent and fiery of action, she gave her suitor a battle for his pains. I'm not sure who won who, but it was an exciting dance. Together again in the Fire Dance from *El Amor Brujo,* the two gypsies danced the familiar rhythms as they have never been danced before. The dancers tore through twisting, turning and wrenching movements, increasing the intensity and speed of their actions until it reached an almost explosive climax; another step and flames would surely have burst forth.

In *Ay, que Tu,* Amaya let her voice wail its eerie flamenco chant while her dancing gestures amplified the meanings of a tough and salty song. Here she chattered with her audience and seemed to improvise her steps as she went along. The *Alegrías* found her turning on the incredible velocity of her heel-beats, creating innumerable rhythms danced at machine-gun-fire speed, while her body spun at equal tempo until some times you could see nothing but a streak of whipping hair, the flash of an evil smile. For her encore, she ordered two of her guitarists to drop their instruments and dance with her. They each lasted a minute or two, while Amaya went on at break-neck speed.

Triana danced his solos brilliantly as always, touching them with the arrogant charm of the Spanish dance. The Amaya sisters and Lola Montes added much to the performance through the skill and pep of their dancing. Sabicas, the guitarist, won encores for his solo, and Norman Secon and Manuel Matos alternated at the piano, each giving splendid support to the dancers. But it was Carmen Amaya's evening, for this human Vesuvius smouldered, flamed and exploded her way through the most exciting evening of dance that this city has seen in many a season.

Appropriately enough, the program ended with a Spanish jam session, *Fiesta in Seville,* in which the entire company participated, each member contributing his own individual styles and rhythms to the whole. And a jam session led by Carmen Amaya is really something to see. The demonstrative audience filled every seat in Carnegie Hall and crowded into every available cranny of standing room for this, the third event in the Hurok Carnegie Hall series. [*New York Herald Tribune*]

Y. M. H. A. Dance Center

January 25, 1942

All dancers struggle. Even the famous ones, excepting those in the highly
subsidized ballet companies, find it difficult to finance tours and New York
recitals. The young dancers are at the bottom of the heap, for when, where
and how do they have an opportunity to present their wares to the public?
The Y. M. H. A. has realized the plight of these young Americans and has hit
upon a way of helping them. For six seasons the Y. M. H. A.'s Dance Theater
series has presented first-rate dance attractions in the modern, comfortable and
well equipped Kaufmann Auditorium at Ninety-second Street and Lexington
Avenue. This year the series' director, William Kolodney, and the dance
teachers' advisory committee of the Y. M. H. A. held auditions for dancers,
and from those auditions six young artists were chosen to appear at the Kaufmann Auditorium under the sponsorship of the "Y." Expenses were paid, the
dancers took no financial risk and yet they had an opportunity to appear professionally in a recognized dance center before an attentive audience.

Mr. Kolodney's new policy of fostering the younger group of native
dancers was inaugurated last Sunday with performances by Naomi Aleh-Leaf,
Eleanor King, Welland Lathrop, Nelle Fisher, Nina Fonaroff and her group
and Elizabeth Waters and her group. From these six dancers and from others
who may care to audition, the committee will select three artists to appear on
another program. If there is a deficit, the Y will pay the bills; if there is a
profit, the dancers will receive it. This aid to American dance may be on a
small scale, but it is a start in the direction of fostering and cherishing an important native art. Certainly all young dancers will look to the Y. M. H. A. as
a source of encouragement, and perhaps Mr. Kolodney will find that his interest in the younger generation of American dancers will be responsible for
the launching of one or more distinguished careers.

Elizabeth Waters and Group   Last Sunday's performance was, theatrically
speaking, a disappointment. The actual dancing was always skillful and sometimes brilliant, but most of the choreography was distressingly inept. Elizabeth Waters and her group accounted for the finest portions of the program.
Miss Waters's solo, *Try, Try Again,* is pure kinetic humor, a hilarious translation into movement of an old and frequently annoying adage, while the group
dance, *They Do Not Accept the Verdict,* captures in its movements the spirit
of defiance, the will of the oppressed to cast off oppression. In *Rite for Rejoicing,* Miss Waters and her dancers place the universal theme of communal
celebration into a Southwestern Indian setting. It is a new work marked by
simplicity of design and colorful costumes and masks. It hasn't quite jelled

yet, for the dynamic growth from the austere rites of prayer to joyous celebration is pretty shaky in spots.

Naomi Aleh-Leaf, in the traditional dances of the Jewish people, was thoroughly delightful. As in most folk dances, the material was theatrically slim and repetition of movements inevitable, but Miss Aleh-Leaf filled them with as many shadings as possible. Her *Awake, Awake! Put on Thy Strength, Oh Zion,* was a highly dramatic and moving use of dance and the spoken word, made especially effective by the dancer's ability to speak and move without breathless effort. Welland Lathrop had some effective moments in *Three Characters for a Passion Play* and Nelle Fisher, with a smooth and masterful technique, danced some beautiful measures in *Mad Maid's Lament* and *Kentucky Mountain Song.* Otherwise, the performance was dragged down by stumbling choreographic patterns.

Choreographic Troubles A few seasons ago many of the young dancers garbed themselves in stark attire and flew about the stage on missions dealing with political and social comment. Now that the modern dance leaders are stressing characterization, humor and colorful staging, the younger dancers are trying similar tactics. The trouble is that they are forgetting to dance. Eleanor King, a skillful dancer, offered *Novella,* which was simply bad Angna Enters, for only a superb mime can make gesture exciting. Welland Lathrop went on interminably with *Harlequin,* posturing with props and not dancing a step. Nina Fonaroff had similar trouble with *Four Dances in Five,* in which she gave impressions of popular entertainers. There was more to her group work, *Yankee Doodle Greets Columbus, 1492.* Here there were many attractive designs and inventive movements, but there was not enough freedom of action and one felt that Miss Fonaroff had forced her ideas into a tight mold rather than allowing those ideas to suggest their own design.

Social comment or satire or character studies are each valid material for any dancer, young or mature. Sunday's dancers either made simple themes pretentious or, in their desire to be novel, tossed in movements that were totally unrelated to the theme at hand. These mistakes are all understandable, for they are inevitable in the trial and error process used by incipient choreographers. I think that young dancers should realize that their greatest dance power is a physical one, for as human beings they are at their physical peak. Subtleties of action, emotional depth will come with maturity when the youthful bounce of physical energy has lessened. Directness and simplicity should be the guides for all dancers and especially the young artists who are still feeling their way along the choreographic road. No themes are barred to them provided they dance them youthfully. The purpose of these performances at the Y. M. H. A. is to give young dancers and growing artists an opportunity to find out these things, to discover what actually happens when a studio effort is placed upon a stage, to feel the reactions of an audience and to prepare themselves for later efforts in the American dance theater of tomorrow. [*New York Herald Tribune*]

Screen Ballet

February 11, 1942

Dance and Hollywood are finally getting together. For years the motion picture musical shows splashed forth with tremendous production numbers which gave us glimpses of beautiful show girls and opulent sets. Occasionally the camera would focus for a moment or two upon ensemble action, the tapping feet of a principal or a ballerina's pirouette; otherwise, the camera made no attempt to capture the action of dance. Soloists fared better. Fred Astaire, Ginger Rogers, George Murphy, Eleanor Powell and their colleagues found their engaging skills translated into good screen entertainment. But dance as a dramatic medium for the projection of story, idea or mood had little opportunity to prove its worth. Dancing was simply incidental embellishment.

The possibilities of collaboration between dance and motion pictures are now being tested by Warner Brothers, who have just completed two ballets in technicolor, *The Gay Parisian* and *Spanish Fiesta*. These short subjects employ the talents of the Ballet Russe de Monte Carlo and both stories are derived from ballets frequently presented by the company. The former is, of course, *Gaîté Parisienne* and the latter *Capriccio Espagnol*. The choices were well made, for both ballets are gay and colorful of scene, filled with peppy action and based upon infectious and comparatively familiar music. If further ballets with other companies are planned, *Giselle* might be attempted, for imaginative, and not literal, translation would surely make for stunning motion picture fantasy. The powerful patterns of human emotion, which make Antony Tudor's *Lilac Garden* one of the great ballets of our time, could be captured by the camera, and Agnes de Mille's *Three Virgins and a Devil,* filled as it is with comic gesture, would be perfect screen material.

With a Spanish Flavor Of the current Warner Brothers productions, *Spanish Fiesta* is far and away the better. The general design of the ballet has been followed, and the camera keeps its focus upon the dances so that the sequences of action are easily understood and permitted to arrive at logical and dynamically forceful conclusions. The directors have wisely interpolated purely atmospheric shots between the dances and have familiarized the audience with certain characters through the use of close-ups which, in these instances, are warrantable, for they are presented as part of the general dramatic scheme. The color is something to marvel at, and because it is given action through the swirl of many-hued skirts and the flash of capes, it too seems to dance. *Spanish Fiesta* is exciting because it is direct and unpretentious; the dances are simple and the camera has caught that simplicity while finding its dramatic effects in the movement of Alexandra Danilova, Tamara Toumanova, Frederic Franklin and especially Léonide Massine.

   The Gay Parisian, on the other hand, is pretentious and far from direct in its approach to ballet. The slight story of a rich Peruvian and his flirting sojourn in Paris has not been noticeably altered, but the dances themselves have lost much of their original flavor due to the nervous camera eye which refused to light on any one spot for any length of time. Just as a dance was beginning to make its patterns and its moods felt, the camera wandered off to view a staircase, a row of bottles or some one's face. One of the major errors was the absence of Danilova from the role of the coquettish glove seller. All balletomanes will quite rightly resent this ignoring of one of the great characterizations in contemporary ballet. Aside from this, Milada Mladova, who dances the role in the picture, does nothing to make the glove-seller the worldly, highly romantic and slightly tough figure she should be. Mladova is beautiful and winsome, but never once exciting. Frederic Franklin's role has been twisted about to the point where the dashing baron emerges as a study in boredom.

Massine—Motion-Picture Star   Léonide Massine's Peruvian comes through with all the gay comics that it possesses in the theater, and Massine obviously saw to it that when he was dancing the camera kept its focus upon him. Because of this, his dances and his characterization are the most effective in the motion picture version of the ballet. The only other highlight is the dancing of Lubov Roudenko as the leader of the cancan girls. The camera focuses without break upon her sequence of spins, allowing her to carry the audience to the cumulative, dramatic peak of this tour de force. In other instances the camera has failed to capture dance movement well. Aside from the fact that the waltz of Mladova and Franklin has been botched by too many scene-seeking digressions, the angles from which the movements have been taken are not effective. Parts of the body are permitted to get out of camera range, the clean line of the dancers in pose is often lost through the use of misplaced close-ups or distance shots and in one instance Mladova's extended leg in one of the adagio lifts is lopped off in mid-air. This lopping business is just as detrimental to dance effect as the cutting off of a Grace Moore high note in a motion picture would be to song effect. *Gay Parisian* could have been a stunning motion picture ballet, but too much decor got in the way and the camera forgot to dance with the dancers.

Warner Brothers proved what could be done in the way of translating theater ballet into motion picture entertainment with *Spanish Fiesta* and they suggested what should not be done with *The Gay Parisian*. I hope that furthe productions are contemplated, for the motion picture, in spite of the use of sound, is primarily a medium of action, and dance is the art of action. A union of the two should make for an unbeatable combination. In a later article I would like to make a few suggestions (from the dance viewpoint) concerning this union of motion picture and dance, and to discuss the experimental dance films recently taken by Dwight Godwin, Thomas Bouchard and other dance photographers. [*New York Herald Tribune*]

Martha Graham—1942

March 1, 1942

What kind of theater dance does a nation at war expect of its performers? Can relief and refreshment be found only in the parading of show girls or in the exuberant rhythms of the tap dancer? Does war time require that dance reduce its scope to the point where it focuses upon nothing but good fun? I think not. Of course, we want the show girls, the tap stylists and the novelty dancers, but more than before we need a dramatic dance that stirs the mind, lifts the spirit and gives spur to the imagination.

Martha Graham supplies a good case for the dance art in war time. Always considered one of the most serious American dancers, frequently called (and she hates it) a high priestess and one whose innovations have, on many occasions, stumped a lay audience, Miss Graham, in war time, is having her most successful season in many a year. On a recent tour she drew an audience of five thousand in Detroit, four thousand in Grand Rapids, four thousand in South Bend and a gathering of a puny three thousand in Columbus, Ohio. Three theater pieces constituted her program: a primitive ritual, a poetic dance-drama and a satire on family life. Huge audiences turned out for this program which promised them no show ladies, no tap routines, not a single popular tune nor even the spinning, leaping, glittering virtuosity of balletic dance. They went to the theater to share with the artist her thoughts and feelings about faith and beauty, romance and squabble, fantasy and reality. Granted that the Graham name is a great one in American dance, the fact remains that her kind of dance is developing a drawing power it never had before and at a time when most people apparently have less time and money for the theater than before the war. This seems to me to be proof enough that the general public, not the dance devotees, is beginning to feel the need of the nourishment which can be derived from a rich theater dance.

The Change in Graham   The increase in Graham popularity can also be traced to the change in her dance. Perhaps it should be called a development, rather than a change, for her fundamental use of dance motion has not altered. At one time Miss Graham dealt with abstractions, or distillations of emotions, rather than with specific characters and dramatic events. *Lamentation* revealed no specific character, nor was the state of mind delineated through stock gestures. It was not the act of lamenting which she presented; but the motor responses to the causes of lament which she disclosed. This sounds very complicated, but it simply meant that you were not to view this Graham dance through your eyes alone but to experience it with your entire body, to relate it to your experiences with sorrow. The eye absorbs the color of a painting and relates it to earlier experiences with color; the ear absorbs the tones of music, relating them to earlier experiences with sound; the entire body should absorb the movement of dance, relating it to personal experiences with movement. This precept of Miss Graham's dance was sound; the only trouble was that almost every one had had more conscious experience with color and sound than with movement.

Martha Graham in her new theater pieces still demands this kinesthetic response, but she makes it easier for the layman to take by surrounding it with easily recognized characterizations, plot, colorful costumes and slick staging. Running a close parallel to *Lamentation* is a dance in *Letter to the World.* You have followed the story of Emily Dickinson, her joys and fears and ecstasies. Then she loses the one she loves, leaving her with the anguish and pain which follow loss. Her body is crumpled, her fists beat against herself as if to obliterate an emotional pain through a physical one. It is not possible to simply look at this dance sequence with your eyes alone; dance trained or not, your body inevitably reacts to the dance action itself. The same holds true for the lifting dances of exaltation, the bouncing jig of frolic, the quiet measure of serenity.

The Power of Theater–Dance   It is this very scientific-sounding element of kinesthesia which makes the current Graham dances great dances and dances which can have a powerful effect upon the tension-laden audiences of the nation. The entire body absorbs some of the sweet simplicity and devoutness of *El Penitente,* a story of people possessed of faith and humbleness and joy. The entire body experiences the richness of thought and feeling which the figure of Emily Dickinson dances in her *Letter to the World.* The entire body

144

reacts to the squabbles and scuffles and domestic hilarity which fill the stage in *Punch and the Judy*. If it is escape from the present you seek in the theater, Miss Graham makes the escape complete, for every one of your muscles is controlled by the imagery of dance. If you seek entertainment or stimulation, the Graham dance is again equally potent, for she entertains and stimulates not merely the eye of the beholder but his entire feeling being. Miss Graham's *Letter to the World* is not meant for reading. Its surface patterns tell a story, but its dynamically varied actions make radio-like contact with the muscles and sinews of the audience. Such an all-out dance is surely the most powerful kind of war-time dance. [*New York Herald Tribune*]

Pillar of Fire

April 9, 1942: Passion in Dance

A great ballet, eloquent and stirring in its relation of human passion, was born last night when the Ballet Theatre presented the world premiere of Antony Tudor's *Pillar of Fire* at the Metropolitan Opera House. Superlatives are inadequate in describing this ballet, for its tremendous dramatic power results from that rare and perfect fusion of inspired artistry and knowing craftsmanship. Even its theme, when told, can give little clue to its greatness. *Pillar of Fire* is a story of frustrated passion as it tells of a girl who, believing the man of her choice loves her younger sister, gives herself to a man she does not love. But there is much more than overt movement and mimed characterizations to *Pillar of Fire*. Every gesture, every pattern of action, every static moment reveal some segment of human emotion, some pulse of human passion. It is gripping, frightening and incredibly beautiful by turns, for it is dance, not born of physical skill, but of inner compulsion. Great theater art *Pillar of Fire* certainly is, and it can boast an equal amount of popular appeal, for last night's capacity audience cheered itself hoarse in the loudest, longest ovation that any theater dance has had within my memory.

A star too was born last evening, for young Nora Kaye danced the leading role of the passionate girl with superb technical skill and with a dramatic eloquence worthy of a Judith Anderson. The throbbing anger of jealousy was seen in her movements, indecision tugged at her spirit, and her body, taut with bitterness, yielded itself to one she did not love. Antony Tudor was splendid as the thoughtless, unseeing man who neglected the girl for a bit of harmless frolic with the younger sister, and who finally, with tenderness and understanding, showed her the love that had always been there.

145

Hugh Laing was splendid as the lusty and dashing lover-of-the-moment, and Annabelle Lyon danced the role of the carefree younger sister to perfection. Members of the ensemble added immeasurably to the power of the piece, for Mr. Tudor used them as a sort of Greek chorus which presaged and reflected the shifting moods of the heroine. To say that the dance movement of *Pillar of Fire* are fresh and inventive is to underrate them. They are that, but more important is that they are dramatically articulate, as clear as the spoken word, but more powerful because the entire body speaks. The music of Schoenberg's *Verklaerte Nacht* and the beautiful settings and costumes of Jo Mielziner united with the Tudor choreography in the creation of the most potent of contemporary ballets. [*New York Herald Tribune*]

April 12, 1942

You can't fool the public. Audiences will accept *Russian Soldier* with its corniness, its rampant sentimentality, its evident sincerity and its smooth staging. They will even bestow affectionate applause upon this work of the always beloved and usually great Michel Fokine. But they reserve their unstinted ovations, their honest cheers for the newest and greatest of contemporary ballets, *Pillar of Fire,* and for its creator, Antony Tudor. *Russian Soldier* had almost everything\on its side; the booming advance publicity of the ballet management, the prestige of Fokine's name, the timeliness of its theme, highly effective staging. *Pillar of Fire* had consummate artistry, flawless craftsmanship of the theater, and *Pillar of Fire* won because of its intrinsic worth.

If I am not stepping too far afield, I would say that *Pillar of Fire* constitutes a great contribution to the theatrical field. Certainly, it is a great ballet, and because of its peculiar brand of greatness, difficult to describe. Like his *Jardin aux Lilas,* Tudor's new ballet is more concerned with the inner experiences of the characters than with surface action. Such dance movement, arising as it does from an almost organic compulsion, is more emotionally potent than the flashiest virtuosity. *Pillar of Fire* is gripping, terrifying, maddening and beautiful, for its story is born of human passion, told in the revealing terms of human movement. The theme is unimportant except for its function of serving as a stimulus to the development of the characters. It tells of a girl who, thinking the man of her choice is more interested in her younger sister, gives herself to a lusty lover of the moment. That is all there is to the theme, yet upon it hinges the frustration, the jealousy, the indecisions and the ultimate agony of a woman, and from it springs tremendously dramatic patterns of human behaviour.

Nora Kaye: American Ballerina   The most difficult role in all ballet, both technically and dramatically, is that of the girl. When Nora Kaye danced it Wednesday evening she raised herself to undisputed stardom as the finest of American ballerinas. Her physical skill was brilliantly realized, for incredibly difficult balletic actions and dynamic sequences of free dance actions were projected with strength and not with strain. But, in every instance, the overt aspects of the movements were made to serve the purposes of characterization, of projection of inner emotion. A static pose was tense with jealousy and fear, a gesture toward the man she loved was filled with confused pleading and humiliation, and as she yielded herself to the first youth who came along defiance and hopelessness and agony were revealed in the dance pulsations of her body.

Reflections of the girl's conflicting, shifting feelings were personalized in the actions of the two ensembles: the lovers-in-experience and the lovers-in-innocence. From a purely technical viewpoint these ensembles offered variety of movement, contrasting the light and the sweet with the earthy and the lustful, but more than that, like a Greek chorus, they presaged events to come. To use another simile, they served as a sounding board for the varying emotional vibrations of the girl. Tudor's fresh and inventive movements were exciting in themselves, but even more exciting in what they said. Virtuosic effects were rightly used at moments of great tension or to give accent to a specific action. The staging was unusually good, for the settings and costumes of Jo Mielziner were in perfect tune with the quality of the dancing. The mobility of the sets, abetted by the best lighting effects of the season, enabled even the backgrounds to reflect the changing moods of the ballet. Still another unit of the production contributed richly to the total effect and that was the music of Arnold Schoenberg's *Verklaerte Nacht*. An impassioned, haunting score, its tonal patterns were expertly woven into the fabric of the ballet.

The Hit of the Season   There is so much to be said for *Pillar of Fire* that it is difficult to know where to end a discussion. As a theater work, it is unquestionably an artistic and a popular success, and that is a rare combination. It is wonderful that the Ballet Theatre has a smash hit in its repertory, but *Pillar of Fire* should also make the powers behind the ballet conscious of something more than immediate box office success. The Tudor work proves what many of us know but which few managers seem to suspect, and that is that there is a vast difference between progress and novelty. It is not enough to produce freshly garbed ballets, based upon an old pattern. Managers, I know, are wary of experimentation, for many experiments fail, but the success of one is worth all of the momentary novelties you can name. When the war is over, *Russian Soldier* will be forgotten, for what excitement audiences

147

experience in its presence is born of their enthusiasm and respect for a gallant, battling, twentieth century Russia and not for a sentimental Fokine ballet of Russia, 1812. *Pillar of Fire* gives its audiences a tremendous emotional experience because it is in itself a great work of art. Ballet Associates, which financed this production for the Ballet Theatre, is to be praised for its support. It is to be hoped that ballet managements will follow a similar path, cherishing the great ballets of the past, commissioning new works from established choreographers and giving young choreographers an opportunity to advance the cause, artistic and popular, of the ballet art. [*New York Herald Tribune*]

Vaudeville Dance

May 10, 1942

Vaudeville is back, and along with its comedians, singers, acrobats and dog acts are the dancers. This is as it should be, for dancers have been vaudeville headliners ever since a Mr. Robertson danced an "antipodean whirligig" on his head in a variety show about the time of the American Revolution. But Mr. Robertson's unique approach to the dance art does not imply that all dancers in vaudeville must be tricksters. Ruth St. Denis and Ted Shawn transplanted many of their Denishawn ballets to the variety stage and Martha Graham toured the vaudeville circuits with great success in Shawn's *Xochitl,* an Aztec ballet. In fact vaudeville has always given a home to great artists as well as to passing novelty acts, and with the return of vaudeville, the policy has been continued, for both *Priorities of 1942* and *Keep 'Em Laughing* devote generous portions of the bill to dance.

Paul Draper is the dancing star of *Priorities,* and dance followers can be pleased that young Mr. Draper shares top billing with such vaudeville veterans as Willie Howard, Lou Holtz and Phil Baker. The aristocratic tap dancer easily holds his own amid the rousing and sometimes rowdy vaudeville surroundings. Encores come thick and fast for a dancer who can win an audience with an elegant dance to the music of the classic Paradies, continue with the hummable folk melodies of America and conclude with a sheaf of improvisations to the tunes that the onlookers call for. All of his dances he performs brilliantly. The taps for the Paradies play a counterpoint to the melody, while the balletic style of his body reflects the nobility of the music. The folk dances are my own favorites for they possess dignity and humor and zest. As danced by Paul Draper, they are truly folk, yet brilliantly theatrical.

148

Another American dancer, Jack Cole, is upholding the prestige and the applause-getting properties of dance in *Keep 'Em Laughing*. You might not take Mr. Cole for an American, at least on stage, for his dances are Oriental and he looks Hindu enough to have been born in the shadow of an eastern temple. But American he is, and his dances have a local twang to them. Hindu gestures are used, and they are certainly derived from the gesture language of India, but the dancer has set them to swingtime. You may not be familiar with this ancient vocabulary of movement, but something about the modern tempo makes everything clear, and Cole's digital conversation with his Oriental girls in one of his dances informs you that an Oriental pick-up is not very different from the Manhattan variety. The three Cole girls are beautiful to look at as well as being adept at swingtime Oriental dance, but it is Jack Cole who walks off with the honors, for he is one of America's finest young dancers, an exciting personality and a dancing star whose muscles never say no to any of his commands.

There is one segment of vaudeville dance which shows its age in the current shows, and that is the dancing of the chorus and the promenading of the show girls. The show girls carry off their assignments with little difficulty, for they are not expected to dance, and when they are attractive to the eye, they have done their jobs well. But the choruses of the two shows display a disarming lack of precision in routines that would hardly inspire any one. Since earlier vaudeville days, Robert Alton has come along to prove to us in his musical shows that chorus girls can be made to dance, and that the chorus routines can be inventive, skillful and the high spots of the show. With a reproving glance at the half-hearted kicks of these chorus girls, we can applaud the return of great vaudeville dancing in the persons of Paul Draper and Jack Cole. [*New York Herald Tribune*]

Jupiter Dances

June 7, 1942

"It is probable that this is the last of the lavish, resplendent musical shows that we shall see for some time, perhaps for the duration," wrote Richard Watts, Jr. in his review of the new Rodgers and Hart production, *By Jupiter.* Adding my bit to my colleague's authoritative discussion, I would like to say that dance helps immeasurably in making *By Jupiter* lavish and resplendent. First of all, the star of the show is a dancing star, Ray Bolger, and if there is a more adept comic dancer than Mr. Bolger, I have failed to see him. Secondly, the dances have been staged by Robert Alton, the top-flight choreographer for the musical comedy field. And thirdly, the ensemble, with the exception of a few members, is attractive, facile of movement and thoroughly worthy of the action designs which Mr. Alton has devised for them.

As a youth made dainty and delicate by a heritage and a lifetime of female domination in the land of the Amazons, Ray Bolger creates a character in dance which is hilariously comic. Through his dances he pokes great fun at the swooning lyricism expected of the underling males of Amazonia, and through his buffoonery he manages to satirize not so much the effeminate male as the wiles of the female herself. Aside from those dance episodes which augment his dramatic characterization, Mr. Bolger turns up with that loose-limbed elasticism which marks his wonderful style. His disarranged anatomy slides down steps, hurtles through the air, tumbles over couches and gets itself thoroughly involved, in one way or another, without ever losing the rhythm and phrasing of good dance. At the end of the show the worm (used figuratively here) turns as the men assert their rights and squash the dominance of their female overlords. Here Ray Bolger displays the art of Terpsichore in its more violent aspects as he dances *Now That I've Got My Strength*.

Robert Alton has staged the dances for *By Jupiter* with his now familiar skill. I believe that the element of integration has a great deal to do with the success of all Alton choreographies. So often in musicals the chorus gives a kick or two, the soloist does her spin and the specialty dancers follow with their isolated acts. But Alton fuses them all together in such a way that the result is actually a ballet in minature, with many changes of pattern and shadings in dynamic action which build to a knock-out finale. The old chorus line is gone, and in its place are myriads of shifting designs. Sometimes the ensemble will work in mass effect. Again the ensemble will be split into smaller groups, each accorded a specific phrase of movement, or a soloist will emerge to vary the focus of dance. It would be impossible to list the techniques employed, for Alton uses whatever style of dance will suit his purpose. Tap there is, but not merely with noise, for body actions and floor patterns are made to augment it. Ballet comes in for its share and in one number the boys of the company toss off some balletic leaps and legbeats in authoritative fashion, while the toe-slippered girls, executing their pirouettes with precision, prove that musical comedy dancers of today actually have to know how to dance.

I don't know the names of all the dancers who have their successful solo flings in *By Jupiter*. Robert and Lewis Hightower, assisted by one of the girls in the company, highlight several of the dance episodes with their muscular, yet always rhythmic, acrobatics. Marjorie Moore, usually a skillful ballet dancer in musicals, was not at her best on the opening night. I noticed that a foot was bandaged and perhaps that accounted for the lack of that quick and sturdy movement which customarily marks her dancing. An unexpected dance hit is to be found in the hoofing of Bertha Belmore, who plays the role of Pomposia, a large and lusty Amazon matron. Miss Belmore is pure dowager in appearance, both as to size and expression, and her expert and good-natured hoofing, time-steps and all comes as an hilarious surprise. You can see from this brief report that dancing, even from unexpected quarters, plays a major role in *By Jupiter,* and because the new Rodgers and Hart musical has been called "lavish and resplendent," I maintain that dance must share honors for the lavishness and the resplendence. [*New York Herald Tribune*]

Final Criticism

July 12, 1942

My critical chastisings and cajolings of dance and dancers cease with this column for the duration of the war. I would like to take this opportunity to review the record of American dance, to examine its current state and to give, in not too Olympian fashion, a few suggestions for its future course of action.

During my seasons with the Herald Tribune I have seen the modern dance make its final emergence from the strangling shrouds of cultism into the bright light of pure theater. The grim countenances, the body-racking movements, the too abstract abstractions, the ear-rending musical accompaniments and the costumes, which always looked as if they had been borrowed from a house of detention, are all gone. In their place we have Martha Graham's eloquent revealing in dance of a great New England lady, Emily Dickinson, in *Letter to the World* and her hilarious analysis of domestic squabblings in *Punch and the Judy*; Doris Humphrey has given us her document of American dance in *Decade* and Charles Weidman has proved the range of appeal for modern dance by carrying his *Flickers* from the concert stage to the Rainbow Room; discarding her occasional and violent editorials on the social state of man, Helen Tamiris has danced the simplest and the greatest editorial of her career in *Liberty Song*. In fact, all of the modern dancers have at last become truly modern, and not simply modernistic. After years of revolt from heritage, they have at last turned to that heritage for the richness it has to offer. Ballet is recognized as a valid and usable technique for those moderns who wish to broaden their range of action, and the achievements of America's own Denishawn organization are beginning to appear again, this time through the productions of the moderns themselves.

151

Along with other styles of theater dance, ballet has zoomed to new heights in America. Each season sees longer ballet engagements, and as this branch of the art has grown in popularity, its standards have been raised by the demands of the public. The old classics are cherished, but they are danced with greater skill and finer staging than before. The twelve-year-old mentality of ballet has sprung to adulthood in the great ballets of Antony Tudor, a choreographer who finds that men and women make more exciting theater characters than do sylphs and enchanted swans. The theory that ballet was the right of the Russian artist has been neatly exploded by Eugene Loring and by Agnes de Mille, who have given the "pirouette" a good American twang. The powers behind ballet have not only unearthed the fact that Americans can choreograph, but they are discovering that modern dance can enrich ballet with new and fresh movements and that names like Kaye or Conrad or Gibson can give the "ovas" and the "skis" a run for stardom. These same powers have yet to learn that there is a difference between progress and novelty, that new dance action or new balletic structure is far more exciting and important than thousands of dollars' worth of costumes bought to pep up an old-style work.

Dance as an educational power has spread through colleges and universities, schools and recreation centers. Some of the teaching is excellent, some mediocre, a great deal of it bad. As yet there is neither system nor standard, and there won't be until America's leading dancers forget their traditional rivalries and mutual suspicions and throw out the charlatans of dance both in the public schools and in those thousands of private schools which flourish without benefit of any guidance or control whatsoever.

In stage show, musical comedy, night club and motion picture, dance has progressed. Discerning audiences demanded better dancing and they got it. Ambling show girls are still ambling, but chorus ensembles now dance through patterns that are inventive and interesting, and miniature ballets, often show-stoppers, replace those weary dance interludes which in the old days were evidently designed to give the headliners a rest. The motion-picture industry has yet to discover the first principles of dance photography, but a start has been made and cinematic dance is decidedly on the way.

American dance, like all other American activities, has been challenged to prove its worth, and dance cannot simply say, "I am an art. I am above all this." If it answers the challenge in such fashion, it deserves to die, and quickly too, until another generation can create a dance that is worthy of enduring. But I feel certain that American dancers will meet the challenge well. In peace time they progressed in their art, and although they did not develop it to the degree that it can be developed, they did their best. Now that it is war time, American dancers must forget their petty bickerings and unite as the rest of the nation is united. They must discipline their actions, and under wise and strong leadership, aim for definite goals. Theater dancers can work through the U. S. O. and other service organizations to bring entertainment and relaxation to members of the armed forces, and to bring momentary relief from tension to large civilian audiences. Dance educators and I mean educators (not teachers of theatrical dancing) can and must map out systems of dance exercises for civilian use in matters of physical fitness, body conditioning, the alleviation of occupational fatigues and recreation—the science of dance action must be put to war-time use. It is also a war-time duty to think ahead to the return of peace, and dancers must not only organize themselves for current action, but they must have a greater dance art ready for the renewal of art life when the war is over. This too, takes courage, the same courage that is shown by Ted Shawn who is helping to keep the flow of dance alive with his American dance festival and university of dance at Jacob's Pillow.

American dance has a great function to perform, as I have tried to show, and I know that it will fulfill that function. If American dancers fail in any way, they will hear about it when the war is over, for this critic will return to them from military service, a far tougher disciplinarian than he was before, still cheering American dance, but demanding more of its exponents. [*New York Herald Tribune*]

1942 — 1945

Give My Regards to Broadway

Leave of absence for World War II military service

Still in the Air Corps—striking a pose near the Pyramids of Giza (1944).

1946

I Told You So!

*Return to "the Trib" from GI service • Dark Meadow offered by
Graham • Angna Enters • Danilova still supreme • Sybil Shearer and Iva
Kitchell, two special ladies, give solo concerts • Shearer, Iris Mabry,
Anna Sokolow, and Merce Cunningham give important recitals • Weidman,
without Humphrey, presents A House Divided • Ballet Society, headed
by George Balanchine, founded • Ballet Theatre judged superior to the
declining Ballet Russe • Bal Nègre presented by Katherine Dunham*

The Native's Return

November 18, 1945

May an ex-GI be granted the privilege of saying "I told you so"? From 1939
until I received my "Greetings" in 1942 I urged the impresarios to foster
American ballets, not the Muscovite *Union Pacific* nor the pointless *New
Yorker* of Leonide Massine, but American ballets by American choreographers.
Ballet potentates and balletomanes presented me with a united front of kind
but firm opposition. Ballet had to be Russian to sell, American idioms were
not generally suited to ballet, companies composed of Continental dancers
could not master American styles; these and other arguments formed the platform of disapproval.

Upon returning to the local scene I find American choreographers and
their ballets almost stealing the show from the Continental wing, and rejuven-
ating the traditional ballet with the lusty action, the fleet tempo of the New
World. Following in the pioneering footsteps of Eugene Loring's *Billy the Kid*
and Agnes de Mille's *Rodeo* came Jerome Robbins with *Fancy Free* and *Interplay*, Michael Kidd's *Backstage*, Todd Bollender's *Commedia Balletica* and
Graziana by John Taras, all produced for major ballet companies and created
by young Americans who had barely finished dancing their way out of the
corps de ballet into solo roles. Whether this welcome change was due to

157

wisdom on the part of directors and managers or was born of desperation inherent in the pursuit of novelty is not worth debating; American ballet was given its chance and won its first laurels, that is the important thing.

What is the value of this new American ballet other than its novelty? Thematically and kinetically it is adding whole new chapters to ballet history. Take *Fancy Free* as an example. Its story of American sailors in search of fun, firewater and females has its source in any one of our harbor cities, and the kinetic approach is as American, but not quite as rude, as the rush, push and job of the subway-goer. In movement, Robbins has used the vocabulary of the traditional ballet, but the new juxtapositions of these familiar dance words, the accent given to them and the native action idioms of jitterbugging and pantomimic gesture with which they are spiced result in a ballet which is purely American. Such a dance vocabulary bears the same relationship to the traditional-Continental one as the American tongue bears to the King's English. They are not at odds; they simply complement each other.

It would be shortsighted and unfair to hail these new native ballets as the cream of American dance or even as the equal of established repertory works. These young choreographers have introduced us to a new idiom of balletic action and they have given us theater pieces which are gay and slick, even richly inventive in matters of pure choreographic design. Ahead of them lies the difficult task of creating works of art which explore, distill and reveal the depths of mature thought, the profundities of adult emotion; they must learn how to disturb and arouse the beholder as well as casually entertain him if they are to achieve for themselves and the American ballet idiom a *Pillar of Fire*, a *Baiser de la Fée* or a *Giselle*. I do not intend to imply that henceforth American ballets must be fraught with philosophical meaning, but I do believe that thought-provoking themes and the patterned web of human emotions must serve as material for American ballets, along with the stories in lighter vein which sparkle but which do not possess the luminosity of great art.

Lest I should be accused of desiring the fall of the traditional European ballet, let me say that the growth of the American ballet style will enhance the whole theater of dance. An enchanted maiden in *Swan Lake* will gain by contrast with her strutting Yankee sister in *Fancy Free*; the acid backstage furies in Antony Tudor's *Gala Performance* make an interesting parallel with the sweet character and gentle satire in Michael Kidd's *Backstage*, and although George Balanchine disclosed infinite dance patterns of great beauty in the storyless *Serenade*, still other facets of pure dance design came into being through the sharp actions and jitterbug seasonings of Robbins's *Interplay*. The American dance idiom will not harm the traditional ballet; it will give it new and, I think, abundant life. [*New York Herald Tribune*]

158

Dark Meadow

January 27, 1946

Martha Graham has been called the high priestess of the modern dance. Sometimes the phrase has been used bitingly, at other times reverently, yet both connotations are accurate from their separate viewpoints. To those who go to Miss Graham's theater of dance with the determined belief that all dances should be pretty and orthodox as to theme and technique or that each movement should be a visual representation of a word or literary phrase, then Miss Graham assumes the role of a priestess of a cult. To those who realize that Miss Graham is not concerned with representation but with revelation, that her line of artistic communication uses the network of the senses rather than the path of literal thought, then she becomes a high priestess who discloses the nature of man, his aspects of divinity and his mortal flaws.

Theme of Renascence   In her new work, *Dark Meadow,* Miss Graham is more of a priestess than ever before since she is dealing with the theme of renascence and since she handles it with fire and the vision of an apostle. As I pointed out in my initial review of *Dark Meadow,* the choreographer selects as the proof of man's immortality the forces of memory, of love and of resurgence. These forces are captured in the form of a ritual, or a series of rituals, and this I think is significant, for man, no matter what his religious denomination may be, invariably seeks contact with his deity or searches for proof of his immortality through the magic formula of ritual. Since Miss Graham does not wish her message of renascence to be associated with a specific race or culture, she has given her work an archaic cast and this in turn creates an impression of agelessness which is admirably suited to the theme at hand.

The enduring qualities of memory are shown through the "ancestral footsteps" of the archaic dancing chorus, for the chorus shows us patterns of human behavior which we have inherited rather than learned, it indicates that loss and despair are inevitably followed by the rebirth of hope, it reveals the unquenchable fire of love and it preaches the tenet that although the mortal properties of man must perish, his spirit must ever be reborn. Participating in this ritual of the mysteries of life is the figure of the One Who Seeks, danced by Miss Graham. In herself, this human figure is lost, without hope and without belief, but through contact with the truths vouch-safed by this instructing chorus and through contact with the motivating figures of She of the Ground and He Who Summons, the One Who Seeks at last finds faith.

Symbols of Rebirth   Aside from its forthright handling of the main theme of rebirth and its supporting themes of memory and of love and the tidelike

159

resurgence of energy, *Dark Meadow* contains many implications of the belief in rebirth; to name but two, one can point to the use of certain phallic symbols easily traceable to antique religious rites or even to modern primitive dances concerned with the fruitfulness of man, beast and the soil; there is also present an indication of the Cross and its promise of resurrection to the Christian. There are other symbologies, all contributing to this pattern of man's concern with his search for renascence and all adding richness to the structure of the work itself. This brings us to still another remarkable attribute of *Dark Meadow* and that is its surface power. If one does not care to journey with Martha Graham into the mysteries of rebirth, he can find satisfaction and visual stimulation in the magnificence of her choreography. The movements of the archaic chorus fall into incredibly lovely and arresting patterns and the dance designs assigned to the principals are rich in invention and virtuosity. Miss Graham's dance in the "terror of loss" episode is a marvel of pictorial beauty and power while Erick Hawkins's solo work is a tour de force of leaps, spins and space-covering actions.

I do not maintain that Martha Graham's dance is easy to understand nor do I think that one can effortlessly enjoy it, but that it has been and is a profound force in the field of theater dance no one can deny. There are those (many of them non-dancers) who consider Martha Graham the greatest creative artist of our day, there are others who deem her a pretentious cultist and there are still others who react favorably to her dancing but can give no reason for their enthusiasm. This last group was represented, along with the other two, at the opening performance of *Dark Meadow*. While sleuthing about during intermission I heard repeatedly such phrases as "I didn't understand it but it was wonderful" or "I think she is terrific even if I don't know what it is all about." I overheard one person say "I didn't understand it, but I felt it," and that was as it should be, for Miss Graham's aim was to make you feel, to arouse in you a sympathetic reaction to her art communication. Immediate response was what she sought; reflection and analysis could come later; Martha Graham had succeeded in her purpose. [*New York Herald Tribune*]

On Angna Enters

February 17, 1946

She is a composer, designer, author, playwright, scenarist, sculptor, scholar and painter, but above all, Angna Enters is a dancer. Her performance last

Sunday at the Kaufmann Auditorium of the Young Men's and Young Women's Hebrew Association, as an attraction of the splendid Dance Theater Subscription Series, served to remind those of us who had not seen her in several seasons what a great dance artist she really is. True, her technique does not stem from any of the established schools of dance movement. Such pieces as *Madame Pompadour,* in which she slowly dons the sartorial impedimenta of the female of 1900, or *Piano Music No. 4,* concerned with a high school graduate who nervously "renders" a number at commencement time, may not constitute dance in the strict sense of the word, if our definition of dance requires the presence of mathematical rhythm, formal pattern and heightened movement in addition to the prime attribute of dancing, which is to communicate through motion. As I suggested in last Sunday's column, there are all kinds of "good dancing and not all of it is orthodox in matters of tradition; as a dancer, Angna Enters is both "unorthodox" and "good."

Although Angna Enters is an American artist, she is not specifically concerned with the American scene. Her sources of interest are human behavior and periods in history, both projected through character, and her selections can and do range from a persecuted Jewess of fifteenth-century Spain through a French gothic madonna to the zany surrealism of the twentieth century. In an Enters program then, one finds the comic, the tragic, the erotic, the gentle and the cruel used not as abstractions but as revelations of man, as clues to the tenor of a period. Her now classic *Pavana* is more than a dance form, more than a surface design of sixteenth-century Spain; through costume it discloses the opulence of the Renaissance and through its movement it reveals the thin veneer of a court etiquette beneath which seethed the evil and cruel impulses governing a still savage and corrupt castle. *Pavana* is not a dance of the Borgias; it explains the Borgias and others of their kind.

Past and Present United   With Miss Enters, a period theme does not necessarily result in a museum piece. *Auto da Fé,* for example, is concerned with the persecution of the Jews in medieval Spain, but the dancer imbues her characterization of a hunted, harmless woman with such anguish and terror that it resolves itself into a denunciation of all those, be they members of the Spanish Inquisition or Nazis or modern intolerants who trample upon the innocent. In *Little Sally Water* there is no definite historical springboard for her characterization. This piece deals with the process of growing up, a process to which we are all subjected. Miss Enters takes the bitterness as well as the humor inherent in the general theme and shows us a happy little girl bouncing her ball and chewing her hair ribbon, then an adolescent aware of her looks and eagerly absorbing the mysteries of a "forbidden" book and finally the grown woman who tastes transgression and pitifully seeks to recapture the innocence of her childhood. In *Auto de Fé* and *Little Sally Water,* as well as in

161

the majority of her other works, Angna Enters shows up characters whose behaviorisms strike perilously close to home, occasionally making us squirm as she requires us to remember the foibles of men.

Although the theater of Angna Enters pulls no punches and although it is frequently shocking, as truth so often is, there is a wealth of entertainment in it. The costumes are wonderful in design, in selection of fabric and in appropriateness to the theme of a given dance. The accompaniments have been chosen with discrimination and originality and are integral portions of a theater piece; examples of this would be the delicate song of Gautier de Coinci, arranged to accompany the *Queen of Heaven,* and the hilarious combining of totally unrelated airs for the surrealist *Dilly-Dally.* Since Miss Enters is a painter of international repute, it is not surprising to find pictorial beauty in her programs, to find stage patterns and body poses which photograph themselves in the mind of the onlooker. If the erotic maneuverings of *Odalisque* or the movements of weary satiety of *Aphrodisiac-Green Hour* disturb the sheltered onlooker's sense of propriety, he may be certain that the husky, bloomered girl of *Field Day,* or the neat and tidy lady of *Vienna Provincial* will soon grace the stage. All four dances are honest representations of character and Miss Enters is generous enough to give pleasant as well as unpleasant truths.

Freedom of Selection   To my way of thinking, the greatest quality about Angna Enters is her unfetteredness. Since she is not an exponent of a certain dance technique, since she is proficient in many of the associated arts, and since her interests are not bound by a specific locale or period in time, one cannot imagine her avoiding a special theme because of unsuitability; if she became interested in a theme she had never danced before, she would most certainly work out the technique necessary to its projection. The theater of Angna Enters is, to use a distasteful word, instructive, but for him who relishes the acquisition of learning as well as the acquisition of more material things, the dance of Angna Enters provides true wealth, for, as we have seen, Miss Enters is avid of interest and she shares the products of her interests with her followers. For the seeker of surface entertainment, Miss Enters is right down in front with things to shock, to delight and to amuse. She is "unorthodox," but she is "good." [*New York Herald Tribune*]

An Outline of Qualifications That Make Danilova Supreme
March 24, 1946

Alexandra Danilova is one of the great ballerinas of our time. In my opinion she is the greatest of those ten or twelve women, currently performing in

America, who have a claim to the title of "ballerina," for in spite of stage show, floor show and motion-picture advertisements which promise "50 ballerinas 50," there are probably hardly more than fifty in the entire world who warrant that rank. In the American theater of balletic operations, Danilova is surely the commanding ballerina, for she possesses qualities and qualifications of schooling, of experience, of skill, of wit and of personal radiance which none of her rivals can fully match. Perhaps a few comments on these qualities and qualifications will not only serve to explain Danilova's greatness but will also supply a definition of the term "ballerina."

Danilova's schooling, commencing in the Imperial schools of Russia and continuing in western Europe and in the United States, has supplied her with an impeccable technique. The great ballerina is by no means a virtuoso in the physical sense, for lesser performers accomplish greater numbers of pirouettes, leap higher or balance longer on point, but with Danilova the result is far greater. Her technique welds together those ingredients of rhythm, pattern, action, dynamics and purpose which constitute dance, so that one is conscious of dance, not technique, aware of the art, not the tools. Her schooling is balletic, but she possesses an instinctive technique for movement, along with Ruth St. Denis, Martha Graham or Egypt's great singer-dancer Om Kalsoum, which makes it impossible for her to execute a kinetically awkward or purposeless movement. If she had been born a Maori, the chances are that Danilova would have become a Maori dance leader, but since she was born to the heritage of ballet, she has become not only a mistress of the technique of ballet but more important, a model of how that technique should be used.

Dance Intelligence   To each of her many and varied roles, Danilova brings experience and intelligence, as well as technique. In the role of the Swan Queen in *Swan Lake,* she is the perfect classic ballerina. There is the personal dignity, the reserve, the poised display of body line which tradition demands of the classic ballerina, but she goes further. In the delineation of the role, one ballerina will accent the swan qualities, another the queen aspects, still another the womanly attributes of the role, but Danilova manages to be all three and in addition to this merger, she somehow succeeds in evoking the air of fantasy and of doomed passion which make *Swan Lake* a theatrical masterpiece and not just another fairy-tale ballet. These technical requirements of the classic ballerina and this power of characterization, Danilova brings to other classic roles, but because of her sensitivity to theme, music and pattern, she is different in each part. An arabesque may be an arabesque to some, but to Danilova it is different as used in *Swan Lake* and in *The Nutcracker,* and it is even different as used at various times within the same ballet. In effect, she gives different inflection to the same balletic word depending upon its place and purpose in a balletic phrase.

163

A listing of Danilova's other roles, and they are many, would be impossible to group within this space; however, mention should be made of a few in order to indicate her versatility. Her dancing of the principal role in *Coppélia* constitutes one of the unforgetable experiences in dance, for not only does she dance the final act, made up of storyless numbers, with exactitude and elegance, but she makes the prankish heroine of the first two acts an utterly winning and highly humorous character. No one who has seen her as the Glove-seller in *Gaîté Parisienne* or the cancan dancer in *Le Beau Danube* will deny that she is also an unparalleled dancing soubrette, and her appearances in the bumpkin-like ballet *Igrouchki* mark her as a first-rate clown. To top it all, she can claim achievement as a mime, for her rare performances of the role of the favorite of the harem in *Scheherezade* disclosed acting skill of high caliber.

A Star's Radiance   In addition to technical skills, knowledge of dance styles, intelligence in characterization and an instinctive command of the dynamics of dance, Alexandra Danilova possesses that personal radiance which is probably the deciding factor in transforming a soloist into a ballerina, or a principal player into a star. Call it personality, "it" or an effective arrangement of body chemistries, this radiance not only lights up the stage but it also lights up the audience and the result is applause, appreciation and across-the-footlights affection. Like all vivid personalities, Danilova has certain mannerisms, and these mannerisms, such as the spirited and rhymically logical flicking of her wrists, dim the view of certain ballet analysts, to her many dancing achievements. Danilova's few personal idiosyncrasies of performing, liked by many and annoying to some, do not mar those dance qualities and qualifications which I have attempted to jot down, for these qualities and qualifications not only make Alexandra Danilova a great artist, they signify "ballerina."
[*New York Herald Tribune*]

Two Ladies—Sybil Shearer and Iva Kitchell

May 4, 1946

In nature, Sybil Shearer seems to find serenity, beauty, grandeur and normalcy, but in her probings of man, she has apparently found him shallow, aimless and close to the border of insanity. Her dance program yesterday afternoon at Times Hall indicated such findings and expressed them sometimes brilliantly, sometimes obscurely but never ineptly. Her choreographic style is very much her own and when it employs cliches of movement they derive, not from other dancers but from her own overuse of certain gestures; and her dance technique is developed to a degree that few other modern dancers of her generation have yet achieved. There is, then, much to admire and respect in Miss Shearer's program and in her dancing, and on occasion she achieves that perfection which will be more frequently hers when further maturity comes.

In a Vacuum, for example, is one of the most perfect dances of its kind to be found on any program. Its riotous, almost hysterical humor is neither mimed nor gestured but is, rather, purely muscular, for Miss Shearer moves her body (and segments of it) in sequences completely devoid of functional or expressional logic and the result is more hilarious than words could possibly describe. In *Sarabande, The Adaptability of Man, O Lost!, Shallow Water* and *Is It Night?* she reveals, bitterly and with touches of ironic humor, the weaknesses and the pettiness of man. *Shallow Water,* for instance, seems to be concerned with the superficialities and the falseness of the demogogue, the bigot, the pessimist and others, while *Sarabande* is a delicious satire on nervous vanity and purposeless being. Among other things, *The Adaptability of Man* is a really funny tour de force in just plain scratching, as Miss Shearer shows us a woman who scratches, claws, slaps and attacks the insects which have found her as their target.

When she is concerned with nature, or with man in nature, the Shearer dances take on beauty and sweetness. *In the Cool of the Garden* succeeds in evoking the qualities promised in the title itself, and *In the Field,* showing man very close to his mother-earth, is as simple and as noble as wall paintings of similar theme which one finds in the ancient tombs of Egypt. *Several Transmutations* in its four parts—*Early Sun, Morning, Four O'Clock, Evening*—manages to reflect not only the qualities of those times but also man's reactions to them; the first is bright and hopeful and filled with promise, the second is buoyant and bustling in its freshness, the third is generally calmer but interrupted with flashes of energy like the sudden colors of sunset and the fourth is serene. In this last work, costume changes for each section marred the flow of the piece, and it was obvious that such changes were unnecessary, since essential change of effect should have come through body movement and not through dress.

Such dances as *Is It Night?* and *Let the Heavens Open That the Earth May Shine* were not fully realized in choreographic pattern nor in expressional clarity. In these and in some of the other dances, even in those that were generally effective, there was too much movement or too much repetition of movement phrases. Miss Shearer uses her hands constantly, and although they are expressive and schooled to the point of virtuosity, they demand too much attention, and with such a brilliant dancer that is a pity, for her torso and her limbs are potentially as articulate as her hands and are equally deserving of focus. The audience was a large one and enthusiastic; it was composed for the most part of dancers from the fields of ballet, modern dance and musical comedy who gave every evidence of enjoying a busman's holiday. The fine accompaniments were provided by Marian Hall and the too dim lighting by Helen Morrison. [*New York Herald Tribune*]

November 11, 1946   Fun at the Dance

Iva Kitchell, who danced at Carnegie Hall Sunday night, provided her audience with a wonderful dose of terpsichorean tonic which seemed to lift every one out of a rainy day depression and into a state of pleasant exhilaration. Whether she was giving accent to the ham instincts of the ballerina or delving into the grim secrets of an esoteric form of dance, Miss Kitchell was a joy and a reminder that there was something amusing to be found in almost anything.

Although the young dancer is far from subtle, concerned more with parody than with satire, she is perceptive, and because she is an exceptionally skilled dancer she has a large field in which to play. Her *Sonatina Rococo* and *Ze Ballet* find her playing havoc with "phony" acrobatics, persecuting a port de bras sequence in unmerciful fashion, giving hilarious twists to pirouettes and poses and striking perilously close to the dance styles of several serious ballet performers one could name. Her pseudo-Oriental tappings and scarf-and-garland dances are just as devastating and her excursions into the realm of modern dance are accomplished with a wonderful air of intense bewilderment, or perhaps I mean bewildered intensity.

Soul in Search, which might have been inspired by Martha Graham's great work, *Dark Meadow,* allowed Miss Kitchell to search vocally as well as physically with richly funny results. There was self-search, search in space, search on the floor as the dancer whipped herself into a final frenzy of desperate action which defied most of the laws of choreographic logic. *Non-Objective* fell into the same category and fell most delightfully.

In addition to those numbers which poke fun at dance styles, Iva Kitchell offers several pieces concerned with certain characters and certain common actions. Some of them such as *Maisie at the Movies, The Gentleman Friend* and *Growing Up,* allow for some engaging pantomime and provide a pleasant contrast with the more strenuous dance parodies. Of her new pieces, only *The Vert Brothers—Intro and Extro,* fails to hit Miss Kitchell's usually superior stride. The movement patterns are fairly obvious with Brother Intro limiting himself to small scale movements and to a minimum of space probings and with Brother Extro dashing about with bravado. The result, however, is not particularly humorous, probably because it lacks the surprise accents, the wrenched stresses which make her other dances generate the laughs.

A large audience, with shoulders shaking a good deal of the time, was in attendance, and it was apparent that Iva Kitchell was able to project even her small-size gestures and necessary grimaces to the far corners of that house. Harvey Brown, composer-pianist, was the excellent accompanist of the evening. [*New York Herald Tribune*]

Four Solo Recitals Here Called Indicative of Future of Dance

May 19, 1946

Four young dancers of uncommon skill, two of them possibly possessed of genius, offered solo recitals in New York on recent dates. Since they are all exponents of the contemporary dance, and since the stars in this branch of the art are approaching or have passed the half-century mark, a survey of their gifts and possibilities seems warranted. Iris Mabry, the least developed of the four young artists, may be credited with a lovely body, a technique which enables her to move with clarity and assurance and a style which is fresh and original. She does not really dance much as yet, for her movements are deliberate and her patterns of dance are arresting to the eye rather than meaningful to the senses. It is probable that if Miss Mabry chose to let an established choreographer create or at least arrange her dances she would quickly become a valuable performer-dancer, but perhaps she feels that being a choreographer-dancer enables her to develop along lines best suited to her basic skills. At any rate, her experimental dances, although they do not constitute good dance theater, serve as heralds of more rewarding and maturer dancing to come.

Anna Sokolow, the most orthodox dancer of the four, has improved enormously over these past few seasons. Her concert at the Y. M. H. A. last Sunday was distinguished not only by her dancing skill but by fine choreography and excellent programming. Although pure comedy was absent from her program, the need for variety was answered by formal dances to music of Bach, folk dances of both Mexican and Jewish derivations, dances which had folk flavor but which were not traditional in step and dances of personal comment. Variety of theme was augmented by varieties in style and in dynamic properties, thus making the program of absorbing interest throughout. Miss Sokolow, who used to appear as a rather ungracious and defiant performer and a rather remote dancer, now fills her dances with warmth and, when the occasion demands, gentleness as well as conviction. I enjoyed her entire program, but particularly moving was "Mexican Retalbo" with its sweet, stiffly

167

moving portrait of a primitive virgin and its later presentation of a devout and emotional supplicant, progressing with a painful and humble gluteal walk to the Virgin's place.

The Goodness of Nature   Superb technical skill, a fresh and eloquent style and a complete awareness of the difference between movement execution and dancing mark Sybil Shearer as one of the finest young dancers of our day. She is irritating at times because she allows her prodigious dexterity of the hands to overshadow the potential articulation of other body movements, but this is probably only a phase in the dancer's self-search. Miss Shearer has real choreographic talent and a refreshing approach to her art. Her program, almost equally divided between the foibles of man and the beauties of nature, already gives evidence of a trend of thought apparent in few dance programs other than those of Ruth St. Denis's. She is not at all like St. Denis in technique or style, but both are concerned with beauty and with a search for perfection. While Miss St. Denis finds beauty of spirit in man himself, Miss Shearer in her dances makes men petty and wasteful of his gifts and in other dances exalts the order, the beauty and the richness of nature. *In the Field,* which shows man uniting with nature to bring forth richness, and *Let the Heavens Open, That the Earth May Shine,* a not very successful hymn-dance, indicate that Miss Shearer is heading for a dance not concerned with homely events of perhaps passing interest but dedicated to the pursuance and revelation of beauty and perfection in a mankind which recognizes the laws of nature. Such pursuit, I believe, will be of inestimable value to the art of dancing.

In his solo program last Sunday evening, Merce Cunningham (of Martha Graham's company) made it clear that his amazing dance qualities and highly personal style cannot be ignored in the dance world of the immediate future. Surely this young man was destined to be a dancer, for five minutes of watching his dancing convinces one that "to dance" is his equivalent of our "to breathe." Some may quarrel with his style, others with his choreography, but I do not believe that his basic dance skill, his kinetic genius, if you will, can be denied. With experience and guidance, he could probably become a dominant and successful figure in American dance, but mis-direction of his talents could just as easily make him a passing figure in an ephemeral cult.

Inner Dance   Such dances as *Root of an Unfocus* and *Tossed As It Is Untroubled* (an "externalization of a laugh within the mind") would have appeared as so much pretentious, psychological nonsense if danced by almost any one other than Merce Cunningham. The young dancer, however, made them both simple, convincing and absorbing. Such subjective material suits him far better than an overt dance as *Invocation to Vahakn,* although it must be reported that *Fast Blues* is danced with openness and prowess. Essentially, however, dances of inner impulse, of instinctive action find Mr. Cunningham at his best. He is not a wide-eyed, radiant stage personality; he is, rather, sullen and self-absorbed, but this absorption he manages to communicate to his audience. The darting, animal-like qualities of his dancing are fascinating, for they are not animal in the sense of "cat-like tread" or "gazelle-like leap," but they seem to disclose the enduring animal properties of man himself. The costumes for his concert were the best I have seen contemporary dancers use in many a season and the program was unrolled without a hitch, but at the close, one tended to remember (in most instances) the dancer rather than the dances. Ultimately, when the choreography of his programs becomes richer in content, and nourishing to the audience participant as well as arresting to his eye, we should be able to remember dance and dancer alike. [*New York Herald Tribune*]

Weidman Recital

May 24, 1946

It was an excellent program of contemporary dance which Charles Weidman and his company offered Wednesday night at the Studio Theater. There was humor, of satiric nature and of the lighthearted brand; there was tragedy, in personal guise and again of national scope; above all, there was the drama inherent in all good dancing. The opening piece, a solo by Mr. Weidman, fused several of these qualities into a single dance work, for *On My Mother's Side* is actually a series of dance portraits of the artist's ancestors and the heritages which they bestowed upon him. Through the pertinent and expressive lines of Mr. Weidman's movements we see the great-grandfather who was the irresponsible yet canny roamer, the great-grandfather who was the sturdy settler, the blind and ever-toiling grandmother, the grandfather who took his own life rather than face disaster, dancing Aunt Jessie and finally Sonny, who grew up to be a dancer. This established favorite of the Weidman repertory remains, after many seeings, a beautiful work of characterization through dance.

David and Goliath, a bubbling Biblical ballet for full company to the seventeenth-century music of Johann Kuhnau, tells the famous story with child-like candor and simplicity. The moral of the piece is completely, and purposely, obscured by the plainly danced facts of the fable. David is utterly boyish, pious when he remembers to be so and distinguished by a delightful teen-age bravado. Goliath is a big oaf who stumbles about frightening the Israelite maidens into a state of tremors, until he is knocked out of the picture by David's well placed stone. The work is just as simple as that, appealing because of its simplicity and hilarious in its characterizations. Mr. Weidman was the bumbling Goliath and Peter Hamilton the buoyant David, both ably abetted by stamping Philistines and a bevy of frightened maids.

For the major offering of the evening, the company offered *A House Divided,* a work based upon the problems of reconstruction following the Civil War and upon the democratic precepts of Abraham Lincoln. It is an effective and moving work, curiously but successfully combining speech, dance action and pantomime. The narrator, who moves about the stage along with the dance figure of Lincoln, speaks the words of the great President as Mr. Weidman, as Lincoln, translates the spirit of the words into dance gesture. These spoken-mimed episodes are followed by dance scenes concerned with the preceding texts, and the whole emerges as an integrated testament to freedom, to equality, to brotherhood. The action touches upon the tragedy of the war itself, the blindness of the people to the need of union, the lot of the Negro slave, the parasites who exist on the labor of others, and throughout it all glows the compassion of Lincoln the man, and the determination of Lincoln the President to make democracy work for all peoples of the nation.

Mr. Weidman, as Lincoln, brought great dignity, warmth and emotional drive to his characterization, while Peter Hamilton, Nadine Gae and Saida Gerrard supplied fine dance passages in the shifting roles assigned to them. The entire company, barring a few minor lapses, danced exceedingly well and with appropriate fervor. The program also offered Mr. Hamilton's *Purcell Suite,* a pleasant version of a gigue, sarabande and hornpipe, danced with physical skill and a nice romantic touch by its choreographer and Nadine Gae. The closing work was Mr. Weidman's *And Daddy Was a Fireman,* one of this distinguished American dancer's best and most popular ballets. It was presented too late in the evening for comment on this occasion, but many will recall that in it Mr. Weidman's forebears come in for further usage and supply the audience with hilarious theatrical fare. The splendid accompanist of the evening was Freda Miller, pianist. [*New York Herald Tribune*]

New Ballet Society Founded with Balanchine as Director

October 27, 1946

A new ballet organization has made its appearance on the American scene, but it is not just another ballet company, not merely a fresh challenger for

170

commercial supremacy in the ballet arena. The Ballet Society, a non-profit making membership corporation, with headquarters at the New York City Center, has come into being for the express purpose of fostering the lyric theater in America through the production of new works. In its initial announcement, the Ballet Society made the following comment: "Since ballet in the United States is relatively new, our interest has been primarily in the revival of productions already famous, or the creation of works based on national themes. Now, with the close of a second world war, broader directions are possible and desirable." In pursuit of those directions, the Ballet Society plans to develop a completely new repertory of ballet, ballet-opera and other forms of the lyric theater through the collaboration of progressive choreographers, musicians and easel-painters.

The Ballet Society's productions will not feature star performers (the manager of a commercial company would have apoplexy at such a notion) nor repertory favorites (a fond farewell to *Scheherezade*) but will concentrate upon "expert musical and dance direction to insure an essential elegance and freshness." Dancers in these presentations will be drawn from the student body or from among the graduates of the School of American Ballet, and the musical artists will be selected from the best trained younger talents. In addition to its theater presentations, the Ballet Society plans to co-operate with other educational and cultural institutions for the purpose of production, exhibition and publication; to publish books, prints and articles concerned with dance; to produce and circulate dance films; to publish record albums of music used in the society's performances, with photographic documentation and full program notes; to award fellowships to talented young dancers and choreographers.

Opening Program   The Ballet Society will inaugurate its first season on Nov. 20 at the High School Auditorium, 225 East Twenty-fourth Street, with the premiere of *The Four Temperaments,* a ballet-pantomime with music by Paul Hindemith, choreography by George Balanchine and scenery and costumes by Kurt Seligman, and the American premiere of *The Spellbound Child,* a lyric fantasy in two parts with music by Maurice Ravel, choreography by Balanchine and scenery and costumes by Aline Bernstein. On Dec. 11 in the Auditorium of the Museum of Modern Art, the society will present "The Classic Ballet," a demonstration with pictures and dancers of the evolution of traditional theatrical dancing.

At the Hunter Playhouse, Jan. 13, the program will offer *Pastorela,* a ballet-opera with book by Jose Martines, music by Paul Bowles orchestrated by Blas Galindo, choreography by Lew Christensen and scenery and costumes by Alvin Colt; *Renard,* a ballet-burlesque with book and music by Igor Stravinsky, choreography by Balanchine and scenery and costumes by Esteban

171

Frances; *Javanese Court and Popular Dances* by Ratna Mohini, Soekaro and Pamoedjo, with music transcribed and arranged by Colin McPhee; *The Nightingale,* with music by Stravinsky, danced as a Javanese ballet in the native idiom. A presentation of Gian-Carlo\Menotti's *The Medium,* with revised score and new staging, will be presented in February at a theater to be announced.

Spring Productions   The program for March 19 at the High School Auditorium will offer *The Minotaur,* a ballet with music by Elliott Carter; choreography by Balanchine, and scenery and costumes by Joan Junyer; *Lady Hamilton,* a ballet with music by John Colman, choreography by William Dollar, and scenery and costumes by Dorothea Tanning; *Zodiac,* a classic ballet with music by Rudi Revel, choreography by Todd Bolender, and scenery and costumes by Esteban Frances. The season's final performance, on May 14, at the High School Auditorium, will be composed of *Highland Fling,* a ballet with music by Stanley Bate, choreography by William Dollar, and scenery and costumes by David Ffolkes; *Northwestern Rite,* a ballet with music by John Cage, choreography by Merce Cunningham, and scenery and costumes by Isamu Noguchi; *Minstrel Show,* a ballet with music by Carter Harman, choreography by Lew Christensen, and scenery and costumes by Robert Drew. There will be no tickets available for single events, only subscription sale in connection with membership application.

Ballet Society's staff is a notable one, including George Balanchine as artistic director, Leon Barzin as musical director, Lew Christensen as ballet master, Lincoln Kirstein as secretary, Paul Magriel as editor of dance books and records, Michael Rainer as executive manager and Jean Rosenthal as technical supervisor. In Mr. Balanchine the society possesses the foremost contemporary figure of the classic dance; where some choreographers merely reset the patterns and the pas of the past and others turn to non-traditional kinetic styles or folk sources for their material, Balanchine maintains the elegance and the refinement of the classic ballet, bringing to it new accents, new directions and even new movements but rarely veering from its established principles. These admirable qualities, although they do not encompass all of the possibilities of creative dance, should bring considerable distinction to his artistic direction.

In Mr. Kirstein the staff boasts a dance leader who has done much for ballet in America, not only through his writings and his school, but through his Ballet Caravan, which bucked terrible odds in an attempt to proclaim the worth of American ballet artists, be they dancers, choreographers, musicians or designers. Although the Caravan is no more, its place in American dance history is established and its spirit, now mature, is perhaps the life-essence of the Ballet Society. We shall know before long and we shall also learn whether such an organization such as the Ballet Society can match or surpass the artistic achievements (some of them admittedly based upon revivals or restorations, but some of them genuinely progressive and innovative) of the commercial Ballet Theatre. [*New York Herald Tribune*]

Ballet Theatre's Performances Disclose New Trends in Dance

November 3, 1946

The rival New York seasons of the Original Ballet Russe and Ballet Theatre made it very clear that the latter was by far the better company. One did not have to look very hard nor very long to arrive at such a conclusion, for in spite of the rich gifts of artistry bestowed upon the audience by Alicia Markova, Anton Dolin, André Eglevsky, Rosella Hightower and a few of the permanent members of the Original Ballet Russe, the Colonel de Basil company was shabby in dancing, in the staging of its old productions and in the choreographic caliber of most of its newer works. Ballet Theatre, on the other hand, was fresh and exuberant and accurate in its performing, bright in its staging and spirited as an organization.

Ballet Theatre, however, is worthy of a higher compliment than pleasant and obvious comparison with a patently inferior company. It is not enough for either the critic or the public to be pleased with something simply because it is better rather than worse, for if art is to develop one cannot be content with anything less than the "possible best," a rule of thumb determined by known or hoped-for standards of excellence. Ballet Theatre, then, is deserving of praise not because it is better than the low-grade ballet vouchsafed on most occasions by the Original Ballet Russe, but because, in its own right, it represents to a considerable degree the "possible best" in ballet today.

The artistic achievements, partially planned and partially intuitive, of Ballet Theatre are achievements in creativeness rather than in mere theatrical smoothness. This creativeness is discernible in the actions of directors, choreographers and the dancers themselves and is traceable, I believe, to a growing discontent with surface prettiness and to a search for real artistic substance. Perhaps the war brought about this change, perhaps American dance artists are basically more concerned with substance than with veneer, but whatever the reason, Ballet Theatre's dancers made it evident that they were not offering the shell of art but were concerned with discovering and revealing the heart of dance, the substance of dance.

Kaye and Alonso In Ballet Theatre's presentation of the classics, one could perceive the search for substance. Neither Nora Kaye nor Alicia Alonso danced the Swan Queen in *Swan Lake* as if she had been coached in a routine, but danced as if she had studied the character, arrived at certain conclusions about her, and as if she had refused to execute a movement until she had determined why it had been choreographed in the first place, and what dramatic, emotional or purely kinetic purpose it possessed. In this and in other roles these two distinguished young dancers sought for the substance of art and found it. In new ballets it was not difficult to find, for the choreographer was on hand to explain his purposes, but it was more difficult with traditional works which had been passed down from generation to generation, with each successive one forgetting more of the basic substance while desperately trying to retain the choreographic shell. Although great dancers in other companies (Danilova in *Coppélia* or Markova in *Giselle*) have also rejuvenated the classics through wise and knowing artistry, it remained for Ballet Theatre to extend the rejuvenation principle to organizational level.

The company's artistic direction gives evidence of a trend toward artistic substance. The merits of the company are stressed rather than the particular attributes of a star, the choreographic material is permitted and encouraged to range from safe classicism to experimental modernity, from the trivial to the profound, from the pleasantly decorative to the artistically challenging, and dead wood, even though it be sacrosanct through tradition, is cut away. An example of this last point would be Ballet Theatre's discarding of obsolete miming passages or at least the restudying of them and the restoring of them to their original meaningful purposes. In these respects, Ballet Theatre is echoing the revolution initiated by the modern dance. Not that Ballet Theatre is turning to the techniques and styles of modern dance, but like modern dance it is concerned with reminding us (and itself) that dance, to be great art, must disclose its motivations, its purposes, its goals and not rely upon surface prettiness nor upon the passing excitement aroused by meaningless, physical virtuosity.

Ballet Substance Occasionally, Ballet Theatre's actions make one wonder whether the direction is aware of the reasons behind its achievements. Certainly *Les Patineurs,* imported from England, and the new and flamboyant decor for *Giselle* suggest that the management is willing to rely upon fresh paint rather than upon solid structure. At any rate, under its own steam or under the compulsion of the times, Ballet Theatre is providing ballet with new substance, with living art-tissues rather than with embalmed beauty. The fact that Jerome Robbins, with four smash comedy hits behind him (two in ballet and two on Broadway), endangered his not yet rooted success as a designer of gay dances by creating the depressing, bitter and not-pap-for-the-audience

174

Facsimile proved that the American choreographer and Ballet Theatre were aware that contrived shadows of past successes could not hope to rival the fresh substance of a new creation. *Facsimile* was a success, but even if it had been a failure, the validity of its artistic premise could not have been denied. In *Facsimile,* in the Tudor ballets and in its dancing of the classics, Ballet Theatre is opening the door to ballet art and not merely allowing us to look at its decorative porticos. [*New York Herald Tribune*]

Katherine Dunham—Bal Nègre

November 9, 1946: Hot!

Stringing together dances from her concert repertory, production numbers from her earlier Broadway shows and several new pieces, Katherine Dunham has contrived a new revue, *Bal Nègre,* which Nelson L. Gross and Daniel Melnick presented at the Belasco Theater Thursday evening. If the Dunham performers can bear up under the very considerable strains and intensities inherent in their choreographic assignments, Belasco audiences should find frenzy of excitement at subsequent presentations. Certainly the opening night audience gave every evidence of responding happily to the stage activities.

If *Bal Nègre* does not represent Miss Dunham at her artistic best, it surely boasts the sure-fire aspects of the Dunham dance. The entire production is brightly staged and brilliantly costumed (by John Pratt), the dynamic intensity of primitive dance propels the show along at a racy clip and the familiar Dunham sensualities of movement, apparent in voodoo rituals, quadrilles and even in plain walkings-about result in an arresting and frequently exciting revue.

Those very qualities which give *Bal Nègre* much of its excitement, however, also constitute its failings, for Miss Dunham has given her revue too much sensuality, too much intensity, too much speed, and before the proceedings are half over, one commences to yearn for something very quiet and very dignified. There is, in Miss Dunham's version of dance, dignity and serenity and lyricism, qualities to be found in much of primitive dancing, but she has failed to employ them to any degree in *Bal Nègre.* It is a pity, for her program would gain in thematic richness and in dramatic contrast by their inclusion.

Miss Dunham and her company danced wonderfully throughout the evening. The star herself was particularly effective as the girl in the ballet *L'Ag'ya,* for not only did she bring warmth of movement to her dance with her lover but she also brought an eerie, hypnotic quality to those movements done under the spell of a voodoo charm. Her most effective moment, to jump back to my earlier comments about the choreography, was one which found her standing almost still as the charm commenced to take effect; here was dynamic control, here was the excitement born, not of muscular explosion, but of muscular suspense. In the same ballet, fine dancing was provided by Lenwood Morris as the shrieking, prancing zombie king, by Vanoye Aikens as the lover and by Wilbert Bradley as the villain. These young dancers together with Lucille Ellis, Eartha Kitt, Othella Strozier, Jean Léon Destine and others supported the star in splendid fashion.

Additional numbers on the program included *Motivos*; *Haitian Roadside,* a pantomimic skit with dance and song; *Shango,* a ritual dance and *Nostalgia,* a collection of early-American dances and songs. The orchestra, which made a great deal of noise along with some fine rhythms, was under the direction of Gilberto Valdes and the Sans Souci Singers were responsible for the singing assignments.

Bal Nègre, then, is loud, flashy and explosive, it offers much that is excellent in the way of dancing and it certainly cannot be accused of lethargy; one could have wished, however, that Miss Dunham had contributed more of her artistic gifts and less of her showmanship instincts to the proceedings, for then *Bal Nègre* might have emerged as a really distinguished program of theater dance. [*New York Herald Tribune*]

1947

Doris & José, Martha & George, Theme & Variations

Doris Humphrey creates Lament for Ignacio Sanchez Mejias and the Story of Mankind for José Limón and Company • Ballet Society's first season offers L'Enfant et les Sortilèges, The Four Temperaments, Divertimento, Pastorela and Renard • Graham, ever-triumphant, in Cave of the Heart, Errand into the Maze, and Night Journey • The brilliant Rosella Hightower • Jack Cole and group at the Latin Quarter • The American Theatre Wing offers dance training for ex-GIs • The Laubins, Indian dance experts, saluted • Ballet Theatre offers Balanchine's Theme and Variations and some outstanding soloists

Doris Humphrey Praised for New Works, Artistic Direction

January 12, 1947

A little over a year ago Doris Humphrey terminated her career as a dancer. At that time in these columns I offered a brief resume of her distinguished contributions, both as a dancer and as a choreographer, to the American dance and suggested that her retirement from the stage, although viewable as immediate tragedy, would permit her to concentrate exclusively upon her enormous choreographic talents. She has done just that and has come up with two magnificent theater pieces, *Lament for Ignacio Sanchez Mejias* and *The Story of Mankind,* both choreographed for José Limón and his company and both given their New York premieres last Sunday.

Ostensibly, *Lament for Ignacio Sanchez Mejias* is a Spanish-flavored dance-drama concerned with the life and death of a courageous and vivid bullfighter, but actually it is an allegory, an elaborate metaphor which speaks of the life and death and immortality of all men through the figures of Ignacio, Destiny and Woman. The bullfighter, Ignacio, moves through those patterns of action which constitute his lot in life and within their framework expresses his own qualities of being, his pride, his courage, his sensitiveness. Destiny, the inexorable choreographer, designs and times his death with unswerving, unemotional precision. Woman, loving him, cherishes Ignacio's life and mourns his death, and through her lament recalls his absent soul and gives it immortality in her memories.

Miss Humphrey has, of course, made Ignacio the central dance figure, while the female figures, who speak the poetry of Garcia Lorca, are given a minimum of dance movement. Yet the sum effect is one of constant, concentrated dance. Miss Humphrey has fused action and speech in such a way that speech seems to be born of movement as movement, in turn, is often born of inner stimulus, as if an inner pang of anguish caused the muscles of the body to contract and the voice to speak. Every movement, whether alone or with accompanying speech, whether large or gestural, is eloquent, and these individual patterns of movement are woven into an overall pattern of stirring beauty, a dance-drama of visual color and of compelling passion.

Atom-Theme Ballet   Miss Humphrey's *The Story of Mankind* is in theme utterly different from the *Lament*. Again, her movements are eloquent and the threads of action woven into sturdy fabric, but she is more concerned with comment than with revelation, with surface manifestations of man than with his inner compulsions. In this hilarious and biting satire, she sweeps man from cave through palaces and castles to a penthouse and back to a cave again, showing us his concern with the architecture of his house rather than with the architecture of his spirit. Miss Humphrey gives her cavewoman marrow-penetrating shivers, her lady of ancient Greece motions of sculptural elegance, her medieval dame wimple-tossing actions, her mistress of a brownstone a well bred prance and her penthouse wife jittery actions, suitable to a jittery age, and fusing into the cavewoman shivers again at the coming of the atomic era. Throughout the piece, the bluff, husky male invents, builds and embellishes for his wife, although he gives the impression that without her nagging he would doze peacefully through the ages. *The Story of Mankind* is quite as wonderful a work in its way as the *Lament*, but instead of being a timeless ritual it is a great cartoon with a spoof and a message of immediacy.

With these two works Doris Humphrey has maintained her position as one of the great choreographers of our day and has contributed immeasurably to the growth of other dance artists, for certainly José Limón and his company members could not have given the distinguished evening of dance they gave without her contributions. Mr. Limón has been a superior dancer for several seasons and has given evidence of considerable choreographic gifts, but Miss Humphrey's works have given broader range to his dance talents and have exploited heretofore latent attributes of personality and physical virtuosity. Through his own efforts and through association with Miss Humphrey, Mr. Limón has become a dancer of manly elegance, of dramatic power and sensitivity, a dancer without peer in his generation of men dancers.

The Director's Hand   As artistic director for the little group which José Limón heads, Miss Humphrey has brought her innate taste and vast experience to bear upon program arrangement and execution. Not only has she aided Mr. Limón to discover and increase his own stature, but she has performed similar miracles on other members of his company. Pauline Koner dances as she never danced before, with new authority and elegance of style and with complete command of every motor inflection. Letitia Ide, Meg Mundy and Miriam Pandor perform their assignments with physical accuracy and full understanding of the dynamic and dramatic implications of their roles.

Miss Humphrey is already at work on a dance for four performers to an Aaron Copland piano sonata and is plotting out two dramatic dance pieces, all for the Limón company. In addition to working with Mr. Limón, it is possible that she will, as she has done in the past, aid other young dancers with their programs. Thus Miss Humphrey, with her dancing days behind her, retains her position as a key figure in the world of dance and as a dominant force in the channeling of such dance activities, at least as far as America is concerned. [*New York Herald Tribune*]

Initial Ballet Society Works
Stress Variety of Form, Style

January 19, 1947

A report on the activities of Ballet Society is due. This organization which came into being last autumn with the stated purpose of fostering the growth of the lyric theater in America already has two programs to its credit and one book publication. The book has been discussed in these columns, the productions have not. If there seems to be something mysterious about the absence of dance reviews following Ballet Society's presentations of its programs, such mystery is easily explained by the following data: Ballet Society productions are not open to the general public upon purchase of single admissions but open to subscribing membership only; there is no press list; the theaters employed are, in some instances, distant enough from the theatrical district to make the meeting of a newspaper deadline difficult; the dance personnel is composed of skilled professionals and promising students, which poses a problem in critical standards for the reviewer; finally, Lincoln Kirstein, Ballet Society's secretary, requested that those newspaper representatives who attended performances as his guests abstain from writing dance reviews because of the student nature of the performing units. Musical reviews have appeared since the orchestra, under the direction of Leon Barzin, was of professional caliber.

Although reasons for omitting critical reviews of Ballet Society's productions seem valid, a few general comments on the enterprises of the organization are, I think, warranted. Let it be said right at the start that balletic chestnuts have been completely avoided, that non-balletic forms of dance have not been neglected, that unusual care has been given to the selection and use of music, costuming and decor and that George Balanchine, the artistic director, has apparently done everything in his power to make Ballet Society's presentations both stimulating and tasteful.

Two Programs   The initial program, presented in November, consisted of *The Spellbound Child,* a lyric fantasy, and *The Four Temperaments,* a ballet by George Balanchine, while the second program, presented last week, offered such varied items as a suite of Javanese dances, two modern dance solos by Iris Mabry, *Pastorela* (a ballet-opera), *Renard* (a ballet-burlesque) and Balanchine's *Divertimento.* Here, then, was the variety which Ballet Society had promised, variety in selection of forms, creators and executants, and here, too, care in production was manifest. The choreographic caliber of the works presented was quite another matter, for although there were a few first-rate examples of the choreographer's art, a number of the offerings were of inferior grade. Since the choreographers concerned were all professionals, a brief discussion of the works themselves would not be out of order.

Of first interest in Ballet Society's current repertory are *Divertimento* and *The Four Temperaments.* In the former work Balanchine has created a completely charming non-descriptive dance piece. It is typically Balanchine in its pattern-weaving arm actions in adagio episodes, in the contrapuntal handling of some of the group movement and in the invention which assembles a corps of dancers upon the stage, suspends the action and permits individuals or small units to emerge from repose, dance a theme or a contributory phrase and return to the sustained pattern. But although these structural devices constitute a sort of Balanchine trademark, they are given fresh and imaginative usage in *Divertimento* and are touched with the wonderfully gracious elegance which distinguishes many of this choreographer's efforts. *The Four Temperaments,* viewed as a non-descriptive work, is almost as rewarding, for its movement designs are arresting and kinesthetically effective, but it fails completely in mirroring those descriptive qualities (choleric, sanguinic, etc.) listed on the program of the ballet. The failure, however, rests upon the composer,

180

Hindemith, rather than upon Balanchine, who binds himself to the musician's outline.

Choreographic Troubles Dependency upon tricky costumes, unless concerned with a fancy dress ball, has never seemed to me to guarantee theatrical success. In both *The Spellbound Child* and *Renard,* the brilliant and often imaginative costumes in no way compensate for choreographic lack. Balanchine has given his mobile chairs, teapots, roosters and foxes a few capers but very little dancing and that on a plane suitable to a minor Sunday school pageant. Lew Christensen's *Pastorela* is also reminiscent of a pageant, and a not very exciting one at that. Granted that it is difficult to transplant a folk ceremony or festival to the stage, to cut it, to give it theatrical accent, to coax dynamic shading out of it, but it can and has been done successfully by others. Mr. Christensen apparently has been content with cutting and the result is a ballet which captures something of the simplicity but little of the earthiness and fervor present (or at least latent) in the Mexican material. The Javanese dances of Soekaro, Pamoedjo and Ratna Mohini are delightful, not merely because of their exotic nature, but because of the wealth of pattern which exists within the small spatial area they employ and because of the delicate dignity with which they are projected.

Although Ballet Society's choreographic record is not yet something to shout about, the organization has made a lusty start and the list of forthcoming productions promises much. Further, the direction will probably learn from its mistakes, if it thinks some have been made, and will clarify its production policy in respect to just what constitutes progressiveness in the lyric theater. The creation of a dance film library (still in the blueprint stage), collaboration with educational institutions, the publication of further items of dance literature should help immeasurably in establishing Ballet Society as a vital and welcome force in America's dance. [*New York Herald Tribune*]

Graham Triumphs—1947

February 28, 1947

It was a genuine triumph which Martha Graham experienced last evening at the Ziegfeld Theater on the occasion of the Broadway premiere of her newest dance work, *Cave of the Heart,* commissioned by the Alice M. Ditson Fund of Columbia University and presented there at a special showing under the title *The Serpent Heart* last spring. The title, the designations for the characters and portions of the choreography have been changed since the preview, but the work is basically the same, only more detailed and more dramatic than it was (and it was brilliant then) as its earlier showing.

Miss Graham no longer terms her role *One Like Medea* and now calls it *The Sorceress,* and the other parts have been similarly altered in their appellations, but the changes are not important to the sense of the work. *Cave of the Heart* is a drama of possessive and destroying love and as such its relationship to the *Medea* of Euripides, or even more to the modern poetic version by Robinson Jeffers, is apparent. Certainly its kinship to the theater of ancient Greece is manifest in the magnitude of its creative power, for here is no petty love but rather flaming passion; here is not simple hatred, but rather destroying venom; here is not merely tragic death, but rather violent destruction.

Through the movements of the Sorceress the very chemistry of expanding hate is revealed. There is first the pleading, the suspicion, the jealousy; then the trembling anger, the plotting, the placing of a poisoned crown upon the head of the girl-victim; later, as the venom of a hating heart bursts from its cave of the breast and binds its own creator in its poisoned strength, vengeful destruction is brought to the loved one, and finally the Sorceress, cleansed by the fire of her evil deeds, triumphant but divested of humanity, stands alone framed, like a tragic goddess, by the rays of the sun.

Cave of the Heart is something of a double triumph for its creator. It never diverges from the Graham tenet that her dance should reveal the inner being, that it should give substance to the hidden passions of man, yet because of its physical power, the grandeur of its choreographic surfaces and the unmistakable surge of its drama it should prove of compelling interest to even the most determined Grahamphobe. It is, then, triumphant dance and triumphant theater and it provides Miss Graham with a role of titanic proportions, at once terrifying and beautiful, majestic and incantational.

Erick Hawkins, who has developed his assignment considerably since last spring, is excellent as the brash adventurer, the one loved by the Sorceress, the one who seduces the young girl, and Yuriko as the victim of the seduction and the poison of the Sorceress is incredibly sweet and innocent, yielding in her femininity, girlish in the lightness and freedom of her actions. To May O'Donnell as Chorus fell the task of reflecting the passions of the players, of auguring and of lamenting, and this task she accomplished in distinguished fashion.

Other commendations are due Samuel Barber for his score, which supports and, at times, impels the action with its passages of heroic grandness, of maddeningly insistent rhythms, of melodic insinuations; Isamu Noguchi for his somber sacrificial altar and his sun-like piece for framing the Sorceress; Edythe Gilfond for the richness and dramatic pertinence of her costumes, and Jean Rosenthal for lighting effects which could not have been more perfect.

The audience was of good size and bestowed prolonged applause and bravos upon Miss Graham as the curtain fell on *Cave of the Heart*. [*New York Herald Tribune*]

March 1, 1947

The final premiere of Martha Graham's season at the Ziegfeld Theater was presented last evening before a capacity audience which heartily applauded *Errand Into the Maze*. This new work, with a title derived from a poem by Ben Belitt, bases its action upon "that errand-journey into the maze of the heart in order to face and do battle with the Creature of Fear." This self-assigned problem Miss Graham succeeds in solving with directness and economy of movement, with her familiar intensity and with a curious air of poignancy which somehow makes the beholder feel that he too is sharing in the battle.

Structurally *Errand Into the Maze* is both pertinent to the theme and ingenious in design, for Miss Graham has constructed her choreography in such a way that a vast area of ominous space is created and threaded with endlessly weaving pathways, and within that space and along those lanes of action the battle with fear is fought; here, in the battle, the movements are those of search, of fleeing, of cringing, of determination, of defeat, or renewed struggle and finally of triumph. Although the structure, like the theme itself, is without period and applicable to every living soul, it is given a quality of classical grandeur through its tenuous relationship to the heroic myth of Theseus and the Minotaur, a relationship easily suggested by the choreographic realization of the maze and by the symbolizing of fear in the figure of a bull-headed man.

If there is any point of argument with reference to the choreography it would concern the use of the Creature of Fear, for he is accorded no movements of a dance nature and is more of a mobile symbol or prop than an actual embodiment of fear itself. However, since we are meant to experience the battle with fear through the figure of the one who makes the errand, perhaps too much action on the part of the symbol would serve only to dim the true focus of the dance.

Miss Graham danced her new role in exciting fashion, her body giving physical articulation to the anguish, the terror, the fierceness and the release which the character experienced, and Mark Ryder, as the symbol of fear, brought to the simple assignment the skill necessary to its realization. The music by Gian-Carlo Menotti was superb for the purposes of the dance, rhythmically compelling, swelling to dramatic peaks in keeping with increased dynamics upon the stage and containing within its structure a repeated beat which seemed to create the terrifying sound of the heart when it booms through a stethoscope. The setting by Isamu Noguchi, beautiful and fantastic, abetted the dancer's creation of space and pattern. *Errand Into the Maze* is a dance of subdued excitement; it is not one which generates violent applause, for it is too personal for that, almost like a secret between the dancer and each individual in the audience, but it is, nonetheless, a distinguished dance work and of particular appropriateness in these times when fear attacks us all.

Of special interest at this performance was the revival of *El Penitente,* Miss Graham's primitive mystery suggested by the rituals of the Penitentes. On this occasion, Pearl Lang assumed the role of the Mary Figure (Virgin, Magdalen, Mother) ordinarily danced by Miss Graham, thus marking the first time that a "Graham" role was danced by any one other than the star herself. Miss Lang danced it nicely, for, although she lacked the intensity of Miss Graham and was girlish rather than womanly as the Magdalen, she was easy and accurate of movement and beautiful to look upon. Erick Hawkins was unnecessarily subdued in this performance as the Penitent and John Butler was not quite strong enough, particularly in back and arm movements, as the Christ Figure. The new Noguchi properties were not nearly as apt as the rough and heavier properties used in the earlier production, but the music of Louis Horst seemed finer than ever. [*New York Herald Tribune*]

March 2, 1947: Ballet Public Unnecessarily Troubled by Graham Dance Art

During the last week two large New York theaters have been busy with dance affairs, the Ziegfeld with Martha Graham and her company and the City Center with the Ballet Russe de Monte Carlo. At this incipient point, our little parallel must come to an abrupt halt, for Miss Graham moves along one dance path while the ballet follows a totally different route. Many devotees of the ballet regard the Graham dance as something resembling an unfortunate artistic quirk, while a goodly portion of the modern dance followers view the ballet as a flossy case of arrested development; a few (and their numbers are growing) are capable of experiencing the beauties of both.

The saw which states that comparisons are odious should be revised to aver that comparisons are devastating, at least where a comparison of modern dance with ballet is concerned. The two versions of dance cannot be compared except in the most general of terms. Both are housed in the theater, both are arts of movement, both are governed by the motor possibilities and limitations of the human body, both, through their choreographies, create discernible and balanced structures, and both exist for audiences. Each, however, builds differently upon those generalities.

Martha Graham's dance is no more difficult to understand than is the ballet, but it is more difficult to enjoy. This difference is simply a matter of conditioning. For many generations we have been conditioned into believing that the long, clean lines of a body in arabesque are beautiful, that balance upon a toe slipper is a wonderful refinement of body skill, that multiple pirouettes and flashing entrechats are both stunning to behold and exciting to the senses. All this is true and such esthetic conditioning is desirable provided we do not use it as a standard by which to judge an equally valid but basically distinct esthetic.

No Arabesques   If we attend a Martha Graham dance event not expecting to see arabesques, entrechats, pirouettes or the motor refinements of the ballet, we will have partially prepared ourselves for the experience by eliminating non-pertinent rules. The next step is to flatter ourselves into believing that we have a boundless store of reflexes practically panting to be conditioned for further useful, self-rewarding purposes and that the horizon of our range of perception can be extended with a bit of exercising. We are now ready to enjoy, for example, Miss Graham's high lateral extension of the leg and to enjoy its beauty as much as we enjoy an arabesque, not by comparison but in its own right. It is a sweeping movement, long, clean and, because it is generated in the great trunk of the body, powerful. It is anatomically correct or the dancer would fall, totter or wrack her body, and it is structurally correct or it could not achieve a pattern in space. Take any other Graham movement and these same physical truths are manifest.

There is more, however, to the Graham dance than its physical power and beauties. Its major function is not to re-create (or even to stylize) overt behavior patterns and characteristics but to give uninhibited physical fulfillment to inner compulsions, to give substance to dreams, imaginings and secret feelings. In following this course, Miss Graham is not being esoteric, she is simply rounding out human biography by reminding us that our secret selves (and let us not pretend to the unsullied heart of a transparent Galahad) are as much a part of us as are the surface beings the world sees. *Letter to the World* provides, perhaps, the best proof of the tremendous worth of this policy. In it, Miss Graham shows us two aspects of Emily Dickinson, one the well bred, gracious and properly inhibited New England lady, and two, the wild, tragic, passionate inner self of the poetess. It is obvious, of course, that the former figure, if her inner self had duplicated her outer self, could not possibly have written such rich and emotionally unfettered poetry as Dickinson wrote and that the biography of the secret self, as danced by Miss Graham, constituted the greater portion of biographical truth.

Mirroring the Heart   Outward revelations of inner feelings are also to be found in the theater of ballet, particularly in the works of Antony Tudor,

Jerome Robbins and Agnes de Mille. Here, however, the conditioned balletomane has an arabesque, a releve onto point or some familiar physical pattern
which he may clutch, figuratively, to his heart and thereby gain courage to
travel with the choreographer into untrodden fields of art. Miss Graham, of
course, does not use the friendly arabesque, and its absence, or the absence of
some other motion to which the beholder has been conditioned, causes most
of the misunderstandings. Martha Graham, her modern dance colleagues and
the choreographers of modern ballet, when they are dealing with the problem
of giving substance to things felt, are actually working with material familiar
to every one. When Miss Graham, as the highly irked wife in *Punch and the
Judy,* jumps onto the back of the figure of Pegasus and soars happily away
from her marital problems she is simply giving expression to what undoubtedly transpires in the heart of any wife so afflicted. Some go home to mother,
some may tipple, some may dream, but it is escape they are after, and Miss
Graham's actions represent not a specific mode of escape but the very escape
urge itself. Modern dance, be it as amusing as the foregoing incident or tragic
or passionate, is just as simple as that. [*New York Herald Tribune*]

May 5, 1947

Cambridge, Mass., May 3.   A new dance work brought to a close the Harvard
University three-day symposium on music criticism when Martha Graham presented *Night Journey,* commissioned by the Elizabeth Sprague Coolidge
Foundation in the Library of Congress, at the Cambridge High and Latin
School this evening. The composition, with a score by William Schuman, is
the latest (and perhaps the last) in a cycle of Graham compositions deriving
their inspiration from the myths and drama of ancient Greece. *Cave of the
Heart* had shown the influence of the *Medea* story and *Errand Into the Maze,*
though not dealing directly with the myth of Theseus and the Minotaur, had
found its roots and form in the legend.
    Night Journey is more specific in its link with Greek drama, for its
major characters, Jocasta, Oedipus and the Seer, are quite definitely the
characters of Sophocles's *Oedipus the King.* It is this close identity with a
specific drama which suggests that *Night Journey* may be the last of the
Greek cycle. Miss Graham is wont to reach for universal elements in drama
and to avoid the use of definite characters. I would guess that the very
closeness of *Night Journey* to *Oedipus the King* augurs a shift to a different
source of dance stimulus.
    The work is not, of course, a movement version of the Greek drama.
The action, though physically placed in Jocasta's room, actually occurs in her
heart at that point "when she recognizes the ultimate terms of her destiny."

As she clutches the cord with which she is to hang herself, her mind rushes back over the incidents which led to her doom and her body reflects in its anguished movements the horror and tragedy which stabbed the spirit of a woman cursed to be, unwittingly, the wife of her own son and the mother of his children.

As Jocasta, Miss Graham at first gives violent expression to the tragedy of her predicament. A leg sweeps high, the figure is suspended for a moment, the limbs part and the body simultaneously sinks and falls to the floor in majestic despair, in full prostration. A tortured run along tortuous paths of escape, trembling hands beating the air in frantic pleas to the deaf gods, all actions of appeal and of evasion fail and Jocasta pauses to lash herself with memories of the past. The Seer enters to convey his prophetic message, trembling as he indicates a dread destiny, and then comes Oedipus to Jocasta, first as her child, then as her hero-husband and finally as the self-blinded cause of her tragedy. Throughout the action of the principals, the chorus, Daughters of the Night, mirror immediate tragedy, augur the remorseless rush of doom.

Miss Graham has created a fine and stirring work in *Night Journey* and her own performance as Jocasta is generally a brilliant one with but passing weak spots which will be cleared up with further performing. Erick Hawkins makes a handsome and tragic Oedipus and dances in less studied manner than normally, permitting his actions to spring easily and logically from the compulsions of the drama. Mark Ryder is splendid as the Seer, for he makes the figure at once inexorable and sympathetic, a link between the decrees of fate and the hopes of man.

Mr. Schuman's score provides a dramatic base for the choreography and serves, admirably to augment, to accent and to echo the course of dance action. The stage designs of Isamu Noguchi also lend form and purpose to the action. I particularly liked the glittering yet distorted bed which focused upon and symbolized the nature of the evil tragedy which beset Jocasta and Oedipus. *Night Journey* has not, on the basis of a single performance, attained its intrinsic excellence. There are weak portions, a blurred transition or two, but they are minor and will undoubtedly be solved by the tightening up process all new works undergo. The audience cheered the premiere lustily and heartily applauded Miss Graham and her company in *Dark Meadow,* which opened the program. [*New York Herald Tribune*]

187

Hightower

March 21, 1947: Surprise Debut

A tradition was broken last evening at the Metropolitan Opera House, when the Original Ballet Russe opened its engagement, for S. Hurok was forced to usher in his season without Alicia Markova in the title role of *Giselle*. As the lights were dimmed Anton Dolin, the premier danseur, stepped forward to announce that Miss Markova was ill and that Rosella Hightower, following a few hours of coaching by Mr. Dolin, would dance the role of Giselle for the first time. There was a concerted groan when Markova's illness was announced, cheers at the mention of Miss Hightower's assignment and the performance was on.

There is no need this morning to present a detailed account of Miss Hightower's interpretation of one of the most difficult roles in the repertory of the traditional ballet. It was, of course, a good performance, for the young American dancer is one of the best artists in the field of ballet, and it was a brave performance, for not only had Miss Hightower learned the choreographic intricacies of the role in a matter of hours but she also was ill, almost too ill to dance. In spite of the difficulties of the occasion, she moved throughout her dance patterns with assurance and, upon occasion, with brilliance. The dramatic implications of the part did not escape her; the initial dances were sweet and gay, the mad scene was accomplished convincingly and without undue melodramatics and the second-act characterization, in which Giselle is a ghost maiden, suggested the eeriness and tragedy implicit in the part.

It is to be hoped that Miss Hightower will be given opportunity to dance Giselle many more times, for her pinch-hit performance was better than those given by some veteran Giselles I have seen. Since she is a superb dancer and a sensitive artist, there is every reason to believe that her Giselle, in time, should become a distinguished portrayal in dance.

Marjorie Tallchief was called upon to dance the Queen of the Wilis, when Miss Hightower relinquished that part for the title role. It was a fine performance of a difficult role, and Miss Tallchief danced it even better than she has in the past. Her leaps, at times, were strained, but her characterization was regal, intense and implacable to just the right degree. In the role of Albrecht, Anton Dolin was again the ardent swain, the sorrowing lover if not always the perfect dancer. However, his support of Miss Hightower was faultless and his solo passages were accomplished in his engaging bravura fashion. The corps de ballet, as the townsfolk of the first act, was lethargic and the ghost maidens of the second act succeeded in obscuring the choreography on several occasions. Mois Zlatin led the orchestra through the Adolphe Adam score in sluggish fashion and evoked a generous quantity of wrong notes from the pit. [*New York Herald Tribune*]

March 22, 1947: Hightower

It was a Rosella Hightower evening again last night at the Metropolitan Opera when the Original Ballet Russe offered the second program of the current engagement. At the opening performances Miss Hightower had stepped into the title role of *Giselle,* with but a few hours of coaching, and had emerged with colors flying. Last evening found her back in two ballets familiar to her and she danced them better than ever. They were William Dollar's beautiful dance piece, *Constantia,* and Edward Caton's *Sebastian,* with book and music by Gian-Carlo Menotti.

In the former work, Miss Hightower danced with a wonderfully cool quality of lyricism, the movements strong yet absolutely unstrained, the patterns of the body in space clearly etched but never suggesting static pose. As a matter of fact, Miss Hightower's interpretation of the part laid stress upon spatial pattern rather than upon floor design or upon the dynamic properties of a body in motion. The arc of a leg rising upward, the spiral of a fouette, the circle of a pirouette and many other explorations of space pathways made of this performance an exciting adventure. The ensemble also, through Mr. Dollar's choreography, pursued these travels in group form. The corps, although frequently far from certain about the best way to travel, danced better than normally, a rather feeble compliment I admit. André Eglevsky was excellent in the leading male role and Yvonne Patterson, who sounded as if she had lead in her toe slippers, contributed some stirring percussive actions to the ballet.

For *Sebastian,* Miss Hightower was called upon to change herself into a courtesan and performed the metamorphosis skillfully. Her character emerged with touches of nervous gaiety, a hint of personal abandon, thoughtlessness and, in the scene of her persecution by witchcraft, sheer terror. It is an interesting role in a spotty ballet and Miss Hightower is constantly finding fresh aspects of her character to reveal. Kenneth Mackenzie assumed the role of Sebastian on this occasion for the first time in New York. His enactment of the Moorish servant, who gives his life for the courtesan, is an appealing one, at once tender and savage. Particularly effective is his neraerotic dance with the courtesan's scarf and his tragic dance of lamentation with the insensible body of his beloved. George Skibine was dashing and courtly as the courtesan's favorite, the Prince, and Yvonne Patterson and Marjorie Tallchief were appropriately malevolent as the evil sisters intent upon murder. [*New York Herald Tribune*]

Dancing in the Supper Club;
Jack Cole and His Dance Group

March 30, 1947

Perhaps it is the sound of mass mastication and sipping or perhaps it is the air
of inattentive gaiety which does it, but whatever the reason, one somehow
does not expect to find superior dancing in a supper club. Usually one does
not find it and must content himself with viewing show girls whose gifts are
of a structural rather than an artistic nature or with a vivid but gaudy production act featuring a "novelty" number. Occasionally, however, night-club
shows present excellent exhibition ballroom dancers, specialty dancers with
real skill and temporary refugees from the concert or theater worlds. On the
other hand, rarely does one discover in a night club a dancer whose work is
specifically designed for such presentation but which is in its own right artistically valid and far more distinguished than many an aristocratically nurtured
ballet offering. In the dancing and the dances of Jack Cole these rare gifts
are made manifest.

Mr. Cole and his company of seven highly trained dancers are currently
playing at the Latin Quarter and I advise any one who professes an interest in
superior dancing to go and see them. Their offerings are three in number: a
dance of jitterbug derivation, a suite of East Indian dances employing adapted
Hindu dance technique and a finale of Latin American actions. Before we
turn up our noses at such material, let us remind ourselves that jitterbugging is
probably a more accurate example of American folk dance than is the hoe-
down and that we bow low before Spanish jitterbugging when we are given it
under the title of "cuadro flamenco." It is the treatment accorded such
material which transforms it into exciting dance art. In his first dance, Mr.
Cole captures and distills the energetic spirit of the jitterbug, codifies and
polishes the movements, gives discipline and form to otherwise rambunctious,
instinctive actions. This very same process is employed to create a *Scheherezade* or a *Rodeo*.

Jitterbug Incantation　　Three young men, dressed in brown suits and pork-pie
hats join the dapperly clad Mr. Cole for the jitterbug dance, a dance which
has both the power and the ritualized quality of an incantational rite. It is,
of course, twentieth century and American, but the intensity of the dancers,
the heavily accented rhythms, the repeated movement figures, the ecstatic
leaps followed by plummetings to the floor seem to convey the same magical
purpose apparent in many of the tribal dances of Africa.

The East Indian dances, performed by Jack Cole with Florence Lessing
and a group of four boys and two girls, are completely different from the

190

jitterbug work. They are filled with action and the tempo is fast, but the accent is placed upon detailed movements, upon Hindu hand gestures, the slight shift of the neck, the meaningful fluttering of eye muscles. The effect is one of sophisticated romance, of amused comment presented in terms of elegant action. The Latin American section is again different. Where the jitterbug dance is intense, magic-making and the Indian suite formal and glittering with precise detail, the Latin dances are like games in which the participants are uninhibited searchers of fun, reveling in the luxury of their own easily moved muscles.

Mr. Cole and his handsome group perform these fascinating dances brilliantly. They are vivid and lively enough to enchant even the most casual observer and their skill should delight the dance follower. Certainly Jack Cole need bow to no one in matters of technical skill or dance authority.

There were other dance happenings at this Latin Quarter program, including a contortionist who writhed to music a young man who bounded pleasantly, a toe dancer who passed a good deal of time in a back-bend (but not as engagingly as Harriet Hoctor used to do it) and a gentleman who danced while fiddling. If this last act seems novel, permit me to say that back in 1793 in New York a gentleman named Alexander Placide was billed as one who would "dance a hornpipe on a tight-rope, play the violin and display the American flag in various attitudes." The current performer neglected his tightrope and his flag. [*New York Herald Tribune*]

American Theatre Wing Offers
Ex-G.I.s Retraining in Dance

June 22, 1947

When American dancers discarded their tights and tap shoes for the uniform of their country's armed forces, they faced not only the sorrows and fears of departure toward an unknown fate but the dread of return to a profession they knew only too well. Theatrical contacts would become tenuous, the "name" might be forgotten but more important, muscles would forget their years of dance discipline, technical facility would withdraw, the entire instrument of dance, the body, would be badly out of tune. Those American men and women of the dance profession who served with the military are back and face to face with the difficulties they dreaded, but through the G.I. Bill of Rights, which has accredited some of the dance schools of the nation, these dancing veterans have been able, without expense, to restore their prowesses and to return to their profession.

The organization most concerned with and most active in the program for retraining of dance veterans is the American Theatre Wing, the organization which brought so much theater and entertainment and fun to the wartime soldiers through the stagedoor canteens and other services. The dance division of the wing's professional training program for veterans provides the returning dancer with courses in modern dance, ballet, tap and such related courses as body building for actors, dance fundamentals for actors and singers, acting, history of theater, technical courses (stage management, lighting, etc.), vocal study, musical theory, voice and diction and make-up. The faculty includes many of the leading figures in the world of dance and the training program is designed to equip the ex-G.I. dancer for a renewed career in any branch of dance activity he desires. It is a professional program for professionals conducted by professionals accredited by the New York State Board of Education and the Veterans' Administration.

Broad Program of Study   The veteran who avails himself of Wing courses has a wide selection of teachers and studios from which to choose his trainer or trainers. He may study modern dance with Martha Graham, Hanya Holm, Charles Weidman or José Limón; ballet with Roland Guérard, George Chaffee, Helene Platova, or at the Fokine or Ballet Arts Studios; tap with Peter Birch or Ernest Carlos, and dance fundamentals for actors with Kathleen O'Brien. It was not possible for me to visit all the Wing's dance classes, but the several I saw clearly suggested that the former G.I.'s were receiving exactly the kind of training the Wing promised, training aimed "to aid veterans returning to the entertainment industry by providing educational and retraining benefits on a professional level" and "to provide training in related fields in order to develop the individual's capacities and his employment opportunities."

Martha Graham felt that the veteran, following his long period of "uniform" service, warranted "consideration as an individual," and that every G.I. returning to the competitive field of theater "deserves an opportunity not to be disillusioned." Alwin Nikolais, assistant to the distinguished dancer, Hanya Holm, gave his all-veterans class an impressive two-hour instruction period in limbering and stretching, technique and pure dance with each member receiving individual attention. The class by Charles Weidman which I attended found the Wing veterans sharing the studio with non-G.I. students, all of them participating in Mr. Weidman's fluid, lively and dramatically eloquent version of dance under this modern dance leader's careful guidance.

Tatiana Piankova's lesson at the Fokine Studio appeared to me to be particularly well suited to the needs of veterans, for the teacher not only insisted upon a rigidly correct execution of movement, but also took pains to explain the relation of each movement to anatomical structure and to dramatic or theatrical effect. Teaching the ballet system of Vaganova, leading ballet instructor in the Soviet Union, Miss Piankova instilled the element of theater into an uncompromising, difficult technique.

Training for Versatility   Kathleen O'Brien's dance fundamentals for actors and singers proved to be an interesting class and of obvious benefit to any one who walks onto a stage, for Miss O'Brien stressed the teaching of body facility and agility, co-ordination, balance, presence, purposeful movement and other aspects of articulation through motion. As a matter of fact, a portion of the Wing's dance students are interested in dance as it pertains to theatrical skills in general and not to the field of dance concert. I would guess that all of the 167 students who have enrolled in the Wing's dance division during this, the first year of its existence, are aware of the growing importance of dance in all forms of theater and that they are eager to prepare themselves for dance theater, for modern dance, ballet or tap assignments in musical shows and for the increasing number of roles in the drama which place accent upon characterization through movement. The fact that the students who take a combination of modern dance, ballet and tap training outnumber those who restrict themselves to one technique indicates that these veterans are preparing themselves for any dance job which comes their way and for the versatility which our theater, more and more, is requiring of its performers. The American Theatre Wing, then, is not only restorative but creative, building former G.I.'s into good dancers, perhaps better dancers than they were before they donned the uniforms of the nation. [*New York Herald Tribune*]

Reginald and Gladys Laubin, the Indian's Dancing Envoys

August 3, 1947

The figure shoots upward, shifting the patterns of his feet in air, descending with lightness to the floor where he traces new intricacies of design. This is not ballet. Another figure sits quietly, narrating a tale with articulate fingers, forming word images with knuckle, palm and fist rather than with the mouth. This is not the gesture dance of India. At another time, a dancer may rush with rhythmic abandon about his area of space, permitting his body to explore new paths of movement humor, or he may, through movements and the manipulation of accompanying symbols, reveal character, passion or search, disclose the inner man. These two aspects of his dance represent neither jitterbugging nor the contemporary expressional dance. Although these brief views of dance action appear to constitute much of the dancing we find in America, some of it imported and some of it but recently evolved, they actually constitute traditional and indigenous American dance, the dance of the American Indian.

The almost forgotten (or never appreciated) riches and wonders of American Indian dance are finding renascence in the dedication, the labor and the skills of two white Americans, Reginald and Gladys Laubin, whose most recent performances in the East occurred two weeks ago at the Jacob's Pillow Dance Festival. No one who attended their program could have failed to generate within himself new respect for America's first citizens and those who had previously been infected with misinformation, with distorted legend of the Indian's dirtiness, his savagery, his ignorance, his primitive culture, must have experienced both guiltiness and wonder in the presence of a dance art characterized by dignity of bearing, classic grandeur, complex vocabulary, spiritual power and extensive thematic scope.

Mirror of a Race   Many will agree that an ethnologic dance mirrors, with unusual accuracy, the character and the characteristics, the cultural level of the nation which gave it being. Since most forms of ethnologic dance or folk dance are derived from the natural actions, the ideas and the ideals of a people rather than contrived by an individual dance genius, one may be certain that the dance of the American Indian reveals neither the genius of an individual Indian nor the decadence of another individual but reveals with honesty the average Indian. The average Indian, thereby, emerges with flying colors. Because Mr. and Mrs. Laubin believe in the truthfulness of dance and because it is their chosen mission to aid the non-Indian American to understand and appreciate the nation's first inhabitants, they are bringing to school, university, museum and concert audiences not only the beaded costumes, the feathers and the ceremonial paint of the Indians but also the Indian's character, imagination, wisdom, dreams and hopes, given substance in dance.

Although Reginald and Gladys Laubin are of the white race, they have lived with Indians long enough to absorb not only the essence of Indian dance but the Indian viewpoint; thus they are in the fortunate position of being objective about the very culture of which they are now a part. As members of the Sioux nation, as adopted son and daughter of the late Chief One Bull, they have specialized, for the present, in the dances of the Plains Indians, learning those dances which are frequently performed and saving from oblivion those which had been forgotten by all but the oldest men. Such is the respect in which they are held that many young Indians, some of them veterans of the recent war and others of them college graduates, are commencing to show interest in the great dance heritage of which they are the heirs. The

Laubins, therefore, are not only serving the Indians by performing their dances for general audiences but also by inspiring the Indians to continue to cherish a dance art which has few if any peers in the world.

Dance Treasures   It is not possible to itemize here the many kinds of American Indian dances which the Laubins present. A hoop dance, distinguished by intricate patterns of action and cumulative dynamic intensity, is as virtuosic as anything I have seen in ballet. A chief's dance, simply conceived, achieves a wonderful portrait in dance through the shuffling but proudful walk, the toss of the head, the gruff facial actions, the assured carriage of the torso. Nature is not only emulated but accorded humorous comment in a prairie chicken dance and deity is invoked with sacerdotal majesty in the openings of a social dance as well as in a more ritualistic buffalo dance. There are dance dramas augmented with song, poetry and sign talk, ceremonials in which a feather blown from a pipe represents both a prayer and the heaven's clouds towards which it is directed. These and other aspects of American Indian dance demonstrate that his range of style is from the basic or functional through the classic to the surrealistic, that his themes are often more mature (both intellectually and spiritually) than those of his white dance-colleagues and that his technique, studded with air turns, complex foot patterns, sign talk, torso actions and innumerable other manifestations of a skilled body, would cause many a Broadway dance artist to pale with self-doubt. Surely this dance of the American Indian is worthy of cherishing by all Americans, for it is obviously not a neolithic hangover, but a great dance of contemporary force and significance as Reginald and Gladys Laubin are reminding us. [*New York Herald Tribune*]

Ballet Theatre—1947

November 27, 1947: Balanchine Triumph

The aristocrat of contemporary ballet, George Balanchine, has created another glittering and handsome work in *Theme and Variations*. Built upon Theme and Variations from Tchaikovsky's *Suite No. 3 for Orchestra* and staged with scenery and costumes by Woodman Thompson, this ballet, presented last evening at the City Center by Ballet Theatre, provides further proof of Mr. Balanchine's skill in deriving new sparkle, fresh nuance from the most traditional of Occidental dance vocabularies.

The new work is highly formal both in choreographic structure and in style, but the pas de deux, the solos, a pas de quatre and other dance divisions are so imaginatively devised that the ballet succeeds in being completely modern. True, the majority of its movements are familiar, but in this instance they are accorded new accent, new sequence and, inevitably and rightly, new dynamic values. There are, of course, twists which are pure Balanchine, such as the interlacings of groups or off-aplomb poses, which are exciting because of their very unbalance, but the whole effect is one of traditional balletic elegance reborn in the mid-twentieth century and not simply resurrected for it.

Theme and Variations, in addition to its formal beauties, possesses another important element, virtuosity. It is, then, also a show piece, and this element will delight those many persons who like tricks or feats of skill in their ballet. For the premier danseur it offers one of the most exciting solo variations in ballet; it provides the ballerina with opportunity to display her speed, her smoothness and her assured agility, and it encourages them to dance together in a manner designed to reveal the ballerina's line and the cavalier's gallant concern for both her loveliness and her balance. It does not neglect the lesser dancers, for they too are presented with handsome and intricate patterns to pursue.

The initial performance of *Theme and Variations* was marred, understandably, by nervousness on the parts of all concerned. This was apparent not only in technical slips but also in manner. The style of the ballet was, I think, intended to be graciously formal, not cooly formal. Such matters will undoubtedly be corrected by further performing of the work. Barring this air of tension, Alicia Alonso danced her principal role commendably. Its fleetness of action, the long, sweeping lines of its patterns were in complete harmony with this dancer's basic gifts. Igor Youskevitch has in this work one of his best assignments and already he is dancing it, particularly the solo, with brilliance. The ensemble as a whole is still a trifle unsure of itself but valiant and sometimes successful in its attempts to do justice to Mr. Balanchine's superb patterns. By the end of the current season or by next spring, *Theme and Variations* should be a high point in Ballet Theatre's repertory. [*New York Herald Tribune*]

December 21, 1947: Young Soloists of the Ballet;
Notes on Achievement, Promise

Not many years ago, some of us were watching with keen interest the dancing of several non-stellar Ballet Theatre performers. What were the qualities which made us look twice, which urged us to glance away from the principals long enough to cast appraising and appreciative eyes upon supporting artists?

It was not virtuosity which attracted us, since virtuosity was normally the province of the stars, but projection of personality, verve, perhaps an innate awareness of line, dramatic power, wit, sparkle and those almost intangible gifts which distinguish dancing from mere movement execution were either apparent or implied. Two of these youngsters, Nora Kaye and Alicia Alonso, became Ballet Theatre's superb ballerinas; another, John Kriza, became a first dancer of enormous value to the company and yet another, Jerome Robbins became not only a gifted principal dancer but one of America's most successful and important choreographers. The list could be continued, but let us, instead, turn to Ballet Theatre's present ensemble.

Among Ballet Theatre's young soloists, there are several who are worthy of notice not merely because they are now good soloists but because greater potentials are implied. Perhaps Diana Adams is too tall to become a ballerina in traditional roles, but with the increased range of ballet material there is every reason to assume that principal parts suited to her long, lean lines, her commanding presence will be created. She already has such a role in the trivial *Helen of Troy*, she is compelling as Medusa in *Undertow* and she is commencing to realize the dramatic qualities of the Queen of the Wilis in *Giselle*. Certainly, her sweeping grace, her accuracy in achieving desired body-line patterns, the interesting manner in which she controls the flow of energy are qualities which deserve outlet in many more roles than she possesses at the present.

Hayden and Fallis There is every reason to suppose that Melissa Hayden will one day be a ballerina. She is already becoming sure enough of her technique to clothe it with the colors of dance, to touch her natural winsomeness with dignity and to search for the most effective accents and phrasings in her roles. Her dramatic range is still small, since she is inclined to project her own qualities rather than the attributes of the character she is enacting, but this, too, should expand with further experience and exploration. Barbara Fallis is another gifted dancer. Except that her elevation is less, she reminds me of Karen Conrad, for she is strong, apparently tireless and enormously alive in all of her actions. Her bouncing strength occasionally gets out of hand and she frequently performs as if she were isolated instead of being a part of a greater dance fabric, but once she controls and channels her energies, she should become an exciting dancer.

Ruth Ann Koesun's progress has been so rapid that her emergence as a principal dancer, provided her progress continues, will be realized in two or three years. She possesses a highly individual quality of movement, shy but not weak, delicate but assured; further, she is aware of the different styles demanded by different ballets and she is, basically, capable of subordinating her own personality in order to bring forth that of the character concerned.

In time she could be, I think, a highly affecting Giselle. Norma Vance, Anna Cheselka, Paula Lloyd and Cynthia Riseley are dancers to watch, although their directions are not yet as clearly defined as are those of the others I have mentioned.

Among the young male soloists, Zachary Solov and Eric Braun offer the greatest promise. Mr. Solov is still too self-conscious about his dancing and the effect he is making upon an audience, but his talent is a genuine one and broad enough to encompass classic, dramatic and humorous roles, although there is still some question about his instinct for the elegance necessary to purely classic dance. Mr. Braun is a strong, clean dancer with flashes of spirit and as yet unrealized attributes of style. Fernando Alonso and Fernand Nault, although they improve with each successive season, are still mainly dependable, likable performers. The company as a whole, speaking of the boys as well as the girls, is a good one, but there are a few of both sexes who appear to me to be hopelessly inadequate to Ballet Theatre's high standards.

Muriel Bentley   In a special category of highly gifted Ballet Theatre soloists, one must place Muriel Bentley. A charter member of Ballet Theatre, she has developed not into a ballerina but into a unique artist of great value to the company and to the dance world as a whole. Miss Bentley is not a classic dancer, nor is she a virtuosic dancer in the accepted sense of the term, yet she cannot be viewed simply as a minor soloist. To her all too few roles she brings authority, accuracy, dramatic projection and a wit which, although often blatant, is absolutely irresistible. The wit, made manifest both in facial movements and body actions, is contemporary American in accent, yet Miss Bentley makes it pertinent to any characterization. Her performance as A Lady No Better Than She Should Be in *Tally-Ho* is a masterpiece of dance, and her contributions to other ballets, some of them serious in nature, are memorable. If she is not a star in the ballet tradition, Miss Bentley is certainly a star in her own tradition, and Ballet Theatre would do well to employ her gifts at every conceivable opportunity. [*New York Herald Tribune*]

1948

CCSD, BT, NYCB

Palestine dances manifest Arab–Jewish cultural bonds • Plans announced for the Connecticut College School of the Dance • After 15 years, Ballet Russe de Monte Carlo's glitter gone • Weidman and Harald Kreutzberg, two enchanting men, give concerts • Ballet Theatre premieres de Mille's Fall River Legend • Helen Tamiris and Valerie Bettis work together in Inside U.S.A. • Florence Rogge's creations still on view at Radio City • The critic criticized • TV dance — a new medium • The Paris Opera Ballet makes a controversial debut • The New York City Ballet's first season

Arab–Jewish Cultural Bonds Are Found in New Palestine Dances

February 1, 1948

In a Moslem house of worship in an Arab land, I had seen a dance of religious ecstasy. The dancer spun in place, one arm directed toward the earth, the other raised toward heaven and his head nestled against the reaching arm. In a modern theater in New York, I saw a concert dancer of Jewish faith spin in place, one arm directed toward the earth, the other raised toward heaven and her head nestled against the reaching arm. This was not a fluke, not a coincidence but a clue to unity, perhaps a very fragile unity but one given substance in the swiftly passing action of dance. The Moslem dancer was a dervish worshipping his God in ancient Cairo. The concert dancer was Paula Padani, a young Palestinian, dancing a piece inspired by her ancient heritage, *The King Saul*.

The power of ethnologic dance, of dance which springs from a people, from land and from heritage, is a power not to be ignored. It probably cannot, in itself, solve international and intranational problems, but it can, I think, contribute to the clarification of such problems. It will reveal differences, but it will also point the way to common ground. The new Jewish dance of a torn and changing Palestine provides, because of its immediacy, a fairly clear picture of the processes of ethnologic dance. Past links between the peoples of India and those of Indonesia are recorded in many enduring similarities in their dances; the half-Balkan, half-Oriental aspects of Cypriot dance tell of shifting cultural and political forces on that island and in the dance of Spain one finds the heritages of the Celt, the Arab and, perhaps, the ancient Egyptian. But all this is history, fascinating history. In Palestine a new ethnologic dance is being formed, almost hot-housed into quick flowering.

Arab-Jewish Dance Links   A few months ago this column presented a brief discussion of Palestinian dance as reported by Hassia Levy, a dancer from that land. Since that time I have seen a performance by Miss Padani at the Y. M. and Y. W. H. A. and have talked with Gert Kaufmann, leader of the folk dance movement in Palestine, about her activities in her country. Each has supplemented Miss Levy's report and the ethnologic aspects of Palestinian dance become clearer, the links between Jewish dance and Arab dance more apparent. For example, the dervish turns in Miss Padani's *The King Saul* and the like turns of the modern Moslem dervish derive, I am sure, from a common source, from ancient semitic ecstatic rituals. In other dances the gentle placements of the feet, the easy freedom of the hips, an air of delicate sensuousness proclaimed an Oriental heritage, a link with those dances of the Lebanese Christians, the Egyptian Moslems and other Arab peoples which I have seen.

Other heritages, other links were also apparent in Miss Padani's dances. The dartings, the nervous tremblings, the desperate racings in the wonderful opening passages of *The Fleeing* told of a European political heritage of terror and oppression while the energetic bounce, the stampings, the skips of *Horra* indicated the absorbing of a Western, a mainly Balkan folk dance heritage. As a young artist of a changing Palestine, it is apparent that Miss Padani must find her material in the many ethnologic dance sources of her widely scattered people. These sources are not only divided into East and West but also subdivided into national heritages and a heritage born of the contour, climate and quality of the land of Palestine itself.

In the folk field this source diversity is also manifest. Mrs. Kaufmann, who has guided the course of folk dance in Palestine, and even created folk dance, makes it perfectly clear that Arab as well as Western influences are embodied in the new folk expression of Palestine. Traditionally there are, she believes, two main sources of Jewish dance, the Yemenite, which is Oriental, and the Chassidic, which is eastern European, but in the last four or five years she has augmented this material through the inclusion of all kinds of folk dances performed through the centuries by European Jews, the revival or

200

creation of Jewish dances using Arab melodies and Arab dance patterns common to the joint Arab-Jewish Oriental heritage and the evolution of new dances mirroring sentiments and conditions in Palestine today.

Holy Land Dance   As head of the Central Cultural Committee of the Workers' Federation of Palestine, Mrs. Kaufmann has trained folk dance leaders for work in every Jewish settlement in Palestine and she has also headed dance festivals in which the inhabitants of Palestine, Moslems, Jews and Christians alike, have participated. Her first festival was held in 1929, the most recent (reported in my previous article on Palestinian dance) was held in June, 1947, on the Hills of Ephraim for thirty thousand spectators. She has, as I have indicated, sought to bring to Palestine all of the many kinds of Jewish dance expression, but she has not ignored, rather has she fostered, dance forms common to Arabs and Moslems alike, common to the Middle East. A new Palestinian dance, *Debka Rafiach,* danced by men who had been in a concentration camp, is obviously strictly Jewish in source, but the Egyptian *Raks Debbkah,* also a dance for men, suggests a link in terminology, in dance custom. Mrs. Kaufmann, her assistants and other dance leaders who are teaching, re-activating dances common to Jew and Arab, who are striving for communal dance activities are contributing, perhaps only in a small way, to the unity of the Holy Land. Such dances should help to introduce Occidental Jewish newcomers to an Oriental culture in which they are to live and they should help to reassure the Arab peoples that there exist at least a few folk bonds between them and the recent arrivals. Solution of Arab–Jewish problems is not to be found in a dervish spin or in a debka, but the hope of friendship may pulse within such common dance actions. [*New York Herald Tribune*]

Summer Dance Center Planned for New London; Teaching, Festival Program at Jacob's Pillow

February 15, 1948

Dancers are optimists. They believe that some day the snow will cease falling, the sun will give forth with increased warmth and audiences will travel into the snowless country in search of summer dance events. In preparation for this season, plans are already being made for dance festivals, educational programs and intensive courses for dance students. This summer a new dance program will be introduced at Connecticut College, New London, Conn., under the joint sponsorship of Connecticut College and New York University. The six weeks' session in modern dance, to commence July 13, will follow plans laid down by Martha Hill of the New York institution and Mary J. Shelly, the two educators who directed the Bennington School of the Dance from 1934 to 1942. Miss Hill and John F. Moore, director of the summer session of Connecticut College, will act as co-chairmen of an administrative board representing the two colleges.

In addition to Miss Hill, the dance faculty of the New York University–Connecticut College School of the Dance will include Martha Graham, Doris Humphrey, José Limón, William Bales, Jane Dudley, Sophie Maslow and Erick Hawkins. Courses in music for dance will be offered by Norman Lloyd, Ruth Lloyd, Louis Horst and Betty Horner Walburg. A course in theater design will be given by Arch Lauterer. Delia Hussey and Shirley Wimmer will be in charge of courses in dance for elementary and secondary schools and Ruth Bloomer will head a course in dance and education. Classes in the use of poetry and speech in the lyric theater and in dance will be given by Ben Belitt and Jo Van Fleet. The school, currently preparing for a maximum enrollment of two hundred, will be open to men and women, students and teachers of dance, professional dancers, musicians and music students, theater designers and theater design students. The minimum educational requirements for admission is completion of secondary school education.

In conjunction with its educational program, the new summer dance school will feature three dance programs each week for the six weeks' season. Performances, which are to take place in Connecticut College's Palmer Auditorium, will be given by Miss Graham and her full company. Mr. Limón and his group with Miss Humphrey as artistic director and the Dudley–Maslow–Bales Trio supported by a new group of dancers. If tentative plans materialize, the festival series will culminate in a final program of new works by the resident artists and their groups. This dance wing's activities, which constitute a part of Connecticut College's regular summer session, will also include a dance seminar series featuring discussions on dance criticism, dance for motion pictures, television and dance and other pertinent topics. The aim of the new school is to provide a center for modern American dance where student and teacher, artist and audience may find "the working contacts vital to an art which is both a force in the contemporary theater and a medium of education."

In Massachusetts, near Lee, Jacob's Pillow will again function under the direction of its founder, Ted Shawn, who relinquished his management last summer for his record-breaking performing-teaching-lecturing tour of Australia. Mr. Shawn is not yet ready to announce his faculty or his festival artists, but he reports that his dance university will have departments devoted to ballet, modern dance, ethnologic dance, folk dance and two special courses, one for teachers and one called dance synthesis designed to provide students familiar with a single technique with an intensive survey of the major dance idioms. The regular session will run for eight weeks during July and August, preceded by the two weeks' course in dance synthesis and followed by the teachers' course also of two weeks duration.

As in other years, Jacob's Pillow will also present a festival of dance performances, three each week, to be held in the Jacob's Pillow Dance Theater. It is Mr. Shawn's plan to have ballet, modern dance and ethnologic dance represented on each program and to integrate the festival series with the educational program, since Mr. Shawn regards the performances not as isolated theatrical events but as opportunities for the Jacob's Pillow students to become familiar with the finished products of dance creation as well as with the techniques, the tools of dance used in the classroom. [*New York Herald Tribune*]

Ballet Russe de Monte Carlo's 15-Year Fame Found Badly Shrunken, Glitter Nearly Gone

February 21, 1948

The Ballet Russe de Monte Carlo has an enviable name. That name connotes fifteen years of constant performing in America; productions which were once brought to glittering life through the services of Danilova, Baronova, Toumanova, Riabouchinska, Massine, Lichine, Shabelevsky and other stars; seasons built upon still unhackneyed works and new works of major proportions. And just where is the Ballet Russe de Monte Carlo now? Where does it stand? Its glitter is nearly gone, its older productions are often shabby, new works are small in scale and its magical qualities rest mainly in its distinguished name and in the person of its prima ballerina, Alexandra Danilova.

It is difficult to say just what has caused the decline in the fortunes of the Ballet Russe de Monte Carlo. Lack of sufficient capital or of dependable subsidies, unwise economies perhaps, contentment with already won laurels, lack of a firm artistic policy or course of direction may be the factors involved. Certainly, the company finds its focus in Miss Danilova; there are no other female stars, no other prepared and promoted ballerinas, although Ruthanna Boris is certainly of ballerina caliber. Frederic Franklin and Leon Danlelian carry the male wing, for the other men, without exception, are not principal dancer material, at least, at the present time. Compare this tiny, albeit distinguished, list of stars with that of the Monte Carlo ten or fifteen years ago.

As for artistic policy or purposeful programming, why is a bill such as *Swan Lake, The Nutcracker* and *Scheherezade* and slight variations thereof offered several times during a season? What kind of an artistic direction is it which permits more than a normal quota of under-rehearsed presentations? The direction is not the one which originally led the Ballet Russe and the company has suffered schisms, but has it not had time to heal its wounds?

One could continue to pose rhetorical queries relative to the lacks in the Ballet Russe de Monte Carlo, but that would be unfair, it would suggest that the Ballet Russe de Monte Carlo is slowly sinking toward an inevitable doom. But doom is not inevitable for the company. The repertory, in spite of several weary and overplayed items, boasts some splendid works, among them some superb ballets by George Balanchine, *Frankie and Johnny, Rodeo* and Miss Boris's recent *Cirque de Deux*. Even the old works, ballet's traditional pieces and masterpieces, would be welcome if they were treated like perennial belles and not like old and important dowagers.

The company itself is by no means hopeless, for many of its members are fine young dancers. It is too small and it needs discipline, but it is basically lively and personable. In Miss Danilova, the Monte Carlo possesses a unique star, unique in her dance gifts and in her ability to evoke adoration from a large portion of the dance public. Miss Danilova, however, needs some ballerina colleagues if the company is to be as strong as it used to be. Perhaps an already established ballerina (or two) could be brought into the company or perhaps the direction would do well to consider the ballerina potentialities of Miss Boris, Mary Ellen Moylan and, at a later date, Patricia Wilde.

Finally, a definite program of production would seem to be in order. We must be grateful for the opportunity accorded Miss Boris to stage her delightful *Cirque de Deux* and all of us look forward to the forthcoming premiere of Ruth Page's *Billy Sunday*, a frankly experimental piece. In recent seasons, the Ballet Russe de Monte Carlo has appeared to pop novelties into the repertory. Some were good and some bad, which is customary, but most of them appeared to be, with the possible exception of the restaging of *Raymonda*, inexpensive-looking, modest, bargain items. I like inexpensive, modest ballets with good choreography and good dancing, but I also expect of ballet something in the field of spectacle, a field in which ballet is unmatched. One also expects a major and modern ballet organization to lend its facilities for the uncovering of new choreographic talent, for the constant exploration of new dance realms.

Perhaps these comments upon the disappointing aspects of an important, and perhaps beloved, organization appear to be unkind or, worse, unnecessary. Because the Ballet Russe de Monte Carlo may be considered as being both important and beloved, a review of the state of the company seems particularly pertinent. All one need do is to recall the initial years of the company's

American phase to know that it is no longer the same company, either in personnel or in caliber. If memory is not to be trusted, a glance at yellowed clippings will confirm the fact that change has occurred. No one likes to see an old friend come upon unhappy days and the Ballet Russe is certainly an old friend to all who love dance. True, it still has its happy moments, magnificent moments of superlative dancing, but those moments are less frequent than they should be. It is to be hoped that the Monte Carlo's leaders will not only look back to the old days for a reminder of what was but also look ahead to a future which must be better than the present. [*New York Herald Tribune*]

Two Enchanting Men—Weidman and Kreutzberg

April 19, 1948: Return of a Favorite

It is a distinct pleasure to have Charles Weidman back on Broadway again. Nine years is much too long a time for Broadway to get along without his inspired clowning, his showmanship, his dance artistry, qualities which have made him one of America's dance leaders. These attributes were very much in evidence last evening when Mr. Weidman and his company opened their engagement at the Mansfield Theater, for the program selected for the occasion was thematically and stylistically varied and the dancing was of the first order throughout.

The evening's major offering, a New York premiere, was *Fables for Our Time,* based upon four stories by James Thurber and produced through the facilities afforded by a Guggenheim fellowship which the dancer was awarded last year. It is a wonderful work, imaginative, witty and as captivating as the Thurber tales themselves. Mr. Weidman has employed a narrator to set the scene and to present the concluding moral in each instance, but he has also worked the narrator into his choreographic plan with such skill that one accepts the speaker as a participant rather than as an outsider. The choreography itself is composed of non-representational dance, theatrical pantomime of a high order and Mr. Weidman's noted brand of kinetic pantomime, of impulsive action which has muscular meaning if not literal sense.

In *The Unicorn in the Garden,* Mr. Weidman gave us an utterly winning characterization of a man who saw a unicorn, fed him lilies, was unimpressed with his wife's disbelief and was happy to see her, rather than himself, carted off to an asylum for telling her tale to a policeman and a psychiatrist. *The Shrike and the Chipmunks,* the second of the *Fables,* was an inspired bit for the star and for Betty Osgood as the female, for here he played an artistic chipmunk who made patterns with nuts while his scurrying, scolding wife stored them away.

The most impressive of the *Fables* was *The Owl Who Was God*. In the title role, Mr. Weidman provided us with a superb characterization which was at once human and owl-like. The blinking of the eyes, the ruffling of the feathers, the puffings and whistlings, the staggered walk, all bespoke the bird, while the pomposity, the blind leadership, the willingness to be followed pointed up the human moral. *The Courtship of Al and Arthur*, the most recently created section of the suite, was the least effective. It had many moments of frolic, of telling movement and of dramatic point, but it was not as fully integrated as the others. However, as a whole, *Fables of Our Time* is a splendid work, its most valuable attribute being its magical fusing of the real and the unreal, bald statement of fact with sheer fantasy, sermon with fun. The star was, as I have suggested, in top form for all of his characterizations and excellent support was provided by Jack Ferris as the pleasantly sardonic narrator, Betty Osgood, Saida Gerrard and other members of the company.

The program also offered a lively performance of *And Daddy Was a Fireman,* a light-hearted account of the dancer's own family in the period of the nineties. Mr. Weidman was Daddy, the intrepid fire-fighter, Peter Hamilton was the darting, flying figure, of Fire; Nadine Gae was the sweet and demure heroine and Betty Osgood was nothing short of perfect (as she is in everything) as a Victim of the Fire. *Lynchtown*, Mr. Weidman's powerful re-creation and revelation of the forces of evil, of self-debasement which accompany the crime of lynching brought Beatrice Seckler back to the fold of the company in a performance of great brilliance, of terrifying power as the chief figure of a blood thirsty mob. Peter Hamilton danced his own *Jesse James* with boisterous humor and virtuosic dash to the accompaniment of Robert Herget's fine, lusty-voiced narration and the evening closed with Mr. Weidman's moving and eloquent study of Abraham Lincoln, *A House Divided*. [*New York Herald Tribune*]

November 1, 1948: Enchanting

An enchanting evening of dance was accorded the audience at the Ziegfeld Theater last evening when Harald Kreutzberg appeared in his first recital of the season. Enchant, I think, is exactly what the Austrian dancer does to those who watch him, for as a whole, his dances are slight, his use of traditional virtuosity is negligible and his choreographic and performing styles change but little, if at all, with the passing years. But these matters are of no concern to any one simply because Mr. Kreutzberg obviously loves to dance and communicates that love and the joys and excitements of movement to the beholder.

The program contained seven new dances. They were all similar in structure and in style to older dances in the Kreutzberg repertory but they were in no sense repetitious, for they varied in accent, in gesture and in the arrangements of movement material. *In ¾ Time,* a little piece without story or specific characterization, opened the program on a pure dance note. *The End of Don Juan,* melodramatic and emotionally exaggerated, would have been foolish if any one but Mr. Kreutzberg had danced it but as performed by him it seemed to have dramatic honesty and considerable theatrical power. In the similar vein of tense dramatic dance was *Job Expostulateth with God* and here the dancer's familiar fusing of straight dance and pantomime, of large-scale body action and dramatic patterns achieved through sudden and sharp hand gestures resulted in a stirring portrayal of a majestic figure.

Notturno, with its Latin flavor but without use of traditional Latin dance technique, was perhaps the freshest, choreographically, of all of the new works. It did not rely upon characterization and it made but passing use of gesture but employed full-body movements, distinguished by remarkable dynamic control, to project its emotional values.

Amusing, good-hearted and hilarious material marked the others of the new dances. *Trois Morceaux Characteristiques,* composed of *Printemps, L'Amour* and *Souvenir,* were charming surrealistic cartoons and *Jolly Trifles,* made up of "Lunch Time," "Exercises at Midnight" and "Dashing Spaniard," had the audience calling for encores. In the latter suite, the first dance concerned a scarecrow which fed the crows, the second dealt with a highly active ghost and the third with the most ineffectual of caballeros ever to appear on a stage. They were all delicious characters but the athletic ghost with his billowing robes and telescopic neck was irresistible. Variations on *O du Lieber Augustin* was the least successful of the new pieces, pleasant but undistinguished.

Li-tai-po, Song of the Stars, From an Old Calendar, Master of Ceremonies and *Selige Walzer,* all familiar to the Kreutzberg public, filled out the program. The handsome and imaginative costumes, the superb masks and the excellent lighting all contributed to a smooth and highly professional evening and Friedrich Wilckens, the dancer's composer-pianist, provided his always study and sensitive accompaniments to a program which I, for one, would be happy to see again. [*New York Herald Tribune*]

207

Fall River Legend

April 23, 1948

Murder, willfully committed but with ample provocation, was the theme of a new ballet presented last evening at the Metropolitan Opera House by Ballet Theatre. Agnes de Mille, the choreographer, has taken her situation and some of her characters, if not her facts, from the unsolved Lizzie Borden case of 1892 and has created a danced melodrama which, according to a program note, "explores the passions that lead to a violent resolution of the oppressions and turmoils that can beset an ordinary life."

The heroine of *Fall River Legend* is first introduced to us as she stands accused in front of a gallows. In this timeless moment of terror, her mind races back over the past and we are shown first the happy girlhood with a loving father and a gentle, fragile mother; then comes the death of a parent and a stepmother, hard and evil, at least in the mind of the child, commences to persecute the girl. The persecutions mount in various ways: parental love is denied, stifling disciplines are enforced, an escape through romance is blocked and the destruction of the symbols of persecutions, the father and the stepmother, ensues.

Miss de Mille has created three engrossing characters for her ballet, the Accused, the Stepmother and the young Pastor who almost succeeds in rescuing the girl from her life of misery. The gestures, body movements and action patterns designed for the Accused clearly reflect her subdued neuroticism, her desperate eagerness for fun and happiness and her mounting determination to rid herself of her oppressors by violence if necessary. The Stepmother is presented as steel-spined, grudging of tenderness, reserved of action but implacable in attitude. In the gentle gestures of the Pastor, in the lift to his body and in the openness of his motions, warmth and loyalty are made manifest.

These are the characters around which *Fall River Legend* revolves and in which the ballet finds its motivation and these are the characters to whom Miss de Mille has accorded her most imaginative choreography. When these three, singly or together, are on stage, the ballet has drive and mounting tension, but when they are absent or merely held in arrested attitudes, the pace of the piece slows down, even seeming to digress. The ensemble, for example, represents the townsfolk of Fall River and their sequences are designed to indicate the youthful frolic which the girl envies and of which she is not a part. But these episodes, although they have dramatic validity, in theory at least, by providing a contrast to the loneliness and misery of the girl, are rather like interruptions. One could have wished that Miss de Mille had achieved greater integration of these contrasting actions and their emotional overtones. Further, these group interludes are not distinguished by Miss de Mille's usual inventiveness and spice, although they do contain several passages of effective dance.

The principal roles in *Fall River Legend* were beautifully danced. Alicia Alonso was completely believable as the Accused and Muriel Bentley was magnificent as the Stepmother. The Pastor was simply and affectingly enacted by John Kriza and others in the ballet who contributed to the drama were Diana Adams as the girl's own mother, Ruth Ann Koesun as the Accused as a child, Peter Gladke as the Father and Crandall Diehl as the Speaker for the Jury. The appropriately melodramatic score was conducted by its composer, Morton Gould, and the costumes by Miles White were in keeping with the period of the work. Oliver Smith's mobile setting and backgrounds were enormously successful and themselves accounted for much of the ballet's aura of oppression, hate and violence. [*New York Herald Tribune*]

Tamiris and Bettis Bring Dance Distinction to Broadway Revue

May 9, 1948

A feeling of smugness was unavoidable. It was the opening performance of a new musical revue, the stars were great and famous the production was lavish and the skits featuring the headliners were hilarious, yet a dancer was able to "stop the show" twice and to generate batches of bravos. In theory, at least, this is not unusual, not a particularly good excuse for smugness on the part of those who are dedicated to the art of dancing. Dancers have always participated in revues and sometimes starred in them, but such dancers have specialized in dancing which is traditionally suitable to revue needs, in eccentric or virtuosic dancing, in skillful hoofing, in tap, toe or acrobatic. Often they have been good, even great dancers, but they have, in the main, been concerned with diversion rather than with the communication of emotional patterns.

The success of Valerie Bettis in *Inside U. S. A.* seems, at first glance, to be unusual because Miss Bettis is a modern dancer and not a revue specialist and because her dance way has led her in the immediate past to the creation of such concert works as *And the Earth Shall Bear Again, The Desperate Heart, Five Abstractions in Space* and other works obviously unsuited to a diverting revue. For *Inside U. S. A.*, interestingly enough, she changed her way of dancing not at all. She did not attempt a hot rumba, a tap number or a balletic show-piece; she danced as she has always danced, but on this occasion she danced not about a woman searching for the mysteries of life nor about a woman searching for the mysteries of life nor about a desperate heart but about a waterfront enchantress and an enticing woman given to homicidal impulses.

The Dancers's Attributes   In her two dance episodes Miss Bettis disclosed those qualities which have given her great distinction in the concert field. These were a remarkably disciplined movement range, action which was both volatile and mercurial, a knowing use of muscular intensities to achieve dramatic and kinesthetic effects and a fine sense of instinctive (not shock) gesture. I am almost certain that the majority of those who cheered her performance were happily unaware of these technical and stylistic details, but they were obviously delighted with the theatrical results which these basic attributes engendered. Of course Miss Bettis is beautiful and glamorous and clearly material for Hollywood, but her success, I like to think, is due to her superb dancing.

One must also go further and say that a good deal of Miss Bettis's success is due to Helen Tamiris, choreographer for *Inside U. S. A.,* and herself a major figure in the field of modern dance. Whether Miss Tamiris choreographed every Bettis gesture and step or not is unimportant. What is important is that Miss Tamiris knew how to use the personal skills of her chief dancer and how to apply modern dance to the needs of a Broadway show. Her choreography for *Haunted Heart,* in which Miss Bettis dances with three successive suitors, is alive with the pulsations of restless romance, with quick thrusts of passion, with an air of loneliness which is both haunting and appealing. She has treated *Tiger Lily,* a little ballet around a girl accused of pushing a swain over a cliff, with great zest and wit. It is a choreographic parody of a tabloid coverage of a sensational trial and through movement (modern dance movement for the most part) she establishes the characters of the girl, the judge, the attorneys and, fittingly enough, tells the sensational story through movement sensations and kinetic overtones rather than through words or obvious pantomime.

Tamiris, Choreographer   In addition to bringing theatrical glory to herself as choreographer and to Miss Bettis as dancer, Miss Tamiris has done a bang-up job of staging the musical numbers and of providing short, frequent and appropriate dance interludes and passages. In *Blue Grass, First Prize at the Fair, At the Mardi Gras* and *My Gal Is Mine Once More* she has, through her dance actions, given body-response to the rhythms of the music, reflected the pictures suggested by the lyrics and done much to establish the prevailing moods of the various scenes. Her dancers in these scenes, headed by a top-notch specialty dancer, Eric Victor, and including J. C. McCord, Rod Alexander and George Reich, have served her beautifully, but it is Miss Bettis, of course, who is the heart of Miss Tamiris's most distinguished Broadway accomplishment to date. This combination of two major modern dance personalities, of two of the nation's most zestful dancers, of two dynamic red-heads has served *Inside U. S. A.* well and given modern dance on Broadway a hearty and healthy boost. [*New York Herald Tribune*]

Radio City Music Hall Ballet: Florence Rogge's Creations

May 30, 1948

There is a tendency in dance circles to regard the corps de ballet at the Radio City Music Hall with mild scorn or at least with kindly condescension. Are not the corps de ballet offerings designed to appeal to more than seven million movie-goers each year? Is it not true that revolving stages, shifting platforms and other mechanical devices share in the choreographic patterns? Is not ballet treated by the Music Hall as an activity contributing to stage show variety, to spectacle? If these things are so, the balletomanes might say, how can one expect to find good ballet at the Music Hall? These things are so and in spite of them, and sometimes because of them, the Music Hall's corps de ballet and many of its presentations may quite properly be regarded with admiration, enthusiasm and respect.

Florence Rogge, associate producer and choreographer for the Radio City Music Hall, has created, over the year, a ballet ensemble which is unmatched in precision and which possesses an academic ballet technique of more than merely serviceable range. The technique enables the dancers to perform with confidence and competence adaptations of such ballets as *Swan Lake, Coppélia, Les Sylphides* and to dance effectively and skillfully ballets created by Miss Rogge. The precision, which is not at all mechanical in quality, gives necessary definition and clarity to the mass patterns which sweep across the great stage. This ballet ensemble, then, need experience no sense of inferiority, for by strictly balletic standards it is admirable and by stage show or variety standards it is most certainly in a class by itself.

Choreographer's Problems　Of the ballets created by Miss Rogge, the majority of those which I have seen constitute examples of first-rate theatrical craftsmanship and, in several instances, of artistically absorbing choreography. It is perfectly true that Miss Rogge is frequently governed, and perhaps limited, by the theme selected for the entire production and that she must remember that

211

the millions who witness her ballets are not all schooled in the fine points, the niceties of ballet technique and of style. It is her duty and her function to make ballet enjoyable to the layman, to accent those aspects of ballet which are of immediate effectiveness and to lead her vast audiences gradually, painlessly into recognizing, accepting and liking areas of the ballet art new to them. Those who have visited the Music Hall from time to time for several years know that under Miss Rogge's direction, both the corps de ballet and the ballets themselves have continued to grow in proficiency and in quality.

Ballet at the Music Hall is still spectacle; it must be, for the theater plant itself obviously demands spectacle. One might also add that spectacle is one of the effects which ballet relies upon even in the most sacred of balletic precincts. This does not mean that only violent actions or big geometric patterns are permitted at the Music Hall. In the ballet for the current stage show, for example, Patricia Bowman, the ballerina, dances with her partner an adagio which is just as lyric and delicately etched as an adagio from practically any of the ballet classics. Further, it does not end in a circus flourish, but in a sequence of dainty frappes which diminish into repose as the music fades to an echo. Preceding the adagio and following it, the corps de ballet creates upon the stage large (yes, spectacular) patterns which delight the eye with their symmetries, their dissolvings, their re-formings, but there is more than geometric interest in Miss Rogge's choreography. The movements of the dancers—the running bourrees, the grands jetes, the poised arabesques—draw upon kinesthetic values and upon linear (as distinct from geometric structure) values. The forms, the qualities and, to a surprising degree, the shadings of the accompanying Chopin music are reflected in this choreography. There are flourishes, admittedly, and there are some purely pictorial posings, but they in no way dissipate the basic excellence of this work.

Expanding Repertory In the current ballet, with Miss Bowman as the star and in the preceding one which featured Genia Melnitchenko and Robert De Voye as the major soloists, Miss Rogge was able to bring to her presentations the stellar accents, the solo highlights usually needed to give focus, to say nothing of variety, to ballet action. With guest stars supporting the home company, the choreographer thus finds the scope of dance at the Music Hall enlarged and variety in repertory possible. Miss Rogge already has an impressive list of varied works to her credit and is contemplating ballet versions of such compositions as Khatchaturian's *Masquerade Suite, Les Preludes* of Liszt and Deems Taylor's *Through the Looking Glass*. As a choreographer as well as a director, Miss Rogge's position in the dance world is secure on the basis of her achievements. To the balletomane her importance may be lost sight of in the vastness of the Music Hall itself, but an investigation of the caliber of her work and the realization of the incredible size of her Music Hall followers should quickly cause him to change his mind and to respect her contribution to American theater dance. [*New York Herald Tribune*]

Dance: Critic Criticized for His Critiques by Those He Criticizes

July 11, 1948

The duties and functions of a dance critic have been discussed in these columns on several occasions. Backgrounds, criteria, methods and critical creeds have been presented in an effort to make clear what a dance critic, or this dance critic at any rate, attempts to do. Such topics were treated with seriousness and with as little reference to personalities as possible and this necessary treatment precluded discussion of a burden which the average critic must bear. It is a light burden, both as to weight and as to importance, but it is invariably present and warrants, I think, light comment at this time.

The burden to which I refer is that some dancer somewhere is almost certain to be highly irritated by whatever a critic writes or whatever a critic does not write and either lets him know about it directly or through a grapevine system which ultimately delivers the message that the critic does not know what he is talking about. Dancers, for the most part, are egocentrics. Even those who are highly spiritual, even those who try to regard their gifts impersonally, even those who are intensely devoted to the universal values of dance are subject to the pangs of a hurt ego. As a group they have little or no respect for writers who lavish praise indiscriminately; they prefer the sterner, stricter critics but as individuals they want these critics to be stern and strict with rival dancers and not with themselves.

If a stern and strict criticism is also honest and pertinent, the intelligent dancer will ultimately take heed and, perhaps, do something about publicly noted flaws but not until a period of irritation and perhaps vituperation has served to salve a bruised ego. On one occasion, I was forced to give a rather harsh notice to a new and major work by a great dancer. Another dance critic felt similarly about the piece. Months later, the work appeared on Broadway in totally revised form and is now considered one of the masterpieces of our time. The dancer-choreographer concerned admitted later that she had been hurt and furious over the initial reviews, but that she herself had not been pleased with the work even before the reviews appeared. She wanted favorable criticism, she said, but if she had received it, she would have been dismayed by approval of a creation which, intellectually, she knew was not worthy of her.

Dancer in a Rage   Another dancer raged and stormed (in person) over a solo
I had thought was quite poor and defended it with every argument he could
muster. A few months later it was removed from the repertory and, as far as
I know, was never danced again. It was never mentioned again, I might add.
At times, dancers, choreographers and even dance organizations accuse the
critic of trying to kill the art of dance in America by keeping audiences away
from the theater through unfavorable reviews and when the critic points out
that if the public had seen the performance in question the same result would
have obtained, he is regarded as more of a beast than ever. Sometimes, not
often, but sometimes a dancer will admit, off the record, that what the critic
said about a performance was true and then add "why did you have to write
it; couldn't you have told me about it at lunch?" The critic mentions that a
newspaper does not engage him to play coach or personal adviser to a dancer,
that he has a duty to his readers and that he does his best, through harsh review or accolade, to be of help and perhaps of value to artist and audience
alike.

      If a dancer receives a series of good reviews, the critic who wrote them
is hailed by the dancer as the greatest critic of his time, the only unbiased
critic, a font of wisdom and a true friend of dance, but let the critic disapprove of or find fault with a cherished new work, he immediately becomes an
inferior critic, biased, dyspeptic, disloyal and a turncoat. Since dancers are
rivals, not only economically but also in matters pertaining to the ego, it occasionally follows that an enthusiastic review of one dancer or dance company
will elicit a diatribe (to the critic) from another dancer or company. I have
been trapped or cornered at meetings or in lobbies by dancers who berate me
for writing a favorable criticism of another dancer. They accuse the recipient
of the criticism of everything from not knowing the difference between fourth
and fifth positions in ballet through charlatanism to creating dances which are
antichrist, and I am not exaggerating. Lack of space is rarely accepted by a
dancer as a valid excuse for omitting mention of a forthcoming performance
or brevity of review, the selection of a photograph to accompany a dance
column or review is an invitation for caustic comment and other actions of
the critic are also subject to sometimes bitter, sometimes hurt denunciation.

The Specialist's Vanity   The critic's burden, however, is light, for there are
dancers who are immediately appreciative of stern reviews as well as of harsh
ones and the majority of dancers, once the initial pique with a critic is passed,
is again friendly and, possibly, hopeful. Further, dancers' egocentricities are
understandable and are by no means to be regarded as faults of character. A
housewife is egocentric too in her own field. She likes the family to praise
her pies and if, on occasion, she turns out an inferior bit of pastry, she prefers
polite fibs or no comment at all. Dancers are probably not much more

214

egocentric than any other specialist, a housewife included, but they are intense and articulate. The critic may not enjoy the impassioned complaints which emanate from their group, but he can understand the reasons and assume the burden. To be truthful, critics themselves are not any more eager than anyone else to receive adverse criticism for their efforts; they are simply more accustomed to it, and since dance is an exciting art and dancers are usually fine and stimulating persons, the critic is amply rewarded for the burden of abuse which temporarily irate artists pile upon him from time to time. [*New York Herald Tribune*]

The State of Television Dance: Some Words on a New Medium

September 19, 1948

Before the ballet and dance concert seasons really get under way and require the undivided attention of these columns, I would like to make a few comments and pose a few questions relative to dancing for television. In recent weeks I have seen television shows featuring Alicia Markova and Anton Dolin, Maria Teresa Acuna with her group of Spanish dancers and Bob Herget and his partner. None of them, it seemed to me, was as imaginatively conceived and as effectively presented as several of those dance programs which Pauline Koner staged for television two seasons ago. Somehow, I had expected to note greater progress in the application of theater dance to television, but perhaps I had not seen enough television dance to judge the situation fairly or perhaps program directors had preferred to avoid experimentation other than permitting a casual array of close-ups and long shots.

The use of close-ups and long shots is, of course, essential to television, to any two-dimensional camera medium for that matter. The focus of the camera must move just as the eyes of the spectator in the theater move to concentrate upon the highlights of performance, and the camera's great mobility must be employed to counteract the loss of depth, of three-dimensional theater. All one asks is that the close-ups and long shots be choreographed, that they be governed not merely by the desirability of having variations in focus but that they be governed by the form and substance of the dance itself. Miss Markova and Mr. Dolin were handsome little figures in their television show, and occasionally the camera wandered in to catch the flutter of Miss Markova's arms in *The Dying Swan* or the romantic facial expressions of the two in a pose, but it failed to seek out the trembling excitement of petits

215

battements, it did not soar with the dancer in his leaps and it did not, in the main, bring the beholder close to the constantly shifting centers of movement. The television camera could make magic, not theatrical magic but visual magic of a new kind, but this it failed to do in those programs which I saw.

This brings us to another point. Can theater dances choreographed for the large stage be successfully transferred to television? Some would lend themselves to translation, others would require certain revisions and all would require what might be called television treatment. To present them straight or with a few sporadic close-ups and long shots would make them just about as stirring as those unembellished motion pictures of dances taken for choreographic record only. Ideally, dances should be created expressly for television; since television is a distinct medium of entertainment. As I recall, Miss Koner did just this and with extremely promising results. Some of Miss Acuna's gypsy dancing was pleasantly reproduced, and Bob Herget brought a welcome air of spontaneity to his televised offering, but on the whole, their dancing and that of Miss Markova and Mr. Dolin seemed pale, remote. It was pretty at times, even interesting in spots, but it lacked punch. It lacked punch not because it was inherently weak but because its energies were not caught by the television director and re-communicated to the audience.

Dancing—all kinds of dancing—is obviously a fine entertainment potential for television. Dancing is action, it is rhythm, it is pattern and often it is drama. Surely those attributes are needed by the new medium. A knowing director and choreographer could, together, avoid making a reflection in miniature of stage dance and could apply the basic attributes of dance to the limitations and potentialities of television. To date it seems to me that the limitations have governed televised dance and the potentialities have not often been realized. Television dance is still young, however, and the next few months and years should find its producers and creators more willing and better prepared to adventure into a still unexplored area of art and entertainment. [*New York Herald Tribune*]

Paris Opéra Ballet

September 24, 1948

The Paris Opéra Ballet offered its second program on the International Dance Festival series last evening at the City Center and the report which I must make this morning is hardly jubilant. The amenities of the gala debut of

Tuesday last, when French and city officials were present to celebrate the French company's participation in New York's Golden Anniversary, are now over and the time has come to analyze the organization not as a visitor but as a professional performing unit. One cannot pretend to pass final judgments on the basis of two programs but stylistic tendencies, technical oddities, choreographic approaches and overall theatrical manner may surely be discussed.

The company's style is courtly and apparently this courtliness is maintained with grim determination throughout all kinds of ballets with all sorts of themes. Even when the dancers are called upon to play at being forest creatures they are courtly. In addition to being courtly, the ballet's members are given to frequent flourishes and I would say that their version of ballet contains five positions of the wrist as well as the customary five positions of the feet. The leg extensions of the ladies are usually high and clean and the small-scale footwork often precise, but the movements appear to be accomplished by the measure rather than by a long and flowing phrase and with the exception of Yvette Chauviré, movement colorings, shadings in intensity are not often manifest.

All of the dancers are gracious and eager. They also perform, in the main, with authority and assurance, so one must assume that they are dancing as they think they should and in keeping with the style established by their long history as a national dance organization. Perhaps not all of us are appreciative of their way of dance and perhaps some of us just do not care for it very much. Certainly, the company is at its most engaging when it concerns itself with ballets basically courtly. Furthermore, one must take into consideration the deficiencies of the City Center as a theater. Without question, the French Ballet would appear to much better advantage in a opera house or theater large enough to accommodate its regular settings and large enough to give perspective to its stagings.

The second program offered only two works: George Balanchine's wonderful show piece, *Crystal Palace,* to Bizet's Symphony in C, and Serge Lifar's two-act ballet, *The Knight and the Maiden,* with music by Philippe Gaubert and decor by Cassandre. This last named piece deals with a knight, a princess who has been transformed into a white-antlered hind and their romantic problems and I cannot think of anything pleasant to say about it. Choreographically it seems to me to parallel one of those endless ballets which come along at dancing school recital time and in which all of the students must have a part. It is all very foolish dramatically, uninteresting as straight dance and not even Miss Chauviré, who danced so exquisitely in *Mirages* on the opening bill, could do much with the role of the maiden. *Crystal Palace,* since it is structurally a magnificent work, fared much better, but its inherent sparkle, its tongue-in-cheek hauteur and its sweeping choreographic line were not often in evidence.

217

It seems, at this point in the engagement, that the Paris Opéra Ballet put its best foot forward on its opening night. It was pleasant, if not exciting, in the eighteenth-century style *Castor and Pollux* and through *Mirages,* it provided Miss Chauviré with an opportunity to bring honor to her company. Perhaps later programs with other works will serve to erase, partially at any rate, the memory of this second program.

Outside the City Center, pickets were carrying placards protesting the participation of Serge Lifar, ballet master of the Paris Opéra Ballet, in a festival sponsored by the Mayor's Committee for the Commemoration of the Golden Anniversary of the City of New York. Handbills which were distributed referred to the dancer-choreographer as a "Nazi collaborationist." The pickets represented the American Dancers' Anti-Fascist Protest Committee. [*New York Herald Tribune*]

New York City Ballet—First Season

October 12, 1948: Resident Ballet

The New York City Ballet Company made its debut last evening at the City Center. To avoid confusion, however, let it be said at once that the debut was one in name only, for the company was Ballet Society and the productions were Ballet Society productions. The new name has significance, nonetheless, since it means that the New York City Center of Music and Drama has added the art of dancing to its community activities.

The performance was a handsome one, even a miraculous one at times, and I should like to share in the celebration by happily eating some of my words of last season. At that time *Orpheus* was given its first presentation and at that time I had strong reservations concerning it. George Balanchine's choreography, I felt, was not comparable in emotional equalities, in colorings, in mysticisms to the score by Igor Stravinsky and that it treated the Orpheus myth neither as a heroic classic nor as an intense and dedicated ritualized legend. This season's presentation brought out, for me at least, those qualities which I had found missing on earlier occasions.

Orpheus is a difficult work to dance because it is not dependent upon the use of feats of skill. It is very simple, for the most part, quiet, even gestural in sections and where it becomes complex in pattern it can easily look to be superficially contrived. Last season, I think, the dancers were not ready to find and project the drama inherent in the formal gestures and processional actions. Now they are ready and the great beauties of Mr.

Balanchine's tender, austere and mysterious recreation of the Orpheus tragedy emerge clearly and luminously. It is a wonderful work and I am happy that I was wrong about the choreography and happy that the dancers are now prepared to give the choreography the theater-life it deserves.

Nicholas Magallanes was again the Orpheus, but what a different enactment from that of last spring! Instead of a negative, beaten boy, Mr. Magallanes showed us a man who maintained his stature even in despair, who gave us tragedy and not simple sorrow. It was a fine performance of a difficult role which demands accuracy of gestural accent and command of body dynamics. Francisco Moncion was again compelling in the part of the Dark Angel and Maria Tallchief was the lovely Eurydice. The superb scenery and stage properties by Isamu Noguchi, the lighting by Jean Rosenthal and Leon Barzin's conducting of the music contributed immeasurably to the total magic of Mr. Balanchine's *Orpheus.*

The evening opened with *Concerto Barocco,* with choreography by Mr. Balanchine to music of Bach and employing setting and costumes created after sketches by Eugene Berman. These were originally designed by Mr. Berman for the American Ballet Caravan's production of the ballet in 1941. The performance itself was a pleasant one, although it was not as incisive nor quite as varied in movement coloring as those usually presented by the Ballet Russe de Monte Carlo, a company which also includes the work in its repertory. It is probably a matter of individual taste, but I prefer the Monte Carlo's version, with its simple black costumes and no decor, to the more ornate version by the New York City Ballet Company, Bach's title to the contrary. Marie-Jeanne danced the principal figure very well indeed, and gallant support was provided by Mr. Moncion. Ruth Gilbert, an attractive dancer, has not yet invested her part with the sharpness and the strength necessary to its full effectiveness.

The closing work was Mr. Balanchine's glittering, virtuosic *Symphony in C* to music of Bizet. The lateness of the hour made it impossible for your reporter to remain for more than the first movement, but that was time enough to see that the company was in fine estate for the assignment, with Maria Tallchief dancing with a brilliance which literally set the stage alight. Mr. Magallanes, Mr. Moncion, Tanaquil LeClercq, Marie-Jeanne, Jocelyn Vollmar, Herbert Bliss and Todd Bolender were others listed as major participants. [*New York Herald Tribune*]

October 19, 1948: Youthful

It was a fresh and youthful performance that the New York City Ballet Company gave last night at the City Center. The virtues of youth—exuberance, eagerness, stamina, bounce—were present and the flaws—self-consciousness, gaucherie, ineptness in covering up an error—were also apparent at times. But the spirit was right and much of the dancing was handsome and bright enough to make one delight in the young company as it is and to anticipate with relish its highly promising future.

To open the second program of its season, the company selected George Balanchine's *Serenade* with music by Tchaikovsky. It is a difficult work to perform because of the complexities of the mass patterns and because innumerable of the musical details of the score, both structural and emotional, must be realized (or responded to) in terms of movement. The corps de ballet members were not quite prepared to meet all of these demands and there were rough edges discernible off and on throughout the ballet, but the spirit, as I have suggested, was right and the dancing alive with youthful charm.

The dancing of Marie-Jeanne in the principal role was, of course, something else again. Although it is in her dance nature to be quick, staccato, even nervous of movement, she brought a fine fluidity of motion to her assignment and gave the ballet, quite rightly, its center of action through her impressive performance. Herbert Bliss, barring an initial suggestion of tenseness, was fine as the partner in the waltz section and Nicolas Magallanes was excellent, both in physical action and in dramatic quality, in the closing movement.

Punch and the Child, Fred Danieli's pleasant little work with music by Richard Arnell and delightfully macabre sets and costumes by Horace Armistead, was given its best (it has been performed by this group under its Ballet Society title) performance to date. It is slight of theme and loose choreographically, but it does sustain a story-book atmosphere and it does boast several engaging episodes.

Beatrice Tompkins was again the vicious, energetic Judy, a role which she performs superbly, and Herbert Bliss was the henpecked Punch. Little Judy Kursch was appealing as the Child who dreams her way into a magic world behind the Punch and Judy show and others of the company did nicely with supporting roles.

The evening came to close with Mr. Balanchine's classic ballet to Mozart's *Symphonie Concertante in E Flat.* It is a lovely work, cool, elegant and pure, like the score which is its stimulus. The company danced it very nicely and Maria Tallchief, Tanaquil LeClercq and Todd Bolender, as the principals, danced it to perfection. The orchestra, led by Leon Barzin, provided the dancers with sensitive accompaniments and the audience with a distinguished musical evening. The program will be repeated tonight. [*New York Herald Tribune*]

Many things went wrong before the curtain rose on last evening's performance by the New York City Ballet Company at the City Center but one never guessed it, for the pinch-hitters were at ease and the regulars in vivacious mood. John Kriza, who was to have made a guest appearance with the company had injured his ankle and André Eglevsky, premier danseur of the Marquis de Cuevas's Grand Ballet de Monte Carlo, had jumped in at the last moment with but a few hours rehearsal. Herbert Bliss, one of the organization's principals, was also indisposed and Francisco Moncion was called upon to dance his and Mr. Bliss's roles in one of the ballets. There were other shiftings but, as I say, it all worked out very nicely indeed.

Aside from casting, the evening's major interest focused upon the season's first presentation of *Four Temperaments* with choreography by George Balanchine, music by Paul Hindemith and scenery and costumes by Kurt Seligman. Several changes have occurred since the work was first presented by Ballet Society. The costumes have been simplified and those which were over-burdened with decorative impediments are now suitable for dancing bodies and one can see not only the outlines of choreography but also emotional and dramatic intents. The whole work has grown considerably both in shape and in performance value and it now may be classed among the company's most arresting works. It is a colorful ballet both as a theater production and as dance, for Mr. Balanchine has devised rich and imaginative movement patterns to give substance to his four temperaments: Melancholic, Sanguinic, Phlegmatic and Choleric.

Of the principal dancers, Maria Tallchief, Nicholas Magallanes and Todd Bolender were unquestionably the best, although Mr. Moncion did some fine work in his own theme and that which he took over from Mr. Bliss. Miss Tallchief, given superb support by Mr. Magallanes, accomplished some of the finest dancing to be seen in these parts and Mr. Bolender as the leading figure of the phlegmatic theme came closest of all to realizing in dance the very nature, the implications of the world itself. In the brief part of Choleric, Tanaquil LeClerq was also effective although this theme does not receive as full a development as the others.

In *Symphony in C,* Mr. Balanchine's elegant and utterly delightful show-off piece, Mr. Eglevsky had very little to do but he did it with his customary suavity and charm. It was good to have him back for an American appearance even if the assignment did not afford him opportunity to display many of his dance skills. Of the others, one must mention Miss LeClercq, Mr. Magallanes, Marie-Jeanne, Mr. Moncion and, of course (and this is getting to be a habit), Miss Tallchief. Jocelyn Vollmar and Mr. Bolender, who were the principals of the last movement, went on too late for me to see. At any rate, the first three movements were danced in lively fashion and a few mistakes here and there in the actions of the corps de ballet caused but minor harm. [*New York Herald Tribune*]

October 31, 1948: The Unique Problems of the Ballet

Like all new dance organizations, the New York City Ballet Company has its artistic, promotional and financial problems. Some of these problems are unique, while others are general. In this latter group, one may list the unfamiliarity of the name, an unfamiliar (since the company does not produce traditional works) repertory and, with the exception of a few of the principal dancers, unfamiliar dance personnel. Further, there is no "russe" in the title, and this commendable omission probably discourages that persistent group, still distressingly large, which cannot utter the word "ballet" without mating it with "Russian." Finally, heavy expenditures must be made not only to promote popular interest in the new company but to maintain and expand the repertory.

As to the specific nature, with its attendant problems and virtues, of the New York City Ballet Company, one may point out that, like its parent organization, Ballet Society, it is dedicated to the advancement of the lyric theater. This means that as a producing agency it will abstain from such box-office favorites as *Scheherazade* or *Giselle* and concentrate upon those aspects of dance, music, stagecraft or book which would seem to foster the aims of the organization. In other words, Ballet Society–New York City Ballet Company is not guided by the rules of the commercial theater. Yet it must achieve financial success if it is to continue. In order to carry out its purposes and still pay its own way, the company, under the direction of Lincoln Kirstein, has elected to test a formula new to major American ballet organizations and that is to establish itself as a resident company. There will be no journeys of one-night stands, no touring as such; instead, the New York City Ballet Company will strive to serve its own city and to build its following from the members of the community.

The next point is to question whether the New York City Ballet Company is worthy of the support of the local citizenry which it seeks. Personally, I believe that the company merits such support. True, it is not the smoothest performing unit in the dance business, but the student-dancers of its corps de ballet are progressing steadily and its principals—particularly Maria Tallchief, Marie-Jeanne, Tanaquil LeClercq, Francisco Moncion and (as a partner, at any rate) Nicholas Magallanes—are not only excellent dancers but arresting stage personalities. The repertory, built mainly around the works of George Balanchine, is small but generally distinguished and if the accent is upon elegance

222

and style rather than upon works of a lusty nature or of American theme, one may assume that Mr. Kirstein, who has contributed so richly to American dance through his earlier ventures and adventures, will see to it that these aspects of repertory will be developed.

To return to Mr. Balanchine, let it be said at once that the inclusion of so many of his works in the repertory of the New York City Ballet Company constitutes, at this point, the company's major claim to distinction. The haunting ritual-mystery which is *Orpheus,* the sparkling, kinetically flamboyant *Symphony in C,* the imaginatively patterned *Four Temperaments* and his many other ballets, classic of form but contemporary in flavor, represent a great dance gift worthy of cherishing. In addition to according lavish and loving production to the Balanchine ballets, the organization has given choreographic opportunity to junior artists of dance and has enlisted the services of several fine composers and painters in order that music and decor may be intrinsic parts of, and not merely necessary adjuncts to, a ballet creation.

It is to be hoped that New Yorkers will find it possible and pleasant to support their new resident dance company, for if they do it is likely that the New York City Ballet Company will be able to fill a fuller schedule than the current one of two performances each week for a season of two months, that it will be able to broaden its repertory and polish its personnel and that it will be able to provide artistic outlet for some of the youthful talent of our day. The organization, as I have indicated through specific examples, is certainly not beyond criticism. There is much to be done before it can match, point by point, the achievements of some of our commercial dance organizations, but it is young and alive, talented and determined and if details of its activities sometimes warrant harsh criticism, its over-all functions and professed goals certainly merit encouragement and nurturing. [*New York Herald Tribune*]

223

1949

Margot: America Falls in Love

On Broadway, Hanya Holm's choreography for Kiss Me, Kate • New York City Ballet's second season offers Balanchine's Firebird, and The Guests and Bourée Fantasque • At the 92nd Street YMHA, Jean Erdman's Perilous Chapel and Valerie Bettis' As I Lay Dying • Limón Company in Humphrey's Corybantic and Limón's La Malinche; Janet Collins in La Creole • Ballet Theatre returns after a year's absence • Fonteyn triumphs in Sadler's Wells Ballet American debut • Les Ballets de Paris presents Zizi Jeanmaire in Petit's Carmen • José Limón, Sophie Maslow, Valerie Bettis and Charles Weidman presented by New York City Dance Theatre • Limón's masterpiece, The Moor's Pavane, has its New York premiere on a program with Doris Humphrey's Invention

Dance: Miss Holm and Her Fine Kiss Me, Kate Choreography

January 9, 1949

Hanya Holm, choreographer for the new musical hit, *Kiss Me, Kate,* customarily conceals her enormous talents in the classroom. Students know of her greatness as a teacher, but until last spring, when she staged the dances for "The Eccentricities of Davey Crockett" in *Ballet Ballads,* her reputation as one of the leading dance figures of our time was based upon her first major American work, *Trend,* first presented more than a decade ago, and upon smaller scale concert pieces which had but infrequent showings. At last Miss Holm's dance is coupled with a smash Broadway success and if the choreography for *Kiss Me, Kate* does not belong in that category which contains *Trend, Metropolitan Daily* or the productions she stages at Colorado College each summer, it represents musical theater dance at its best.

The Holm admirers may, quite possibly, be disappointed in the new musical's dances, disappointed not in the quality but in the quantity and in the degree of importance accorded them. There is no ballet as such in *Kiss Me, Kate,* but there is dancing, all of it firmly integrated into the show to contribute to the achieving of a total theatrical impression. The dancing gives flow to the musical, it provides the means for transitions in pace or in mood or in style, it aids in the definition of character and it accounts for the production's necessary flashes of physical virtuosity.

The choreographer might have interrupted the course of the show with a full dance work which would have given her opportunity to disclose her full dance gifts. She might, if she had been more of a veteran in the musical comedy field, found somewhere in the book a valid excuse for a complete, but contributory, ballet. Miss Holm did neither. Instead, she served a theatrical plan with the craft of dance and did the job in distinguished fashion.

If there was no ballet in Miss Holm's choreographic scheme for *Kiss Me, Kate,* there were arresting dance passages, movement details of wit and beauty and an amazing array of styles. As a matter of fact, Miss Holm and her assistant, Ray Harrison, at appropriate moments provided the show with classic ballet, modern dance, jitterbugging, soft-shoe, acrobatics, court dance, folk dance and episodes which might be described as rhythmic playfulness. This was rich dance fare, even if the portions were small, and the shrewd Miss Holm left us wanting more, not less.

It would be difficult to say which of the scenes employing dance was the best. The first, "Another Op'nin', Another Show," permitted the dancing ensemble to enliven a backstage scene with spurts of practice-action, fragments of formal dance and a good deal of frolic. Later in the first act, Shirley Eckl, a lovely dancer, and a small ensemble gave visual form and beauty to the song, "Were Thine That Special Face." Harold Lang, one of the principals of *Kiss Me, Kate,* had a charming, boyish solo in the play-within-a-play sequence of the opening act. It was not a show-stopping type of dance, for it was lyric, unpretentious in its occasional use of virtuosity and without smashing climax, but it accomplished its purpose as an engaging incident. Mr. Lang, at the performance I attended, did not dance it as easily as one would have wished, but elsewhere in the show he was in fine fettle.

In "Too Darn Hot," Fred Davis and Eddie Sledge danced a rousing specialty number in which they were ultimately joined by Mr. Lang, who turned on his technical skills full force and brought down the house. For background in this scene, Miss Holm devised some non-intruding but atmospherically effective jitterbug passages for the ensemble.

The rousing first act finale, a tarantella, and the second act finale, a handsome court dance, together with other movement passages augmenting primarily musical scenes constituted still further dance joys for the dance follower. Miss Holm must, of course, receive first credit for the success of her dance passages and movement details, but her dancers too deserve praise for bringing her choreography to zestful life.

Now that *Kiss Me, Kate* is set and Miss Holm presumably happy about it all, the choreographer will busy herself with the incidental dances and movement direction for Garcia Lorca's *Blood Wedding,* to be produced by New Stages late this month. After that, one may hope, that Miss Holm will have opportunity to stage the dances for another musical, one which will permit her to take over the stage for a work comparable in scale, say, to the superb Civil War Ballet which Agnes de Mille choreographed for *Bloomer Girl.* [*New York Herald Tribune*]

New York City Ballet

January 21, 1949: Modern Classic

The Guests, a classic ballet by Jerome Robbins with a score by Marc Blitzstein, was given its world premiere last evening at the City Center by the New York City Ballet Company. It is truly a classic ballet, for all its contributory modernisms, and it is a ballet implicit with drama in spite of the absence of specific plot. If *The Guests*, in its current form, is not a great ballet, it is, nevertheless, an absorbing one which adds stature to its young choreographer and which augurs new directions for classic dance.

Mr. Robbins has, for the most part, employed not only the traditional vocabulary of ballet but also many of its established forms and courtesies. With these he has constructed a work which is architectural in proportions rather than flatly decorative, and he has achieved dimension by breaking up his ensemble into two or more groups, by dispatching these groups in varying directions and along numerous paths. In other words, he has used the drama of space, and he has used it rather like Hanya Holm has done in her group compositions, but he has built his choreographic structure in space, not in Miss Holm's modern dance terms but in ballet terms. The result is a work which has dimension, formal strength and freshness of pattern.

The details of the choreography for *The Guests* also constitute a point of interest. By inflection, through movement attack and by shrewd juxtapositions of steps and ensemble actions, Mr. Robbins has invested his classic pas with dramatic purpose. Some gesture, some touches of purely expressional movement have, of course, been used to transmit the emotional colorings of the work, but in the Pas de Deux, for example, he communicates tenderness and latent passion in almost purely balletic terms.

There is no story to *The Guests*. It is, I would say, incident without circumstance; it implies situation without explaining condition. We are shown one figure—perhaps he is a host or perhaps he is a monitor—and we are shown two groups, two castes, two societies or any two opposing units. A girl from one and a boy from another come together by chance and while unaware of each other's identity experience desire for unity. When their masks are removed, opposition, conflict, defiance and ostracism result. The circumstances, the conditions are not told, but the incident, the situation is conveyed through abstraction.

The Guests has its unsatisfactory aspects. The abstract nature of the choreography and the definitiveness of the Blitzstein music are not always happily mated; the early sections of the ballet, though of architectural interest, are weak in dynamic range and there are moments (perhaps due to the performing as well as to choreographic flaw) when too much seems to be happening at once. But on the whole, *The Guests* is a fine composition and its central Pas de Deux is a miracle of beauty.

The company, all things in the way of a premiere considered, danced the Robbins work nicely and will unquestionably disclose more of its retails and inherent values with further experience. Maria Tallchief and Nicholas Magallanes as the principals were splendid in every way, technically, stylistically and dramatically, and Francisco Moncion as the host (or arbiter) was impressive.
[*New York Herald Tribune*]

October 28, 1949: Exciting Revival

What could be pleasanter than to have an old classic, which had been showing the unkind ravages of time, reborn into a new (or almost new) classic sparked with contemporary vitality? Such a happy rebirth occurred last evening at the City Center when the New York City Ballet Company presented Igor Stravinsky's *Firebird* with new choreography by George Balanchine and scenery and costumes by Marc Chagall.

The story of the ballet remains, inevitably, slight if not altogether pointless. It still concerns a prince who captures the Firebird and is given one of her magical feathers in return for her release. Later, when he is interrupted in his wooing of a princess by a band of demons, the feather is waved, the firebird comes to the rescue and the hero weds his heroine. So much for that. Now let us get on to the dancing, for herein lies the excitement of the new *Firebird*.

Mr. Balanchine has devised some magnificent movements for the title figure. They are fluttering, flashing, soaring and, at the proper moments, they fairly flame with dynamic tension and speed. In his own miraculous way, Mr. Balanchine has again taken the academic ballet for his basic stuff of dance and through freshness of sequence and of accent, through the incorporation of freely created but related actions, has made this traditional language of dance seem contemporary without in any way marring its classic nature.

It required, I would guess, a Maria Tallchief to dance Mr. Balanchine's difficult measures for the Firebird and to reveal their beauties in full. Miss Tallchief, thankfully, was present and gave a performance of historical proportions. I have never seen a more brilliant Firebird (and we are not talking about choreography now) and I doubt seriously that there will ever be a greater one.

The Firebird is, of course, the central figure of the ballet but Mr. Balanchine has not neglected the others of the story. The prince has a part which is small but which allows him to become more fully drawn as a character than did the Fokine version of the work. He has some fine dancing to do in the pas de deux with the Firebird, a pleasant sequence with his princess and her maidens and a lively bit with the demons. Francisco Moncion, turned out in a really superb Tartar makeup, made a splendid prince.

The folk-like episodes of the princess and her ladies have been pleasantly devised and seem not only less interminable than those of the original version but quite entrancing. The magicians and demons are not, it must be confessed, very frightening, but they are lively, and Mr. Balanchine has accorded them some unusually effective group patterns to accomplish. A slight irony seemed to touch this section, for Mr. Balanchine gave his demons just a hint, the merest hint, of jive and an adapted Charleston movement or two. Very engaging and right, I would say, since no one seemed to take the demons seriously.

There were wild bursts of applause for Miss Tallchief throughout the ballet and an ovation for her, Mr. Balanchine, Leon Barzin and his orchestra and for the others of the cast at the finish. [*New York Herald Tribune*]

December 2, 1949: A Sheer Delight

Bourrée Fantasque, the New York City Ballet Company's latest work, is sheer delight. Last evening's audience at the City Center guffawed, sighed and cheered as the ballet progressed along an unexpected route from horseplay through tender romance to a flamboyant, circus-like finish. George Balanchine, whose ballet it is, must have had the time of his life creating it, for the fun is spontaneous and not at all contrived, the romantic section is fresh yet easy in its movement patterns and the closing polonaise incorporates practically every known trick for bringing down the house.

Mr. Balanchine's new work is by no means an example of elfish mayhem. It is listed as a classical ballet and it is just that. It spoofs ballet and it takes a fleeting jab at the choreographer's own tendency to wind dancers into daisy chains and it tosses in activities which border on the acrobatic, yet its vocabulary, both balletic and gestural, is primarily academic and its choreographic form is as flawless as that to be found in any one of Mr. Balanchine's pure-dance masterpieces.

Much of the opening movement, which bears the title of the ballet itself, finds its humor in pure kinetics. There is no plot here, but the dancers commence a familiar balletic enchainment and instead of arriving at a normal resolution culminate their activities in pleasantly zany actions which have a muscular and ironic logic if not an academic one. If the ballerina extends a hand, why grasp it? why not lay your head upon it. If male partners have wondered what the ladies are doing with their feet in an adagio, why not let them function on their own for a moment while the gentlemen lie on the floor where proper analysis may be achieved?

Tanaquil LeClercq and Jerome Robbins headed the ensemble for this initial section and they were nothing short of triumphant in their assignments. Miss LeClercq's wide and innocent eyes and her long legs projected the wit of her sequences to perfection, and Mr. Robbins, agile as a leprechaun and twice as mischievous, created a character which must be classed with his immortal Hermes in *Helen of Troy*. The ensemble, too, was fine and very funny indeed.

Just to prove it could be done, Mr. Balanchine jumped from this frolic to the sweetly sentimental Prelude, which starred Maria Tallchief and Nicholas Magallanes, and made us not only accept but be captivated by a totally new mood. It is a lovely section, wistful and searching in quality, a reverie of romance. Miss Tallchief was completely winning in it and Mr. Magallanes supported her through the big and difficult yet soft movements of their duet with gallantry of manner and considerable beauty of movement.

The Fête Polonaise, which brought the work to a close, appeared also to bring every dancer in New York upon the stage. What with runs, leaps, beats and swiftly moving mass patterns, the stage seemed about to burst, but by some miracle, form remained discernible and the curtain came down upon a choreographer's dream (or maybe nightmare) of a sure-fire finale. Janet Reed and Herbert Bliss launched this section in spritely fashion, but were soon lost, along with the other principals, in the whirl of group action.

The score, an arrangement of selections from the works of Emmanuel Chabrier, provided the choreographer with a perfect base for his ballet and, as played by Leon Barzin and his orchestra, proved charming in its own right. The costumes by Karinska, set off by a simple backdrop and gracefully draped white curtains of filmy material, were handsome and chic. [*New York Herald Tribune*]

Two New Works: Dance–Drama by Bettis, Erdman Group Piece

January 30, 1949

Valerie Bettis has done a remarkable job in transporting the characters—their overt actions and their secret sensibilities—of William Faulkner's novel, *As I Lay Dying* to the stage. Her work might be termed, if one insists upon placing it in a category, a dance–drama. In truth, however, it is more than a dance–drama; rather it is a creation, with its own integrity and identity, which exists in the theater and which uses the technical tools of dance movement, acting, speech, music and portrait-like composition to achieve its purpose.

Commissioned and first produced by the Choreographers' Workshop, *As I Lay Dying* was accorded excellent staging in its presentations at the Y. M. and Y. W. H. A. last Sunday. Miss Bettis, heading the cast, surrounded herself with as fine a company of actors-dancers as one could desire. Together they established the quality of bitter weariness, relieved by moments of assuaging beauty, which pervades the Faulkner novel and individually each gave clear definition to the outer behaviour patterns and to the inner portraiture of his character.

Two Kinds of Time   In constructing *As I Lay Dying* Miss Bettis has made vivid use of the element of time. In fact she uses two "times." One is chronological time, which carries along the surface narrative of Addie Brunden's dying, the making of her coffin, her death, her funeral and the related actions and reactions of her family and neighbors. The second is non-sequential time, a time which, because it exists only in the heart and mind, allows fragments of the past to be reborn into the present and to be very real, if unseen. The choreographer, of course, permits us to see these remembered bits of the past and she fuses them with the narrative easily, logically, without apology.

The surface story of the dying of a weary, worn Southern farm woman, although inherently tragic, is commonplace, even dull theatrically. Miss Bettis has permitted this picture of poverty, of lethargy, of homely domestic action to take over the stage too frequently and for periods too long in duration. The picture, naturally, is needed to establish condition and situation, and it must recur from time to time, but not, I think, in such attenuations. Into this barren landscape, with its superficially commonplace figures, Miss Bettis has thrust the vivid and compelling forms of the inner beings, the remembered beings: the young and passionate and searching Addie of long ago; Jewel (superbly acted by Richard Reed) of the tempestuous heart, sensitive, defiant, alone; Brother Whitfield, fearfully yet ecstatically experiencing illicit union with the Addie of the past, and the others, each revealing his secret heart.

231

Lest any one assume that the employment of several art forms and the use of two "times" make for false pretension in *As I Lay Dying,* let me assure him that Miss Bettis's work is as simple, as forthright and as naturally poetic as the best of those folk dramas produced by the Carolina Playmakers. It does, as I have suggested, permit excessive use of folk landscapes, but it is otherwise a masterwork. The star has directed and lighted her production beautifully in addition to choreographing it, writing the scenario and dancing in it. One hopes that it will be given many more presentations, particularly with the present cast, which features not only the exceptional performances of Miss Bettis and Mr. Reed but also compelling characterizations by J. C. McCord, Beverly Bozeman, Hugh Riley, Doris Goodwin, Duncan Noble and, in fact, by each member of the company.

Jean Erdman Program   Another fine young modern dancer, Jean Erdman, also danced last Sunday (at Hunter Playhouse) with her company. This program, built in concert form as was Miss Bettis's, was composed of solos, short ensemble pieces and one new composition of major proportions, *The Perilous Chapel.* Miss Erdman danced beautifully, as she always does, throughout the evening. Her solo, *Ophelia,* was particularly stirring on this occasion and her group was dedicated in spirit even if it did not always convey the choreographer's intentions to the fullest.

The Perilous Chapel, finding its motivation in "and I saw a new heaven and a new earth: for the first heaven and the first earth were passed away; and there was no more sea" (Revelation), is not at all Biblical in flavor nor dramatic in form. It seeks, I think, to give dance image to the poetry implicit in the quoted text; thus, without stating, representing or moralizing, *The Perilous Chapel* is concerned with spatial patterns, with designs in flux, with an atmosphere of questing, with a structural sweep not unlike that which one finds in the drawings of William Blake. In its present state the work is too long and its dynamic gamut too small, but it is an interesting composition nonetheless, curiously restful (without being dull) and generally satisfying as pure dance design. The score, by Lou Harrison, is both suitable and pleasant. I haven't the faintest notion what Roxanne Marden's decor signifies, either dramatically or spatially, but it will hold up a leaning dancer, that I know. [*New York Herald Tribune*]

Three Days of Dance Magic Given
by José Limón, Janet Collins

April 10, 1949

In a short span of three days—March 31, April 1 and 2—New York witnessed what were probably its finest and certainly its most exciting dance events of the year. José Limón and his company, directed by Doris Humphrey, danced at the Ziegfeld Theater on those dates, and on April 2 Janet Collins gave her first full-length recital in our city. At all these performances, superior technique, style, taste and imagination were in evidence, but what made these events an illuminating experience was the presence of a quality which I can best describe by using the word of the art itself, "dance." Mr. Limón and Miss Collins danced. They did not execute. They did not attitudinize. Whatever they did, whatever their theme, they succeeded in presenting not only the form of dance, but also in communicating to the beholder the urge to dance.

Mr. Limón never danced better in his illustrious career than he did during his brief engagement this season. There were new aspects of dance substance to be found even in those works which he had, one supposed, been dancing faultlessly for several seasons. There was new grandeur in his realization of that masterpiece, *Lament for Ignacio Sanchez Mejias,* there was greater tenderness and warmth to his dancing in *Day on Earth* and the sharp and noble *Chaconne* was as impressive an example of highly formalized dance action as I have ever seen.

Limón and Company   The wonders of his performances were not exclusively Mr. Limón's. His company, composed of the tremendously gifted Pauline Koner (as guest artist), the irreplaceable Letitia Ide, the talented Miriam Pandor and Betty Jones and the three who specialized in one role each, Jo Van Fleet, Melissa Nicolaides and Lucas Hoving, gave breadth and individual illuminations to Mr. Limón's productions. How many of the Limón dance wonders are due to Miss Humphrey would be hard to say. Her choreography does, obviously, account for several of the wonders for she is, perhaps, the greatest dance creator of our day.

There were two new works presented during the Limón season, Miss Humphrey's *Corybantic,* set to Bela Bartok's Sonata for Two Pianos and Percussion, and Mr. Limón's *La Malinche,* with a wonderfully pertinent score by Norman Lloyd. The former is another triumph for Miss Humphrey. It is a frightening, inquiring, warning work in which the choreographer presents the predicaments and the perils which beset modern man in terms of those "wild and destructive dances" from which the title derives its name. *La Malinche* is still, I would say, in a state of incompletion. Its basic conception is fine as are many of its passages but this folk-like treatment of a Mexican legend is not yet on that plane where one finds those other dance works in Mr. Limón's repertory.

Miss Collins's Debut   Janet Collins, who had had a rousing success with the one or two dances presented on variety dance programs earlier in the season, easily fulfilled the hopes that had been held for her with her first solo recital. Miss Collins, dancing at the Y. M. and Y. W. H. A., provided her audience with classic dance, modern dance, racial dance and regional dance. As a dancer, she was completely successful in all categories, although as a choreographer, her major modern dance offerings were open to criticism. She is such a remarkable performer, however, that one really doesn't care much what she dances. This does not mean that she is a careless composer or that her compositions are of little count, to the contrary, but it does mean that she moves so exquisitely, so tellingly and with such radiance that one is content to bask (if that can be done kinesthetically) in the sheer beauty of her movement. Like Ruth St. Denis, it seems impossible for Miss Collins to make a wrong motion or a movement which jars one from dance reverie. Such a gift, although the result of hard work and careful nurturing, is also magical and as such, it is inexplicable. One simply accepts the magic and believes in it.

Miss Collins's magic was, as I have indicated, disclosed in many guises. The little *Blackmoor* suite was bubbling, puckish and elegant; the *Eine Kleine Nachtmusik* selections were elegant, bubbling and genuinely aristocratic; the *Spirituals* were filled with wonder and passion, sensitivity and remembrance; the *Juba* was witty; *Protest* and *Credo,* disappointing in substance and form, were rich in isolated movement beauties and *La Créole* and *Après le Mardi Gras* were utterly irresistible. In *La Créole,* subtitled Dreams of the Quadroon Ball, Miss Collins did little more than sprawl on the floor and wiggle her feet in the air, yet I do not mind going on record as saying that it constituted a dance experience which I have rarely seen equaled for pure movement compulsion. The tipsy *Après le Mardi Gras* also represented an unforgettable dance experience. In fact, Miss Collins herself, with her technique, her stylishness, her scope and her magic, was so unforgettable that those of us who saw her performance will probably badger those who did not into going to her next program by way of finding out what unforgettable dance really is. [*New York Herald Tribune*]

234

The Ballet Theatre

April 19, 1949: Happy Return

Ballet Theatre returned to New York Sunday evening and everyone was happy. Here at the Metropolitan Opera House, after a year's absence, was the youthful company which dances with the zest of a basketball team, with the natural vivacity of friends at a party and with the artistry of those who are compelled, by a magnificent repertory, to explore and to discover and to describe a rich range of dance. These perennial Ballet Theatre attributes have undergone but little change in spite of many changes in personnel. There were rough spots at this first performance of the season and some of the regular principals have probably danced closer to perfection in the past, but the best of the ballet companies was back and lacks could be forgiven, at least for the gala opening.

The brightest aspect of the occasion was, I think, the performance of Ballet Theatre's great ballerina, Nora Kaye, in the principal role of Agnes de Mille's *Fall River Legend*. As the tragic heroine in this story suggested by the Lizzie Borden case, Miss Kaye provided a characterization eloquently realized in terms of pure dance, dramatic movement and gesture. In the sustained turns in arabesque, one sensed the reaching out for escape from anguish; in the bent and twisting body, in the nervous grinding of the torso, one knew of the turmoil and the anger which was to lead to drastic action, and in the gestures of terror and of hate, of hopelessness and desperation, one recognized the heralds to the coming madness.

Aside from Miss Kaye's melodramatic, yet sensitive and sympathetic enactment, there were superb performances by Muriel Bentley as the satanic stepmother, by Diana Adams as the sweet and kind mother who had died, by John Kriza as the pastor and by Ruth Ann Koesun and Peter Gladke as the heroine in childhood and the father, respectively.

The performance opened on a traditional note with a presentation of *Swan Lake*. Nana Gollner, beautiful to behold and technically impressive was the Queen of the Swans. Miss Gollner has danced the part with greater warmth and a better sustaining of the dramatic thread on other occasions, but physically her performance, with its swift and accurate turns in multiple form and the wonderfully sustained arabesques, was an exciting one. Igor Youskevitch as the Prince was perfection itself. His support of the ballerina was unaffected and sure and his brief solo variation was accomplished with the stylishness one expects in classic ballet and with the pleasant exuberance of a folk dance.

The corps de ballet in *Swan Lake* behaved, for the most part, as a Ballet Theatre corps is expected to behave. This means, of course, that it had a group spirit and an awareness of choreography as opposed to the all too frequent concern of a corps with a desperate "what comes next?" air. There were off moments, one must admit, but none which was fatal. Wallace Seibert was agreeable as the Prince's Friend and Edward Caton was the most interestingly malevolent sorcerer we have seen in a long time.

Fancy Free, lively and exuberant again, following a period of occasionally pedestrian performances, was excellently danced by John Kriza, Paul Godkin and Eric Braun as the three breezy sailors and by Janet Reed and Muriel Bentley as two of the three girls. Bambi Linn as the third strolling lady was just that, a lady, and there is no place for a lady in *Fancy Free*. Miss Bentley, entering to an enormous burst of applause, was particularly wonderful as a tough tart and Mr. Kriza and Miss Reed danced their sweet and jazzy pas de deux as beautifully as it has ever been done. [*New York Herald Tribune*]

First Reactions to a Great Dance Group, the Sadler's Wells Ballet

October 16, 1949

The production of *The Sleeping Beauty* with which the Sadler's Wells made its American debut at the Metropolitan Opera House is as magical as is its source material. There is kinetic magic in the dancing of Margot Fonteyn, there is the magic of style combined with discipline in the performance of other members of the large company and there is visual magic in Oliver Messel's towering sets and gorgeous costumes and in stage effects which cause protective forests to spring up around a sleeping castle or which permit an evil fairy to race onto the stage in a macabre, rat-drawn carriage.

Although *Sleeping Beauty* is an elderly ballet, it is new to us, for it has never before been presented in its entirety in New York. Within the framework of this aged novelty, the Sadler's Wells introduced us to new aspects of traditional dance. This may seem paradoxical, but it is not. Traditional ballet, rules and regulations to the contrary, is inevitably colored by the characteristics, both racial and personal, of those who dance its measures.

Dance Differences   Where the English artists concern themselves with grandness of manner, our own dancers tend to reflect grandness of size in movement. Musically, where they define beat and phrase, we (perhaps instinctively) convey the phrase's inner rhythms and accent (sometimes merely through the slightest pulsations) off-beats. Finally, with respect to traditional ballet, the

236

English performers devote their attention and their enormous skills to the faultless execution, technically and stylistically, of an enchainement while Americans would invariably impregnate the same classical sequence with dramatic colorings attained through the application of the body's dynamic powers.

These differences between English ballet and American ballet are in approach rather than in quality, and as long as the approach is a valid one, the magic of theater dance may be realized. The Sadler's Wells Ballet, then, enchants in matters of pure dance as well as through aspects of production and the supreme exponent of English ballet as it has been made manifest in *The Sleeping Beauty* is Margot Fonteyn, the company's prima ballerina.

Miss Fonteyn, Ballerina   As Princess Aurora, Miss Fonteyn is completely lovely. Several ardently balletic individuals reproached me for speaking of Miss Fonteyn as merely "lovely" in my review of the opening performance and suggested that "fabulous" would have been amply justified. Somehow, "fabulous" belongs to a flamboyant Aurora, such as Tamara Toumanova used to give us and not to the gracious, girlish and impeccable Aurora of Miss Fonteyn. The English ballerina's dancing of the role is, in my opinion, an unforgettable experience. Not only is the overall performance a miracle of beauty but the dance details are endlessly fascinating and, I insist, lovely. The simplest of movements—a lifting of the foot, the exactitude with which a gesture is placed in a phrase of action, the tilt of the head, a miniature glissade—are as hypnotic as are her precise accomplishment of multiple turns or the light darting (she neither sweeps nor swoops) of her leaps.

Miss Fonteyn's way of dance is a pure distillation of the dance style of other members of the company, of English dance. Her colleagues and her assistants bring to the rest of *The Sleeping Beauty* the same devotion to mannerliness, unhurriedness, correctness of detail and a narrow, delicate, but in the case of this particular ballet acceptable, dynamic range. In whole and in part, the Sadler's Wells production of *The Sleeping Beauty* is something which the dance follower, and even the general theater-goer too, should not miss, for even the basically corny sections, such as the garland dance, and passages of attenuated pantomime are so exactly done that one cannot fail to appreciate the craftsmanship involved. Furthermore, these sections are few and for the rest, the ballet is absorbing by any and all standards of theater dance.

The other ballets—*The Rake's Progress, Symphonic Variations, Facade* and *Hamlet*—which were also presented during the first week of the engagement, have given us opportunity to see examples of contemporary English choreography and the ways in which the English approach to traditional dance may be adapted or expanded to project modern themes of great diversity. A discussion of these and other works in the repertory must wait until a later date, but let it be said here and now that the Sadler's Wells Ballet has, in its first week, convinced most of us that it is one of the great dance companies of our time and that its prima ballerina, Margot Fonteyn, is irresistibly . . . lovely. [*New York Herald Tribune*]

Roland Petit's Carmen (Ballets de Paris)

October 7, 1949: Sex and More Sex

The sex impulse may, with perfectly scholarly propriety, be accepted as one of the fundamental stimuli of the dance art. There are other stimuli, of course, spiritual or cerebral, but les Ballets de Paris, which made its American debut at the Winter Garden last evening, obviously considered the first named stimulus of paramount importance. This, naturally, made for a program which ranged in subject matter from the wistfully romantic and the emotionally charged through material which suggested that the company might be referred to as "les Ballets de Minsky" to a ballet of animal passion, of frenzied and tawdry love.

The major production of the evening was Roland Petit's much heralded dance version of *Carmen* and it turned out to be pretty terrific stuff. Mr. Petit, who is director and principal dancer for the organization as well as the chief choreographer, has not concerned himself with the non-passionate parts of the operatic tale. He has, indeed, dispensed with much and added something, notably a bedroom scene which is by all standards the high point of the ballet, choreographically, artistically, architecturally and, need one add, physically. In this sense, the normally elegant and refined movements of the traditional ballet are used with sardonic brilliance to project a situation dealing with primitive, even feral lust.

The whole of this balletic *Carmen* is motivated by the element of physical desire. This condition is manifested not only in the dances of Carmen and Don José but in the supporting actions of a supercharged ensemble which surrounds the couple with pounding rhythms, mass lust and lustiness.

Obviously, if the ballet were to be a success, the title role had to be entrusted to a performer equipped with sturdy dance technique, dramatic skill and vivid personality. The company has such a star in Renée Jeanmaire. Her Carmen is a remarkable, if not very profound, characterization. Her facial expression is, for the most part, limited to a sexy snarl but her movements are rich in dynamic color and the shifts of her emotional interests, the degrees of intensity with which she meets varying incidents are clearly revealed in her actions.

238

Mr. Petit makes an impressive Don José. There is more than a touch of hamming in his realization of the part, particularly at those moments when he attempts to draw Don José as a suffering hero, but he accomplishes the love scenes in forthright manner, permitting expressional movement rather than stock attitude to convey his meanings. The members of the corps, cast as bandits, cigarette girls and such, were all excellent, the settings (five of them) and costumes by Antoni Clavé were nothing short of inspired, and Jean Gitton led the orchestra in spirited fashion.

The program's other, and lesser, offerings were Mr. Petit's *Le Rendez-vous* and *L'Oeuf à la Coque* and William Dollar's pas de deux, *Le Combat.* Of these, *L'Oeuf à la Coque,* a ballet which could be transplanted with no trouble at all into a musical revue, was the most entertaining. Showing hell as a wild kitchen and the cooking ingredients as pretty girls decked out as chicks, it combined bits of ballet and general horseplay with acrobatics and burlesque-type struts. It was all great fun and Colette Marchand was entrancing as the cook's most delectable ingredient. Miss Marchand also danced very nicely, as did her partner, Milorad Miskovitch, in *Le Combat,* but the work, aside from some isolated passages of choreographic interest, is pretentious in style and cursed with one of the longest (or so it seemed) death scenes in all ballet.

Last night's audience was large and enthusiastic and suggested through its responsiveness that the Messrs. Shubert who, in association with Arthur Lesser, brought the company to America, would have every reason to antici-pate a pleasant run for les Ballets de Paris and *Carmen* at the Winter Garden. [*New York Herald Tribune*]

New York City Dance Theater

December 15, 1949: Dance Milestone

A major milestone in the progress of American contemporary dance was reached last evening at the City Center when several of the leading artists and groups of modern dance joined forces to create the New York City Dance Theater. Here, at last, one saw the first attempt in more than a decade (aside from special festival occasions) to assemble the incredibly rich but scattered repertory of American dance into a single repertory and to present a program featuring not one but several stars. America's indigenous theater dance was, in this way, making a bid to rival the ballet, not in techniques nor in styles, but in theatrical magnitude.

239

If the New York City Dance Theater's first performance may be viewed as an honest omen, it is safe to say that the project is destined for success and that contemporary dance, by uniting its choreographic and performing talents, will surely win popular support—all in good time, of course—comparable to that accorded the ballet. Certainly the initial bill outlined in brilliant fashion the tremendous scope of modern dance and filled in that outline with innumerable dance details of absorbing interest.

Sophie Maslow's *Folksay,* already a classic in the field of contemporary dance, was an ideal choice for an opening work. It is as simple, as sweet and as emotionally penetrating as the Carl Sandburg lines (from "The People, Yes") which provide its motivations. It has sweep and tenderness, virtuosity and poetry as it tells of the fun, the foibles, the romancing and the dreams of everyday folk. It was beautifully danced on this occasion by Miss Maslow, William Bales and the New Dance Group with Tony Kraber and Pete Seeger as the loquacious accompanists.

If modern dance had a system of ranking its performers, Valerie Bettis would surely wear the insignia of a prima ballerina. For the new company's inaugural program, Miss Bettis danced her great solo, *The Desperate Heart* and how magnificently she danced it! Not only were the implications of the title, the suggestions aroused by the accompanying poem reflected in the dynamic shadings of her dancing but the sheer perfection of muscular command manifest in every movement made her performance a memorable one.

The highlight of the evening was a revival of Doris Humphrey's masterpiece of other years, *Shakers.* It is, as many will recall, an exciting work of cumulative intensity, a theater piece which derives its stimulus and theme from the ecstatic dance of a sect which forced sin from the body through shaking motions. It is in every way a glowing work. The group patterns are richly inventive, the dynamic gamut masterfully traversed, the purposefulness of the action clearly defined. Miss Humphrey, who used to dance the principal role of the Eldress, was replaced by the lovely Letitia Ide and although no one could hope to erase the memory of Miss Humphrey in the part, Miss Ide accomplished her assignment with beauty of movement and strength of bearing. One missed too the rather haunting accordian accompaniment formerly employed, but the new hymn-like chorus provided the work with stirring, appropriate support.

Next came José Limón's *La Malinche,* with Mr. Limón, Pauline Koner and Lucas Hoving in the three roles of this Mexican legend. It is a superb work which tells, through the medium of a village festival or a folk celebration, the story of the Aztec girl who betrayed her countrymen to the conqueror and found peace only when, as a repentant spirit, she returned to help her Indian brothers fight for liberation. The three artists were in top form and the orchestra and chorus, conducted by Simon Sadoff, presented the Norman Lloyd score faultlessly.

The evening closed, as it should, on a gay note with Charles Weidman (the greatest humorist in modern dance) and his company in *Fables for Our Time,* a suite inspired by the writings of James Thurber. It was, as always, a hilarious experience. Mr. Weidman had the principal roles in the four fables of the suite and Jack Ferris was the ideal narrator, sardonic and calm while all sorts of inanities occurred around and about him. [*New York Herald Tribune*]

Invention by Humphrey and Limón's The Moor's Pavane

December 16, 1949

The first male dancer of our era, directed by America's most distinguished choreographer, presented a memorable evening of dance last night at the City Center on the second program in the New York City Dance Theater's current repertory season. José Limón was, of course, the dancer and his company's artistic director was Doris Humphrey. I am not at all sure that there is such a thing as dance perfection, but if there is, Mr. Limón achieved it last evening. He and Miss Humphrey and the company achieved it in terms of pure dance action, in terms of choreography, in terms of compelling performance, in terms of great direction.

To begin with, Mr. Limón has a magnificent body. If this, at first, seems like a rather superficial remark, let us remember that the instrument of dance expression is the body. Mr. Limón also has a commanding presence. The perfection of the body instrument, this commanding presence together with the motor disciplines and sensitivities essential to the dancer make it apparent that the dance which Mr. Limón creates is of matchless caliber. Under Miss Humphrey's direction, the others of the company—Pauline Koner (first soloist), Letitia Ide, Betty Jones, Ruth Currier and Lucas Hoving—extend the artistry of the star into an artistry of group proportions. With such dancing and with choreography of comparable excellence, by Miss Humphrey and Mr. Limón, it is small wonder that this little organization achieves that dance perfection I have mentioned.

The program, composed of four works, featured the first Broadway showings of two. These were Miss Humphrey's incredibly beautiful *Invention,* with music by Norman Lloyd, and Mr. Limón's *The Moor's Pavane,* to music of Purcell arranged by Simon Sadoff.

Invention is pure dance. That is, there is no dramatic theme, no specific characterization. There are emotional overtones and human colors as there must be in any dance concerned with even the most abstract relationships of human bodies, but the work is mainly what its title suggests, invention. Miss Humphrey's dance inventiveness carries her through theme and variations in movement pattern, through contrasts and parallelisms in action and through a myriad of absorbing dance details predicated upon differences in leaps and jumps and turns, variations in tempo and rhythm, shifts in direction and in spatial designs, surges and ebbs in dynamic intensities and upon the numberless potentialities of human motion and dance form.

The Moor's Pavane, on the other hand, has plot, characters and turbulent emotions to contrast it with pure dance. It is, however, completely formal in conception and therein lies its tremendous dramatic force. The entire work, or all but transitional passages of it, is governed by pre-classic dance forms, colored by contemporary theatrical movement and distorted at times, but still clearly related to the pavane and other courtly forms. Within this formal and elegant structure exists the drama involving Othello, his wife, his evil friend and the friend's emotionally tortured wife.

Insinuation, the planting of lies, the birth of doubt, the creation of false evidence, the denunciation, the murder and the despair are threaded into this fabric of formal dance. The result is a theater piece of terrific impact, for passions are implied and violence simmers below the surface, breaking through only at inevitable, uncontrollable moments. There is no wallowing in melodrama here, although the plot is basically melodramatic, rather is there an adventure into great drama where the unexpected occurs and where the expected is treated with originality and inexorable logic.

As I have suggested, Mr. Limón and his colleagues danced all of their assignments brilliantly. The star, Miss Koner, Miss Jones and Mr. Hoving were superb in *The Moor's Pavane* and Mr. Limón, Miss Jones and Miss Currier danced *Invention* as it deserved to be danced. *Lament for Ignacio Sanchez Mejias,* with Mr. Limón, Letitia Ide and Ellen Love, was accorded a luminous presentation and the evening closed with Mr. Limón and Miss Koner in the hilarious and biting *Story of Mankind.* The fine little orchestra was led by Mr. Sadoff and Jean Rosenthal worked miracles with the lighting. [*New York Herald Tribune*]

242

With Nora Kaye in a lecture-demonstration at New York's 92nd Street YM-YWHA, 1950. Photo: Saul Goodman.

With Ruth St. Denis, Doris Humphrey, Charles Weidman, and John Martin at Capezio Dance Awards honoring "Miss Ruth," 1954. Photo: Louis Melançon.

A party at the apartment of Arthur Todd, critic, historian, collector. Left to right, Merce Cunningham, Nik Krevitsky, Leon Danielian, Helen Dzhermolinska, Walter Terry, and John Butler, 1950. Photo: Arthur Todd.

Walter Terry arranged for TV star, Arlene Francis (center), hostess of the *Today* show, to present a kinescope of an interview and performance by Ruth St. Denis to Genevieve Oswald (left), curator of the Dance Collection, New York Public Library, 1954.

With Maria Tallchief in a lecture-demonstration at New York's 92nd Street YM-YWHA 1956. Photo: Ted Tessler.

With Melissa Hayden (left) and Maria Tallchief (right) at a lecture-demonstration on "The Art of the Ballerina" at New York's 92nd Street YM-YWHA, 1956. Photo: Saul Goodman.

With Fredbjørn Bjørnsson and Inge Sand of the Royal Danish Ballet. Rehearsing for a lecture-demonstration, New York City, 1956. Photo: Radford Bascome.

Junior soloists, Royal Danish Ballet. Seated: Walter Terry, Stanley Williams (Dance Instructor), 1958. Photo: McWilliams.

Diana Adams rehearsed by George Balanchine as Walter Terry looks on, 1957.
Photo: CBS.

Emily Coleman (dance-music critic, *Newsweek*), Ted Shawn, Walter Terry, Martha Hill at Capezio Dance Awards honoring Shawn, 1957. Photo: Joe Engels.

With Greer Garson, Alexandra Danilova, Anatole Chujoy at the Capezio Dance Awards honoring Danilova, 1958. Photo: Jack Mitchell.

With Lucia Chase at the publishing party for Walter Terry's *Ballet: A New Guide to the Liveliest Art.* Edward Villella, right, 1959. Photo: Jack Mitchell.

With Ted Shawn at Jacob's Pillow, 1959.
Photo: John Lindquist.

Nina Popova, Nicholas Magallanes, Walter
Terry. At a party given by Ballet Theatre's
Charles Payne, 1958.

With Jerome Robbins, 1958. Photo: Saul
Goodman.

A dance critic lifts Alexandra Danilova as Thomas Andrew (left) and Alicia Markova, Jacques d'Amboise look on. Publishing party for *Ballet: A New Guide to the Liveliest Art,* 1959. Photo: Jack Mitchell.

1950

Dancing the Human Condition

*Jerome Robbins creates Age of Anxiety for New York City Ballet •
Frederick Ashton's Illuminations for NYCB • Ballet Theatre presents
Herbert Ross's Caprichos • Uday Shankar and Hindu ballet • Limón's
The Exiles premiered at Connecticut College's American Dance Festival •
Letitia Ide superb in Doris Humphrey's Day on Earth*

Triumphant Quartet

February 27, 1950

That potent triumvirate which made ballet history close unto a decade ago
with a rollicking theater piece called *Fancy Free* has done it again. This time,
however, Jerome Robbins, choreographer, Leonard Bernstein, composer, and
Oliver Smith, scenic artist, must share their triumph with the poet, W. H.
Auden, whose Pulitzer Prize-winning work, *Age of Anxiety,* constituted the
base of that ballet by the same name which was given its world premiere last
evening at the City Center by the New York City Ballet Company.

    Age of Anxiety is not, of course, rollicking. It deals with—and I quote
from the Auden poem—"Sad hunters of Perhaps" and it takes them on
"peregrinations of lies and loves," "into dream wishes, vert and volant" as "the
approximate man" seeks for his faith in an *Age of Anxiety.* There is no obscurity in Mr. Robbins's treatment of a complex theme. Probing, yes; fantasy,
yes; questioning, yes, but of obscurity of idea there is no hint.

    Through his choreography Mr. Robbins outlines the life and thought
patterns of his four protagonists, three men and a girl. They are not as distinct individuals as are their counterparts in the poem, but that is all to the
good here, for they are no longer characters in literature but dancers instigating
patterns of action which will ultimately extend beyond themselves and into
the actions of a group. He has, however, followed the sectional developments

of the poem and of the Bernstein score and has collaborated, in the truest sense of that word, with his associates.

Collaboration is manifest not only with respect to music and choreography—where dynamic, thematic and stylistic aspects are matched—but also with respect to dance and poetry. The alliterative nature of the poem finds its counterpart in Mr. Robbins's skillfull use of repeated gesture and the descriptive backgrounds of the poem, the dreams of individuals are, in the ballet, the province of the dance group.

If I have, thus far, given the impression that *Age of Anxiety* is interesting mainly because of its excellence in collaborative craftmanship, it is because such craftsmanship is rare and to be honored. But *Age of Anxiety* is more than a successful etude. It is an enormously compelling work of art. I cannot offer a synopsis, for it is not a story; it is an experience. The four who guide its course are the frightened souls of an anguished era and we share in their experiences, both real and imagined, as they find solace in passing proximity, as they recall and reject various ages of a lifetime, as they travel into dreams which melt into nightmares or nothingness, as they cry for a father-brother-dictator-superstition image to protect them, as they throw themselves into joyless revel and as they finally find faith, or perhaps it is merely the promise of a faith to come, in their own frail beings. It is not, then a story. It is an emotional experience communicated through dance, through Mr. Robbins's perceptive and eloquent dance.

For those who refuse to be burdened with an age of anxiety, either their own or someone else's, let me add that the choreographer has created dance designs of sufficient physical beauty, power and imaginativeness to rouse those who would ignore the theme. Mr. Robbins is a man of the theater and profundity of idea is not going to cause him to neglect the surface polish of dance.

The record, one supposes, requires it to be said that there are a few barren moments, an awkward or unclear dance fragment or two in *Age of Anxiety,* but I will cease quibbling here and now, for minor flaws are inevitable in first performances. The cast, headed by Mr. Robbins, Tanaquil LeClercq, Francisco Moncion and Todd Bolender, was superb. Mr. Bernstein's score, his "Symphony No. 2," is an ideal one for dance. Rhythmically, structurally, dynamically and, with respect to tonal pulsations essential to a union of dance and music, it is tremendously successful as an integral part of this collaborative effort. Oliver Smith's cold and distant designs are admirably suited to the work and Jean Rosenthal's lighting may be regarded as an invaluable aspect of the decor. A large and distinguished audience received the new work with cheers and dozens of curtain calls rewarded the artists for their efforts. [*New York Herald Tribune*]

244

Double Gala

March 3, 1950

It was a gala occasion last evening at the City Center and on several counts. From the dance viewpoint, the major item of interest was the world premiere of *Illuminations,* a work especially staged for the New York City Ballet Company by one of England's foremost choreographers, Frederick Ashton, of the Sadler's Wells Ballet. The performance also served to inaugurate "International Theater Month," sponsored by the American National Theater and Academy, and Rosamund Gilder, an ANTA official and chairman of the Panel on Dramatic Arts of the United States National Commission for UNESCO, was present to speak briefly on the aims of this theater month.

The audience for this double gala was a distinguished one. United Nations officials were present, members of ANTA and UNESCO were on hand for the occasion and the British guests were headed by Sir Oliver Franks, British Ambassador to the United States. The American and British national anthems were played by Leon Barzin and his orchestra at the start of the evening's festivities.

And now to Mr. Ashton's new ballet, inspired by the life story and poetry of the Frenchman, Arthur Rimbaud, and set to music by Benjamin Britten for string orchestra and voice. Scenery and costumes were designed by Cecil Beaton. The English choreographer has chosen to treat his theme in terms of (and I use his own words) "danced pictures or charades." It follows, then, that the ballet has little opportunity for dramatic development, for cumulative choreographic effect. It must inevitably find its theatrical unity in the figure of the poet who participates in or beholds the successive charades and in the mood of fantasy which pervades the work as a whole.

In the main, Mr. Ashton has been successful in providing his "danced pictures" with unity through the actions given to his principal figure and through his sustaining of the element of fantasy. It is a rather fragile unity, to be sure, but it is there and revisions will, no doubt, strengthen it. Viewed in its parts, rather than as a balletic entity, *Illuminations* is frequently enchanting, occasionally exciting and constantly interesting. The English choreographer has used his American dancers quite wonderfully—even shrewdly— by designing for them movements which make use of the American dance performer's physical strength, dramatic flair and intense dynamism. This, perhaps, has led him into some awkward choreographic contrivings and unnecessary acrobatics, but aside from a few passages in this vein, his designs are fresh, structurally admirable and, in keeping with the ballet's title, "illumined."

In *Illuminations* we are shown a poet, a youthful rebel who seeks to experience life quickly, violently, avidly. The scenes suggest, sometimes specifically and again elusively, a few of those experiences of sacred and profane love, dreamy solitude, pagan adventure, beauty, ugliness, falsity. As in the poems from which the ballet draws its inspiration, fragments of adventure, glimpses, hints are given rather than episodes and so *Illuminations* emerges as a series of fragments, some eloquent, others teasingly misty and a few disappointing.

Nicholas Magallanes in the principal part of *Illuminations* was in every way perfect. His characterization, subtly yet richly drawn, was notable for its emotional hues, for beauty and strength of style and motion. His poet was sensitive but not sappy, passionate but not melodramatic, youthful but not juvenile. It is a difficult role and Mr. Magallanes deserves cheers for realizing its potentialities so completely on the occasion of his first appearance in the part.

Melissa Hayden also gave a tremendous performance in *Illuminations* as the figure of Profane Love. It was wild, pagan and free in character and Miss Hayden danced it for all it was worth. Tanaquil LeClercq in the paler role of Sacred Love and elsewhere in the ballet danced beautifully as did the other members of the large cast. Mr. Barzin led the orchestra and William Hess was the tenor soloist. There were many curtain calls and many bravos for the new work, for its dancers and for Mr. Ashton. [*New York Herald Tribune*]

Distinguished Addition

April 27, 1950

A terrifying theater piece, touched with macabre beauty and trenchant irony, was given for the first time by Ballet Theatre last evening at the Center Theater. It is called *Caprichos,* for the choreographer, Herbert Ross, has based his ballet upon Goya's commentaries to his own Caprichos etchings and has, furthermore, captured the artist's flavor and composition in his dance designs.

Mr. Ross, whose work was first produced by the Choreographers' Workshop, has changed it slightly—or so it seemed to me—in order to make full use of the heightened gifts of Ballet Theatre's artists. Alterations have in no way lessened its basic simplicity of plan, but they have served, rather, to sharpen, to accent its dramatic points. In its Ballet Theatre version, *Caprichos* is a distinguished and distinctive addition to a repertory already notable for its dance range.

Caprichos is in four episodes, unrelated thematically, but closely knit through mood, style and the continuing presence, as vulture-like spectators, of

246

the two girls who dance the opening episode. In the initial scene, the two "have seats enough and nothing to do with them better than carry them on their heads." This they do in a series of movements of lush slothfulness, of aimless play as they indicate the purposelessness of both energy and repose.

The second episode—"No one ever escapes who wants to be caught"— brought forth Nana Gollner as the woman whose inviting dance and provocative behavior instigated the chase by two men (Eric Braun and Peter Gladke) and led, inevitably, to a wild and disordered fleeing, capture and conquest, with the two do-nothing girls as delighted onlookers to a scene of ravishment.

The third scene, in many ways the best of the four, is an incredibly difficult and theatrically hypnotic adagio. It is danced by John Kriza into whose arms falls an inert female form and the entire episode deals with his attempts, through a series of fantastic movements, to lift her, to coax her, to shake her, to frighten her, to seduce her into life. Mr. Kriza performs this difficult part magnificently and Ruth Ann Koesun, as the girl, gives a performance (lifeless though the figure seems) which is little short of miraculous. The theme here, by the way, is "If he were more gallant and less of a bore she would come to life again."

The final scene, with Mary Burr as the principal figure, is a ritual of torture. The woman is burned at the stake while priests toss their branches, one by one, to replenish a fire which seems to lick her feet and legs, causing limbs and body to withdraw and contract in agony while the presence of dignity remains to death.

Caprichos is, as one can see, not a diverting piece but it is an absorbing one. There is bitter humor, as there should be, in the presence of caricature and there is emotional power behind the caricature. Ballet Theatre has staged it brilliantly from the inspired dancing of the principals through the perfect costuming by Helene Pons to the sensitive, revealing lighting of Peggy Clark. The score, Contrasts for Piano, Clarinet and Violin, by Bela Bartok was played, and beautifully, by Broadus Earle (violin), Joseph Levine (piano) and David Weber (clarinet). [*New York Herald Tribune*]

Shankar, Dancing Envoy, Mirrors the Heritage of India in Dance

June 1, 1950

Our immeasurably rich dance season has already provided us with stunning and artistically impressive examples of imported and native ballet, American contemporary dance and ethnologic forms and further ballet, modern and ethnic dance activities are to be expected during the remainder of the winter and the spring. At the moment, ethnologic dance is of prime importance for its major representative in the Indian wing is the great Uday Shankar, currently making his first American appearances in more than a decade with his Hindu Ballet.

The initial Shankar program, presented last Tuesday at the Forty-eighth Street Theater, was an exemplary one. It clearly established for the onlooker the Oriental approach to dance and its component parts made manifest the enormous scope of Indian dance in particular. Here, in this way of dance which shuns extroversion, we were invited to share in those serenities, both spiritual and muscular, which characterize much of Hindu dance and to experience conflict, passion and humor through the implicative (rather than the explicit) movements of the Indian dancer's art. For those unaccustomed to a theater form designed for illumination as opposed to simple diversion or even stimulation, Mr. Shankar's program provided sufficient in the way of surface beauty and entrancing exoticism to satisfy, I believe, all but the most determined proponents of the crash-bang-zowie school of entertainment.

The distinguished dancer's offerings for the first week of the run included, among other items, ancient dances of invocation to deity, folk episodes, pure dance expressions and dance dramas with roots in mythology but with pointed purpose for the contemporary scene. Through these examples of Indian dance one became aware not only of heritages in techniques, styles and themes of Hindu dance but also of the continuing force which these heritages exert upon the culture of a modern nation.

Eternal Melody, a new work, provides a good example of the ageless, universal, non-eral approach of the Indian to his dance. It is based upon a Sanskrit legend and it tells of Brahma's creative achievements, among them man and woman, and of the strangely beautiful and frightening (to say nothing of ironic) process by which woman was devised. The simple tale reports that woman—composed of the roundness of the moon, the velvet of the flower, the cruelty of the tiger, the warmth of fire and the chill of snow, among many other things—enchanted her husband and also drove him to distraction. She goes home to Brahma (since being the first woman she cannot go home to mother) only to return to the man and the succeeding generations of men who find that life with her is trying but that life without her is impossible.

Not only *Eternal Melody* but also a pastoral piece concerning the god Krishna and his weary flirtation with some dairymaids, a mighty epic of Shiva the divine dancer and other works of the program were, of course, presented through dance terms alien to the art experiences of many Americans. Perhaps few among those present on opening night knew the meanings of the hand gestures and perhaps the leisureliness of the action, the strangeness of the music, the delicate intricacies of rhythmic patterns confused the average on-looker. But I am inclined to think otherwise, for Shankar presents his traditional dance in such a way that its general meanings, its dramatic values and its pure dance beauties—if not its specific details—are projected with surprising clarity.

Mr. Shankar, in preparing the ancient dance of his people for the contemporary theater, has not compromised with the major precepts of tradition. No new, no easier movements are incorporated into his works and no themes are barred because of profundity or because of their archaic nature. He has, rather, simply applied modern theatrical principles to his staging of Hindu dance. Needless, or at least non-essential, repetitions of gestural or rhythmic passages have been eliminated; gesture sequences composed of finger motions of such similarity that only a tutored eye could detect differences, have been rephrased (still with authentic and appropriate gestures) to give visual variety to the pattern and variation in dynamics, a necessary attribute of contemporary theater, has been given greater definition.

That the traditional dance of India, rooted in four schools—bharat natyam, kathakali, kathak and manipuri—and constantly fed by the folk expressions of many regions is equipped to supply the theaters of the world with an endless repertory of dance masterpieces is immediately apparent. Shankar, however, envisions still broader uses for his nation's dance. In his recent film, *Kalpana,* he presented two ballets, *Labor and Machinery* and *Rhythm of Life,* both realized in terms of traditional dance movement with no freely devised actions permitted to infiltrate. In future tours of America, these two contemporary works will be seen and as the years pass, this great dancer and art leader plans to include in his repertory other ballets on social and political themes, each employing exclusively the techniques of Hindu dance tradition. The *Ramayana* will not be forgotten, nor the exploits and adventures of gods and ancient heroes, but contemporary India will use its ancient dance tongue to speak of its immediate present as well as of its enduring heritage. [*New York Herald Tribune*]

José Limón's The Exiles

August 13, 1950

New London, Conn., Aug. 11. The premiere of a new work by José Limón was the major item of interest on this evening's program of the American Dance Festival series. This new dance creation, employing Arnold Schoenberg's

Second Chapter Symphony, arranged for two pianos by the composer, is a duet for Mr. Limón and Letitia Ide and one would be almost tempted to say that the mere presence of these two fine artists would be sufficient to assure the success of any composition. This, however, is not quite the case with *The Exiles.*

The theme of *The Exiles* is, of course, indicated by the title. Mr. Limón has not taken a specific incident nor an actual period. Rather has he left it up to the beholder to apply his own specifications to an abstraction. Perhaps one may see in it the expulsion from the Garden of Eden or, in a more contemporary vein, the displacement of a man and his wife from home and land.

The dramatic substance of the work, its emotional patterns find their reflection in movements designed to communicate the lostness of those who seek solace in remembrance, of those who continue the search for a new Eden. At times, Mr. Limón has been successful in communicating these aspects of exile. There is much, in the initial passages, which is stirring and touching and portions of that episode which deal with the desperate need of the two for constant physical proximity are rich in pathos. Passages in the section concerned with reverie, with recollections of what may have been a paradise, are also affecting.

For each freely flowing phrase, honest and forthright in the conveying of the dance plan, there seemed to be one which was labored, forced, even contrived. There were also times when the Schoenberg music tended to overpower the dancers but instead of submitting to its passing dominance, they appeared to battle it for supremacy. Admittedly, not all of the disappointing properties of *The Exiles* should be blamed upon the choreography. Often awkward passages smooth out as the performers become more familiar with the work itself and coloring, dramatic and dynamic, emerges with frequent performing. I would guess, however, that choreographic revisions will be as necessary to the eventual success of *The Exiles* as will be the need for further opportunities to dance it.

Mr. Limón and Miss Ide performed their new piece with strength, assurance and considerable beauty and, as I have suggested, once they have mastered its drama as well as its technical surfaces, they will surely have a theater composition more nearly worthy of their enormous talents. The music was played, and excellently, at this performance by Simon Sadoff and Russell Sherman. [*New York Herald Tribune*]

Letitia Ide, a Dancing Woman,
and Her Role in Day on Earth

August 20, 1950

Girl dancers, spinster dancers and just plain female dancers abound in the
world of American dance. A woman dancer is rare, for she glows rather than
shines, warms rather than excites and mirrors maturity of being and not simply
maturity of intellect or of physical skill or the presence of Miss Ide. She is
even of emotional experience. These are delicate and, perhaps, intangible qualities and I am not certain that I have described them, or will be able to do so,
clearly. It would be wiser, then, to name a specific dancer in this category
and to tell about her dancing of a specific role. The dancer is Letitia Ide; the
role is that of the Woman in Doris Humphrey's *Day on Earth*.

Miss Ide is not a virtuoso and there is nothing remarkable, in the academic sense, about her dancing. I am told that she is honestly surprised by
the hearty delight with which the public greets her performances, by the eagerness of choreographers to have her dance in new works and by the enthusiasm
of fellow dancers, who are rarely enthusiastic about any dancing other than
their own. Perhaps she wonders why any one cares to watch the dancing of a
young matron, albeit a very beautiful one, with two children (the older is
twelve) when slimmer and more athletic girl dancers are to be seen or mature
female dancers of international renown to be found. The answer is simply
that this woman-matron-mother supplies a dance quality which is absent, or
partially so, in the dancing of others of her performing sisters.

Miss Humphrey's *Day on Earth,* a major creation in the repertory of
José Limón and his company, could not possibly communicate all of its emotional and, yes, even pictorial values without not the central figure—the central figure is the Man—but she is essential to the pattern and to the purpose of
Day on Earth.

Most dance followers are familiar with *Day on Earth* and they will recall
that its day-span is actually a distillation of a life-span and that the protagonists (there are no seen antagonists) are Man, Young Girl, Woman, Child. The
Man, danced by José Limón, traverses this span which encompasses such
activities and experiences as toil and play, youthful dalliance and adult love,
fatherhood and family life with its joys and tragedies, death and the promise
of rebirth.

To the part of Woman, Miss Ide brings her unique dance womanliness.
Her slower, more expansive and tenderer movements provide perfect contrast
to the impulsive, coltish actions of the Young Girl. In the very modesty of
her bearing, one senses a commanding presence, commanding because of its
emotional dependability. There is hurry only when hurry is needed by the

demands of husband and child and there is lovely eloquence in those strong yet caressive gestures and motions directed toward or involving the cherished ones. In passages suggesting a too-soon departure, the Woman indicates a fearful unwillingness to leave through hovering, hurrying movements which might suggest that she is attempting to rush counter to the moving treadmill of time.

Miss Ide's dance characterization is, I think, the most impressive in a foursome of impressive performances. At least this was so during a recent presentation of *Day on Earth* on the American Dance Festival at New London, Conn. The reason for this, as I have tried to indicate, is to be found in the very rarity of her dance approach. In other dance works she has, quite naturally, very different roles; one in particular, that of the figure of Destiny in *Lament for Ignacio Sanchez Mejias,* requires her to be implacable, remote, cold. Yet Miss Ide is always a woman dancer—in figure, in beauty of face, in action and in the communicating of emotional values—and if she is not a star, she is, nevertheless, one of the most important and valuable dancers of our day. [*New York Herald Tribune*]

1951

La Mort, L'Amour, and a Li'l Cakewalk

The impact of Jean Babilée in Le Jeune Homme et La Mort and L'Amour et son Amour at Ballet Theatre • NYCB has two hits in Ruthanna Boris' Cakewalk and the Balanchine-Robbins Tyl Ulenspiegel

Violence, Brilliance in Ballet:
Mr. Babilée as Le Jeune Homme

April 15, 1951

He sprawls across the vermillion coverlet on a narrow bed. A raised foot presses against the wall. The body is motionless. Yet dance, great dance is implicit in the highly charged inaction of this figure as a young man in a Paris garret awaits the coming of the love which is to be his death.

It was this very scene which introduced Jean Babilée to American audiences last Monday at the Metropolitan Opera House. Could it have been pictorial impact, created by the somber setting and the dancer's pose, which made one feel that the celebrated French artist had triumphed before he had commenced to move? Or could it have been, as I have suggested, the dynamic impact of one who could project, even through repose, the promise of violent movement? The latter, I think, is the likely explanation.

Melodrama for Two The work selected by Ballet Theatre as a vehicle for the local debuts of Mr. Babilée and his wife, Nathalie Philippart, was *Le Jeune Homme et la Mort,* a melodramatic duet in which the two had won renown abroad. Violence and passion, in situation and in physical incident, swell as the ballet progresses. The waiting boy moves. He looks at his watch. Restlessness gives birth to sharp, brusque gesture. Angry impatience drives the body into fretful spins, into tensions of torment.

With the entrance of the girl, the young man, unknowingly, faces death.

253

The spurning of his pleas and advances is harsh and cruel. A kick, a shove, a contemptuous glance merely drive him to abject pleading as he crawls trembling across the floor or leaps to a table top to press an embrace upon his love, perched like a fierce queen upon the rude furniture.

The violence increases further as the passionate battle continues. The boy threatens suicide and the girl, with malicious co-operation, fixes the noose and departs. Chairs are hurled and a tortured mind tortures the body, directing it to crash despairing to the floor, to thrust harshly into the air, to race in hopeless circles, to hang itself. Then, shafts of light center upon the figure dangling by his neck. The apparition of death enters. The mask is removed, revealing the girl who had been loved in life, and is placed upon the head of the dead youth. The walls disappear and the woman, love and death combined, leads the boy to an unnamed heaven or hell across the rooftops of Paris.

Spectacular Dancer   This is the ballet which stars a phenomenal dance artist, which provides theatrical expression for an intense personality and a commanding virtuoso. As this is being written, Mr. Babilée has appeared only in *Le Jeune Homme et la Mort* but this dance characterization alone is sufficient to establish him as a superb and uniquely endowed artist and for America, the dance sensation of the season. Miss Philippart also is deserving of resounding applause, for she too performs with fire and force a role which, though subordinate to that of the young man, is dramatically and technically demanding. Together, the two make *Le Jeune Homme et la Mort* a tremendous theatrical experience.

The ballet itself, by Jean Cocteau in collaboration with Roland Petit, is a stunning theater piece. Perhaps it is not strictly a ballet in the formal or technical sense but it is theater dance of a potent kind. Ballet actions, both pure and adulterated (by impulsive movement), are combined with gesture, acting and a kind of apache-like genre of violent motion. The use of music of Bach (Passacaglia in C Minor, orchestrated by Respighi) as accompaniment to brash melodrama may be startling but its nobly flowing beauties provide, I believe, a wonderfully satiric counterpoint to the frenzied patterns of this choreography.

The comments of the music, the fine setting by Oliver Smith, the dance designs of Mr. Petit all unite in giving theatrical substance and dimension to Mr. Cocteau's melodramatic plan. And the plan itself affords Jean Babilée an opportunity to display his uncommon gifts as dancer, as actor and as a stage personality of glowing and glowering power. [*New York Herald Tribune*]

A ballet of delicate beauty and fleeting fantasy, *L'Amour et Son Amour* was given its American premiere last evening by Ballet Theatre at the Metropolitan Opera House. The choreographer and star was Jean Babilée, the French artist who has been appearing with phenomenal success in another French importation, *Le Jeune Homme et la Mort*. The new work is totally different. It is not as dramatic, not as explicit in its projection of emotion as is *Le Jeune Homme* but for those willing to pursue its elusive patterns of loveliness, it is equally rewarding.

Mr. Babilée's creation, his first to be seen in America, does not pretend to a representational telling of the story of Cupid and Psyche. It is a poem metered by the designs of moving bodies, it is the echo of a song in space. It is as distant from the myth as that, yet it captures the mystery, if not the details, of the myth.

Psyche is seen first with two men, two figures who suggest in their liquid movements the flow of water, the gentle insistence of some natural pressure. The girls, as zephyrs, carry the insistence further and Psyche is borne heavenward. Here, set off by a heavenly panorama of deep blue sky and shining stars, is Cupid, ready to receive His Love, to dance with her, to guide her steps toward a union of a sky figure with one of the earth.

"Love has no explanation—do not seek a meaning in love's gestures," writes Jean Cocteau, the man who designed the superb settings and costumes for this ballet. No more can the beholder seek to explain each gesture, each pattern of action in *L'Amour et Son Amour*. The gestures—and they are hauntingly beautiful in this work—hint, but they do not expound, just as the larger actions speak as a dream rather than as an essay.

Mr. Babilée is the winged Cupid in his own ballet and he dances his part with grandeur and yet, in the passages with His Love, with tenderness. Nathalie Philippart as his Love is splendid in a demanding role and the ladies of the corps are fine as the urging zephyrs. William Burdick and, particularly, Ralph McWilliams were effective as the initial escorts. The music—drawn from Cesar Franck's "Psyche" Suite—has been used with imagination and taste by the choreographer. *L'Amour et Son Amour,* in spite of its choreographic beauties both for group and soloists, will quite probably not win the success achieved by Roland Petits' *Le Jeune Homme,* for it is remote, distant, far from reality. The journey, however, is very worth the effort expended. [*New York Herald Tribune*]

Cakewalk, an Ebullient Example
of Dance Americana by Miss Boris

June 17, 1951

Ruthanna Boris's first ballet for the New York City Ballet Company strutted into the City Center last week to give the repertory a new hit production. And *Cakewalk* is very much of a hit, for who could resist the flourishes and pleasantries of the grinning Interlocutor; the facile prancing of the End Men; numbers dealing with a pretty Wallflower, Venus and the Three Graces, a Wild Pony and Hortense, Queen of the Swamp Lilies; hoofing, comic pantomime and a rousing cakewalk?

Although balleticized variations on the handful of authentic cakewalk steps provide the movement motif for this work, the ballet itself actually encompasses much of the materials used in the minstrel shows of a half-century ago. *Cakewalk,* however, is not merely a reproduction of a minstrel show or an olio of old acts. It is a true ballet, for the choreographer has employed the vocabulary of ballet—even to the using of "pointes"—for the creation of a contemporary theater piece.

The delicious characteristics of the minstrel show, then, are not to be found so much in the basic technique used in *Cakewalk* as in the coloring of that technique with the accents, the rhythms, the gestures and the stances of folk forms. This knowing and imaginative treatment of the theatrical figures and forms of an earlier period has resulted in as fine an example of dance Americana as one could hope to find.

Miss Boris's *Cakewalk* does need some trimming and tightening here and there and this choreographic surgery it will no doubt receive shortly. But only a carper of the lowest order would dwell upon the passing flaws of an ebullient ballet which is surely the American answer to *Gaite Parisienne.*

Not only is the choreography for *Cakewalk* unfailingly lively and almost always witty but the score, arranged and orchestrated by Hershy Kay after music by Louis Gottschalk, is delightful from start to finish. There are also handsome costumes and settings by Robert Drew—these were originally designed for a ballet called *Blackface*—and most important of all, *Cakewalk* has a cast which is a dream.

Janet Reed, as a forlorn belle, is wonderful in the Wallflower Waltz and her pas de deux with Herbert Bliss, in which they play Hortense, Queen of the Swamp Lilies, and Harolde, the Young Poet, is movement filigree of the loveliest sort. Then we have Tanaquil LeClercq and Beatrice Tompkins as the high-stepping, joshing End Men; Frank Hobi as the fleet-footed, gracious Interlocutor; Patricia Wilde as the Wild Pony, a rival to Roy Rogers's Trigger if I ever saw one; Yvonne Mounsey as a Venus with streamers and Three Graces, and finally there is the ensemble which participates lustily as an audience for the soloists, as supporting performers in some of the acts and as the mass star of the grand finale, the cakewalk itself. [*New York Herald Tribune*]

November 15, 1951: A World Premiere

Jerome Robbins, the dancer, triumphed—if George Balanchine, the choreographer, did not do so—in the new dance version of *Tyl Ulenspiegel* which was given its world premiere last evening at the City Center. The New York City Ballet's production of *Tyl* is an elaborate one—possibly over-elaborate with respect to properties—and visually handsome, but as striking as the decor is and as pictorially arresting as the Balanchine ensemble designs are, it is Mr. Robbins' performance which captures and revitalizes the spirit and the purpose, the wit and the warmth of a great legend.

Inevitably, comparisons will be made between this *Tyl* and the one created and danced by Jean Babilée and recently on view in New York. There is little point, however, in comparing the two, for their approaches to the figure of Tyl differ in numerous ways. Where Babilée gave us an episodic resume of the man and his legendary characteristics, Mr. Balanchine and Mr. Robbins have selected a specific period and a special theme for the presentation of Tyl. In this later version, he is still the prankster, still the mercurial doer of mischief, but his pranks and his tricks are devoted to the cause of liberty as Tyl aids in the repelling of the Spanish invaders from the soil of Flanders.

Neither Mr. Balanchine in his choreography nor Mr. Robbins in his characterization has sought to transform Tyl into an unsullied hero. He remains a raffish, gleeful, vulgar, partly cruel but fundamentally joyous fellow, and one is led to believe that he enjoys the havoc created by his liberating techniques as fully as he cherishes the cause of freedom.

Mr. Robbins permitted us to see these contradictory elements of Tyl's nature. He made us love him and laugh at him, disapprove of him and weep for him as he capered disrespectfully and irresistibly throughout his fantastic adventures. He made a myth into a human being, an unlikely one perhaps, but human nonetheless.

Mr. Balanchine's choreography for his principal figure was, of course, superb or Mr. Robbins could not have achieved what he did. Elsewhere, however, the distinguished choreographer was less successful. Other characters—the King of Spain, a Duke and his Duchess, soldiers, peasants—rarely came to life, scarcely had dimension. They were backgrounds and their movements were mainly pictorial rather than dramatic. True, Tyl is the focal figure, but because his antagonists tend to be cardboard, the magnitude of his conflicts is somewhat lost.

257

There are striking moments here and there in the choreography for groups or ensembles or even smaller units, but a sort of cluttered posturing mars many of the passages. No one would wish for an ensemble to take over, for it is Tyl's story, but the group designs seem to intrude—without being dramatically purposeful—rather than to augment and extend Tyl's own saga. So if parts of this *Tyl Ulenspiegel* are disconcerting, one can, at the very least, cheer Mr. Balanchine for his choreographic conception of Tyl himself and hail Mr. Robbins for his total realization of that conception.

The scenery and costumes by Esteban Frances were marvelous not only to view but also for their great contribution to the evocation of an era and its legends of strength and fantasy and hard, bright beauties. Jean Rosenthal's lighting was, as always, magic-making and Mr. Barzin and the orchestra played the Richard Strauss score beautifully indeed. [*New York Herald Tribune*]

1952

Ashton Gives City Ballet a Magical Picnic

Ashton creates Picnic at Tintagel for NYCB • Gene Kelly dances in MGM's Singin' in the Rain • Isadora Duncan drawings given to The New York Public Library's Dance Collection by Abraham Walkowitz • The Dancers of Bali debut • Bambi Linn and Rod Alexander dance on TV • Ballet Theatre's two Alicias — Alonso and Markova

Picnic at Tintagel, a Fantasy and Tense Love Drama in Ballet

March 9, 1952

Successful narrative ballets or dance works composed of dramatic episodes are not uncommon. They present difficulties, however, to the choreographer, for the classical unity of time in drama is a safety device which, if ignored, may possibly lead the dramatist or choreographer into attenuations or constrictions. The urgency of a dramatic situation may become less urgent with the extension of the time period, supplementary plots may steal energy from the main power line of drama or, in transplanting a time-covering narrative to the stage, the stage artist may be forced to make each episode so sketchy that the work as a whole becomes sketchy, a resume of a drama and not a drama itself.

Dance, fortunately, is one of those arts which can do pretty much what it wants with the element of time, and some of its most illustrious products are those works which explore and expose the drama of a single moment. Martha Graham's *Night Journey*, built entirely around that instant when the heroine first becomes aware of the enormous tragedy of which she is a part, is a superb example of the dance's mastery of time for dramatic purposes.

There are other instances in which a specific situation, an incident or an immediate conflict, provides the core of a theater piece. In this category one

259

may place Frederick Ashton's captivating new ballet, *Picnic at Tintagel,* staged for the New York City Ballet. Scenically, it jumps from the twentieth century back a thousand years into legend, but the drama itself is based upon a single situation which transpires in a matter of minutes.

Passion at a Picnic   The situation Mr. Ashton has selected is simple, immediately recognized for what it is, even familiar, but it is his choreographic treatment which makes it seem new, fresh and of concern to an audience. A husband, his wife, her lover, his rivals for her favors and servants visit the ruins of Tintagel on the Cornish coast for a picnic. As the lovers lift their glasses in a toast, an ancient parallel of their plight is renewed and they find themselves, ensorcelled by the atmosphere of the place or perhaps by the mysterious actions of the strange caretaker, transported to the Tintagel of old and into the bodies of Tristram and Iseult. The husband becomes King Mark and the others find their counterparts in the legend.

As the ballet closes, the original scene is restored and the central characters, frightened and disturbed by their joint dream, hurriedly depart as the caretaker lifts from the ground two gleaming swords, relics of the dream or omens of what is to come. Mr. Ashton's drama, then, is concerned with that ominous moment preliminary to crisis. At the picnic, desire of the lovers for each other and the swelling anger of the husband draw close to catastrophe. The same situation, lived to its completion in fulfilled passion, betrayal and death through the fantasy of Tintagel revisited in antiquity, is but a second of thought in the minds of the distraught trio. The drama is of the instant; only implications of drama are permitted to span long reaches of time.

Not only has Mr. Ashton used well the dramatic urgency of time but he has also choreographed with craftsmanlike shrewdness and considerable artistry. Except for the duet of Tristram and Iseult there seems to be a minimum of dancing in *Picnic at Tintagel.* Actually this is not so, for if Mr. Ashton has employed mime as his method of communication, he has rhythmicized it expertly and has extended it into dance action with each spasm of dramatic tension.

A Love Duet   The love duet itself is a work of great beauty. Even its prelude is remarkable, for he has given the waiting Iseult movements which proclaim her yearning for Tristram, her impatience in awaiting his arrival. The steps are classical—little running bourrees on point—but the hips move ever so slightly with each step and the result is unbelievably sensual. The duet is an extension of this into wider, freer movement, into patterns which celebrate the sought-for wonders of proximity.

To dance his demanding measures, the choreographer has selected a perfect cast. Diana Adams as the wife (Iseult) gives, I think, the very finest performance of her career. She is lovely to behold, beautiful of movement and wholly successful in communicating the emotional meanings of the ballet. As the lover (Tristram), young Jacques d'Amboise (he is only seventeen) creates a sturdy figure, tender but pleasantly gauche, impetuous and boyish. Francisco Moncion as the husband (King Mark) is also splendid, as are Robert Barnett as the caretaker (Merlin) and the other members of the small cast.

And just to carry this theatrical excitement a step further, Cecil Beaton was commissioned to do the settings and costumes. They are marvelous. The ruined Tintagel is shadowy, mysterious, fascinating, and the way in which it resolves into the restored castle of many columns and arches is pictorially magnificent. Jean Rosenthal's masterful lighting serves not only the transformation scenes but also the costumes which, in the Tristram–Iseult scene, glow and glitter with rich color and brightness. The costumes for the opening and closing episodes, motoring apparel for the year 1916, are also delightful. The score (The Garden of Fand) by Sir Arnold Bax serves the formal and dramatic needs of the ballet exactly, and *Picnic at Tintagel* becomes—musically, pictorially, choreographically, dramatically—a theater piece of which the New York City Ballet may be justly proud. [*New York Herald Tribune*]

Kelly's Exhilarating Dance Tonic for April: Singin' in the Rain

April 13, 1952

For those who were left disappointed, irked or downright angry by the recent performances of the Sadler's Wells Theatre Ballet at the Warner—and there were many bitter complaints which came to my attention and with which I generally concurred—permit me to recommend a tonic. Go to the Radio City Music Hall and watch the buoyant, amusing, skillful and highly professional dancing in the new film, *Singin' in the Rain.*

The new Gene Kelly picture is filled with wonderful dancing. The numbers, with the exception of the Broadway ballet sequence, are comparatively short and deceptively modest in the sense that one does not look upon them as production numbers. But they are superb dances, nonetheless and represent the most appealing choreography to come from Mr. Kelly. Although they are richly inventive with respect to steps, body actions, rhythmic variations and space-effects, much of their charm derives from their impulsiveness. They grow easily and naturally out of scenes and incidents because to use the words of one of Mr. Kelly's numbers, "Gotta Dance."

261

"You Were Meant for Me," a danced song which the star performs with Debbie Reynolds, commences with acting, develops into song, extends into rhythmic advances and retreats indicating cautious romancing and expands, ultimately, into sweet and tender dancing. Romance alone, love remembered and dreamed of, find dance form in Mr. Kelly's performing of the film's title song. Here, the young man, oblivious of the elements, dances and splashes his joyous way along a rainy street. The umbrella becomes a toy and not a protection, puddles are meant for churning by irrepressible feet and mere rain cannot dampen the spirits of one who has "gotta dance" his happiness.

There are two fine numbers which Mr. Kelly and Donald O'Connor, one of his co-stars, dance together. In "Moses," they put up with the inanities of a speech instructor for just so long and then, taking a tongue-twister as a guide, they jump into a dance romp, a bit of rough-house perhaps it is, which is great fun. The most hilarious offering is a dance which the two, as vaudeville hoofers in a flashback scene, perform in the great tradition of eccentric dancing. They tap, shuffle, strut, kick, clown, exude enthusiasm and play violins in a sequence certain to bring a smile to the lips of even the most determined grouch.

Mr. O'Connor has his solo fling in "Make 'Em Laugh," a number which combines dancing and comedy tumbles expertly. The three—Mr. Kelly, Mr. O'Connor, Miss Reynolds—also unite in a pleasant sequence which contributes yet another segment of skillful dance invention to the film. It can be noted, at this point, that the accent is upon comedy or upon lightness of mood. But *Singin' in the Rain* also provides examples of dance satire and of fantasy.

The Broadway ballet episode, although it contains comic hoofing and general spectacle, finds its high point in a dance performed by Mr. Kelly and Cyd Charisse. Here two figures, one elusive and inviting and the other enchanted by a vision, dance through a vast, undefined space. A mysterious breeze choreographs the actions of an incredibly long white scarf worn by the girl and, on occasion, the scarf itself spans the separateness of the two by touching, caressing, even embracing the figure of the man. The effect is not only visually beautiful but utterly sensual, quite as sensual as those fleeting moments when the pair actually achieves physical proximity.

In the Kelly-Charisse duet especially, Mr. Kelly, the film's choreographer and (with Stanley Donen) co-director, has exploited that element of space which the camera can explore so excitingly but which it does not always do when dealing with dance. Here, then, is dramatic situation heightened by the use of distances, visual perspectives; here is incident made more fantastic through the awesomeness of a seemingly limitless background of space; here is camera dance, not flat in design but rather with patterns which plunge deep into space.

And to round out the dance virtues of *Singin' in the Rain*, Mr. Kelly has provided bits and pieces which satirize—in style, form and camera angles—the dance ensemble effects arrived at in those early versions of the motion-picture musical. Need I add that Mr. Kelly's dancing is worthy of his choreography throughout and that his colleagues and assistants are expert and personable in the sequences, sometimes simple and again difficult, assigned to them?

"Gotta dance" is the motivating spirit which pervades the dances in *Singin' in the Rain* and because this spirit is communicated with gusto and imagination and fine craftsmanship, the dance sequences of the film provide the onlooker with the most pleasant spring tonic imaginable. [*New York Herald Tribune*]

In Memory of Isadora, Walkowitz Drawings To Be Shown at Library

August 24, 1952

The car moved forward, a scarf fluttered with the breeze and caught in a turning wheel, a fashionable decoration became a noose and one of the world's great artists was dead by strangulation. It was twenty-five years ago, Sept. 14, 1927, that sudden death came to Isadora Duncan, weary, worn and impoverished. And with the announcement of the tragedy, the whole world seemed to realize anew that Isadora had been a genius, that the declining years were as nothing in a career which had brought new beauty and artistic revolution to the theater of dance.

Writers and poets, artists and laymen dug into their files and their memories for the means to record and commemorate a tempestuous life and a great career. Their offerings remain in libraries, in galleries, in archives and on bookshelves and from them the student can come close to the genius of Isadora. Yet do any of these memorabilia actually recreate the way in which Isadora danced? A word or phrase describes a reaction, captures the force of her presence, records a gesture but the sequence of her dance is missing. As far as anyone knows, motion pictures of her do not exist and her art, ephemeral as dance ever is, comes to us of today in teasing fragments.

Of all the many artists who have celebrated Isadora with camera and brush, none has been more successful, I think, in capturing the flow of her dancing than Abraham Walkowitz. His voluminous collection of sketches and paintings done from life give those of us who never saw Isadora a feeling that here she is once more moving for us. One sketch will not do it but hundreds of them will, for as the eye moves quickly from records of a jump, a run, an extension of the arms, a thrown-back head, Isadora almost dances again.

263

Collection Given to Library   Mr. Walkowitz has given 257 of his water color and pen sketches of Isadora to the New York Public Library, 42nd St. and Fifth Ave. (a separate collection of fifty has been given to the library's music branch on East 58th St.) and next month an exhibition, arranged by the library's dance curator, Genevieve Oswald, will be opened in commemoration of the anniversary of Isadora's passing. And it is a fabulous collection.

Today, the dance world reveres Isadora Duncan, recognizing that many of her dance concepts support our own contemporary dance. We know, from her own writings, what she felt about dancing, what she believed in, what she was attempting to do. Mr. Walkowitz, through his drawings, suggests how she went about it. Looking at his fine works, one realizes that Isadora had developed a remarkable range of movement. Her full, feminine body is shown lashing through space or poised, one would guess, upon an echo of music; leaping, running, skipping; bent in sadness or erect with triumph. Sometimes the arms seem to float or again they invite or repel or hail.

In one view the body is twisted, again its mirrors a series of arcs (arms and head, back and torso, legs and feet); sometimes the chest slumps into an attitude of defeat or the knees seek the ground in supplication; again, the majesty of Isadora is caught in the reproduction of a stance with feet spread far apart, arms upraised and head thrown back in ecstasy. Tunics and togas and scarves add their patterns to the designs of the movements themselves.

Portraits of Dancing   Mr. Walkowitz's drawings of Isadora are faceless, for they are portraits of dancing. His sharp and easy lines, rather than stopping the body in space, suggest continuing movement and, in the color sketches, the white halos around a movement pattern seem to suggest the actual displacement of space by a moving being.

The colors themselves help to create a mood or enhance an action. In flaming red, with arms upraised, she proclaims; in flowing draperies of blue, with head lowered and arms cupped upward, she is like the source and the very flow of water; in green, with a cape of brown, one hand seems to bless the earth while the lifted head and an arm raised aloft praise the heavens; in a short lavender tunic, she leans in reverie toward the sound of music no longer heard. Thus, Isadora almost dances again although a quarter of a century has passed since her movements were stilled forever. Mr. Walkowitz has given his wonderful clues to her way of dance to an organization which can and will, shortly, make them available to the public and with these clues, charted in line and color, the seeking eye will find, perhaps, the genius of the divine Isadora. [*New York Herald Tribune*]

Dancers of Bali

September 19, 1952: Beauty Plus

William Saroyan once wrote a play called *The Beautiful People*. The same title fully describes the event which took place last evening at the Fulton Theater where the Dancers of Bali with their Gamelan Orchestra, from the little Indonesian village of Pliatan, made their American debut. For there was beauty everywhere. Beauty of movement and beauty of sound, beauty of color and beauty of spirit. From temple doorways, etched against a deep blue sky, came tiny dancers in golds and crimsons and purples, in costumes of breathtaking loveliness and in the wonderfully monstrous garbs of demons.

The tinkle and boom and vibrato of gongs, xylophones and drums filled the air as the dancers sculptured the unseen volume of space with movements which told stories of warriors and bumblebees, legendary heroes and simple human beings in search of fun. It mattered little that not all of the gestures were understandable to a Western audience or that ethnic dance symbols eluded the untutored eye, for perfection of form, meticulousness of movement and the love of dancing were clearly transmitted.

The dances of Bali, as represented by this company which is visiting us under the auspices of the Cultural Department of the Republic of Indonesia, are lively but leisurely, that is to say that the breakneck pace, the cumulative surgings toward climaxes usually required in our own theater are absent. But the Balinese, if they do not race or surge, provide innumerable contrasts to stir the interest of the viewer. Their dance appears to have a far more simple vocabulary than that of India (from which many dance influences are derived), but they give it scope through rhythmic and thematic contrasts and through a thorough exploitation of every detail of that movement range upon which their dance is based.

As this evening of enchantment progressed, one came to recognize with warming familiarity certain movement idioms of the Balinese artists. Almost all actions were accomplished in a position which the ballet would term a "plié" and this knee-bend not only provided the dancer with a firm base from which to work but also gave all motions a quality of resilience, of gentle bounce. The torso swayed from side to side, leaning, tilting and sometimes dipping dangerously. Toes were often upturned, elbows were held shoulder-high and fingers fluttered messages of emotional excitement or sensuous tranquility.

The eyes, as in Hindu dance, laughed or implored, invited or disclosed fear; the cheeks trembled with laughter or arrogance; heads shifted laterally on supple necks and the masked mouths of demons gnashed triumphantly. In *Oleg*, two little maidens, dressed in red and gold, searched the air with

265

tapering fingers, sat comfortably on space and rubbed noses amicably while in *Ketjak,* a large male chorus, sitting in a circle around a clown, danced the transformation of an ensemble of mortals into an army of monkeys to the irresistible accompaniments of their own shouts, hisses and chattering cries.

The stars of the company, twelve-year-old Ni Gusti Raka (a real baby ballerina) and Sampih, the chief male performer, appeared first in *Tumulilingan,* a courtship dance involving a lady and a gentleman of the bumblebee family. Miss Raka, as the flitting female, was utterly lovely. The gold-sheathed cylinder of her child-body flickered from side to side, the little feet carried her fleetly across the stage and her sudden shifts in rhythm were truly like those of the bee in quest of many blossoms. Sampih, too, was excellent in this, but his most stirring offering was *Kebyar,* a solo built upon emotional responses to music. His magnificently schooled body moved with incredible ease and virtuosity throughout the extremely difficult patterns of this crouching, swooping, mercurial dance.

The highpoint of the program was, of course, Bali's most celebrated dance, the *Classical Legong.* Here the performers were three little girls, led by Miss Raka, and one could see why this dance is performed exclusively by children. Only a child, muscles and bones made of rubber and free of the growing flesh of adolescence, could accomplish such hairpin back and side bends, could sit on the heels and bound upright with never a tremor of effort, could move with such fluid speed. This was an absorbing Balinese ballet and it built in story and in movement intensity to the finale in which Miss Raka, as a bird with golden wings, danced with magic-making fury.

But there were still other numbers to delight the onlooker. There were the folk dancers of *Djanger,* a sort of cousin to the American square dance; *Ende,* with its fighting clowns; the nymphs, heroes, comics, gods and gorgeously masked demons of *Baris* and the *Barong* with the most glorious dragon in all the world and a witch that not even a Grimm could have envisioned for fairytales.

Then there were the superb playing of the orchestra under the direction of Anak Agung Gde Mandera, mayor of the Balinese village of Pliatan; the expert performances by every member of the company; the sumptuousness of the costumes; the perfect setting and expert lighting of Richard Harrison Senie; the contributions of the story-teller, Miss Winarti Partaningrat, and, in truth, the entire production conceived by John Coast. The beauties of Bali, then, are fourteen thousand miles nearer to us than they have ever been and we of America are indeed fortunate that a fine bit of Bali is now housed at the Fulton. [*New York Herald Tribune*]

A Joyful Dance for Television

September 21, 1952

Autumn was approaching, but suddenly it seemed like spring again. There was freshness, there was newness, there was sweetness. Of course it wasn't real. It was actually Sept. 6 of this year and this pleasant little miracle occurred only on television. It seemed like a miracle mainly because television dance is so often distressing, a state of affairs usually engendered by unimaginative camera direction, by tired choreography or by a choreographer required by someone in authority to choreograph tired themes, by a tendency to use dance merely as a visual aid to instrumental music or song. Bambi Linn and Rod Alexander, appearing on the season's first "Your Show of Shows" program, worked the miracle.

The superb duo danced the *Younger Than Springtime* number which had enchanted supper club audiences last spring and again, this time in a wholly different medium, they triumphed. A hit on the stage is not necessarily (nor frequently) a hit on the screen. This is especially true of choreography, yet *Younger Than Springtime* had the same beauty of form, the same patterns of romantic excitement that it disclosed when danced on stage. Perhaps the camera director fell in love with the dance and was eager to explore and convey its centers of loveliness. At any rate, the camera work was the best that I had ever seen on this particular program with respect to dancing.

With Mr. Alexander's choreography handsomely reproduced on the televised screen, it was possible to savor fully the technical expertness and the emotional sensitivity of the performers themselves. And how exquisitely they danced. They were smooth and not merely slick; they were fresh and not simply tricky; they managed to create a romantic dewiness without resorting to schmalz. In the small confines of a TV setting, they created space, freedom and an air of aloneness as they danced their song of love with sweet vigor and soaring spirit.

Commencing in January, Miss Linn and Mr. Alexander will return to "Your Show of Shows" for thirteen weeks and it is devoutly to be hoped that they will not succumb to a formula, either because of the success of a given dance or because of the awful pressure placed upon those who must choreograph something new each week. Not even *Younger Than Springtime* could hold up under too many variations but if this remarkably gifted couple can retain that fresh skill, that unforced imaginativeness which went into the making of this duet and apply them to new numbers, their dances will surely continue to be as young and as alive as spring.

All of this may sound as if Bambi Linn and Rod Alexander were the hope of television dance. This is not quite accurate. There are innumerable skillful dancers on television and the medium has engaged several expert choreographers, among them such individuals as Tony Charmoli, John Butler, James Starbuck, but a good many of them must experience frustration since they are, for the most part, captives of a formula. Mr. Starbuck's ensemble dances for *Your Show of Shows* (at least in the presentations which I have seen) are uninterestingly viewed by the cameras and, I fear, are often uninteresting choreographically. His dance direction of Imogene Coca, on the other hand, is masterful.

Mr. Charmoli's numbers for the Lucky Strike show are superb camerawise and when he is accorded sufficient program time, usable music and an acceptable theme, he turns out some fine examples of television dance. The truth of the matter is that Mr. Chamoli, Mr. Starbuck and the others can create and have created dance excitement on television but to do so they must have the cameras, the music, the ideas and the artistic authority (they have the dancers) on their side; otherwise they are likely to emerge with dance doggerel, with hurried dance fill-ins while the real stars, singers and comics, are gargling or changing costumes. At least, that is how it has seemed to me and that is why *Younger Than Springtime* seems so wonderful. [*New York Herald Tribune*]

Two Alicias and Two Dance Ways
Enrich Ballet Theatre's Season

October 12, 1952

Both are classical, lyrical and theatrically experienced; both are famed for their enactments of two traditionally significant roles, Giselle and the Queen of Swans; both are named Alicia. Neither, however, rivals the other. It is true that Alicia Markova has legions of admirers who have jammed the Metropolitan Opera House this season to see Ballet Theatre's great guest star and it is equally true that Alicia Alonso, the company's prima ballerina, has been accorded and has earned ovation after ovation during the engagement which ends tonight. They are not contestants, not sparring partners. They are ballerinas.

There is no one in the theater of dance quite like Alicia Markova. Although she possesses that power of projection essential to every star, she is almost always removed from reality, cool and remote, lost in an era of spiritual romanticism. For Miss Markova seems to belong to the Romantic Age of ballet, to a theater world of enchanted beings so fragile that one note of harshness would, apparently, destroy them.

268

In her long and illustrious career, the English ballerina has played all sorts of roles, modern as well as traditional, comic as well as tragic. At one time, she was a technical virtuoso and she can still (when the occasion demands) kick high, accomplish plural turns, jump, stamp and cut through space with sharp actions. But she is, at the moment, a specialist. Her specialty is period style (nineteenth century romanticism) combined with a personal delicacy of movement that is without parallel. She does not excite the onlooker with either physical or dramatic tensions or urgencies but she does, through her matchless style of dance, evoke a sense of wonder in her gentle exposition of elusive beauties.

The Markova Giselle   In her most celebrated role, Giselle, Miss Markova evades almost all opportunities for technical display and concentrates upon style and the building of mood. Even the mad scene is subdued and the contest between mortal desire and the destroying forces of death, which provides the motivation for the second act, is treated with extreme daintiness. Yet Miss Markova's Giselle remains a thing of wonder. As a theater piece, old *Giselle* is pretty foolish but that it is rich in fantasy and in poetry is incontestable. Miss Markova chooses to accent these attributes and through her lighter-than-air motions, the incredible beauty of her arms, the arch of her exquisite neck and steppings so light that they would not bruise a petal, she becomes a creature of fantasy, a silent conveyor of poetry.

In *Swan Lake* and *Les Sylphides,* she pursues a similar line of performing. There are, of course, differences necessitated by the varying requirements of the ballets themselves but in the main, Miss Markova celebrates the ethereal in dance, the vision, the dream, the sweet illusion. In the *Nutcracker* pas de deux, which she also danced this season, Miss Markova introduced the element of glitter. She knew, of course, that this was primarily a ballerina-display piece and she behaved accordingly. She was still light and effortless, still Markova, but her miniature flourishes were apt and her action sparkling. But it is in such ballets as *Giselle, Swan Lake* and *Les Sylphides* that she is incomparable, for in the realm of poetic fantasy she is truly "the one and only."

Alicia Alonso excites the onlooker. By the time she has completed her first variation in *Giselle,* the house is roaring its approval, for although she too is concerned with style, she is not one to minimize the glory of physical action. Her legs sweep ear-high and her sustained balances cause one to hold his breath; her way of drama is colored by Latin fervor and in her conception of this ballet's second act, the power of earthly love is indeed a force to be reckoned with.

269

The Alonso Approach   This approach to *Giselle* is just as correct as Miss Markova's and just as important to the art of ballet. The same may be said for Miss Alonso's treatment of *Swan Lake*, for where Miss Markova is a bird-like figure with womanly characteristics, Miss Alonso is a woman touched by the characteristics of a bird. Ballet Theatre's Cuban star, then, is a classicist and even a lyricist but she believes in communicating the heat of drama, the warmth of a very real femininity and the excitement of physical effort to her public.

In George Balanchine's *Theme and Variations,* Miss Alonso moves softly through adagio passages and sharply through allegro sequences and in both one is aware of the sensuousness of movement. A leg, for example, may float easily upward but the exhilaration of stretching is also present in its execution just as the daintiest of steps speak of the pleasure of contact as well as of lightness. Miss Alonso is not often ethereal and her poetry is usually passionate rather than romantic, for she is the kind of ballerina for whom the art of balletic display was invented, a feminine virtuoso, an actress, a vivid personality.

If it were a different day and age, fans would probably unhitch the horses from the carriage and pull Miss Alonso in noisy triumph through the streets, and for Miss Markova they would strew her pathway with the rarest of blossoms. [*New York Herald Tribune*]

1953

Homage to Two Queens

Ballet finances — New York State legislation allows New York City to lease City Center Theatre for $1 per year • Lester Horton's company makes its east coast debut • "American Dance" presents Graham, Limón and Pearl Lang • Robbins' Fanfare for NYCB celebrates coronation of Queen Elizabeth II • Virginia Tanner's Children's Dance Theatre of Salt Lake City debuts at Jacob's Pillow • The Slavenska-Franklin Ballet presents Bettis' A Streetcar Named Desire and Danilova in Mlle. Fifi • Fonteyn in Swan Lake during Sadler's Wells third American visit

Legislature to Act upon a Bill Affecting City Ballet Finances

February 22, 1953

Good news for American ballet, and for the New York City Ballet in particular, is that two public servants of the State of New York have come to the aid of one important enterprise in our city's cultural life. Senator MacNeil Mitchell, R., Manhattan, chairman of the Senate Committee on Affairs of the City of New York, and Assemblyman John Robert Brook, R., Manhattan, chairman of the Assembly's New York City Committee, have introduced in the Legislature an enabling act which would permit the City of New York to enter into a long-term, dollar-a-year lease with the New York City Center of Music and Drama.

The Legislature will probably act on the bill sometime next month and then a final decision must await action by the city's Board of Estimate. But hopes are high at the financially hard-pressed City Center, for acceptance of the bill will help to assure the continuation and expansion of the Center's ballet, drama and opera seasons. Under the terms of the present lease, which expires in 1955, the rental fee to the City of New York, owner of the building on W. 55th St., equals 1½ per cent of the City Center's gross receipts.

271

To some, this rental fee may seem modest, but it must be remembered that the New York City Center of Music and Drama functions without benefit of subsidy, that its production and operating costs are high and that tickets for performances are scaled at popular prices. The rent now amounts to approximately $23,000 a year but, as Senator Mitchell and Assemblyman Brook point out, . . . "$23,000 a year is a relatively small sum for the world's greatest city to invest in its cultural future."

Municipal in Name Only Morton Baum, chairman of the executive committee of the City Center and the man who had requested the introduction of the bill, notes that despite its name, the New York City Center of Music and Drama is actually a private, non-profit making organization which, through the titles of its performing units (New York City Ballet, New York City Opera, New York City Drama Company), reflects credit upon the City of New York. Last year's enormously successful European tour by the New York City Ballet would be a case in point.

Elimination (to all practical purposes) of the rental, Mr. Baum feels, would give the city valid reason to believe that it was contributing to the maintenance of a municipal ballet-opera-drama center, would make possible further physical improvements at the plant itself (these and repairs cost the organization about $10,000 a year) and would enlarge the scope of activities of the three performing-producing wings.

As far as the New York City Ballet is concerned, the passage of the bill would mean more productions, longer rehearsal periods (essential to a company with a large repertory) and a partial alleviation of financial pressures. The rent item in the City Ballet's budget for its recent season at the City Center was $6,000 and for the year's ballet schedule the amount would range between $10,000 and $15,000. With this money, now going for rent, allocated to other functions, the ballet could mount two major works with scenery and costumes, enjoy extra rehearsals and, in the words of Betty Cage, the City Ballet's executive manager, "help us in general because we're so poor."

And why is the New York City Ballet poor in spite of the handsome grosses earned by its magnificent seasons? Because ballet is expensive to produce and to maintain. New works come high, a repertory must be maintained (well rehearsed, freshly washed, sometimes newly costumed) and a large company of dancers and a full symphony orchestra (with occasional soloists) must be paid. Other necessary expenditures round out a pattern of financial agony for the organization daring enough to assume responsibility for one of the most expensive of theatrical endeavors.

The Rise of a Ballet It seems to most of us who are associated with the field of dance that the New York City Ballet merits whatever help it can get.

272

Without subsidy and in a few short years it has risen to a plane of equality with the great ballet companies of the world. Under the general direction of Lincoln Kirstein and the artistic direction of George Balanchine, it has, through its tours abroad, enhanced American prestige in Europe and served New Yorkers faithfully by taking on the responsibilities of a resident organization.

Our own Ballet Theatre receives the support of its Ballet Theatre Foundation and the major ballet companies of Europe, among them the Sadler's Wells Ballet, the Royal Danish Ballet, the Paris Opera Ballet and the state ballets of Russia, all receive financial support. Yet the New York City Ballet has had to travel its path to national and international renown without benefit of continuing subsidies. As an entity and as a part of the New York City Center of Music and Drama it has surely earned tangible help as well as hearty, but unbudgetable, praise. [*New York Herald Tribune*]

Dancing Guests from California: The Horton Company in Local Bow

April 5, 1953

New York, recognizing the fact that it is the nation's dance center and pretty certain that its dance events are superior to those anywhere else in the land, sometimes tends to be patronizing and kindly, rather than envious, in its attitude toward dance enterprises centered outside of New York. Last weekend, New Yorkers, dancers and dance followers alike, had no reason to assume a patronizing air; rather, had they cause for pride in the dance achievements of another city, for the Lester Horton Dancers, a group from the Lester Horton Dance Theater in Los Angeles, brought vigor and polish and imagination to their programs at the Y. M. and Y. W. H. A.

Four thematically varied works, all with choreography, decor and costumes by Mr. Horton, were given on the program which I attended. These were *Dedications in Our Time,* danced tributes to three dance pioneers (St. Denis, Wigman, Graham), to a poet (Lorca), to a painter (Orozco) and a memorial to Hiroshima; *The Beloved,* a violent duet treating with the cruelty of a double standard of moral behavior; *7 Scenes With Ballabilli,* a delicious romp, somewhat in the manner of the commedia dell'arte, and *Prado de Pena,* based upon Lorca's *Yerma.*

In all, the basic technique was that of modern dance and it seemed to me that movement idioms associated with Martha Graham's distinguished style

273

tended to prevail. But this was all to the good, for the emotional intensities of three of the four creations required the sort of movement stress and dramatic sweep for which Miss Graham is renowned and, furthermore, Mr. Horton colored such movements with gestural accents, rhythmic responses and pattern-sequences of considerable freshness and, frequently, apt ingenuity.

Best of all, Mr. Horton's choreography and his staging of it was whole-heartedly theatrical. Dramatic development, dynamic contrasts, movement surprises and clear expositions of plot or mood or joke were, with few exceptions, maintained throughout the program. There were, I think, theatrical exaggerations. Some of the falls were harsh and some of the pullings and pushing and wrenchings were violent. But many of us in New York have become weary, at certain (not all) modern recitals, of thematic obscurity, underplaying, choreography which tarries too long in the limbo of unresolution. So the Horton zest, forthright pictorialism and dramatic directness were especially welcome.

A Flaw or Two   Choreographically, the major flaw was attenuation. The opening episode (to the dance pioneers) of *Dedication,* although it contained some stunning movement, was unnecessarily long and the Hiroshima section, danced with force and feeling by Misaye Kawasumi, weakened its choreographic impact by straggling along beyond its peak of effectiveness. The Orozco sequence was, undoubtedly, the finest in the suite.

The Beloved, on the other hand, was comparatively compact. Certainly it was intense, the most violent duet (and I include the pas de deux for the Poet and Profane Love in *Illuminations*) I had ever seen. Its melodramatic treatment of the theme of the erring turn-of-the-century wife and the brutal punishment administered by her husband was, if not subtle, tremendously exciting. *7 Scenes With Ballabilli* was prankish and fun (perhaps a trifle too long) and indicated that this gifted group was as at home in comedy as it had been in drama, melodrama and in the sturdy lyricism of the opening dance.

Prado de Pena, a sort of ritualized version of Lorca's play about the tragedy of a barren wife, Yerma, found Mr. Horton, as choreographer, and his dancers at their best. Each of the six scenes was tightly knit, each extended the thread of drama and each communicated a specific emotional state. With Carmen de Lavallade and James Truitte in the leading parts, *Prado de Pena* exploited handsomely the expressional, physical and theatrical resources of modern dance.

Carmen de Lavallade   And this brings us to the performers themselves and to Miss de Lavallade in particular. She is a beautiful dancer. The body-instrument is strong yet fluid, excellently disciplined technically and wonderfully responsive to musical and dramatic nuance. As a matter of fact, she is the most exciting dancer to come out of California since Janet Collins (her cousin) made a spectacular and (as subsequent events proved) successful New York debut in the same auditorium several seasons ago.

There was also fine dancing by Mr. Truitte, Miss Kawasumi, Lelia Goldoni, Norman Cornick and, indeed, by every member of the company. Some, of course, were more stirring than others with respect to personal style or expressional power but all were well trained, thoroughly rehearsed, vital.

Thus, the local debut of the Lester Horton Dancers gave cause for pride in the modern dance efforts of Californians and brought freshness of idea, new faces, fine dancing, theatrical verve and even, perhaps, a healthy dash of envy to the New Yorkers who attended. [*New York Herald Tribune*]

"American Dance"

April 17, 1953: Miss Graham's Evening

Martha Graham's tender testament to an Appalachian springtime and her re-creation of the monumental tragedy experienced by the Jocasta of antiquity were the major offerings on the third program of "American Dance" presented last evening at the Alvin Theater. There were also two Broadway premieres—Helen McGehee's *La Intrusa* and Nina Fonaroff's *Sea Drift*—on this modern dance festival program but the evening belonged to Miss Graham.

As the Wife in *Appalachian Spring*, Miss Graham brought to the role a wonderful radiance which dominated the entire ballet. Her starry-eyed devotion to her Husband, her piety, mother-tenderness, the cherishing of the threshold, courage and gaiety were present in her characterization. And loveliest of all was her light and joyous dancing in the duet with her Husband. In vibrant action or in arresting immobility, Miss Graham demanded the attention of the onlooker through a performing splendor which remains unequaled in the world of dance.

Stuart Hodes was impressive as the sturdy Husbandman and Natanya Neumann did nicely with the part of the Pioneering Woman although the expansiveness of movement and gesture inherent in the role tended to escape her. As the Revivalist, Bertram Ross had similar difficulties, for although the danced sermon came through with vigor, the intensity of fanatical faith which other performers have brought to this assignment, was not always fully sustained. Nevertheless, it was a fine performance of a beautiful work. The ensemble danced expertly and the Copland score, as played by the orchestra under Simon Sadoff's direction, was exhilarating indeed.

275

As Jocasta in *Night Journey,* a wholly different Martha Graham was revealed, for here were violence and unutterable anguish, the shattering of a soul and the death of a spirit. In that sweeping kick which culminates in a combined sinking and falling movement—an oft-repeated pattern in this work— Jocasta's majestic despair was symbolized, distilled. For this was not petty sorrow or hurtful ache but the enormous agony of a heroine learning in one awful moment that she had wed her son and born him children.

It was a tremendous performance which Miss Graham gave and she received faultless support from Mr. Ross as the handsome, heroic and tortured Oedipus; from Mr. Hodes as the fateful Seer and from the superb chorus, Daughters of the Night, led by Helen McGehee. Here again, this time with William Schuman music, Mr. Sadoff conducted with vigor and sensitivity and the Noguchi setting was lighted to perfection by Jean Rosenthal. [*New York Herald Tribune*]

April 18, 1953: *Electrifying Premiere*

An electrifying new work, in its Broadway premiere, was the principal presentation of the fourth program of "American Dance," the festival series currently at the Alvin. And last evening's large audience was quick in responding affirmatively to the creation by a young and at this point, more than promising choreographer. Pearl Lang's *Rites,* built upon music by Béla Bartók, is the most absorbing and satisfying theater piece to emerge from the workshop of a junior modern dancer in many a day.

Miss Lang, an important member of Martha Graham's company and comparatively well known to musical comedy audiences, has used the Graham technique as her base in *Rites* but there is nothing Grahamesque either in the style of her dancing or in the kinetic flavor of her choreography. All is fresh and vital, for although she owes her superb training and her dance tools to Miss Graham, *Rites* is wholly her own and her creative independence is unwaveringly evident.

Rites, as its title suggests, is a series of ceremonies treating with Aloneness, Beginning of Belonging, Celebration, Slaughter of Innocence, Lament, Fall Into Chaos and Renewal. But Miss Lang has achieved a wonderful and extremely rare effect in her exposition of ritual. Rituals, because of their archaic heritage, are often remote or, if they are contemporary and lustily primitive, they tend to obscure the individual in mass action. Miss Lang, while retaining an aura of inexorable timelessness and filling her stage on frequent occasions with group movement, has, nevertheless, succeeded in communicating the dignity of the individual, the passion of the person, the feelings of single and separate beings.

There is, then, human warmth as well as group incantation to *Rites* and one draws close to the rich humanity which Miss Lang projects through measures dealing with love and fear, trial and defeat, sorrow and reborn hope, all of them common experiences but here illumined by the selectivity of dance.

Miss Lang, possessed of a magnificent technique, commanding presence and a glowing beauty, danced superbly in her new work. Bertram Ross and the adult ensemble were also splendid and performed the extremely difficult and highly inventive lifts and falls and, indeed, all the movement designs to perfection. Particularly remarkable were the two children, Carol Dellaglio and Bruce Marks, whose dancing aplomb, highly skilled technique and emotional sensitivity left one open-mouthed with amazement. The Julliard Quartet, which played the Bartok score, completed the beauties of a truly beautiful dance occasion.

The program also offered repeat presentations of Doris Humphrey's *Fantasy and Fugues* and her new masterwork, *Deep Rhythm,* both danced by José Limón and his company, and Mr. Limón's *The Visitation* (Arnold Schoenberg) in its first Broadway showing. *The Visitation* has been discussed in these columns before on the occasions of its performances at the American Dance Festival at New London and at the Julliard School of Music. It remains one of Mr. Limón's most touching and tender creations, a warm and simple telling in dance of the legend of the Annunciation.

Mr. Limón, Pauline Koner and Lucas Hoving danced it with enormous power and, I think, with even greater refinement of emotional detail than ever before. As the Man, Mr. Limón gives accent to the protectiveness and the rough-tender adoration of Joseph for his wife and as the Wife, Miss Koner gives us a Mary who grows from a shy and carefree girl to a heroine aware of that awesome glory which has been visited upon her. Mr. Hoving's Stranger is, in gesture, in lightness of motion and in authoritative mien, unmistakably the messenger, the Angel. [*New York Herald Tribune*]

New York City Ballet

June 3, 1953: Coronation Ballet

Across the seas from London, the celebration of a queen's coronation continued as an American dance organization lent its joyous spirit and performing skill to a program honoring Queen Elizabeth II of England. For last evening was "Coronation Night" at the New York City Center where the New York City Ballet presented a new work, *Fanfare,* and danced in other ballets representing the collaborations of British and American artists.

277

Honor was due in more ways than dancing. Gorgeous emblems flanked the stage, the anthems of the two nations were played and at the third intermission, Newbold Morris, chairman of the board of the City Center, introduced a guest speaker, Major General William Alfred Dimoline, head of the Service of Advisors to the United Kingdom and representative on the Military Committee of the United Nations. Replicas of some of the crown jewels and coronation regalia were displayed and "The Orb and Scepter March," composed by Sir William Walton for the coronation, was given its New York premiere by the orchestra under Leon Barzin's direction.

Balletically, the high point of the evening came with the world premiere of *Fanfare,* choreographed by Jerome Robbins to Benjamin Britten's *The Young Person's Guide to the Orchestra,* consisting of variations and a fugue on a rondeau by Henry Purcell. It is a gay and frolicsome work employing the distinctive talents of thirty-four dancers divided into groups—woodwinds, strings, brass, percussion—and subdivided into individual instruments. The plan has provided Mr. Robbins with magnificent opportunities for the creating of mass action and of delicate detail and he has functioned in both areas with wit and brilliance.

Peppered with Mischief   *Fanfare* is courtly but its courtliness is suffused with good humor and peppered with mischief. Not only has Mr. Robbins selected and invented movements and, particularly, rhythmic phrasings which appear to be visualized characteristics of the instruments portrayed and the themes allotted to them but he has also found the special brands of fun associated with, say, the tuba, the double bass or the bassoons. One sees speed and lightness in the dancing of flutes, gliding legate in the celli, soaring in the clarinets, ripples and sweeps in the harp and fine pomposity in the percussion.

The whole of *Fanfare* was a delight but certain passages stick in the mind. First, Todd Bolender and his colleagues in a hilarious and superbly choreographed percussion episode. Then, perhaps, one would speak of Yvonne Mounsey's beautiful re-creation of the harp, the aerial actions of Roy Tobias and Carolyn George as the clarinets, the easy bravado of Edward Bigelow's tuba. But one could go on and on, naming the sections which delighted and the dancers who made them delightful.

Drama of Space   The dance details, fine as they were, did not obscure totality, for when Mr. Robbins uses the full ensemble or segments of it, he again disclosed his remarkable understanding of the drama of space with its lanes of adventure, its invitation to design. The handsome costumes and decor, uncredited on the program but reportedly designed by Irene Sharaff, carried out the musical themes and providing the occasion with a cue-giving source was a Major Domo, acted by Robert Fletcher, who delivered the text by Eric Crozier in impressive and friendly fashion.

There were laughs and murmurs of approval throughout the entire work
and as *Fanfare* ended, applause and cheers, flowers and curtain calls indicated
the addition of a new hit to the repertory of a great company. [*New York
Herald Tribune*]

A Dance Pilgrimage

July 26, 1953

Twenty-three girls, ranging in age from eight to eighteen, joined hands, bowed
their heads and prayed. A few moments later, the curtain rose upon what was
to be an unforgettable experience in dance. These were not professional
dancers preparing to give elaborate ballets or complex dances in recital form.
They were children, members of Virginia Tanner's Children's Dance Theater
and they had come with their teacher and their parents all the way from Salt
Lake City, Utah, to make their debut in the East at Jacob's Pillow, the famed
summertime dance center near Lee, Mass.

At times, it had seemed as if the trip to Jacob's Pillow and, subsequently, to the Connecticut College School of the Dance at New London, would be
impossible. Funds for such a project were non-existent. But the children
themselves earned money; parents made cakes, cookies, dolls and quilts and
held rummage sales; the Church of Jesus Christ of Latter Day Saints contributed money to these of their children whose dance education at the McCune
School of Music was under the jurisdiction of the church's own Brigham
Young University and finally the Mayor of Salt Lake City provided the last
sum needed for this pilgrimage.

And it was to be a pilgrimage, for not only would Miss Tanner and the
children bring the freshness of their dance way to others but they would visit
those shrines commemorating the great westward trek of their Mormon forebears. The faith of these children and the faith in them held by others made
the journey possible and such faith was renewed in the church services held in
their bus while en route and in that prayer which was the prelude to their performance at Jacob's Pillow.

Children's Dance From the first, there was beauty. The great doors at the
back of the stage had been thrown wide and the children danced against a
background of trees and hills touched with moonlight. But more important
than the loveliness of the setting was the vital innocence of the dancers themselves. They looked like children and not like miniature adults; they danced

themes of their own choosing and of their own creation; they dressed simply, for no spangles were needed for those whose eyes shone brightly and their bodies, some babyish and other adolescent, some plump and others long and slight, were wonderfully disciplined yet gloriously free in movement.

What did they dance? Well, first they merely echoed with clapping hands a series of rhythmic patterns established by Miss Tanner. Soon, however, the rhythm was invited to spread from hands to the body and each girl, improvising, found her own dance mould in which these pulsing patterns of rhythm might be contained. There were runs and leaps, turns and falls and combinations of them, all devised by the girls themselves under Miss Tanner's guiding eye. Dreams were danced, folk airs were given physical outlet, carols were celebrated in movement and a little dance of eventide, in which kittens and kangaroos and babies turned from action to rest, brought the program to a close.

Other children have danced such themes and there are other children, quite certainly, who have performed with greater brilliance, with far more precociousness of a technical nature but none, I think, have conveyed so perfectly the bright (not palid) purity of child-dance. It is difficult to describe even the most potent intangibles and the best I can do is to say that the children danced as if they had faith in themselves, had love for those of us who were seeing them, actively believed in their God and rejoiced in all of these.

An Audience Cheers There was nothing namby-pamby, molly-coddle, goody-goody about any of them. They were strong and alive, filled with humor and mischief. They were real but so too was this quality of faith which illumined them and their every action. At the end of the program, the audience at Jacob's Pillow stood and cheered. Eyes on both sides of the footlights were moist.

Students, the harshest judges of all, gathered to discuss faith and its place in their busy-with-technique training programs. One young dancer with tears in her eyes turned to some of her colleagues and said, "Why don't we go and drown ourselves" and a great star murmured, "I am ashamed of myself. I have been dancing for money, for adulation, for the propagating of art ideas and I had forgotten why I had become a dancer in the first place. These children have reminded me." And Ted Shawn, the Pillow's director, said softly, "I feel that God has danced in this theater tonight."

Before the pilgrimage back commences, Miss Tanner and her young dancers will appear tomorrow at Connecticut College where Doris Humphrey, José Limón and Martha Hill, who saw them in the West and urged them to make the difficult trek, will be on hand to greet them. Whether the Jacob's Pillow experience can, should or will be duplicated is difficult to say but those who visit Connecticut College's Palmer Auditorium tomorrow night will surely discover a new dance beauty, a new dance testament created by children in whom faith and vigor function in unity. [*New York Herald Tribune*]

Slavenska-Franklin Ballet

July 28, 1953

The elegance of courtly etiquette, so often associated with the art of ballet, was temporarily banished last evening at the Lewisohn Stadium at that point in the program when Mia Slavenska, Frederic Franklin and their ballet company turned their energies to the emotional and physical violences of *A Streetcar Named Desire.* Valerie Bettis' dance treatment of the Tennessee Williams play had been an immediate hit upon the occasion of its New York premiere last winter and a Lewisohn Stadium audience, overlooking the stadium's inadequacies as a dance site, received it with fine enthusiasm.

The performance itself was splendid in almost every respect. Miss Slavenska as Blanche, Mr. Franklin as Stanley and Lois Ellyn as Stella repeated their vital and expertly detailed characterizations and the supporting dancers were effective in lesser parts. As a matter of fact, I think the work has probably improved with respect to performing smoothness since last it was given here. Certainly the three stars never faultered in the suspenseful building to the ballet's tragic denouement and surely Alex North's haunting score, adapted and orchestrated by Rayburn Wright, was never more stirringly played than by the Stadium Symphony Orchestra under Otto Frohlich's direction.

But the evening was not all devoted to violence and passion. The evening opened with a divertissement from the classical *The Nutcracker* and here Miss Slavenska, Mr. Franklin and their associates comported themselves with elegance and grace. True, the two stars encumbered their courtly phrases with some unnecessary flourishes, with some near-circus accents (perhaps provided for the benefit of the stadium's most distant viewers) but on the whole, they, Lee Becker, Shirley Weaver, Sally Seven and Ronald Colton, accompanied by other soloists and members of the ensemble, offered a *Nutcracker* which was stylistically quite respectable and physically lively.

The evening's guest artist, and a very special one at that, was Alexandra Danilova, who has now been performing with this company for a year. The great Russian-American ballerina was first seen with Mr. Franklin in the Waltz from *Le Beau Danube,* a ballet with which they are closely identified in the hearts and memories of all dance lovers. Once again, dancing together, they worked their familiar magic as they moved, sometimes gently and sometimes exuberantly but always romantically to the strains of the Strauss music.

To close the program, Miss Danilova returned in the title part of *Mlle. Fifi,* a ballet especially created for her by Zachary Solov. Here, her celebrated legs were given ample opportunity for display and her gifts as one of the most delicious of contemporary soubrettes were properly exploited. The ballet is slight but, in its breezy way, it is a perfect vehicle for Danilova the comedienne as distinct from Danilova the prima ballerina.

An audience of 11,000 was present for the stadium's second and final dance program of the summer season. [*New York Herald Tribune*]

Sadler's Wells Ballet

September 14, 1953

With suitable pomp and circumstance, together with much splendid dancing, England's celebrated Sadler's Wells Ballet returned to the Metropolitan Opera House last evening for its third American visit, its first in three long years. The seating arrangements in the old opera house had submitted to changes and on stage, the venerable *Le Lac des Cygnes* was presented in a brand new production which included new scenery, a new Neapolitan dance and some new choreographic arrangements. From the festive air and enthusiastic response of the audience, one would say that the changes worked on both sides of the footlights were successful.

Unchanged—well not quite, for great artists never stand still—was Margot Fonteyn, the company's prima ballerina and one of the world's most distinguished dance stars. Unchanged also were the graciousness and eagerness-to-please of our dancing visitors, the unhurried lyricism of their lucid pantomime, the technical and stylistic exactitude of the corps de ballet, opulence of production and those manifestations of careful direction which we have come to expect from the organization's director, Dame Ninette de Valois.

But shining over all was the dancing of Miss Fonteyn. Performing the dual role of Odette-Odile, the enchanted Swan Princess and the magician's evil daughter, the ballerina clearly defined through movement the distinctive characteristics of each while at the same time retaining sufficient similarities to make believable the hero's acceptance of Odile in her disguise as his betrothed Odette. Confusing? Perhaps. But not when Miss Fonteyn carries us into a world of romance and of sorcery.

Even within the framework of each rule, the ballerina detailed many varying characteristics. As the Swan Princess, she indicated the specific nature of her enchantment not only through fluttering arms but also in the tremor of the shoulder, the arch of the neck and poised alertness contrasted with mercurial speed. Authority—for she was a princess—was disclosed in imperious gesture and womanliness found its form in those gentle, loving actions which brought her into proximity with her Prince.

As Odile, the black swan, Miss Fonteyn discarded much of the softness characteristic of Odette, accenting the bravura, the glittering. A harsh coquetry marked her facial expressions and sharpness of attack alternating with moments of false gentleness provided her actions with dramatic purposefulness. There was some wavering in the long sequence of fouettes in Act III, but for the rest, Miss Fonteyn performed superbly the most difficult role in classic ballet, a role in which she quite probably has no peers.

As the Prince, Michael Somes accorded the star impeccable support, mimed his role pleasantly and danced (something he hardly gets around to doing in this ballet) adequately. There was a beautiful performance by Pamela May in the acting part of the Princess-Mother and Anne Heaton provided a delightful bit of very stylish dancing as a Peasant Girl. The Pas de Dix in Act I was also realized with polish and accuracy, but the Pas de Trois in the same act was pretty bad. Brian Shaw danced his part in it stirringly and with engaging buoyancy, but his two lady colleagues labored and toiled, endeavored and executed but never got close to the spirit of dance.

Julia Farron and Alexander Grant came close to stopping the show with the new Neapolitan Dance choreographed by Frederick Ashton, and there were other striking performances by other principals. There were also less fortunate moments, some due to the performers and some to the choreographic nature of this old masterpiece, but there was no question but what Dame Ninette's new production (with the assistance of Mr. Ashton) of a work created more than half a century ago by Marius Petipa and Lev Ivanov and lately restaged for the Sadler's Wells by Nicholas Sergeyev was the best we have yet seen.

Leslie Hurry's settings and costumes were big and splendid and the wondrous Tchaikovsky score, as played by the orchestra under Robert Irving's direction, was also big and splendid, to say nothing of being very, very loud. [*New York Herald Tribune*]

283

1954

Balanchine Begins a Yuletide Tradition

NYCB premieres Balanchine's Nutcracker, Western Symphony and Ivesiana • Hungarian refugees Kovach and Rabovsky make American debut at the Broadway Theatre • In Canada, the rise of two fledgling companies — the National Ballet of Canada and the Royal Winnipeg Ballet • Connecticut College commissions its first work — Limón's The Traitor

New York City Ballet

February 3, 1954: Magic

The skyscrapers seemed to disappear, the roar of subways was hushed, surly looks vanished as New York, or a small part of it at any rate, was transformed into a fairyland of music and smiles and glorious magic. The magician responsible for this brief and delightful dream world was George Balanchine, whose new, evening-long production of *The Nutcracker* was given its first performance last evening at the City Center by the New York City Ballet.

But Mr. Balanchine, choreographic genius though he is, was not the only magician at work, for there was magic in the dancing of the company itself, in the sweet performing of forty children from the School of American Ballet, in the voices of the boys' choir from St. Thomas Episcopal Church.

And there was sorcery of the finest grade provided by Karinska, who created the fabulous costumes; by Horace Armistead, who designed the soaring scenery; by Vlady, maker of masks, and by Jean Rosenthal, who illumined this fairyland with her own magical lighting, just as Tchaikovsky had illumined (and he still does) the original "The Nutcracker" with his shining music more than sixty years ago.

In all respects, this new mounting of *The Nutcracker* constitutes a major event, for it represents the first program-length ballet produced by our own resident company—a sister company, the San Francisco Ballet, has its full-length *Nutcracker* and other such productions in its repertory—and it's the most lavish ballet yet attempted by the New York City Ballet. It is, indeed, a real spectacle, rich in excitement, impeccable in taste and by all indications of audience response, a roaring hit.

Since American dancers rarely treat with the element of spectacle, it is appropriate to report first on such matters. Among other wonders, there is a transformation scene in which a living room fades from view and a sturdy Christmas tree commences to grow to gigantic proportions and while we are watching this with mouths joyfully agape, the little toys we have seen at the Christmas party become larger—including the wonderful Nutcracker itself—and giant mice invade the scene to do battle with the valiant toy soldiers.

Again there is a change and even the Christmas tree disappears to give way to a fairyland of snow in which flakes gently fall upon great branches already laden with whiteness. Later, we are carried to the Kingdom of Sweets, supervised by the Sugar Plum Fairy herself, and here we meet dancing candy canes and marzipan, a lady with a hoopskirt so large that she can house a batch of children beneath it, flowers free of restraining roots, a flashing dewdrop and other enchanting creatures.

Karinska, with her indescribably beautiful costumes; Mr. Armistead, with his scenes and transformations, and Leon Barzin and the orchestra, giving bright renewal to the Tchaikovsky score, cannot steal the glory away from the dancing. Once again, Mr. Balanchine has worked that miracle of using the traditional movements of the classical ballet and making them seem wholly new through the freshness of his sequences, through the imagery of his mass designs, through the evocation of hidden rhythms, through balancing dance with silly humorous pantomime.

And the dancers do justice to Mr. Balanchine and his colleagues. Maria Tallchief, as the Sugar Plum Fairy, is herself a creature of magic, dancing the seemingly impossible with effortless beauty of movement, electrifying us with her brilliance, enchanting us with her radiance of being. Does she have any equals anywhere, inside or outside of fairyland? While watching her in *The Nutcracker,* one is tempted to doubt it.

And briefly, but with enthusiasm, one must note the charming performances of Alberta Grant, whose dream *The Nutcracker* is about, and Paul Nickel, the Nutcracker himself and a perfect little cavalier; Yvonne Mounsey and Herbert Bliss, who led a group in a Hot Chocolate episode with a distinctly Spanish flavor; Francisco Moncion, as Coffee, in a lazy Arabian dance; George Li, as the chief figure in a Tea pas de trois, unmistakably Chinese; Robert Barnett, as the mercurial leader of the Candy Canes; lovely Janet Reed, good enough to eat as a Marzipan Shepherdess; Edward Bigelow, wearer of the mammoth hoopskirt; Tanaquil LeClercq as the Dewdrop and Nicholas Magallanes as the Sugar Plum Fairy's gallant and expert partner.

The children were also irresistible in their several dances and a group of the adult professionals was superb in the most beautiful Waltz of the Flowers I have ever seen.

There were, one must report, a few production hitches but they were surprisingly few for such an elaborate affair and the first night audience minded them not a bit. Spurts of loud applause peppered the performance, cheers greeted special numbers and, at the close of the evening, rousing ovations were accorded Mr. Balanchine, Miss Tallchief and in truth, everyone concerned with the New York City Ballet's newest, biggest and most spectacular presentation. [*New York Herald Tribune*]

September 8, 1954

It may seem hard to believe but a classical dance technique born in medieval courts and nurtured as an aristocrat of the theater can speak, through movement, the language of the cowboy and can sing, again through movement, the songs of America's folk. George Balanchine, eminent classicist and Russian-born artistic director of the New York City Ballet proved this last evening. The proof? *Western Symphony*, which was given its premiere at the City Center.

As every one should know by this time, major elements of the classic dance have been used before in the making of American ballets. The enormously popular ballets of Agnes de Mille, Eugene Loring, Jerome Robbins—to name three—attest to this. But these were story ballets, pieces on American themes, dances which fused folk action and popular American steps with ballet technique.

Western Symphony has no story to tell and its Americana is limited to a cowboy hat, western boots (dance practice clothes are worn in lieu of regional costumes) and the pantomimed strumming of a guitar. Nonetheless, it is a completely American ballet not merely in those choreographic patterns which owe something (as far as shape is concerned) to the squares and rounds, the star formations and the swing-your-partners of our own native dance but also in the application of classical steps to an evocation of American spirits, humors, rhythms, colors.

Here in *Western Symphony* are steps and attitudes and enchainements which you will find in *Swan Lake* or *Coppelia* but in the new Balanchine work, they have lost their European accent. Mr. Balanchine, whose movement responses to music constitute one of the miracles of contemporary choreography, has let the American tunes which form the ballet's score give specific character to his dance actions without blurring their classical origins.

Furthermore, the choreographer has found in the vocabulary of the classical ballet movement equivalents for those steps, gestures, antics and by-plays characteristic of American folk and game dancing. So expertly has this been achieved that *Western Symphony* seems just as classical as the same choreographer's *Concerto Barocco* and just as American as Miss de Mille's *Rodeo*.

Of equal importance to the success of *Western Symphony* is the composer, Hershy Kay, who has written a symphony based upon American folk tunes. It is a great score, witty, nostalgic, lovely and lively (superbly conducted by Hugo Fiorato) and it would be impossible not to dance to it.

The form of the choreography follows the form of the music: an introduction and four movements (Allegro, Adagio, Scherzo, Rondo) and each movement has its own special set of dance leaders. In the first, Diana Adams and Herbert Bliss led their unit through patterns suggesting the zestful good humor of a barn dance and both stars danced beautifully, singly, together and with the ensemble.

In the second, Janet Reed and Nicholas Magallanes gave dance substance to a ballad with its hints of courting, female elusiveness, male mooning and the hurdles of romance. Patricia Wilde and André Eglevsky raced joyously and effectively (on earth and in air) through the Scherzo and with the Rondo, Tanaquil LeClercq and Jacques d'Amboise wrapped up the Western excursion with a fleet and hilarious sequence of action for the ballerina and a dance for her cavalier which contained all the exuberance and the bravado of an outdoor man of muscle and spirit.

It was, indeed, an exciting, diverting and superbly molded ballet which Mr. Balanchine and Mr. Kay presented and which the dancers performed with vigor and dash (if not always with ensemble accuracy). Applause was loud and long and the bravos shattering as multiple curtain calls were demanded. [*New York Herald Tribune*]

September 15, 1954

Genius is always surprising and the genius of George Balanchine contains more surprises, perhaps, than that of any other choreographer. He has been a prolific dance creator for many years, yet staleness never touches his work; again and again, he has given new sequences, new colors, new kinesthetic meanings to the ancient steps of classical ballet; he has built dances upon gesture; he has given impeccable physical substance to great music and he has departed violently from his own, specific dance heritage.

With *Ivesiana,* which was given its world premiere last evening at the City Center by the New York City Ballet, Mr. Balanchine has turned his genius to violent departure. True, his mastery of choreographic form is present, toe slippers are in evidence, certain traditional movement discernible and climaxes are shrewdly theatrical. But for the most part, *Ivesiana* treats with newly invented movement, strange and unexpected sequences of action, unanticipated body distortions and an air of eeriness.

The score of *Ivesiana* has, of course, determined the choreographer's style and form. The music is made up of several unrelated compositions by the late Charles Ives, a New England composer controversial during his lifetime and, until comparatively recently, hailed as a genius by only a small number of musicians.

The difficulties in following either choreographically or in dance performing, the rhythmic complexities of Ives' music constitute a challenge and Mr. Balanchine (if not always the dancers) has met the challenge brilliantly. In certain episodes, he ignores the beat completely and builds his choreography upon mood and long phrases. Elsewhere he has created swiftly shifting actions to conform with the metric nature of the accompaniment. In both treatments, he has been strikingly successful in a formal, if not continuously in a theatrical, sense.

Ivesiana is not a narrative ballet but each of its six episodes conveys a particular mood and certain images indicative of dramatic incident and each has a title. Of the six, the most powerful was a nightmarishly beautiful adagio called "The Unanswered Question," superbly performed by Allegra Kent and Todd Bolender, assisted by an ensemble of four.

In this section, the display of the girl, borne about as if she were a goddess-lure, her elusiveness, her physical desirability were projected through actions which hinted at eroticism but which were tempered by the coolness, the remoteness of dreams. Here, indeed, Mr. Balanchine's amazing fund of invention was tellingly exploited.

Excellent also was the initial number, "Central Park in the Dark," macabre, slithery, ominous in its placing of a swift and violent romance between a boy and a girl amid surrounding figures of evil cast. Janet Reed, partnered by Francisco Moncion, brought her great skill in the communication of emotion to bear upon a difficult role and achieved the clearest and most stirring enactment in the whole ballet.

In "Halloween," Patricia Wilde and Jacques d'Amboise moved with fine strength and skill, but the result seemed to be more of an exercise than a scene in dance. Even less effective, despite the presence of the lovely Diana Adams, was "Over the Pavements." This seemed to be moodless and not particularly interesting in its movement sequences. Herbert Bliss, usually a stalwart dancer, was of little help here.

"In the Inn" had some engaging moments provided by Tanaquil Le-Clercq and Mr. Bolender and with some sharpening of the potential humorous aspects, episode. "In the Night," performed by the whole company moving slowly on their knees, concluded *Ivesiana*.

Whether *Ivesiana,* with its arresting choreography, its remarkable score by Ives and its sensitively designed lighting by Jean Rosenthal, becomes a popular success is debatable. It is not glittering ballet in the traditional sense and it is not pretty but despite some weak sections, it is undeniably the product of a choreographic genius. [*New York Herald Tribune*]

Kovach and Rabovsky

February 10, 1954

Two electrifying young performers, who recently made a courageous and daring escape—an event which has since been well publicized—from behind the Iron Curtain, made their American stage debut last evening at the Broadway Theater. As guest artists with Roland Petit's Ballets de Paris, Nora Kovach and István Rabovsky offered their version—and a spectacular one it is—of the Grand Pas de Deux from *Don Quixote,* choreographed by Guszev after Marius Petipa, set to the familiar Minkus music and with new costumes by Karinska.

The Hungarian-born dancers have appeared as principal artists at the Maryinsky Theater in Leningrad and at the Bolshoi in Moscow and it follows that their dance style varies from those—American, English, French, Canadian—with which we are familiar. Hints of this style have been conveyed by Russian ballet films but in person, its flavor is even more distinct.

If the dancing of this young couple is typical of the style (in works similar to *Don Quixote*) current in the ballet theaters of Russia, then it must be classed as bravura. Certainly, the accent is upon virtuosity, occasionally at the expense of what we have come to regard as good balletic line, and the flourishes which introduce, pepper or conclude a particular daring passage have a circusy air about them. But this is not condemnation; it is description and individual taste will be the deciding factor.

There is no argument, however, about Mr. Rabovsky physical prowess. His soaring, suspended leaps, his jet-speed turns, his spurting ascents and facile descents (often to kneeling positions) have never been equaled by any male dancer that I have ever seen in the ballet. As a matter of fact some of the movements he accomplishes seem to be brand new. He is not subtle but he is gracious; he drives his actions hard but his dancing is exciting in the extreme, exciting enough to lift one right out of his chair.

Miss Kovach is less spectacular than her partner-husband, but her energy, her dash and her own sturdy flourishings are quite a match for his. Her pointes are strong, the whipping fouette spins cause her no trouble, her balance is good and her general movement behaviour tells of authority as well as sturdiness. She and Mr. Rabovsky make a dashing pair as they invite danger through the zip and bravado of their actions, as they introduce us to a way of dance charged with energy and rich in physically stirring feats of skill. They will be seen in the same offering on all of the remaining—through Feb. 27—performances of the Ballets de Paris in New York.

It is also worthy of note that the Ballets de Paris company itself, which had a near-disastrous opening a few weeks ago, due to lack of rehearsals and scenic problems, is now performing with the speed, accuracy and chic expected of such a group. Not everything on the program is of great artistic moment but it is now neatly presented and it is all thoroughly (or pretty thoroughly) entertaining. Last evening, Mr. Petit, Violette Verdy and George Reich were particularly good in *Le Loup* and Leslie Caron, beautifully partnered by Serge Perrault, was in fine, impish form in *Deuil en 24 Heures*. *Carmen,* with Colette Marchand, completed the bill. [*New York Herald Tribune*]

Canadian Ballet Accomplishments

February 14, 1954

The Canadians, these days, are busy with ballet. In recent years, major cities from one coast to the other have established ballet companies, some of them professional, others semi-professional and still others of amateur status, and there have been ballet festivals also through which the citizens of Canada have come to recognize more fully their national accomplishments in dance. Last summer, the National Ballet Company of Canada traveled to the United States to give a series of successful performances on the Jacob's Pillow Dance Festival at Lee, Mass., and last week the Royal Winnipeg Ballet of Canada displayed its special dance gifts at the National Theater in Washington, D. C.

Neither company is the equal of England's Sadler's Wells Ballet or of our own Ballet Theatre or the New York City Ballet nor is such equality pretended. Both are modest, junior organizations with ambition, taste and a desire to contribute to the international art of ballet the distinctive colors, in performing and in choreography, of Canadian dance skills. The two are rivals, and their rivalry is said to be exceedingly sharp, but they are different in many respects.

Two Major Groups The National Company of Canada, which has, I think, the stronger dancers, is concerned almost exclusively with what might be called a standard repertory composed of traditional ballets, classical pas de deux and such modern masterworks as *Lilac Garden*. The Royal Winnipeg Ballet, on the other hand, is not as much interested in traditional ballets—other than a few pas de deux and longer excerpts from the classics—as it is in building a repertory of new creations, several of them treating with Canadian themes and materials.

The opening night program in Washington contained two new ballet abstractions—or shall we call them non-narrative compositions?—choreographed by Arnold Spohr, the company's chief (although his technique is limited) male dancer and two works on indigenous themes by Gweneth Lloyd, artistic director of the Royal Winnipeg Ballet. Miss Lloyd's offerings were the more impressive not only because of their maturer choreography but also because the somewhat inexperienced (but that is not to say undisciplined) dancers were on safer ground with lusty, dramatic activities than with assignments demanding movement exactitude and stylistic precision.

Miss Lloyd's *Shadow on the Prairie,* with a striking score by Robert Fleming, was almost consistently successful in its fusing of folk dance movement with a kind of free style ballet. Particularly eloquent was an extended solo designed for the young bride in which her growing terror of the unfamiliar prairie emptiness was clearly and touchingly conveyed to the point that her ultimate madness and death seemed inevitable. Incidentally, this piece was especially well danced by the company with Carlu Carter giving a splendid performance as the heroine and Gordon Wales excellent as the husband.

A Folk Ballet   Lots of fun was Miss Lloyd's rough and gawdy treatment of *The Shooting of Dan McGrew,* a work which has its thin moments but which also boasts passages of inspired comedy and of lusty action. Every one, including the handsome and spirited Eva von Gencsy, Roger Fisher, Bill McGrath and Mr. Spohr, danced it with that communicable vigor which is one of this youthful company's happiest characteristics.

And this brings us to Mr. Spohr in his capacity as choreographer. His two ballets, *Intermede* and *Ballet Premier,* are clearly the work of a fine craftsman, for their abstract designs are sequentially clear and imaginative in movement detail. But craftsmanship is not necessarily, nor often, artistry.

Mr. Spohr makes stage pictures, and they are good ones, but because he tends toward photographic moments of such sharpness a series of abrupt finales ensue, his ballets lose their potential sweep and their exploitation of a given movement pattern is obscured. Mr. Spohr's choreographic gift, however, is a genuine one, modeled (by coincidence and not by direct training) after that of George Balanchine, the master of pure movement sensitized through music.

The young Canadian choreographer will, without question, develop into an imaginative, sensitive and tasteful dance creator of which Canada may be proud, just as the omens indicate that the Royal Winnipeg Ballet itself may, in all likelihood, grow from a junior company of fine promise and great charm into an adult dance organization capable of sharing the burdens, the duties and the joys of the major ballet groups of the New World. [*New York Herald Tribune*]

American Dance Festival

August 20, 1954: World Premiere

New London, Conn., Aug. 19.   The thematic grandeur, the rich and royal colors and the dramatic immediacy of the religious painting of the Italian renaissance had temporary renewal in dance this evening when Connecticut College, on the occasion of the opening of the seventh annual American Dance Festival, presented José Limón and an all-male company in the world premiere of *The Traitor*.

The new work, the first dance production to be commissioned by this college, treats with the tragedy of history's most notorious betrayer, Judas, for although Mr. Limón, the choreographer, does not specifically identify the traitor as Judas or the leader as Jesus, their identities are clear and the drama of betrayal, including the scene of the Last Supper, is instantly related to its Biblical source.

In every respect, *The Traitor* is a tremendous creation for the theater. Paul Trautvetter's setting of narrow archways suggests the labyrinthine beauty and mystery of Jerusalem's ancient streets. Pauline Lawrence's costumes, though modern in cut, proclaim their heroic colors with boldness. The score by Gunther Schuller (symphony for brasses) services the various characters and the conflict with dramatic pertinence and the striking lighting by Tharon Musser establishes atmosphere, seeks and reveals the particular beauties of choreographic pattern.

But for a dance drama, these contributory elements are not enough to compose a successful theater piece. Choreography must dominate. In *The Traitor* it does just that. Mr. Limón has created group designs and single-body patterns of enormous sculptural and pictorial splendor, but as majestic as these are in outline they are never merely pictures. Each is the result of a dramatic drive. One may be the climax, the final statement in a phrase of action or a point of drama held captive in a moment of arrested motion.

Clearly, frighteningly, the consuming jealousy of Judas is portrayed in angry gesture, great exhortations, twisted insinuations and clearly and strongly the unquenchable fire of Jesus' mission glows through actions revelatory of purpose, dedication, faith and a strangely appealing kindness steeled with sternness. The ensemble of six men serves first as the followers of the Jesus-figure, later as a general chorus which carries off the crucified one and torments the traitor as he hangs in death.

Although the entire work possesses cumulative dramatic power, particularly stirring is the episode of the Last Supper, powerfully conceived both with respect to stage design and to movement characterizations. Here, indeed, one could not fail to recall the great paintings of the past while at the same time responding to the instant urgings of contemporary, living theater.

In the title part, Mr. Limón gave a portrayal notable for its communicable passion and for its penetrating definition of details of character and key points of drama. Lucas Hoving danced the role of the leader with a dignity which was never drab, never self-righteous but at all times vital, urgent, commanding. The supporting parts were splendidly cared for by Charles Czarny, Richard Fitz-Gerald, Michael Hollander, Alvin Schulman, Otis Bigelow and Jon Coyle, several of them excellent as individual performers, all of them superb as members of an impressive dance unit. [*New York Herald Tribune*]

1955

A Merry Markova

Ballet Theatre presents Alonso as Giselle, Markova as Juliet, and Nora Kaye and Erik Bruhn in the Black Swan Pas de Deux • The ANTA American Dance Series offers Anna Sokolow's Rooms • The Royal Danish Ballet debuts at Jacob's Pillow • Sadler's Wells returns with Fonteyn in Tiresias and Firebird and Svetlana Beriosova in Rinaldo and Armida • Carmen Amaya and Katherine Dunham still light up the stage • Ruth Page presents Markova on Broadway in The Merry Widow

The Ballet Theatre

April 15, 1955

The perennial nature of the ballet *Giselle* is, in certain respects, a cause for wonder. By modern dramatic standards, its story of an inconstant love, of death from a broken heart and of ghostly girls haunting dim glades at night time does border on the foolish. Yet *Giselle* has served the world's ballet companies for more than a century, and it has been a constant favorite in the highly contemporary repertory of the Ballet Theatre since the company's inception fifteen years ago.

Last night at the Metropolitan Opera House, the Ballet Theatre presented *Giselle* for the first time this season and the reason for this ballet's staying powers was immediately apparent. It may be foolish as unadorned narrative but as a ballet it is miraculous. And when there is a truly inspired ballerina to enact the role of Giselle, even the story seems reasonable, poignant, emotionally compelling.

The Giselle on this occasion was the Cuban ballerina, Alicia Alonso, who has long since established herself as one of the great Giselles of our time. Through her impeccable classicism glows a Latin warmth which, in turn, suffuses the entire ballet with a rich range of dramatic colors. Her peasant girl of Act I, though physically fragile, is spirited, incurably romantic and given to

295

sudden shifts of mood. Pleasure and doubt, ecstasy and despair alternate swiftly as she suspects and then learns that her handsome suitor is not a country boy but a nobleman and, indeed, is engaged to another.

Thus does Miss Alonso prepare for the coming mad scene. Her delicateness, her bright innocence, her emotional instability are so clearly defined that we can and do believe that the betrayal has driven her from her senses, pushed her toward suicide and, finally halted forever a too trusting heart.

In Act II, as a Will or spirit, Miss Alonso succeeds in creating an air of ghostly fantasy while at the same time permitting us to see that her love for the now contrite Albrecht has spanned the barrier between life and death. Here, in this act, she is incredibly light, elusive, swift of movement.

It was, then, a memorable performance which Miss Alonso gave. For the record, I suppose I should note that there were about three minor mishaps of a technical nature but they really didn't matter much in the light of a total characterization which was as illuminating as it was exhilarating.

As Albrecht, Igor Youskevitch was splendid, injecting humor where humor was appropriate and coloring the rest of his enactment with varying degrees of gallantry, tenderness, passion and remorse. Needless to say, his pure dance passages were brilliantly realized.

The Queen of the Wills was played and danced with enormous power and pertinent arrogance by Lupe Serrano, one of the Ballet Theatre's most valuable members, a girl who possesses unusually fine elevation and accomplishes all her movements with authority and exactness.

The corps de ballet, I thought, danced well indeed, for despite some uneven lines in the formal dances of Act II, unity in style, in rhythm and in dynamics prevailed throughout. [*New York Herald Tribune*]

April 16, 1955

Alicia Markova, guest artist with the Ballet Theatre during the company's fifteenth anniversary season, now being celebrated at the Metropolitan Opera House, returned last evening to a role she created for this same troupe more than a decade ago. The occasion was the revival of Antony Tudor's *Romeo and Juliet,* to music of Delius and with lavish scenery and costumes by Eugene Berman.

Miss Markova was not the only "original" in the cast. In addition to her heroine, there were Hugh Laing as Romeo and Nicolas Orloff as Mercutio, both participants in the 1943 premiere.

The English ballerina's conception of Juliet is a sweet but compelling one, for although she gives accent to the delicate and gentle nature of the girl, a radiance pervades her actions and her stillnesses, illuminating a shy but genuine passion.

296

Actually, there are no virtuosic steps with which the ballerina may invite attention. This Juliet, to come alive, must convey her emotions through subtle gestures, a loving glance, an eager run, a melting responsiveness to the approaches of her beloved. Miss Markova does just this and her Juliet, though vocally mute, communicates its poetry through lyricism of motion.

Mr. Laing has always been a superb Romeo, impetuous, sometimes sullen, tense and passionate, and Mr. Orloff, though small of stature, manages to seem dashing and full of devil-may-care bravado. The smaller roles were nicely played, especially by Vernon Lusby as Paris, Charles Bennett as the Friar, Darrell Notara as Tybalt and Catherine Horn as the Nurse.

Aside from one or two moments of rhythmic disunity in the opening men's dance, the large ensemble danced the exceptionally difficult (though they are not often spectacular) measures well. Indeed, this *Romeo and Juliet* is rarely spectacular in its movements—its spectacle is in the staging—but it is quietly moving and handsome to behold.

After the leisurely beauties of *Romeo and Juliet*, the Ballet Theatre zoomed into a rousing performance of Agnes de Mille's *Rodeo*, a ballet which, as every one should know by now, is bursting with action, comedy, romance and all kinds of free-style movements which seem as fresh now as they did when Miss de Mille invented them.

Heading the cast—and a marvelous one it was—were John Kriza as the Champion Roper, James Mitchell as the Head Wrangler and, in the ballet's key part, Jenny Workman as the Cowgirl. I don't suppose any dancer could make one forget how marvelous Miss de Mille was in this role, but Miss Workman is certainly next best to the choreographer herself. She is brash and funny and enormously appealing and she makes every one on both sides of the footlights fall in love with her.

Mr. Kriza was in top form for one of his best roles and Mr. Mitchell played the Wrangler with such physical strength and dramatic color that it emerged as the co-starring role it was always intended to be.

For this program *The Black Swan* pas de deux, which had been performed earlier in the week, had Nora Kaye and Erik Bruhn as its protagonists and what a performance it was! Together and separately, the two were electrifying in their flashing journey through a maze of intricate steps.

Miss Kaye, who has always found this a fine outlet for her virtuosity, tossed off her multiple turns, her balances and her hoppings on point with physical ease and stylistic glitter and Mr. Bruhn, a member of the Royal Danish Ballet, made it clear that in him we may well find a new contender for the title of first classic male dancer of our day. He may not yet have the polish of his seniors but he is, in a word, terrific. [*New York Herald Tribune*]

American Dance

May 16, 1955

Anne Sokolow's *Rooms*, which has had a few off-Broadway showings, was presented yesterday afternoon at the ANTA Theater on the American Dance series. Those who attended the earlier performances had circulated enthusiastic reports about Miss Sokolow's new group creation, a procedure which sometimes invites too great expectations. However, the prophets were right. *Rooms* is a powerful, deeply penetrating exploration of man's aloneness (as distinct from loneliness, which is something else again).

On a dimly lit stage, furnished only with a scattering of plain, straight chairs, nine episodes are given. In the first, which establishes the point that aloneness does not mean the absence of others, eight persons move on or near their special chairs. Despite proximity, each is utterly alone in his room, in his little area, in himself.

Subsequently, Miss Sokolow defines specific examples of aloneness. There is the dreamer who has space to himself, unobstructed but also unattended in his dreams. There is the lonely woman who fabricates a lover, social companionship and gaiety and finds she cannot fill the emptiness and there is the boy, struck by panic, who searches out and begs for help and assurance, only to be turned down by the cold, unresponsive dismissals of those to whom he appeals.

There are other sequences, including one called Going in which a young man soon becomes "real gone" as he submits to hypnotic, self-mesmerizing rhythms of jazz. Even in Desire aloneness is manifest as three boys and three girls achieve brushing contacts—a leg against a leg—but fail in replacing solitude with romantic union.

It is obvious, from the foregoing comments, that *Rooms* is hardly a cheerful work of the theater, but it is the function of any theater art to disturb and to stimulate as well as to divert. Miss Sokolow has given her subject stunning theatrical treatment through movements which are striking as pure dance action but also revelatory of the individual dreams of each of the participants or groups of participants. Indeed, she makes you care about her characters to the degree that their problems replace your own. And what more effective magic can a choreographer work?

Miss Sokolow's company, composed of experienced dancers and performers sensitive to their director's style, danced *Rooms* with technical authority and dramatic force. Of the soloists, Jeff Duncan (Dreams), Beatrice Seckler (Escape), Jack Moore (Going) and Donald McKayle (Panic) were particularly impressive and in Daydreams, Eve Beck, Judith Coy and Sandra Pine performed their flowing measures beautifully.

A fine jazz score, expertly tailored to the ballet's theme and its many variations, composed by Kenyon Hopkins, was excellently played by a small ensemble of musicians under the composer's direction. [*New York Herald Tribune*]

Dance World: Series in Review

May 22, 1955

American Dance, during a three-week season at the ANTA Theater, proved that modern dance, as an independent theater art, is still very much alive. We have known, of course, that it has been a lively participant in television and musical comedy dancing, in movies and, of course in the field of education. As dance theater, its leaders have found difficulties in obtaining Broadway houses, thus making it seem as if the modern dance movement had entered a lull.

Actually, modern dance has creative as well as financial problems and it may be said that certain of its junior exponents have yet to find themselves as choreographers (most are pretty good performers or, at least, technicians). But the American Dance season, sponsored by the B. de Rothschild Foundation, brought together something more than seventy dancers in forty productions, many of them new.

As I have pointed out before, the key figures of modern dance would do well to pool their choreographic resources and performing skills into a single modern dance repertory company. It is easier to sermonize about it than to do it, I realize, but it is a goal that the artists themselves and imaginative managers–bookers might consider more seriously than they have in the past.

Miss de Rothschild   Bethsabée de Rothschild, the foundation's guiding force, gave us the next best thing to this dreamed-of company in the American Dance series which ended yesterday. All of the companies, all of the dancers were highly expert and although not every selection was of top caliber, the repertory as a whole was on a plane worthy of the highest standards of modern dance.

It would be impossible to offer more than capsule summaries of major events in the American Dance season. Martha Graham, the most illustrious of modern dancers, danced with undiminished technical power and, perhaps, greater luminosity of spirit than ever before. And the dancing of her company was something to marvel at.

Of Miss Graham's new choreographies, *Ardent Song,* a lush, Oriental-like ritual of the mysteries of the night, was notable for its beauties of design and for its genuine capturing of a variety of romantic, erotic moods. *Seraphic Song,* another group piece in which Miss Graham did not appear as dancer, was based on the character of Saint Joan and was impressive more for its elaborate staging, for its air of pageantry than for its actual dance patterns. However, the second performance indicated that, as the dancers dug deep into their roles, there was more dramatic richness to the ballet than was apparent at the premiere.

Miss Graham's Voyage   The same thing happened to *Theater for a Voyage.* Miss Graham, three of her men dancers and the choreography itself were disappointing at first but at the second performance, when the orchestra's tempo was faster and the nerves of a premiere gone, *Theater for a Voyage* commenced to convey its emotional messages more clearly.

In such enduring pieces as *Cave of the Heart, Every Soul Is a Circus* and *Appalachian Spring,* Miss Graham and her company gave us theater dance of the highest order.

José Limón and his company, sharing the major performing duties of American Dance with Miss Graham, shared honors as well. He appeared in his own works and in those by his artistic director, Doris Humphrey, one of the world's great choreographers. Of special significance was his all-male work, *The Traitor,* a dramatically stirring and wonderfully sensitive treatment of the betrayal of Jesus by Judas.

Humphrey and Limón   Miss Humphrey's *Felipe El Loco,* though improved since its premiere last summer, still disappointed but her comparatively new *Ruins and Visions* was magnificently danced and acted by the Limón company and the star and his assistants gave particularly telling performances in *Day on Earth* (Humphrey), *Lament for Ignacio Sanchez Mejias* (Humphrey), *Night Spell* (Humphrey) and *The Moor's Pavane* (Limón).

Anna Sokolow, using a group especially assembled for the occasion, was represented by *Rooms,* a work which treated the state of being alone with beauty, uncommon tenderness and heartdeep understanding. Valerie Bettis, also supported by a company created for the season, offered a fine revival of her Faulkner-inspired *As I Lay Dying* and, as a soloist, gave us a masterful example of that difficult idiom, the dramatic solo, in *The Golden Round,* a vivid characterization of the ambitions and emotional turmoils of Lady Macbeth.

John Butler and his dancers, one of the best of the contemporary dance units, highly theatrical but with genuine modern dance integrity, gave the series one of its most joyful highlights in *Three Promenades With the Lord* while Pearl Lang and her company brought a more subdued but gently flowing version of joy to the ANTA stage in *And Joy Is My Witness.*

The Soloists   As to the soloists, Paul Draper earned laurels for everything he danced as the series' only tap artist; Ann Halprin's whirling, ecstatic *The Prophetess* was exceptionally good; Iris Mabry fared well in her comic moments and Pauline Koner fared brilliantly in her dramatic solo but poorly in her comedy; in her older pieces, Janet Collins was nothing short of magical but her new solo, though flawlessly performed, was fluff of the fluffiest sort and Daniel Nagrin, sharp and biting in his dance attacks, danced as he always does, with splendid prowess.

There were, as I have noted, some disappointments but Miss de Rothschild's season made one point, and an important one it is, brightly clear: that the range of modern dance is bounded only by the range of man's experience. [*New York Herald Tribune*]

Jacob's Pillow Festival

July 8, 1955

Lee, Mass., July 7.   A royal debut took place yesterday evening amid rustic New England surroundings as ten leading dancers of the Royal Danish Ballet made their first American appearance in the Ted Shawn Theater on the Jacob's Pillow Dance Festival series. A large audience was present for this major dance event and the visitors were greeted at almost every turn by warm applause, by bravos and, at the close, a hearty ovation.

Those Americans who had seen the Royal Danish Ballet, one of the oldest continuously active dance organizations in the world, on home ground wondered whether lack of elaborate production facilities and the smallness of the touring unit could possibly do justice to the great traditions of Danish ballet.

They need not have worried, for although we did not see Danish ballet at its fullest, we were able to savor its special dance flavors, enjoy more than a passing glimpse of its hitherto unfamiliar choreographies and capitulate to the charm and vitality of as delightful a group of performers as we Americans have seen in a long time. And how do the Danes dance? Well, they are much stronger technically than rumor had predicted. True, they are less polished in accomplishing turns than ballet dancers of other school heritage but they are joyous aerialists bounding skyward frequently and gleefully.

The men are, perhaps, more effective dancers than the women, a state which may certainly be attributed to the great nineteenth-century ballet master, August Bournonville (the real father of Danish ballet), whose own dancing

301

prowess and the teaching influence of the great French dancer, Auguste Vestris, apparently convinced him that the male dancer could be more than a prop for the ballerina.

The Danes also have a wonderful freedom of action in the hip socket, enabling them to swing their legs in high and easy arcs of action and because their spines are also trained in mobility, the dancers seem to have a body-lilt not often found in Russian-trained dancers. Rhythmically, they like to end a phrase with a sturdy accent, with a sort of kinetic flip which is rather like using an exclamation point at the end of a sentence.

Choreographic interest in their initial program quite naturally centered in the Bournonville ballets and extracts and in other works unknown to the American theater. The company opened with Bournonville's *Konservatoriet*, a delightful piece serving to establish the Bournonville style which, after a century, still is the governing system in Denmark, and the technical range of the Danish performer. It is simply a dancing lesson with steps and patterns increasing in difficulty and complexity as the work progresses.

Also of interest were the extracts from *Coppélia*, with choreography by Hans Beck after the original of Saint-Léon. The dances were completely different from those seen in the *Coppélia* productions mounted in America. They were less virtuosic, perhaps, but highly inventive, piquant and admirably related to the Delibes score.

In these bits from *Coppélia*, Inge Sande made an irresistible Swanhilda and there were fine, virile actions supplied by Fredbjørn Bjørnson, Fleming Flindt and Stanley Williams.

Kirsten Ralov and Mr. Bjørnson were seen in a completely winning Pas de Deux from Bournonville's *Flower Festival of Genzano* and in Emilie Walbom's *Dream Pictures*. Mona Vangsaae was particularly lovely in two lyrical dances, one romantic and the other slightly satirical, and there were pleasant passages by Miss Sand as Columbine, Frank Schaufuss as Harlequin and the assisting soloists.

In the Grand Pas de Deux from *The Nutcracker*, Miss Vangsaae and Mr. Schaufuss, both exceptionally gifted dancers in other assignments, were not consistently effective in this Russian-style duet. Miss Vangsaae's arm movements left much to be desired and both of them lacked, in certain passages, that lightness of action, the movement precision and that exactitude of body-line essential to this creation.

Elof Nielsen, pianist, provided the dancers with rhythmically helpful accompaniments, which were occasionally distressing tonally, and John Christian and William Thomas were responsible for the fine lighting and the excellent settings (particularly *Coppélia*). But all interest centered on the Royal Danish Dancers themselves and, with the exception of the ill-advised *Nutcracker*, they did honor to their great ballet heritage and brought to all of us, I think, a memorable dance experience. [*New York Herald Tribune*]

302

Sadler's Wells Ballet

September 17, 1955

The woman's lot is the happier one. Or is it the man's? That is the argument of *Tiresias,* the Frederick Ashton ballet, which was given its first American presentation last evening at the Metropolitan Opera House by the Sadler's Wells Ballet. It is a pretty interesting argument, too, if you stop to analyze it, which I fear Mr. Ashton did not.

I bow to no one in my profound admiration for Mr. Ashton's awesome choreographic gifts, but I cannot turn that admiration toward *Tiresias.* In his *Daphnis and Chloe,* the distinguished choreographer has taken an ancient classic myth and given it contemporary impact, infused it with that vitality which belongs only to immediacy. In *Tiresias,* he has taken another ancient tale and given us little but pictorial pomp and practically no circumstance at all.

His story is that of a Cretan athlete who, upon seeing two snakes engaged in sinuous courtship, strikes the female and is instantly transformed into a woman. Somewhat later, after experiencing womanhood for an unspecified spell, the female Tiresias is confronted with the snakes once again. This time, striking the male, Tiresias is changed back into a man. In the third and closing scene, he is brought before Zeus and Hera and asked to settle the argument—which he is well equipped to do—of which is the happier, the male or the female. Tiresias decides upon the female, Hera strikes him blind in her fury and Zeus gives him the gift of prophecy.

This is, no doubt about it, a marvelous story and it should be hair-raising when told in terms of dance action. Unfortunately, Mr. Ashton has, in his choreographic defining of character, merely skimmed the attributes of masculinity and femininity.

We are shown a Tiresias who is physically stronger than the girl athletes he bests in a minor contest. But what of his behavior in the face of peril, of passion, of boredom? How does his maleness color his conduct? And we may ask the same of Tiresias the woman. We are shown her female form and certain patterns which appear to be feminine but that is all. One may say that it is impossible to characterize the male and the female with anything approaching philosophical depth in dance terms. In modern dance, Doris Humphrey accomplished it brilliantly in her *Ritmo Jondo.* It could also be done in ballet.

Well, Mr. Ashton tells the story, superficially, and one finds himself far less concerned with the outcome than with, say, the fate of the Sleeping Beauty and her Prince Charming, two extremely familiar figures in an equally familiar fairytale.

At any rate, *Tiresias* has been lavishly mounted. Isabel Lambert's settings, with the accent upon the Cretan bull motif, are exceptionally handsome and certain of her costumes are striking, although I did feel that Hera resembled the Hindu goddess Kali and Zeus had his Wotan aspects. The score, by the late Constant Lambert, seemed heavy, plodding.

Michael Somes as the male Tiresias and Violetta Elvin as the female Tiresias were visually handsome and probably got just about as much out of their roles as it was possible to get. Pauline Clayden and Brian Shaw were the Snakes but even their activities, though accomplished horizontally, seemed more playful than passionate. [New York Herald Tribune]

September 21, 1955

English balletomanes engaged in a reportedly lively controversy last year when their own Sadler's Wells Ballet presented its revival of Michel Fokine's forty-five-year-old classic, *The Firebird*. Last night at the Metropolitan Opera House, American dance followers had their first opportunity to see and to exchange their own pros and cons on the subject. Discussion there will be, but I doubt that any raging controversy will ensue.

The current production was restaged by Serge Grigoriev and Liubov Tchernicheva, both former members of the Diaghileff ballet which first mounted the Fokine–Stravinsky work, and Margot Fonteyn, the prima ballerina of the Sadler's Wells, was directed in her part by Tamara Karsavina, creator of the title role. It was Miss Fonteyn's characterization around which much of the controversy centered.

The Fonteyn characterization should cause little controversy here. First of all, few Americans will be able to compare her interpretation with that of other ballerinas (certainly few can say they saw Karsavina in it); secondly, for those who have seen several Firebirds, the typical American reaction is likely to be the more varied characterizations there are afoot the better.

If there is any argument, it will probably concern itself with which is the more enjoyable production, the shortened and totally rechoreographed version by George Balanchine (a hit in the repertory of the New York City Ballet) or the longer, old Fokine original freshly mounted. Well, we'll get into that in a moment. First to Miss Fonteyn.

Miss Fonteyn (and I'm not going to compare her with any other ballerina) is a proudful, flashing, beautiful Firebird. There was a regal fierceness about certain of her actions, a quality totally in keeping with a free born creature of the air, and there was a marvelous communication of the sense of desperation as she found herself a captive of the huntsman Prince.

Indeed, Miss Fonteyn succeeded in fusing her make believe movements with tremendous emotional reality. The flutterings, the preenings, the soarings, the dartings, the swiftly beating gestures as she attempted escape seemed not merely bird imitations, for through Miss Fonteyn's performing magic, they revealed the heart of this wild and powerful creature of the air.

As to the production itself, one must say that Fokine's choreographic force and sensitivity shine brightly in the passages designed for the Firebird herself, in the mass groupings of dancers and in gestures revelatory of human warmth and romance.

There are, however, barren patches and they seem barren to me not because of any lack of pleasant stage design, but because of lack of pace. Perhaps some of us demand an overdose of speed in this era of rushing, but I for one got a trifle weary with the ball game played by the Enchanted Princess, with the extended activities (still beautifully designed) of the magician's retinue and with that endless finale in which nothing happens.

The settings and costumes by Gontcharova for this *Firebird* are nothing short of sumptuous and, in the inactive last scene, one can watch the gorgeous background and the horde of brightly clad dancers with something of the same interest one finds in seeing a particularly good illustration in a book of fairy tales. And finally, Igor Stravinsky's great score is always there when things bog down on stage.

Supporting Miss Fonteyn in *The Firebird* were Michael Somes as the young hero, Svetlana Beriosova as the maiden of his choice and Frederick Ashton, who gave a striking performance (in a miraculous makeup) of the evil magician.

The program opened with the first American performance of Frederick Ashton's *Rinaldo and Armida,* a four-character tale involving a warrior and an enchantress, their ill-starred love and her death.

It is a short work which does not allow much time for detailed characterization, but Mr. Ashton has come up with a thoroughly entertaining and excitingly composed theater piece. Mr. Somes was properly amorous as the warrior and Miss Beriosova danced like a dream as the Enchantress. Anne Heaton and Ronald Hynd accomplished their lesser roles well, the score by Malcolm Arnold was properly lush (and fraught with emotional suspense) and the scenery by Peter Rice, enhanced by John Sullivan's lighting and some fine steam effects, provided the perfect setting for this fleet and absorbing drama in dance. [*New York Herald Tribune*]

Carmen Amaya

November 21, 1955

That supersonic, dynamite-laden Spanish gypsy, Carmen Amaya, is back in town. A few weeks ago, Miss Amaya had played four performances in

Carnegie Hall, her first American appearances in more than a decade, and had the old house shaking with the storms of applause. Last evening, Miss Amaya and her company of Spanish gypsy dancers and musicians returned to New York for a three-week engagement at the Holiday Theater and again the shouts of "Ole!" and "Bravo!" echoed past the portals and out onto Broadway.

Basically the program is the same as that presented at Carnegie, although a few new numbers have been added, for aside from a regional jota and a classical dance with balletic flavor, everything was dedicated to flamenco. And this is as it should be, since Miss Amaya and her colleagues are superb exponents of the wild and passionate, sad and mischievous dances of the gypsies.

Of the new numbers, *Ritmos Carmen Amaya* was of major interest, for it not only permitted the star to sing with her fascinating gravel-throated tones but it also gave her rich opportunities for lusty comedy. She mugged outrageously, she told jokes in pantomime and she made fun of her own explosive style of dance. It was all extremely broad, but wholly Spanish in its humor and it serves to present a delightful side of an artist whose dancing is normally incantational in power, in concentration, in dedication.

Elsewhere on the program, Miss Amaya gave us of her incantational forces. There were the passionate invitations and protestations of the *Soleares*; the immeasurably tragic yet fiery rhythms of her great *Siguiriya,* through which the voice of the gypsy people seem to cry and to sing, and the closing *Alegrías,* in which Miss Amaya's feet made unbelievably beautiful and exciting patterns of sound, thunderous, again whispering, sometimes slow and again faster than a hail of bullets.

Again supporting Miss Amaya were Goyo Reyes and Pepita Ortega as the stirring principal dancers; Sabicas, featured guitarist; Domingo Alvarado, flamenco singer; Alfredo Speranza, pianist; three other guitarists and a fine ensemble of dancers, among them Diego and Curro Amaya, both of them impressive performers. At all times, at the Holiday, it is a good Spanish dance show but when Carmen Amaya is on stage, it becomes an event capable of raising your hair, your blood pressure and your spirits. [*New York Herald Tribune*]

Katherine Dunham

November 22, 1955

Katherine Dunham, beautiful, casual of movement and an astute performer, and her contrasting company, exuberant and virtuosic, returned to New York last evening after a five-year absence for an engagement at the Broadway Theater. And let it be said right at the start, before we turn to critical details, that Miss Dunham presents one of the handsomest productions you are likely to see in these parts.

The revue has been costumed by John Pratt and not only has he given Miss Dunham an array of costumes which enhance her own notable charms but he has also dressed every member of the company superbly for each of the varied numbers in the show. The colors are brilliant, the styles imaginative, some are wonderfully funny and others are extravagantly beautiful. Mr. Pratt has also designed the settings and these together with his costumes, make the Dunham show an eye-filling delight.

But what of the choreography and the dancing? Well, much of it is very good indeed—some of it highly distinguished and enormously exciting—and parts of it are mighty thin, slender with respect to choreographic invention and slight with respect to action. At its least impressive, the Dunham revue consists of a parade of picturesque costumes and characters.

Brazilian Suite, the opening work, probably falls into the casual category. Miss Dunham looks lovely, sings a bit in her sweet, small voice and dances hardly at all and her company, though energetic, is confined to the business of creating atmosphere rather than engaging in dances which surge toward climaxes. There are, of course, exceptions and among them I would like to list *Choros 1 and 4,* two delightful variations on the nineteenth-century Brazilian quadrille.

With the Argentine *Tango*, Miss Dunham stepped up her own dancing intensity and in *Veracruzana,* one of her most popular numbers, she returned to work which, though dramatically casual in the manner of the *Brazilian Suite,* is alive with colorful and humorous incidents and inspired passages of choreography. In this number, one of the most unforgettable of Dunham images is to be found, the sight of the star herself dressed all in white and lolling on an enormous white swing which spans the stage.

Miss Dunham's most impressive choreography is to be found in her *Rituals,* including the rites celebrating puberty, fertility, death and religious possession. In the first two rituals especially, Miss Dunham has created movements which are physically brilliant, dramatically pertinent, powerful in the projection of emotion. And her company dances these rites in electrifying fashion.

The men dancers, as is appropriate to most primitive rituals, are given the greater opportunities. They all dance well but Lenwood Morris as the youth and Vanoye Aikens as the warrior in the puberty rite are magnificent. In the fertility dance, Lucille Ellis is splendid and in the rite of death, Miss Dunham gives a highly sensitive performance of the widowed queen who must seek another mate so that renewal of life may be omened even as a death is mourned.

In the closing section of the program the Dunham dancers turned to Americana, starting first with some beautifully sung Negro Spirituals (one was attractively danced) and continuing with popular dances such as the shimmy, black bottom, strut and cakewalk.

The marvelous *Barrelhouse,* in which Miss Dunham and Mr. Aikens do a Florida swamp shimmy, had to be encored and deservedly so, for this is an insinuating, sexy and delightfully humorous dance which every Dunham fan cherishes in his memory. [*New York Herald Tribune*]

A Merry Markova

December 21, 1955

Ruth Page deserves a medal. She has reminded American audiences that Alicia Markova need not always be associated with sylphs and dryads, with fragile heroines, with mistiness. Miss Page had the vision to cast the famed English ballerina in the title part of her ballet, *The Merry Widow,* and to see her judgment justified, first in performance in Chicago and now in a New York engagement which opened last night at the Broadway Theater.

In the early phases of her long and distinguished career, Miss Markova was to be found doing snake-hips in a contemporary ballet as well as dancing the classics. Later, America saw her in a diversity of roles, but her legend of ethereal grace and fragility led her to be identified as the frail Giselle, the delicate Juliet, the re-creation of the floating Taglioni.

In *The Merry Widow,* Miss Markova is far from frail. She is tiny, she is light, she is even gentle, but she exudes very feminine fire, coquettishness and a smooth worldliness which are captivating. She dances far more vigorously than usual, letting her legs kick high, spinning easily and fast, tossing off folk-like measures with brio and leaping with girlish ease.

She is, of course, still Markova, and we wouldn't have it otherwise. Her lightness and deftness are there and so also are certain of her own artistic idiosyncrasies. But this is a Markova in a new light, facing a fresh challenge and coming through with colors flying. [*New York Herald Tribune*]

1956

Bournonville Makes It Big

NYCB presents Maria Tallchief in Pas de Dix; the premieres of Allegro Brilliante, Todd Bolender's Souvenirs, and George Balanchine in Jerome Robbins' The Concert • The Royal Danish Ballet makes its New York debut at the Met • The Yugoslav State dancers make their American debut

New York City Ballet

March 1, 1956

An old-style movie vamp and an aristocratic ballerina, a strange combination, pretty much shared the spotlight at the City Center last evening. The ballerina was, of course, the New York City Ballet's brightest star, Maria Tallchief, who fairly flooded the stage with movement grace and shimmering beauty as she danced the leading part in George Balanchine's *Pas de Dix*.

In this *Pas de Dix*, to music of Glazounov, Miss Tallchief is given opportunities to disclose her mastery of delicate and subtle steps as well as to display that virtuosity for which she is renowned. In both areas, she was all that any one could ask of a ballerina. Her solo variation, exceptionally difficult technically (although it may not seem so), was danced with great stylishness and faultless musical phrasing. Elsewhere, the feet flashed through sparkling patterns, the arms were moved with the dignity of a queen (but with the flowing loveliness of a dancer) and all was radiant.

Because Miss Tallchief is one of the world's great ballerinas (who number no more than a dozen at the most), it is difficult, and almost purposeless, to look at any one else when she is on stage. The *Pas de Dix*, however, is so designed that others have their moments of command. André Eglevsky, for example, not only partnered Miss Tallchief well, but he also turned in some solo measures which revealed him for what he is, a top premier danseur (also a rare breed). The eight supporting dancers—four girls and four boys—danced with vigor, with stylishness and, for the most part, with technical accuracy.

The evening's vamp was Irene Larsson, the most captivating creature in Todd Bolender's *Souvenirs,* a pantomimic spoof on the dress, manners and activities of a group of guests registered at a resort hotel in the year 1914.

Miss Larsson, who created the role of the vamp last season, writhed, slunk, snarled, hissed and tangoed her way through her scenes in hilarious fashion, making short but pleasant shrift of an ardent wooer and demonstrating various methods of using a couch as a springboard to seductive activities. Others in the cast contributed pleasant bits to this highly flimsy but engaging charade but it was Miss Larsson who gave the ballet its moments of gaudy grandeur.

The opening work was Jerome Robbins' *Interplay,* one of the most delightful of all contemporary ballets. The New York City Ballet has never been fully at ease in this brisk and jazzy work—the Ballet Theatre dancers capture its style perfectly—and last evening the same uneasiness was apparent. Every one danced hard but the air of improvisation, the sporting instincts were missing. Carolyn George and Herbert Bliss danced the tender pas de deux beautifully and of the ensemble, Barbara Fallis and Arthur Mitchell alone caught the ballet's feeling of fun. For the rest, this performance of *Interplay* substituted smiling effort for genuine liveliness. [*New York Herald Tribune*]

March 2, 1956

George Balanchine's new ballet, *Allegro Brillante,* is a choreographic exercise. It has no story, no characterization and, actually, no specific mood (other than a general air of pleasantness). Yet it possesses a special kind of fascination as if it were saying, "Here are some classical dance steps and this is how they look when they are paired with musical notes and phrases." Naturally, Mr. Balanchine's new work, which was given its world premiere last evening at the City Center by the New York City Ballet, is not quite as simple as all that.

Allegro Brillante is, in fact, complex. It is rich in steps, in fresh arrangements of steps, in gesture and in patterns of movement. And one of its prime virtues is that it presents Maria Tallchief not as an imperious queen, not as a glittering figure of fantasy but as an exceptionally attractive girl who moves like an angel.

The very exercise-nature of *Allegro Brillante* permits us to concentrate upon Miss Tallchief as a flawless executant of any movement assigned to her, from a simple raising of the arms through a chain of rapid turns across the stage to perilous actions with her partner requiring split-second timing. One does not have to consider what character she is portraying nor does one have

310

to check up on her command of dramatic coloring. One simply watches her move gloriously and it is an exciting experience.

But if Mr. Balanchine has provided his star ballerina with a show-case for the classical purity of one artist, he has not neglected the other dancers in his troupe. Nicholas Magallanes has some impressive duties to perform as Miss Tallchief's partner and dances his own modest measures with facility. The eight supporting dancers also enliven this highly attractive dance exercise as they pursue the imaginative and pictorially agreeable choreographic paths Mr. Balanchine has laid out for them.

Allegro Brillante, set to the single movement of Tchaikovsky's unfinished Third Piano Concerto, was played by the orchestra under Leon Barzin's direction with Nicholas Kopeikine as the distinguished piano soloist. The two musicians joined Miss Tallchief, Mr. Magallanes and Mr. Balanchine on stage for a series of rousing curtain calls which indicated that the audience approved highly of a new work, modest in its theatricality but rich in pure dance values. [*New York Herald Tribune*]

March 7, 1956

An analogy might be drawn between the little girl who had a little curl right in the middle of her forehead and Jerome Robbins' new ballet, *The Concert,* which, when it was good, it was very, very good and when it was bad, it was horrid. For there were moments last evening at the City Center which suggested that the New York City Ballet had come up with the comedy hit of the season (or a decade, for that matter) and there were other moments when one felt that a consistently successful and brilliant choreographer had stumbled.

Mr. Robbins calls his new work a charade and it is at its feeblest when it is just that and at its most inspired when its jokes are told in dance. The choreographer's idea is that at a concert, the individual is free to create images in his mind about the music itself, about its implications and about the trains of thought or reverie which the music may stimulate. For his dance purpose, he has selected music of Chopin and sometimes he has come up with a literal reaction to the Minute Waltz and sometimes his own fancies have led him to create a delicious series of anticlimaxes to the little prelude always so popular in *Les Sylphides.*

The Concert starts with the pianist on stage and a group of varied persons—dreamers, gum-chewers, a bored husband, a culture-seeking wife and the like—as the audience. These figures, augmented by an ensemble from time to time, people the ballet and enact its charades.

Things got off to a fine beginning when Tanaquil LeClercq, stirred to

311

the depths by the music, launched herself into a whirlwind of action, with hair lashing, her face and her feet trying desperately to keep pace with the music until complete collapse struck her.

Another hilarious sequence had to do with a group of dancers unable to agree on steps and rhythms as they went grimly about the task of destroying choreographic form. Here was a dance joke, defying literal description, which had the audience shrieking and choking with laughter. Robert Barnett's Minute Waltz, during which he spun wildly around the stage, was also good fun and there were superb comic moments when the men dancers, picking up the dancing girls in an array of unlikely and unlovely positions, carted them on and off stage.

There were some passing humors to the Butterfly Etude, which involved two armies of angry butterflies (a delightful notion), and there were several pleasantly lyrical and nostalgic passages for Miss LeClercq and for the umbrella-carrying dancers in the Rainbow Prelude. But a series of cartoons in which a wife attempted to polish off her husband with gun, poison and T.N.T., fell flat and there were other pantomimic gags which were equally lifeless.

But in spite of its empty episodes, *The Concert* (amusingly costumed by Irene Sharaff) is certainly worth salvaging, for its best scenes are as funny as anything to be found in the theater of dance. Generous cutting revisions and complete reworking here and there should find Mr. Robbins with another hit to his credit.

Miss LeClercq, Mr. Barnett, Todd Bolender, Yvonne Mounsey and the supporting players danced well and clowned hard and were always effective— upward and downward—as their material. Nicholas Kopeikine was the patient and skilled piano soloist and Hugo Fiorato conducted those portions of the Chopin music which had been orchestrated by Hershy Kay. [*New York Herald Tribune*]

March 9, 1956

The New York City Ballet had its own special surprise party last evening at the City Center when George Balanchine, the company's artistic director, filled in (and quietly unannounced) for one of his ailing dancers, Todd Bolender. It was a surprise enough to have Mr. Balanchine, who has not been an active performer for a good many years, appear on stage but it was doubly surprising to see him in a ballet, *The Concert,* newly created by another choreographer, Jerome Robbins.

Mr. Balanchine, of course, has many talents other than his renowned choreographic skill. Occasionally, he conducts the ballet orchestra and he has, thoroughly bearded and robed, mimed the role of the father in his own *The*

Prodigal Son. In Mr. Robbins' madcap ballet, which had had its premiere on Tuesday, Mr. Balanchine enacted those portions of Mr. Bolender's role which were mainly pantomimic and left the more active sections to the buoyant Robert Barnett.

It was fun to see Mr. Balanchine perform and he was good, a comedian with fine timing. And the ballet itself was improved, for Mr. Robbins had cut it drastically and given it better pace than it had had at the opening. Then, much of it was hilarious but some of it was pretty feeble. The revisions have helped enormously but there is still more work to be done before its really great comic qualities are sustained throughout. [*New York Herald Tribune*]

The Danish Ballet in Review

October 7, 1956

The Royal Danish Ballet, in its American debut at the Metropolitan Opera House, enjoyed a rousing success. To pass over interesting but highly commercial matters briefly, it should be noted that every seat for every performance of the two-week engagement was sold (the gross was approximately one quarter of a million dollars) and that, with a few exceptions, standing-room capacities were reached for the presentations. Furthermore, the Royal Dancers are being met with such fine advance enthusiasm on their present tour (limited in length and area), that Frederick Schang, president of Columbia Artists Management, would like to see the company fly the polar route from Denmark to the West Coast next year for a tour of the West-of-the-Mississippi cities.

The organization's box-office successes were certainly matched by the artistic accomplishments. Choreographically, the repertory ranged from ballets created in the late eighteenth and early-middle nineteenth centuries to creations of the present, from works of Danish choreographers to those of other lands. Obviously, not every one liked everything.

The old *Napoli* (1842), for example, is fairly leisurely for the first two of its three acts. In fact, a Danish ballet official described one of the long pantomimic sequences as "relentless" but then went on to point out that a century ago, no one was in much of a hurry, either on stage or off. Nonetheless, *Napoli* retains a charm, boasts a quaintness, exploits the elements of spectacle and preserves an otherwise forgotten but exceptionally important genre of dance theatre. To watch it is frequently a pleasure, to study it is a unique privilege.

313

The Past   With *La Sylphide,* one was in the presence of a historical master-piece, as enchanting today as it must have been one hundred and twenty years ago and surely the wit and lilt of the oldest of still performed ballets, *The Whims of Cupid* (1786), have not diminished with the years.

But the Royal Dancers did not center their skills entirely upon the choreography of their favored master, August Bournonville (*La Sylphide, Napoli, Konservatoriet*), for they gave an impeccable and glowing performance of Fokine's *Chopiniana* (known to us as *Les Sylphides*) and the same choreographer's *Petrouchka* found new life and color and dramatic impact in the Danish production.

The peak (and a tremendous peak it was) of the Royal Danish Ballet's twentieth-century achievements came with the evening-long *Romeo and Juliet,* created for the Danes last year by England's Frederick Ashton. Here was fabulous production, a ballet version of the great story far better than any I have ever seen and, indeed, a telling of the tale which caused one to forget that it had ever been done in other media. Here, in this Ashton masterpiece, was a Danish triumph.

And, of course, the Danes triumphed not only because of their remarkable repertory, their lavish staging and their royal (always fascinating to Americans) status but also because of their splendid dancers and their wonderfully schooled dancing. Officially, the company is starless and perhaps it is this policy, combined with the fact that the dancers are together in classroom, rehearsal and performance from childhood through retirement, which results in the most faultless ensemble dancing I have ever seen in ballet.

The Soloists   The huge company possesses, naturally, a national style as well as command of the varying Bournonville, Fokine or Ashton styles required by specific periods or themes. But although the Danes can move as one when called upon to do so in unison action, they also can preserve ensemble integrity while at the same time projecting individual detail clearly. Thus, a physically active corps of young adults, a unit of soloists, a group of children and associated mimes can present color, variety and contrast within the framework of perfect unity.

Despite the lack of classifications for ballerinas and premiers danseurs and the accent upon company work as a whole, the Royal Dancers have produced individuals with special talents and exploitable powers. Margrethe Schanne, for example, may be moved from the title role in *La Sylphide* (of which she is the unrivalled delineator) to a brief solo in *Napoli* but her individual artistry preserves its identity in the small, as well as in the large, assignment.

Certainly, the eye quickly finds the long and lovely line, the lightness of action, the quiet radiance of Mona Vangsaa or moves on to the vivid and vital motions of Kirsten Ralov. In Inge Sand, we submit to the ebullience of a joyous soubrette, dashing happily through *Coppélia* or bounding with glee in *Graduation Ball* while the mysterious, floating grace of Kirsten Simone (haunting in *La Sonnambula*) or the girlish rapture of Kirsten Petersen (an irresistible Juliet) or the shining speed of Mette Mollerup (a glowing Rosalind) invite us to forget the ensemble momentarily and cherish the artistry of the individual.

The Royal Dancers abound in strong and highly skilled men. Henning Kronstam, the company's great Romeo, is a genuine danseur noble (in spite of his youth) and a romantic actor–dancer of uncommon powers while Fredbjørn Bjornssøn, whether he is enacting the role of Franz in *Coppélia* better than it has ever been done before or cutting capers in *Graduation Ball* or stopping the show with his zestful and high-flying variations in either *La Sylphide* or *Napoli,* is easily recognizable as a demicaractere dancer with few rivals anywhere in the world.

Dance Actors   Borge Ralov, listed as first solodancer, is the Royal Danish Ballet's top dramatic dancer, a magnificent Petrouchka, and Niels Bjørn Larsen is its great mime, ranging from the enraged Tybalt in *Romeo* to the evil witch in *La Sylphide.* An invaluable member is Stanley Williams who moves from dancing bouncy Bournonville variations through romantic or character leads to excellent and elegant miming and although Frank Schaufuss' duties as ballet master come first, his dancing of Mercutio places him among the organization's most impressive artists.

The Royal Dancers have come and gone but their season at the Metropolitan was such a stirring experience that one prays that Mr. Schang will not only bring them back to America for visits to Western cities but also right back to the Metropolitan for a second and longer engagement. [*New York Herald Tribune*]

Yugoslav State Company

October 12, 1956

With prancing feet, happy smiles and the occasional flash of a sword or a dagger, the Yugoslav State Company of dancers, singers and musicians made its American debut last evening at Carnegie Hall under the management of S. Hurok and with the official sponsorship of the Yugoslav government.

The huge company, generally referred to as *Kolo,* the name of a popular reel dance from its native Serbia, gives as much variety as possible to the folk materials of its nation. Dances and songs from the six Yugoslav Republics are represented and the themes range from communal reel dances through measures almost Oriental in flavor to a dramatic dance of the outlaws or a mock sword dance accompanied by the boom of a drum.

There is rich variety also in costuming and in the very steps themselves, for although this is folk dancing, there are opportunities, especially for the men, to display agility, strength and complexity of movement design, usually at a rapid clip. Nonetheless, the easy-going nature common to folk dancing prevails and the key steps which link the more exciting passages are charming but tend to lull the onlooker. However, if one can do without the incisiveness of straightforward theatrical dancing, these folk artists can delight and, frequently, excite the onlooker.

As for the performing level of the Yugoslav State Company, it is on the highest professional plane, even if the choreographic substance is of folk fabric. The ensemble work is brilliantly executed, for small units or the large company move through the fleetest of steps with unerring precision and accomplish tricky patterns of turns, twists, jumps, kicks or foot-beats in perfect unity. In this respect, it is a remarkable company deserving of the highest praise.

The Carnegie program, listed as *Slavonic Rhapsody* and directed by Olga Skovran, the ballet mistress, choreographer and artistic director, was at all times colorful but some of the numbers were, inevitably, more stirring than others. Among the many highlights, I would like to mention the rousing dance of the outlaws, introduced by a crouching, furtive walk, characterized by alertness as well as vigor and boasting the strongest dramatic thread of any of the dances.

The unaccompanied *Kolo* was also a delight, what with its swift patterns and the rhythms made by the tread of many feet. The sword duel in which the drummer himself participated as dancer as well as musician; the dances of Dalmatia, joyous, big of design and sturdy, and a stunning Macedonian dance for men, built upon catlike steps, wonderfully controlled balances on half-toe and long sequences of slow-motion actions done in unison, were among the other appealing offerings.

The engaging music—a sense of sameness was noticeable in sound as well as in dance action—was provided by an onstage orchestra under the direction of Zarko Milanovitch, by the tambouritan players and by the dancing singers themselves. [*New York Herald Tribune*]

316

1957

Milestones: Ballet and Broadway

John Butler's The Unicorn, The Gorgon and the Manticore premiered by the NYCB • Les Ballets Africains debut at the Martin Beck • Two Spanish dancing stars — Roberto Iglesias and José Greco • Robbins makes history with West Side Story • Square Dance and Agon — two Balanchine masterpieces premiered within one week

New Menotti Fable Triumphs as Ballet

January 27, 1957

There is a pale blue Manticore, with droopy spines (they couldn't hurt a soul) and a sad, affectionate mien, who symbolizes old age. There is a fierce and glittering Gorgon, assured of stance, a trifle arrogant, ready for all comers, who represents manhood. And there is the prancing, skittish, endlessly exuberant, unpredictable Unicorn, the mirror of youth. These are the key, but not necessarily the principal, figures in Gian-Carlo Menotti's madrigal-fable for chorus, dancers and orchestra, produced in New York (it had its premiere in Washington at the Library of Congress) by Ballet Society and performed by the New York City Ballet at the City Center.

There are some cubbyhole worshippers who may argue that *The Unicorn, the Gorgon and the Manticore* is not a ballet in the strictest sense of the term (although the term has never been very strict during the last three centuries) but whether it is a pure ballet (and I happen to think it is) or not, there is no denying that it is pure theater, a brilliantly conceived and faultlessly executed integration of dancing, gesture, poetry, song, instrumental music and visual spectacle.

Laughter, Tears Mr. Menotti's music, as my colleague, Jay Harrison, has pointed out in some detail, is remarkable in texture, in its ability to make one

317

laugh or cry, in its tunes and in other musical matters. The composer's libretto is equally appealing, for it too can lead one to laughter or to tears, as sentiment, wit and passion pour forth in singable, danceable words. Finally, the choreography by John Butler gives stage image and action to music and words so skillfully and vividly that a total theater creation, fusing the powers of several arts, is the happy result.

In this enchanting allegory–commentary (poetry and satire move side by side), which is now at home in the New York City Ballet's current repertory on view at the City Center, Mr. Menotti has presented us with a Poet, a gentle non-conformist, who avoids the society of the townsfolk, "yawns at town meetings" and even refuses to let "the doctor take his pulse." Still, he fascinates the villagers, including the local Countess, as he strolls on succeeding Sundays first with a Unicorn, next a Gorgon and finally a Manticore.

The envious Countess must not be bested by the Poet so she also, and other ladies with her, obtain a like sequence of pets and destroy them in sequence as they presume the Poet has done with his. But when the townspeople rush to the Poet's castle to punish him for his suspected murders, they discover him dying, surrounded by his three devoted monsters, "the pain wrought children of my fancy."

In the beautiful setting designed and illuminated by Jean Rosenthal and wearing Robert Fletcher's stunning costumes (executed by the one and only Karinska), the dancers enact the fable with movements which not only project overt behaviour but which also pare the figures down to their petty or noble, their raging or serene, their envious or happy hearts. Mr. Butler has seen to it that each of the three mythical pets reveals his specific symbolism clearly in carefree (Unicorn), commanding (Gorgon) and gentle (Manticore) actions and he has characterized the Poet through pacings (slow and easy), phrasings and gestures suitable to the dreamer, the pursuer of visions.

The Countess is asked to storm and stamp, to gesticulate, to plead, to dissemble as she harries her mild but doting husband, the Count, into submitting to her whims and obtaining duplicates of the Poet's pets for herself. The Mayor and the Doctor are extensions of the troubled Count and their wives are, for the most part, nervous slaves of the Countess' trend-setting maneuvers.

There are splendid moments of movement virtuosity in *The Unicorn, the Gorgon and the Manticore* and there are great sweeps of choreographed hilarity for the beautiful but waspish Countess. Indeed, the undefeatable wiles of a willful woman have rarely been so amusingly caricatured in dance as in Mr. Butler's choreography. But there is heart-penetrating sadness also, especially in the ballet's closing passages when the Poet is borne from his castle by his pets to die among these creatures of his fancy, these milestones of his life.

The act of creating a masterpiece is, of course, not enough for the theater. It must be performed to live and the New York City Ballet's artists have brought Mr. Menotti's work to vibrant life. Janet Reed, in a performance which reaches the heights of great comedy, is triumphant as the Countess and Roy Tobias is not far behind her in the less demanding but important role of the bedeviled Count. Nicholas Magallanes, not always as bright of motion and dramatic accent as he might be as the Poet, enacts the death scene, however, with wonderful sensitivity and beauty of phrasing.

Trio of Beasts   Arthur Mitchell, Eugene Tanner and Richard Thomas, as the Unicorn, the Gorgon and the Manticore, dance and mime their measures perfectly and John Mandia, Wilma Curley, Jonathan Watts, Barbara Milberg make their supporting roles colorful and enormously effective elements in the overall plan of the fable. Together with the chorus and orchestra, these dancers contribute richly to the swift and continuing dramatic impact inherent in Mr. Menotti's irresistible theater piece.

Lincoln Kirstein, director of the New York City Ballet, has long fostered the development of the lyric theater in America, a theater in which the arts of dance, mime, drama, song, poetry and fantasy, separately or collectively, would be tenderly and, sometimes, daringly nurtured. With his decision to present *The Unicorn, the Gorgon and the Manticore* in the New York City Ballet's repertory, he has once again furthered his cause and, at the same time, given his audiences a fresh and provocative theatrical experience which they will surely treasure in the most selective areas of memory. [*New York Herald Tribune*]

Les Ballets Africains

February 17, 1957

Les Ballets Africains, with a striking array of costumes, wonderfully chic (but appropriate) decor, ritual dances, play dances and, among other embellishments, selections of bare bosoms, made its New York debut last evening at the Martin Beck Theater. About half way through the program, a friend asked me if it was "really ethnic." Well, I have been to Africa and comparing what I saw there and what is on view here, I would say it is quite ethnic in that it is wholly African in flavor, spirit, rhythm and in movement style.

But if it is ethnic, that does not necessarily mean that all the dances are traditional. Along with ancient jungle ceremonies and work dances are songs and dances which clearly reveal the influences of the Arab, the French, the Portugese and, I would say, the American or European serviceman.

Furthermore, the material, both ancient and contemporary, has been edited for the stage. The company, founded in 1952 by Keita Fobeda (presently the Minister of the Interior for the Republic of Guinea), has its headquarters in Paris and whatever screening process occurs there most certainly colors staging, pacing and selection if not the actual dance movements themselves.

At any rate, ethnic or part-ethnic, the members of the troupe are highly professional and the program itself, aside from the fact that certain repetitions of steps and choreographic patterns occasionally lead to lulls, provides for a variety of songs (some richly primitive and others almost flamenco-like), some fine music played by fascinating musical instruments (drums of all kinds, guitars, logs, horns, boxes and a huge gourd-type instrument which sounds like a harp) and dances which range from initiation ceremonies through market scenes to fire-swallowing numbers.

Actually, there is a good deal of virtuosity present to raise the audience right out of their seats. Both the men and the women move their torsos with that remarkable fluidity which seems to be the special province of the African. The step patterns also are exceptionally light, swift and accurate. The men, of course, have the leaps to do and they do them with an elevation and a spring which are enormously exciting. In addition to all manner of jump, there are flying turns, rollovers, aerial tackles and fine variations of these.

The ladies of the ensemble are pretty generally grounded (but this is quite ethnic) and display their brand of virtuosity through the suppleness of the body and in rhythmic agitations (including theme and variations) of the posterior.

Now, I suppose, we must get to the matter of nudity above the waist with respect to the girls of the company. In Africa, naturally, this would not even invite comment, but New York, which is chillier most of the year, does not recognize such methods of dress. The first time the girls appear with bosoms bare, it is in a simple, decorous ceremony. It seems wholly suitable and no more inflammatory than, say, a lovely color photo in the *National Geographic*. Later in the show, however, guilelessness is not always present, for one number, though not really naughty, is nothing more than a not-very-ethnic strip. (I have seen this also in Africa, but I always suspected that outsiders encouraged such choreography.)

All in all, then, Les Ballets Africains offers a diverting evening in the theater and, indeed, moments of rousing vigor and striking action. In addition to the fine corps of dancers, singers and instrumentalists, all of whom merit praise, one must not overlook Bernard Daydé's superb decor and costume designs (Ralph Alswang has supervised the scenery and lighting for the American tour), an integral and delightful part of this African revue. [*New York Herald Tribune*]

Two Spanish Dancing Stars —
Iglesias and Greco

May 20, 1957: Roberto Iglesias

A new and vivid dancer, with a highly virtuosic technique and an intensely dramatic personality, has come along to add his name to the list of the important male Spanish dancers of our day. The name is Roberto Iglesias and he made his New York debut as an independent artist with his own company Saturday evening at Carnegie Hall. Mr. Iglesias has been seen by American audiences in other seasons as a junior performer, and even then he showed great promise, but he has returned now as a dancing star, as a director of his own ensemble and as a choreographer. Thus, the event may properly be called a debut.

And an exciting debut it was, in spite of the fact that dear old Carnegie is hardly ideal for dancing and in spite of dreary lighting effects. Mr. Iglesias managed to triumph over his surroundings and by the end of the show, he had the audience clapping wildly, shouting "Olé!" and even tossing hats into the air.

First, to the dancing of the star himself. His stance is elegant, yet charged with electricity; his heel-beats define a vast array of rhythmic designs, clamor furiously or diminish beautifully to pattering sounds as gentle as raindrops on a roof; his turns are fast, his lunges deep and, when he dances with a partner, the sizzle of sex is in the air.

As a choreographer, he has worked effectively within a somewhat limited area. His sources are almost all regional dances of Spain or flamenco, and in the former he adheres closely to those which bound and bounce, although he achieves some variety through the use of self-accompaniments, such as sticks, blocks, triangles, tambourines and the like. His own early ballet training also shows up in his choreographies, for although they have been Hispanicized to a degree, the lifts, the extremely high kicks, the air-turns, the beats smack from time to time of ballet. It is true, however, that Spanish dance does boast equivalents of these ballet actions.

The least ethnic of his choreographies was also the least effective. This was *Idolos de Arena,* a little ballet based on the bullfight. It had its pleasant moments but the emotions were a trifle sticky and posturing, at times, took the place of dance.

Among the program's many high spots were *Fiesta en la Isla*, a lively and joyous suite of dances from the Canary Islands; *Zorongo Gitano*, an impressive gypsy duet for Mr. Iglesias and Esperanza Galan; *Theme and Variations*, a highly inventive and exuberant arrangement of the jota; *Point and Heel*, zapateados, danced with brilliant foot-work by Mr. Iglesias and Aida Ramirez; the comic peasant courtship dance from Mexico, *El Palomo y la Paloma*, charmingly performed by Lupe García and Antonio Espanol; the hot, heavy, fiery and erotic *Soledad* for the star and Miss Galan (this literally stopped the show and small wonder), and the closing *Duende y Solera* for full company.

Almost everything, as I have indicated, was bubbling peasant or darkly gypsy, with few minor exceptions, yet the program had a cumulative force and carried its audience to increasing peaks of enthusiasm. Mr. Iglesias was the star, the center, the bright focal point of the occasion but his assisting dancers and musicians were excellent. Miss Galan was especially impressive and there were welcome contributions by Maria Merida, singer; Rafael Jerez, guitarist, and Marina Alonso and Ramon Vives, pianists (although they banged the pianos occasionally). [*New York Herald Tribune*]

May 22, 1957: José Greco

José Greco's Spanish dance revues have long been distinguished for variety, taste, great polish, excellent staging and flamenco fire neatly balanced by Spanish elegance. His newest revue opened a three-week engagement at the Playhouse Theater last evening and it is certainly one of his best. New dances and new dancers joined with favorite artists and numbers from other seasons in a program which included gypsy, classical, folk and period dances; comic interludes, little ballets; simply presented dances and songs and brightly mounted production numbers.

Indeed, not since the days of the late, great Argentinita, with whom Mr. Greco was associated as a very young man, has a Spanish dance star so thoroughly exploited the riches of Spain's incomparable dance. The tendency has been to specialize, with the accent on flamenco, and so it is a joy to have Mr. Greco back with an array of dancing treasures.

The star himself is, as almost every one knows, a versatile performer and an expert technician. In flamenco, he is not given to snarling or snorting, concentrating instead upon intensity and upon the projection of body line, clarity of pattern and aristocratic bearing for which he is renowned. He can cut loose, of course, and he did in several of his selections.

Among the highpoints of his own contributions were *Soleares y Seguiriyas*, danced with the lovely Lola de Ronda, in which the curious brooding

322

quality of the Seguiriyas was wonderfully blended with the passion of romance. In this number, there was a fascinating sequence which called for a tonal duet between castanets and heelbeats, as the lovers spoke in the code of musical sounds.

Then came the charming *Los Amantes de Sierra Norena* (set to that captivating song, "Anda Jaleo") with Mr. Greco and Miss de Ronda; Argentinita's enduring regional dance comedy, *La Castellana,* with Mr. Greco, Miss de Ronda and Margarita Zurita; the dashing, prancing, virile *El Cortijo* for the star and three assisting male dancers, and production numbers such as the bullfight ballet (*Lamento y Retorno*), the spritely *Fantasia de Valencia y Aragon* (a splendid first-act finale composed of a classical duet, a bouncy jota for the company and a tambourine jam session), and other works in which Mr. Greco shared honors with his company.

And not only is the company a magnificently trained unit but it is also an aggregation of splendid soloists, both dancers and musicians. New to America was Rosario Caro, a singer–dancer with shattering heel-beats, a powerful and husky voice and an energy in her actions which made a red dress and white petticoats fuse into a turmoil of flame and foam. Matching her was the marvelous Gracia del Sacromonte, a flamenco singer who tears herself nearly to shreds, rotates her head madly and clowns engagingly as she sings.

A quiet and gracious flamenco artist was Manuela de Jerez, who sang with great beauty just as Miss de Ronda provided wholly refreshing contrast to the gypsy dancers in such numbers as her gentle and lyrical *Córdoba*. Also featured were the Bronze Gypsies—José Mancilla Gitanillo Heredia, Maribel de Cirez, Margarita Zurita—who brought fine frenzy, splendid technique, good humor and, of course, gypsy fire to many of their offerings.

The balletic bounce, the leg-beats and the split jumps of *Bolero del Pescador y Verdiales* were executed with verve and skill by a gifted and personable young dancer named José Molina, and Pepita Sevilla and Mr. Heredia clearly stopped the show with their tempestuous and brilliantly executed *Bulerias de Juanene.*

Words of praise are also due the solo guitarist, Carlos Ramos; the pianist, Lydia Del Mar, and the assisting guitarists and ensemble dancers. Norina, a classical singer, was pleasing in some of her offerings but not in all. And a final word of praise for Mr. Greco, not only as a great dancer, but also as an imaginative choreographer, an astute director and a producer who knows how to put on the best Spanish dance revue to be seen here in a long time. [*New York Herald Tribune*]

Hungarian Ballet Dancers
Who Fled Reds Make Debut

July 27, 1957

Ellenville, N. Y., July 27.   Two Hungarian ballet dancers, Vera Pasztor and
Erno Vashegyi, who escaped from Budapest during the Russian invasion of
their homeland last fall, made their American debut last evening at the Empire
State Musical Festival.

Supported by five male dancers recruited recently in New York, the two
offered three ballets, *A Summer Day* to music of Prokofieff, Debussy's *The
Afternoon of a Faun,* and Béla Bartók's *The Miraculous Mandarin,* all with
choreography by Miss Pasztor and Mr. Vashegyi.

Of the three works, *The Miraculous Mandarin* was far and away the most
impressive presentation. This tremendous musical creation, which has had an extremely checkered career in the theater because of the licentious aspects of its
theme, tells the story of a prostitute and her three male procurers. First an old
roué and then a youth are seduced and robbed in the woman's garish quarters.

But with the coming of the mandarin, all is changed. He refuses to die,
although he is beaten, stabbed and hanged. The procurers flee in terror and
the girl tearfully clasps the miraculous mandarin to her and she experiences
true love, immortal love for the first time.

The choreography, except for some disturbing details here and there
(such as a tendency to make steps and gestures abject slaves of musical beats)
was inventive and wonderfully melodramatic. The lurking actions, the violent
attacks of the prostitute's helpers were superbly staged and the patterns designed for the prostitute herself were expertly realized as they ranged from indifference through calculated sensuality to fear and final repentance.

The choreographers clothed the mandarin in movements which were imperious, cool, mysterious, providing him in the battle scene with motions
which clearly defined his superior strength, both physical and spiritual. Mr.
Vashegyi, in the title part, gave a fine performance, aside from some unnecessary flailings. He made the mandarin a figure of terrifying stature. Miss
Pasztor, as the prostitute, danced with remarkable skill, giving us movement
passages of great beauty while at the same time investing her actions with the
varying emotional hues essential to the role.

The ensemble of men was excellent throughout, with José Gutierrez and
Kenneth Gillespie giving brief but vivid enactments of the old rake and the
youthful libertine, respectively, and with Robert Brett, Donald Martin and
Gayle Young doing brilliantly as the procurers. Of these last three, I felt that
Mr. Martin was particularly effective in bringing an animal furtiveness and cat-
like strength to his actions.

Because of the sudden illness of Laszlo Halasz, the conductor, Tibor Serly, the distinguished Bartók authority, led the Symphony of the Air, after only a few hours' rehearsal and gave a brilliant performance of this masterful, almost overwhelming score which evoked cheers from the audience.

Before now, *The Miraculous Mandarin,* Miss Pasztor, Mr. Vashegyi and the ensemble appeared in *Summer Day.* Although they danced acceptably, the choreography captured nothing of the wit and the engaging moods of the Prokofieff score. Indeed, it was all pretty pedestrian, often awkward and, at times, absolutely devoid of interest. The dancers' version of *Afternoon of a Faun* had nothing to do with the Nijinsky original, for this duet treatment detoured possibly effective archaisms, eluded any quality of soft and subtle, sensuality and settled for a kind of characterless romancing. Sheldon Soffer, however, conducted both scores skillfully. [*New York Herald Tribune*]

The West Side Dance Story

October 20, 1957

The controversies swirling about *West Side Story*, the new musical at the Winter Garden, are in themselves complimentary, for no one cares to waste energy arguing over something inconsequential. Furthermore, it is pretty generally agreed that *West Side Story* is an enormously important theater creation. Some think it is a precedent-setting masterpiece (I do); my distinguished colleague, Walter Kerr, has found it to be "the masterly work of some clear, imaginative, adventuresome minds" but finds a major flaw in its "heartless" craftsmanship; others are shocked by the brutality of its characters, members of two city gangs of delinquents; a few stuffy souls may possibly grumble, "what's happened to the old time musical comedy?" (*Happy Hunting* anyone?)

There are those who may feel that since musicals are usually comedies that all musicals (unless they are quarantined by the walls of an opera house) must be light and cheery. Yet the basic form of the American musical may possibly be the most exciting and potentially fertile development in the theater since the Greek drama emerged from the danced poetry of the dithyramb. The musical theater, then, may quite properly treat with tragedy as well as with comedy. *West Side Story*, deriving its theme from *Romeo and Juliet,* is obviously a tragedy and because the Montagues and the Capulets have been changed to the teenage gang called Jets and to the Sharks (Puerto Ricans), the tale has disturbing significance for viewers of today.

325

But a musical which disturbs, instead of amuses, faces much the same problem which ballet met when it emerged from an era of sylphs, dryads, princesses, ogres (who always got their comeuppance in time for a happy ending) and pretty creatures doing pretty things. I remember once chatting with a charming lady who confided that she adored ballet but didn't like Antony Tudor's works "because they disturb me." Frankly, I thought she could do with a bit of disturbing and I believe that *West Side Story* is by no means devoid of such stimulating therapy.

Jerome Robbins, who conceived the idea for *West Side Story,* directed it and choreographed it, has, in a sense, rediscovered something old and achieved something new. With the co-operation of his collaborators, Arthur Laurents (book), Leonard Bernstein (music), Stephen Sondheim (lyrics) and Oliver Smith (scenic production), he has restated for our times the necessity of action for drama and the power of dance as the fullest manifestation of action in drama.

Dance-Drama-Song   The chief concern of this column is, of course, the position of dance in *West Side Story* but dance cannot be disassociated from the other elements in this musical for the simple reason that all are inseparable parts of the same creative idea. For some time, our musical theater has been reaching toward the form achieved in *West Side Story.* Many seasons ago, Helen Tamiris expounded on her dream of a theater in which a playwright (or some other creator) could call upon all the arts to serve the theme, not sequentially (with turns for this and that art expression) but collectively.

Since Agnes de Mille made history with her dances for *Oklahoma!* the duties of dance in musicals have grown enormously and many shows which have called upon the talents of Mr. Robbins, Miss Tamiris, Miss de Mille, Michael Kidd, Hanya Holm and others have come close to achieving a synthesis of the arts. But here, in *West Side Story,* a new high has been reached, for the theme is serious and deadly pertinent to our times, and dancing is not used as a release from tension but as a vivid symbol of it, as a desperate, sometimes evil and sometimes hopeful voice speaking through the body.

Choreography   The great wonder of *West Side Story* is that realistic action flows into dancing and out of it again without hitch or break, just as speech swells or snarls its way into poetry and song. But it would be ungrateful to overlook the individual values of the choreography itself. Mr. Robbins, assisted by Peter Gennaro, has done a superlative job. The opening dance immediately establishes the temper, the characteristics of the gang members; the Dance at the Gym, where Tony (of the Jets) meets Maria (sister of the Sharks' leader), is a vivid and harshly touching evocation of the ball in *Romeo and Juliet,* and the rumble itself, swift and vicious, captures all the tragedy of mistaken heroism.

Beauty comes to the vision scene as the hoodlums, drawn from their sordid surroundings and savage life, escape briefly into a dream which can never come true. But throughout the story, Mr. Robbins gives us dance passages which fleetingly reveal the tenderness and innocence of young love amid the rush of fighting figures, bodies tensed for attack, flashing switchblades, and tough, jazzy dances which display the fear-covered bravado of the delinquents.

Proudly, we may note that this show could not have been done without a dancing cast and that is exactly what it is. Almost every member of it is a dancer and all of them are called upon to perform the toughest and most demanding choreography which, perhaps, Broadway has ever seen. And they are splendid dancers. As the principals, Larry Kert and Carol Lawrence, are dancing actors of great skill and sensitiveness and there are powerful and memorable dance enactments by Chita Rivera, Lee Becker, Tony Mordente, Mickey Calin and, indeed, by the other dancers, each of whom is a distinct dance personality.

For those who do not care to be disturbed when they attend the theater, perhaps one should recommend some other musical, but in this day when the Russians are boasting of an intercontinental ballistics missile and already have a moon of their own, perhaps the rumbles, the switchblades and gang fights of *West Side Story* would seem to represent sheer escapism. But disturbing or not, *West Side Story* is not to be missed by those responsive to the powers, physical and dramatic, of dance.

If the elements of tragedy, shocking brutality, delinquency and biting social comment (as manifested in the ironic, thought-provoking danced song, Gee, Officer Krupke) are controversial in certain quarters, there surely can be nothing but the highest praise for the flawless fusion of dance, music, lyrics and narrative. And in the event that the continuous presence of dance action may "disturb" a few, permit me to murmur again that both poetry and drama were born of the rhythms of dance; that Thespis, the first known actor (who gave his name to the profession), performed in the midst of dance; that the great classical dramas of Greece cherished the movements of the chorus and that the core of drama was, and remains, action. [*New York Herald Tribune*]

Balanchine: Petipa to Square Dance

December 1, 1957

George Balanchine, artistic director and chief choreographer of the New York City Ballet, has made the phenomenal leap from basic training in the Russian

Imperial Ballet to the non-imperial rhythms of American folk dancing. What is even more remarkable, he has been able to retain the shining classicism of Russia's great nineteenth-century choreographer, Marius Petipa, of whom he is the artistic heir, while at the same time doing full justice to the folk heritage of his adopted land. This singular achievement, first tested successfully in his *Western Symphony,* is even more fully manifest in his new *Square Dance.*

It is pretty generally admitted that Mr. Balanchine wears the Petipa crown and, through his creativeness, has burnished it to a new brightness. An exceptionally modest man, he slyly suggests that almost all the movements he uses in his ballets are extracted from Petipa works. He does, however, admit to adaptation. What he refuses to brag about and what we all know is that although his classicism is in the line of Petipa, he uses traditional steps and gestures in wholly new sequences, provides them with new accents and colors, invests them with new musical, emotional and dramatic meanings and, in brief, proves himself to be a genius of dance.

Petipa's Heir In his *Ballet Imperial, Concerto Barocco, Serenade, Symphony in C, Theme and Variations, Pas de Dix, Sylvia Pas de Deux* and a vast array of other masterpieces, the line of succession from Petipa to Balanchine is apparent but it is equally clear that if the junior respects the senior, he is by no means a copyist. Rather is he an art-evolutionist, one of the greatest the ballet has ever produced.

That Mr. Balanchine is also equally successful as an experimenter, an innovator, is proved in his *Prodigal Son, Orpheus* (both dramatic works), *Ivesiana* and others. In matters of rechoreographing noted works from the past, he has won laurels for his enormously popular *The Nutcracker,* a one-act *Swan Lake* and the vivid *The Firebird.* Last week, with *Square Dance,* he tried something still different from all his previous creations and compositions and gave the New York City Ballet the first hit of its current season.

With *Western Symphony,* Mr. Balanchine had set basically classical steps to American folk tunes, arranged and orchestrated by Hershy Kay. The result was a strictly American ballet. In *Square Dance* he has used music of Corelli and Vivaldi, continued his employment of classical ballet steps and, by some miracle, turned up with a ballet unmistakably American. The key to this union of European classicism and Americana is, of course, the introduction of a square dance caller into the framework of the ballet.

Ballet Caller On stage is a bandstand with a string ensemble and beside it stands Elisha Keeler, one of the country's top callers. As Mr. Keeler issues his homely instructions, using typical square dance terminology and occasionally egging the performers on with pretty compliments, the dancers move through the classical measures designed by Mr. Balanchine.

328

Movement, music and calls are skillfully related. To begin with, Mr. Balanchine has found traditional steps and fresh patterns which match the calls, sometimes exactly and often with slight humorous departures. Nothing is forced, all is swift and facile, yet the formal structure of the ballet is quite as strong and as richly imaginative as any Mr. Balanchine has evolved for more serious themes.

The Corelli-Vivaldi score fits both the balletic action and the folk elements of the work. This may seem unlikely but the logic is apparent when one stops to realize that fiddling is the customary accompaniment for square dancing, that Vivaldi and Corelli were violinists and composed generally with the violin in mind and that in their day, musical compositions were still closely allied to the dance forms of the period (seventeenth and early eighteenth centuries). Furthermore, the dances themselves—gavotte, sarabande, gigue, etc.—though associated with courtly life, had their roots in peasant dances.

Patricia Wilde and Nicholas Magallanes, who head the cast, and the assisting dancers have caught on to Mr. Balanchine's purpose and respond to perfection. They retain the elegance and the dignity of traditional ballet while reflecting the joyousness and good-nature of folk dancing. Mr. Keeler calls them Pat and Nick yet Miss Wilde succeeds in behaving both like a ballerina and a charming young girl out for a good time. The two stars have a stunning pas de deux (without calls) but for the rest, they bound about with the other dancers or take over the stage for exuberant flashes of virtuosity.

Pat and Nick   If Miss Wilde is the brightest figure in *Square Dance*—Mr. Balanchine has put her prowess to the test with many brilliant steps—Mr. Magallanes is completely winning as her beau, both as dancer and companion, and the ensemble of boys and girls moves with infectious vitality. As for Mr. Keeler, he is the catalytic agent which unites the gracious aristocracy of ballet with the easy-going dignity of the folk. A marvelous job, an irresistible ballet and Mr. Balanchine is a wonder. [*New York Herald Tribune*]

Agon

December 2, 1957

A George Balanchine–Igor Stravinsky collaboration is always an occasion but the newest joint creative effort of one of the world's great choreographers and one of the greatest of contemporary composers is, in many ways, the crowning achievement of their long artistic association. *Agon*, which had its world premiere last evening at the City Center (a preview presentation for the benefit of the March of Dimes had been held last week), is not as poetic as *Orpheus,* not as heroic as *Apollo*, not as sensual as *The Prodigal Son,* but it is triumphant in its exposition of pure movement, movement inextricably and perfectly related to the composer's complex score.

Indeed, for sheer invention, for intensive exploitation of the human body and the designs which it can create, *Agon* is quite possibly the most brilliant ballet creation of our day, at least in that area usually described (although not quite accurately) as "abstract dance." For *Agon* has no plot, no specific emotional coloring, no dramatic incident. It does, of course, mirror the rhythms, the dynamics and the witticisms of the music but it does have a character of its own, for the movements are not only extensions of sound into physical substance but they also comment upon the score, occasionally tease it, race with it, rest with it, play with it.

But if *Agon* has no narrative to spin, it does have form. The individual dancer has his own patterns to pursue, duos and trios have theirs as do the larger groups. Sometimes they work in unison but more often they are called upon to thread their separate and independent movement designs into a larger fabric of choreography encompassing all the dancers.

It is difficult, if not impossible, to describe an abstract work and perhaps I have given the impression that *Agon* (which means "Contest") is primarily an exercise in action, an etude. Nothing could be further from the truth. True, *Agon* is not warm, not overtly human, but its very coolness is refreshing and it generates excitement because it totally ignores human foibles, dramatic situation, and concentrates wholly upon the miracle of the dancing body.

And if the miracle of skilled and sensitive dance action is not enough for some, let me say that *Agon* is rich in humor. It is not literal humor but, rather movement fun. It comes when a dance step or gesture makes an absurd but somehow pertinent comment on a note or phrase of music, it comes when an involved bit of activity bounces swiftly into an extraordinarily simple resolution and it comes when we are led to expect a bravura bit and are presented instead with a flippant or gracious gesture.

The dancers of the New York City Ballet, as they move through solos, pas de deux, pas de trois, pas de quatre and even through modern treatments of the ancient sarabandes, galliards and branles, perform their individual feats and collective duties with vigor, a crystal purity of line, magnificent phrasing and wonderful wit. Since Mr. Balanchine has elected to use classical ballet movements, free-style dance and swift interjections of gesture in his choreographic plan, the dancers have no easy task but they fuse these different but related elements so superbly that one is conscious of only a single method of expression.

330

All of these dancers deserve praise, but the soloists merit special comment, for they are the leaders of this contest. Melissa Hayden, accompanied by Roy Tobias and Jonathan Watts, fairly stops the show with her glittering and amusing dancing in the branles; Diana Adams and Arthur Mitchell make fabulous designs in their pas de deux and Todd Bolender, Barbara Walczak and Barbara Milberg are delightful in the sarabande, galliard and coda.

Agon was, naturally, the featured event on this all-Balanchine–Stravinsky program, and it received a rousing welcome, but a revival of *Apollo* was also an occasion in itself. Young Jacques d'Amboise danced the title role for the first time and turned in a performance which surely marks him as one of the top male dancers of our era. Not only did his proven virtuosity find new and electrifying outlet in this ballet but his characterization of the boy-god was also impressive in its integrating of youthful strength and exuberance with the authority of a deity.

Mr. d'Amboise, striking as he was, did not alone make this *Apollo* a rich experience. As the Muses, Maria Tallchief, Miss Hayden and Patricia Wilde contributed beautiful performances, with Miss Tallchief the radiant central figure of Terpsichore. *Orpheus,* in a fine performance by the principals and a fuzzy one by the corps, and *Firebird* (starring Miss Tallchief) completed this history-making evening in the theater of dance. [*New York Herald Tribune*]

December 8, 1957

The major event of the current ballet season at the City Center took place last Sunday when the New York City Ballet presented a program of theater masterworks (four), created over the years (thirty) by George Balanchine, choreographer, and Igor Stravinsky, composer. Obviously, this was an occasion but it was an extra special one, for the bill included not only a brilliant revival of *Apollo* but also the premiere of the newest collaborative effort of the two masters, a pure dance creation called *Agon* (The Contest).

The premiere of *Agon* attracted not only a distinguished audience but also an intensely enthusiastic one. Yet the overwhelming response cannot be regarded as a blanket approval. In fact, a few dissenters, all eloquent and literate, have taken me to task, pleasantly but firmly, for the unqualified enthusiasm expressed in my review of the opening. Equally stubborn, and comfortably backed by majority support, I would like to say a few more words about *Agon,* which I believe is a masterpiece in its particular area of dance creation.

Agon is without story, without dramatic incident, without scenery and formal costumes, without specific emotional colorings. I agree that it has very little human warmth about it. Usually, I lean toward those dance works

331

which are born of the urgencies of the human heart. But *Agon* does not pretend to mirror the frailties and the nobilities of man's character. Rather does it exploit and celebrate the movement miracles of which the skilled dancer's body is capable.

Movement Miracles   In his specially commissioned score, Stravinsky has supplied (perhaps "challenged" would be a better word) the choreographer with an incredible array of complex rhythms, phrasings, tonalities, statements and resolutions. With these as stimuli, Mr. Balanchine has invented movements—balletic, free dance, gestural—as complex as the score itself. But if the Balanchine actions are inspired by the music, they are not helplessly fettered to it.

The choreography of *Agon* is, of course, a physical–visual complement to the score at the basic level. It does more, however, than translate sounds into movements. It has a life and a form of its own as it grows out of and comments upon the rhythms, qualities and rich witticisms of the music. Through solos, pas de deux, pas de trois, pas de quatre and larger units, Mr. Balanchine floods the stage with a tremendous wealth of design as his dancers pursue individual patterns which suggest the excitement of a contest but which are arranged with such mathematical precision that flawless dance architecture is maintained throughout.

It would be impossible to describe all of the stirring sequences of movement—novel, surprising, virtuosic, amusing—which constitute the choreography of *Agon*. If the heart is not moved, the mind and the muscles are, for the choreographic invention is prodigious and the actions of the dancers serve to remind us that here are very special beings trained to project the glorious powers and beauties of the human body in motion.

Of the ballet's many highspots (there are no lows), I would mention the three modern style treatments of the old Bransle in which Melissa Hayden, ebulliently abetted by Roy Tobias and Jonathan Watts, dances superbly; the wonderfully ingenious Pas de Deux, expertly performed by Diana Adams and Arthur Mitchell, and Todd Bolender's engaging Sarabande, paired with the lively Gailliard of Barbara Walczak and Barbara Milberg.

Cool Brilliance   And so if *Agon* does not have the passion of *Pillar of Fire,* the winning warmth of *Rodeo* or the heartfelt anguish of *Age of Anxiety,* it has an almost nuclear-age brilliance about it. Further, it is alive with muscular humor. One could not and should not compare it with ballets born of other premises, for in its own sphere of abstraction, it is, I believe, the finest ballet of our era and the greatest of the Balanchine–Stravinsky collaborations. [*New York Herald Tribune*]

332

1958

Russians Blaze — Stars and Stripes Waves

Inbal Dance Theatre of Israel at the Martin Beck • Balanchine's Stars and Stripes premiered by NYCB • Graham's monumental Clytemnestra and Embattled Garden premiered • American Ballet Theatre rising from its ashes offers American debut of Violette Verdy in the American premiere of Cullberg's Miss Julie, with Erik Bruhn • Verdy makes her debut with NYCB in Divertimento No. 15 and the American premiere of Cullberg's Medea • Allegra Kent and Lotte Lenya triumph in NYCB's production of Balanchine's The Seven Deadly Sins • The Moiseyev Russian Dance Company makes blazing debut at the Met • New York is a Jerome Robbins Festival

Inbal: New Theater Born of Dance Past

January 7, 1958

The ecstatic dances of the ancient Israelites, the vision of David dancing before the Lord "with all his might" are familiar to most of us through the words of legend and of history. But one would have thought that only the record remained. Not so. The ecstatic dances, religious in spirit and wonderfully primitive in the exploitation of energy, have survived three thousand years in the isolated culture of the Yemenite Jews and have been brilliantly re-created for the stage by Inbal, the Dance Theater of Israel, which opened a three-week engagement last evening at the Martin Beck Theater.

The all-Yemenite company, composed of Jews restored to their homeland a few years ago following an exile of 2,500 years in Adab Yemen, brings to the theater a rare dance treasure in which Oriental flavors, African vitality of action, Hebrew and Arabic tongues are combined with Jewish ceremony and never-forgotten Jewish lore. In itself, this is fascinating enough for the ethnic scholar. But Inbal is more than a repository of the past. It is superb contemporary theater.

Sara Levi-Tanai, the founder and director, has accomplished the incredibly difficult task of transforming folk dance—which is generally of limited interest to any one except the participant and his neighbors—into theatrical dance with form, pacing variety and impact. As in her stated goals, she has kept alive the spirit of improvisation while at the same time demanding of her dancers complete theatrical discipline. In her capacity as choreographer, she has demanded the same things of herself and thus she has combined heightened folk dance steps with vivid patterns, dramatic gesture and edited ritual to make true ballets.

Almost all forms of ecstatic dance call for the inclusion of song, shouting, speech and instrumental support (we in America have returned to this in such powerful creations as *West Side Story*) and it follows that the Inbal productions employ all of these elements of expression. Hebrew and Arabic words, chanted or spoken, are fused with the Oriental wail of voices, the murmur of the flute, the beat of drums, the jangle of tambourines as the performers re-create the ebullient dances of shepherds (*In the Footsteps of the Flock*); communicate the passion of prophecy in *Song of Deborah*; gently, humorously, tenderly capture the age-old rites of a *Yemenite Wedding* or evoke still other colors in the remaining dance–dramas in their program.

The bearded men are not only exuberant in their actions but technically adept as they move in exactly defined lines or circles, bound high over watch fires in the desert or gambol deftly for the Queen of Sheba. The women, lithe and dark and lovely, are headed by Margalith Oved, a superior artist who can communicate the pitch of intense passion as Deborah, enchant the viewer with her commentary for *Yemenite Wedding* or play the coquette as Sheba.

But all of the performers are splendid (their vitality alone is enough to make one jump out of his seat) and so also are the colorful costumes, the effective settings, the expert (well, its very modern but pertinent) lighting and the musical arrangements of ancient airs. Special gratitude for this event must go to Mrs. Levi-Tanai, the creator of Inbal; to Jerome Robbins and Anna Sokolow, two American choreographers, who provided the dancers with technical and theatrical disciplines but no artistic interferences, and to S. Hurok and the America–Israel Cultural Foundation, responsible for Inbal's American appearances.

It was an exciting evening, of course, with national anthems played and a distinguished audience in attendance but the true excitement was generated by Inbal itself as it communicated to another age the ancient ecstasy of dancing. [*New York Herald Tribune*]

In the Footsteps of the Flock, the title of the opening suite of dances presented by Inbal, the Dance Theater of Israel, in their program at the Martin Beck, is wonderfully descriptive of the company itself, its origins and its goals. For although the title is merely a poetic way of announcing a series of shepherd dances, it also tells us something about a group which is faithful to 2,500 years of tradition. But if such footsteps mirror fidelity, they suggest, equally, action and Inbal is most certainly moving forward supported by the memory of what Martha Graham once called (in a dance) *The Ancestral Footsteps.*

Intellectually, it is fascinating to see what Inbal has wrought from history. We know, of course, that the Yemenite Jews who compose the company are members of a community recently returned to Israel from Yemen where their ancestors had fled five hundred years before the birth of Christ. In their program, we see traditional steps and ceremonies long preserved in isolation and we see also strong Oriental influences, Arab colors, even African pulsations. Here, indeed, we discover long hidden treasures of rhythm, ritual, custom.

Ecstatic Dance   Intellectual discovery, however rewarding it may be, is by no means the only factor in Inbal's splendid success. Two other attributes, one ancient and one modern, give special luster and depth to one of the finest dance groups to visit our shores. The first is the spirit of ecstasy which leaps forth from the group just as it surely emanated from the dancers' Biblical ancestors when the prophets "spoke in a great voice" or when David danced "with all his might."

The second impressive quality inherent in the company is the excitement of discovery, not simply on the part of the audience but with the dancers themselves. It is a feeling not easy to describe but it does exist and it is explainable. The dancers have discovered, through the direction and choreography of Sara Levi-Tanai, that they not only have a rich past but also a future. They are in the midst of creativeness; old dances and ceremonies are assuming theatrical guise; new ideas are seeking form in dance; immediate feelings find voice in newly devised action. And this excitement of self-discovery is communicated to the audience with just as much fervor as the ecstasy inherent in their religious dancing.

Choreography   For the adamant balletomane, Inbal's basic simplicity of movement may appear too elemental to arouse his interest but in the choreography, one comes upon striking invention and richness of texture. Dance steps are but a part of this choreographic fabric. Gestures, ritual, song, declamation, shouts and the shrill, trilling cries of the women are major ingredients in this wonderfully refreshing theatrical plan.

Mrs. Levi-Tanai, fusing these expressional elements into disciplined and eloquent theater form, has thus been able to project both the awesomeness and impact of prophecy in *Song of Deborah*; the vitality, the joyousness, the bounding strength of shepherd folk in the Arab-flavored *Leaping Flames* and *In the Footsteps of the Flock*; the shy dignity of a blessed romance in *Shabbat Shalom*; broad humor in *Queen of Sheba* and the sweetness, anticipation, incidental fun, wonder and ageless ceremony which go into the preparation for a *Yemenite Wedding*.

The Dancers   But if the chief creative honors go to Mrs. Levi-Tanai for her vision of a new theater dance derived from the materials of a very special heritage and gratitude goes to Jerome Robbins and Anna Sokolow for their technical assistance, the dancers themselves deserve unqualified praise for bringing the vision to life.   The men, with their short black beards and flashing eyes, are technically expert in all that is demanded of them by the choreographer and, further, amazingly skilled in communicating the exuberance of dancing.

The beautiful girls, with Margalith Oved as the principal dancer, are as strong and as vital, within the framework of their winning femininity, as the men. Miss Oved, indeed, gives a tremendously powerful portrayal of Deborah but can and does, in other dances, color her actions with coquettishness, shyness and even the guarded sensuousness of a girl in love.

Inbal, with its gifted dancers, with its exhilarating music and handsome settings and costumes has quite obviously won the approval of New Yorkers, for the engagement at the Martin Beck, originally scheduled to end Jan. 26, has been extended through Feb. 1. And that is good news indeed. [*New York Herald Tribune*]

New York City Ballet

January 18, 1958

If the Russians have done a pretty thorough job of jarring our morale with their sputniks and related activities, a Russian-born American named George Balanchine has come up with a morale-builder guaranteed to make any one feel that there is indeed nothing like the good old U. S. A. And last night's audience at the City Center shook the rafters as they cheered the world premiere of the New York City Ballet's newest production, Mr. Balanchine's *Stars and Stripes,* a roaring hit if I ever saw one.

Just before the curtain went up, I happened to run into Mr. Balanchine and asked him if his new ballet had a story. He replied "Yes" and I said "What is the story?" His answer was "the United States." And it is, in a way, a story about the U. S. A. but it has no plot. It is the story in movement of our vast energy and exuberance, our love of show, our speed, our rhythm and, perhaps most of all, that sense of humor which makes it possible for us to laugh at ourselves while we are laughing simply because it's great to be alive.

There's no telling what non-Americans would think of this glittering, splashy, uninhibited spectacle but for us, it is a ball. If one finds the marches of John Philip Sousa irresistible, and most of us do (how else did many of us stagger through basic training in the Armed Forces?), then he will be delighted with the score fashioned by Hershy Kay on Sousa's music. And if you are one to cheer a simple parade, you will quite probably jump out of your seat at Mr. Balanchine's combination of a parade and all the technical fireworks, tricks and formations which ballet has to offer.

In fact, Mr. Balanchine divides his ballet into five "campaigns," instead of the customary movements, and has whipped together three "regiments" to dance them. Even a classical grand pas de deux does not omit salutes!

What Mr. Balanchine has devised in his five campaigns is nearly indescribable, so much happens so fast. There are precision high kicks which rival those of the Rockettes; whirling circles of action; soldiers doing multiple air turns instead of about-faces or cutting perilously through each other's ranks with high, stabbing leaps; intricate steppings which remind the viewer of perky drum majorettes.

The grand pas de deux is very grand and very classical in its traditional roots but the cavalier is a handsome officer, his ballerina is really a Liberty belle and their activities have the brusqueness and the brilliance of a fabulous maneuver. Indeed, the choreographer's invention here and in all other sections of the ballet is absolutely stunning not only with respect to steps and designs but also in its encompassing of humor and enormous vitality.

Co-starring with Mr. Balanchine is a premiere couturiere etoile (to coin a phrase), Madame Karinska, who designed the resplendent, gaudy and gorgeous costumes and executed them with the authority of a master engineer. Dashing uniforms, star-spangled skirts, plumed helmets and other blazing costumes were handsomely framed by David Hays' setting which, at the close of the work, displayed a huge American flag.

All of the dancers got right into the high spirit of this happy jamboree. Because of the complexity of the choreography and the speed of the movement there were some near mishaps in the ensemble but not enough to worry

337

about and the stars gave of their best. Allegra Kent, Robert Barnett and Diana Adams were delightful and Melissa Hayden and Jacques d'Amboise brought down the house with their wonderful pas de deux.

Well, maybe *Stars and Stripes* isn't actually our answer to Sputnik, but it is an answer to depressed feelings and it is a lusty tribute to American high spirits, fun, endurance and unquenchable good humor. There were three other ballets on the bill, all superbly danced, but on this occasion, *Stars and Stripes*, quite properly, rode high over all in this ballet dedicated to the memory of Fiorello H. LaGuardia. [*New York Herald Tribune*]

November 26, 1958

The New York City Ballet, currently celebrating its tenth birthday, opened the second (and longest) of three engagements for the 1958–1959 season last evening at the City Center. There were no new works on the program but, appropriately enough, the four offerings were all by the company's artistic director, George Balanchine, who is also celebrating an anniversary of his own: his twenty-fifth year in the United States. Double congratulations, therefore, are in order and to them one must add congratulations on the high level of dancing seen last evening.

The opening *Divertimento No. 15* (Mozart) is one of Mr. Balanchine's pure dance creations, a ballet which has its very being in the exquisite movement inventions born of the rhythms, phrases, formalities and colorings of the score itself. This ballet, conducted with a wonderful feeling for the inherent grace of the music by Robert Irving, was beautifully danced by the large corps de ballet and the soloists, five ladies and three gentlemen.

Of particular interest, of course, was the dancing of the French ballerina, Violette Verdy, familiar to American audiences through her appearances with other companies, who was making her debut with the New York City Ballet. Miss Verdy, an absolutely enchanting dancer, moved into the Balanchine style with no trouble at all and danced her measures with beauty of line and with a pertness of manner which is quite her own.

There were highly agreeable contributions by the other soloists—Melissa Hayden, Allegra Kent, Patricia Wilde, Judith Green, Jonathan Watts, Nicholas Magallanes, Roy Tobias—with Miss Hayden edging out her friendly rivals to a degree through the vitality, technical accuracy and authoritative elegance of her dancing.

Orpheus, a tenderly conceived, ritualized telling of the lovely legend of Orpheus and his lost Euridice, was second on the program. And once again, the poetic choreography (containing much superbly designed gesture fused with full-body patterns of action), the glorious Stravinsky score and the

338

fascinating decor (magically lighted by Jean Rosenthal) of Isamu Noguchi worked their gentle wonders. Mr. Magallanes (Orpheus) and Francisco Moncion (Dark Angel) were splendid in roles with which they have long been associated and Diana Adams was appealing as Euridice.

For frolicsome feats of skill there was the *Pas de Trois,* to music of Glinka, in which Miss Hayden, Miss Wilde and Jacques d'Amboise swept through this aristocratic contest with fine verve and, of course (since we expect it of them), technical skill. Mr. d'Amboise, understandably, brought down the house with his high leaps, facile and flashing batterie and multiple spins, but the ladies also had their moments of highly effective virtuosity. *Symphony in C,* conducted by Hugo Fiorato, who had also led the orchestra in the lilting Glinka, brought the program to a close. [*New York Herald Tribune*]

November 27, 1958

Medea, a ballet by Sweden's best known choreographer, Birgit Cullberg, was given its first American presentation last evening at the City Center by the New York City Ballet. A distinguished audience, headed by the Secretary General of the United Nations, Dag Hammarskjold, was on hand to cheer the new ballet (first given by the Royal Swedish Ballet in Stockholm) and its distinguished choreographer. I only wish that I could continue the cheering in print but I find myself alternating between bravos and sighs of disappointment. *Medea* had its sterling moments but the cumulative effect of a remorseless tragedy was, I think, unachieved.

The work, set to piano pieces (mainly, Mikrokosmos) of Béla Bartók, orchestrated by Herbert Sandberg, boasts a stunning opening tableau in which Medea and Jason emerge from their marriage bed with their two charming children linking them together, and a brilliant pas de deux mirroring the terrible tensions between the couple when Medea learns of her husband's infidelity. In these two sections, in Medea's anguished solo and in the horrible moment when Medea drags the bodies of her slaughtered children on stage, the ballet projects both movement power and dramatic passion.

Elsewhere, the choreographer seems to have been content to devise patterns which barely suffice to tell the tale itself, without digging deep into motivations. Oh, yes, the designs for the principals and the chorus were generally inventive—Miss Cullberg is a mistress of balanced stage pattern—but those brilliantly choreographed emotional tensions which characterized her creativeness in *Miss Julie,* a ballet presented earlier this year by another company, were not consistently present.

Some of the blame for the pallid moments in *Medea* must be laid to the score, for it was overorchestrated to the point that the music absolutely overwhelmed the action on several occasions. But much must be laid to Miss Cullberg herself. The movements designed for Creusa, Jason's new love, were brassy rather than seductive and Jason himself emerged as little more than a handsome but characterless figure (I admit freely that Jason, in almost any version of the Euripides play, never seems quite bright). Nor did the chorus on all occasions (there were exceptions) fulfill its classical duty of omening and commenting upon the course of drama with vivid authority.

So, in brief, there were admirable and even exciting moments in this *Medea* but there were not quite enough of them to make the ballet match the play in force or (and perhaps I should not make this comparison but it seems inescapable) to rival the hair-raising power of Martha Graham's dance treatment of Medea, *Cave of the Heart*.

The dancing in *Medea* found its peak in the performance of Melissa Hayden in the title part. Miss Hayden, a superb actress–dancer, wrung every bit of passion, fury, hatred and revenge out of the role as it was choreographed and when she headed the action, all was well. Jacques d'Amboise, heroic of mien and stalwart, did what he could with the part of Jason and the lovely Violette Verdy did her best work as Creusa in the short but poignant death scene. Delia Peters and Susan Pillersdorf were winning as the hapless children, and Shaun O'Brien did as well as he could, I suppose, in the empty role of Creon. [*New York Herald Tribune*]

December 5, 1958

The critics, this morning, are in something of a dilemma, for the New York City Ballet has produced an operetta or, perhaps, one should describe it as a music-drama with dancing. Further along in these columns, Jay Harrison is discussing the music. It is my duty to comment upon the dancing. Both of us lean toward the notion that our colleague, Walter Kerr, the Herald Tribune's drama critic, might well have covered the event as a piece of popular theater.

This does not mean that I did not respond joyously to every moment of *The Seven Deadly Sins* which had its American premiere (twenty-five years after its Paris bow) last evening at the City Center. The production, with a score by Kurt Weill, revised choreography by George Balanchine (who staged the original production), lyrics by Berthold Brecht in a new translation by W. H. Auden and Chester Kallman, and marvelous scenery, costumes and lighting by Rouben Ter-Arutinian, with the costumes executed by the peerless Karinska, is an absolute knockout. It isn't a ballet by a long shot but it is, in my opinion, superb theater.

The story of Anna I, sung and acted by Lotte Lenya (Kurt Weill's widow and the star of the original presentation), and Anna II, danced by Allegra Kent, is a gayly sordid exposition of remunerative adventures in the big city which help to build (and we see that building going up stage right during the course of the play) a home in Louisiana to which the weary girls will ultimately return.

The Seven Deadly Sins presents, with wit and bite, a scroungy, tawdry, bawdy, occasionally degenerate group of characters headed by our girls who move from low-grade pan-handling and pickpocketing through strip teases, love for sale and similar activities until the funds for the homecoming are earned. It is all brash and evil but it is hearty in the manner of the dance and the musical theater productions of post-World War I Germany.

Now to the dances and the dancing. Miss Lenya, as an actress, moves wonderfully, with an easy, careless grace which characterizes Anna I's quality of unashamed dissipation. Miss Kent, of course, actually dances. In one fabulous scene, in which Miss Lenya informs us that not an ounce must be gained, Miss Kent goes through a delicious array of stretches, acrobatics and balletic warm-ups and is rewarded for her efforts by a quick lick of the ice-cream cone held temptingly by Miss Lenya.

Later, Miss Kent, stripped to legal minimum, is borne in on cellophane-wrapped platter as the most delectable dish in a night club. Still later, she is forced by Anna I to divest herself of her finery (all is carefully deposited in a handy sack), for these are earnings, and to start again from what is literally scratch. Throughout the work, the dancer is called upon to combine mime and fetching poses with out-and-out dance and in all categories, she is enormously provocative. Actually, however, there is no real dance solo as such, for dancing here, both for Miss Kent and the ensemble is purely contributory. The story is the thing.

The movement of the masked dancers of the chorus, the action style of the whole work, even most of Miss Kent's patterns hark back to the semi-balletic modern dance of Central Europe some thirty years ago. In fact, the Jooss Ballet's *The Big City* kept coming to mind. But where the Jooss work has aged sadly, *The Seven Deadly Sins* has succeeded in projecting a nostalgic commentary upon another period, upon a half-forgotten form of theater, sound and movement.

The Seven Deadly Sins, in its belated American premiere was, obviously, the event of the evening. The audience cheered it and I would not be surprised if non-balletomanes flocked to the City Center in droves to see this brassy theatrical delight. [*New York Herald Tribune*]

Graham: Monumental Dance

April 2, 1958

The monumental tragedy of the sinful, cursed figure of classical Greek legend, Clytemnestra, served to bring Martha Graham back to Broadway for her first New York appearance in three years and her first local repertory season in five. The current engagement, which opened last evening at the Adelphi Theater under the auspices of the B. de Rothschild Foundation, has also brought with it another "first" and that would be the noted dancer's first program-long theater piece in a dancing career which has spanned almost forty years.

The four-act *Clytemnestra,* which had its world premiere last night, is not a dance duplication of either the myths or the ancient dramas in which Clytemnestra plays her evil role of infidelity, murder and vengeance. Rather, does Miss Graham seek to penetrate the soul of this woman as she strives to assess her sins and to discover the cause of her awful damnation.

We see her first in Hades, dishonored even among the dead, and then in the summoned visions of her past and those who played their parts in the drama of her life: Helen, whose beauty led to the fall of Troy; Agamemnon, Clytemnestra's warrior-husband, whom she betrayed and killed; Aegisthus, her lover; Orestes and Electra, her children, who avenge their father's death through matricide and the murder of the lover; Iphigenia, sacrificed to the gods; Cassandra, Paris, the Furies and figures of fate and death. Finally, the visions end, Clytemnestra finds herself once more in Hades, having discovered her strengths and her weaknesses and knowing that rebirth may provide the hope of ultimate escape from the doomed family of which she was once a part.

Through almost ritualized movements, through choral patterns, solos, duos, trios, Miss Graham unfolds the inexorable course of tragedy in a work which is unhurried but enormously theatrical in its bursts of passion and in its cumulative power.

Indeed, the tension is almost unbearable in those scenes in which Agamemnon is readied for murder and Clytemnestra suffers the nightmare which omens her own doom. The fencing, dissimulating dances of the plotters are rich in irony and suspense and the appearance of the giant-size ghost of Agamemnon is awesome.

But such is the length and magnitude of the choreography that more than one seeing is essential to discover, explore, remember and record its special powers and theatrical sorceries. It is not, of course, an easy work, but then, Miss Graham is not given to compromise of any sort, but that it is intensely theatrical is inarguable and that it provides the receptive onlooker with a shattering dramatic experience is unquestionable.

The score by the Egyptian composer, Halim El-Dabh, is by no means easy (or even comfortable) to listen to. In fact, with the exception of some airs of jubilation and wistfulness, it is monotonous in beat and tonality but this very monotony serves Miss Graham well for it is a floor upon which her dancers make their melodies, declamations, sonorities and stillnesses in terms of movement. That this music for orchestra and voice could stand alone seems highly questionable but that it is an integral part of a dramatic, choreographic plan is apparent.

Supported by the El-Dabh score and physically enhanced by Isamu Noguchi's striking decor and Miss Graham's inspired costume designs, the dancers, soloists and corps alike, give brilliant performances. Miss Graham herself, whether frozen into terrified immobility or making an anguished gesture with a hand or spinning in anger and frustration, is tremendously effective in the title part. She is, naturally, the focus of the whole work and there is never a moment when she is not in full command of the stage.

Of the splendid company, only a few may be listed here for their very special contributions. Outstanding were Helen McGehee, Yuriko, Matt Turney, Ethel Winter, Bertram Ross, Paul Taylor, Gene McDonald and David Wood, several of them dancing more than one role, and each of them bringing to their assignments fire, polish and dramatic authority, to say nothing of high technical prowess, worthy of the great star with whom they are associated.
[*New York Herald Tribune*]

April 4, 1958

A restlessly erotic new dance work, *Embattled Garden,* with choreography by Martha Graham and a specially commissioned score by Carlos Surinach, was given its world premiere last evening at the Adelphi Theater as the second new production in Miss Graham's current repertory season. The scene is the Garden of Eden and the characters are Eve, Adam, Lilith and The Stranger (who could quite conceivably be the serpent).

Miss Graham's view of activities in Eden is one of highly charged amorousness, rather than of Biblical solemnity. This is not to say that her creation is a comedy. Far from it. It is a tale of experienced love invading the province of more innocent (or, at least, more disciplined) love. Lilith, with her ancient knowledge, and The Stranger, with experience gained beyond the confines of the Garden, introduce their violent passions to Adam and Eve and the scene becomes the background for flaunted charms, for newly released desires, for jealous clashes between the men, for sensual explorations.

Urgency of action is the key to *Embattled Garden.* There is no time for courtship, for The Stranger, with a tremendous, muscularly taut leap from his perch in the tree, sets the pace for the ardent caresses which are to follow. Miss Graham's choreography, containing some wonderfully inventive designs, great bursts of virtuosity and gestures potently evocative of her theme, is skillfully integrated with Isamu Noguchi's setting which includes not only the highly stylized tree but also a slightly elevated (and tipped) maze-like ramp crowned with a forest of supple poles.

In addition to threading her love-frenzied dancers through the patterns of the maze, Miss Graham has also responded brilliantly to the brightness, the rhythmic insinuations, the brash sensualities of Mr. Surinach's highly stirring score.

As for the performances themselves, there is nothing but the highest praise. Glen Tetley, new to the Graham company this season, danced with marvelous technical brio and superior dramatic power as The Stranger and Bertram Ross was at all times impressive in action, acting and in his commanding stage presence as Adam. Yuriko was splendid as the alluring, eager and excitingly adventuresome Eve and Matt Turney did a fine bit as the watchful, sophisticated Lilith. The orchestra, under Eugene Lester's direction, did handsomely with the Surinach music. [*New York Herald Tribune*]

April 6, 1958

One of the world's great ballet artists, currently deep in rehearsal, telephoned me last Tuesday evening as I was writing my review of Martha Graham's new *Clytemnestra,* apologized for the interruption and asked if I had enjoyed the new Graham creation. I murmured something to the effect that "enjoy" was not quite the word and the immediate response was, "Ah, you were upset. It is important to be upset in the theater. Too much is simply amusing." Earlier, I had overheard a junior soloist of the ballet, who was attending the performance, say, "Well, it's not entertainment in the usual sense of the word but it's fascinating, disturbing and I wouldn't have missed it for the world."

Martha Graham, ever since she left her post as soloist with Ted Shawn and later, the Denishawn Dancers and completed a highly successful stint with the *Greenwich Village Follies,* has achieved that presumably paradoxial position of being an intensely dramatic and highly theatrical performer without being an entertainer. *Clytemnestra,* which opened the Graham repertory season at the Adelphi Theater, is upsetting, disturbing, stimulating and utterly absorbing dance–drama. It is not merely diverting, but then, neither is *Death of a Salesman* or Richard Strauss' *Electra* or the great Oresteia (from which *Clytemnestra* derives some of its material).

Revelation Indeed, Miss Graham's new, evening-long creation (in four acts) is, in a very real sense, a monumental summation of her vivid and demanding approach to dance. It is a revelation of "things felt," it is a dramatic analysis of evil and the forces which permit evil to work, it is a psychological portrait of a woman damned.

Like her Medea (*Cave of the Heart*) and Jocasta (*Night Journey*), her Clytemnestra is not simply a dancing version of a classical figure as it moves throughout the course of a drama or myth. Rather, does Miss Graham concentrate upon one aspect of the character—Clytemnestra's necessity to discover why she is dishonored and damned even among the dead of Hades—and upon this single aspect, she builds her work. And by dancing, she can communicate certain details of passion for which words are inadequate.

The choreography is cast in the style of a mighty ritual, unrushed, often symbolic, relentless in its exposition of every factor pertinent to the fate of the doom-ridden heroine. In fact, even elements of the Trojan War are introduced, for the war itself had had a distant but inescapable (and disastrous) effect upon Clytemnestra. But throughout her work, Miss Graham has not sought to present only the acts of violence. She has presented us with causes, preludes and plottings. Thus, the watcher, may wait impatiently (and suspensefully) as preparations are made for the inevitable. But then, when the inevitable comes, its impact is both climactic and releasing.

The archaic formalities of the work by no means obscure the vivid immediacy of Miss Graham's highly personalized movements. The crouched running steps speak of terror, the turns with a leg held high in back and the head close to the floor tell of restless waiting, the back falls to the floor are mirrors of despair and the trembling hands and roving eyes reveal suspicion and doubt. These and other actions familiar to followers of Miss Graham are found here recharged and released to lay bare the elements of faithlessness, sacrifice, vengeance, murder and revenge which mark the life, death and doom of Clytemnestra.

Score, Decor Ageless in its ritualized form and in its theme and wholly contemporary and brilliantly theatrical in its method of presentation, this *Clytemnestra* would, I think, be as at home in an ancient Greek amphitheater as it is in a Broadway house. Part of this dual potency is due to the remarkable score by Halim El-Dabh, to the wonderfully stylized decor by Isamu Noguchi and to Miss Graham's costume designs, based on drawings by one of her dancers, Helen McGehee.

The choreography, of course, comes first but the score is of importance because it serves that choreography. As independent music, it is often monotonous, and it wails, throbs, moans and shrills, interrupted but rarely by snatches of luminous melody. But this is as it should be—in this case at least—for the dance itself demands neural sounds, music played upon the trembling nerves of the human body.

Obviously, in a creation of such size, in concept as well as in duration, not every moment of movement was equal to others. The first act seemed unnecessarily long, the very end (in which Clytemnestra finds hope in the promise of rebirth) was weakly keyed and there were some other arguable elements.

Inarguable, however, was the majestic and dynamically vibrant performing of the star herself and the absolutely expert performances turned in by Yuriko, Helen McGehee, Matt Turney, Ethel Winter, Bertram Ross, Paul Taylor, Gene McDonald, David Wood and other members of the company as they brought dance life to the figures of Electra, Orestes, Agamemnon, Aegisthus, Helen, Iphigenia, Cassandra, Paris, the Ghose of Agamemnon, Hades himself, the Furies and others involved in a tragedy of heroic dimensions. Fine also were Bethany Beardslee and Robert Goss who spoke, intoned, sang, trilled and cried out their notes in the El-Dabh score.

Given carte blanche (and sufficient newsprint), the critic would be tempted to write a book about this *Clytemnestra* but succinctness will have to suffice and I will close by saying that Miss Graham has reached a new peak of achievement in a long career in which triumphs have been the rule rather than the exception. [*New York Herald Tribune*]

Ballets de Paris

April 8, 1958

If you're chic and sexy, how can you miss? Well, the famous French dance troupe, Les Ballets de Paris, which returned to New York last evening (after several years absence) for an engagement at the Broadway Theater, possesses those agreeable qualities in good measure.

Furthermore, the company is unashamedly a purveyor of ballet a la show business with no nonsense about the niceties of the ballet d'ecole. Of course, the arabesques, the pirouettes, the cabrioles, the fouettes and their balletic relatives are all there but Roland Petit, the organization's founder-director and choreographer, has mixed them up (sometimes successfully, sometimes not) with materials right out of vaudeville.

The best production of the current bill is Mr. Petit's justly celebrated and enduring dance version of *Carmen,* with which he electrified theatrical circles a few years ago. With Jeanmaire in the title part and Mr. Petit as a sullen, passionate Don José, this is a treat not to be missed. Whether she is flashing her black eyes over the edge of a fan, flashing her legs in intricate patterns across the stage or flashing her provocative smile, Jeanmaire is utterly irresistible.

And Mr. Petit is by no means to be overlooked. When he is dancing the Habanera (obviously, this has no connection with traditional operatic sequence) while the raffish habitués of the café chant "l'amour" insinuatingly, he is enormously effective. But so also are the other members of the company as they move with vigor, sensuality and a neatly disciplined lewdness against the stunning sets by Antoni Clavé (who also designed the equally striking costumes).

The novelties of the program cannot hold a candle to *Carmen* but one of them, *La Dame à la Lune,* a Petit ballet to music of Jean Francaix and elaborate decors and costumes by Edouard Dermite, has its moments. Chief among these is a rousing cancan in which the girls swirl their foamy skirts, grab hold of a foot and stretch the limb skyward and zoom to the floor in a dandy selection of splits. Mr. Petit, as the male cancan star, goes with them the whole way, splits and all and the total effect is pretty exciting stuff.

Other highlights of *La Dame* include the dancing and, I might add, the mere presence of a beautiful young lady named Veronica Mlakar; lusty performing, but with a pleasant degree of polish, by Dick Sanders and a let's-shoot-the-works duet by Jane Laoust and Rino Adipietro. Far less amusing were some activities by a batch of commedia dell'arte characters and the dance of the butterflies I still don't believe. If it was supposed to be funny, something went awry en route.

Not much can be said for *La Rose des Vents,* a ballet about a waitress who was really a mermaid and who was graciously tossed back in the sea by an accommodating sailor. It was rather like a neighborhood treatment of *Ondine* and not even the dancing of Jeanmaire and Mr. Petit could save it. As a matter of fact, I thought they danced it with something less than enthusiasm for Mr. Petit's labored and far from inspired choreography. Anyhow the settings by Bazarte were effective and there was music of Milhaud to listen to.

The opening ballet, *Contre-Pointe,* though it contained nothing to make you grip your hands in ecstasy, was filled with Mr. Petit's flashes of movement inventiveness, particularly in the matter of lifts. The boys hoisted the girls over, under and around themselves skillfully and elsewhere, both groups rolled about the floor, engaged in some mild acrobatics and gamboled energetically about the stage.

Energetic is perhaps the best word to use in describing *Contre-Pointe.* There is practically no mood at all and Mr. Petit's movement departures from standard ballet action, though frequently effective as isolated designs, seem contrived. I guess you would call them clever but beyond that, the word empty would apply. However, Miss Laoust, Mr. Adipietro, Ariel Auclerc and

Mr. Sanders turned in nice performances. Very energetic. The music, incidentally, was by the orchestra's director, Marius Constant. The practice costumes worn by the dancers in this work became swiftly soiled (during the floor rolls) because of the quantities of skid-averting rosin on the floor, rosin which also caused the dancing slippers to squeak continuously.

If there were downs as well as ups, there was no denying the fact that Mr. Petit, Jeanmaire and their Ballets de Paris put on a swiftly paced, smooth-running, handsomely mounted revue in dance form with *Carmen* as the prize of the evening. [*New York Herald Tribune*]

Dance: Russian Blaze; America on Fire, Too

April 20, 1958

The Metropolitan Opera House nearly burst its aging seams last Monday when the Moiseyev Dance Company from Moscow made its American debut. On stage, approximately one hundred dancers performed with explosive exuberance and stunning virtuosity while on the other side of the footlights, the audience exploded with applause and cheers. At the close, every one applauded every one else and a fine Russian–American rapport was achieved as the result of the new cultural exchange agreement between our country and the Societ Union, an agreement which made it possible for S. Hurok, the indefatigable impresario, to present the Moiseyev dancers in America.

One need not delve deeply into the political implications of the visit to come up with the simple fact that the Russians have made a mighty effective move in sending us a mass of smiling, richly talented ambassadors. For it is quite impossible not to like these spirited folk dancers. Indeed, one can go a step further and say that we appear to have certain traits and characteristics (perhaps only superficial but nonetheless real) in common. Both Russian and American dancers display vast amounts of energy and good nature, move spaciously, respect precision and, with an easy air of bravado, enjoy showing off in feats of physical skill.

Ambassadors   Obviously, the next thought to cross the mind is that if the Soviet government has made both a shrewd and pleasant move in sending the Moiseyev dancers here, could we not return the compliment by sending our own dancing ambassadors, representing our culture, our characteristics, our achievements, to Russia?

348

Well, we should and we can. But who shall we send? I overheard some rather panicky remarks, following the Moiseyev debut, to the effect that we should round up our own folk dance group and pack it off to Russia. And what, may I ask, do we use for material? The Virginia Reel? A square dance? For the truth of the matter is that America's folk dance heritage is barely three centuries old (with the exception of the ceremonial dances of the American Indian), while the Russian folk dance draws from many nationalities and many centuries of accomplishment.

Furthermore, our folk dances are fundamentally recreational and rarely provide (although there are exceptions) for the flashes of individual and group virtuosity which make Russian folk dances innately theatrical.

But we are not lost. Our simple folk flavors and, more important, our heritage of freedom as a people are incorporated in many of our theater dance works, ballets and dance–dramas by Agnes de Mille, Jerome Robbins, Michael Kidd, Doris Humphrey, José Limón, Martha Graham and many others.

In fact, speaking of Miss Graham, who recently concluded a local engagement luminous with the highest standards of dance artistry, it should be pointed out that Igor Moiseyev, in an interview with your reporter, spoke highly of Miss Graham, noted that "there is no modern dance in Russia," continued by saying that Miss Graham's artistry was "peculiar to America" and explained that modern dance has not made a stand in the Soviet Union "because it does not apply to our point of view choreographically."

American Dance   It seems to me that if our side of the American–Russian cultural exchange agreement is going to be effective, instead of making up something which does not exist (a folk dance troupe comparable to the Moiseyev), we would do better to export what we do have. And what we have is pretty wonderful.

Under the auspices of the President's Special International Program for Cultural Presentations, Miss Graham has already made a history-making tour of the Orient; Mr. Limón has cut through the Iron Curtain to win ovations for American modern dance in Poland, and both the American Ballet Theatre and the New York City Ballet have represented their homeland with great distinction in other lands.

No, there is no paucity of dance riches in America, but, paradoxically, these riches require cold cash for proper exploitation. Only the United States government, if it recognizes the ambassadorial powers of the dance art (and it should by this time), can see to it that the Russian people enjoy as stirring a glimpse of us as we have of them in the persons of the Moiseyev artists.

And to return to the Moiseyev Dance Company's first performance in America, let me say that if the dancers brought down the house, they richly deserved it. First of all, under Mr. Moiseyev's direction, these folk dancers from many regions of the Soviet Union have been disciplined into a highly professional unit and their dances have been slickly tailored (without losing any folk sturdiness or color) to the needs of the theater. The girls move with the precision of the Rockettes in numbers requiring exactitude of step and formation and with an infectious joyousness in passages festive in nature.

Russian Males The boys, of course, are much more brilliant (but the male is invariably the spectacular figure in ethnic dances). Their jumps and leaps boast the excitement of genuine resilience, their pirouettes and air-turns run into the multiples and when they get to work on those incredible full knee-bend activities, with kicks, turns, twirlings and a host of variations, they fairly lift us out of our seats. "Wow!" probably best describes these virtuosi of the Russian "prisyadka."

Although the dancers receive ballet training in addition to instruction in their folk specialties, the program itself is not at all balletic. Even the little story dances are by no means ballets. Rather are they theatricalized "images of a people's art," as Mr. Moiseyev described them to me. Touches of corniness, repetitiousness and vaudeville antics are present but do minor harm, for the show itself is skillfully wrought, expertly composed of the most attractive or exciting "images" of folk dance.

And the "images" which the Moiseyev dancers have transferred to our minds and memories are many. We might recall the charming, unaffected and delicate entrance of the maidens in the opening number; the wonderfully amusing *Yurochka,* in which a youth cannot make up his mind which lass to choose and winds up losing them all to other swains; the exquisite plastique and ritualized gestures of *Mongolian Figurine* or, in *Partisans,* the cloaked figures of scouts moving like the wind as they skimmed (seemingly without benefit of ambulation) across the stage.

Folk Fun Great good fun was to be found in *Soccer,* a near-slapstick but highly active satire on the sport, and also in the dance called *Two Boys in a Fight*, a number executed by a single dancer bent double into two costumes and battling with himself. The closing *Ukrainian Suite* of Spring Tide Ritual Songs ranged from the lyrical dances of the girls through a real Radio City Music Hall tableau with sun flower props, to a roaring finale in which every one cut loose with sheafs of virtuosity, including a male dancer, catapulted by a hidden assistant, right over the heads of the girls.

A splendid company, this Moiseyev unit, and heartily welcome they are. We cannot duplicate them in the very special area of dance which is their heritage but, when it is America's turn to repay this dance visit, we can match them in both skill and artistry with dances and dancers unique to our historically youthful but incredibly fertile heritage. And this, I think, is the

350

particular value of cultural exchanges: in addition to amicable and inevitable competition for "laurels," there is the exciting exposition of differences, art differences which invite not conflict but admiration and, perhaps, ultimate understanding. [*New York Herald Tribune*]

A Ballet Company Is Rising From Its Ashes

August 17, 1958

"Morale is high, possessions low," wrote Lucia Chase to her New York office as the American Ballet Theatre, of which she is co-director, began the final lap of an extended European tour. Miss Chase's somewhat cryptic comment is understandable to those who have read of the disaster which struck the company in late July and of the troupe's resumption of the tour after missing only two performances.

The disaster was in the form of a fire which destroyed twelve full ballets, four pas de deux, costumes, scores and the personal belongings of the dancers. Trucks, carrying the equipment from Cannes, where the American Ballet Theatre had performed, to Switzerland, where performances had been scheduled for Geneva and Lausanne, caught fire. Only a charred souvenir program remained. Only one ballet production—ironically, its name is *Pillar of Fire*—which had been shipped to Brussels for the engagement at the World's Fair, was preserved out of the whole touring repertory.

Heroine Miss Chase, who had been in New York briefly to arrange for the company's three-week season at the Metropolitan Opera House (starting Sept. 16), was put through some rough paces within a matter of hours. The plane on which she was travelling back to Europe was forced to make an emergency stop at Gander after ditching seemed inescapable. Exhausted on her arrival in Cannes, she was met with the news of the fire. Instead of swoons or hysteria, Miss Chase got to work.

Five thousand toe slippers had to be replaced, so Miss Chase got on the transatlantic telephone and ordered these items and other dance dress essentials from home. Then she asked for production assistance. From England's Royal Ballet, the Ballet Rambert, the Royal Danish Ballet and from other European companies and groups came loans of settings, costumes and scores for standard classics and costumes which could be adapted to certain of the works exclusive to the Ballet Theatre repertory. Even commercial firms, both here and abroad, contributed makeup, hosiery and the like.

Somehow, Miss Chase managed to assemble three full programs and the company opened at the Brussels World's Fair on schedule. The fire had caused damage estimated at $400,000 but an advance of $10,000 from the United States Department of State, which had sponsored the tour through the agency of the President's Special International Program for Cultural Presentations (administered by the American National Theater and Academy), and Miss Chase's refusal to give up had turned the tide.

New Ballet Although the American Ballet Theatre's financial future seemed far from rosy even before the fire, Miss Chase is obviously not worrying about future disasters. She has ordered replacements for the main sets and costumes destroyed by the fire and, in addition, has announced that three new ballets and five revivals will be given during the New York run as well as the regular repertory and the novelties originally announced.

The new works are Anton Dolin's *Variations for Four,* a work for male dancers only; a new classical ballet by Herbert Ross to the music of Tchaikovsky's Violin Concerto in D and a new Pas de Deux by Mr. Ross.

The revivals include Mr. Dolin's staging of the Victorian *Pas de Quatre*; *Helen of Troy*; *Petrouchka,* rehearsed under the direction of Leon Woizikovsky (one of the world's great interpreters of the title role) in Warsaw recently; Antony Tudor's *Jardin aux Lilas* and the same choreographer's *Judgment of Paris.*

Other premieres, announced at an earlier date, are the Swedish ballet, *Miss Julie,* created by Birgit Cullberg; Herbert Ross' *Paean* and Kenneth MacMillan's *Journey. The Blue Elephant,* originally planned for the Metropolitan season, has been dropped. [*New York Herald Tribune*]

September 19, 1958

Sweden's most famous contemporary ballet, *Miss Julie,* based upon the play by August Strindberg and choreographed by Birgit Cullberg, was given its American premiere last evening at the Metropolitan Opera House by the American Ballet Theatre. Happily, the production and the performance of this distinguished dance–drama compared favorably with the Royal Swedish Ballet's own presentation which I had been fortunate enough to see on home territory in Stockholm.

The story, well known to drama lovers, deals with a beautiful, petulant, oversexed and somewhat sadistic young lady of high family who taunts her fiance beyond endurance, seduces the butler of the household and then, shamed and terrified by the images of her disapproving ancestors, forces the butler to kill her. It is, obviously, a sordid tale but one in which details of character and colors of incident give the work a poignancy and a classical air of tragic inevitability which lift it out of the area of mere sensationalism.

Miss Cullberg, in translating the play into movement terms, has captured these details and colors admirably and if her choreography occasionally falters (mainly in the last and somewhat drawn out closing scene), the ballet as a whole has a powerful drive to it, a remorseless surge toward self-gratification, panic and disaster.

The movement style is that of modern ballet in its fusing of classical actions with dramatic gesture. And Miss Cullberg makes shrewd use of the virtuosity of classic dance to generate excitement while making it serve, along with emotional gesture to forward the plot. Thus, great leaps, spins, balances, extensions are not only exciting as isolated phenomena of body prowess but also as expressions of desire or urgency or invitation.

If one must put Miss Cullberg's choreography in some familiar category— and this might be helpful because her other ballets are not known in America—it might be said that she works in that same area as does Antony Tudor. Her personal style, however, is quite her own and both her craftsmanship and her artistic approach appear to be uninfluenced by any particular person.

The present cast for *Miss Julie* is ideal. Violette Verdy, small but commanding, with a lovely little figure and a saucy face, dances the title role superbly. She moves, as the character must, from fiery arrogance to provocative licentiousness, from restless authority to despair with compelling logic. Indeed, Miss Verdy omens the dreadful fate of her character from the very start of the ballet. She makes us know that retribution is inescapable.

Erick Bruhn, departing from his customary roles as a gallant cavalier or tragic hero, gives a magnificent enactment of the butler. His personal virtuosity is present to stir the onlooker to enthusiasm but what is more important is that his characterization is brilliantly conceived as he draws a figure which is falsely servile, physically passionate, alternating between fear and confidence. It is a great part for a very great dancer.

Excellent also were Scott Douglas as the brutally treated fiance, Sallie Wilson as a cook and Susan Borree as a fun-loving peasant. The ensemble was equally fine, for although it moved as a disciplined group, each individual projected special characteristics. The music by Ture Rangstrom served the dramatic requirements of the ballet skillfully and the costumes and scenery by Sven Erixon were fine. [*New York Herald Tribune*]

New York is a Jerome Robbins Festival

August 31, 1958

The name Jerome Robbins meant little, if anything at all, to the theatergoing public of fifteen years ago. Discerning balletomanes attending performances by Ballet Theatre (now the American Ballet Theatre), however, did not overlook a vivid young dancer whose superb rhythm, wit and energy transformed even minor roles into something of importance. Indeed, it was often more exciting to see this youth "dance" his way through a technical mistake than to see another "execute" coldly a feat of skill.

A year later, in April of 1944, Jerome Robbins was somebody. He had created a ballet called *Fancy Free* for Ballet Theatre and it was, in simple Broadway parlance, a smash hit. Bewildered and happy, he perhaps wondered if he could ever do it again. Well, he did it again and not only in the medium of ballet but also in musicals, movies and television. In fact, some sort of a record will be established next month when Mr. Robbins finds himself represented in no less than five Broadway theaters.

The Robbins Production List   Starting Thursday, his own company, recently returned from triumphant appearances at the Festival of Two Worlds at Spoleto, Italy, and the Brussels World's Fair, will open an engagement at the Alvin in Jerome Robbins' "Ballets: U. S. A." On Tuesday, the New York City Ballet, of which he is associate artistic director, will begin its fall season at the City Center in a repertory which includes several Robbins ballets. On Sept. 16, the American Ballet Theatre, still giving an honored place to *Fancy Free,* will open at the Metropolitan Opera House. And currently playing are two hit musicals, *Bells Are Ringing,* which he directed (and co-choreographed with Bob Fosse), and *West Side Story,* which he conceived, directed and choreographed. With more than a little justification, then, one might paraphrase our city's summer slogan and say that "New York is a Jerome Robbins Festival."

There is no pat formula to account for the fourteen years of theatrical success. It is obvious, of course, that Jerome Robbins has enormous talent (many would call it genius, as did Germany's great dancer, Mary Wigman, when she saw *West Side Story*), tremendous energy and imagination. But there are other clues, some involving the artist's creed; others, shrewdly practical. "What really interests me," he says, "is the conduct of man, the rites he performs to face the mysteries of life." But he goes on to explain that one of his new ballets, *N. Y. Export: op Jazz* is a teen-age ritual just as his *Age of Anxiety* (produced by the New York City Ballet) is a ritual of adults searching for pattern and purpose of living.

354

Popularity   He does not hold with the theory that there is a distinction between so-called "artistic" theater and "popular" entertainment. "It is either interesting or it is not, no matter what you call it. If a piece of theater makes an audience say, 'I wonder what will happen next?' it will be popular." Furthermore, he does not believe that the absence of dialogue in ballet should cause any communications problems for the non-dance follower. He points, as an example, to his own *The Cage*, a fantasy rich in violence and suspense. "It's pure movement," he says, "and there is no pantomime but you don't expect any one to talk."

But talk does interest him, for he not only prefers the "live" theater to any other medium but he also finds greatest satisfaction in working on a production that brings all the arts together, such as *West Side Story,* which best represents that synthesis of the arts with which he is deeply concerned.

No Favorites   Another clue to his success in various fields of the theater is that Mr. Robbins does not play favorites, nor does he feel that there should be any lowering of quality for a musical as compared with a pure ballet. "The situation," he states, "dictates form and method but not quality. The effort I put into *The King and I* was equal to that expended on any ballet. It is true that in ballet you have freedom of choice in theme, in music, in style, in many things; but what I learned in ballet is to be found in *West Side Story*, and what I learned in musicals is now found in my ballets."

This interrelation of ballet and musical comedy is by no means a new experience for Mr. Robbins. Actually, it started with *Fancy Free* itself, his first collaboration with Leonard Bernstein, the composer, and Oliver Smith, the designer. For out of *Fancy Free* grew the musical *On the Town*. Thereafter, the Robbins bounding from ballet to Broadway and back again became the rule rather than the exception.

Now, about to be surrounded by so many of his theatrical ventures, his first impulse is to shout "Wow!" But on the echo of this expression of understandable exuberance comes an eagerness to explain how he feels about each event and how he happened to wind up on Broadway with his own company in "Ballets: U. S. A." Naturally, he has a very special place in his heart for the American Ballet Theatre and its production of *Fancy Free*; his official association with the New York City Ballet is matched by his affection for that company; *West Side Story* he loves unashamedly; but, as he says, "what you are working on at a given time has your first interest" and so "Ballets: U. S. A." is commanding his thoughts and energy.

Mr. Robbins never planned to have a company of his own, and the thought of presenting such a company on Broadway never entered his mind. The group was formed when Gian-Carlo Menotti invited him to present some of his works on the Festival of Two Worlds. Originally, two other

355

choreographers were to have participated in a program directed by Mr. Robbins (hence, the title, "Ballets: U. S. A.") but changes occurred and only one other choreographer (Todd Bolender) was represented on this program. (For Broadway, a new Robbins ballet will replace the Bolender work.)

Because of the tremendous success achieved in Spoleto and Brussels, Mr. Robbins felt that the dedication of his sixteen dancers should be rewarded by continuing their performances at home. The enthusiasm of the dancers and of European audiences for the Robbins ballets was shared by Leland Hayward, the producer, who, for the first time in his career, decided to present a dance event on Broadway. Thus, New York will see ballets—classic, jazz, comic— which served to introduce many Europeans to American dance flavors.

From all reports, the Europeans were both delighted and awed. Says Mr. Robbins: "Our American dancers were treated in Europe as the Moiseyev Dancers from Moscow were treated here. No one could believe that the company had been in existence only three months and that the same sixteen dancers performed in the several styles of ballet the program demanded. At Brussels, Russian visitors asked if they all trained in one school, how long they had been in training, admitting freely that they had never seen anything like it before."

But Mr. Robbins told them that his dancers, though essentially ballet-trained, came from a variety of schools, from various parts of the United States and ranged in national origins through Korean, Irish, Negro, German, Italian, Puerto Rican, Scottish, Russian and a few others. These, then, were the dancers who, in an extremely modest total of nineteen performances (their twentieth will be on opening night at the Alvin), had electrified visitors to the festival and the fair.

"People at home are not aware of the great effect our dancers have abroad, that American dance can and does serve our country brilliantly in other lands," says Mr. Robbins. Starting Thursday, however, Americans will be able to see for themselves the American dance program hailed by our neighbors across the sea. And, if they care to spin around to four other theaters some time during September, they will also find why Jerome Robbins has become SOMEBODY in the American theater of dance. [*New York Herald Tribune*]

356

1959

The Bolshoi Invasion

Doris Humphrey — a eulogy and tribute • Tudor and Ross create for the Metropolitan Opera Ballet • Ulanova and Plisetskaya triumph in the Bolshoi's spectacular debut at the Met • Episodes — a Balanchine and Graham masterpiece • Gagaku, the Dancers of the Japanese Imperial Household, make American debut with NYCB • Britain's Ballet Rambert debuts at Jacob's Pillow • Bayanihan, from the Phillipines, and Slask, from Poland, make their American debuts • 92nd Street YMHA offers the premiere of Talley Beatty's Road of the Phoebe Snow

Doris Humphrey: Servant, Leader

January 11, 1959

Doris Humphrey, a devoted servant and impassioned leader of American dance, died young. She was only sixty-three when death came Dec. 29, 1958. Behind her she left not only her personal family (her husband and son) but also those innovators (Martha Graham, Charles Weidman, Helen Tamiris, Hanya Holm) who shared with her the task of building America's modern dance and even her illustrious predecessors and former teachers, Ruth St. Denis and Ted Shawn. But if her death was untimely by standards of longevity, her forty years-plus of dancing, choreographing, directing, teaching were immeasurably rich.

Her name, of course, is secure in the annals of the theater, in the histories of dance, in the memories of those who prospered artistically by her guidance. But her personal courage, as well as her dance genius, deserves recording, for it was this courage which made the last fifteen years of her life among the most fruitful.

Before she retired as a dancer, shortly before World War II came to an end, she had been performing with her customary lightness and technical exactitude while suffering extreme pain. Arthritis in the hip shortened one leg,

357

yet she concealed this and the accompanying pain even from her close associates until after she had given her final performance. The pain grew worse, a cane was necessary to walking, yet she turned to teaching, choreography and direction with fierce vigor, driving herself relentlessly, driving her dancing charges with care and patience.

A complicated hip operation a few years ago relieved the pain to a degree but locomotion was still not easy. Yet Miss Humphrey went to almost every modern dance event in New York, conducted rehearsals daily, created new works for the theater, attended meetings concerned with the welfare of dance and dancers, traveled to Europe, uncomplainingly climbed stairs to see studio auditions, directed several major dance enterprises, planned and fought for the establishment of a modern dance repertory theater. An incredible way of life for a well woman, an awesome one for a woman battling sickness and pain.

During her last illness, which necessitated two operations and kept her bed-ridden, she not only carried on many of her activities by letter and telephone, but she also wrote a book, *The Art of Making Dances*, to be published by Rinehart & Co. this year. In 1949, Miss Humphrey had received a Guggenheim Foundation grant to write this book on choreography but she had delayed work on it, giving the explanation, "I'm still learning about dance." But not more than a week before her death, she wrote to a friend on a Christmas card, "Well, at last it is finished."

Courage This courage was an essential part of Doris Humphrey and it aided her in facing adversities in her career as well as in health. But she had reason to plumb these resources of courage, for she was devoted to her seafaring husband and to her son (family life was adjusted to, but not subverted by, the theater) and she was possessed by that compulsion of genius which makes creativity, anguished or ecstatic, inescapable.

And what, with courage, did Doris Humphrey accomplish? As a girl in her home town of Oak Park, Ill., she studied every kind of dance—ballet, ballroom, "interpretive"—that she could find. With her fantastic kinetic memory, she could reproduce every step and every gesture of an entire dance program she had seen but once. Restless, searching, she left home to join the then greatest dance company in America, the Denishawn troupe and school, headed by Ruth St. Denis and Ted Shawn, where she became a very special protégée of St. Denis and rose to stardom under the Denishawn aegis.

But ten years of Denishawn (1917–1927) were enough and she left behind her a successful career as an interpreter of exotic dances and music visualizations to try to discover, at least to her own satisfaction, the core of dance. She stripped away the theatrical aids of elaborate costuming, representational mime, helpful music, scenery and, with her body alone, sought to find the drama of action. She stood and she moved experimentally for months in front of a mirror and she found that the materials of dance were born of gravity and that the range of dance lay within the action of fall and recovery, an area she termed "the arc between two deaths," death in vertical rigidity, death in submission to gravity.

Arc of Action   On this idea of the "arc," she built the drama of her dances, for not only were there physical daring and virtuosic perils as the body swayed or whirled or dipped away from its safe verticality but there were, inherently, comparable adventures in emotion, in thought, in drama, in adventures from the safe to the exciting, even to the terrifying. In two of her early solos, *Circular Descent* and *Pointed Ascent,* this technique served to create stirring dances with mainly kinetic meanings but, in other works, the same technique could reveal the despair, the passion of man himself and project specific conflict and incident and theme.

Later, to this organic action of dance, she added the great vocabulary of human gesture, both inherited and instinctive, to her patterns of dance. She experimented, and successfully, with unaccompanied dance, with noises rather than music, with poetry, with ramps and steps and huge blocks rather than with flat scenery, with color, with abstractions as well as with drama.

But no short article can even begin to summarize her achievements; her lovely dancing at Denishawn; her fruitful years with her partner and close friend, Charles Weidman; her brilliant direction of the José Limón Company; her choreographies for the Humphrey-Weidman troupe, for Limón and for others. Perhaps, the necessity of Doris Humphrey to the American dance scene can best be described in the simplest and most modest way: endless numbers of struggling young choreographers, stumped by a problem, would simply say, "Let's ask Doris." And Doris Humphrey, a great and revered choreographer, listened and helped. [*New York Herald Tribune*]

Met Opera Ballet

March 23, 1959

The Metropolitan Opera Ballet, entirely on its own and unflanked by singers for the first time in the Met's history, presented a program of four new ballets by four different choreographers last evening at the Metropolitan Opera House. The great theater, jammed to the doors, housed an audience which seemed like a dance "Who's Who" and on stage, the resident company, headed by its own two stars and three guest artists, performed as if to say, "You see? We can do it!"

And do it, the Met did, for the all-ballet night was an important affair. This is not to say that every new work on the bill was a masterpiece or that every performance reached perfection. There were, inevitably, weak spots but genuine creativeness and imagination characterized the occasion. It was, then, more than a good "first try"; it was, rather, a distinguished effort which gave promise of an even better ballet future for the Metropolitan Opera.

Of major interest, of course, was the new ballet—his first large-scale effort in some years—by Antony Tudor, the Met's ballet director. Titled *Hail and Farewell* (a rather breezy name for a highly poetic work) and set to Richard Strauss' Festival March, Serenade and Four Last Songs, it turned out to be the best Tudor choreography in a good many years. It is without story but is, at least in the Four Last Songs, rich in mood.

The opening sections, March and Serenade, of *Hail and Farewell,* are not particularly impressive. In truth, the choreography here resembles slightly a dancing school recital bit and the actions in Serenade lean dangerously toward the "yearning" style of esthetic dancing. But with the Songs, Mr. Tudor came into his own and gave us four gentle, tender but gloriously styled solos.

Here, Mr. Tudor created glowing choreographic images, haunting and exquisitely lyrical and they were brought to superb dance realization by Nora Kaye (guest artist), Lupe Serrano (the Met's ballerina), Edith Jerell and Audrey Keane. Unforgettable was Miss Kaye's dancing of the closing song, a triumph she shared with the singer of the songs, the noted soprano, Eleanor Steber, who performed on stage placed high on a platform behind the dancers.

But the evening did not belong exclusively to Mr. Tudor and his artists. The opening ballet, John Butler's *In the Beginning,* is also a fascinating treatment of a temptation of Adam and Eve. Choreographed to Samuel Barber's Symphony No. 1 and strikingly enhanced by decor and costumes designed by Jac Venza, the ballet starts and closes with stunning tableaux of enormously inventive design. At times, perhaps, Mr. Butler's inventiveness leads to pictorially effective but dramatically halting moments midway in the work and makes the ballet more episodic than cumulative in quality.

In the Beginning, however, is intensely theatrical and filled with vivid scenes of tenderness, passion, temptation and terror. Bambi Linn was a touching, lovely figure as Eve and Bruce Marks was physically strong and manly but dramatically pallid as Adam. As the male Tempter, symbol of the snake, Thomas Andrew performed with splendid dynamic impact, communicating stunningly the glittering and sinister aspects of the role. And Sondra Lee, the female equivalent of the serpent, colored her characterization with bright strokes of slyness and evil.

360

The program's only really gay and carefree number was Alexandra Danilova's short, classical essay, *Les Diamants*, elegantly costumed by Karinska and set to the tuneful music of Charles Beriot's "Scène de Ballet." It is a pleasant little piece for ballerina, danseur and four girls and its choreographic high spots are, naturally, for the ballerina.

In the principal part, Miss Serrano danced brilliantly, giving us both regality and virtuosity in her performance. She was a joy but the kindest thing one can say about Mr. Marks was that he was dreadfully miscast. In the modern dance field, he is a remarkable young artist but in classical ballet, he has a long way to go, at least in roles as demanding as that given him by Mme. Danilova.

The fourth work, Herbert Ross' *The Exchange,* set to Francis Poulenc's "Concerto for Organ and Orchestra," was expected (in some quarters, at least) to be controversial, since its theme was derived from a story called *The Sin of Jesus.* However, nothing shocking took place on stage, for although the figure in red was presumably Jesus, Miss Kaye conceived her own role in such a way that the events and the characters seemed to be dream-images, the images of a naive, simple peasant girl.

Actually, I am not too clear about the plot of *The Exchange,* so let me say that it appeared to be about an innocent girl who prays for an angel (at least I believe it is an angel) and, in her radiant excitement in finding him, inadvertently harms him and is not granted, at first, forgiveness by the figure in red. In any event, Mr. Ross has given Miss Kaye a part which exploits her skills as an actress, a communicator of mood and behaviour and he has given some beautiful passages to Scott Douglas (the company's premier danseur) as the angel. There are also some highly effective measures for José Gutierrez (in red), Mr. Andrew and the large and extremely well disciplined corps.

Conductors for the evening were Ignace Strasfogel, George Schick, Walter Taussig and Martin Rich; the organist was Edmund Shay and the violinist for the Beriot, Raymond Gniewek. John Ward created decor and costumes for Mr. Ross and the Tudor costumes were by Motley. [*New York Herald Tribune*]

Bolshoi Ballet Hailed in Debut at the Met

April 17, 1959

An event of historic significance took place last evening when the world-famous Bolshoi Ballet from Moscow made its American debut at the Metropolitan

Opera House. The huge troupe of dancers—the largest ever to visit our shores—and its almost legendary prima ballerina, Galina Ulanova, had literally aroused floods of excitement long before the opening.

Near-sellouts for all performances had been achieved, disappointed balletomanes who had been unable to get tickets had stormed the offices of the company's American manager, S. Hurok, as the dance world prepared to receive a celebrated ballet company which had toured outside of Russia only three times before in its two-hundred-year-old history.

Opening day in New York simply added to the excitement. Expectant standees gathered at dawn outside the Met, a bomb scare was reported in the early evening and a police search revealed nothing ominous, curiosity-seekers crowded 40th St. by the stage door to see the Soviet dancers arrive for performance and a glittering audience, liberally sprinkled with American dancers of note, crowded into the theater for the 7:30 curtain which was to rise on the three-act spectacle, *Romeo and Juliet.*

And then, at 7:40, the house lights dimmed, the orchestra played the national anthems of the United States and of the Soviet Union and the curtain rose.

And what did New York's most expectant audience see during the three and one-half hours which followed? Well, in *Romeo and Juliet* they saw unquestionably the largest spectacle in dance form which they had ever seen on the Met stage (indeed, the company had to scale its production down to fit an area smaller than that which they have at home), a spectacle composed of huge, solid and elaborate settings; many lavish (although not necessarily chic) costumes; crowds of persons on stage; some absolutely fabulous fencing episodes, very hearty and old-fashioned acting and some dancing.

Of the dancing which took place, the spotlight shone on Galine Ulanova, whose radiance of presence, whether in repose or in exquisite motion, was such that special lights seemed quite unnecessary. It is no secret that Mme. Ulanova is nearing fifty yet her Juliet is a girlish creature, impulsive, unsure, questing and eager.

For those looking simply for physical tricks, Mme. Ulanova did not give them what they sought. The choreography allotted to Juliet is comparatively simple and not very varied but Mme. Ulanova makes every gesture a poem in dance; her very walk is like a thermometer of emotional changes; her runs are alive with urgency; the line of the body in arabesque or other poses is flawless, and when she moves on pointe, always without effort, always with joy, you know she is in her own special world.

Ulanova's Triumph   Ulanova was, in fact, the glory of last night's occasion. She was, for this program at least, the Bolshoi itself or, at any rate, what we expected the Bolshoi to be. For the ballet of *Romeo and Juliet* is heavy, ponderous and, at times, dull.

Leonid Lavrosky, the choreographer, has chosen to treat the Shakespearean play in a combination of mime, realistic street scenes and dancing with the accent on the first two ingredients. The style is broad—there are bodices ripped in anguish, fists shaken and eyes ogled—but the scenic production itself is of a like style, opulent but not really beautiful. The dancing, in turn, is held to a very small collection of classical steps, to some lively folk dance sequences and to a short batch of demi-caractere activities for troubadours, jesters and the like. Whatever impact *Romeo and Juliet* may have as a theatrical spectacle, it contains little of choreographic interest.

The Other Dancers Interest in the performance was, as I say, centered in Mme. Ulanova and the shattering bravos were reserved for her. However, a word or two about her chief associates. Yuri Zhdanov, the Romeo, appeared to be of a wrestler's build and heft but he moved with surprising lightness and partnered the great ballerina not only with strength but with skill. Yaroslav Sekh's Mercutio was suitably lively and, I thought, possessed of considerable charm. Vladimir Vasiliev as Benvolio, Alexander Lapauri as Paris and Irina Makedonskaya as the nurse all performed with authority.

Konstantin Rikhter's Tybalt seemed superficial in its villainy and I couldn't find anything particularly stirring about the semi-acrobatic and not terribly neat activities of the street dance soloists. Marina Kondratieva, however, as Juliet's friend, danced her brief passages with a becoming lightness and lyricism.

The great Prokofieff score was conducted with what seemed to me to be a heavy, heavy hand by Yuri Faier but then, Piotr Viliams' settings were heavy also.

Important Occasion But, whatever reservations one may have about the merits of the Bolshoi's first production here, there can be no reservations about Mme. Ulanova nor about the importance of the occasion. Mme. Ulanova has already won us and the chances are that subsequent ballets will hold much more interest for an American audience.

As to the occasion itself, all one needs to recognize is that the Bolshoi Ballet comes to us, under the auspices of S. Hurok and the American National Theater and Academy, as the Soviet Union's greatest ballet company and that its heritage, derived from the old Russian Imperial Ballet, is the same balletic heritage which, adapted over the years, has formed the base of our own younger, different but burgeoning ballet.

Thus, it is a very special privilege for us to see a company whose immediate predecessors gave so much of immeasurable dance treasure to the entire world. And we may be sure that the present company, in the days and weeks to come, will provide us with new experiences in the theater of dance.
[*New York Herald Tribune*]

The Bolshoi Ballet from Moscow had two very special treats in store for the huge audience which assembled last evening at the Metropolitan Opera House. The first was the American debut of Maya Plisetskaya, who had never before danced outside the Soviet Union with the Bolshoi (not even London and Paris saw her), in one of her most celebrated roles. The second was the American premiere of the Bolshoi's own version of one of the international ballet classics of all time, *Swan Lake,* in four acts.

The Bolshoi production is, of course, big and lavish. It is also quite different choreographically from the four-act staging which Britain's Royal Ballet has brought to us on various occasions and the second act, which American companies present as an entity and call *Swan Lake* is also different in choreographic treatment except for the famous adagio, the Swan Queen's solo and her coda (there are minor alterations even here).

The Bolshoi style also varies, as is right and natural, from our own. But all of these differences constitute only one hurdle for the local balletomane; he must not let familiarity be his nostalgic guide. This hurdle crossed and he is ready to cheer a masterful performance of a great ballet and hail a new (to us) and remarkable ballerina.

Miss Plisetskaya, as is the custom, dances a dual role. She is Odette, the gentle and tragic Queen of the Swans who can be released from the spell cast upon her by a magician only by the true love and faith of a man. She is also Odile, the Black Swan, the magician's daughter, who must lure Odette's Prince away from his vow.

Miss Plisetskaya's Odette is a wonderfully lyrical figure. It is quietly regal, very delicate (almost elusive) in its romanticism and miraculously bird-like with respect to fluidity of the arms and the mercurial mobility of back and neck. Other Odettes, and there are several (both American and European) who deserve to be described as "great," give far more accent to movement glitter and mimed passion but the Soviet ballerina, with her cool and beautifully poetic Odette, is preparing a stunning contrast for the Odile to come.

In Act III, Odile appears and with her come glitter, incredible brilliance of brittle movement and a passion laden with venom. Here, Miss Plisetskaya not only turns in an enactment of telling power but gives her audience all those tricks of virtuosity which evoke bravos and squeals and cries of delight. There were split leaps, long sequences of turns (although this version omits the famous sequence of thirty-two fouettés), stunning balances, high leg extensions and a fine array of other sharp and shining actions.

Not every one, I suspect will like Miss Plisetskaya's conception of Odette–Odile—every aficionado has his own favorite ballerina for a given role—

but the real point of the matter is that here is a vivid interpretation, brilliantly danced by a ballerina who belongs in the top roster of stars.

The large company of soloists and corps provided Miss Plisetskaya with first-rate support. The ensemble of swan maidens in Act II moved with both grace and precision, but particularly impressive was the dancing of the divertissements of Act III. Here, the Bolshoi dancers, so well trained in character dance forms, came up with stirring, richly vital presentations of Spanish (my! those backbends!), Neapolitan, Hungarian dances and other brief numbers, including a charming dance by the Prince's possible brides (he turns them all down).

Among the featured performers, I would mention Nicolai Fadeyechev's nicely acted Prince, supplemented by some dance measures agreeably performed; Vladimir Levashev's expert performance as the Evil Sorcerer; Georgi Soloviev, who had some splendid passages as an acrobatic Jester; Elena Iliushchenko, regal as the Princess–Mother, and, in various dance assignments, Maya Samokhvalova, Natalia Taborko, Lidia Shein, Liudmila Bogomolova, Marina Kontratieva and Lev Evdokimov.

I must say I have several reservations, here and there, about the choreography created by Alexander Gorsky and Asaf Messerer with a nod or two toward the original creators, Lev Ivanov and Marius Petipa, and I have some reservations about performing style. But there is no argument about the fact that the Bolshoi's *Swan Lake,* with its big settings and bright costumes (designed by Simon Virsaladze), its big and superbly disciplined cast and its Maya Plisetskaya (who won a tremendous ovation at the close of the evening) as Odette–Odile, is something to see. [*New York Herald Tribune*]

April 24, 1959

The Russians, last evening, primed the pumps, pulled out the stoppers, turned on the taps and flooded the stage of the Metropolitan Opera House with just about every twist and trick at their command. Heretofore, the Bolshoi Ballet from Moscow has shown us only program-length dramatic ballets, *Romeo and Juliet* and *Swan Lake.* Last night, the program was composed of thirteen short ballets or ballet excerpts and was most accurately tiled Highlights Program I (Number II turns up next week).

The evening started modestly enough with a very agreeable performance of Michel Fokine's *Chopiniana,* which we know as *Les Sylphides.* The great Galina Ulanova was the central figure here and she danced exquisitely, especially in the duet with Nicolai Fadeyechev, but this work by no means displays her very special gifts as an actress–dancer nor does its purposeful blandness allow Mme. Ulanova to communicate that wonderful radiance present in her Juliet or her Giselle. But it was, of course, a treat to see her.

After *Chopiniana,* we had the Grand Pas de Deux from *The Sleeping Beauty* in unfamiliar choreography by Asaf Messerer, danced to the hilt by Raissa Struchkova, who flirted, hammed and carried on to a fare-the-well. Technically, she was fine and her bravura wiles delighted the audience. Boris Kokhlov was her steady, but understandably obscured, partner.

And then came the highlight of this program of highlights, the magnificent Maya Plisetskaya as the flamboyant Bacchante in the Walpurgis Night scene from *Faust.* Miss Plisetskaya, ballet's answer to the opera's Maria Callas in matters of personality, presence, grandeur, temperament and virtuosity, can best be described in the good old American slang expression "Wow!"

The Walpurgis affair is corny beyond belief (why is crouched skipping in a Bacchanale supposed to be sexy?) but Miss Plisetskaya makes you forget everything but the marvels of her body in motion, sailing through air to be caught by strong male arms, hoisted aloft in fetching poses, spinning with electrifying brilliance, balancing on pointe with stunningly arrested action, leaping, bending, darting. What shall I say? A great dancer. A great performer.

The youngest of the Bolshoi ballerinas, nineteen-year-old Ekaterina Maximova, appeared with Gennadi Lediakh in the Pas de Deux from *The Flames of Paris,* and showed herself to be not only a beautiful girl with a lovely figure but also a splendid little dancer. Mr. Lediakh, given some spectacular actions for the male, executed them superbly and served notice that he is one of the best of the Bolshoi men dancers, particularly with respect to the fact that he can not only do feats of skill but, unlike some of his colleagues, do them without a touch of heaviness.

We Stalingraders was a soldier tableau but I guess every dance company has some kind of a choreographic memorial to war-time courage. The dances from Igor Moiseyev's *Spartacus* were also of warlike cast but a far earlier period involving, as weapons, a flashing broadsword and a trident. The dances from *Spartacus* were flamboyant and of little depth but they served to promote the agility of the men dancers in fine fashion.

Dance Suite, an etude choreographed by A. Varlamov, turned out to be a charming bit. It was mainly a series of short studies in pattern for groups of various sizes and it was excellently danced by Liudmila Bogolomova, Vladimir Vasiliev and their associates.

Other items in this balletic medley included *Etude, A Bashkir Dance, A Blind Woman* (danced by Mme. Ulanova), *The Flight of the Bumblebee, Bulgarian Dances* and, to close the evening, *The Waltz,* in which Miss Struckkova and Alexander Lapauri participated in all those lifts, jet-propelled tosses and related spectacular actions for which the Russians are famous. An ovation, naturally, ensued and the finale had to be repeated for an audience which had loved every moment of a program which pretended to be nothing more nor less than a sort of Soviet "Hit Parade" in dance form. [*New York Herald Tribune*]

May 17, 1959

No doubt about it, the Soviet company's Metropolitan season was a great occasion, an enormously important one for which we must thank that persistent impresario, S. Hurok, who had been striving to get the fabled Bolshoi to America for years and years. And what we saw was one of the world's finest dance organizations, headed by such superlative artists as the gentle Galina Ulanova and the blazing Maya Plisetskaya, in a repertory which ranged from beautifully staged classics through mutilated classics to contemporary works which, in turn, ranged from the ridiculous to the interesting.

Discernment A vast section of the public and, I am sorry to say, some American dancers seemed incredibly intemperate in their reactions to the Bolshoi performances. They screamed in delight over everything. Now there was plenty to cheer, much to admire, moments when one quite naturally wanted to weep because of the sheer beauty of, say, a Ulanova performance. But lack of discernment led many to cheer inferior choreography and some very bad dancing. This, I think, was not only unfair to ourselves as creators of dance, but also to the Russians who, I presume, prefer knowing appreciation to blind adoration.

When some overawed American dancers gasped, "I haven't seen anything like it!" as they watched examples of Russian virtuosity, especially in the Highlights Programs, they were telling the truth. They hadn't seen the Bolshoi until this season. And they can be expected to repeat the phrase when some other first-rank company with a style of its own visits our country for the first time.

But, as a matter of fact, such hysterical reactions are not new to us. We did it when the Royal Ballet (then the Sadler's Wells) first came to America. Nitwits in the audience started applauding, on one occasion, when some unknown damsel stepped forth from the corps to hand a bouquet to a prince charming and were stopped by a perhaps jaded, but more discriminating, voice from the audience which boomed, "Good heavens! What do you suppose they'll do when someone gets onto pointe!" And we did it again when the Royal Danish Ballet first appeared here and I guess we'll go on doing it.

Ulanova There is more fun, however, as well as good sense, in grading one's responses to the product offered. For example, any one who did not respond with enthusiasm to Mme. Ulanova's *Giselle*, to the quite unequaled ensemble dancing of the corps de ballet in the second act of the same ballet or to the glorious acrobatics of Raissa Struchkova and Alexander Lapauri in *The Waltz* should certainly have his head examined. On the other hand, it was clear to any one who had been exposed to dance at all that the Bolshoi version of *Swan Lake* was much inferior choreographically to that of Britain's Royal Ballet, that its treatment of the Rose Adagio from *Sleeping Beauty* was much less effective than our own and that *The Ocean and the Pearls* Pas de Trois was one of the silliest items any troupe outside of vaudeville (circa 1920) ever tossed at the public.

Perhaps a good way to examine the peaks and the low points of Soviet ballet art would be to discuss *Stone Flower,* a new work (less than a year old in its present form), the final novelty of the Bolshoi season. It is a big, lavish, three-act ballet based on a Russian fairy story. It has a score (his last for ballet before his death) by Serge Prokofieff which my musical colleague, Jay Harrison, says is very inferior Prokofieff. My only comment, and this from the dance viewpoint, is that it is danceable.

On the credit side, it may be said that *Stone Flower* boasts more extensive and integrated dancing than does *Romeo and Juliet* (which is overburdened with realistic action and very old-fashioned pantomime). The folk dance sequences are exciting and the gypsy sequence is stunningly choreographed. But more important is the presence of a clue to what future Soviet choreography might develop into. There is an utterly charming duet for the heroine and a fairy Fire Girl in which Russian folk dance steps are interrelated, with fine movement logic and freshness, with classical ballet movements. Elsewhere in the ballet, this fusion of folk and classical occurred briefly and always effectively.

Folk and Classic　　And perhaps this bringing together of folk and classic or, rather, adapting folk movement to the classical mold or finding classical equivalents for folk steps and gestures will open up a whole new choreographic area for Russian creators. Certainly, our own ballet has grown in scope because of Agnes de Mille's infusion of folk materials into ballet, Jerome Robbins' use of jazz in ballet or the modern dance's invigorating contributions to ballet. At any rate, such elements in *Stone Flower* gave the work a special significance.

Also on the credit side one would list the dazzling dancing of Miss Plisetskaya as the snakelike but all-woman Mistress of the Copper Mountain. What a performer! Unafraid of bravura tactics, magnificent of body, mistress of technique, the ballerina is really a marvel. Almost as exciting is the young, still somewhat gauche but wonderfully vigorous Vladimir Vasiliev. With fine agility and power, he can and does surmount the physical hurdles of his role in *Stone Flower* with a dash and a boyish brilliance which makes cheers very much in order.

On the debit side of *Stone Flower,* I would name scenery and costumes in bad taste and so cluttered of color that it was difficult to see the movements which took place. I would also note that the choreographer gave the Mistress of the Copper Mountain a very limited selection of movements which were repeated until they were drained of all effectiveness and that except for the little duet I have mentioned, treated the heroine, Katerina, to a like paucity of invention.

The tableaux in *Stone Flower* were contrived. One could even see dancers darting (not dancing) into place for the final "living pictures." Tableaux can be pretty or even dramatically effective but one would like them to be the unforced result of the preceding action.

But enough of *Stone Flower.* It had its magnificent moments, its naivetes and its artistic nadirs.

Ballet Institution Without being chauvinistic or ungrateful for the offtimes overwhelming experience attendant upon the Bolshoi programs, it is perfectly possible to probe the strengths and weaknesses of both Soviet and American ballet. Immediately apparent is the fact that any state-supported company has the advantage of permanence and of security. We do not have a corps to match in size, in schooling and in discipline that of the Bolshoi whose members have trained together since childhood.

In our various corps, there is always a turnover each season as dancers move on to Broadway shows and newcomers, in limited rehearsal periods (because of finances), must learn anywhere from twenty to thirty ballets. We also have the problem of a limited number of first-rate male dancers for ballet mainly because little boys rarely start ballet training at the same age as little girls; they grow up first and start ballet lessons dangerously late.

The Bolshoi has a great and an old tradition but creatively, it has worked, until recently, in an artistic prison. This has nothing to do with the communist regime per se. Fokine, Diaghileff and others left Russia before the revolution in order to find freedom of artistic adventure. Balanchine left later and for the same reasons. Here, if we do not have institutional traditions, such as the Bolshoi has, we do function in an atmosphere of free creativity and we have, I think contributed more to an ever-expanding ballet tradition than any other nation of the present.

Art Exchange But all this boils down to the simple fact that we can learn from each other. The undiscriminating shouters for the Bolshoi have done a disservice by clouding this important issue. Certainly, the Soviet artists have given us unforgettable aspects of the ballet art which we have every right to enjoy, to hail, to study and, where pertinent, to emulate. They have not, on the other hand, destroyed our own ballet by comparison. They have helped to point up our genuine failings but they have pointed up our virtues also and from these, perhaps, they will find certain stimuli for their own progress.

An artistic exchange between nations calls for neither a chauvinistic onslaught nor a self-deprecating submission. It calls, rather, for the grasping of an opportunity to see and to discover, to accept and to reject and, most important of all, to understand. In this light, the visit of the Bolshoi Ballet to America is of immeasurable significance to all who cherish the art of ballet. [*New York Herald Tribune*]

A New Dance Masterpiece
by Graham and Balanchine

May 15, 1959

American dance, whatever else it may or may not do or accomplish, does not stand still. It is restless, it is experimental, it is searching. Sometimes the result is disastrous or, better, intellectually interesting. Sometimes the quest ends in triumph. It did just that last night at the City Center when the New York City Ballet presented the world premiere of *Episodes*, set to the music of Anton Webern (a seemingly unlikely choice for ballet) and combining the choreographic talents of George Balanchine, the foremost classical choreographer in America, and Martha Graham, the nation's greatest modern dancer (also an unlikely collaboration).

But the unexpected union of three prodigious talents—Webern, Balanchine, Graham—worked. The union, however, was not literal, for Miss Graham and her dancers, augmented by members of the New York City Ballet, were responsible for only one of the episodes and danced entirely in the Graham style. Mr. Balanchine, aside from presenting the modern dancer Paul Taylor in a solo, used his own ballet dancers exclusively in the episodes which he had choreographed. Yet there was unity. It is obvious, of course, that both choreographers were united by the music of the same composer, but what was more important was that unity was manifest in the theatrical eloquence of dance itself, be it balletic or modern.

Miss Graham elected to use her Webern music as a stimulus for drama. In her tense and touching scene, she gave us the last minute of Mary, Queen of Scots before she placed her head on the executioner's block. The Queen, in her final memories, summons up images of herself in the royal robes of independence; clad in white, in a love duet with her beloved Bothwell who sought her crown; in an ironic game of badminton with Queen Elizabeth,

370

whom she never had met, but who had plotted against her and sealed her doom; swift glances at others who had failed her.

There were terrifying moments when Mary, the woman, seemed ready to cry out for mercy only to be stopped by the vision of her stiff, discarded dress of regality, the symbol of her duty. There was anguish as she reached out toward Bothwell, Darnley, Riccio, Chastelard, standing in ghostly ranks, and in the withdrawal of her hand as she knew that none could save her. And there was majesty as, dressed in red (so that spilled blood would not show upon the raiment of a queen), she mounted the scaffold and bent her head toward the block.

Miss Graham, looking radiantly beautiful, danced the role of the Scottish Queen with that power that has long characterized her performing. The large-scale movements were wonderfully molded but even the smallest gestures, a glance, the lift of the head, or charged stillness communicated vividly the terror, the pride, the warmth of a queen facing death.

As Elizabeth, the New York City Ballet's Sallie Wilson made an imposing symbol of cold supremacy, softened briefly by passing moment of self doubt. Bertram Ross, of the Graham company, was a rough and dashing Bothwell and the other members of the mixed troupe were excellent.

For his shorter but more numerous episodes, Mr. Balanchine eschewed plot entirely. For him, the project was to mirror in movement and in form the phrasings, tonalities, silences and, very definitely, the wit of the music. To do this, he not only employed a great many gestures not previously used in classical ballet but he also altered, adapted and distorted traditional ballet actions to suit his needs. Thus, we frequently saw toe-slippered feet flexed into angular lines or port de bras woven into new and strange designs. Indeed, we saw ballet stepping in and out of the realm of modern dance.

It is not possible here to describe each of the Balanchine episodes. Some, I thought (at least on first seeing), were more successful than others. Among the best, was a pas de deux, danced superbly by Diana Adams and Jacques d'Amboise, in which the two seemed to miss presumably romantic connections by misplaced calculations of who would be where and when. In between, the silences in the score were amusingly used as if the dancers, like boxers between rounds, were thinking out new strategy.

There was another stunning section, filled with humor and surprises, danced by Allegra Kent, Nicholas Magallanes and an ensemble and the closing section, led by Francisco Moncion and the ever-exciting Melissa Hayden, reverted to classicism in movement patterns which were cool, flowing and noble in cast. This last episode, it seemed to me, might have been more effective in modern dance form just as Paul Taylor's absolutely pure modern dance solo, brilliantly executed, seemed interpolated rather than an integral or, at least, linked part of the whole conception.

But these are small quibbles (which another seeing may conceivably erase) with respect to a work which is not only a successful experiment but also one of the most stirring theatrical ventures to come our way since the New York City Ballet commenced its distinguished career a decade ago. *Episodes* makes history and it is not to be missed. [*New York Herald Tribune*]

Gagaku

May 27, 1959

The brilliant, breathtaking extroversion of Western ballet was replaced, for a brief period, last evening at the City Center when Eastern dance presented to the public episodes dedicated to the beauty of serenity, to the elegance of ceremony, to the celebration of exquisite detail. The occasion for this strange (to us) but rewarding (also to us) change of pace was the formal American debut of Gagaku, the Musicians and Dancers of the Japanese Imperial Household, an event jointly sponsored by the City Center of Music and Drama and the Japan Society of New York.

The Imperial troupe, sharing the program with the New York City Ballet, brought to our stage a tradition, both musical and dance, extending back into time for more than one thousand years. And this in itself was a history-making move for not only did it mark the first time that Gagaku had been presented outside of Japan but it also represented the first time that this non-theatrical art form had been seen outside of Japan's Imperial Palaces and Shinto Shrines.

Since Gagaku does not have its home in the theater, the New York City Ballet, with wisdom and taste, arranged to duplicate the elevated platform, carpeted in green and embellished with black and red lacquered steps and railings, upon which Gagaku performs for the Emperor and his guests. Through this setting, the stage, as we expect it to be, was erased; we were, rather, at court to witness ancient ceremonies in sound and movement.

The troupe offered four selections, three dances (one dating back to the seventh century A.D.) and one instrumental work. And it would be inaccurate to pretend that both music and motion were not strange to us, for they were. Untutored eyes and ears could not be expected to comprehend every detail of phrasing, every gestural meaning.

Yet there was no reason to become either bored or lost. In the dance sections, there were no examples of that physical virtuosity or even that

372

emotional projection which we, quite rightly, admire. But watching the movements of the Gagaku dancers, one suddenly realized that a step might not necessarily be the preparation for a run or a leap but that the step itself, executed in slow motion with perfect definition, was a thing of beauty.

Further, one noted a peculiar air of accomplishment in the manner in which a foot caressed the ground, stamped upon it with aristocratic arrogance or, perhaps, merely planted itself there with authority. I found too that a knee-bend was not irrevocably destined for resolution in a jump or a bow but that, as a simple body gesture, it could achieve subtle movement perfection even within the circumscribed area of the action itself.

I would not wish to give the impression that the Gagaku dancers did nothing but step and bend. There were other movements, all quite simple, and the choreography was simple also. But the manner in which a dancer lifted a coiled, golden snake to his lips; knelt to place a shield upon the ground; lifted spears into the air with leisurely exactitude or even marched onto and off of the platform invited admiration. There is nothing more deceptively simple than that form of Japanese poetry called the hokku (or haiku), yet the hokku, to be successful, must communicate a single perfect image. Gagaku does just that, for the images in each step and gesture, are perfectly molded.

As for the music, one picks out at first a sound which resembles a bagpipe, another which is almost organ-like, yet others which are immediately identifiable as the pipe of the flute, the throb of drums, the plucking of stringed instruments. Ultimately, they find some sense of union in our ears and, if we cannot hear all melodic progressions or harmonizations, we can respond, at the least, to exotic sounds and, at best, to an incipient appreciation of forms new to us.

But whatever difficulties the Western novice may have had in absorbing all of the values of Gagaku dance and music, he had no trouble at all in relishing the absolutely magnificent costumes of the artists, the striking masks, the shining swords, the gleaming lances and, of course, the replica of the Imperial platform designed by David Hays and lighted by him.

In a city where practically every one is geared to the tempo of the IRT, the pacing of Gagaku may seem slow but observation of their impeccably studied rhythmic leisure reveals a startling fact: if to move in dance is a joy, then there are times that to dwell upon the beauty of a single movement, a perfect pose, constitutes another, if distinctly different, pleasure. Gagaku dwells upon the beauty of the instant.

In addition to the *Stork Dance, The Snake Dance, The Military Dance* and the instrumental number (*Heavenly Music*) by Gagaku, the program also included George Balanchine's *Serenade, Pas de Dix* and *Stars and Stripes,* all danced by the New York City Ballet. In subsequent performances, all of which Gagaku will share with the ballet artists, the Japanese troupe will offer this and three other different programs, with program number two slated for tomorrow evening. [*New York Herald Tribune*]

Britain's Ballet Rambert: Tradition, New Adventures

July 26, 1959

The Ballet Rambert, which Ted Shawn has imported from England for his Jacob's Pillow Dance Festival at Lee, Mass., starts its third and final week at the Pillow Tuesday with a program devoted to a full-length production (in three acts) of that classic comedy-ballet, *Coppélia*. To date, the British company, under the direction of Marie Rambert, has given us a splendid *Giselle* and six contemporary ballets spanning a period of slightly more than twenty years.

Perhaps a final estimate should not be made until *Coppélia* has been viewed but the character of Mme. Rambert's repertory and the stature of her company have been pretty well established in the two weeks of performing at the Pillow. First to the repertory.

New Talent It is a fact well known to the dance world that Mme. Rambert, over the years, has continuously fostered new talent, both performing and choreographic. In certain instances, she has produced new works and, in other cases, she has given a home in her repertory to ballets previously staged by temporary or short-lived groups. Naturally, she could not give us a total repertory season in three short weeks at the Pillow, but she did give us a cross section of fully-mounted productions ranging, in the contemporary area, from early ballets by Antony Tudor to a brand new work (his first) by Norman Morrice, a member of her company.

Three of the Ballet Rambert works were new to the American public. Kenneth MacMillan's *Laiderette,* used as a curtain-raiser on the *Giselle* program, turned out to be a rather murky piece in which a Pierrot-like theme was given a macabre twist. It contained some of that fine invention and air of poignancy with which Mr. MacMillan creates but the work as a whole possessed little impact. Walter Gore's *Simple Symphony* was better, not very exciting but lively, good-natured and, perhaps, a trifle forced in its exposition of folk dance exuberance.

Norman Morrice Mr. Morrice's *Two Brothers,* on the other hand, was something to invite both attention and admiration. It is quite youthful (the choreographer is only twenty-three) and, reasonably enough, it mirrors the forces and the weaknesses of youth. The Tudor influence is very much present, the Dohnanyi music to which it is set is not ideal as a base for the choreography (it also invites Tudorims) and certain of the highly emotional passages are super-charged to the degree that brings to my mind a line from a Carolina folk play I saw years ago: "Ma, I'm all black and bitter and twisted inside."

Nonetheless, Mr. Morrice has brought to his first choreographic effort fine movement, imagination, dramatic conviction, a good sense of form, a direct (but not superficial) telling of his story and a communicable enthusiasm for what he and the characters in his ballet are doing.

Here, in this ballet built upon the violent jealousy a boy feels for his older brother's fiancee and the disastrous results of this triangle, Mr. Morrice has revealed himself as an impressive young talent.

It is difficult to assess the performing of the Rambert dancers mainly because certain of the ballets exploit their talents and other works disclose, and sometimes cruelly, their shortcomings. Strangely enough, *Giselle,* an enormously difficult ballet, presented the company to good advantage. Mme. Rambert's staging, as I noted in previous columns, is masterful and she has drawn excellent performances, especially from Beryl Goldwyn (the Giselle), from her dancers, Ulanova, Markova, Alonso, Kaye and their various partners are still quite securely in charge of this ballet in other productions but the Rambert version is thoroughly distinguished.

The company, at the other end of the scale, fared less happily in Mr. Tudor's *Gala Performance.* The technical demands of the work were too much for certain of the dancers, although Gillian Martlew was splendid as the Italian Ballerina, and in other ballets, the youthfulness and inexperience of the hard-working and disciplined performers made one feel that this was a talented workshop rather than a mature, professional company. *Two Brothers*, however, was just right for the capabilities of the young artists and wonderfully suited to their freshness of presence and movement exuberance.

Woman of Vision Mme. Rambert, who has had a constant struggle to keep her company going without benefit of dependable financial support, keeps losing her dancers to larger and more secure dance troupes so it is something of a miracle that her present group is as good as it is. I would think, then, it is best to look at the Ballet Rambert not as a rival to Britain's Royal Ballet or to our own American professional companies but, rather, as an important institution devoted to the constant nurturing of new talent. In this light, Ballet Rambert may be seen as a wonderfully vital organization of young dancers and choreographers, filled with the spirit of discovery and promising its audiences a heart-warming adventure with youth, its present skills and its dreams. [*New York Herald Tribune*]

Bayanihan Creates a New Dance Art

October 18, 1959

Bayanihan, the enchanting Philippine dance troupe presently playing at the Winter Garden, provides us with yet another important example of the transference of folk art to the theater. The dances of India, Japan, Indonesia and Spain are theatrical to begin with and need little more than pruning to make them as attractive on stage as they are in the traditional temple, courtyard or cafe. Even a great many Russian folk dances are fundamentally display pieces for the skilled individual rather than mild participation dances.

But in many quarters of the world, the ethnic dance materials, no matter how rich, are of the participation brand, fun to do but not terribly exciting to watch, at least outside of their natural surroundings. There is no reason, however, to deprive the theater of the splendid stuff of folk dance. But someone must do the job of selecting, formalizing, enhancing these materials for theatrical presentation. Haiti, for example, had a fine folk dance heritage and an exciting tradition of voodoo ceremonial action but it took a Jean Leon Destine to make the Haitian dance an art form.

From the Source In Israel, Sara Levi-Tanai has done the same thing with Inbal (which will be appearing in New York shortly), for she has taken comparatively simple Yemenite and related Oriental movements and molded them into an art expression which retains a racial and cultural integrity while at the same time meeting the requirements of a universal theater.

This procedure, of course, applies to ethnic dance arts specifically. Israel has produced dancers who work in the non-ethnic modern dance idiom, Japan has its own groups performing classical ballet and all nations, in one way or another, foster international dance forms. But the preservation and the development of an ethnic dance heritage is important not only to the culture concerned but also to the world which would wish to see, admire and learn from the unique dance expressions of a given people.

Bayanihan is one of the newest examples of an ethnic dance culture which has gone beyond simple preservation (as important as that is) and into creative growth. The program which the Philippine company is performing here is skillfully ordered so that one sees in swiftly paced, contrasting suites the varied steps, costumes and customs of a wide area of the Philippines. We are carried from the elemental, wild and free dances of primitive mountain peoples to the refined actions of those touched by Spanish culture, from the Orient-slanted gestures of the Moslem inhabitants to a wide selection of regional dances and rural scenes of work and play.

Leticia Urtula   As fine as this arrangement is from the geographical point of view it would not be enough if the dances themselves had not been subjected to choreographic arrangement and adaptation. Leticia Reyes Urtula, Bayanihan's choreographer and dance director, has done a superb job in giving form, substance and shading to comparatively simple folk dances or harvest scenes and in exploiting to the fullest the very real virtuosity inherent in the *Tinikling,* during which the dancers step in and out of bamboo poles held close to the floor and struck together in syncopated rhythms.

Actually, Mrs. Urtula might well have given more attention to the need for climaxes in the primitive section but elsewhere she has guided with taste and brightness the choreographic course of a variety of fascinating episodes. In fact, the simple walk of the girls in the Spanish-style suite flowed into designs of great charm and loveliness, patterns which were as arresting in a lyrical way as were the flashing steps of the *Tinikling* and the Moslem *Singkil*; the swift measures of the men with their coconut shell harnesses as they clapped out rhythms on themselves and on each other; the suspenseful balancing acts in which the girls moved while bearing flickering lamps on heads and hands or, at a celebration, two men descending to the ground and turning over while crowned with glasses of wine.

Mrs. Urtula, although she merits unstinted praise for her direction and choreography, cannot take full claim for the success of Bayanihan. This she shares with the dancers and singers, a group of handsome, smiling, utterly engaging artists. They are professionals all but they seem, somehow, rather like neighbors and one loves them on sight. The costumes are stunning, the music is fascinating but the performers are, to put it succinctly, irresistible. [*New York Herald Tribune*]

Polish Folk Ballet

November 4, 1959

The Polish State Folk Ballet, drawing its singing and dancing members from among the shepherds and goose girls and students of Silesia, made its New

York debut—and, incidentally, gave its five hundredth performance—last evening at the City Center. This troupe of some one hundred performers is in no sense a classical ballet company. It is, rather, a handsome and personable folk dance and song unit, disciplined for the theater but retaining the simplicity, even the naivete of the mountain villages from which it springs.

Inevitably, S. Hurok's newest importation will be compared with his recent Russian folk attractions. So let us say right off that "Slask," the popular name (it means Silesia) for the group, boasts neither the performing virtuosity nor the choreographic elaborateness of the Soviet companies. All right, that is settled and now we can concentrate upon the many charms and very special characteristics of these exuberant artists.

So engaging and inviting are these Polish singers and dancers that one really wishes that the barrier of footlights did not separate us from them. How wonderful it would be to see them dancing on the green in Central Park, recapturing the natural background of their rural festivities, or, perhaps, performing in-the-round. But if the stage is not always fair to their delightful air of intimacy and spontaneity, we can, nonetheless, dismiss the sophistication of the theater and join in the spirit of communal exuberance which marks their folk art.

The girls, in an array of colorful costumes, swing their long pigtails high into the air as they spin gleefully across the stage, revealing, under bright skirts, several modest petticoats which look like spinning mushrooms. The young men, in bright peasant garb or dashing uniforms, kick up their heels in joyous jumps, slide to their knees by their ladies' sides or, as the cock of the walk might do, show off their special prowesses by hurdling back and forth over staffs they hold in their hands or by performing those leaps with noses close to the floor which are sometimes called butterfly turns.

In such dances as *Kujawiak and Oberek,* the girls also show off by supporting the men (it is an illusion but effective) in lifted leaps. Well, they are strapping girls but they are utterly feminine even when aiding their men to soar into space.

In addition to patterns calling for zest and bounce, there are those demanding dignity and elegance. There is, for example, an entrance to a number in which nine men and nine girls move like liquid across the stage and, of course, there are the lovely measures of Poland's national dance, the *Polonaise*; the *Mazurka,* which Poland may also claim as her own, and the marvelous *Krakowiak,* born in the city of Krakow. And what, one might note in passing, would the great classical ballets of the nineteenth century do without one or more of these national dances?

The program also contained many songs, some of them choral pieces sung with great beauty and vitality by the ensemble; others such as the *Heli, Helo,* an echo song of mountain shepherds, spiced with humor, and still others devoted to the special solo colors of a deep basso, a penetrating contralto or a sweet soprano.

In a folk program such as this, certain numbers were, understandably, more interesting theatrically than others. Some of the songs and dances seemed to saunter to an end rather than reach for a climax while others built to peaks of excitement. Basically, the choreography, designed by Elwira Kaminska to formalize to a degree the folk patterns, was simple. Most of the plans were circular or lateral but within this directional simplicity, charming effects were achieved. To be truthful, I think Mme. Kaminska could extend her folk actions still further into theatrical idioms without losing the improvisational air of the dances. But that, of course, is just a guess.

The orchestra was under the direction of Stanislaw Hadyna, founder of the company, with Edward Weyman and Arthur Lief as his assistants. The traditional folk costumes were stunning and every one of the performers, from the lovely brunette who could really belt out a song across the mountains to the fair-haired young man who danced with the resilience of a rubber ball as he pursued the girl of his choice, was a charmer. They charmed us in their native songs and dances and they wound up by charming us with their rendition of "America the Beautiful." And, fortunately for us all, they will be with us at the City Center for three weeks. [*New York Herald Tribune*]

New Dance Suite by Talley Beatty

December 20, 1959

Talley Beatty has long been known as an unusually gifted and exciting dancer. As a choreographer, he has come up with several theatrically vivid pieces but by far his finest work is the new *The Road of Phoebe Snow,* which had its premiere at the 92nd St. Y. M. and Y. W. H. A. on Nov. 28. Because of illness, I was unable to attend but, fortunately, saw a second presentation just the other day.

The new creation, which derives its title from the railroad slogan which was related to a legend (Phoebe was exceptionally neat and the Lackawanna boasted of its system as "The Route of Phoebe Snow"), is neither a story ballet nor a choreographic portrayal of Phoebe. It is, I would say, a mood piece or, rather, a work comprising many moods. The railroad is indicated by the flashings of red and green lights and by certain sounds in the score but otherwise the piece concerns itself with boys and girls dancing near the unseen tracks.

Dance Episodes   And what do they dance about? At first, it would seem that they are simply dancing, channeling energy into the rhythms and patterns of dance but then a heightened air of excitement introduces romance, lust, antagonism, battle, cruelty and terror. The episodes are nameless and unnumbered but they have a cumulative relationship which is apparent as the ballet progresses.

And the word "ballet," incidentally, is pertinent, for Mr. Beatty has used a great many actions from the vocabulary of the classical ballet. There are arabesques, attitudes, pirouettes and many lifts associated with ballet but the choreographer has altered them so that they seem to be instinctive manifestations of emotion rather than calculated courtliness.

Mr. Beatty hasn't stopped there. Modern dance, jazz dance, a somewhat frenetic mime and touches of primitive dance are all a part of his choreographic material. Peculiarly enough, all of these ingredients, instead of clashing, fuse into an overall theatrical style beautifully suited to the themes of Mr. Beatty's work. Furthermore, the work itself, aside from a few repititious figurations near the beginning, is absorbing and genuinely rousing theater fare.

Impact   Not only does the increasing intensity of mood in *The Road of Phoebe Snow* hold the attention and invite growing concern for the unspoken dramas of the participants but the physical virtuosity of the piece is also a major factor in giving the work great impact. The slides, splits, lifts, tumblings, leaps and turnings are used with splendid originality of sequence, for although they are used with logic, they contain frequent elements of surprise. And one of the pleasantest surprises was the stirring dancing of a girl named Candace Caldwell, although each member of Mr. Beatty's group performed admirably.

This fine new creation in the field of contemporary dance, with its score composed of selections from Duke Ellington and Billy Strayhorn, was made possible by a grant from the Lena Robbins Foundation. [*New York Herald Tribune*]

With Maya Plisetskaya, 1966. Photo: V. Sladon.

With Rudolf Nureyev, Margot Fonteyn, Rebekah Harkness on the Harkness penthouse terrace, 1963. Photo: Ira Rosenberg.

With Frederic Franklin in dressing room Boston's WGBH-TV for *A Time to Dance* television series, 1960.

With Amalia Hernandez, founder-director Ballet Folklorico de Mexico. Before a TV interview, 1968.

1960

Weaving, Waltzing, and a Wonder Boy

George Balanchine gives an interview • Maria Karnilova, on Broadway in Gypsy, reflects on a career in dance • NYCB offers the premieres of Figure in the Carpet and Liebeslieder Walzer and the debut of young Patricia McBride in Robbins' Afternoon of a Faun • ABT's 20th anniversary year • Graham creates the delightful Acrobats of God • Helen Tamiris and Daniel Nagrin unveil a new company • Edward Villella discusses his triumph in Prodigal Son

George Balanchine

March 20, 1960

"Inspiration? No!" said George Balanchine, "that is for the very young. For me, a ballet is not the result of inspiration, it is not born in child-like dreams. Necessity, rather than inspiration, is the source of choreography. As a professional dance-maker, I want to create but what I do is to assemble ingredients—it is like opening an icebox door and you look inside to see what you have stored away—and then I select, combine and hope that the results will be appetizing."

The New York City Ballet's artistic director and principal choreographer, in describing his methods of work, invariably employs similes related either to cookery or horticulture. Among his friends, he is known as a superb chef and he and his wife, Tanaquil LeClercq, a former ballerina whose career was cut short by poliomyelitis, love gardening, particularly the cultivation of roses. Thus, it is hardly strange that Mr. Balanchine, for whom gesture and speech are inseparable, appears to be measuring out the materials in a recipe when he talks about choreography or changes his gestures to indicate a growing, blossoming plant as he speaks of the evolution of new movements.

The Russian-born dance master is universally recognized as one of the great choreographers of our day and for many, he is the greatest. But although unis small, lithe, bright-eyed gentleman is soft-spoken and exudes kindliness, he is capable of generating controversy. He has been married five times (if that is considered controversial), he has put an end to the star system in the company he heads, he disapproves of ballets with elaborate plots, he feels that ballerinas tend to distort choreography to their own end, he feels free to change from pure classical movement to the most modern action and his answer to the criticism that many of his ballets are cold and that he seems to prefer coldness to warmth in his dancers is simply, "Some like it hot and some like it cold. I like ice cream."

He Is Our Own   Mr. Balanchine also likes American dancers. And he has, over the years, played a great part in molding our dancers of today. Although the New York City Ballet, which opens its twenty-sixth engagement at the City Center March 29, is not quite twelve years old, Mr. Balanchine has been occupied with the training of American ballet dancers for twenty-seven years, since 1933 when he came to America to help in the founding of the School of American Ballet and to guide the course of a succession of companies which eventually flowered into the New York City Ballet.

Although George Balanchine was a major force in ballet before he came to his new homeland and although his international stature has grown with the years, his devotion to his American company is such that we may rightly think of him as our own, as a master whose opinions, learned or seemingly quixotic, profound or pleasantly satiric, we should know about.

His Job   He does not, as we have seen, have any patience with inspiration. None of his wives—Tamara Geva, Alexandra Danilova, Vera Zorina, Maria Tallchief, Tanaquil LeClercq—inspired him to choreograph. "It is my job to create a ballet and I simply use the dancers in the ways they move best. Different bodies have different shapes, different qualities. Some dancers are strong on pointe; others are not. In a ballet, I give them what they can do."

Not even music—although he is intensely musical—actually inspires Mr. Balanchine to create. He must choreograph a ballet so he goes to his musical "icebox" to see what is on hand that he would like to use. "But music," he says, "is essential. Music gives you timing. Movement without time means nothing. Look at our world? It exists in time and in space. The same is true of dance. The proportion of movement to the time of the music is what makes choreography."

His interest in abstract ballets actually began in 1933. "When I first came here," he says, "the dancers available were not very good. I not only taught them in class but I also created ballets that would make them dance. No story to lean upon. Just dancing."

382

But there is a reason for his continuing interest in abstract ballets (although he has several dramatic ballets to his credit and good ones at that). "I don't think you should have to read a program to follow a ballet." Picking up a magnifying glass, he pretended to look at a program. "Who is that character? What is going to happen to her?" And, Balanchine added, "She'll probably be killed in the last act. But why waste time trying to figure out who is who on stage in a story? When the curtain goes up on ballet, I want to see dancing." Then, throwing his arms out, he said, "Dancing needs no explanation. We have our own means of communication, the poetry of gesture. A garden of flowers is so beautiful that no one needs explain it. Dance is like a flower garden, isn't it?"

"Mr. B.," as he is known by his dancers and students, does not object to a story line "if it is simple. But Shakespeare? Why should I take a Shakespeare play as a theme? Shakespeare is already taken, by his own magical words."

And how does Mr. Balanchine feel about the dancers who perform his works? What does he expect of them? What does he demand? "Choreography exists only when the dancers perform it. Further, they are at least half of the choreography themselves, for they are people and each is different from the other. I am using living things as my materials and they become a part of my choreography."

The Right Kind "But although dancers are essential to my choreography," he continued, "they must be the right kind of dancers. I believe that teaching and choreography should be closely related. I don't like to take dancers from various schools and audition them for our company. That is why most of our dancers come from the School of American Ballet where I teach and where my colleagues teach my ways and needs. I'm not a megalomaniac at all, but I was trained in the St. Petersburg style of classical ballet, that's what I give our pupils and that is the style in which I, as a choreographer, work best. And, by the way, I'm not talking about old steps or specific movements, but, rather the drive and energy which characterized the St. Petersburg school."

The man who dislikes the star system and avoids dependence on ballerinas says: "A ballerina is a personality and a personality means improvisation. The personality feels she owes something special to her public and what the choreographer has given her is not quite enough, so she adds things; thus, choreography becomes merely atmosphere for the ballerina. I like best young, well trained dancers, eternal students always learning. Shaw once wrote that most prima donnas play Carmen as if she were a female Mephistopheles. I think that might apply to prima ballerinas."

"Besides," the choreographer continued, "how can you tell which is the greater star or ballerina? Do you like a coloratura soprano or a mezzo? Do you like this ballerina for her speed or that one for her line? Basically, on a technical plane, I think there is very little difference between the capabilities of a ballerina and a well trained young dancer. Thus, I prefer the latter, but if a part calls for the special talents of a ballerina, I certainly wouldn't put a less competent younger performer in the role. Too often, though, a ballerina, once she gets the title becomes a museum piece, a figure in a setting."

Outrage If Mr. Balanchine finds, and he certainly does, many who disagree with him on the value of the ballerina, he also meets up with those who, loving his classical works, are outraged by movement distortions, modern dance inclusions and strange inventions which characterize his recent *Agon* and, even more, the sections he did for *Episodes*. His answer is simple. "Movements should look like the musical sounds of the accompaniment. With Tchaikovsky, the sounds make for one kind of action; with Webern, another.

"And another point. Movements grow and different kinds of movement can be related to each other." With gestures describing grafting processes, he continued, "One kind of a flower can be made a part of another plant, perhaps a vine. The two retain separate identities even while they are united in a new form. With movement, it is the same."

The future? "I think of my next ten or twenty years as the present. I'm working on them all along. There will be, I think, few fundamental changes in ballet in the years to come. Just steady growth. But if I had unlimited funds right now, I would change a few things. I would build a theater for ballet. I would have a great orchestra in permanent attendance. I would have a school where students could study both ballet and their academic subjects daily under the same direction. And I would certainly see that dancers got a great deal of money. They are terribly underpaid, they work hard yet they never complain; they always smile."

Opening his arms in a wide, expansive gesture, he concluded, "And I would give weekly free performances for underprivileged children. They are a fantastic audience. I've seen their responses. Without any preparation for ballet, they always applaud pure dancing. They applaud the true thing."

With a happy smile of remembrance for a recent performance for underprivileged children by the New York City Ballet, "Mr. B." jumped to his feet and headed for a rehearsal of a new work. "Are you excited about it?" he was asked. "Yes," he said, "but don't think I live dancing around the clock. When I leave here, I leave it behind. There's cooking to be done and Tanny [Mrs. Balanchine] and I have more than two hundred rose bushes to look after. That's a job, too." [*New York Herald Tribune*]

Maria Karnilova: Ballet or Bumps

April 3, 1960

"I think every one does bumps and grinds at one time or another," said Maria Karnilova. By casually lumping the whole world in the bump business, Miss Karnilova was merely trying to explain that she had had no formal preparation for her role of Tessie Tura, the rough, tough, good-natured stripper in the hit musical, *Gypsy*, starring Ethel Merman and directed and choreographed by Jerome Robbins.

Miss Karnilova, who regularly stops the show with her hilarious characterization as well as with her bumping prowess, points out that she modeled Tessie after a burlesque performer whose photograph she had seen in a book. "I'm not voluptuous," said Miss Karnilova, "and she—I forget her name—was not voluptuous. In fact, she was the ugliest girl in the book. But show biz was written all over her. So with Tessie, we settled for show biz."

Ballet Background Strangely enough, Maria Karnilova, although she has danced in a number of Broadway shows, is not the product of show business. "I started out as a ballet dancer and, except for a course in modern dance taught by Hanya Holm, I have never had any training other than classical ballet. At fifteen, I was a member of an opera ballet troupe which toured South America. I danced in the Mordkin and Fokine ballets which used to be given in summertime at various stadiums. I danced in opera ballet at the Hippodrome—Nora Kaye was in the company, too—and I remember that Nora and I had to rehearse the ballets in the lavatories, the only practice space they'd give us."

To the dance world, Miss Karnilova is best known for her long and distinguished association with the American Ballet Theatre. She was a charter member of the company when it made its debut twenty years ago. At first, she was simply a corps de ballet dancer but it was clear even then that Miss Karnilova, in addition to fine ballet technique, possessed, perhaps by instinct or perhaps by Hippodrome exposure, the bright, sometimes brash, friendly qualities, the perfect timing of a real show business pro.

Memories Who can forget her as the leader of the coryphees in Antony Tudor's ballet satire, *Gala Performance,* in which she flirted outrageously (as she was supposed to do) with the audience? Or do you remember her as the Pious Virgin (there were bumps here) in Agnes de Mille's *Three Virgins and a Devil,* as the lusty sixth wife in *Bluebeard,* as A-Lady-No-Better-Than-She-Should-Be in the de Mille *Tally-Ho!,* as the lovely heroine of *Helen of Troy* or as one of the weary entertainers in Mr. Tudor's *Judgment of Paris*?

385

Appropriately, Lucia Chase, co-director of the American Ballet Theatre, has invited this important alumna of the company to take part in the organization's gala twentieth anniversary season opening April 19 at the Metropolitan Opera House. Ironically, though perhaps suitably, Miss Karnilova will dance in *Judgment of Paris* in the role of the ravaged saloon entertainer. The date is April 30, and after doing her weary grinds at the august Met early in the evening, Miss Karnilova will dash over to the Broadway Theater in time to do more of the same in *Gypsy*.

But Miss Karnilova cannot be classified as a ballet dancer with a superb comedy technique or as a brassy comedienne with good ballet training. In serious vein, she has danced in the William Butler Yeats play, *The Only Tragedy of Emer*, and as a minor figure in Tudor's *Lilac Garden*, she drew a characterization rich in sympathy, tenderness and understanding. As the forsaken, desperate, aging woman in Donald Saddler's *Winesburg, Ohio* (based on the Sherwood Anderson stories), she gave a tremendous performance notable for its projection of heart-deep tragedy. And, when she was ballerina of the Metropolitan Opera, she gave us, among other interpretations, an exquisite enactment in Zachary Solov's ballet for *Manon*.

Versatility   Miss Karnilova, then, is a very special artist. She has never been permanently classified as a ballerina, yet she has always been important to the ballet world. She has been featured on Broadway but she has never been a star. Her home life—she is devoted to her husband and children—has caused gaps in her theatrical career. The name "Karnilova," however, remains a constant both in the area of ballet art and in the field of show business and this happy state has occurred because she combines the qualities of both in her performing.

"Marusha," as she is known to her friends, has always made contradictions seem complementary. She loves comedy; she is delighted that she is often thought of as a comic and one of her favorite roles is that of the goofy music lover in Jerome Robbins' uproarious ballet, *The Concert*, yet she would skip a well-paying comedy job to do a serious dance role in an experimental production. As a person, she combines brisk humor with a kind of screwball practicality. For example, the slim, vivacious blonde admits she's thirty-nine. "I really am," she says, "but no one believes that any one is thirty-nine so I just say I'm forty and that saves me all those 'oh, really?' with raised eyebrows, cracks." In ballet or show biz, there's no one quite like her. [*New York Herald Tribune*]

New York City Ballet—1960

April 14, 1960

A lavishly mounted new ballet, with gorgeous costumes, a sparkling fountain, courtly elegance and enchanting dances, was given its world premiere by the New York City Ballet at the City Center last evening. This five-scene creation, *The Figure in the Carpet,* was created especially in honor of the Fourth International Congress of Iranian Art and Archeology which is to open in New York City later this month under the patronage of President Eisenhower and the Shah of Iran. In fact, the ballet's sequence of scenes was suggested by the congress' director, Dr. Arthur Upham Pope.

But *The Figure in the Carpet* is by no means an Iranian ballet, for although a stunning Persian carpet design is employed as decor and although the shifting sands of a desert land are remotely and charmingly symbolized in the actions of the dancers, much of the work is cast in the mold of a French court spectacle ballet as it was seen during the Louis XIV era. As we know, the magnificent court productions were peopled with characters representing every one from classical Greek divinities to Incas, Blackamoors, Turks and other distant folk, all of them idealized (or Frenchified) to suit the taste of the times in Paris.

Actually, George Balanchine, the choreographer, has by no means limited himself to the basic format of the court ballet. Obviously, he has used the elaborate ballet technique of today and not the simplified measures of the 1600s; furthermore, he has used as his musical base, music of Handel ("Royal Fireworks Music and Water Music") rather than that of, say, Lully and, finally, in "The Sands of the Desert" episode and in "The Weaving of the Carpet" scene, he has designed choreography evocative of the forces of nature and of the creative industry of ordinary man.

In the three later sections, Mr. Balanchine has turned to the court style as he introduces in the divertissements for "The Building of the Palace" portion, sumptuously clad dancers from France, Spain, America (West Indians), China, Africa, Scotland and, of course, Persia. The appropriate excuse for this divertissement is the presentation of foreign ambassadors to the Persian court and although each of the separate dances hints slightly its land of origin, none is at all ethnic, for all are balletic, courtly and elegant.

The finale, "The Gardens of Paradise," and the Apotheosis, "The Fountains of Heaven," replace, for the most part, dance action with the visual spectacle of scenic transformations, just as the old court entertainments employed machines to create fanciful tableaux.

This, then, is the over-all plan, and an enormously effective one it is, of *The Figure in the Carpet.* But what of the actual dancing? Well, Mr.

387

Balanchine has used a large ensemble of girls, dressed in flowing sand-colored costumes, to represent the desert and he has come up with some stunning choreography. The figures, headed by the wonderful Violette Verdy, suggest through balletic runs, turns and dippings, the swirling sands, the unseen breezes of the desert.

An interlude evocative of night leads into the "Weaving of the Carpet" in which maidens and nomad tribesmen, bearing multicolored streamers, indicate the bright patterns which one day will emerge into glorious carpets with their bright-hued symbols of living things.

As the walls of the palace slide into place and the hanging carpet takes on its full design, the divertissements commence. And here too, Mr. Balanchine has devised some beautiful and existing measures.

Edward Villella, bounding high and moving with the quick brilliance associated with the almost legendary Vestris, danced the French variation, ably assisted by Susan Borree and Suki Schorer. Judith Green and Francisco Moncion were superbly regal as the Spanish duke and duchess and Francia Russell and her West Indians had an amusing bit. Patricia McBride and Nicholas Magallanes, heading the Chinese delegation, had their brief antic moments and Mary Hinkson and Arthur Mitchell, representing Africa, had a striking duet, exceptionally lively but very majestic.

Scotland was assigned to Diana Adams, along with four lairds, and this lovely dancer had a variation, utterly delightful, which included steps which might conceivably have cousin-movements somewhere in the highland dances. And Melissa Hayden and Jacques d'Amboise, comporting themselves with the grandeur, and a touch of hauteur, associated with the French court, were the Prince and Princess of Persia. Their pas de deux, the most extended of the divertissements, was a beauty and they danced it handsomely.

Since this was a first performance, little roughnesses and insecurities and uncertainties were occasionally noticeable and these caused a few subdued moments in the work but with further rehearsing and performing, Mr. Balanchine's masterful conception should emerge clearly and his superb choreography should receive consistently sensitive projection by the dancers.

No small part of the dazzling beauties of the new ballet are due to the scenery, the lighting and the costumes (executed by the great Karinska), designed by Esteban Frances, for they are stunning indeed. The Handel music, as conducted by Robert Irving, was also a contributing joy and the whole affair, spectacle, dancing, music, choreography, was received with enthusiasm by a large and distinguished audience. *Pas de Dix* and *Stars and Stripes,* completed the program. [*New York Herald Tribune*]

November 12, 1960

Patricia McBride, a fast-rising junior member of the New York City Ballet, danced one of the two leading roles in the season's first presentation of Jerome Robbins' *Afternoon of a Faun* last evening at the City Center. As the girl in this contemporary treatment of the Debussy music, Miss McBride was not only lovely to look at but she also communicated the curiously remote air of romance which characterizes the work. Francisco Moncion, who created the male role in this extended duet, was, of course, as compelling as always.

Together the two, playing the roles of dancers who meet, study themselves, discover each other and become enamored of their decorative propinquities as reflected in the invisible mirror of a ballet studio, convey exquisitely that delicate dramatic conflict which sees self-admiration invaded by the potential of love. Although *Faun* is a cool work, the latent passion inherent in the situation gives it tenderness, a strange elusive warmth. [*New York Herald Tribune*]

November 23, 1960

An enchanting new ballet of ineffable loveliness, *Liebeslieder Walzer,* was given its world premiere by the New York City Ballet last evening at the City Center. This gay yet strangely haunting work, evocative of an elegance rarely experienced in contemporary living, has been choreographed by that master of elegance, George Balanchine, to Johannes Brahms' love song waltzes (Opus 52 and Opus 65); its breathtakingly beautiful costumes for the ladies have been created by Karinska and its setting, by David Hays, serves not only as an exquisitely appointed ballroom but also is transformable into a star-crowned night.

Liebeslieder Walzer is presented in two acts. In the first, the four couples who are the cast for the entire ballet, move in the style of the social dance. The girls wear heeled slippers and long, gently billowing gowns. But if this is basically simple ballroom waltzing, Mr. Balanchine has heightened it ever so subtly, relating the etiquette of the classical ballet to the deportment of the ballroom.

Charmingly schooled coquetry, just the hint of an invitation to an amorous but highly refined chase, controlled ardor in becoming embraces, flashes of exuberance and glimpses of dreams are all contained in these sequences of short, simple but perfectly modeled dances. And then the dream itself takes command.

In the second episode, the ballroom candles have been dimmed, the doors have been opened to the night, the chandelier has become a halo of stars and the young couples have moved into a world of their own imaginings. The ladies, now in gossamer dress and wearing toe shoes, rise on to pointe and, moving to another plane, become the elusive, desirable creatures of men's dreams.

The ballroom steps and the etiquette of the first scene are also heightened and find their ultimate forms in the sweep, the precision, the physical excitements and stylistic grace of the ballet. The change from one aspect of dance to another is perfectly achieved, for a delectable reality has given way to the ecstasy of the dream.

And at the close, in dimness, as if the dancers returned politely but unwillingly from reverie, the stars fade, the lights go up and the ladies are once again in their formal attire.

Mr. Balanchine has, in *Liebeslieder Walzer,* not only created a ballet of uncommon beauty but he has also worked something of a miracle in sustaining and, indeed, developing interest in a storyless theme, patterns and forms which never once hurry toward a climax or rush to make an effect. Naturally, even in the simplest measures, his choreographic invention does not desert him and the viewer finds himself sighing as contentedly over a delicate touching of hands as over swirling lifts and turns.

No one dancer should be singled out for special mention for they all— Diana Adams, Melissa Hayden, Jillana, Violette Verdy, Bill Carter, Conrad Ludlow, Nicholas Magallanes, Jonathan Watts—served the ballet handsomely. But remember, it was the ladies who reigned, with the gentlemen, the honored cavaliers.

Also on stage were the musicians, Louise Sherman and Robert Irving at the piano and Angeline Rasmussen (soprano), Mitzi Wilson (contralto), Frank Porretta (tenor) and Herbert Beattle (baritone) grouped around as the singers of the Brahms songs. And these artists also contributed richly to the total joy of a truly elegant and lovely work of theater.

The performance itself, which also included presentations of *Interplay* and *Western Symphony,* was held as a benefit for the New York City Ballet Production Fund and the fund for free performances for children. [*New York Herald Tribune*]

Miss Chase and Her Ballet

April 20, 1960

The American Ballet Theater, twenty years ago, burst upon the New York theatrical scene as one of the most refreshing and exciting dance attractions to be seen in years. Last evening at the Metropolitan Opera House, the company celebrated its very special anniversary with a performance inaugurating a three-week engagement, a prelude to a European tour, including the first appearances by an American ballet troupe in the Soviet Union.

Between 1940 and 1960, the American Ballet Theatre, directed by Lucia Chase and Oliver Smith, has had its ups and downs. It has produced more than one hundred ballets, it has enlisted the talents of many of the world's greatest dancers and choreographers, it has raised stars from its own ranks and it has had, on frequent occasions, a superlative corps de ballet. But, because of financial difficulties (common to all American art enterprises), it has had layoffs, the most recent, of more than a year's duration, just ending.

Thus, last evening, the American Ballet Theatre returned to us as a company composed of a fine group of young veterans and new, and sometimes raw, recruits. But the newcomers, mainly corps de ballet members, are unusually good looking and, at one seeing, one would say technically adept. All they need is to dance together (with constant direction) over a brief period of time until they get the feel of "company." This they will surely achieve during the coming weeks.

As to specifics, the program opened with a mild performance of William Dollar's *Chopin Concerto* (Piano concerto No. 2 in F Minor), with new costumes by Karinska. It is basically a lovely work, lyrical, sometimes sunny, again sweetly sad. The corps executed its technical demands but failed to capture its lilting graces.

Of the principals in *Chopin Concerto*—Lupe Serrano, Erik Bruhn, Ruth Ann Koesun—only Mr. Bruhn, dancing superbly, caught the poetry of the work in his actions. Miss Koesun was cute as can be but a little brittle and Miss Serrano, a splendid technician, settled for coldness of attack.

The real American Ballet Theatre came alive the instant the curtain rose on Nora Kaye as Hagar in Antony Tudor's masterpiece, *Pillar of Fire.* Miss Kaye, who earned immediate stardom when this ballet was first produced in 1942, again gave us her dramatically powerful, emotionally deep and wonderfully appealing enactment of a near-spinster who gives her body in desperation to a lecherous stranger before she finds her true love.

Although Miss Kaye's remarkable artistry shone above all else in *Pillar,* there were excellent performances by Miss Chase in her regular role of the prissy Eldest Sister and by Glen Tetley, making his first local appearance with this company, as The Friend who ultimately brings peace and love to Hagar. The Friend's role is subdued, almost self-effacing, but Mr. Tetley invested it with simple tenderness and quiet manliness.

Less successful, though promising in the part, was Ady Addor (also dancing in New York with the company for the first time) as the flirtatious Youngest Sister. Miss Addor did not seem quite sure whether the character

391

should be simply capricious, innocently mischievous or childishly evil. And even less effective was Tommy Rall, returning after a long absence, as the libertine. He was, I fear, more concerned with physical feats than with characterization. He was boyishly brash but nothing of the decadence of the figure emerged.

The novelty of the evening was a new pas de deux importation, *Pas et Lignes,* choreographed by the French Serge Lifar to music of Debussy and with Claude Bessy (guest artist), ballerina of the Paris Opéra Ballet, and Royes Fernandez as the dancers.

During a musical pause and a choreographic pose in *Pas et Lignes,* two bellowing boos echoed through the Met, to be countered immediately by wild applause for the performance. Presumably, the boos were intended for Mr. Lifar, either for his choreography or because he remained active in Paris during the Nazi occupation. Well, the choreography was certainly boo-able, since it was pretty formless, unmusical, unimaginative and terribly affected. But Miss Bessy was gorgeous and danced delightfully and Mr. Fernandez was admirable as her cavalier.

The evening closed with Michel Fokine's ballet bouffe, (to music of Offenbach and with scenery and costumes by Marcel Vertes), which years ago boasted a cast (Markova, Baronova, Dolin, Skibine, Kaye, Jerome Robbins, etc.) which would make your head spin. Last evening, John Kriza, Miss Serrano, Miss Addor, Scott Douglas and, in his original role of Count Oscar, Boris Runanin, headed the list of principals in a long, involved and occasionally funny ballet about Bluebeard and his wives and Queen Clementine and her lovers.

The orchestra, under Kenneth Schermerhorn's fine direction, and Jean Rosenthal's lighting contributed handsomely to an evening which started the American Ballet Theatre on its third decade, not in its finest fettle opening night but promising brightly for the immediate future. [*New York Herald Tribune*]

May 15, 1960

"The Strange Case of the American Ballet Theatre" seems, perhaps, more like an Erle Stanley Gardner title than it does a departure point for a discussion of the world-famous American dance company. Nonetheless, there is a case and it is strange. The troupe recently completed an engagement at the Metropolitan Opera (prior to a European tour) celebrating its twentieth birthday and the offerings ranged from the inept to the brilliant.

One of the difficulties, as previously reported in these columns, was that the company itself was almost wholly new, for there had been a year's layoff while re-financing and re-organization took place. There was, then, an excuse for some of the ragged dancing since there had been no preliminary New Havens or Bostons, such as Broadway shows enjoy, before going-on-cold (other than a few performances in Havana, Cuba) at the Met.

Positives But the American Ballet Theatre has long experienced ups and downs. On the "up" side, it has presided over the creation of the most varied ballet repertory in the history of ballet; from its ranks have emerged such dancing and choreographing luminaries as Jerome Robbins, Michael Kidd, Nora Kaye, Alicia Alonso, and more recently, Lupe Serrano and Scott Douglas. Furthermore, under the leadership of Lucia Chase, who co-directs the company along with Oliver Smith, important dance experiments have been presented through a workshop division.

The faults of the American Ballet Theatre are generally pinpointed to the fact that there is no real artistic director, experienced, authoritative, imaginative. Oh, yes, Miss Chase is really a general director and Dimitri Romanoff a capable regisseur and Miss Chase is the first to admit that there are problems but she points out, and with some validity (but not inarguably) that there is no one person who could, artistically, direct a repertory composed of traditional classics, modern classics, dramatic ballets, Americana, a French wing, etc.

Miss Chase's plan is to have the choreographers rehearse their own works and a recognized expert on the traditional ballets rehearse these productions. Sometimes these creators are available; at other times, no. The results vary accordingly. During this last season, the Agnes de Mille ballets, coached by the choreographer herself, were splendid. Eugene Loring's *Billy the Kid,* which he supervised, was almost as good. Miss Kaye, in the absence of Antony Tudor, helped out on the Tudor works with which she is intimately associated. And the regisseur did excellently with two classical pieces, *Les Sylphides* and *Theme and Variations.*

Novelties Of the novelties, Birgit Cullberg's *Lady From the Sea,* created expressly for the American Ballet Theatre, was a successful ballet, beautifully danced and polished to a sheen by its creator. Herbert Ross' *Dialogues* was a disappointment but no one could deny that it was expertly danced under Mr. Ross' direction.

But criticism of the American Ballet Theatre invariably centers on Miss Chase. For years, the cry has been for her to get an artistic director whether he is an expert in all aspects of the repertory or not or, as in the early days of the company, when Richard Pleasant was in charge, hire three, one for the classics, one from dramatic works, one for Americana.

A second criticism of Miss Chase is her ideas on casting. In fact, within the profession itself, one hears such disparate comments on her selection of dancers at auditions as: "I've never been able to figure out how she chooses dancers"; "she is uncommonly shrewd in picking out dancers with the right techniques and styles for her repertory"; "I think Lucia's criterion for selecting dancers is that they must look as if they came from 'nice' families."

Whatever Miss Chase elects to do at auditions, it is a fact, and one uncomfortably noticeable during the past season, that she can cast unsuitable persons in various roles. For example, she gave the attractive little Ady Addor parts that this youthful dancer could not cope with at all; she let Christine Mayer, a valuable soloist, flounder in the ballerina role of the Queen of the Wilis in *Giselle*; she assigned the technically glittering Miss Serrano to the lyrical lead in *Chopin Concerto* instead of casting her as the dark, sharp, allegro-moving associate in the same ballet.

Ups and Downs　But whatever obvious directorial faults Miss Chase may possess, the record is clear that she has presided over the building and continuation of a great company. Whether the American Ballet Theatre is "up" (and it is climbing up rapidly again) or experiencing a "down," it is an art enterprise essential to American culture. Many balletomanes prefer the wonderfully disciplined, elegant New York City Ballet. Its strength lies primarily in the genius of its artistic director and chief choreographer, George Balanchine. But to most Europeans, the troupe is not referred to by name but as "the Balanchine company." This is both an advantage and a limitation.

To have a theater devoted to Balanchine and to have it function under his brilliant hand are facts to be cheered. But this is not all of ballet. And the American Ballet Theatre's special value is that it celebrates not one but many.

The styles of both companies, the production aspects, the repertoires, concepts on the importance (or unimportance) of stars differ. Both are needed along with the contributions of still other ballet groups and individual artists, to give total representation to American Ballet. Thus, if the American Ballet Theatre's recent engagement at the Met was a strange case of dance dash combined with dance drivel, it remained perfectly clear that here, in essense and often in fact, was one of the world's most important dance institutions. [*New York Herald Tribune*]

Martha Graham

April 28, 1960

Demons, tragic heroines, martyrs are generally the personnae in the great theater of Martha Graham. Occasionally, she brings us happy innocents and once in a while, she turns the mask of theater so that we may see the smile of comedy. Last evening, at the world premiere of *Acrobats of God,* she gave us joyousness and comedy combined in her exhilarating and incredibly ingenious tribute to the dancer and his world.

Taking her title from the name given to early churchmen who subjected themselves to the disciplines of desert life, the "athletae Dei," Miss Graham set out to celebrate, as she says in her program note, "the trials and tribulations, the disciplines, denials, stringencies, glories and delights of a dancer's world . . . and of the world of the artist."

From the nature of the choreography itself, it is clear that the "trials and tribulations," if they occurred at all, must have taken place before the curtain rose on *Acrobats of God,* for on stage, Miss Graham has revealed the "glories and delights" of dancing. With rare humor, she has indicated that difficulties do certainly exist; the presence of a whip-lashing taskmaster (he's really quite good-natured) and Miss Graham's own marvelous gestures of irritation and impatience, as he gives his orders, point out that all is not frolic in the dancer's life.

Furthermore, hints of initial training, both balletic and modern, point to the years of daily preparation and the tremendously virtuosic, varied and complex actions she has created for her dancers establish clearly the fact that none of this could have happened without discipline. But Miss Graham has placed the accent on results, while poking retrospective fun at the wearying behind-the-scenes preparations, and these results add up to masterful comedy and superlative dancing.

Since *Acrobats of God* has no plot, it is difficult to describe, especially since it is made up of one surprise after another. At one point, the girls, placed upon a high, curved ramp, do knee bends while the boys, lying beneath, and with their feet against the underside of the ramp, mirror the action upside down. The taskmaster (this is my title for him, for he is whatever drives the dancer to dance) commands some spectacular lifts which would startle the Bolshoi Ballet; institutes spins, runs, leaps and falls and quite frequently permits technical prowess to be pleasantly mated with male–female proximity.

Miss Graham's ensemble of dancers, the best she has ever had within my memory and certainly one of the best companies in the world today, gave the brilliant choreography of *Acrobats of God* the living birth on stage it merited. As for the star herself, well, there is no one like her and in the new work, although she does not indulge in virtuosity, she commands the entire situation not merely through the power of her presence but also through the superlative timing of movements and gestures which define, with consummate wit, the knowing position and worldly attitude of a mature and successful artist.

Isamu Noguchi's decor, which includes the graceful ramp and a screened chair behind which Miss Graham retires, from time to time, with great hauteur when the taskmaster gets too obnoxious, is an integral part of the choreographic plan and the specially commissioned score by Carlos Surinach, which involves the presence of three mandolinists on stage, has both Spanish color and drive and a gay theatrical exuberance perfectly suited to Miss Graham's joyful scheme.

Acrobats of God is, then, a marvelous work. It is exciting, therapeutic (washing all cares away), amusing, stunningly inventive and I love it. [*New York Herald Tribune*]

Tamiris–Nagrin Company

November 22, 1960

Helen Tamiris, for many years a successful choreographer for the Broadway theater, recently returned to her first love, the concert dance. Omens have been pointing to this step in the career of one of the important pioneers of America's modern dance. Three years ago, Miss Tamiris staged an independent dance work for a festival in the West. Last year, she was represented in other modern dance events. This year, with her husband, Daniel Nagrin, she has launched the Tamiris–Nagrin Dance Company with herself as artistic director and Mr. Nagrin as the star dancer. Following out-of-town appearances, the new group performed in New York for the first time last evening at the Phoenix Theater.

The program was composed of four works, three of them new to local audiences, choreographically divided between Miss Tamiris, who no longer dances (more's the pity), and Mr. Nagrin, who does dance (and that's a pleasure). All but one I had seen and reviewed in these columns before. The new piece, *Women's Song*, choreographed by Miss Tamiris to music of Norman Dello Joio (Concerto for Harp and Orchestra), is Tamiris in a milder, quieter mood than one usually expects of this once militant and always brightly theatrical creator.

Women's Song is a plotless piece which suggests the basic resilience of women no matter to what changes they may be subjected. The choreographer has made her intentions clear but although there are hints of sadness, of joy, of determination and of gentle fortitude, the colorings are pale and the impact slight. There are, of course, some first rate Tamiris groupings and movement inventions but not enough to give consistent force to a dynamically bland piece.

Miss Tamiris' *Memoir* (to music of Carlos Chavez) is something else again. Here, in a partly autobiographical work, one finds power and passion and dramatic contrast as the choreographer demolishes the obscuring walls of a great city to show us the evils and terrors of the streets and a loving memory of affection, tradition and safety in a Jewish home. In this imaginatively staged work (the audience actually sees the silhouette of the city fall apart), Eleanor Shick was wonderfully poignant as the girl exposed to the brutalities of the alleys who sought brief refuge in memory, and Mr. Nagrin was excellent as the vicious leader of a gang and, in a second role, as the devout and gentle father.

Mr. Nagrin also performed as a soloist in his own *Indeterminate Figure,* a work previously seen locally. Both as dancer and actor, he gave a marvelously amusing and biting portrayal of a man—any man—indulging in fanciful thoughts of what he might be, only to be rudely interrupted by reality. The delightful sound effects score was by Robert Starer.

The closing work, *An Entertainment,* with music of Béla Bartók, choreographed by Mr. Nagrin, was first performed, under the title *Theater for Fools,* two years ago at the American Dance Festival at New London, Conn. In this satire, the principal part were taken by Mr. Nagrin, Sylvia Dick, Florence Peters and William Constanza.

The new company's ensemble is not only excellently disciplined but also loaded with vitality and it was, therefore, a joy to watch not only the highly accomplished and experienced Mr. Nagrin but also his fine supporting cast. Incidentally, in this ensemble, I noticed the presence of Miss Tamiris' nephew, Bruce Becker, a talented youth, who will probably see to it that the Tamiris dance skills move on into another generation. [*New York Herald Tribune*]

A Masterly Performance of a Ballet Masterpiece

November 27, 1960

A great portrayal in dance—that of Edward Villella in *The Prodigal Son*—quite probably will not be seen again during the New York City Ballet's ten-week season at the City Center. This comparatively old (1929) ballet by George Balanchine, to music of Prokofiev and with decor by Rouault, was scheduled only three times (and the three have been completed) for this engagement. Yet *The Prodigal Son* has never seemed more vital and theatrically potent and Mr. Villella's dancing of the Prodigal has been resoundingly hailed as one of the high points—and maybe the high point itself—of a brilliant ballet season.

Why no more performances? The New York City Ballet's direction reports that *The Prodigal Son* is not a box-office attraction, that along with *Four Temperaments, Orpheus* and *Illuminations,* it captivates an audience once assembled but it does not in itself lure the public to the theater of ballet. No one knows why. The titles, perhaps. At any rate, the company usually schedules three performances of such ballets for the benefit of their presumably limited but obviously devoted followers.

Fresh, Inventive   This paucity of performances for *The Prodigal Son* is indeed a pity. To begin with, the New York City Ballet's repertory has few story-ballets and, secondly, though *Prodigal* is an early Balanchine work, it is unquestionably a masterpiece of choreography which still seems fresh, incredibly inventive. And Mr. Villella's portrayal itself warrants as much publicity exploitation as any new production, bright novelty or guest star, for it is tremendous.

Any balletomane knows that Mr. Villella has an electrifying technique and there is a tendency to think of him as a rhythmicized, stylized Olympic champion. But he is also an artist, just as his slightly senior colleague, Jacques d'Amboise, is a brilliant virtuoso and highly accomplished actor–dancer. Incidentally, the two are so different in quality that by praising one, the other is by no means automatically demoted to second place. But today, it is the Villella Prodigal with which we are concerned.

The twenty-three-year-old dancer brings to *The Prodigal Son* his fantastically high leaps and vertiginous spins, his superb muscular control and his correct placement of the body in motion. But all of these aspects of physical prowess have been sublimated to the dramatic line of the ballet, to characterization, to the varying intensities present in various situations. These elements, of course, are inherent in the choreography. Mr. Villella, however, has realized them more fully than any Prodigal I have ever seen.

Mr. Villella's Prodigal, through brilliantly physical action or the simplest of gestures or anticipatory stance, is an enormously appealing figure. The Son's brashness and bravado, while hardly commendable, are made to seem both pitiful and daring, excitingly dangerous. Haven't we all rebelled against authority, or wished to? And the repentance scene, when the Son, broken in spirit and weary of body, crawls to his father's arms, bring tears to the eyes. Between the defiant departure from home and the remorseful return, Mr.

Villella gives us a tremendously absorbing, dramatically cumulative portrayal of a youth as he experiences the delights of adventure and the lure of sex; evil, debauchery, betrayal and retribution.

"Universal Youth"   Because of my admiration for his *Prodigal,* I asked the young dancer whether he thought of the Son as a Biblical figure or as any youth and how he himself related virtuosity to characterization. "To me," says Mr. Villella, "the Prodigal is a universal youth of any age, a youth with desires who undergoes a series of experiences which culminate in a forced maturity.

"As for combining virtuosity with characterization, I simply thought about the role in great detail ever since I first danced it less than a year ago, next I did every step over and over again until it was technically and musically right, until it became a natural reflex. Now, I don't think of technical matters on stage. The Prodigal's first big jump is not only a burst of action but, to me, it is a climax to the boy's angry, and maybe desperate, determination to get away."

This leap that Mr. Villella mentions and all the actions which precede and follow it add up to one of the great contemporary performances in dance. There is a slight chance that a later change of program will allow for one more *Prodigal Son* this season. If so, storm the box office for tickets. A masterpiece masterfully danced is not to be missed. [*New York Herald Tribune*]

1961

The Kirov Invasion

Leningrad's Kirov Ballet makes its American debut • Tap dance star
Eleanor Powell at the Latin Quarter • Four moderns — Paul Taylor,
Alwin Nikolais, Eleo Pomare and Midi Garth • Balanchine's "space age"
ballet, Electronics premieres at NYCB

Paul Taylor

January 16, 1961

Paul Taylor, one of the most fascinating, intriguing, gifted and, at times, infuriating of modern dance performers–choreographers, appeared with his ensemble in a program of his own divising Saturday night at the Hunter
Playhouse.

There can be no argument about the quality of Mr. Taylor's performing.
He is a superb dancer, the possessor of perfect body control, a highly individual style of almost hypnotic power, a curious grace even in the most contorted of movements and a marvelous awareness of the inherent beauty of
space as it relates to dance. By this last, I mean that as a dancer he does
more than invade space with movement; rather, does he treat it as an invisible
temple, for whether his gestures are sharp or lanquid, whether a foot darts
swiftly outward or an arm raises skyward, these gestures appear to be motivated by spatial reverence and not arrogance.

I'm not at all certain that this quality I have just noted can be described
clearly in words but it is present and it, along with Mr. Taylor's prodigious
technique and his rather animal-like litheness, are the chief characteristics of
an unusual dance artist.

Mr. Taylor's little company is also unusually fine, artists all. For Akiko
Kanda, Maggie Newman, Pina Bausch, Elizabeth Walton and Dan Wagoner are
not only technically expert but they also, while adapting themselves to Mr.
Taylor's choreographic style, retain their own personal dance traits.

And now we come to the choreography. It is wonderfully inventive, often ingenious and frequently touched with sardonic humor, with playful jabs at human foibles. Yet Mr. Taylor's choreography is strangely inhuman or, rather, lacking in that aspect of the human which has to do with the spirit. Now this is perfectly proper. Many of George Balanchine's ballets, for example, are purely abstract (or as abstract as mortals can get) in the sense that form and design, rather than feelings, are the goals.

The trouble with the Taylor program at Hunter was that the offerings, though varied in movement, were all pretty much in the same vein with the possible exception of *Fibers,* a new work (commissioned by Ballet Society), which hinted, not very clearly, at conflict, aloneness, fleeting togetherness. One simply wished that Mr. Taylor's program had had greater emotional range, that it had not been so dedicated to the dancer as an instrument instead of as a person. But Mr. Taylor has come a long, long way in his choreographic growth and search since that recital some few years ago when he stood still for an entire number and barely moved in another.

At any rate, even if the heart (corny but still vital) were neglected here, there could be nothing but admiration for this impressive dancer and his gifted associates as they moved through the cool, highly original and generally fascinating formal intricacies of *The Least Flycatcher, Tablet, Epitaphs, Meridian* (all with moments of brilliant kinetic humor) and the somber *Fibers.* [*New York Herald Tribune*]

Alwin Nikolais

January 28, 1961

Stratus and Nimbus, two new avant-garde works choreographed by Alwin Nikolais, were performed by Mr. Nikolais' Playhouse Dance Company last evening at the Little Henry Street Playhouse, freshly and attractively redecorated.

The two pieces plus the concluding work, extracts from *Kaleidoscope,* an older creation, are in that special Nikolais vein which requires equal use of movement, color, sound and design and with the movement pretty thoroughly divorced from emotion or individual personality. Mr. Nikolais not only choreographs but also designs the costumes, determines the elaborate lighting effects and prepares the sound score.

It would be easy to say that all Mr. Nikolais' creations are alike. Well, they are in the sense that their basic ingredients are usually the same and in

402

the effect—rather cool and detached admiration—they invite from the beholder. But Mr. Nikolais is inventive, so one must also report that aspects—I said "aspects"—of movement, color, sound and form vary from work to work. In all, the dancers never really go it alone, for their motions are done in partnership with costumes, some of them very odd, and properties.

The opening *Stratus* was actually a sort of mass duet between the living dancers and the properties and light pools to which they were related, and the score incorporated gamelan-like sounds with effects which ranged from almost everything from the rasp of what seemed like communal whispering to snores and roars.

Although *Nimbus,* of course, made use of props, the accent here was more on the designs created by the dancers, singly and collectively, and the sound track employed tones emanating mainly from musical instruments rather than from other noise sources. In this work, the closest hint at human contact, as distinct from the clinical contiguities of dancing bodies, was in a duet performed by Murray Louis, a superb dancer, and the youthful Albert Reid.

All of the dancers, headed by Mr. Louis, Gladys Bailin and Beverly Schmidt, moved expertly through Mr. Nikolais' unemotional but visually interesting designs. The thought did occur to me that a solo by Miss Schmidt, in which she manipulated a gauzy and colorful skirt, had its ancestry in one of Loie Fuller's moth or flame dances and that some of the tableau-like group patterns represented a highly intellectualized version of some of those June Taylor precision routines for television (remember the old Jackie Gleason show?). But I dismissed these notions, for Mr. Nikolais does a brilliant job of what he sets out to do and his works, though limited in communicativeness, are very much worth seeing. [*New York Herald Tribune*]

Eleo Pomare

February 6, 1961

A modern dance program of serious intent, commendable dancing but of uneven theatrical effectiveness was presented by Eleo Pomare and his company yesterday afternoon at the 92nd St. Y. M. and Y. W. H. A.

The young choreographer, although his movement style seems to be strongly influenced by both Graham and Limón, has many fresh ideas of his own. In his works, one finds interesting group designs, a rather agreeable use (in his non-narrative pieces) of theme and variations and a most welcome spiritedness about it all. But interspersed with the pleasant inventions are some very trite activities, mainly in the gestural line and on the emotional plane.

Mr. Pomare, in this program at least, is given to soul-searching and, directionally speaking, to sky-searching. This is fairly dangerous territory, for it takes a highly experienced choreographer to translate an investigation of self into forms which invite universal concern. Of his pieces in this self-look genre, Mr. Pomare's *Cantos From a Monastery* was the most successful but because it came late in the program after three previous searches, its effectiveness was considerably reduced. But Mr. Pomare danced it excellently.

As a matter of fact, Dudley Williams, in one of the earlier pieces, also contributed some expert dancing to the program but he too was bogged down with a theme of yearning and further undermined by an accompanying poem (a beautiful work by Dylan Thomas), for the poet's images and those of the choreographer were but feebly related.

Alienations, a long suite for soloist and ensemble, made good use of an ominous chorus. Here there were telling patterns, including some interesting lifts. Peculiarly, the lifts for the soloists were awkwardly planned. In one sequence, for example, a male dancer, moving across the front of the stage, lowered his partner to the floor three or four times in a design which was not only clumsy but noisy as the girl was almost dropped to the floor.

With *4 A. M.,* well executed by Mr. Pomare, we were back to the old soul-search again.

Such works as *En Rondeau, Construction in Green* and *Rites,* concerned with dance expressiveness rather than undisciplined self-expression, were, in the main, pleasant adventures into design and mood (heroic, lyrical, bright or gentle, as the situation demanded).

In addition to Mr. Pomare and Mr. Williams, mention should be made of Zenaide Trigg, a lovely young dancer whose movements are clearly defined in space and whose free and open style of action and zestful presence characterize a dancer worth watching. Other members of the company, too numerous to name, also performed nicely. As for Mr. Pomare as a choreographer, I think, at this point, that we will have to settle for the word "promising."
[*New York Herald Tribune*]

Midi Garth

March 13, 1961

"Way out" would seem to be a perfectly usable term with which to describe the activities of experimental or avant garde artists. "Way in," however, is more pertinent in the case of Midi Garth who gave a recital Saturday evening at the Hunter Playhouse. For Miss Garth, who moves quite beautifully, appears to be motivated by an inner stillness rather than by an inner urgency. Her arms, often winglike, seem to be resting on the unseen density of space and on many occasions her feet touch the floor with a sort of weightless caress.

The end result of her style, theatrically speaking, is a way of dance which is poetic in its overtones but strangely detached. Of course, she doesn't float all the time; she can tread the floor with firm step and use her arms to thrust forth but still and all her dynamic range is not extensive. Thus, her dances lull instead of stir and by the time the program is over they tend to merge in the mind as a single dance essay, interrupted from time to time by occasional departures from her mildness.

One of these departures was a number, *This Day's Madness,* in which Miss Garth and two assisting dancers (Elizabeth Rasumny and Linda Stallman) offered a biting and highly effective satire on the world of screaming headlines, deadly routines of work, empty reactions to jazz as it affects and finally infects one woman.

Juke Box Pieces, another departure, did not make the grade with either bite or humor and the closing *Voyages* (a new work) simply never made port. Elsewhere, in several of her solos (there were eight solos by Miss Garth and two ensemble dances), the dancer moved with that gentle, cool authority which is her mark and, as I have said, it was interesting if one made a genuine effort to pay attention. For Miss Garth was "way in" and it was not easy to reach her. Sybil Shearer works in this same general area of dance, but with Miss Shearer, even the most delicate inner pulsations are extended over the footlights. Miss Garth has not yet achieved this communication. [*New York Herald Tribune*]

A Launching Pad on Mt. Olympus

March 23, 1961

The first major space-age ballet arrived last evening at the City Center when the New York City Ballet presented the premiere of *Electronics,* choreographed by George Balanchine to an electronic score by Remi Gassmann and Oskar Sala and with scenery and lighting by David Hays.

The word "space" was used as a generalization, for this work might just as well have been set in the center of the earth as well as on a distant planet.

405

The point is that the fantasies inherent in the scientifically tonalized music and in the stark but glittering crystal decor mirrored the adventures of a new age. True, one could say that *Electronics* was cyclically inevitable, for its ancestors were obviously the "ballets mechaniques" of the last generation but, nonetheless, in designs, in harmonies and cacaphonies, in choreographic accents, it spoke for today.

The ballet itself has no story line, although relationships among living creatures and even conflicts are clearly indicated. But the whole is rather like some fascinating science fiction-style rite. Against the crystal backgrounds, some symmetrical and some brilliantly jagged, the dancers move in snowy white, body-tight costumes (there is a brief and dramatic intrustion of black-clad figures) with the girls of the ensemble wearing shimmering white hair pieces and the two principal girls, silver and gold.

Visually, then, it is a striking work, harsh and uncompromising to the eye but hypnotic, just as the score is harsh yet mesmeric in its relentlessness.

Mr. Balanchine's choreography for *Electronics* is, oddly enough, quite classical in form and in movement detail. There are, of course, certain grotesqueries—a foot flexed instead of pointed, some non-traditional lifts and supports, a culminating body-wrapped-to-body roll down to the footlights— but the solid base is classical dancing with leg-beats, arabesques, pirouettes and the like, all ordered into fresh sequences as Mr. Balanchine always does. But it is as if the choreographer were saying that no matter the age, no matter the setting that the disciplines and the beauties of ballet would prevail, adapted perhaps, but eternal.

Then again, there was something profoundly classical (in the antique sense of the word) about the bearing and the relationships of the figures. In fact, I even thought of Olympus, abode of the gods, for the chief male figure made it clear that he exerted power, the second male figure was like a lesser god (Hermes, perhaps) and the two ballerinas had their Greek myth counterparts. The white and black figures might well have symbolized the forces of light and darkness, good and evil. But space age or antiquity, such symbols are without era.

The leading dancers were Jacques d'Amboise, Diana Adams, Violette Verdy and Edward Villella and each danced superbly. Mr. d'Amboise was a commanding figure, both in virtuosic flight and in gentler action, and Mr. Villella whirled through the air as if he were the restless Hermes (or a space cadet). Miss Verdy brought her lightness and swiftness to a comparatively brief part and Miss Adams' length of limb and loveliness of line were handsomely exploited in both the classical and off-beat adagio patterns. [*New York Herald Tribune*]

The unknown, along with its imagined inhabitants, has fascinated the layman and inspired the artist since the beginning. Adults as well as children are genuinely curious to know what or who may possibly inhabit distant planets. Today, the comics, science fiction and movies attempt to take us to outer space or through the center of the earth.

This is not new. As a child, I felt I knew Thuvia, the maid of Mars, quite well, courtesy of Edgar Rice Borroughs. Before that, there was Jules Verne. And centuries before him, playwrights, choreographers, poets and painters of the great age of world exploration depicted Africans and Incas, sea monsters and Loreleis with exhilarating inaccuracy.

Greeks and Romans   The ancient Greeks, of course, created the gods of Olympus and thus attempted to solve the mysteries of thunder and the seasons and love, along with other inexplicable phenomena. The Greeks, however, combined science and fiction so smoothly in their mythology, their theater, their philosophies that they achieved a classical formula in this area not matched by other cultures. That the Greek mythology was almost exactly reproduced by the Romans and that the gods and their involvements with mortals provided the themes for ballet-banquet fetes and classical ballets for nearly 300 years cannot be put down to mere chance.

It is not at all strange, then, that a brand-new ballet should combine Olympian figures with the fancies of modern science fiction; the most classical action, balletically speaking, with some "way out" designs.

The particular ballet to which I refer is *Electronics,* choreographed by George Balanchine to an electronic score by Remi Gassmann and Oskar Sala and produced March 22 by the New York City Ballet at the City Center.

The score, created through purely electronic means (no natural sounds or musical instruments were used in its making), is not as weird as one might expect. From time to time, one hears what seems to be the electronic equivalent of familiar musical sounds but they possess strange qualities, as if one were listening to the music of the spheres. There are both melodies and cacophonies and there are also some rather terrifying whimpers and roars of eerie sound.

The marvelous setting by David Hays is of glittering crystal, perhaps a temple of jagged ice on Olympus or a grotto of magical glass, and the costumes designed by Mr. Hays are white and body-fitting (other than for a few dressed in black who appear but briefly), topped by metallic streamers of gold, silver or white attached to the head.

With such a score and such a setting, Mr. Balanchine might have adventured in almost any direction. He elected, however, to pool the mysteries of today with the one-time mysteries of a classical age. Thus, the first figure to appear is most surely Zeus asserting his power with the toss of thunderbolts; the two leading females are, perhaps, lovely goddesses with special attributes or the breed of nymphlike mortal with whom the gods enjoyed dalliance, and the second male principal, fleet of foot and aerial of action, might well be Hermes. The invasion of the black-clad figures could certainly mirror the ageless battle between good and evil or the fight for power between the Titans and the followers of Zeus.

But these elements would be equally suitable to the space age, would they not? A crystal cavern on (or in!) an unknown planet, the leader establishing his fearsome dominance and repelling the invader, creatures nearly human but not quite? And Mr. Balanchine has indeed, with the assistance of the music and the decor, fused the ancient and modern ages of mystery to make a science fiction ballet unconfined by era.

Real and Unreal   *Electronics* is not, I think, a Balanchine masterwork. It does not possess the tenderness, passion and dramatic impact of, say, his *Prodigal Son,* nor the incredible beauty of design to be found in *Serenade,* nor the moments of theatrical terror which characterize passages in *Ivesiana.* But *Electronics* is by no means minor Balanchine. Its air of unreality bordering on reality (the secret of science fiction) is fascinating and, from the purely choreographic viewpoint, Mr. Balanchine has mated the conventional with the non-conventional just as his score has done.

Here, in *Electronics,* is a space-age ballet but instead of starting out from Cape Canaveral, Mr. Balanchine has launched it from Olympus. [*New York Herald Tribune*]

Time Taps Lightly, Too

July 9, 1961

Hoofing is slipping away from us. Yet not too many years ago, this was the kind of dancing that one expected to see in musicals, vaudeville, movies. Our dance scene, however, has changed. It has broadened. It is richer. Ballet is no longer an art for the few but, rather, for the vast general public. Modern dance is no longer esoteric. And the dances of India, Bali, Africa are no longer strange to our globally oriented eyes.

Classical and contemporary ballet can be seen on television, musicals have for their choreographers names associated with ballet or modern dance and even in jazz numbers for TV, movies, musicals, one sees a style of dancing strongly influenced by both ballet and modern dance. Fifteen years ago, the pattern was already shaping up. I recall taking a poll of the classes which the American Theater Wing offered World War II veterans under the GI bill. Of the three major dance techniques for theater, ballet, modern and tap, tap was at the bottom of the list, separated by a wide margin from the other two forms.

A Place for Hoofing   But there is no reason to let hoofing fall by the way, for it is a delightful, wonderfully entertaining, joyous area of dance. We need its relaxing, diverting properties just as we require for full dance experience the challenge of the avant-garde dance, the inner perceptivity of modern dance, the esthetic revelations of ballet, the knowledge which we may gain from ethnic dance forms.

There is, and always should be, a place for the true hoofer. And if Fred Astaire is the master hoofer of our day, certainly Eleanor Powell is the mistress of the form. There are a few balletic actions (a tour jete or chaine turns) that both incorporate into their work but both are first and last tap dancers, rhythm dancers, hoofers, for their dance is centered in their feet.

Miss Powell, who ends a highly successful engagement at the Latin Quarter this week, recently emerged from a fourteen-year retirement to prove to her teen-age son, as she laughingly told her audience, that his mother was something more than an oldtime movie star.

In Youthful Trim   The "oldtime" dancing star looks almost as young and dances with as much zip as she did in her movies of two decades and more ago. Her figure is so trim that she can wear tight-fitting trousers or an abbreviated, beaded leotard without revealing a single bulge or an untoned muscle. As a matter of fact, figure-wise and leg-wise, she is more than a match for any of the young Latin Quarter show girls and dancers. And dance-wise, she's a knockout.

In her current act, she rolls out her unfailingly accurate and crystal-clear tappings in everything from a simple and quiet rendition of the "Blue Danube Waltz" to a rousing rhythm contest with her virtuoso drummer, Steve Dweck. Actually, she is not a noisy tap dancer but she does invest her tap patterns with changes in dynamic colors as well as with rhythmic variety and every tap, no matter how swiftly done, is without blur. Indeed, she almost trills with her feet.

Her use of hands and arms is in the oldtime hoofing tradition. There is nothing balletic about them. She almost seems to let them move as they will, except for a gesture or two to give accent to a phrase. And her turns, in place or traveling across the stage, though derived from ballet, show nothing of the ballet dancer's concern for line, rather are they embellishments or conclusions to an elaborate tap phrase.

Nostalgic Memories Curiously, while watching Miss Powell dance, one experiences a feeling of nostalgia. This is not due to her appearance, for she is both youthful and loaded with vitality, nor to the fact that this is a comeback of a popular star of an earlier day. What is it, then?

The nostalgia comes not because we are watching Eleanor Powell but because we are seeing live, on stage, first-class hoofing and we suddenly realize that we haven't seen it in a long, long time. Yes, we see the incomparable Mr. Astaire or the superb Gene Kelly (who adds many ingredients other than tap to his dance style) in the movies or on TV. Occasionally, in stage shows there is a brief hoofing interlude, usually by a promising young dancer or a corps (such as the adorable Rockettes).

But Miss Powell is giving something more. She is giving us a star act in the old variety tradition and it is a hoofing act. Thus, does the nostalgia return. At first thought, the impulse is to wish for more hoofing acts, for old-time's sake, in our variety theaters and clubs but then sense prevails. Do we really want a spate of hoofing acts all over town? Certainly not. What we want is the star act and, after all, there is only one Eleanor Powell so let us happily and gratefully settle for her and for whatever worthy hoofing successors may materialize in the future. [*New York Herald Tribune*]

Leningrad Kirov Ballet

September 12, 1961

It took an audience a fast five minutes (perhaps less) to start cheering the Leningrad Kirov Ballet on the occasion of its American debut last evening at the Metropolitan Opera House. An oppressively warm theater invited the shedding of dinner jackets but not a drop in the unflagging enthusiasm of the public. True, the ovations were not as wild as those which greeted the Bolshoi Ballet from Moscow when it first performed here nor as exuberant as those which welcomed the Moiseyev folk dancers. But the Kirov Ballet, more refined, more reserved, more elegant, made its mark here with no trouble at all.

Most of us had expected that the Kirov Ballet would differ in some degree from its greatest rival, the Bolshoi, for the Kirov was once the famed Maryinsky, Russia's oldest ballet, attached to the court of the czars and noted for an elegance which made Maryinsky-trained dancers look on the Bolshoi as a "circus" group. And, in last evening's audience, there were famous graduates of the old Maryinsky, child-students in the last days of the Imperial Ballet and no doubt the floods of Russian that were being bandied about by these Russian–Americans had something to say about whether the great traditions had been preserved.

For an American ballet goer, it was immediately clear that the Kirov Ballet was different from its Bolshoi rival. In the four-act *Swan Lake* which introduced the group, the choreography was not a carbon of the Bolshoi production and the manner of dancing, though virtuosity was present, was rarely flamboyant. The extravagantly arched back of the Bolshoi dancer was almost consistently absent as were the gestural flourishes.

Inna Zubkovskaya, for example, who danced the dual role of Odette-Odile in this ballet masterpiece, first presented in Leningrad (then St. Petersburg) in 1895, employed a balletic line familiar to us (most of our teachers in the West are from the old Maryinsky) but occasionally, in a final pose, would lunge into a flashy Bolshoi position . . . and it looked just fine.

Interestingly enough, Vladilen Semenov, a dancer of excellent elevation and brilliant batterie at his command, occasionally did leaps in a style used almost exclusively by the Royal Danish Ballet, that is, with a bent knee for the back leg, but then one recalled that Christian Johansson, a pupil of Denmark's immortal August Bournonville, was for years one of the most influential teachers at the Maryinsky.

But let us leave, for now, the matter of divergent and related dance styles and take a look at this *Swan Lake*. As I say, it was reserved and elegant, more like Britain's Royal Ballet, possibly, than the Bolshoi and it was expertly danced but not danced with as consistent a level of excitement as I have seen produced by other companies, both American (which does a one-act version) and European.

Miss Zubkovskaya is by no means the most ideal Odette-Odile. She moves well and she rarely meets up with technical difficulties but her Odette, the heroine Swan Queen, is cold and rather unromantic and her Odile, the machinating magician's evil daughter, is fairly harsh but not especially malevolent.

Mr. Semenov is a bland Prince but he moves so beautifully that one can forgive his dramatic lacks. Just to see him do a double air turn into a flawless and fantastically controlled arabesque is in itself something to see.

Among the highlights of the performance were the first-act Pas de Trois, danced by the light, aerial and exciting Yuri Soloviev and two attractive partners, Alla Sizova and Natalia Makarova; the soarings and prancings of the Jester, performed by Alexander Pavlovsky; the precision dance of the four little swans and the elegantly conceived national dances of Act III.

On the debit side, I would list the foolish costuming of the possible Brides for the Prince—they were in wedding attire, practically ready for the altar, a mass omen that might frighten any young swain; the awkward actions of the Prince's male attendants in Act I and a very real tendency to let dramatic sense and force fall by the wayside.

I think this last lack explained a rather peculiar reaction. As I say, the audience burst into intensely enthusiastic applause throughout but none of it held over to the curtain calls. The audience, then, had applauded the part—the very, very good part—but not the whole.

But the Kirov, with its admirable aristocracy of manner, is with us and it is a privilege to see its long-established dance characteristics as they are manifest in the present company. With other repertory items yet to be seen, we shall surely find other facets of its cool and beautifully schooled artistry. [*New York Herald Tribune*]

1962

A Dream, a Defector, and a Dancing Bear

Balanchine creates his lavish spectacular A Midsummer Night's Dream, revives La Valse for Patricia McBride, and collaborates with Stravinsky for TV on Noah and the Flood • Graham's controversial erotic Phaedra • Ruth Page offers the American debut of Russian defector Rudolf Nureyev at the Brooklyn Academy of Music • Moiseyev Company represents dominating figure of Russian dance • Ballet Russe de Monte Carlo in its 25th year • Glen Tetley • Bruhn and Nureyev — superstars in London • Bolshoi returns with Plisetskaya and the epic Spartacus • Ballet Folklórico de México

The City Has a Royal Ballet in Dream

January 28, 1962

America does not have, of course, a royal ballet company but the New York City Ballet has, in its sumptuous new production of *A Midsummer Night's Dream* at the City Center, given us a theater creation which is as royal as anything you are likely to see. Its pictorial splendors include cool and sweetly mysterious (not frightening) forest scenes in which butterflies and the essential Puck dart about; a leafy bower, for Titania, which shields the Fairy Queen's dainty bed, a huge, pink shell; ground-mists which roll through the glades as Puck goes about righting the errors he has committed in mixing up batches of young lovers; a glittering, golden palace scene for Act II which, at the close, fades away and returns us to the forest with Puck, a green broom in hand, sweeping his woodland home.

The beauties of David Hays' scenery and the marvels of Karinska's costumes are a major aspect of this spectacle-ballet but they by no means

413

outshine the choreographic wonders that George Balanchine has wrought, especially in Act I. For in Act I alone, Mr. Balanchine has given us in dance form the entire plot, along with the major and complex sub-plots, of the Shakespearean drama. And he has worked this magic not by using pantomime but through dancing itself coupled with danced gesture.

Depth of Characterization This first act is also remarkable in that Mr. Balanchine's choreography not only conveys the story clearly but also provides for depth of characterization, along with many exciting formal dances. Thus it is that Puck is seen as a mercurial, mischievous, irresistible creature, half elf, half boy; that Oberon is every inch a king and Titania undeniably the lovely but spoiled Queen of the Fairies and that the characters of Helena and Hermia, Demetrius and Lysander are separate and defined as distinct individuals. Helena's forlorn trailing of Demetrius, for example, is totally different from Hermia's bewildered, baffled search for a lover swept up in an enchantment that has ensnarled them all.

Act II is given over to a lavishly mounted divertissement held in celebration of the marriages of the two sets of lovers (their amorous mix-ups now untangled) and of Theseus (at whose Athenian court the nuptials are held) and Hippolyta, Queen of the Amazons. The choreographer has evolved many engaging dances—pas de deux for the two principals in this divertissement, ensemble dances for the boys and girls and even separate dances for the girls alone and the boys alone—but a sameness pervades all until the very close of the ballet with the return of Oberon, Titania, Puck and their fairy retinue.

The sameness I speak of could be laid to two difficulties. One is that there is little variety in costumes, rich as they are, in the closing act. Gold and flesh colors predominate and they are placed against a background which is gold. Thus, the dancers seemed to fade into the setting. (Mr. Balanchine now reports that he will have these costumes changed—introducing bright peasant dress into the proceedings—by the time the next season at City Center rolls around.)

Movement and Music The music also invites, if not monotony, repetition. The score is composed of all of Mendelssohn's incidental music for the drama itself plus five other Mendelssohn compositions. It is, of course, lovely to listen to but where the actual dramatic elements of Act I provide varying colors and intensities to the stage action, the abstract movement in Act II must rely for richness of hue not on dramatic incident but on the music alone. This richness of inspiration the music for the second act does not provide, at least consistently.

Still, these are comparatively minor, correctible bits in a work which represents an important step in the staging of ballet in America. And certainly, one could not ask for a finer palette of color than that displayed by the chief performers, the actors–dancers of Act I.

Arthur Mitchell is not only the most perfect Puck I have ever seen but I couldn't imagine a better one. As he trots about with his magical flower that will induce love, uses it on the wrong persons, unscrambles his mistakes, grins roguishly, leaps with the shimmer of a moonbeam among the leaves, Mr. Mitchell leads us into a world of delightful fantasy.

A New Kind of Part for Villella   Edward Villella (and one might have thought that he would have been cast as the aerial Puck) was assigned the role of Oberon and performed it superbly. As always, his dancing was of the most exciting brand but here, in this new kind of part, he gave us a characterization which was remarkable, particularly for one so young. As a king, he showed a stature, a presence of authority he had not disclosed before (he seemed as tall as Jacques d'Amboise) and he projected with a neat combination of subtlety and vigor, Oberon's irritation with his Titania, his amusement when she finds that she has been in love with a man wearing an ass's head and his regal, manly charm when he receives Titania back into the royal fold.

Melissa Hayden is sweet and playful, a little pettish and charmingly imperious as Titania (you should see her curled up in her pink shell) and, naturally, glorious as a dancer, and Patricia McBride is excellent as the harried Hermia. Fine too are Jillana (Helena), Bill Carter (Demetrius), Nicholas Magallanes (Lysander) and Suki Schorer (commander in chief of the butterflies). In the divertissement, Violette Verdy and her cavalier (Conrad Ludlow replaced an injured Mr. d'Amboise at the first performances) have no dramatic duties to perform but much attractive dancing to do and there is an ensemble of child dancers in this ballet which adds much to the lightness and winning charm of a glittering new ballet. [*New York Herald Tribune*]

New York City Ballet

May 2, 1962: La Valse

That superbly elegant ballet of decadence, death and doom, *La Valse,* was restored to the repertory of the New York City Ballet last evening at the City Center after a six-year absence.

And its restoration was in itself something of a marvel, for it had not been recorded in Labanotation (dance script) nor had it been filmed. For six years it survived only in the memories of those who had last seen it or danced it.

Naturally, the chief burden of recollection fell upon its creator, George Balanchine, but many of the dancers recalled passages and the greatest aid came from the ballerina for whom the work was created, Tanaquil LeClercq (Mrs. Balanchine), who has not danced since she was stricken with paralyzing poliomyelitis six years ago. According to Mr. Balanchine, Miss LeClercq "remembered every step" and described them to the dancers.

And all who have contributed to this revival of a major Balanchine work earn the highest praise, for it is a remarkably vivid, touching and intensely dramatic recreation of a ballet which suggests ever so subtly that mankind—of this era or, perhaps, on the eve of a great social revolution—is dancing blindly on the rim of disaster.

Those who have seen the ballet will remember that the first half, set to Ravel's "Valses Nobles et Sentimentales," is a series of short dances in which terribly aristocratic creatures, both male and female, move with exquisite step, mannered gesture and a faint air of uneasy haste through duets, solos and little ensemble sequences.

Part II is a ballroom scene (the music is Ravel's "La Valse") lighted by muted chandeliers and set off by black columns suggesting funereal pomp. One of the whirling dancers is a girl dressed in white. She dances with her lover but the ominousness of the decor and the sounds of muted terror which introduce the scene are realized when a figure in black, Death himself, enters and provides necklace, gloves and dress of jet for the girl. He leads her into a dance of death and the ballet ends as the men at the ball hold aloft the inert body of the girl while the desperate revelers rotate around her.

Patricia McBride, in the role created by Miss LeClercq, acquitted herself handsomely, for she did not attempt to imitate her brilliant predecessor, but, rather, found her own accents and qualities and moods within the framework of the part. Nicholas Magallanes (the lover) and Francisco Moncion (Death) were, of course, excellent in roles which they had originated.

In the earlier part of the ballet—actually it is an extended dramatic prelude—Bill Carter gave a memorable performance, for not only did he partner Jillana to perfection and execute a series of turns with a spiral rotation to the upper part of the body (each ending in a kneeling position) with stunning ease but he also retained throughout the mien and manner of a gentleman whose only world was that of romance (governed, of course, by impeccable etiquette).

Jillana also danced to fine effect and there were excellent contributions by Carol Sumner and Richard Rapp, Victoria Simon and Michael Lland and by Suzanne Farrell, Susan Kenikoff and Marlene Messavage who, in their dancing together, suggested the three Fates in the guises of courtesans. And further praise, naturally, goes to Karinska for her glorious costumes and to Robert Irving for his conducting. [*New York Herald Tribune*]

The dancing in *Noah and the Flood* is frankly incidental but the sequences of action and even the fragments of gesture which George Balanchine has created contribute handsomely to the tenth and the latest collaboration between Stravinsky and Balanchine. For example, when we hear the words describing the molding of man in the divine image, we see Jacques d'Amboise, in profile, his gleaming headdress suggesting a warrior-god and the closeups of the finger and arm gestures mirroring the miracle of the human hand, an instrument capable of strength and of elegance.

A moment or so later, we see d'Amboise as Adam and Jillana as Eve and, again, a striking moment is achieved as the two simply touch each other's extended fingertips. Balanchine uses this gesture in his *Apollo* but it is especially effective here as seen through the medium of the camera.

There are, of course, larger scale movements as Mr. d'Amboise (who also dances Lucifer) hurtles from heaven, as Satan in his serpent's guise (Edward Villella) slides and slithers into a doomed Eden and as the corps of the New York City Ballet gives visual form to the building of the ark and to the flood itself.

Mr. Balanchine does not treat the building of the ark in terms of representational movement or pantomime; rather does he present his dancers as celebrants at a dedication and only through their patterns of interweaving do we find a hint of the act of creating or building.

The movements here are classical in base but with some sharp and sudden distortions such as the choreographer has used in his *Agon* (also by Stravinsky) and *Electronics.*

For the flood episode, on the other hand, he is more literal in that the dancers, moving under shiny and wet (perhaps simulated) materials, suggest the roll of the sea, and the individuals, dressed in white, who emerge from the waves make one think of creatures—sometimes fantastic—of the deep.

There are also some mime passages—the dancers wear masks—and at the close of the work in the "Covenant of the Rainbow" section, there is a very brief but stunning adagio passage. But then, *Noah and the Flood* is a short work and, it follows, the dancing comes in quick, episodic fragments.

Incidentally, one of the most charming dance sides of this TV occasion followed the actual presentation of the new work itself, for not only did we catch a glimpse of Stravinsky rehearsing but also Mr. Balanchine working in the studio with his dancers. I was especially delighted to hear Balanchine inform one of the dancers who had had difficulty mastering a flowing, sea-like movement, "I guess I'll have to take you to Atlantic City."

Choreographically, *Noah and the Flood* does not represent the most exciting and meaty of the Stravinsky–Balanchine collaborations but, during its

417

brief course, it gives us a few very special images of movement beauty which only Balanchine could devise. [*New York Herald Tribune*]

Martha Graham

March 5, 1962

The destructive forms of love, or passion, have long provided intensely dramatic conflicts for the dance theater of Martha Graham. She has, of course, given us tender love, spiritual love and even sweet romance but it is love's terror which has inspired her to create some of her most suspenseful dance dramas, many of them distilled from the plays, myths and legends of classical Greece.

Last evening at the Broadway Theater, as Miss Graham and her company opened a two-week repertory season, the dancer–choreographer gave us a new version of a doomed heroine in *Phaedra,* based upon Greek sources, with a specially commissioned score by Robert Starer and with setting by Isamu Noguchi.

In Miss Graham's *Phaedra,* which is more closely allied to the primitive Greek legends than to the Racine play which originally aroused her interest in the theme, the actual villainess is Aphrodite, goddess of love. For it was Poseidon, piqued, who caused Phaedra's mother Pasiphae, to lust for a bull and give birth to the dreaded Minotaur and it was Aphrodite, emulating Poseidon's evil, who caused Phaedra, wife of Theseus who had slain the Minotaur, to lust for her stepson.

The Graham *Phaedra* is truly, as the choreographer herself described it, "a phantasmagoria of desire," for the whole work is that nightmare instant in which Phaedra sees in erotic vision only the near-nude loins of Hippolytus (Theseus' son), seeks his love, is rejected, accuses him to his father of having violated her and brings about his death while the ghosts of Pasiphae, beautiful and ardent, and the stalwart Bull-Dancers haunt her mind.

Miss Graham's new work is heady stuff, tremendously sensual and highly dramatic. Aphrodite is seen as a beautiful wanton, almost flip but also cruel as she writhes prettily, watching the terrible fruits of her spells. Pasiphae is bright, glittering, lustful and the all-male ensemble of Bull-Dancers celebrates in movements of marvelous invention the strength, the litheness, the prowess of youths dedicated to the worship of the bull. Only Artemis, of the figures in the play, remains cool, chaste and, actually, neglected, for although Theseus and Hippolytus are victims of a misdirected passion, they are not its instigators.

418

Miss Graham, in the title part, gave a strong performance, evoking both the lustfulness, the anger and the vengefulness of the heroine fevered by Aphrodite's power. Although she acted the role well and brought her ever-potent presence to bear upon the proceedings, she was not in her best dance form. First-performance nerves, perhaps, was the cause.

Ethel Winter was superb as the lovely, demonic Aphrodite; Linda Hodes was a vivid creature in the small role of Pasiphae and Helen McGehee was appropriately aloof as Artemis. Bertram Ross was fine as the figure of the unsuspecting, ultimately shocked Hippolytus and Paul Taylor was tremendously impressive as the senior hero, Theseus, led to believe through Phaedra's lies that his own son had dishonored the home. And of equal dance value to any of the solo parts was the chorus of the Bull-worshippers who were composed of Richard Kuch, David Wood, Dan Wagoner, Robert Powell, Richard Gain, Clive Thompson and Peter Randazzo.

Mr. Starer's score served the dramatic needs of this powerful drama, near-melodrama it actually is, handsomely and the Noguchi setting, with a stylized pink shell for Aphrodite; a multi-dutch-door panel, which could reveal Hippolytus's physical attributes in piecemeal and teasing fashion to Phaedra's eyes, and, of course, a bed for Phaedra herself, is most imaginative. The costumes, presumably designed by the star herself, were geared to the work's physical desire. [*New York Herald Tribune*]

Russian Defector in Dazzling U. S. Ballet

March 12, 1962

Brooklyn, not Manhattan, was the scene of a tumultuous reception for a dancer new to the American stage. Rudolf Nureyev, the Soviet dance star of the Leningrad Kirov Ballet who defected to the West last June, made his American stage debut (he had appeared earlier in the season on television with Maria Tallchief as his partner) Saturday evening as guest artist with the Ruth Page Chicago Opera Ballet at the Brooklyn Academy of Music.

The big theater was jammed to the doors by those who had come to see the twenty-three-year-old dancer not in a full-length ballet but in a comparatively brief duet, the Grand Pas de Deux from *Don Quixote,* as familiar to ballet-goers as the Mad Scene from *Lucia* is to opera-lovers. Looking at the faces in the audience, one realized that here was a "Who's Who" of ballet, many of the great American dance stars of our day, among them, celebrities who had defected to the West years before, Balanchine and Danilova, to name but two.

And Nureyev, obviously, captivated the audience. With Sonia Arova, the Bulgarian-born ballerina of Miss Page's company as his partner, he evoked such storms of applause that following numberless curtain-calls, he was forced to encore, alone on stage, a portion of a solo sequence from *Don Quixote*.

Hailed in Paris and London as phenomenal, compared favorably with Nijinsky and most recently cheered for his performances with Dame Margot Fonteyn and Britain's Royal Ballet, Nureyev had a cosmopolitan audience, assembled in Brooklyn, literally yelling ecstatically. Did he deserve it?

Nureyev is, unquestionably, one of the most compelling dance figures of our era. In *Don Quixote* he displayed altitudes in leaps and jumps which recalled the legends of Nijinsky. His leg beats were brilliant—muscle beating against muscle in air—and his partnering of Miss Arova was both technically secure and elegant. Indeed, Nureyev seemed to be a remarkable combination of a classical danseur noble, a tender partner and a dancer who defied category.

Actually, it is in the last-named area that he is unique. Erik Bruhn, of the Royal Danish Ballet and the American Ballet Theatre, is equally virtuosic and more polished, France's Jean Babilée is more dynamic but Nureyev, in addition to his thrilling virtuosity, possesses an animal magnetism which invites something very close to hypnotic adoration. He is not so much an attractive and gifted young man as he is a creature, a mysterious being who works magic on the stage whether he is soaring through space, awaiting explosive action or, in curtain calls, permitting a boyish grin to dissolve an otherwise enigmatic expression.

Rudolf Nureyev, in Brooklyn, made his impact upon a discerning American audience and perhaps that is all he wanted. Surely, few stars could expect the ovation he received. Yet to the dance follower, a single pas de deux is little more than a teaser. There is no chance here for characterization or for an extended interpretation of a part, be it dramatic or abstract. One wished that his local debut could have been associated with a production. Why not Albrecht (one of his best roles) in *Giselle*? Should he have waited for such an opportunity.

He chose, however, to leave temporarily his present duties in London with the Royal Ballet to fly to America and dance a duet in Brooklyn on a bare stage. And no matter what those of us feel about his choice and about the benefits of a full-scale production to surround his debut, it is now a fact that he was triumphant. For here, in truth, is the most fascinating new dancer to appear in our midst. And let me hasten to add that he is not just a novelty. This is an artist, already brilliant, who is at the threshold of what could be the most phenomenal dance career of our age.

It was, of course, Mr. Nureyev's evening but gratitude and admiration are due Miss Arova, who performed superbly and won resounding cheers for her own sparkling dancing, and thanks are due Miss Page, who knew full well that her own company and her own ballet creations, *Camille* and *Die Fledermaus,* would be pushed into the background for the sake of a dazzling debut by an electrifying new dance figure, Rudolf Nureyev. [*New York Herald Tribune*]

Dancing Bear Is Everywhere

April 22, 1962

Cultural exchange has become lopsided in the dance field. Russians are dancing all over the lot in the U. S. and that's fine, but where's the reciprocity? It's not their fault; it's ours. Isn't it high time we got on our toes?

The Russians are whizzing along on their art-propaganda program, S. Hurok is reaching new and enviable peaks of success as an unrivaled impresario, but where on earth is the reciprocity in the cultural exchange agreement recently renewed between the United States and the Soviet Union? At least, where is the reciprocity on the dance level? For when Mr. Hurok brings the Ukrainian Dance Company to the Metropolitan Opera House this Tuesday for a three-week pre-tour stand, he will have had six Soviet dance troupes (not counting a huge Russian Festival of Music and Dance) in a period of four years and six days. It was just that long ago that the Moiseyev Dance Company from Moscow made its sensational bow at the Met.

In that period, how many American dance companies toured the Soviet Union? One.

Yet we cannot blame this lopsided state of affairs on a gang of cunning Russians, much as we might like to, nor can we accuse Mr. Hurok of neglecting American artists (actually, he is something of a hero in the exchange field except for dance). No, our government is insistent on seeing that there is a reasonably equitable exchange of performing artists, although it is true that Soviet officials are pretty picky and choosy about whom they will let into their country, while we tend to be sensibly curious and carefree about any and all performers from the Soviet Union.

On the surface, the exchange appears to be working well. Under the agreement, Mr. Hurok, for one, has sent twelve American attractions to Russia and brought twenty Soviet attractions (including the six dance troupes) to the U. S. Other independent managers (such as Columbia Artists) have also worked under this government-approved arrangement.

But why is American dance the forlorn stepchild, the Cinderella, the orphan in this otherwise lively example of cultural reciprocity? Is it that our dance art is inferior to Russia's? Is it that dance is not a good medium of communication and understanding among peoples? A resounding "No" to both queries.

In ballet, we can equal the Russians (and often surpass them), in modern dance and jazz and free dance forms (including the uncensored avant-garde) we are way ahead. They have the edge, and by a wide margin, on brilliantly theatricalized folk dancing not only because their folk dance resources are far more vivid than ours but also because time and expense are no object in creating such troupes as the Moiseyev and the new arrival, the Ukrainian Dance Company.

As for the communicative powers of dance, there can be little argument that an art which transcends the barrier of language and which celebrates the prowess of beautiful, disciplined, healthy, rhythmic bodies is universally understood and admired, despite differences in costume and steps.

No, American dance has lost its reciprocity in the exchange program not because of any inherent artistic lacks, not because the Russians are leading us by the nose, but because the Soviet government has untold funds to spend on the export of its superb performing arts while the United States government can export only through the very limited funds allocated by the Congress to the President's Special International Program for Cultural Presentations (administered by the American National Theater and Academy). In its eight years of existence, this program has sent seven American art attractions to the Soviet Union: three major orchestras, two college orchestras, *My Fair Lady* and one ballet, the American Ballet Theatre.

A Matter of Money   The program's first project was a dance event (José Limón and company to South America) and it has sent a few other dancers and companies all over the world and with enormous success, but ballet troupes are tremendously expensive to transport and the small funds at the disposal of the State Department for this purpose must be shared with music and drama groups. The independents cannot afford to send big dance companies overseas and thus it is that Mr. Hurok's American attractions going to the Soviet Union are mainly solo musicians.

So what do we do? Do we let the Soviet public think that the American Ballet Theatre, splendid as it is, *is* American dance? Should they not know that the New York City Ballet, with a totally different performing style and repertory, featuring a treasury of Balanchine ballet masterpieces (far ahead of any Russian choreography) exists? And what of the incomparable Martha Graham and her company (Soviet dancers who have toured here are wildly enthusiastic—even Igor Moiseyev himself got into trouble at home for his enthusiasm—about her)? Or Jerome Robbins' *Ballets: U. S. A.* and others?

422

Welcome Mat Is Out   Do we let Soviet dance troupes (and believe me, they are warmly welcomed by every one who loves great dancing) dance all over us and around us simply because we are such stupid, unthinking tightwads that we won't supply our dancers with the few thousands of dollars of traveling expenses that would take them right to the heart of the Soviet empire where dancing Americans, without firing a shot, could triumph again as they did with the single visit of the American Ballet Theatre?

The Soviet government has, by agreement, opened the door and laid out a welcome mat to American artists and we, poor things, don't have the carfare to send over all eligible, under the exchange pact, Americans, principally the neglected dancers, who are superbly equipped to speak with the silent eloquence of dance to the Russians.

Indeed, the head of state of a neutral power said to an American dancer performing in his country under our President's Program, "You have done more for your country during your tour here than all the plane-loads of diplomats that you have sent us." And in Indonesia, Martha Graham's performances convinced a violently anti-American newspaper that America was not the land of "dollars, gadgets and bombs" that they had supposed but that, through the artistry of Graham, "America's soul" was clearly discernible. These and other accolades for our dancing ambassadors have been duly reported. Still, the Soviet Union sends us six ecstatically received dance companies of mammoth size (two companies will have had return tours by the end of this year) and we send them one. Reciprocity? [*New York Herald Tribune*]

Twenty-Five Years of Ballet Company

April 29, 1962

Birthday time has rolled around for the Ballet Russe de Monte Carlo. Well, in a way, two anniversaries are involved, for anyone who recalls the 1937–'38 season knows that there was a mad scramble of opposing directors, choreographers, dancers and others and that what had been one company became two. Thus it is that the present Ballet Russe de Monte Carlo is celebrating its 25th year under the direction of Sergei Denham, although the Ballet Russe de Monte Carlo itself, historically speaking, came into being just 30 years ago. Whatever the anniversary, a look at the present status of the company is certainly in order.

423

The company, which rarely performs on Broadway any more and busies itself with the road, arrived at the Brooklyn Academy of Music recently for two performances. This American troupe (yes, despite its name, it is now American and has performed regularly in this country since 1933) has had some artistic ups and downs in the past 15 years but if reviewers around the country have often given it a rough time (and with good reason), the public keeps coming back for more. The magic word "Russe" might have something to do with it.

A Matter of Style   At any rate, both performances in Brooklyn attracted huge audiences, including many dancers, and what happened on stage was a mixture of the good and the bad. The corps de ballet this season is composed of good-looking girls and boys who are well schooled, well rehearsed and spirited. The neatness of action of the corps is surely due to the efforts of the ballet mistress, Nina Novak, also the company's first ballerina, who was unable to dance on this occasion because of an injury.

But that the corps moves with admirable precision through arrays of choreographic designs does not mean that it has been equally well coached in matters of style—such as in the national dances in *Raymonda* or the frothy French goings-on in *Gaîté Parisienne*—or in dramatic gesture and characterization. Supervision in these areas is in order. Truthfully, certain of the principals could use knowing direction in matters of style and dramatic impact. In Massine's perennial *Gaîté Parisienne*, only George Zoritch really knew what this lively, elegant ballet was all about. Certainly, Yelle Bettencourt played the girl-ogling Peruvian as if he were still in rompers and neither Helene Trailine (Glove Seller) nor June Wilson (Flower Girl) invested their roles with that coquettish lilt which once made *Gaîté* irresistible.

Still and all, there was some excellent dancing provided by members of the upper echelon. In addition to the stylish and elegant performing of Mr. Zoritch, the Ballet Russe offered us the highly virtuosic and exciting dancing of Juan Giuliano, the lyrical and line-lovely movements of Paula Tennyson, the strong and dependable and zestful dancing of Eugene Collins, the sure and attractive performing of Andrea Vodehnal and some dynamically bright characterizations in Spanish style by Gail Israel and Mario Ignisci in Leon Danielian's new *Espana.*

High-Grade Ham   But there is another performer I must mention, the guest star, Nina Vyroubova, whom I had seen with the Paris Opéra. You have to see her to believe her. Oh, yes, she is an excellent technician, definitely a ballerina but I haven't witnessed such hamming since Tamara Toumanova last chewed up the scenery here. Vyroubova who, in profile, looks surprisingly like a Mayan glyph, flirts with her partner and her public, indulges in all manner of mannerisms, from rhapsodic flourishes to minxish coquetries. She's outrageous, especially when she manipulates the fan in the *Don Quixote* Pas de Deux, and she is unintentionally funny, but her dancing powers are considerable, she knows the stage and the ham she proffers is delectable and of the highest grade.

As for the programs, they were clutters. Five ballets—or, rather, parts of ballets—on each. The lure of quantity instead of the promise of quality? Grand pas de deux are, of course, acceptable, standard and pleasant. The one-act *Swan Lake,* an entity in itself without the other three acts, is fine. But the Ballet Russe's divertissements from *Nutcracker* and *Raymonda* are fragments of the traditional selection of divertissements in the actual ballets themselves. At any rate, Mr. Bettencourt, if he was a miserable actor in *Gaîté,* was a knockout as the leader of the Russian dancers in the Trepak from *Nutcracker.*

By way of celebrating this anniversary, Mr. Denham engaged three famous alumni of the company—Frederic Franklin, Leon Danielian, James Starbuck—to create three new ballets. Mr. Starbuck's *The Comedians,* set to the Kabalevsky music, makes a stab at liveliness but winds up as rather routine stuff, thin and not at all stirring.

For his *Tribute* (music, Cesar Franck), Mr. Franklin has turned up with an abstract work that is pretty, peppy and pleasant to watch. The tribute of the title, I would say, concerns not only the Ballet Russe but others as well, for Mr. Franklin has passages suggestive of Balanchine's style, others which echo the precarious lifts of Soviet ballets and, most important of all, a quality which exudes the zip and the spiritedness of Mr. Franklin's own unmatched characteristics as a longtime dance favorite.

Mantilla and Cape Mr. Danielian's *Espana,* with a score using music by Breton, Chapi and Granados, has some kind of a plot requiring the presence of a Lady with the Black Mantilla and the Man with the Black Cape. I couldn't follow it at all but it didn't matter much because both these mysterious creatures danced attractively the choreographer's equally attractive designs and the steps and formations created for the corps were bouncy and vital and touched with a chuckle or two.

So it is that we find the Ballet Russe de Monte Carlo celebrating its anniversaries with performances which display an ensemble of well trained dancers, not always aware of period styles, in a repertory which is neatly rehearsed but subjected to occasionally tasteless abridgements both with respect to cutting out dances in a given ballet and cutting corners by using the same setting for different ballets. Bargain basement ballet: some excellent buys along with materials destined for the rummage sale. *[New York Herald Tribune]*

425

Glen Tetley

May 7, 1962

A dance program of serious artistic intent, superbly mounted, was presented
Saturday evening (and again last evening) in the auditorium of the Fashion
Institute of Technology. The program, titled "An Evening of Theater Dance,"
was performed by three of the finest dancers in the business—Glen Tetley,
Linda Hodes, Robert Powell—and the four works, all new, were choreographed
by Mr. Tetley.

Everything seemed auspicious. Mr. Tetley, a successful dancer highly experienced in both ballet and modern dance, had spared no effort and, certainly,
no expense in preparing for an event that was to be something more than the
usual modern dance recital. Not only had he engaged two of the finest dancers available as his colleagues but he had also selected four musical scores (two
of them in their first performances) and engaged a small orchestra and soprano
soloist to perform them. Furthermore, especially designed decors and costumes
were imaginative and, where suitable, sumptuous.

Everything, as I say, promised an exciting evening. Indeed, everything
went smoothly—other than incredibly long intermissions—and the three danced
beautifully. But an element was missing. Just what was it? Was it that some
of Mr. Tetley's themes were not always easy to follow? No, for choreographers of the avant garde are far more obscure. Was the performance too
slick? No. Was it pretentious in theme and treatment? Possibly. Did the
music and decor overwhelm choreography which was not consistently substantial? Probably.

At any rate, that "urgency of action" which Martha Graham has referred
to as a dance essential, was not present to sweep us, the viewers, into a concern for what Mr. Tetley had to say. Nor was the bright insistence of balletic
virtuosity in its modern dance equivalent a part of this performance. It was
difficult, then, to make oneself care about the feelings of the stage characters,
to be caught up in the life of a dance. But one could look, respect and admire, for Mr. Tetley devised actions which had fine pictorial worth if little
emotional glow. He also gave himself and his dancers some incredibly difficult
movements which they accomplished with ease and polish but most of these
were isolated motions and few were permitted to build to climaxes.

The opening *Gleams in the Bone House,* to music of Harold Shapero
(String Quartet Number One) and decor and costumes by Peter Harvey, presented the trio, singly and together, in a series of episodes which disclosed,
attractively, their movement skills.

The second piece, suggested by a Japanese Noh play, was *Birds of Sorrow*, which evoked interest chiefly because of a fascinating new score by

Peter Hartman (one of the percussionists had to dash so swiftly from instrument to instrument that he got as much exercise as the dancers), striking decor by William Ritman and absolutely glorious costumes by Willa Kim.

As for the dancing, sequences of vertiginous spins by Mr. Powell were among the highlights but then Mr. Powell is such a remarkable dancer that anything he does becomes invested with special kinetic magic. Mr. Tetley and Miss Hodes, of course, also danced excellently but the choreographic material they used was of less interest.

How Many Miles to Babylon, with an engaging new score by Carlos Surinach and amusing costumes by Beni Montresor (who also designed the pleasant panel drapes), was a comedy in which the humor, I fear, though intended to be biting, was pretty forced. Miss Hodes had some effectively projected lurchings and kickings as a trampish and waspish Titled Lady, Mr. Tetley worked hard and Mr. Powell, underplaying the role of a Servant, was funnier in gesture and in stance than were the others who were careening a bit too heavily.

In the closing work, *Pierrot Lunaire* (Arnold Schoenberg music) with its stunning set and costumes by Rouben Ter-Arutunian, Mr. Tetley came closest to reaching the heart of the watcher. It is much, much too long as a theater piece but the choreographer himself does let us see the age-old anguish of poor Pierrot and his choreographic conception of the movement qualities and pantomimic characteristics for Columbine and Brighella are fresh and interesting. His skillful use of Mr. Ter-Arutunian set piece—a skeleton of iron pipes rising to various levels such as are found in children's playgrounds—also added to the pictorial interest of an evening which, despite the known dancing accomplishments of its trio of performers, found its success mainly in the dancing pictures it provided the eye.

The Gramercy Chamber Ensemble and a specially augmented orchestra directed by Robert Cole and Jan De Gaetano, soprano, were the program's skilled musicians. [*New York Herald Tribune*]

Teen-Age Squeals for Two Ballet Stars

June 10, 1962

London. A beatnik and a prince have taken London by storm. They are alike in that both are artists of the ballet, both tremendously potent box-office material and both responsible for bringing (especially in the demonstrative

427

balcony areas) a whole new audience to the ballet. The two, who have just completed a series of guest appearances with Britain's Royal Ballet at the Royal Opera House, Covent Garden, are Rudolf Nureyev, the young Kirov Ballet dance star who defected to the West a year ago, and Erik Bruhn of the Royal Danish Ballet and associated for several seasons with the American Ballet Theatre.

Their dissimilarities spring not from the roles they play but from how they play them. Each, for example, has acted the part of Count Albrecht in *Giselle* and the Prince in *The Sleeping Beauty*, each is thoroughly trained in classical ballet and each is a virtuoso of uncommon brilliance. But meticulously executed entrechats, pirouettes and grands jetes and elegance of deportment to the contrary, they are amazingly un-alike.

The Wild Side   Nureyev, with his shock of unruly hair, his sullen expression, seems indeed, at first glance, like a beatnik in ballet tights. When he begins to move, it is with the swift dexterity, the alertness of the ever-watchful youths of *West Side Story* or, perhaps, with the seemingly uncalculated, instinctive spring, turn, twist, darting of an animal. But there is nothing crude or gauche about this animal. He is catlike in both his elegance of action and his enigmatic expression. The discipline of a premier danseur appears to cloak a creature of wild and beautiful movement impulses.

During the Mad Scene in *Giselle*, Nureyev gives the impression that he too is going mad as Giselle sinks ever deeper into a state of dementia, and when he is forced, in Act II, by the magic of the Wili Queen to dance to exhaustion, the anguish and desperation of emotions are strangely paired with impeccable execution of classical steps. At his curtain calls, he stands looking out over the great house. His hair is tousled, his eyes are expressionless as they wander from balcony to boxes to orchestra and suddenly he raises a hand and a smile touches his otherwise sulky lips. For a moment he is a boy, but then the creature, tough-looking and strange, returns to glower.

The Princely Way   For Nureyev's final appearance in *Giselle* before the Royal Ballet left London for festival appearances in Coventry, the audiences stamped, applauded, yelled. Those in the orchestra were enthusiastic and appreciative, but the teen-agers in the balconies squealed and shrieked for their idol until the viewer lost track of the number of curtain calls.

For Bruhn's final appearance of the season in *The Sleeping Beauty,* the audience responded similarly with respect to enthusiasm. The sophisticates in orchestra seats lingered longer than they had for Nureyev and the teen-agers in the high balconies pelted him with flowers. But then, Bruhn is a prince or, rather, he behaves like one. At all times, he is perfectly groomed. No matter how many vaultings into space he may make, not one fair hair moves out of place and the costume never has to be adjusted (as Nureyev does, acting as if shirts and jackets were too confining for a wild and free creature—true, he dramatizes these gestures to superb effect). But this is not to say that Bruhn lacks passion.

In the forest scene, Act II, of *The Sleeping Beauty,* Bruhn, more than any dancer I have ever seen, makes one feel that his reason for not participating in the games and gambols of his courtly friends is not due to either ennui or princely pettishness but that he has, through the power of magic, been exposed to a vision of the sleeping beauty herself. Soon, of course, he and we actually see the Princess in a vision, but Bruhn anticipates this scene magnificently.

Can't Be Compared   And when he dances his demanding measures, he also soars with ease and strength into space and tosses off his multiple turns with dash and zest. But it is a prince, not a mysterious creature, displaying prowess. And so it is that Bruhn and Nureyev, for this London season, have come close to stealing the scene from the ballerinas. Each has his ardent following. And, one might ask, which is the better?

Certainly, there is no greater premier danseur-noble today than Bruhn and, surely, there is no more vivid male dancer of extraordinary personality and striking physical skills than Nureyev. They cannot, of course, be compared. The senior of the two has maturity and its virtues (polish, authority, graciousness and shining virtuosity) on his side, and the younger has the explosive impact of youth, bravado and daring with which to excite the public.

But these two superb male dancers had better not believe for one moment that they have displaced the ballerina. In permanent letters beside the box-office window at the Royal Opera House, three price categories are listed: for matinees, evenings and Fonteyn performances. One of the world's great ballerinas, Dame Margot Fonteyn, numbers both Bruhn and Nureyev among her celebrated partners, but for the practical souls in charge of the box office, there is one enduring, dependable name, "Fonteyn." [*New York Herald Tribune*]

Bolshoi at Met: A Royal Performance

September 7, 1962

The proletarian-minded Russians, whether they like it or not, have a queen on their hands. Oh yes, last night at the Metropolitan Opera House, when the

Bolshoi Ballet opened its month's engagement, there were a real live Prince and Princess (Juan Carlos of Spain and Sophie of Greece, newlyweds) in the audience and make-believe princes and princesses on stage in *Swan Lake*. But reigning supreme was Maya Plisetskaya, one of the world's great performing artists, who well deserves a title once bestowed on her dancing ancestresses of two centuries ago, "queen of the dance," at least as far as Soviet ballet is concerned.

Miss Plisetskaya, as she did three years ago when the Bolshoi Ballet first came here, had an audience of ardent balletomanes (one had been standing in line outside the Met since Tuesday), dance celebrities (Alexandra Danilova whose international career began with the Russian Imperial and Soviet State Ballets, Agnes de Mille and others), movie stars, diplomats (the Soviet Ambassador to the United States, U Thant of the United Nations, Adlai Stevenson) cheering her every move as she danced the demanding double role of Odette, the heroine transformed into a Swan Queen, and Odile, the malevolent Black Swan.

And this great star dominated the entire evening. The lavish sets and costumes, the glorious corps of thirty swan maidens, the colorful executants of national dances were but trimmings for the intensely dramatic, vivid, even extravagantly projected art of Plisetskaya.

As Odette, she brought the wondrous flow of movement, including the rippling arms which had fascinated us first in 1959, and the gentleness of action that give dramatic pertinence to her characterization of a creature part bird and part woman. And it seemed to me, on this occasion, that she invested the part with a romantic tenderness absent before.

Her Odile, of course, was the glittering manifestation of evil that many of us had remembered. Her steppings, which had been so delicately placed as Odette, became harsh and her arms metamorphosed from the sinuosities of the swan-like Odette to the writhings of the cruel Odile.

Terrifying—almost melodramatically so—was that moment in the Black Swan Pas de Deux when Odile, realizing that she has not been completely successful in convincing the prince that she is his betrothed Odette, emulates the rippling arms of the forsaken heroine all the while her face betrays her soulless guile.

It was, then, a Plisetskaya occasion. I cannot imagine that anyone complained because she did not do the traditional (with the West) thirty-two whipping fouetté turns in the coda of Black Swan (she can do them, of course, and does in other ballets), for her sequence of two piqué turns alternating with four jet-speed chaînés were as dazzling as one could wish.

Nicolai Fadeyechev, wearing an appallingly ugly costume and not dancing his solo episodes with any brilliance (though neatly) was a superb partner (the Prince) for Plisetskaya, and Vladimir Levashev was superb as Rothbart, the sorcerer who is the father of Odile and the one who transformed Odette and her maidens into swans.

Other major moments included the first act Pas de Trois, exquisitely danced by the adorable Ekaterina Maximova, the charming Marina Kontratieva with not much help from the male of the trois, Valdimir Nikonov, who didn't point his feet, didn't leap very well, didn't . . . just didn't. Much more effective was Georgi Soloviev as the Jester, for although he didn't deserve the wild applause accorded his agreeably executed turns in air and on the ground, he deserved hearty but modest commendation for a job well done.

The performers of the national dances—Spanish, Hungarian, Italian, etc.—in the divertissement section of Act III were first-rate, as the Russians usually are in character dances. But the choreography here and elsewhere in the four-act ballet—the first three are by Alexander Gorsky and the last by Asaf Messerer, Plisetskaya's uncle—is not nearly as good as that used by Britain's Royal Ballet and other companies. Some sequences—the great adagio for the ballerina and her cavalier in Act II and part of the Grand Pas de Deux of Act III—are very similar to those we have assumed derived from the Petipa–Ivanov original but most of the choreography (admittedly of a later date) is pretty pedestrian.

But the opening night was by no means earth-bound, thanks to the "queen of Soviet ballet," Maya Plisetskaya. And, of course, the great ballerina will be seen again during the engagement arranged by S. Hurok, for not only will she dance other *Swan Lakes* but she will also be seen in roles new to American audiences.

It's safe to wager that other Plisetskaya appearances will attract the legal quota of standees, for last night not even the lowering of the asbestos curtain could stem the wild applause. It was halted half way as the audience accorded Maya Plisetskaya an ovation—cheers and rhythmic applause—which lasted almost to the half-hour mark. [*New York Herald Tribune*]

The Bolshoi: Spartacus

September 13, 1962

You'll have to see it to believe it. *Spartacus,* that is, the wildy extravagant production which the Bolshoi Ballet presented for the first time in America last evening at the Metropolitan Opera House. And I use the word "extravagant" to apply to every thing about *Spartacus.* The staging itself marks it as pure extravaganza, from enormous sets to a lavishly dressed cast numbering more than two hundred dancers and extras. It is extravagant also in its acting style which recalls the eye-battings, lurchings and gesticulations of silent movies.

As a matter of fact, although *Spartacus* is a brand new ballet, it will be enjoyed especially by silent-film buffs, by those who wish the old Hippodrome had never been torn down and by those who relish, perhaps with a sardonic smile, the outrageous in the theater. Well, don't you think a whole Roman arena filled with sword-wielding gladiators is pretty damn exciting? And what's wrong with a bacchanale in which a bored courtesan tempts to the point of desperation a handsome male slave who, permitted a few racy thigh-strokings, is quite naturally put to the sword?

And what is wrong with a drama in which the hero triumphs over insurmountable odds to the very end when the catharsis of tragedy takes over?

To communicate this story of a Thracian slave who leads a furious revolt against the Roman oppressors of 73 B. C., the choreographer has relied heavily on pantomime, dramatic action (such as the swordplay) and an amazing number of tableaux, living pictures of arrested action which tell us first where we are and, secondly, what happened during the blackout.

Spartacus is not as non-dancy as the comment overheard at the end of the first act would lead one to believe: "Look, Ma, no dancing!" There is dancing, pseudo-Roman, pseudo-Oriental, pseudo-Isadora Duncan and pseudo quite a few other things. But there are some wonderfully athletic measures for the warriors and some lively passages for a clown and his companions. The truth is that the dancing gets lost in the bigness of it all. Only the unrestrainedly emotional acting manages to hold its own with the massive towers and statues and with costumes that knock you senseless.

Yes, Leonid Yakobson's choreography, built upon a libretto by Nikolai Volkov, and augmented by the settings and costumes of Vadim Rindin and V. A. Klementiev, seems to belong in the era of silent movie spectacles. Even Aram Khachaturian's specially composed score is silent movie stuff. He has written music to writhe by, gloat by, run by, pose by, along with music for fighting, love-making, praying, loathing and being noble to.

Well, as I say, it is all marvelous if you go for this sort of thing. Certainly, you couldn't ask for a more extravagant extravaganza and if you can combine your sense of humor with a nostalgia for the fanciful improbabilities of the old screen spectacles, you will have a whirl.

At the premiere, it was the mass, the aggregate which starred. The Bolshoi's incomparable Maya Plisetskaya played the role of Phrygia, devoted wife of Spartacus, and somehow, through her performing magic, made the part—which is really one big cliche—believable and Dmitri Begak, wearing a beard and flashing the fanatic rebel's eye (such as one might find in portraits of Lenin), made it quite clear that he is ballet's answer to Steve Reeves of the modern extravaganza movies. [*New York Herald Tribune*]

432

From the Village Green to the Theater

November 10, 1962

"The minute folklore leaves its place of origin, it is folklore no longer," says the beautiful Amalia Hernandez, part-Indian, part-Spanish director general and choreographer of the Ballet Folklórico de México, which opens a three-week stand Tuesday at the City Center. Mme. Hernandez, whose company enjoyed a tremendous success in New York a year ago, continued: "That is why folklore should be taken only as a source of inspiration and developed to create spectacle.

"There are only two reasons in Mexico for the folk dance: for a religious purpose and for fun. A certain village on a certain day will honor the Virgin or a saint and the people will dance for endless hours, doing maybe one or two steps over and over again, as their sacrifice. If the villagers have gathered simply for fun, again they will repeat the same step or pattern. This just won't do for the theater. You can't transplant the steps only. To re-create the emotions behind those simple steps, you need the technique of choreography—selection, amplification, rhythm changes, contrasts, varying formations."

Mme. Hernandez's method of transforming folk material into theater is illustrated by her new piece, *Los Tarascos*. She studied intensively in the region where Mexico's Tarascan Indians live. They are people who still speak only their native tongue and who were never conquered in pre-Hispanic Mexico (although they did pay tribute to the Aztecs). Mme. Hernandez assembled their authentic steps, designs, rhythms, songs and ceremonies, and molded them into a ballet about the periods in a day as related to the life-span of a man.

The seven-part theater piece opens at dawn with a lullaby to the newborn, moves on to a dance of the silver fish by the children, reaches noon with the adolescents in a vigorous stick dance or mock battle, slips into the afternoon with a majestic dance of maturity, enters twilight with little old men in a rollicking but stiff-jointed dance, and ends its course at night with a candle-light ceremony in a graveyard where the living honor their dead. But an epilogue promises another day, another life.

The Aztec Gods, a second new work, posed another problem for Mme. Hernandez. No written notes were used by the Aztecs but their tunes have survived in remote villages and these, augmented by other pre-Columbian airs, make up a score which utilizes such instruments as drums, sea shells and flutes, and a chorus singing in Nahuatl (the Aztec tongue) and Mayan.

The choreographer took for her theme the Aztec legend of the creation of the world. "I picked," she said, "the most theatrical of their gods, the most dramatic of their legends."

433

Mme. Hernandez is only one of the contemporary choreographers who have turned to folklore for inspiration. The Soviet Union's Igor Moiseyev uses a similar approach. True, many of the folk dances in the Soviet Union's several republics and regions are virtuosic and highly colorful—hence theatrical—to begin with, but even these need choreographic editing. Moiseyev's genius lies in his ability to select, weed out, re-arrange and even create appropriate new steps.

Moiseyev, Hernandez and their colleagues in the growing folk-to-theater movement strive to retain authenticity of step and gesture, sound and dress while bringing the spirit, be it gay or sad, of a specific folk expression to the theater. Repetition, monotony, drabness and the amateur standing they leave to the village green.

Folk dancing as such is basically something to *do* and not to *see*. Some folk dances are fun to look at—an American Indian hoop dance, for example (but if you've ever seen one on a reservation, you know that they go on too long); or highland dancing from Scotland (but look how Agnes de Mille adapted it, and to great dramatic effect, for the theater in *Brigadoon*); or a Bavarian slap dance. But who wants to see a square dance? No one really, not until it has been theatricalized by a de Mille or a Balanchine (he did a delicious *Square Dance* ballet with ballet steps, a folk caller and music of Corelli and Vivaldi!).

Some of the highest levels of folk dance fall into a different category. They become ethnic dance or the art dance of a race or culture. The four great classical dance styles of India are unmistakably Indian (and not international, like ballet) and they require professionals to dance them. The same holds true of Japan's Kabuki dance-drama or the royal ballets of Thailand and most of the dances of Spain, but even these need to be adapted to the requirements of the Western theater.

The dance phenomenon of our age is the manner in which highly gifted dancers–choreographers have created an ethnic dance art where none existed. Haiti, for example, had no ethnic art dance—only simple folk dance and related folklore materials. Jean Leon Destine single-handedly created a Haitian dance art from the basic material supplemented by voodoo gestures and other native steps and movements. The Bayanihan Company has achieved a similar feat for the Philippines (where only folk dance and no art dance existed before). Their imaginative directors and choreographers have sought to adapt the folklore of their lands to the needs of the theater: Bulgaria's Koutev; Poland's Mazowsze; Yugoslavia's Kolo; and many, many more.

As the peoples of the world come to be more and more curious about each other and as their leaders seek to find pathways to understanding, the arts serve increasingly as a means of communications. Dancing, free of the barrier imposed by language, speaks eloquently, and when it speaks through

434

folklore terms, it speaks for a people. The village green, the barn, the thresh-ing floor, the cathedral steps cannot be transplanted to the theater but the color, the action, the spirit and the purpose of folk festivals, edited by a knowing hand, can be transformed into theater, a dance theater for the whole world to enjoy. [*New York Herald Tribune*]

1963

America Loves Margot and Rudi

Fonteyn and Nureyev triumphant with Royal Ballet • Ice Capades '64 the best ever • Patricia McBride's dancing • The financial reality underlying the boom in ballet

Royal Ballet—1963

April 29, 1963

Shattered ear drums must have been a dime a dozen last evening at the Metropolitan Opera House as the audience (the standing room line outside the Met had formed early in the morning) beat its palms and cheered wildly for an elegant ballet duo who might also be classified as the hottest little team in show biz. They were, of course, the Royal Ballet's great ballerina, Dame Margot Fonteyn, and her current cavalier, Rudolf Nureyev.

In the third act with the famous *Swan Lake* Pas de Deux, the two stopped the show with the brilliance of their dancing. The plot just had to wait as a good five minutes of bowing took place following Dame Margot's dazzling sequence of thirty-two whipping turns and Nureyev's near-orbital leaps.

Now all this may sound as if the two stars simply settled for a fine array of ballet tricks, of feats of skill. Not so. Naturally, when bravura was called for, they delivered, but great artistry, sensitivity and, yes, even delicacy of gesture were essential to characterizations which were never cheap, always aristocratic.

The vehicle for Dame Margot and Nureyev was the Royal Ballet's four-act-staging of the great classic, *Swan Lake* in which the Russian defector played the role of the Prince and the ballerina the double part of Odette-Odile. The two had performed earlier in the season in *Giselle* but this was their first *Swan Lake* together in America.

Dame Margot gave a magnificent portrayal as Odette, the enchanted Queen of the Swans. Poignancy, gentleness, the glow of romance pervaded every gesture. In sharp contrast was her Odile, dark and sharp and sinister. Both were wonderfully regal but Odette, by the nature of the role, required not only the presence of a queen but also of a warm woman and a bird-like creature. Dame Margot brought all three aspects of revelation to Odette.

Act I was considerably altered, in spots, around Nureyev. In this production, the Prince does not dance at all in the opening act (he simply mimes) but Nureyev did a solo (and a not particularly interesting one) and a fragment with two girls (this is used in the Stanislavsky Ballet's version). Even the mime was altered in the scene for the Prince and his mother, the ruler of the principality, and given a new twist.

Nonetheless, Mr. Nureyev's characterization as a whole was carefully drawn and credible dramatically. The moody-looking, tousled-hair, slight-of-build Tartar dancer is not only an artist but a vivid personality. Thus it was that he and Dame Margot, in addition to providing the audience with two remarkable portraits in dance and displays of formidable ballet skill also gave the audience exactly what it had come to see: Fonteyn and Nureyev, ballet's biggest box office stars.

There were other excellent performances last evening—indeed, this presentation of *Swan Lake* was on the highest level in all respects—but attention was focused on the famous pair to the near-exclusion of other artists. And Fonteyn and Nureyev were not found wanting but their ardent followers. My echoing, aching ear drums attest to that.

The Royal Ballet's two week-end matinees at the Metropolitan Opera House featured major cast changes of more than passing moment. Yesterday afternoon, for example, New Yorkers saw a new ballerina in the dual role of Odette–Odile in *Swan Lake* as Antoinette Sibley performed the part for the first time in America. And she was superb, especially as Odile.

To the part of Odette, the Queen of the Swans and the ballet's heroine, she brought beauty of movement from the lyricism of her port de bras to the lovely steppings, runnings, turnings, balancings of her exquisite feet. I think she needs to deepen her characterization, to make it more romantic, but this is a matter of dramatic coloring which she will no doubt attend to.

Her Odile, the ballet's villianess, is brilliantly drawn, for it is sensual as well as glitteringly evil, and in the famous *Black Swan* Pas de Deux the young ballerina makes you believe that every spectacular movement she performs is designed to enchant, excite and mesmerize the Prince into believing that she is really Odette.

In addition to Miss Sibley's impressive performance, this *Swan Lake* boasted a fine Prince in Desmond Doyle (he was excellent in *Black Swan*), a delightfully amusing acting bit by Stanley Holden as the tottering old tutor and some agreeable dance passages by other soloists. The Tchaikovsky score also was first-rank in the hands of Robert Irving, guest conductor, who used to be chief conductor of this company but is now musical director for our own New York City Ballet and the Martha Graham Company.

Saturday afternoon brought another performance of Frederick Ashton's wholly charming *The Two Pigeons*, on this occasion with Merle Park as the Young Girl who loses her lover (temporarily) to a gypsy miss and Kenneth Mason as the errant youth. Miss Park was most engaging in the part and Mr. Mason was just about perfect in making the lad's behaviour seem worthy of sympathy and quite understandable in one so filled with restless, boyish vigor. A really top-flight characterization in dance. Monica Mason was very good as the sexy gypsy girl and Robert Mead was again highly effective as a jealous gypsy boy. [*New York Herald Tribune*]

May 5, 1963

"Policy, not politics, is the explanation," said Sir Frederick Ashton, associate director and chief choreographer of England's Royal Ballet, now in repertory at the Metropolitan Opera House. Sir Frederick was replying, in effect, to a mass query posed by thousands of balletomanes. Why had Dame Margot Fonteyn and Rudolf Nureyev danced the second *Giselle* and the second *Swan Lake* of the season and not the first performances? Those who had, way in advance, bought tickets for the "firsts," assuming that the company's prima ballerina and its premier danseur would appear, were understandably disgruntled.

Rumors had raced about that pressure had been brought to bear either on S. Hurok, the impresario, or the direction of the Royal Ballet itself by the Soviet government, which had already demanded (successfully) of the French government that Nureyev, the Soviet defector, be banned from appearing at the state-run Paris Opera.

Steering a Troika "Policy," Sir Frederick had said, and he was right, for he and Dame Ninette de Valois, the director of the Royal Ballet, had promised the three top-echelon ballerinas a first performance each. Thus it was that Dame Margot selected *The Sleeping Beauty*, a ballet with which she is most closely identified, and Nadia Nerina and Svetlana Beriosova then chose their full-length vehicles. Nureyev, who dances mainly with Fonteyn (and rarely in *Beauty*) was therefore required to wait until Dame Margot's first *Giselle*.

But all of this popular concern over the Fonteyn–Nureyev partnership and who's doing what when simply pinpoints the fact that the major dance news in America right now is centered in the juxtaposition of two names, Fonteyn–Nureyev. Newswise, everything else in ballet seems minor, at least temporarily.

439

But what about artistically? There can be no argument that Dame Margot has danced more beautifully this season than ever before. The youthful Nureyev, almost 20 years her junior, has given her new theatrical inspiration. This she acknowledges herself. In technique also, she is even more authoritative. The 32 fouettés in *Swan Lake* which used to give her trouble a decade ago are now under regal control. Fonteyn continues to grow as a great, great artist.

What About Nureyev? What of the highly publicized Nureyev (at 25 he is the author of an autobiography)? Many dancers don't like him. Some, I believe, think he is something of a fraud: an adequate but flashy dancer, with an inordinate ego, unorthodox performing style and, in a tousled, near-beatnik way, an arresting personality.

Of course, he's outrageous in many respects and there are those armchair conservatives who dolefully report that he won't last, that he's being over-exploited, that he isn't properly disciplined. Pooh! Noverre and Perrot, Taglioni and Elssler, the later Pavlova and Nijinsky, the still later Danilova and Markova (both recently retired) and the Bolshoi's current star, Plisetskaya, have all been eccentrics.

I just couldn't stand seeing *Swan Lake* over and over again (for hundreds of times) if it did not vary in interpretation from performance to performance. And *Swan Lake* can provide differences only through its performers. Unchanging exactitude of step and gesture and even flights of virtuosity can be found duplicated a thousand-fold in ballet classrooms around the world. Nureyev is not a student, he's a star.

There have been tut-tut-tings (by ballet followers, not the general public) because Nureyev changes ballets to suit either himself or what he was accustomed to in Leningrad. He even had the plot slightly altered in Act I of *Swan Lake.* I don't think it was for the better, but that's a matter of taste. A matter of pure fact is that Rudolf Nureyev has tremendous impact whether he is giving us spectacular leaps in *Black Swan,* glorious leg-beats in *Giselle,* occasionally over-acting, glowering moodily into space or adoring Fonteyn through the most tender and lovely balletic attention you have seen in a long time.

Nureyev is *somebody.* You and I know this; the entire public does and they would rather watch him stand still on stage than see a beautifully drilled student move impeccably and impersonally. This is true of a Martha Graham, a Ulanova or that most noble of all danseurs nobles, Erik Bruhn.

A Policy Vindicated Combine the smolder, the mystery, the dynamic presence, the great streaks of vivid movement which Nureyev gives us with the beauty, the radiance, the womanliness, the queenliness and the shining movements of Dame Margot and the cheers that have shaken the old Met to its foundations are explained.

440

It was a matter of company policy to be fair to all artists—to postpone the first joint appearances in New York of Fonteyn and Nureyev. But policy was forgotten when the two united their remarkable artistries. This is what the public had waited for; this, rightly or wrongly, was the Royal Ballet; this, while Fonteyn and Nureyev were representing the most ephemeral, the most fleeting of all the arts, *was* ballet itself. [*New York Herald Tribune*]

Peril of Hitching a Ballet to Stars

May 12, 1963

Full houses have been the norm for the Royal Ballet at the Metropolitan Opera House principally when Dame Margot Fonteyn and Rudolf Nureyev were promised to the public. Thus it is that during the five-week engagement in New York, programs which did not include ballet's most popular team were lightly attended on more than one occasion. And this is a pity, for Britain's Royal Ballet, as a performing unit, has never been better in its illustrious, ascendant career of 32 years.

Despite the Royal Ballet's current high level of performing skill, even in its homeland the magic name of "Fonteyn" and the double sorcery of "Fonteyn–Nureyev" are almost essential listings if a capacity house is to be attained.

A Danger, Too Last week I wrote about this remarkable pair and the wonders they bring to the stage, as well as making ballet more newsworthy than it would be without them. They would seem to be essential to the Royal Ballet itself and yet for all the luster and artistry they bring to it they also constitute a danger: which is more important, the Royal Ballet or its fabulous duo?

Dame Ninette de Valois, the company's director, would have been considered batty if she had not engaged the phenomenal Nureyev for her troupe and paired him with her own popular prima ballerina whom she had hot-housed to fame within the framework of the Royal Ballet. Any director or manager would have done the same, for aside from the fact that these two dancing properties were highly exploitable at the box office, as a pair, they have brought a new charge, a new impact and, indeed, new inspiration and artistic challenge to a comfortably running institution.

Now there are rumbles just below the surface of the Royal Ballet. Naturally, some of the dancers are understandably miffed at the attention showered upon a newcomer, Nureyev. But it goes deeper than passing

441

jealousy. They point out, as has the English dance critic, Clive Barnes, that an institution cannot hitch itself to two stars. Dame Margot, at the peak of her powers at 43, has only a few performing years left to her. And Nureyev, the dazzling Soviet defector with the vivid personality, will he remain loyal to the Royal Ballet or will he streak on, like a comet, to other starring opportunities?

The dancers, the critics, the ballet scholars point to the fact that in Europe, the Royal Danish Ballet enjoys tremendous popularity as a company not dependent upon any single name, including that of its own internationally famous Erik Bruhn, and that America's New York City Ballet's box office does not rely upon any one ballerina or danseur, although it does boast one great name, Balanchine (its director–choreographer).

Only a Showcase?   Yes, the Royal Ballet, in its finest estate, could well be in trouble, for if it becomes only a showcase for Fonteyn and Nureyev, it will face difficulties when they are gone. Still, Fonteyn and Nureyev must dance somewhere and even if they do shake an institution, they also attract attention to it.

I'm sure that those who have attended performances of the Royal Ballet here in New York and did not see either Dame Margot or Nureyev were understandably disappointed but I am equally sure that once the ballet began, they settled back and had a great time watching one of the world's great corps de ballets and an enviable roster of ballerinas, danseurs, character dancers and young and bright soloists.

There are many non-Fonteyn–Nureyev images which all of us will retain (in addition to memories of the matchless pair) and just a few would include the absolutely perfect dancing of the ladies of the corps in Act II of *Giselle*; the vigor of the ensemble of men dancers as lusty gypsies in *The Two Pigeons* (time was when this company's male wing was weak; now it is one of the best); Svetlana Beriosova's flawless body "line" in action or at immobile anticipation, a model for all female dancers; David Blair's smooth-as-silk air-turns to the knee in *Swan Lake*; Alexander Grant's jetlined Neapolitan dance in *The Sleeping Beauty*; Nadia Nerina's virtuosity, and Antoinette Sibley in just about any thing you care to name.

And speaking of Miss Sibley, is it possible that she might one day step into Dame Margot's shoes, not as an imitator but as a successor?

So, perhaps, one could look at the situation which prevails in the Royal Ballet today from three different but, perhaps, complementary viewpoints: (1) how fortunate it is that the Royal Ballet can present two of the most important ballet stars of our era to its international public; (2) how superb the Royal Ballet itself now is, with or without Dame Margot and Nureyev, boasting as it does an enviable roster of first-rank artists at all echelons and a remarkable repertory which includes many masterpieces of the past and many modern masterworks, chiefly those created by Sir Frederick Ashton; (3) how bright the tomorrow can be if both dancers and the public remember that if a Fonteyn followed a Markova, then there are certain to be worthy successors of Fonteyn, of any star.

Thus, should not the dancers themselves accept the challenge of the reigning personalities and seek to better not their techniques merely but their performing impact? And should not an audience be adventuresome enough to go to the ballet no matter who the star of a given Royal Ballet performance might be, and see if he can spot an heiress to Fonteyn, a rival to Nureyev? They're there, if you'll look. [*New York Herald Tribune*]

Ice Capades of '64— A Show Par Excellence

August 29, 1963

In his *Ice Capades of 1964,* John H. Harris offers the best ice show I have ever seen. The new edition, which opened an engagement last night in Madison Square Garden, contains all the familiar ice extravaganza ingredients: lavish costumes, skating by champions, ballet on ice, something for the kids, comedy, even audience participation. But somehow, the current show possesses perfect pacing which makes it race along with the easy grace and speed of a spread eagle.

Although the new Ice Capades does not have Ronnie Robertson as its star (and he is an unforgettable performer on skates), it has an array of top-notch acts. In the *Kiddie Circus* production number, every one present fell in love with Spanky, a chimpanzee who combines incredibly skillful use of skates with magnificent hamming, and when he races and jumps six barrels (which spell out his name) he has the audience all to himself (a word of praise to Spanky's manager and modest partner, Dave Pitts).

This same *Kiddie Circus* episode also featured Johnny Lebrecque and George Bussey in a sketch which was funnier than any clown act I've seen in a real circus, some pleasant skating, with air splits, by the vivacious Brigitte, and a selection of charming creatures, including a camel and some kangaroos.

For skating which combined the grace of ballet with some pretty smashing acrobatics, we had Phil Romayne and Kathy Steele, and for breathtaking virtuosity, there was Doug Austin to do multiple turns in air and dizzying spins on the surface of the ice. Right up there with him in the display of skating tricks was the light and lithe Japanese star, Hisashi Kuchiki.

In a show fairly bursting with glittering highlights, it is difficult to pick an absolute winner. It might well be the brother-sister team of Maria and Otto Jelinek, Czech-born, Canadian-raised world champions, for their great skating prowess they have brushed with an old-world charm and graciousness; they are, in brief, dancers–skaters with the lilt of Vienna in all they do.

But I cannot stop even here or I would be neglecting other splendid acts and turns. For example, Jan I. Tors did a marvelous *Doll Dance* in which he actually did a duet with himself. It was comic but there was humor throughout the show. Ice humor is actually low comedy (clean but low) but the low comedy in this Ice Capades is on a high level. The three Bruises, for example, tear up the ice and break up the audience with their perennial and ever-hilarious charwomen act, in this instance, placed in Hawaiian setting.

The Bruises have another comedy number to contribute to a show which also included the antic action of a great badminton player, Hugh Forgie, beautifully assisted by Shirley Marie, as he skates, clowns, mugs and plays the game with virtuoso brilliance. Han Leiter also supplies some laughs and Allan Konrad some brisk bright skating.

But could it be that the real highlight is the great precision number for the full ensemble, *The Annapolettes* (sailors, Waves and even an admiral in the audience loved it), staged by those masters of precision, Rosemarie Stewart and Robert Dench (now retired, unfortunately for us all who love ice shows). It's a marvelous set of ice maneuvers that they have invented and it wins bravos. It should.

Then there is Cathy Machado, a headliner, who is a handsome girl, not at all graceful by dance standards but enormously skillful in her execution of feats of skating skill.

Still others deserve bows—Ron Fletcher, the choreographer; the conductor, James Peterson, and certainly Billy Livingston who designed the opulent, wildly extravagant, cute and often amusing costumes. But I guess highest praise must go to our friend Spanky, a real chimp (not a skater in costume) and a real ice pro. [*New York Herald Tribune*]

Patricia McBride's Dancing

September 25, 1963

A memory of Massine's *Symphonie Fantastique,* in which the figure of the Beloved turns into a monster; a hint of the cold evil of the Wilis in Act II of *Giselle*; a touch of the concealed terror of Balanchine's *La Valse* contribute

444

more than possible flavors to John Taras' new ballet, *Fantasy*, which was given its world premiere by the New York City Ballet last evening at the City Center.

The new piece, set to Franz Schubert's Opus 103, orchestrated by Felix Mettl (originally, it was a piano work for four hands), has a cast composed of three couples and an ensemble of girls called Watchers of the Night. And it is these Watchers who recall the Wilis, the implacable death-maidens of *Giselle* whose duty it is to drive the male to exhaustion and death through dancing.

Their leader is the girl of the first couple, at first disguised as an aristocratic and radiant woman who is transformed into a creature of evil (as in *Symphonie Fantastique*) destined to lead her partner to sorcery and death.

The other two couples appear to escape the inexorable calls of the Watchers of the Night, so one may presume that Mr. Taras is suggesting that with three pretty faces, one can never be certain which one masks the soul of evil.

As a ballet, *Fantasy* has moments of great dynamic impact and of pure dance beauties. Patricia McBride, for example, as the gloriously lovely creature who turns into a witch, not only excites the viewer with her powers in projecting the macabre but also dazzles the eye with a series of tours en attitude which are nothing less than fabulous.

There are also some striking passages for Edward Villella as the damned youth, a role the young dancer acts with conviction and performs with technical élan.

Even the Watchers succeed in evoking an aura of ominousness. But Mr. Taras has them going on far too long as Macbeth-type witches, for once their deadly nature is established all they can do is to repeat that fact. As for the supporting couples, they move with lightness and innocence and make no impact whatsoever.

Fantasy, then, is an uneven work, one which boasts sequences with punch, point and vividness of dance action but which also suffers from attenuations and phrases which are thin to the point of being almost nonexistent. The music is to blame in part, for certain of its episodes are too long for the needs of dance exposition.

At any rate, *Fantasy* did one great service in supplying the increasingly brilliant Miss McBride with a role which added still further dimension to her artistry as a performer, as a technician and as a theater person with stage presence.

Carol Sumner and Robert Rodham and Marlene Mesavage and Earle Sieveling were agreeable enough as the other couples. The attractive costumes were not credited to any but a spokesman for the company said that they were composed of "bits and pieces from this and that." [*New York Herald Tribune*]

A sudden change of cast last evening at the City Center permitted Patricia McBride to dance her first *Swan Lake* of the season, and although the New York City Ballet's switches in programming and in casting this fall have aroused howls of protest from ballet followers, no one could be anything but grateful for Miss McBride's spur-of-the-moment appearance as the Queen of the Swans. She was heavenly!

Miss McBride was called upon to replace the scheduled Melissa Hayden who, of course, is quite irreplaceable, but once the change was announced, Miss McBride came on stage and in her own lovely dance terms, took over completely. Since she first performed the role last spring, the young dancer has deepened her portrayal, added even greater refinements to what was at the very outset an arresting interpretation.

The dancer is beautiful in body and in face and she moves with incredible poetry of motion as she defines, swiftly or with superb legato, breathtaking designs in space with the gentle elevation or the kick of a leg, a spurt of spins, a folding or unfolding of the arms, a lift to the head, a gesture of invitation or one of command.

It is the policy of the New York City Ballet to avoid stars and to list its principals alphabetically. Miss McBride cannot help the fact that she is (as are others in the company) breaking rules—she is a ballerina in face, in form, in technical authority and in that elusive quality which makes the viewer know that he is in the presence of something very special, in this case, a ballerina.

The Prince in this *Swan Lake* was Edward Villella (replacing at the last moment his distinguished colleague, Jacques d'Amboise) who danced with brilliance, as he always does, and who gave us a characterization more subtle, more suitable than he had in his first association with the part last week. Miss McBride and Mr. Villella, then, gave us a truly memorable *Swan Lake,* and assisting them handsomely were Mimi Paul, the leading dancer in the Dance of the Little Swans (the Pas de Neuf), and the corps. [*New York Herald Tribune*]

After The Boom Is Over

September 29, 1963

Ballet in America is booming today as never before but the boom may very well be building up to a bust. The danger signals, which are flying more and more insistently, are not esthetic but financial. Yet, paradoxically, ballet today is big business. The trouble is that the people who take in the money are not those who found or head a company, often the truly creative spirits in ballet.

Thirty years ago, no one dreamed that ballet would ever account for much at the box office. In 1933 S. Hurok, the most celebrated of impresarios, brought the Ballet Russe de Monte Carlo to America for a short New York season and a modest tour. He lost close to $100,000 on the venture. In this year of 1963, his gross income from his dance attractions alone will easily hit the $4,000,000 mark.

What happened in those 30 years to lead ballet in America to the peak of success, and also the brink of disaster?

Actually, 1933 was an investment year not for Hurok alone. It was something of a magical year, auguring a resplendent ballet future. In that year, a talented young man by the name of George Balanchine, who had recently come from Europe, in association with a determined American dreamer, Lincoln Kirstein, presented his American students in new ballets which he had devised. From these modest beginnings has grown one of the great ballet companies of our age, the New York City Ballet.

Today, the New York City Ballet, with Kirstein as its general director and Balanchine as its guiding genius, performs for about 20 weeks a year at the vast City Center and, on a recent tour into the Soviet Union, made such an impact that Soviet cultural officials quickly took a look at their own ballet laurels and found them to be a bit tarnished. So it was that Balanchine, trained in the Imperial and Soviet State Ballet Schools and a refugee (in 1924) from his homeland, saw the day when his achievements in America, personified in the accomplishments of the New York City Ballet, shook the Russians right down to their toe shoes and instituted an agonizing reappraisal in Soviet ballet circles.

It would appear, then, that in 1963, the New York City Ballet is solidly perched on the pinnacle of success. Next year it will move over to the New York State Theater in Lincoln Center as a resident company guaranteed 20 weeks of performances a year. Its contract runs for two years.

But how secure is the New York City Ballet? New productions have to be postponed because of lack of funds, bills are sometimes paid just at deadline time, money has to be raised to pay deficits. Ballet companies, no matter how successful they are, cannot pay their own way. It costs more to produce and run ballet than the ballet can possibly take in at the box office.

So it is that an organization called Ballet Society came into being to assist ballet, with its chief support now going to the New York City Ballet. But the clue to the impermanence of a given ballet company may be found in the preliminary discussions relative to the planning of Lincoln Center for the

Performing Arts. Planners knew that the Metropolitan Opera and the Philharmonic were coming to the new Center as established institutions and that if their present leaders should retire or die or move off, the two institutions would go on. With some justification, the planners asked, "Is there a permanent dance institution in America?"

Dance followers, right in the midst of this tremendous dance boom, began to think over the query posed by Lincoln Center planners. Did not the heartbeat of a single woman determine the life span of one of the nation's great ballet companies, the American Ballet Theatre? Could this distinguished company, founded in 1940, and often debt-ridden, survive without its director-benefactor, Lucia Chase, who has spent a rumored $4,000,000 of her own to build a major company and who has attempted to organize a foundation (the Ballet Theatre Foundation) which would raise funds to keep it going?

Would even the seemingly secure New York City Ballet last long without Mr. Kirstein, who has contributed funds and wisdom and taste to his ballet over the years, or could it live without the presence of Balanchine himself, since the New York City Ballet is almost a one-man enterprise?

No, there is no American dance institution equivalent of that of the Met or the Philharmonic to give permanence to American dance companies. What is even worse, there is no subsidy from the government, and without such subsidy, American ballet on a large scale could well disappear.

The non-balletomane might possibly ask, "Is ballet worth all the trouble? Is it worthy of subsidy? Who goes to see it?" The answer is: millions of Americans go annually. It has even been estimated that ballet outdraws baseball at the box office.

In 1933 American ballet first began to go regional in a big way with the founding of the Atlanta Civic Ballet and the San Francisco Ballet, which, under Lew Christensen (long associated with Balanchine), has grown from a one-town company to a troupe that has toured abroad with tremendous success under State Department auspices. Today there are some 160 community ballet groups scattered from coast to coast.

The ballet boom in America includes, of course, performances by other than American troupes. Importations, ranging from the very special (classical Hindu or Japanese or other ethnic dance forms) to the popular (the Bolshoi, Britain's Royal Ballet, the Kirov Ballet from Leningrad, the Royal Danish Ballet), attract audiences not on Broadway alone but in major cities, towns, colleges and universities. The irony here is that every one of these visiting ballet companies is subsidized by its government. They are enjoying our ballet boom while our American companies, unsubsidized, are in terror of the bust which is inescapable, if not today then tomorrow, unless subsidy is forthcoming.

Right on our own continent there is a telltale, ominous shift in ballet personnel immigration–emigration. Until a very few seasons ago, young

Canadian dancers came to the U. S. to make their careers and Canadian dance followers complained that we were taking their best (among them, the great ballerina-to-be, Melissa Hayden) away from them. The Canadians came because there was no financial security at home in a ballet career. Today, all is different; our dancers are going to Canada.

Why to Canada at this late date? Because while the bust was already striking some of our major ballet companies—the Ballet Russe de Monte Carlo was inoperative all last year and the American Ballet Theatre is barely functioning this year—the Canadian government was allocating funds to support its swiftly rising ballet organizations. American dancers and choreographers travel in a steady stream northward to work with the National Ballet of Canada, the Royal Winnipeg Ballet or Les Grands Ballets Canadiens.

Governmental subsidy is all around us. Even poor nations support their arts, including the dance, but the richest nation on earth does not provide subsidy for its arts at home. It has funds for propaganda and it has sent American ballet and modern dance troupes to many countries to let our friends, our enemies and the undecided know that we have a culture. But when it comes to culture at home, "subsidy" is a controversial word. Members of Congress might well hesitate to tell their constituents that some of the taxpayers' money is going to buy pink toe shoes, tights, tutus and to pay for something called "art."

Certain of our dance companies are surviving and some actually advancing because of funds obtained from foundations, guilds and wealthy patrons. But this can only be a stop-gap arrangement, as wonderful as it is now, for our government must come to look upon our dance art not as a luxury for the few but as a national resource of great value to our own citizens and to citizens of other lands.

Meanwhile, the foundations, large and small, are helping to promote the ballet boom while staving off the ballet bust for as long as they can. The Rockefeller Foundation has aided the New York City Ballet and other dance enterprises. Without the Bethsebee de Rothschild Foundation for the Arts and Sciences, one of the greatest artists of our era, Martha Graham, could not afford to create her masterworks or to perform. The Rebekah Harkness Foundation has given financial help and sponsorship of the most generous sort to several dance groups, among them, the Robert Joffrey Ballet. And it is through Harkness support that the Joffrey troupe has zoomed from sound but modest beginnings to a company which has earned international renown and has already served the United States brilliantly through unprecedented successes in last year's tour of the Orient under the auspices of our State Department but with essential Harkness backing.

But the foundations, the ballet guilds, the patrons and the patronesses cannot possibly support all that is worth nurturing on the American dance

449

scene. Only government funds can keep up with the artistic dance boom which has made us the liveliest, most versatile and most creative dance nation of today. Our vast dance talents have helped to usher in a Golden Age of Dancing, but the gold to pay for it is fast disappearing. [*New York Herald Tribune*]

1964

Ford Blows Up a Storm

Ford Foundation's multi-million dollar grant to Balanchine and affiliated companies creates stormy controversy • The Pas de Deux analyzed • NYCB's no-star policy versus the public • Gower Champion's success with Hello, Dolly! • African dance at the New York World's Fair • TV turns to ballet • American Dance Theatre, the first modern dance repertory company, debuts at the New York State Theatre

Ford Blows Up a Storm
January 12, 1964

The cries of protest and of anger which were raised a month ago when the Ford Foundation announced its $7,756,000 program "to strengthen professional ballet in the United States" are still with us, not only echoing loudly but mounting in resentment. The cause of it all is that the largest grant ever to be given to a single art form in this country has been allocated, in the main, to an exclusive few. All forms of dance—other than ballet, have been ignored, thus excluding such an imposing dance figure as Martha Graham, as well as the major male modern dancer–choreographer, José Limón; two of the founders of contemporary American dance, the near-legendary Ruth St. Denis and her long-time husband and partner in Denishawn, Ted Shawn, who has done and is doing a superb job of fostering the art of dance in all its aspects on his Jacob's Pillow Dance Festival and at its school.

These modern dance leaders and their associates have been dismissed by the Ford Foundation, although all are in need of subsidy to varying degrees. But what is equally infuriating to many is that even within the framework of ballet itself, only a single balletic line has been granted recognition. Not only will more than $4,000,000 of the grant go to the New York City Ballet and the School of American Ballet, both headed by George Balanchine and Lincoln Kirstein, but the remainder will go to ballet schools and companies linked in various ways with Balanchine.

451

The Ford program is, indeed, almost a bequest to one artistic family, including close relatives and the equivalent of a cousin or two.

The San Francisco Ballet, for example, which has been granted $644,000, is headed by Lew Christensen, who was a dancer in earlier Balanchine companies for many years and whose own company has had an exchange program of ballets with the New York City Ballet. Another Christensen, William (a brother), heads the Utah Ballet, which is to receive $175,000. With respect to the other recipients (the Pennsylvania Ballet, the National Ballet, the Houston Ballet and the Boston Ballet), Mr. Balanchine is either an artistic advisor, or the company is headed by a former Balanchine pupil or dancer, or, in some cases, both.

Beneath this surface, there are some real shockers. For example, the Pennsylvania Ballet, headed by Barbara Weisberger, was given $295,000 just five months after its first performance (true, Mrs. Weisberger had worked with a semi-professional group in Wilkes-Barre earlier), while the internationally famous American Ballet Theatre was awarded not one cent!

The blame for this shockingly one-sided grant lies not with Mr. Balanchine, one of the great ballet figures of our age, nor with Mr. Kirstein, who has served ballet with tirelessness and taste for many years. They have their splendid dreams and they apparently asked the Ford Foundation to help bring them into being. The idiocy of the situation lies with the Ford Foundation itself which, in the dramatic words of an angry Ted Shawn, allowed the "true American dance to be crucified on a cross of Ford Foundation gold!"

Mr. Shawn's statement, because of its dramatic imagery, may seem to be an exaggeration, but there is no exaggerating the naivete of the Ford Foundation's Humanities and Arts division, headed by W. McNeil Lowry. Mr. Lowry himself acknowledged that the Ford Foundation had no permanent dance advisor or advisors, but said that various teachers and ballet figures across the country had been consulted in general about the project. Yet Jerome Robbins, a close associate of Balanchine, was not consulted, although he reports he would have approved of any grant to Balanchine; Graham, St. Denis, Shawn, Agnes de Mille and other major dance leaders were ignored.

Only absurd naivete would have led Mr. Lowry, who admits he is a dance layman though an ardent supporter of ballet, to believe for even a fraction of a second that the grant allocated by the Ford Foundation to ballet would go unquestioned. Who misled him into believing that the whole dance community in America would cheer? Cheer the recognition of ballet every one has, but the cheers would have been far louder if the grant had, in the words of Martha Graham, been "inclusive" instead of "exclusive."

And it would have been so easy. If the Ford Foundation, without permanent dance advisors, had arrived at the conclusion that Balanchine was the alpha and omega of American dance, which this soft-spoken, modest-toned dance master would surely be the first to disclaim, it could have carried out the project shrewdly by giving a small sop to the American Ballet Theatre, to modern dance leaders and to other qualified dance figures in all techniques. There would have been grumbles, of course, but not the sense of outrage that the arrant disregard for non-Balanchine-oriented ballet has engendered. As it is, the battle lines are drawn, the fight is on and the Ford Foundation is going to have an impossible time getting itself off an esthetic hook.

Mr. Lowry says that the present ballet program does not mean that, in the future, modern dance will be ignored. But he also admits that the multi-million-dollar grant represented the Ford Foundation's long-range contribution to dance. All subsequent projects in dance, he has said, would be of short range. A belated grant to Graham, to Jacob's Pillow, to Limón, to the American Ballet Theatre or to other worthy individuals or institutions will not get the Ford Foundation a full pardon. Its Humanities and Arts division is giving away millions of dollars with a total disregard for the American dance landscape and its needs.

But enough of this aspect of dance ignorance. Another is that a great amount of money is going for scholarships, faculty increases and the like with respect to ballet instruction. That the favored institution is the School of American Ballet in New York City (which the Ford Foundation's official announcement on the grant views as ultimately becoming "a national institution") is but part of the problem. Once an increasing number of ballet pupils are given financial aid for the furtherance of their studies, where are they finally going to earn salaries for their livelihood once their scholarship days are over?

It is apparent that the Ford Foundation has not taken into consideration the fact that there are more good ballet dancers than there are ballet jobs. It is true, of course, that the grant will enable some of the regional groups to increase both personnel and length of performing seasons but this increase by no means parallels the number of new dancers being trained for no purpose but to glut the ballet market. One of the bitter commentaries on the financial conditions of dance in this country, where we have no governmental subsidy for dance activities at home, is that many dancers earn their livings by teaching a new generation how not to earn a living. The Ford Foundation has not helped this state of affairs at all.

Let it be said, in conclusion, that there is absolutely no question that Mr. Balanchine and Mr. Kirstein and their immediate enterprises should have received attention, maybe major attention from the Ford Foundation's program. But that they should have received more than half of the grant for their own uses and that the rest should go to those linked with them, while other major dance efforts were wholly ignored, cannot be explained away by innocence alone.

The grant represents flagrant favoritism, even if born of ignorance (as distinct from innocence). It is nothing short of a scandal that a major foundation has contributed to the potential creation of what Martha Hill, one of the nation's most experienced and respected dance educators, has referred to as "an unhealthy monopoly." [*New York Herald Tribune*]

The Imperishable Pas de Deux

January 19, 1964

What the aria is to grand opera, the pas de deux is to ballet. Just as the opera buff, although he may relish every note of an opera, cherishes especially the Mad Scenes, the Bell Songs, the "Sempre liberas," the "Habaneras" or the "Vesti la giubbas," so does the balletomane eagerly await the glittering Grand Pas de Deux (Black Swan) in Act III of *Swan Lake*, the tender adagio in Act II of the same ballet, the Bluebird duet or the dazzling pas de deux for Princess Aurora and her Prince Charming in *The Sleeping Beauty* or even in such a modern work as George Balanchine's *Apollo,* the pas de deux for the young god and Terpsichore.

These duets in dance, and others like them, may be performed successfully out of context as independent dance creations, just as arias find their happy ways into solo recitals by singers. In both instances, the glamorous extracts are invariably more popular than other numbers, perhaps more profound of dance or of song.

In a program of short (or one-act) ballets, which are usually four in number and which frequently include a pas de deux, it is invariably the old pas de deux war horse or the virtuosic new duet (such as Balanchine's *Sylvia* or his Tchaikovsky *Pas de Deux*) which evokes storms of applause. Esthetic niceties simply have to go by the boards when a first-rank ballerina and her danseur turn on the old razzle-dazzle in, say, *Black Swan*, with its aristocratic contests of physical endurance (32 fouettes, multiple pirouettes, turns in air, breath-taking balances, leaps into space, high lifts and daring catches).

The pas de deux, then, is obviously inescapable and very probably—unless one is a terrible snob—quite desirable. For the special characteristic of the pas de deux is that it packs the highlights of ballet virtuosity, the element of romance, the glamor of personality (and the protagonists of a classical pas de deux had better forget it if they lack glamor and dash), contrasts in speeds of sound and action, and other exciting ingredients—into what emerges as a ballet in capsule form, running anywhere from five to ten minutes.

454

When a grand pas de deux is performed outside the context of the ballet for which it was originally created, it inevitably changes. The Black Swan, for example, exists for dramatic reasons and actually serves the progress of the plot in *Swan Lake*. When done as an independent duet, its dramatic purpose disappears completely, even though an echo of the dramatic may remain. Basically, however, it and other classical pas de deux when extracted from their mother ballets become brilliant examples of physical prowess and balletic style.

The music for the old-time pas de deux need not be first-class by the standards of a musician. Indeed, it is usually better if the music does not intrude an excellence of its own. It's there solely for support of dancing. So it is that the Grand Pas de Deux from *Don Quixote*, with its music by Minkus (who has a record library of gems from Minkus?), is a perennial favorite, partly because the dancers couldn't go off-beat to the music if they tried and also because the Minkus beat and airs give zestful, flashy, dependable support to the performers. In a case such as this, Minkus is far better than Bartók.

The need for the independent pas de deux, with respect to both the desires of the public and the arranging of a balanced program, has often exceeded the supply. Most ballet troupes (not all), both native and foreign, return again and again to *Black Swan, Don Quixote, Nutcracker* (the three most popular ones) and a few others. For us, the recent introduction of the dazzling *Corsair* pas de deux from the Soviet Union and the bubbling *Flower Festival in Genzano* duet from Denmark has witnessed a welcome addition to the pas de deux fare for both stage and television.

The most prolific creator of new pas de deux is, of course, George Balanchine. In recent years, he has done several notable ones—the *Sylvia* and the Tchaikovsky *Pas de Deux* are already near-classics—and it is interesting to note that during the current eight-week season (ending next Sunday) of the New York City Ballet at the City Center, the only new works were two pas de deux by Balanchine and the only revival, *Waltz Scherzo,* also a duet and also by Mr. B.

But Balanchine is not interested in making replacements for the venerable pas de deux born in other eras. He is interested, obviously, in the challenges of the duet and in its potential range.

So it is that his two latest pas de deux, *Meditation* (to music of Tchaikovsky) and *Tarantella* (to music of Louis Gottschalk as reconstructed and orchestrated by Hershy Kay), are in marked contrast, each to the other. Both are superb examples of the choreographic art, both require a cast of only two, yet the two are poles apart with respect to mood, color, flavor, and emotional content, while retaining firm balletic bases.

Meditation represents a surprising new side of Balanchine in the pas de deux idiom. It is not one of his marvelously bright and cool and brilliantly

455

paced creations; rather is it a haunting poem in movement, a dance which finds its power not in feats of muscular skill but in the deep, dark mood of romance which it conveys. As danced by Jacques d'Amboise and Suzanne Farrell, *Meditation* seems to be a distillation of all of literature's young lovers, ardent but ill-starred. A lovely, lovely pas de deux.

Tarantella, as danced by Edward Villella and Patricia McBride, is just the opposite. Its Neapolitan-colored steps are conceived with stunning virtuosity, and if its speed is that of the jet age, its exuberant quality is that of the sturdy and tireless lad and his lass dancing to their hearts' content in a village festival.

If opera has needed more contemporary composers capable of writing independent arias (or excerptable ones) for singing stars, the dance world has needed choreographers to create pas de deux which would relieve the strain on the oft-performed chestnuts, beloved as they are. In this area alone, Balanchine has done a great service to ballet and to the public. He once said that the activities of a ballerina in a show-piece pas de deux were not too distantly related to the vocal displays of a coloratura.

He further suggested that a coloratura trilling like a bird was at once both a little foolish and quite marvelous. Perhaps he feels the same about the antics in a bravura pas de deux. But whatever his exact opinions, he has enlarged the horizon of the pas de deux form, invested it with new vigor and imagination and provided the pas de deux-oriented public with up-to-date companion pieces for the indestructible Black Swans, White Swans, Bluebirds and other still adored balletic fauna from the last century. [*New York Herald Tribune*]

New York City Ballet vs. the Public

January 26, 1964

Reason for praise and cause for complaint are both pertinent to the New York City Ballet's 35th and final (for two years, at least) engagement, which ends today in its long-time home theater, the City Center. In the spring, the company, headed by Lincoln Kirstein as general director and George Balanchine as artistic director and chief choreographer, becomes the resident ballet at the new New York State Theater in Lincoln Center. There, it will perform 20 weeks each year on the basis of a two-year agreement.

Praise is in order on many scores for the season now ending. The New York City Ballet, as one of the world's great companies, has been performing

456

superbly for the most part. There have been a few under-rehearsed ballets and some "off" nights. But such times were rare during an eight-week stand which witnessed the predominantly Balanchine repertory unfolded with cleanness of line, stylishness and technical brilliance.

One of the special virtues of Balanchine's artistic direction is that he provides challenging performing opportunities to the junior dancers as they move up through the ranks. All of us have watched with delight the progress of long-limbed Patricia Neary, who has a remarkable technique and a highly personal style; Suzanne Farrell, small, fair, wistful; the bounding, bright-visaged, zestful Gloria Govrin (she and Miss Neary, both tall, are marvelous to behold when their assignments call for them to move side by side) or Patricia McBride, adding still further laurels to her already considerable accomplishments as a dancer with a poetic-dramatic flair.

In the contingent of young men dancers, one might take note of Anthony Blum, for although he is by no means a newcomer to the company, in the last year he has made greater strides than before in his career. He has even progressed to the point that he is often cast as Maria Tallchief's partner.

As for Miss Tallchief, she and the other senior ballerinas—Melissa Hayden, Violette Verdy, Patricia Wilde—have been performing as none of the youngsters can hope to perform (for a while, yet), thus making it quite clear that stars such as themselves, or, in the male wing, Erik Bruhn, Jacques d'Amboise, Edward Villella, constitute a very special breed which brings tremendous prestige to a company which fights for starlessness.

And now we come to the cause for complaint. Mr. Balanchine and Mr. Kirstein long since instituted the no-star system. The New York City Ballet has principal dancers, soloists and ensemble dancers. No one is named prima ballerina or ballerina or premier danseur. Neither artistic priority nor seniority prevails in matters of billing. All listings are done alphabetically. When the alphabet first became the yardstick, the leading dancers were understandably irritated (some left the company) and some balletomanes were infuriated. But the management was adamant and the public and the dancers had to accept the new ruling.

Still, the popular interest in stars was not stilled and audiences could find when their favorites were performing by consulting the weekly program listings (including casting highlights) in their newspapers. Now even that has changed and the management of the company has stated that no casting details for a given program will be announced until the day of the performance itself.

The reason given for this is that unanticipated injuries, which plague all dance companies, cause last-minute shifts in cast and, sometimes, even in program. Betty Cage, general manager of the New York City Ballet, said with sad wryness, "It would be easier for us to list who is *not* dancing than who is." This because of a series of dancer-indispositions which had beset the company.

Injuries, of course, do affect the presentation of a program. The substitutes may be not as good as those originally scheduled or they might even be better but this does not solve the problem of those who attend the ballet in order to see it through the interpretations of their favorite dancers.

A further deterioration in the relationship between the New York City Ballet management and the public has occurred during the last two City Center engagements. This has taken the form of inadequate announcements for apprising the assembled audience what changes in cast or program have been made. Sometimes no announcements are made at all and newcomers to the ballet, looking at their printed programs but seeing something else, could well be confused about who was doing what in which.

The management's lack of concern for the public which supports it and which, presumably, it is in existence to serve, actually works hardships on many devoted New York City Ballet followers whose funds are limited. Letters come to this desk complaining bitterly that hard-earned money has been spent to see a specific program or a particular artist or both and that a last-minute change has caused the ticket-buyer to see ballets he has seen before (and maybe doesn't want to see again) and dancers who are not the ones of his choice. Out-of-towners are particularly angry at such changes.

The very least that the New York City Ballet could do would be to report last-minute changes on cards in the lobby and from the stage. Anything less seems to me to indicate an attitude contemptuous of the tastes of the public. The alphabet listings have long made it clear that those who head the New York City Ballet feel that the public should attend the ballet without concern for the individuals who are performing. Perhaps this is, esthetically, an ideal goal, but the average person is interested in and attracted by performing personalities and no alphabet in the world is going to change them.

During the Christmas holidays, it was almost impossible to find out when Tallchief and Bruhn were dancing together. Yet is there any one who cares about ballet who would not prefer to see these two great dancers together than two lesser performers? Or maybe one need not even use a yardstick of artistic comparison and simply say that Tallchief is better known nationally and internationally than any other ballerina in the company and that the public is curious to see her. This may come as a terrible shock to the New York City Ballet direction, but it is the public's right to come to see Tallchief and not to see a Balanchine ballet.

The New York City Ballet is different from all other companies in many ways in its repertory, its special style, its Balanchine imprint and in other matters—but its duties are not different from those of other companies. If the American Ballet Theatre, Britain's Royal Ballet and, when they visit this country, the Soviet state ballets can list programs and casts, so can the New York City Ballet.

Perhaps the direction of the New York City Ballet does not care that it is losing the faithful support of balletomanes both here and out of town. Perhaps they feel that Hayden fans or Villella fans should be converted into balletgoers willing to take anything and any one provided on stage.

Well, the company's management is now in a position to ignore complaints with even greater hauteur than before. For this is the company which will move into Lincoln Center at a period paralleling that of the New York World's Fair and this is the company which has just been granted $2,000,000 from the Ford Foundation. [*New York Herald Tribune*]

Broadway Choreographer

March 1, 1964

Hello, Dolly!, the musical comedy at the St. James, gives scrupulously equal billing to two individuals. Carol Channing, of course, is the Dolly of the title and she is both funny and irresistible. Gower Champion, the second individual, never appears on stage, but a great deal that is funny and irresistible is due to his combined talents as a director and choreographer.

To star a choreographer in the credits of a musical is a true sign of our times. At the turn of the century, when Ruth St. Denis introduced to New York City a new concept of the art of dance, the word "choreography" was not used. "I didn't even know what it meant—if I had ever heard it—because I simply 'made' dances," she says today. Decades later, when George Balanchine staged the dances for *On Your Toes* and Agnes de Mille revolutionized the musical comedy theater with her dances for *Oklahoma!*, the words "choreography" and "choreographer" became standard, not esoteric, descriptions of a theatrical function and its executant.

The next step was for the choreographer to prove his mettle as a director, to bring his knowledge and imagination to bear upon the linking of dance action with non-dance action in a musical show. Of these choreographers–directors, Gower Champion is one of the greatest, although he says with disarming candor, speaking of Jerome Robbins, that "Jerry is the best."

Direction and choreography. What is the line which separates them? What is the process which links them? "The choreographer," says Mr. Champion, "is more dictatorial than the director. The very nature of his work requires him to tell dancers exactly what to do. Yes, you *tell* the dancer. As a

459

director, you *point* the actor in a direction and let him carry it from there and if it doesn't work, you start again or revise or adapt.

"The choreographer requires that his dancers be expressive in dance terms while the director, in working with actors, tries to elicit the inner feelings of a character through both speech and gesture. The middle ground—not the dividing line—between choreography and direction is what I call staging. This is what links dancing and acting and I think that the choreographer, in the role of director, can bring something special to the business of staging."

If *Hello, Dolly!* offered its director–choreographer many marvelous opportunities, it also presented some problems. "On the road, Act II with the Waiters' Gallop and the "Hello, Dolly!" were stylistically right and at the same time brought a sort of harum-scarum life to the show. Act I, by contrast, turned out to be too placid and it had to be reworked so that we could give it the same vitality that the other act had.

"We found too that David Burns was bringing a wonderful quality—the funniness of a W. C. Fields acting like a curmudgeon—to his role. So we dropped certain songs originally planned for this character in order to channel David's special talents into the show, to utilize his great gifts and to exploit his way of building wonderful comedy out of expressions of anger and exasperation."

Mr. Champion, as choreographer–director–stager, spoke of the show's star: "Carol and I worked closely and for a long time. We worked on her performing style in terms of both character and period—for example, Dolly had to have a 'pulled-up' look which is totally foreign to Carol, but it was necessary and she got it. Then, I set the numbers for Carol. After each one was set, I'd turn her over to Marge, who would rehearse her and work on the details. I called Marge the 'woodshed coach.'" The "Marge" of whom Mr. Champion speaks is, of course, his wife and longtime dance partner, although Marge Champion has retired from public performing in order to spend more time with the Champion family.

How did Mr. Champion, briefly resting on the stack of laurels he has just earned for his work with one of the best musicals in many years, feel about the stature of musical comedy dancing as compared with that of the dance theater itself? "I think it's equal but different. For musicals, the choreography has to be simpler, more direct. For pure dance, it should be more complex and it should explore.

"But I guess I don't think of myself as a true choreographer. I'm a musical comedy dancer and choreographer and the musical is my field. I create especially for the musical theater and I couldn't cross over to the City Center and do a ballet like Jerry can. I wish I could—Hanya (Holm), Helen (Tamiris), Jerry (Robbins) and some other choreographers can move back and forth between musicals and dance theater—but I can't. My talents lie elsewhere. I suppose you could say that they lie not in pure dance but purely in musicals."

Mr. Champion is by no means alone in his specialization. True, Robbins, Holm, Tamiris, Balanchine, de Mille, Saddler and Ross (though not lately for Mr. Ross), are among those choreographers who are just as at home with ballets or modern dance works as they are with musicals, but choreographers such as Kidd (once closely associated with ballet), Fosse, Gennaro, Layton, Haney, Krupska (who has also done ballets), Mattox, Cole and a few others are almost exclusively associated with musicals or some form of show business. Indeed, Mr. Champion reserves special admiration for the work of the late Robert Alton, who introduced a fresh choreographic concept into the musical theater many years ago.

And there will have to be a continuing search for new approaches to musical comedy dancing, Mr. Champion believes. "I think modern jazz has about had it. Besides, where is there to go in this direction after *West Side Story*? And I think ballet, as ballet, has had it too in the musical field. *Dolly*, because of its period, harked back to an archaic style, to rhythms and movements suitable to that period."

Where will the new influences come from? "Curiously enough," says Mr. Champion, "they could evolve from something as seemingly simple as the Twist. I don't mean that every one will start doing the Twist on stage but what I mean is that in that popular dance and those related to it, new materials are present. From this source, something may come which would possibly jell into a new musical comedy dance style. I don't know yet just what it is but I feel that it's there and I know that we must find a new way to go."

The future of the director–choreographer lies not only in the musical comedy field. "There is a place," says Mr. Champion, "for the choreographic touch in plays too. Of course you've got to forget—or push aside—a lot of dance habits. You can't ask actors to move on such-and-such a beat. But I do believe that the choreographer can contribute, as a director, a good deal to a play, especially if it is a heightened or exaggerated kind of theater. The farce comes immediately to mind and, naturally, any form of fantasy."

At the moment, however, Gower Champion is doing little more than musing. "Here we've been talking about new forms and styles for musical comedy dancing and new choreographic touches for the theater and when you ask me what I'm doing, I have to come up with the oldest cliché in the business—'I'm reading scripts'—but that's it. That and that Marge and I are excited about living in New York again after all this time. And there is one other thing too. We both keep in dance shape but since we've been here, we have procrastinated about going back to class and exercising regularly. We're resting a bit after *Dolly* but we'll get started any day now."

What kind of dance classes will Marge and Gower look for? Says the director–choreographer, "easy modern jazz." And it seemed to me, listening to him, that there was an ever-so-slight accent on the word "easy." But with *Hello, Dolly!*, he's earned it. [*New York Herald Tribune*]

461

From Africa to the Fair

March 29, 1964

Auditions are held under all manner of conditions, many of them exceedingly trying, but Ralph Beaumont must surely have established a new record for an auditioning choreographer by having to conduct auditions in the midst of political unrest, wars and threats of massacre. Mr. Beaumont has recently returned from a five-week journey, from east to west, through Africa. The African Pavilion, representing 24 African nations, had engaged him to audition and select African dancers and dance groups to appear daily at the New York World's Fair, beginning April 22.

Mr. Beaumont was picked for the job not only because of his experiences as a choreographer of musical shows, television and industrials, but also because he is thoroughly trained in primitive dance and is a product of Katherine Dunham's teaching.

Mr. Beaumont's first exposure to African and Afro-American dance came in San Francisco, where, following an Army hitch, he was enrolled in college. Miss Dunham and her company were performing and young Ralph attended 14 performances. He went backstage at the close of the run and said to Miss Dunham, "Where can I learn to dance like this?" The reply: "In New York." Four days later, Ralph had quit college and was on his way to New York, where, under the GI Bill, he entered the Dunham School and threw himself into a training schedule that called for 25 classes a week.

With this Dunham schooling and his years of theatrical experience, Mr. Beaumont set forth on his first African adventure early this year. "Yes, there were times when I was frightened," he reports. "Once, because of bad communications, the advance party I was supposed to meet didn't find me for five days. I was all alone in a strange land and it all felt like a nightmare involving Stanley and Livingston.

"It was inevitable that I should occasionally be exposed to violence because in certain countries there was political unrest and tribal conflict. At certain borders or customs, I was not made to feel welcome, but once I reached the dancers, there was marvelous rapport. The auditions of the African dance groups had been expertly organized by the American embassies and by the cultural departments of the U. S. and the African governments.

"I found great variety in both movement and costume as I went from country to country. For example, in one area, I was surprised to find that the women—absolutely beautiful women, they were—dance more vigorously than the men. This is unusual, for the African women, like American Indian women, customarily take a back seat in dancing, allowing the men to display prowess while they clap and sing and sometimes shuffle.

"In another country, the dances were amazingly Oriental in gesture and in costume. I could have sworn that I was in Thailand.

"But although there is tremendous variety in African dance from country to country and region to region, there is one wonderful unifying characteristic. It is that African dance movement seems almost impossible to teach to outsiders—it has to be passed down, it is 'built in,' perhaps. The Africans truly communicate through dance.

"In their dances they tell of a hunt or of a hero, they tell a story or a history. I noticed too that the climate tends to destroy painting and statuary—they just don't last. So it seems to me that to the African, his dancing displays his present prowess and his dances contain his past."

Mr. Beaumont, who plans to make three more scouting-auditioning trips to Africa (he could not visit all 24 countries on the first journey), notes that the African Pavilion felt that importing various forms of African dance was essential to authenticity. The dancers will perform out-of-doors on a stage area of packed dirt in a setting suggesting an African village compound which would include a lake area, tree houses, birds and animals.

Three or four African dance groups of contrasting styles, numbering about 50 dancers and drummers in total, will perform daily for 20 minutes out of every hour. Divided up, this would call for one group to dance for only five minutes out of each hour. After a certain period of time, these particular groups will return to their homes in Africa (although there may be holdovers occasionally) to be replaced by other dancers from other countries. This relay pattern will prevail from the opening date next month through Oct. 22 and for the equivalent period of six months in 1965.

In auditioning the various African groups, Mr. Beaumont found the dancers not only warm, friendly and artistically devoted, but also enthusiastic about performing at the World's Fair. There was, he reports, one amusing delay in an audition. At one place, the drummers simply mimed their rhythms soundlessly. The visitors didn't know why. Then, a paper was delivered to the lead drummer and the sounds began to burst forth. The paper had contained permission from the king for them to play—they were royal drummers and played only upon royal command.

Would the giant Watusi, famous for their dancing, be present at the fair? Mr. Beaumont expressed the hope that they would be included in a later edition. Explanation of their absence comes from Geoffrey Taylor, a newspaper man who, by accident of travel, journeyed briefly with Mr. Beaumont's party in Africa. Mr. Taylor, writing in the British *The Guardian,* stated that one of new Africa's problems of self-government included the preventing of "a recurrence of the panic which led to the massacres of Watusi." It has been estimated that some 25,000 Watusi have been slaughtered by tribal enemies and that survivors have found refuge in Red Cross camps.

Mr. Beaumont, then, was called upon to conduct auditions in lands in which upheaval was sometimes in effect or was imminent. As Mr. Taylor wrote: "In the Congo, one cannot name a tribal, political, or economic problem which is not acutely obvious to even the most casual observer." And later, "However much we are worried by Africa, Africans of experience and ability are worried much more."

Despite problems and perils, Mr. Beaumont in his first auditioning job away from New York, London, Rome or Hollywood, responded enthusiastically to his assignment for the African Pavilion. He can't wait to get back to Africa and to see more of the vast dance wealth of the 24 nations. [*New York Herald Tribune*]

When Television Turns to Ballet

April 12, 1964

Television, as far as dance is concerned, can be alternately lauded and lambasted. When it employs choreography as mobile decor for a singer, it usually does the job agreeably, for its aim is not set too high—the esthetic level is simply that on which aural interest in a star is matched, or at least supplemented, by rhythmic action of some kind.

Too often, because of the similarity of musical numbers from show to show, a given choreographer will find a helpful formula and the constant viewer gets to the point where he can predict "here comes that step again!" There are exceptions, of course. Over the years, Tony Charmoli, one of the top choreographers for the top variety shows on TV, has consistently maintained a top level of achievement in terms of choreographic inventiveness, vitality and pertinence to the musical number involved, relating them to the gifts and limitations of the singing star who must be served.

But there is a great deal more than dance decorations to be found in TV. Networks and programs (even some which are commercially backed) have actually commissioned important choreographies. John Butler, for example, who is kept thoroughly busy year after year "staging numbers" for TV's revue-type shows, has had many opportunities to create and produce dance works of stature, avant garde and even experimental, for television.

Other choreographers have been given similar opportunities to bring both a creative and adventuresome spirit into TV dance. Among these, one might note that Alwin Nikolais' avant-garde works for the stage have been successfully adapted to the TV screen; that Donald Saddler, for a "Bell Telephone

Hour," was not only engaged to choreograph a new ballet on the Romeo and Juliet theme but was permitted to have the human voice (that of Sir John Gielgud), reading poetry of Shakespeare, serve as the accompaniment for a pas de deux.

CBS' Repertoire Workshop commissioned Norman Walker to create its very first presentation, a modern dance work called *Reflections,* which subsequently made a successful transition—the reverse of the usual order—from TV to the stage.

Naturally, TV is interested not only in entertaining and, sometimes, in stimulating dances for its popular screen but also in dancers, especially star dancers. So it was that American television could boast that it presided over the American debut of one of the most electrifying dancers of our time, Rudolf Nureyev.

Nureyev, since that historic occasion more than two years ago, has not only performed "live" in this country but has returned again and again to dance various pas de deux on "Bell Telephone Hour," a program which deserves the highest praise for its continuous concern in presenting its public with many of the most glittering ballet artists—Maria Tallchief, Eric Bruhn, Edward Villella, Dame Margot Fonteyn, Sonia Arova and many others—of our time.

Praise for the intent and for the act is one thing; methods of presentation are quite another. Returning to Nureyev, for example, it can be said that certain of his TV appearances have captured the dazzle of technique and the vivid personality one finds when seeing him in the theater. But more do not. The reason? Camera work which fails to compensate for losses sustained when transferring the dance and the dancer from stage to screen.

To begin with, the physical stature of the performer is drastically reduced for the TV screen and if the camera never moves in close to the dancer, all one ever sees is a tiny figure, with indistinguishable features, making miniature movements in the distance. The camera, however, is mobile, which a seated audience is not, and through this magic it can move right into the center of interest.

By this, I do not mean that the dance and the dancer should be chopped up. But there are always pauses and poses in ballet. Let us see—and more than once—Nureyev's face, for the face dances—its movements mirror what the dancer himself feels about what he is dancing. In the drama of the dancer's face one may see passion or compassion, animal alertness or moodiness or any of a number of emotions pertinent to the dance he is performing.

And the closeup need not always be concerned with a face. Sometimes a body, poised for flight or merely at dance rest, remains immobile while port de bras, the movement of the arms, becomes for that moment dance itself.

How can one ever forget—certainly I never shall—that superb moment in the televised version of the Royal Ballet's *Cinderella* in which the camera focused upon Dame Margot's feet as she sped forward, executing the most perfect bourrees on pointe, right into the eye of the camera and into our own centers of motor response to the miracle of dance.

Usually, three or four cameras are involved in filming a TV dance but unless transitions are controlled by a director who knows something about dancing, these can chop up the dance. When Dame Margot, with Michael Somes, danced an excerpt from *Firebird* on TV, only a single camera was used. This, when well handled, can be an advantage, for the camera, then, almost dances with the dancer.

There is still another problem which television doesn't always solve when its performers are dancers. Nureyev is famed for his spectacular elevation. This doesn't always show on the TV screen. We need to see some subtle suggestion of a hurdle—a baseboard or a ledge or the like—so that when Nureyev takes off, we literally have a frame of reference in space.

The ballerina's most famous tours de force are multiple fouettes, those whipping turns on one leg, as the dancer rises from flat to pointe and back again, which are especially celebrated in the *Black Swan* pas de deux from *Swan Lake*. But the key to their excitement is balance and the key to that balance is the dancer's control of full body weight sustained (and perilously) by a tiny toe tip. The TV screen cannot reflect this sense of weight—most of the time we see not only miniature figures but also silhouettes—but it can compensate for this by moving in, as it did with the Fonteyn bourrées, for a close view of the centrifugal force which keeps the spins going.

Actually, some of the best camera work for dance has been found in shows with modest budgets, particularly those in which choreographic experimentation has been invited. Here, choreographer and director work closely. On some of the big shows this also occurs but one cannot help noticing the sliding scale of film standards which prevail.

For example, with Nureyev's several appearances on the "Bell Telephone Hour" the sliding scale has prevailed. In a few, his art was stunningly projected; in others, it was only fitfully revealed. Now this, of course, can be avoided. If you are going to present a great dancer, use every bit of power the TV camera possesses to exploit that dancer's talent to the fullest.

One can offer nothing but heartfelt thanks and, when deserved, deep praise to Bell Telephone for its showing of ballet. But one can ask for even more from this and other programs: when transplanting dance from stage to screen, let the directors take cognizance of the limitations and the potentialities of the TV medium and make their adjustments accordingly. If one aspect of the magic of dance must be lost in transition, replace it with another bit of magic, TV magic. It's there to be used. [*New York Herald Tribune*]

A Company of Moderns

December 6, 1964

"I guess you might say that my job is to lose money wisely," said John Hightower, the young executive director of the New York State Council on the Arts. "And I think we were wise in our support of the new American Dance Theater. As a matter of fact, we didn't lose as much money as we had planned."

The American Dance Theater, which made its bow with two performances, Nov. 18 and 19, at Lincoln Center's New York State Theater, represents an initial endeavor to establish a permanent modern dance repertory company. Thirty years ago, leading modern dancers, galvanized by Helen Tamiris, brought their companies together for repertory performances. But over the years, the companies have remained independent and, except for occasional festival appearances, each of the moderns has gone his own way.

Thus, we have had Martha Graham and her company (the most determined lone wolf of all), José Limón and his company, and so on along the line. The American Dance Theater broke precedent in that its first performances were not given by a temporary aggregation of dance groups but by a new assembly of modern dancers, selected by audition, engaged to dance in creations by the late Doris Humphrey (whose dream it was to establish just such a repertory company), Limón, Anna Sokolow and Donald McKayle, all first-rank modern dance choreographers.

Was this first try by the new American Dance Theater a success? Mr. Hightower noted that the Council did not lose as much as anticipated. The budget had allowed for an expenditure of $35,000—a modest sum considering that a new company had to be brought into being and rehearsed for four weeks; that a new work had to be mounted, and that the operating costs of the New York State Theater are far from low—but such was the popular response to the new enterprise that every seat in the big house was sold for both performances and some had to be turned away at the box office. The Council's costs dropped to $20,000.

In a very real sense, the American Dance Theater owes its launching to the New York State Council on the Arts, but now it must steer its own course. "We would like to see the American Dance Theater become a going concern, a legal entity on its own," said Mr. Hightower. "Then, the Council would consider providing contributory financial support, when appropriate, as it does to other established art institutions."

In the hope that the two performances in New York would attract other support for the American Dance Theater, a letter addressed to modern dance choreographers and signed by Mr. Hightower, José Limón (the artistic director

467

of the first presentations of the new group) and Roger Englander (the producer), told the choreographers that this was their company and that their participation was solicited.

What the Council hopes is that a new non-profit organization, with an energetic board of directors knowledgeable in the ways of fund-raising, can be established in order to give permanence to the American Dance Theater. The two performances were arranged and supported for just this purpose. But were they good enough to warrant continuation of a project which would give performing permanence to masterworks from the past in modern dance and new creations? The answer is "Yes," but with qualifications.

The new piece, *Workout*, by Donald McKayle, was a bomb, a bad echo of Jerome Robbins' *Interplay* and filled with low-grade balleticisms having no place in modern dance. Mr. McKayle is, of course, one of the major figures in today's dance—he's a Capezio Dance Award winner and choreographer of the musical *Golden Boy*—but *Workout* was a miss (even Balanchine and Graham have them).

The established pieces on the first program of the American Dance Theater naturally fared much better. Miss Humphrey's *Lament for Ignacio Sanchez Mejias,* with its cast composed of Louis Falco, Letitia Ide (the most beautiful grandmother in the dance world) and Patricia Hammack in itself symbolized the wisdom of establishing a repertory company for the presentation of American modern dance. Here were movement and drama and poetry and color and passions; here was dance theater.

Anna Sokolow's *The Question* is not an easy piece but it is a challenging and disturbing one. And one of the purposes of modern dance is to challenge and to disturb, rather than to divert or simply amuse. Except for a very few pieces with a comic touch or a satiric comment, Miss Sokolow's works view humanity by a standard which makes Medea seem like Little Nell. Her *Dreams* is really a nightmare, her *Rooms* (a masterpiece of theater dance) is sinister and her *Metamorphoses* almost induces suicidal thoughts. *The Question* won't make you happy (indeed, it does go on too long) but it has power and purpose to it. Miss Sokolow is essential to the American Dance Theater.

However, I do feel that on the American Dance Theater's first program, one elaborately mounted modern dance work should have been included just by way of indicating that, physically, contemporary dance can be as eye-filling as ballet. A Graham work would have filled this need superbly. But this is not to say that *The Question* or other Sokolow works cannot serve the American Dance Theater. They can, but subsequent presentations should take into consideration that scenery and costumes—pretty or beautiful, macabre or fantastic—are desirable, too.

The closing piece on the inaugural program was Limón's tribute to Miss Humphrey, *A Choreographic Offering,* based upon themes and variations from many of her choreographic masterpieces. In size of cast alone, it served to equate modern dance with ballet and that is an important point, for in America we are all too often inclined to confuse quantity with quality—that's why we use phrases such as "50-showgirls-50" or "company of 100" (including electricians, carpenters and local wardrobe help)—and if modern dance is to establish itself in repertory forms, it's got to be big (not just good).

Where the American Dance Theater will go from here remains to be seen. The New York State Council on the Arts gave it a boost and will, undoubtedly, assist it in the future, but it must now find its own support if it is to continue. The initial program had to be predicated upon availability of choreographers and dancers and much was missing. Ideally, a Graham work, pieces and performances by Paul Taylor, Alvin Ailey, Merce Cunningham, Alwin Nikolais, Pearl Lang, Norman Walker and others would have been desirable, but these will surely come—they must—if this new modern dance enterprise is to find a deserved permanency.

How it should be organized, directed and managed, as well as supported, constitutes a problem. We are living in a ballet age. Before her death in 1958, Miss Humphrey discovered this when she and Miss Tamiris sought foundation support for a modern dance repertory venture. Fortunately, the officers of the New York State Council on the Arts have counteracted, through its support of the American Dance Theater, the esthetic naivete of those foundation officials who turned down the carefully prepared modern dance repertory project of one of the great choreographers of our age, Doris Humphrey.

And this leads us to a matter of continuity. If Tamiris, one of the founding leaders of modern dance in America, shared the work of planning a modern dance repertory project with Miss Humphrey, why should she not be asked to continue to serve in such imperative matters of organization and direction?

But although the future of the new American Dance Theater is, at present, undecided, the omens are certainly good. The New York State Council on the Arts not only lost less on its initial venture in this field than it had anticipated but felt "wise in our support." Take it from there, modern dancers!
[*New York Herald Tribune*]

1965

Teamwork: McBride & Villella, Fonteyn & Nureyev, Harkness & Money

James Waring at Judson Church • Balanchine's Harlequinade, starring Villella and McBride, a hit at NYCB • Agnes de Mille's American Heritage Dance Theatre • ABT at 25 • Merce Cunningham's strident work, Winterbranch • An analysis of the greatness of Fonteyn and Nureyev • NYCB premieres Balanchine's spectacle, Don Quixote • Rebekah Harkness and her new company • Maria Tallchief parts company with NYCB • Royal Danish Ballet returns to New York

The Avant Garde Looks Instead at the Past

February 2, 1965

The avant-garde turned nostalgic last night, particularly in a show-biz spoof, when the Judson Dance Theater presented James Waring and his company in a program made up chiefly of new numbers.

In fact, "memory" was a keynote, for the event took place in an improvised theater in the Judson Memorial Church, the opening *Three Symphonies* was dedicated to the memory of the late Fred Herko, an avant-garde dancer, and other sections were in memory of Gracie Allen and Jeannette MacDonald.

The work labeled "to Gracie Allen" was called *Musical Moments* and was, suitably a comedy. The zaniness which characterized Miss Allen's adored and enduring art was echoed here in the actions of the dancers, in their expected and unexpected responses to music or sounds or props.

Some of the comic episodes in *Musical Moments* were a trifle childish or forced and some could have been done just as easily by vaudeville comics as by dancers . . . but, in general, there was lots to laugh at.

471

I think the highpoint came when Mr. Waring and other members of the cast went wild to the "William Tell Overture." I can't describe it in detail but the performers leapt frantically, ran, marched and, as a sort of nutty leit motif, stooped down to scrub areas on the floor (in rhapsodic Rossini meter, of course).

A vamp bit, with David Vaughan and Deborah Lee, was a delight and so also was a 1920 nightclub satire with a slick, man-about-town, his empty-headed flapper friend and a girl who moaned her torch songs while sitting on the piano a la Helen Morgan. And there were other amusing items, including a ridiculous toe dance, in this suite.

After it was over, it passed my mind that, shortened, tightened and slicked up a bit, this Waring piece would be right at home in a club such as the Upstairs at the Downstairs.

I'm not certain that Mr. Waring was living up to his reputation as a choreographer of the avant-garde in this number, but who cared?—he gave us all a good time.

The opening number—which I saw sideways—was a serious, lyrical and rather tender piece (dedicated to Mr. Herko) called *Three Symphonies* and set to very interesting electronic scores by Richard Maxfield. The patterns, occasionally sculptural in effect, were attractive and a recurring movement motif was the vibrating or trembling of a foot, a leg, a hand.

I saw this first piece from the side simply because the curtain went up earlier than announced and because the only way to get to one's seat was across the stage floor itself. If the program had been based upon the choreography by chance theory, we in the wings would have felt quite free to move through the dancers while wending our way seatwards. Still, from the side, *Three Symphonies* was interesting.

After a second intermission, the program closed with further episodes in the extended *Musical Moments* parodies. [*New York Herald Tribune*]

Harlequinade—A Hit

February 5, 1965

The stolen kisses, the chases, the pratfalls and all of the amorous antics of the commedia dell'arte have been delightfully recreated in the New York City Ballet's utterly winning new ballet, *Harlequinade*, a two-act production which was given its world premiere last night at the New York State Theater.

George Balanchine, its choreographer, had been inspired by his own memories of *Les Millions d'Arlequin* and by its score by Riccardo Drigo whom Balanchine, as a child, had known in St. Petersburg.

And in his brand-new version of the story, Balanchine has done honor to his own memories, for although his remarkable choreographic invention is ever present, he has tampered in no way with the immortal and beloved figures of the flirtatious Columbine, the prancing Harlequin, the mournful Pierrot, the perky Pierrette, the bumbling Leandre and all of the other essential characters, including, of course, the Good Fairy, without whose magic Harlequin would have wooed in vain.

Dancing, rather than pantomime, is the chief ingredient, naturally, in this ballet version of commedia dell'arte, but Balanchine has used pantomime artfully and wittily, where necessary, to make the plot clear and to disclose through clowning the frailties of certain of the characters.

He has not, of course, presented all of the high jinx in pantomimic form. For example, there is a marvelous number for a night patrol in which every member is inebriated. But there are vivacious dances everywhere. In these, Balanchine has not only provided his principal dancers with sparkling actions and great bursts of virtuosity but he has also designed some ensemble dances which bubble along and even seem to chuckle muscularly.

To his delectable dances and his wonderfully integrated bits of broad pantomimic humor, Balanchine has added the use of various stage effects: Transformations, substitutions, statues which come to life and a shower of gold (the millions for Harlequin) from a cornucopia. This is indeed not only a splendid ballet but also a stunning show.

These staging effects, the scenery itself and the costumes are the work of Rouben Ter-Arutunian. The basic setting is an adaptation of his earlier designs for the New York City Opera's production of *La Cenrentola,* but he added a house to it and made still other changes. So well has he done his work as a designer, that the very spirit, the brightness as well as the tradition of commedia dell'arte are present in his production. For a moment or two, I thought I was in Copenhagen's famed Pantomime Theater in Tivoli Gardens.

The Drigo music is delicious. You'll know some of the airs and will be happy to become acquainted with others. It is sweet, lively, rollicking, noble and effervescent by turn, and, last night, Robert Irving and the orchestra made it a joy to hear.

As for the dancing, well, it was superb. Edward Villella was the bounding hero, and not only did he cut loose with some fabulous feats of skill, but he also played the role of Harlequin with a fine awareness of both the ardor and the humor inherent in the part.

He was matched by the lovely Patricia McBride who also acted as skillfully as she danced and that, I might add, is something to shout about. And there were shouts of approval in order for others in the cast, among them Suki Schorer (Pierrette), Deni Lamont (Pierrot), Gloria Govrin (the Good Fairy, who looked just a trifle like a show girl), Shaun O'Brien (Leandre), other principals and also an ensemble of talented children from the School of American Ballet.

Yes, there were shouts, loud and long, at the curtain calls as the audience welcomed the New York City Ballet's brand new smash hit to the great stage of the State Theater. [*New York Herald Tribune*]

Agnes de Mille's Repertory of Americana

March 12, 1965

The busiest choreographer in New York (and, perhaps, in America) at this very moment is Agnes de Mille. This particular lady, who is equally at home in ballet, musical comedy, movies and television (and she has had successful whirls into the recital and night club fields), is presently devoting her remarkable energies to the American Ballet Theatre. The company is celebrating its 25th birthday with a gala season at the New York State Theater, and Miss de Mille, who was active at its inception, is still one of its major figures.

She is one of 18 choreographers (ranging from the early 19th-century's Coralli, creator of *Giselle,* to today's youthful Glen Tetley) represented in the American Ballet Theatre's matchless repertory. But the de Mille responsibilities are enormous for this current season since she will be represented by four ballets (more than any one of the other choreographers) and these will be given 16 times during the 32-performance run.

Furthermore, two of the de Mille ballets are brand new—*The Wind in the Mountains* and *The Four Marys*—and one, *The Frail Quarry,* is a revival and restaging (at least half of it is wholly new choreography) of her earlier *Tally-Ho!* And the fourth is her enormously popular dance-drama of the Lizzie Borden murder case, *Fall River Legend,* but with a new leading lady in the role so long identified with the now-retired Nora Kaye.

Miss de Mille, in spite of her current pressures, is looking way beyond the American Ballet Theatre's season toward the fulfillment of a dream, the establishment of her American Heritage Theater. "It would be the American equivalent of Russia's Moiseyev," she says. "I've started work on it. I've raised some money for it. I've commissioned two scores, Laurence Rosenthal's for *The Wind in the Mountains* and Trude Rittmann's for *The Four Marys*—yes, I've done studio work on these ballets over the years.

474

"What I need to bring the American Heritage Theater into being is money. Give me a quarter of a million dollars, and then we'll talk. I want a real patron."

Miss de Mille went on to say that she is "giving those pieces of Americana suitable to a ballet company" to those troupes including the American Ballet Theatre, which are equipped to do them. But eventually, when the American Heritage Theater comes into being, these and other Americana pieces by de Mille and by other choreographers will be pooled into the repertory.

What will be the cast of this American Heritage Theater? "It will have no stars," says Miss de Mille. "It will be a people's ballet. With repertory, we'll concentrate first on our Anglo-Irish-Scottish folk heritage along with the heritage of the Negro. Later, we would expand to include the American Indian, the Hawaiian and other traditions. In fact, I want every type of native rhythm and native dancer represented."

Would the American Heritage Theater build its repertory in terms of folk chronology or geographical regions? "No," says Miss de Mille firmly. "I don't care if there are 18 New England ballets and none from Idaho! I don't mean that literally, of course. I just mean that the first concern must be authentic folk roots.

"I'm not going to tell you the details of my *Four Marys* except to say that it's interracial and that although the subject is Mary Stuart, the source is an American ballad. The *Wind* ballet is really a country calendar divided into Traveling Weather, Wind, Ice, Rain, Natural Catastrophe, All Clear and Apotheosis.

"When I do folk ballets, I don't believe in rupturing tradition but I do expand folk steps into theatrical terms. What I can't stand is to see Russian Imperial Ballet forms planted on American folk action."

For all of her ballets and for the coming American Heritage Theater, Miss de Mille requires that her dancers be accomplished actors. "Most of them don't know what acting is," she says. "I guess we don't have the pantomimists we once did. But we need them. At least I do.

"Just the other day I told a bunch of dancers—they were very correct and great at technique—that the situation called for more than steps. I said to them, 'You should sound like a bunch of young bulls bellowing after the female instead of sounding like virgin butterflies.' That got 'em! And I got what I wanted—acting."

In her American Heritage Theater, then, Miss de Mille will have actors as well as dancers, every kind of native rhythm, authentic American roots and no Russian Imperial influences, thank you! But one major influence will be inescapable. It will be Agnes de Mille's own taste and talent, drives and desires.

"The repertory of Americana pieces by myself and by other contributing choreographers will be based, as I say, not on chronology or region but upon what each creator of ballets wants to say. In my own case, I guess it boils down to what *I* am, rather than what is strictly American folk!" But it will be Americana, even if de Mille-flavored, for the creator of the dances for the history-making *Oklahoma!* and the choreographer of *Rodeo* and *Fall River Legend, Hell on Wheels* and a battery of other ballets has already served her own American heritage as brilliantly as Igor Moiseyev has celebrated the folk marvels of the Soviet Union.

Miss de Mille has yet to achieve her American Heritage Theater. Every one, including government officials, thinks she should have it and that America needs it, but so far the incoming funds have been far smaller than the $250,000 she needs.

"It's hell," says Miss de Mille, "but we'll make it some day. But then this whole business of choreographing is hell, sheer torture. I remember once getting stuck midway in choreographing a new work. I didn't know what to do. Every thing I tried was terrible. I went to bed. I went to sleep. I woke up at 4 a. m. and decided to cancel out the ballet entirely and leave America. I decided to move to Chile. But at 5 a. m., I had an idea for the ballet. I decided to cut out the scene that had thwarted me. I finished the ballet. I didn't go to Chile."

Miss de Mille will have equal tortures as she builds her American Heritage Theater, and she's prepared for sleepless nights. But she promises to see it through and *not* go to Chile, except, maybe, for a vacation. [*New York Herald Tribune*]

American Ballet Theatre—
Twenty-five Triumphant Years

March 17, 1965

There were times, during the past years, when many of us feared that the American Ballet Theatre, one of the world's truly great companies, would not survive another season.

Financial problems, rehearsal lacks, no available Broadway theaters of the right size and other difficulties beset the company. Indeed, there were even year-long layoffs. But the American Ballet Theatre has made it. And triumphantly. For last night it celebrated its twenty-fifth anniversary with a gala opening at Lincoln Center's glittering State Theater.

476

This remarkable company, envisioned by the late Richard Pleasant and led over the years by its indomitable co-directors, Lucia Chase (its devoted patroness and a top-notch artist of the theater) and the stage designer, Oliver Smith, has built a repertory which encompasses ballets which span nearly two centuries of time and which include abstractions, romantic works, dance-dramas, lusty Americana, sophisticated importations and the avant garde.

Last evening, then, was not merely an occasion for heady nostalgia; it was an occasion for celebrating first-rank dance achievement.

Nostalgia, of course, did have its proper place in the proceedings, for the initial program in this month-long engagement at the State Theater began with Michel Fokine's ever-beloved *Les Sylphides,* the very ballet which, under the late master's personal direction, opened Ballet Theatre's first program a quarter of a century ago. It made history then, for it proclaimed the birth of a major American ballet company. And it made history again last night as it made clear that another 25 years—at the very least—lie ahead of this company. We need the American Ballet Theatre. Our dance culture cannot do without it.

There is no reason to compare the two *Sylphides,* for while one lingers lovingly in the memory, the other is of today. And the American Ballet Theatre presents the best *Les Sylphides* you are likely to find at home or abroad. The current company defines its wonderful patterns inpeccably and the dancers invest its gentle, lyrical measures with vitality. They don't resurrect it; they dance it.

Last evening, the corps was superb and the principals were fine, especially Sallie Wilson in the leaping Mazurka, Ruth Ann Koesun in the delicate but glowing Prelude and Royes Fernandez and Miss Koesun in the lilting Pas de Deux.

If there was nostalgia in the selection of the opening work, there was also the essential display of the ballerina's right to bravura. The shrewd choice here was the *Black Swan* Pas de Deux, a real rouser which allows outlets for both technique and temperament. Lupe Serrano, the company's prima ballerina, danced it and built her part—also shrewdly—to a dazzling finish.

Throughout, she displayed her fine aplomb, her sure balance on one tiny pointe and she gave us some stunning suspended turns but when she came to the coda and the traditional sequence of thirty-two fouettes (to the ballerina, what a cadenza is to the coloratura), she started them slowly (a feat in itself) and increased her speed right into the flash finish. Every one in the audience roared, and well they should have.

Since *Black Swan* is a duet, Miss Serrano was obviously not alone, and her cavalier on this occasion was Scott Douglas, a dancer of elegance and skill, who also built his performance up to a finale which displayed to excellent advantage his control of technique and of style. Kenneth Schermerhorn

477

conducted (as he had *Sylphides*) but his variations in tempo and in intensities might well have given the composer, Tchaikovsky, quite a turn.

But the American Ballet Theatre's test by fire in its first program in the State Theater (the home of its only rival, the New York City Ballet) came with Harald Lander's *Etudes,* a brilliant creation and one which throws every balletic trick in the book not only at stars and soloists but at every gentleman and lady of the ensemble. I'm happy to report that this performance of *Etudes*, beautifully mounted and beautifully rehearsed, brought down the house.

Etudes, as the balletomane will recall, is literally a series of studies, for it commences with the simplest of classical exercises at the ballet barre, moves to the essential disciplines for turning and gliding and leaping, and culminates in a fabulous burst of action in which, seemingly, all of ballet's technical ingredients, the result of a recipe compiled over a three-hundred-year period, are present. Well, it's a dish fit for a king and it contains far more than those blackbirds baked in that celebrated pie.

Toni Lander, heading the female contingent of the cast, was in electrifying form—her split leaps around the stage had the audience cheering and her balances were breathtaking—but she shared honors with Mr. Fernandez and Bruce Marks, both in fine estate.

But *Etudes* stands or falls by the total dancing of the total cast. Last night, it stood up proudly.

To end the opening program, nostalgia, suitably, was brought back, this time, in the guise of Jerome Robbins' first ballet, *Fancy Free.* And one member of the original cast (the ballet had its premiere in 1944), John Kriza, was on hand to share the stage with such newcomers as Lawrence Gradus and Basil Thompson as the other fun-seeking sailor in the Robbins–Bernstein–Smith ballet classic.

So it was quite a birthday party, ballet style, last night. And waiting ahead for balletomanes are performances which will include not only the varied and splendid works of the American Ballet Theatre's notable repertory but also some major new creations by some of America's great choreographers. The birthday celebration, then, is not over. It's just beginning. [*New York Herald Tribune*]

Show a Little Mercy, Merce

March 28, 1965

"Dance Triumph of Cunningham" read the headline of a review in the Herald Tribune last month. "Boos, catcalls and roars of derision . . ." introduced a review (of Merce Cunningham) this month in this paper. How, in one month, can such extremes occur? Who changed? The choreographer and the reviewer were the same on both occasions. But I report to you duly that I did not change in any way but that Mr. Cunningham provided us with a program of stimulating, moving, delightful, challenging nature in February at the Hunter College Playhouse, and that in March, in one new number, *Winterbranch*, he outraged and tortured the majority of those present at the New York State Theater.

This brings up a point of esthetics—or, if you prefer mere theatrical sensibility. Is there a stopping point in experimental dance or is it no-holds-barred all the way? For in using the word, "tortured," I'm not kidding, and I mean it in the physical sense. Yes, yes, I know our consciences should be tortured in this terrifying age; I also know we should be exposed to unpleasant themes and visions of death and degradation. This is the function of the artist as analyzer, as prophet.

But I do think ticket-purchasing dance followers should not be physically tortured by amplified sounds that literally pain the eardrums or by blinding lights suddenly turned upon them, without warning, from the stage. In *Winterbranch,* both these methods of torture are employed.

Let's get it straight right now that Merce Cunningham is one of the most important dance figures of our day—both here and abroad—but it does not mean he is infallible, nor does it mean he can have his way with a captive audience (as the villain did with our Little Ermintrude).

The play *Death of a Salesman* is hardly a barrel of laughs; the opera *Wozzeck* is touched with terror, and I doubt any one has wished, over a period of 2,000 years, that Klytemnestra would come home with him. But none of these works, although disturbing (as they are meant to be), confuses or physically assaults those present. They have terrifying, horrible things to say, but they say them, they communicate them. Today, Martha Graham's remarkable theater of dance is centered around both heroines and demons, heroes and destroyers (and she lets us know they overlap at times), and the inexorable sweep of destiny over the ages, is her sermon.

Dance progress, however, does not end with Miss Graham, any more than it did with Isadora Duncan, Ruth St. Denis, Ted Shawn or Mary Wigman. It goes on, but the dividing line between experimentation and self-indulgence needs to be explored.

Oh, yes! I know from European reviews of *Winterbranch* that some felt that it represented man emerging from primeval ooze or trapped in a concentration camp or any of a series of images of the fight for survival, but if you couldn't see this, you could hardly respond. George Balanchine, product of the Russian Imperial Ballet, has been more successful with related themes and with an avant-garde approach in, say, his *Ivesiana.* Is this because Balanchine never forgets he is creating for the theater?

479

No matter how far out the choreographer may be, I feel that certain conventions—or, let us say, limitations and possibilities—of the theater cannot be ignored. Obscurity is the chief curse of the experimentalists, aside from delight in torturing the public. Most of Mr. Cunningham's pieces are effectively lighted, and, some (though by no means all) have interesting or pertinent sounds as musical (?) backgrounds, but *Winterbranch* (one of a cycle of seasons) is done in near obscurity. If stage lighting offends his scheme, and if amplified noises are essential to his concept, should he use the stage? Should his dancers not be outdoors in ooze or mud or in trenches peppered by machine-gun fire?

If his creative independence is such, why does he submit to performing in the old-hat theater with a proscenium arch? And why, pray, does he, and his company, at the end of a performance walk down to the footlights and bow like traditionalists of the theater?

Mr. Cunningham, of course, is by no means alone in his excursions into non-theatrical obscurities or shock areas. Paul Taylor once did a duet (with a partner, you'll be happy to know) in which there was no movement at all. Just this month, Bertram Ross, the leading male dancer in Martha Graham's company, tried his hand at choreography and confused almost all of us in his intent and in the identity of the characters on stage. I don't mean simple things like having two people in a number called *Triangle*—one could have been the wife, the other the mistress of one who had been murdered or committed suicide or died or gone to Weehawken—but deeper obscurities.

Members of the Judson Dance Theater have performed nude (this is hardly avant-garde) or run through the audience (Olsen and Johnson stooges did this) or mixed word-association sequences with gestures.

Some of this is fun, some stimulating, some revealing, but some of it is either self-indulgence or fraud. Much of it is vital to the growth of dance expression, but some of it is guilty of dance repression. "Why don't they dance?" was a sad query heard during the absolutely static moments of Mr. Cunningham's *Winterbranch* and pantomimic vagaries and posings in Mr. Ross's works. Well, one could argue endlessly about what dancing is, where it starts and where it stops.

But I pass on a comment I overheard at Lincoln Center following *Winterbranch*. There had been boos and hoots (and, possibly, a lonely bravo or two), but one member of the audience said quietly to his companion, "One may say that this is a form of personal expression, but one does not necessarily say that it is art."

Carolyn Brown, a principal in the Cunningham company and one of the most accomplished dancers you will find anywhere, has taken me to task in a letter defending *Winterbranch*. And this she should do—because she works for Mr. Cunningham and because she believes in him (I believe in him, too). But though she explains *Winterbranch* and its place in the choreographic scheme of Mr. Cunningham's output, and quotes the foreign press, and reports that a stranger in the subway considered Mr. Cunningham "courageous and brilliant," she never says whether he has the privilege to hurt (and maybe permanently impair) hearing and vision in order to project "a form of personal expression."

At the second performance of *Winterbranch* at the State Theater, the bombardment of sound was reduced, the lights, which blinded sections of the audience, changes and the stage lighting increased so that one could view the goings-on. The producer of the modern dance series at the State Theater tells me these changes "were mutually agreed upon." So this means Mr. Cunningham must have concurred that certain excesses were not essential to his dance, that their alteration did not harm his concept; otherwise, he would have refused to perform.

So on one occasion, Merce Cunningham—and other avant-garde dancers-choreographers—can instruct, divert, describe, reveal, mystify and arouse the onlooker with works of genuine merit, while on another occasion indulge himself in treating an audience, through obscurities or physical tortures, with contempt. What Mr. Cunningham does in his own studio or backyard for an invited group is his own business; what he does in the theater is theatrical business. There is such a thing as a paying customer, and that customer is sometimes right, especially if he doesn't find it an unalloyed delight to be abused. Mr. Cunningham, as I've said, is a major dance figure. He has a responsibility—not only to himself but to the public. [*New York Herald Tribune*]

Fonteyn and Nureyev: Why They Are Great

May 9, 1965

The publicity? In this case, you can believe it, for today's dance world has seen nothing quite like Fonteyn and Nureyev. The names alone promise sold-out houses around the world, tickets purchased at scalper's prices, teenage pleas of "I've just *got* to get a ticket or I'll die!"

Of course, they are personalities. Rudolf Nureyev, with his shock of long hair, his mysterious Tartar face, his magnificent muscular prowess, made a dramatic dash for freedom from the Soviet ballet to the West.

Ten years ago, Margot Fonteyn announced that she would retire at 40. Today, at 46, she is at the peak of her powers as one of the great ballerinas of our age. While in her 30s, she had said that 40 was a sensible age for retiring as a dancer since she would not be in danger of going on for that "one year too long" as some of her predecessors had done. "Maybe," she said, "I'd still be dancing well at 45. But you can't really be sure. I'd rather stop too early than too late."

Circumstances in her life caused her to change her mind and to continue as a dancer. But the magnetic factor which lifted Dame Margot onto a new level of achievement as she was nearing the close of an already fabulous career, was represented by the dazzling and enigmatic Nureyev. He in his 20s and she in her 40s found untapped dance powers through their association, and they have explored and exploited them.

In the minds of the public, Dame Margot and "Rudi" (as teen-agers, and also his friends call him) seem to represent the epitome of an unusual romance in which closeness of rapport, despite a wide age differential, makes for a unique association. All of the fans know, of course, that Dame Margot is the devoted and dedicated wife of Roberto Arias, a Panamanian politician who was almost fatally wounded by a would-be assassin's bullet many months ago. But in their work, a royal romance is present, for Fonteyn and Nureyev share a passion for their art.

So it is that the top stars of Britain's Royal Ballet (now in the final week of its season at the Metropolitan Opera House), are far more than provocative personalities. They are artists of uncommon magnitude. Dame Margot has said that she has learned a great deal about ballet from the youthful Nureyev. He, in turn, has learned from her. She has become more vivid as a stage presence, warmer in attitude, more profound in her probing of a meaningful movement or a musical phrase. The occasional dramatic excesses in which Nureyev once indulged are gone. The passion is there but it is controlled. Each, in relating his personal art to the other, has created a new art, a duo art quite unequalled in our time.

The difference in their ages offers no hazard at all. And it is not simply that Dame Margot looks surprisingly young, off-stage as well as on. It is not a matter of being well preserved. It is that her radiant maturity is in glorious harmony with Nureyev's air of impetuosity, the just province of youth.

They are, therefore, perfect as the adolescent lovers in the Royal Ballet's opulent production of Kenneth MacMillan's *Romeo and Juliet*. Ever since I saw Dame Margot's Juliet on the opening night, I have been trying to recall the source of an enlightening statement about Juliet. I haven't been able to track it down but I believe that it was Jane Cowl (and many mature actresses have played Juliet) who said something to the effect that "only at 40 do you know the wonder of being 14."

Nureyev, as Romeo, was the impetuous dashing youth. But he was something more, for just as Dame Margot, through her maturity, made silent,

482

eloquent comment on youth, so did Nureyev let us penetrate beyond the love-touched cavalier.

I shall never in all my life forget their first *Giselle* here during this season. It was a miracle, plain and simple—and that is the only kind of miracle that one can easily believe in. To the roles of Giselle the tragedy-touched heroine, and to Albrecht, who deceived her only to prove everlastingly faithful upon her death, the two brought their superb insight into characterization. Indeed, Dame Margot's Mad Scene represents one of the great acting achievements of this or any era—and I'm not exaggerating when I say it would equal the art of a Sarah Bernhardt or a Judith Anderson.

Nureyev too was a marvel in his revealing of conflicting emotions, of his reaction to his own duplicity—which begins in innocence and ends in monumental tragedy. He gave us a nobleman, falsely disguised as a peasant (and he clued us to these falsifications with the subtlest of gestures) and in one passage, during which he is almost in the background, he delineated the metamorphosis of a boy into a man.

But even more than their portrayals mirror the unity of Fonteyn and Nureyev. When they dance together—sometimes in unison as they do in Act I of *Giselle*—every movement contour is in flawless accord. They move through space as one—the spring into a leap is simultaneous, the extensions of the legs thrusting into space are absolutely parallel, the arcs of traveling bodies are as one in timing and design. I thought to myself how often cameramen have inadvertantly taken pictures of unflattering moments—preparations for a feat of skill, recoveries and the like. The camera could have taken Fonteyn and Nureyev at split-second intervals and never recorded anything that was not beauty, perfection dualized.

Finally, one may ask, and with all justification, "But aren't there any other good dancers in the Royal Ballet?" Of course there are. There are first-class interpreters of *Romeo and Juliet* and of *Giselle* and of all the other ballets in the repertory. There are, within the ranks of the company, very probably tomorrow's glittering stars, preparing and praying for that tomorrow.

For today, however, Fonteyn and Nureyev bring to the theater of ballet an extra glamour, an extra excitement, yes, and an extra mystique. The Royal Ballet is smart to use them, to make much of them. Even their whims (if any) and their huge salaries are not worthy an argument. As stars, Fonteyn and Nureyev are too valuable to quibble about.

Our own New York City Ballet, great company that it is, does not understand such tactics. Under George Balanchine's direction, it focuses upon a company and upon an individual (Balanchine), who is a choreographer, not a dancer. But this does not necessarily stir the public. I cannot imagine that the Royal Ballet's performances of *Romeo and Juliet* were jammed to the doors because thousands of persons said to themselves, "Kenneth MacMillan! Kenneth MacMillan!"

These thousands had two other names in mind—the most magical names of ballet today: Fonteyn and Nureyev. [*New York Herald Tribune*]

Don Quixote: Stunning, Lavish
. . . But Not Much of a Ballet

May 28, 1965

America's least-known professional dancer was the undisputed star of a glittering gala held last evening at Lincoln Center's New York State Theater. The occasion was a benefit preview of the New York City Ballet's new three-act spectacle, *Don Quixote.* And the little-known dancer who portrayed the title role was none other than the choreographer of the new ballet, George Balanchine, the world's most celebrated creator of ballets.

"Mr. B.," as he is known to all of his dancers and to countless numbers of students in the coast-to-coast ballet schools in which he has a guiding hand, is not a novice performer by any means, although he almost never appears on stage and then, usually unannounced. As a product of the Russian Imperial Ballet (as a child dancer, he won the attention of Czar Nicholas II) and the Soviet State Ballet (he fled Russia, along with Alexandra Danilova and Tamara Geva, more than forty years ago), he became a highly proficient dancer but he was destined to win international renown as a choreographer.

Balanchine, as the choreographic architect of the New York City Ballet, has little time and inclination for returning to the art of performing. He has, however, donned a patriarchal beard and long robe to play, on rare occasions, the role of the Father in his famous staging of *The Prodigal Son* and has brought tears to the eyes of those present through the beauty of his biblical-inspired gestures and the tenderness with which he forgives the errant son.

Mr. B., an expert musician, has also been known to take over the podium and conduct the New York City Ballet Orchestra to brilliant effect, and usually at such a clip that his dancers find it almost impossible to keep up with his tempos.

Last night, as the errant-knight of the great Cervantes tale, Balanchine assumed—and for one night only—what is quite probably the biggest performing role he has taken on since he left Russia.

How was he? Well, since the event was a private preview for the benefit of the New York City Ballet Fund (designed to hold the seats at low price levels for the rest of the year), Balanchine asked that this preview not be reviewed. So I won't review him. I'll simply *report* that he was wonderful, absolutely wonderful!

484

Tonight, *Don Quixote* will have its official premiere, with Richard Rapp in the title part, at the State Theater and will continue to be performed through June 5. For Saturday, then, I will review this production (said to have cost close to half a million dollars), choreographed by Balanchine to a specially commissioned score by Nicolas Nabokov (an old-time Balanchine colleague) and with scenery, costumes and lighting by the Spanish artist, Esteban Frances.

Today, I must defer to Mr. Balanchine's wishes, and not review a performance in which he participated only to help the fund-raising campaign (tickets were priced from $5. to $100. each).

But I think it quite proper to report that this new *Don Quixote* is not only a lavish ballet—the most extravagant that the State Theater has ever seen—but that it has transformation scenes involving fantasy effects, that it has a live horse and donkey, that a cast of close to one hundred (including child dancers) are in it and that the fashionable and enthusiastic preview audience applauded the effects and the dancing frequently and delightedly.

I also wish to report (and I'm not reviewing, mind you!) that this practically unknown dancer, George Balanchine, gave such a tender and touching portrayal of the Don, in which the classic fusion of the comic and the pathetic was brilliantly achieved, that I wish he would reconsider his decision of making this a one-time affair and, instead, permit other audiences to see a master of choreography excel as a master actor–dancer on the stage itself. (If the foregoing is not actually a report, it is a suggestion, but definitely, Mr. B., not a review!). [*New York Herald Tribune*]

May 29, 1965

It's big. It's expensive. It's eye-filling. But it isn't a very good ballet. This, I think, describes the New York City Ballet's lavish production of *Don Quixote*, a three-act ballet which was given its world premiere last night at the New York State Theater.

There is no arguing that the enormous settings (including an entire village square and an elaborate throne room among the several changes of scene) are stunning indeed. Esteban Frances, who designed these, also created the costumes, executed in the most sumptuous materials by the fabulous Karinska. Indeed, the black-and-gold motif of Act II is quite probably the most elegant image ever brought to a New York stage.

All these are solid virtues, decorative virtues, but they cannot fill vast expanses of choreographic inaction.

For a good deal of this newest version of *Don Quixote* relies on pageantry, on bits of pantomime and on such novelties as a live horse and donkey, cute interludes by child dancers and fantasy effects. All these are just fine in themselves but they are not well (although not nearly as brilliantly as Balanchine had done it the night before).

True, Mr. Balanchine has introduced some attractive variations—particularly for Suzanne Farrell, who moves exquisitely—here and there but they are tiny oases in a desert of routine action. The village dances of Act I, though the costumes give an illusion of brightness, are pretty dull, and the dance of the maidens of Act III is very bland indeed. This is not first-class Balanchine, despite the excellence of the brief, fleeting variations.

On the positive side is the choreographer's conception of the character of Don Quixote. He has done it entirely in terms of mime but he has designed it, molded it, enkindled it with poignancy and deeply felt comic tragedy. Last night Richard Rapp acted this role genuinely activated by imaginative choreography.

Don Quixote in its newest guise (and it has been the subject for ballets many times over the centuries) may well be the most opulent ever staged. As such, it is eminently worth seeing simply as spectacle. But if you go to the ballet to see ballet, you will very likely be disappointed, for the art of ballet dancing is the weakest ingredient in this staging of the Don's sad tale. [*New York Herald Tribune*]

The Harkness Credo: Talent Must Be Served

July 18, 1965

"The people who stay in the middle don't interest me," said Rebekah Harkness, composer, sculptor and patroness of the arts. "It is the artist or the delinquent I care about—the point is to do something for the two extremes: on the one hand, to give the artist opportunities to release his talent; and on the other hand, to help the delinquent find himself through the disciplines of art."

To this end, Mrs. Harkness, through her own Rebekah Harkness Foundation and the foundation established by her late husband, William Hale Harkness, has provided desperately needed funds (totaling millions of dollars) to the arts, and to dance in particular. Harkness sponsorship aided Jerome Robbins' *Ballets: U. S. A.* in a European tour, promoted the Robert Joffrey Ballet from a small national company to one of international stature, and made possible free dance events, in collaboration with the New York Shakespeare Festival, in Central Park's Delacorte Theater.

A year ago, the Harkness dance enterprises embarked on new and expanded programs. The Harkness Ballet, which now numbers approximately 30 dancers, was founded with George Skibine and Donald Saddler as its artistic and assistant artistic director, respectively. The initial tour, which began in 1965, was booked in Europe and provided the new company with a sort of glorified New Haven in which to try out its new works and to discover its incipient strengths and passing weaknesses.

At the same time, Mrs. Harkness purchased the old Thomas Watson town house and launched the long and expensive process of having it converted into the Harkness House for the Ballet Arts in New York City. When it opens in the fall, as the home of the Harkness Ballet and as a center for ballet seminars, workshops, lecture–demonstrations, art exhibits related to dance, its many studios will foster not only ballet but music, design and literature as they relate to ballet.

"It has," says Mrs. Harkness of the new ballet house, "the airs and graces of a palazzo. Maybe I'll be criticized for its elegance but I do think that beautiful surroundings are important to the working artist. And I'm serious when I use the word 'working.' I mentioned earlier, didn't I, that I'm not concerned with those individuals who stay in the middle? Well, this means I'm interested in the worker-artist. For example, there is the professional—the real pro—who does a fine job on the equivalent of the good old nine-to-five basis. I care about the one that works to 5:45, that works extra. The former is a 90-per-center. He rarely does anything memorable. It's the extra 10 per cent which counts. I guess it's the difference between the adequate and the inspirational.

"No, I'm not enough of a nut to believe that time heals all wounds nor that time creates talent. I'm not even certain just what makes for talent in the individual—chemical factors? inspiration? love?—but if talent is there, it needs time to grow. Nobody can put talent into another being. My job, and my privilege, is comparatively simple and that is to give release to talent that is already there. Maybe it's a minor talent—although we pray it is major—but it too deserves a chance. To put it bluntly, at our Summer Workshop at Watch Hill, R. I., and, later, at our headquarters in New York, the plan is to give choreographers, composers and designers the time to work out their ideas and if they have that mysterious thing, if they have something to say, this is the opportunity provided them in which to say it. It doesn't always work out. But it might. And the 'might' is worth all the expense and the effort."

This summer, at Mrs. Harkness' arts center in Rhode Island—a firehouse converted into two large studios, other studios in her own house, a complete inn for the many married couples in her troupe—the creative opportunities for a wide range of artists are being given the time and the release that Mrs. Harkness believes are the right of the potential holder of talent.

Donald McKayle (represented choreographically on Broadway in *Golden Boy*) is working on a new ballet with an Israeli theme; Sophie Maslow is restaging her successful *The Dybbuk*; Alvin Ailey, who has already created two successful works for the Harkness Ballet, is at work on *Macumba,* with a score by Mrs. Harkness herself; and the Henry Street Playhouse's Alwin Nikolais is moving out of his own distinguished home for a rare occasion to create a new work for the Harkness Ballet.

Other choreographic highlights of the summer workshop at Watch Hill include a new version, by John Butler, of Gian-Carlo Menotti's *Sebastian*; Mr. Saddler's new American Indian ballet, *Koshari,* with a score by the Indian composer Louis Ballard; a piece by Mr. Skibine to a new score by Carlos Surinach; Stuart Hodes' *Free for All,* to music of Paul Bowles, and other ballets by Mr. Saddler (an *Alice in Wonderland Through the Looking Glass* piece), William Dollar, Leon Fokine, Karoly Barta, Richard Wagner and others.

The ambitious program—the Workshop at Watch Hill, Harkness House in New York, a second Harkness Ballet tour of Europe in 1965-1966, a Rebekah Harkness Foundation Dance Festival in Central Park this fall—are but a part—albeit major—of the Harkness plans. "I think it's important," says the slim, supple (she takes ballet class and yoga exercises daily), youthful mother of three grown children, "to help dancers develop secondary talents. Why should dancers have to fear that awful moment when the muscles just won't do the job any more? I'd like to see them ready with another skill—maybe design, perhaps music, teaching, therapy—which will extend their earning capacities for many years."

A long-range project has to do with men in the ballet. Mrs. Harkness recognizes the fact that dancing for men is subjected to the incontrovertibly erroneous notion that dance is a feminine art but, more important, that the all-American "pop" is worried that his son won't make a dependable living. For this outmoded attitude, Mrs. Harkness has a campaign in mind.

"My idea," says Mrs. Harkness, "is to send lecture-demonstration programs out to as many schools as possible. Whom do we want for male dancers in American ballet? We want the types you find in high school gymnasiums. We need to win them over at that vulnerable age—and their parents, too. For these boys from our gymnasiums, given the training, can do anything that the Bolshoi Ballet wonder kids can do.

"And, I guess, this brings us back to where we started, my function. I'm a composer and I work at it hard. I'm also a sculptor—I've got a figure, in the next room, with all its muscles lying about and I'd better get 'em into place—but my own foundation and Bill Harkness' foundation have set out to help ballet in America. Mistakes will be made, that is inescapable. But the artists of the ballet have, over the years, brought so much to us that I feel that my job is to bring to *them*—in time, in opportunity, in release, in

encouragement, in financial help and stimulating surroundings—what I can."
[*New York Herald Tribune*]

Tallchief Tells Why She Bowed Out

October 31, 1965

"A true ballerina," says S. Hurok, the master impresario of our era, "is like a true artist in any field—a great pianist, a great opera singer, a great actor. They project. They possess a magical quality which electrifies audiences, which moves the public. Such gifts are really few and truly far between, and when found, they must be cherished and they should be presented in the best possible circumstances and conditions."

The status of the ballerina in America received a serious jolt earlier this month when Maria Tallchief, one of the world's most illustrious ballerinas, announced her withdrawal from the New York City Ballet's season, which closes today at the New York State Theater.

Miss Tallchief, who had not appeared at all during the engagement, explained that she was dissatisfied with the way her performances had been scheduled and with the repertory assigned to her. At the time, she remarked that the New York City Ballet did not need a ballerina and did not want a ballerina. Tallchief is a ballerina.

The directors of the New York City Ballet made no announcement of the Tallchief withdrawal (from that particular season, not from her long-time association with the company). However, the unexplained absence of someone of Miss Tallchief's prestige could no more go unnoticed than if Dame Margot Fonteyn had suddenly failed to turn up for a season with England's Royal Ballet at Covent Garden. The public would hardly have said, "Bye, bye, baby," and let it go at that.

The lessening use, by the New York City Ballet, of Miss Tallchief's undisputed position as the best known American ballerina has been apparent for some seasons. Three of her close friends and colleagues on the international ballet scene—Dame Margot, Rudolf Nureyev, Erik Bruhn—have even teased her during a New York City Ballet season with a "Maria, when *do* you dance?" The general rule, when she did dance, was to have junior soloists in the company take precedence over her in seasonal "firsts" and to give her, as she says, "early bird" matinees.

It came to pass, then, that she found her chief artistic outlets with other companies as a guest star.

489

In guest appearances such as these, Miss Tallchief continues to break box office records from Ted Shawn's Jacob's Pillow Dance Festival in the Berkshires to Honolulu. The New York City Ballet, under the artistic direction of George Balanchine, is disinterested in stars (casts are never announced in advance) and places the accent upon the junior performers in the troupe.

A few seasons ago, when Bruhn himself (now touring America with the Royal Danish Ballet) was guest with the New York City Ballet, he found the experience an unhappy one—indeed, he and Tallchief had to argue the management into letting them dance together!—and in a recent interview with dance critic Jean Battey in *The Washington Post,* he said, "I adore Balanchine, I have tremendous respect for him. But he also bores me." Mr. Bruhn disapproves, of course, of Balanchine's liking for "anonymity" in his dancers.

As for Miss Tallchief, born in 1925, she says, "I resent the definition that a ballerina is an 'old bag,' for ours is a life of dedication. Ballet in America has come into its own in our time—people have accepted it. Of course, we need new dancers, new bodies, new souls on stage, but we need the youngsters to master the classics.

"We also need these youngsters, these newcomers, to respect and learn from those who have achieved stature in their art, be it ballet, music or design. New ideas are essential, but we must retain respect for the art of ballet—and that means the artist too—or else it is no longer an art form and becomes something anyone can do."

As for her decision to withdraw from the season now ending, Miss Tallchief said, "I did not complain about a company I love and admire. What finally happened was that I was not given the kind of support I needed as a performer—I was not given a chance to serve. Also, my dignity was imperiled—this, perhaps, was the all-important factor in my decision. Ballet is an aristocratic art, and with it goes dignity as well as responsibility."

Says Tallchief of the responsibility of the ballerina, "You study technique and style from childhood. You don't say, 'I'm going to be a ballerina'; rather, you try to become expert in your craft. Then, one day, you find you are accepted by your colleagues and peers. Then, as the younger dancers come along, you accept a responsibility to guide them.

"But if these youngsters are brought up in a climate in which they are not expected to have respect for any dance artist of experience, they will wind up having no respect for themselves. I remember when I first saw Ulanova, it was a mystical experience. This was dance. This is what I had been trying to do.

"Responsibility, yes. As an artist you demand more of yourself as you mature, more of yourself as you strive to communicate the art essence to others. Being a ballerina is to be a person of responsibility. It's not just work, it's your life, a way of life."

Miss Tallchief then listed some of the requirements of a ballerina: (1) "She requires roles. You cannot create an aura unless you have the material with which to do it"; (2) "A ballerina is not just a toe dancer. She is special, she needs promoting, not just for herself but to serve her company"; (3) "She should have a wide range of opportunities to interpret a variety of roles, for she takes steps given to her and makes them her own. Each individual brings something different to the same role. As an American, I believe in great individualism. That's the way I was brought up."

Rather than reiterating the attributes essential to a ballerina—technical skill, style, versatility, musicality, dramatic range and the like—Miss Tallchief suggested that, perhaps, "mystery is an important quality. The viewer should not be able to anticipate what is coming next, for then the excitement, the revealing are gone. So what we have to guard against in ballet is peopling the stage with a bunch of machines."

The ballerina, the woman of individuality and of mystery, has an historic place in the development of ballet. It was Philippe Taglioni who created *La Sylphide,* but it was Marie Taglioni, his ballerina daughter, who made it the enduring symbol of the Romantic Age. Camargo of an earlier era, Elssler, Cerrito, Grisi and Grahn of Taglioni's era and Pavlova of the first part of this century exerted influences of immeasurable force in the history of world ballet.

The ballerina—and her age does not matter, for she can be young in years or mature, as long as she possesses those essentials which make up the ballerina: dedication, responsibility, dignity, individuality, technical disciplines, mystery—is truly *someone.*

Maria Tallchief, in her odd position as a world-renowned ballerina who is not really wanted by her own company, now stands at the threshold of what could be the major performing years of her life, just as Dame Margot has achieved unparalleled pinnacles of popularity and artistic accomplishments after reaching forty.

Tallchief, who bears no resentment toward Mr. Balanchine, once her husband and her longtime mentor (he created many ballets just for her), or to the company's general director, Lincoln Kirstein, or to the company itself, says simply, "It's just their policy that has no place for someone like me, for a ballerina."

As for her own future, she says, "In the next few years, if I'm given the proper roles, I feel that I can recapture the wonder of dancing. . . ." For one of the great ballerinas of our time, the next step, the direction she takes in the tomorrows, are all important, not only for herself but for our world of dance. [*New York Herald Tribune*]

In Ballet, There's Nothing Like a Dane

December 12, 1965

The Royal Danish Ballet, now in the final week (it closes next Sunday) of its month's engagement at the New York State Theater, is unique. Every one in the world of dance knows this. But what makes it unique? Is it repertory or a special dance style or appearance or schooling or a sort of Danish mystique? Let's have a go at it by beginning with the most obvious facet of its uniqueness, repertory.

The Royal Dancers' choreographic inheritance, historically speaking, are the ballets created by the great 19th-century Danish ballet master, August Bournonville. Until about a decade ago, this treasurehouse of the choreographic art belonged almost exclusively to the Danes. It still does, for although other companies in other lands (including America) now perform Bournonville pas de deux (such as the *Flower Festival in Genzano* duet or that from *Kermesse in Bruges*), Bournonville suites (the third act of *Napoli* is a favorite) or even the full-length Bournonville staging of *La Sylphide,* created in Copenhagen in 1836, just four years after the Taglioni original (now forgotten) had its premiere in Paris, Denmark continues to present more Bournonville ballets than any other country and the Danes continue to dance them better than any one else.

Aside from inheriting and preserving (sometimes in exact detail and occasionally in outline) Bournonville's stage masterpieces, the Danes have received another legacy—and this is truly unique—from Bournonville, the ballet master, a master teacher as well as a master choreographer.

There are Bournonville classes conducted by Bournonville experts in Copenhagen's Royal Theater. Traditionally, there are set classes for each day of the week (although now it's possible to give Monday's class, say, on Thursday). And we know that Bournonville is present, for the master not only wrote down his sequences of exercises and combinations of steps but also incorporated into every class generous excerpts from his repertory of ballets.

So this brings us, through repertory and schooling, to style. Obviously, this dancing style is unique. True, the students in the Royal Ballet School and the members of the Royal Danish Ballet receive training in other, more modern styles of ballet, but the Bournonville style is there when needed. The old man himself, in his dancing days, was a great jumper; his ballets demand elevation; it is not surprising, then, that the Danes' jumping prowess is very special.

The uniqueness of this style is to be found in the bigness, the expansiveness of its movement. The Danish port-de-bras is more sweeping than that evolved in Russia and passed on to the rest of the world; indeed, it is almost

492

like the invitation to an embrace, but that is as it should be, for this style stems from the Romantic Age of Ballet (preserved only in prints and books, except for the Danes).

This expansiveness in the arms, shoulder and torso is to be found even in the leaps. These leaps, in Bournonville style, are done with the back leg bent, that is, in "attitude." The Russians do "attitude" leaps also but not like the Danes who soar toward you, with opening arms, from behind the footlights.

Repertory, style, schooling and preserved history (the Danes possess the oldest, unaltered ballet extant, the 1786 *Whims of Cupid and the Ballet Master*), all make the Danes unique. But what else does? Appearance? Perhaps. One might be forgiven for laboring under the delusion that all Scandinavians are blond; they are not. Naturally, there are a good many of the Royal Dancers who are golden of hair and fair of complexion, but there are others with jet black hair (not dyed) or brown or red.

Some of the Danish dancers are tall while others are short, most are slim (the men especially) and the girls range from the svelte to the curvy (and quite a few of them are). The curves of some of the ladies have surprised our American dancers (not the general public) chiefly because our dance followers have become conditioned to the very thin, almost pre-adolescent female bodies which George Balanchine favors for his New York City Ballet.

But almost all companies have places for tall, short, medium, slim, curvaceous beings as long as they are good dancers. Still and all, the Royal Danish Ballet does have an appearance which is its own. The dancers—or almost all of them—have trained together since they were seven years old; thus, when they are called upon to move in unison, they are so thoroughly attuned kinetically, that they truly move as one. The exactitude of their steps, arms placements, mass formations in, for example, Jerome Robbins' *Fanfare,* positively puts to shame the ensemble efforts of the New York City Ballet (which is going through a rough-around-the-edges period anyhow) in the same work.

More than physical contours, more than the individual differences in physiognomy which are apparent in any company, there is an appearance to the Royal Danish Ballet. It is an appearance difficult to define, for it is the physical manifestation of an inner spirit. And this spirit is that of exuberance. In joyous ballets, such as *Napoli* Act III, this lovely energy touches not only smiling lips and shining eyes but the bounding limbs and those embracing arms I have noted.

This brings us to the final uniqueness of the Royal Danes, and perhaps it is the almost untranslatable "mystique" which explains itself in French. We have considered the unison effectiveness of Danish dancers who have been together since childhood; we have touched upon a spirit which finds fulfillment in muscular outlet; we have reviewed the wellsprings of a remarkable dance past and noted the accomplishments and challenges of the present. The "mystique," I do believe, represents a combination of these and other qualities and it is unique.

American dancers, especially ballet dancers, are living in an age when technique is the goal instead of the means. Many of these young Americans have found themselves critical of certain aspects of performing in the Royal Danish Ballet. One doesn't balance enough, another is too plump, a third doesn't do this or that. But the irony is that not one of them—or maybe only a few—can do what the Royal Dancers do (with the probable exception of the dancers of the American Ballet Theatre) and that is to establish illuminating individuality within the framework of total accord. This is the "mystique," the uniqueness.

Some of our American dancers have expressed the opinion that in the ballet of *Carmen,* only Erik Bruhn, one of the great dancers of our age, is deserving of unbounded praise. True, Mr. Bruhn brings an intensity, a total commitment to the role of Don Jose which transforms him from Bruhn into the tortured, tempestuous Spaniard. But that is not all that there is to the Danish staging of Roland Petit's *Carmen*, originally a French ballet by a Frenchman for Frenchmen. The Danes do it better. Why?

In the Royal Danish Ballet's *Carmen,* every character is more than a choreographic figure. Each is a personality. In the opening scene, each girl walks differently, each boy stands differently, yet there is total rapport. The three bandits are individuals also, for although they work, as the plot requires, in consonance, each is a person unlike the others—they rob, push, dare, adore, defy, tease and react to danger differently from each other. They are actors as well as dancers; they are no longer in the classroom, they are on the stage.

American dancers, probably the most hard-working dancers in the world as far as constant physical training is involved, are so concerned with the exactitude of execution of their tendus, fondus, cabrioles, entrechats, the five positions of the feet and on and on, that they sometimes forget that these disciplines exist only to transform them into other beings. Most of them could not meet the theatrical (not technical) standards imposed by the Royal Danish Ballet. For the Royal Dancers, from the fabulous Bruhn down to the youngest member of the corps de ballet, have channeled a unique past into a unique present. They are not necessarily better than other dancers—Russians, British, Americans—but they are different and, hence, unique, for their special mystique has been exploited to make a special dance magic. [*New York Herald Tribune*]

1966

Toni Time

Toni Lander triumphs with ABT • Eugene Loring's These Three premiered by the Joffrey Ballet • The spirit of the late Helen Tamiris • Bad deal for the Metropolitan Opera Ballet

The Triumph of Toni

February 6, 1966

This has been Toni time in New York City. The clapping, the shouting, the awed gaspings and the bravos at the New York State Theater attest to this. The object of such enthusiasm is, of course, Toni Lander, now in her sixth year with the American Ballet Theatre.

Why hasn't this matter come up before? No one can say for certain but there is that time when some one really makes it, and there is no predicting. Miss Lander is no stranger to American audiences. She has evoked admiration in the past and large applause for her technical prowess—she is a genuine virtuoso. She was indisputably a ballerina, a versatile artist and, as a dividend, a handsome blonde. But I think the average balletgoer settled for an "oh, yes, she's very good" or cheered her dazzling display of technique in her husband's *Etudes* but did not decide immediately to see as many Lander performances as possible.

This year, the magical one, it has changed. One hears in the vast lobbies of the New York State Theater, "It's Lander tonight!" or "I've never seen her and I can hardly wait!" Then, as the curtain rises, there is a hush of anticipation; as Miss Lander enters, there is a burst of applause; as the curtain falls, the yells of approval are deafening. Yes, it has been Toni time.

All of the performing attributes which have stirred New York audiences during this American Ballet Theatre season have long been present in Miss Lander. We had read that the Danish ballerina was highly praised when only

495

in her teens, we knew that her repertory ranged from the classical through the romantic to the intensely dramatic. We had even seen her accomplish so much, but suddenly it took hold of all of us, the art of Toni Lander.

Suddenly, through the alchemy of time and talent and exhaustive labor, the many qualities which made up Toni Lander—or any human creature, for that matter—jelled. The admirable had become the extraordinary; the enormously gifted had become the unique.

At 35, Miss Lander has commenced the most ideal decade of her career. She is young enough to retain the spring of youth and she is mature enough to analyze, probe, capture and reveal new facets of characterization, of style, even of technique.

Let's investigate the physical accomplishments first. I mentioned "spring." In ballet, this is called "ballon" and it doesn't mean how high you go but the manner in which you get there and, most important, stay there. Miss Lander has both "ballon" and "elevation," so when you see her split-leaps across the stage in *La Sylphide* or the adorable boundings in place (as the Sylphide claps her hands in innocent ecstasy) or the aerial sorties in *Swan Lake* or the space probes in *Etudes,* you will feel a similar lift within yourself.

She possesses velocity, too, a beautifully controlled command of speed which finds one of its most breathtaking outlets in *Etudes* when she starts a series of turns, in diagonal, across the stage and, imperceptibly, increases the tempo of execution until her actions assume the force of jet-propulsion.

The balances on pointe are strong and secure, the leg extensions are high, the turns come fleetly or slowly as the music demands, the swiftly running bourrees (at the close of *Swan Lake,* Act II) resemble shimmers of moonlight on the water. But there is no need to dissect Miss Lander's technique any further. The technique is that of a glittering virtuoso, and the use to which it is put is that of a sensitive artist.

As a mistress of style, the ballerina transforms herself from the authoritative *"reine de la danse"* in *Etudes,* in which she is required to prove her superiority to every one else, to the virginal, elusive fairy of the forests in *La Sylphide* to the wanton and tragic heroine of *Miss Julie.* In all three ballets, she must be an aristocrat, but each is totally different from the other.

You think the ballet dancer performs only with her feet? Look at her head. In *Etudes,* the head is held imperiously but with charming condescension for the lesser beings around her; in *Miss Julie,* the head tosses imperiously but, this time, with arrogance; in *Swan Lake,* it mirrors in its gentle turnings and quiverings an enchanted bird; in *La Sylphide,* the head is held with pride but with a certain shyness, a modesty which reminds you of lovely lithographs of ballet's Romantic Age of more than a century ago.

The feet, the head, the arms—one could describe in detail how Miss

Lander uses them differently not only for each ballet in which she appears but also for each episode, each scene, each mood, each measure.

Her training has had much to do with the emergence of this striking artist. She was a product of the Royal Ballet School in Copenhagen and she rose to the rank of soloist with the Royal Danish Ballet itself. Here, then, she was exposed to techniques and styles which spanned the centuries, from the early 19th century through the great Bournonville era (*La Sylphide, Napoli,* etc.) to this century's Fokine and the contemporary choreographies by her own countrymen and other Scandinavian experimenters.

After leaving Denmark, her performing duties in Europe and, subsequently, with the American Ballet Theatre simply served to challenge her already recognized gifts and to hasten her advance from "a being" to "personality."

To achieve personality on stage may have once been a problem. Anita Loos has said that gentlemen prefer blondes. This may well be true, but in ballet, the majority of great ballerinas (there have been exceptions) have been dark-haired. The black hair, the black eyes just naturally project—such a girl can just stand there and be noticed. The blonde, unless she works extra hard at projection, seems pale (no matter how pretty she is) and almost fades away unless she asserts her presence in some other manner.

Remember when Toumanova and Baronova were rival ballerinas? Toumanova, the "Black Pearl," was a dazzler to begin with. The fair Baronova had to strive for impact in other ways. Toni Lander had to emulate Baronova. For a while, she was a stage figure who seemed remote, pretty, pale, perhaps even a little icy. No more.

For Toni Lander has made her blondeness gleam, she has taken her command of technique and made it command the attention of the public, and she has managed, while changing style and character and mood from ballet to ballet, to retain a presence which is uniquely Lander.

Why all this should have happened in 1966, I do not know. True, for the American Ballet Theatre's 25th anniversary season last year, Miss Lander was working with an injured foot. But no, there is more to it than that. It was time for the hidden magic to burst through and for a valuable and respected dancer to become a real star. Promotion and publicity had nothing to do with it. The American public went, looked and, by its ardor, proclaimed its opinion that this has truly been Toni time in New York. [*New York Herald Tribune*]

Dance Me a Dance
with Social Significance

October 2, 1966

America's dance of social comment has come back to us full force. It has returned in the form of a new ballet, *These Three,* choreographed by Eugene Loring (famed for his *Billy the Kid*) and produced by the City Center Joffrey Ballet during its recent New York season.

I say "has returned" because America has had a unique tradition in its dance of social comment. The new *These Three* is a distillation of the conditions and attitudes which led to the murder of three civil rights workers—two whites and one Negro—near Philadelphia, Miss. But its antecedents go back to the 1930s, to the period of the Great Depression, when dancers and choreographers made their fervent, and often highly emotional, protests against social injustices.

More than 30 years before *These Three,* the late Helen Tamiris had created her *How Long Brethren,* an enormously successful work which was made up of the following episodes: "Pickin' Off de Cotton," "Upon de Mountain," "Scottsboro," "Let's Go to de Buryin'" and "How Long Brethren."

Indeed, it would seem that the militant, fiery Tamiris put in motion a trend which was to see the theater of dance flooded with works of social comment. As far back as 1929, she had composed *Revolutionary March* and *Dance of the City.* In quick succession came *Cycle of Unrest, Monumentum* (made up of "Unemployed," "Sh! Sh!," "Legion," "Nightriders," "Diversion," "Disclosure") and *Adelante,* a protest against the cruelties of the Spanish Civil War.

Tamiris was by no means a long figure in the dance of social comment. Martha Graham, the late Doris Humphrey, Charles Weidman, Hanya Holm— the leaders of America's modern dance movement—also raised their dance voices in protest against man's inhumanity to man, but such themes were much less frequent with them than with Tamiris or with that spate of dancers-choreographers who imitated them.

One of the major works of the 1930s which explored the plight of the Negro and flashed a blazing light on a horror-filled subject was Weidman's *Lynch Town* (originally from his *Atavisms* suite but often done as an independent work). Here, Weidman revealed not only the explosive frenzy, the blood lust of the lynchers themselves, but the equal guilt and evil of the onlookers who, vicariously, shared the thrill of murder.

Weidman has always been viewed as the comedy genius of American modern dance, a great clown, and he has often used his wit (buffered by a bit of suitable venom) to disclose the foibles of man, but he has created dance works of deadly seriousness, such as *Lynch Town*. He returned to the Negro theme again in his great portrait of Lincoln, *A House Divided*. Other deeply rooted problems of the times were probed by Weidman and his colleagues and, as I say, by lesser lights.

It seemed as if every young choreographer was rebellious. Anna Sokolow, destined to become one of the major choreographers of our time, was angry and unhappy (she still is, choreographically speaking) about evils, inequities, insecurities. Those whose names have long since been forgotten tortured the public with highly personal, dreadfully choreographed cycles of unrest, of protest, of revolution as they clambered aboard what might be described as a "ban"-wagon.

I don't need to dig out from my 1930 files any of the programs of these minor protesters. The format was almost always the same: Statement, Conflict, Resolution, Revolution, Affirmation. Small wonder that a rash of such pieces inspired Fanny Brice to create her hilarious satire on modern dance, *Rewolt!* Even the usually practical Doris Humphrey was worried about this. "How will we ever make it if people like Fanny Brice make fun of us?" she said. To which I replied, "You've already made it or a star like Fanny Brice couldn't be bothered with modern dance."

When the period of self-indulgence was over, one could look back and assess what modern dance had achieved in the field of social comment. Once the excesses had been pared away, the strong bone of social conscience and human consciousness remained to become an important part of the skeletal structure of American dance.

This era of the dance of social comment (it was paralleled by the drama in such plays as *Let Freedom Ring* or *The House of Connelly*) belong to the art of American modern dance rather than to ballet. True, the Jooss Ballet's masterpiece, *The Green Table,* an anti-war ballet, was created in 1932, but it must be remembered that Jooss was closer to the Central European modern dance than he was to traditional ballet.

Later, the world of ballet, as its creative horizons expanded, found sources of inspiration in the field of social comment. Jerome Robbins explored it in *The Guests,* a much underestimated ballet which was ahead of its time (or behind, from the modern dance position). This was a ballet of ostracism, of the separation of communities, ethnic or religious (Robbins did not turn literal), by unseen but potent barriers.

The choreographic treatment which Robbins used with *The Guests* is of paramount interest to us, for it was a distinctively American choreographic concept. This has to do with distilling, with procuring the essence. Modern dance had known this for a long time (there were no cowboys nor Indians in Martha Graham's monumental classic, *Frontier*). Robbins did not give us the

499

geographical location, the time, the names of the antagonists in *The Guests*. He gave us the core of conflict and the characteristics, the individual and the mob, with which it was met.

Loring, in the newest of social comment ballets, *These Three*, uses the same distinctively American choreographic treatment. He does not say that this is Philadelphia, Miss. Why should he? It could have happened anywhere, and the choreographer need not be a geographer. He does not tell us when this happened. For the choreographer need not be a chronicler. He does not even say that the three of the title are civil rights workers per se. Naturally, we assume they are, and also, because we know recent history, we tend to identify the three with front-page newspaper reports. But we would be doing Loring an injustice if we stopped right there, for he is saying in dance that in man's battle against injustice, three who have dedicated themselves to fraternity may be destroyed by an insensate, fearful mob, but that hope, in the image of four, will emerge to take their place.

The force of Loring's *These Three* lies in the fact that the choreographic treatment incorporates all forms of dance (ballet, modern, jazz, gesture) and that its viewpoint is universal rather than provincial; of the essence (and the essential) rather than the literal. *These Three* is in the finest tradition of the dance of social comment. We have, as we should, many great ballets predicated upon the premise of "let me entertain you." Eugene Loring is reminding us that one of the functions of the artist of the dance is—"let me disturb you." [*New York Herald Tribune*]

The Tamiris Spirit

November 6, 1966

"Chairman-in-Chief in Absentia"—this is an honorary title which America's renascent modern dance owes to the late Helen Tamiris. Just a very few weeks ago, when the National Dance Foundation was brought into being to produce as well as present modern dance in extensive Broadway seasons and subsequently across the land, more than one of its founding members murmured, "Helen would have been all for it."

The exuberant, fiery, often controversial dancer–choreographer–leader died this summer. Less than a year ago, she was busy with plans to create a major new work and, perhaps, revive her historic *How Long Brethren* for the American Dance Theater, a fairly new repertory theater, currently quiescent, which gave two seasons at the New York State Theater. Then the fatal disease suddenly struck the lustiest of all the founders—the others being Martha Graham, Doris Humphrey, Charles Weidman and Hanya Holm—of America's modern dance.

Before the new National Dance Foundation, headed by the dancers-choreographers Alvin Ailey, Merce Cunningham, Murray Louis, Alwin Nikolais and Paul Taylor, was even dreamed of, Tamiris was a veteran of earlier enterprises.

Yes, even before the American Dance Theater, with José Limón as its artistic director, planned its first season, Tamiris and the late Doris Humphrey had pooled their talents and their influences on a project to establish a big modern dance repertory company which would present the modern dance masterpieces of the past as well as produce new works. They made budgets and plans, they besieged foundations for money, they hoped. Then Humphrey died and the project waited until the American Dance Theatre was launched.

But way before the Humphrey–Tamiris blueprint, Tamiris herself had led the way in starting a modern dance repertory season on Broadway. In 1930, when modern dance was barely five years old, Tamiris helped organize the Dance Repertory Theater (she was its first president) which, for two years, presented seasons featuring works by Graham, Humphrey, Weidman and herself (Holm, the fifth modern dance leader, had not yet left her native Germany for America).

Tamiris' indomitable spirit patently pervades the new and vital National Dance Foundation; it can be a guide to the American Dance Theatre and to yet other dance projects.

The coming generation of American dancers will know Tamiris only as history. Many today never saw her dance and knew her only as an exceptionally beautiful woman with a dazzling smile, a roaring laugh, inexhaustible energy and a fierce determination of Whitmanesque proportions, "to see America dancing."

The volatile spirit was there from the start. It was even in her name. For Helen Becker, born in 1905 of impoverished immigrant parents in New York's Lower East Side, found her name and, curiously, her special characteristics in the first line of a poem about a Persian queen: "Thou art Tamiris, the ruthless queen who banishes all obstacles." Tamiris didn't banish them all, but she came close.

Her father disapproved of the child's urge to dance; besides, he couldn't afford lessons. So little Helen danced in the streets. There is a story, perhaps apocryphal, that a handsome woman, driving by, ordered her car to be stopped and said, "My child, you will be a dancer." The woman? Isadora Duncan. But her brother, however, saw her dancing in the streets and urged his father to enroll the eight-year-old in Irene Lewisohn's dance classes at the Henry Street Settlement. The career had begun.

At Henry Street, she studied free dance forms (a precursor of modern dance), but subsequently passed an audition in ballet at the Metropolitan Opera and earned her first salary along with free lessons. She was soon restive with conventional ballet forms and moved on to study with the liberal Michel Fokine, but still felt that "ballet, imported from abroad, could not speak for America in American terms."

Briefly, she went into show business as a specialty dancer and scored with a Chinese number ("I twirled my braids to great applause," she said) in *The Music Box Revue* and saved enough money to pay for her first concert in a program of her own choreography and using her own personally developed dance technique. *Dance Moods,* which she called her debut program given at New York's Little Theater, Oct. 9, 1927, was a success and opened the way for her to banish other obstacles.

Her first programs included movement idioms associated with the prize fighter, the American Negro, the citizen of the jazz age, the ordinary man. Her dancing of Spirituals, her Walt Whitman dances and, soon, her dances of social protest heralded her future course.

Tamiris, the first American to dance at the Salzburg Festival (1928), during the depression became the director of the Dance Division of the Works Progress Administration's Federal Theater Project here in New York, but she continued to dance, choreograph and protest while she directed. In her most violent dances, she was described as "a dynamo of energy and blunt force, fearless, direct and propulsive," but with her Negro Spirituals, "not translation but illumination." Nobody ever matched her impact.

It was no secret that Tamiris, during the thirties, was an ardent left-winger. But when she moved from the poverty of concert dancing to choreographing for Broadway musicals (*Up in Central Park* in 1943 and, later, the revival of *Showboat, Annie Get Your Gun, Inside U.S.A., Plain and Fancy* and many others), the comfort of a mink coat and a bank balance seemed to make her much more conservative, if no less robust and opinionated.

She has, I think, too often been underestimated in the place she held in the birth and growth of American modern dance. She did everything with such gustiness and urgency that when she did a bad work, it really was a blooper, but she also turned out some stunners, among them, the radiant *Liberty Song.*

A re-appraisal of Helen Tamiris' great contribution to America's dance triumphs would find her in the top echelon as a dancer, a choreographer (the bloopers to the contrary), a pioneer, a leader, an organizer, a fighter. Tamiris is no longer here to help banish the obstacles which, say, the new National Dance Foundation faces, and that is to raise money to buy or lease a theater on Broadway for American modern dance and to attract funds to keep such a project going into the tomorrows. But the Tamiris spirit is right there with the organization's directors. And they had better do honor to their absent chairman or they may well hear some celestial rumblings of disappointment and, of course, protest. [*World–Journal Tribune*]

Bad Deal for Ballet at the Met

December 4, 1966

The poor old Met. In its new Met home it is still having troubles with its ballet enterprises. Indeed, ballet deterioration has set in during the very first season of the Metropolitan Opera in its glittering new house at Lincoln Center.

Just a few weeks ago, I discovered that the Met's annual ballet night, originally slated for next April, had been cancelled. This fact was not announced—it had to be unearthed. Now this seemed mighty strange, since new union agreements had provided year-round security for the opera's dancers, since ballet performances by the resident troupe had proved successful at the box office (not only at the old Met but at outside events), and since the stated policy had been that the opera ballet would be encouraged to expand its activities.

What's the trouble?

Presumably, when the Metropolitan Opera, three years ago, engaged Dame Alicia Markova to be its ballet director, the goal was to build ballet. Or was the world-famous ballerina, recently retired, to be merely window-dressing? After all, an illustrious professional name and a title royally bestowed could do no harm to the Met's over-all prestige.

Dame Alicia has presided over two all-ballet nights at the Met, stadium appearances at Lewisohn, Jacob's Pillow Dance Festival events and even happy excursions into Brooklyn's Prospect Park. Not all was perfect, not by a long shot, for it takes time for a stellar performer to become a decisive, fast-moving, shrewd, ruthless director.

The "Dame," of course, has her weaknesses. She tends to see dancing through the eyes of one who was a performing artist celebrated for delicacy, gentleness, mysticism, and I have been told that at audition she leans more to the dutifully correct dancer of refinement than to the flamboyant hoofer. Still and all, Markova knows more about ballet than any of her bosses at the Met, and given, in equal qualities, both a chance and a prod, she could probably carry off what she would like to do.

But let's look at the status of ballet at the Met today. In the past two seasons, through extra performances, the Metropolitan Opera Ballet has improved noticeably, the standards are higher, the possibilities are endless. True, bad casting and poorly conducted rehearsals made the new *La Gioconda* ballet a shambles (the leading male dancer should have been dismissed summarily, such was his monumental inadequacy).

The cancellation of the single ballet night and the basic attitude of the management toward ballet are not going to help the cause of ballet at the Met. What ambitious dancer, in his right mind, would want to be with the Met? Oh, yes, if you are run-of-the-mill and know it, the financial security it provides is dreamy. But if you want to be someone, forget it.

And the Met, because it neglects its opera ballet, keeps losing its best dancers—not all but some. Hans Meister, Edith Jerell, Katharyn Horne and other good dancers have left. More will follow, for there seems to be, at the moment, no future.

The cancellation of the ballet night was determined by lack of funds (as Dame Alicia pointed out, the ballets of last season were designed for the new theater and were instantly available) and, according to rumor, by lack of dance talent. If there is a lack, it's the Met's own fault for not offering performing opportunities to dancers.

Rudolf Bing, the Met's general manager, and his assistant, John Gutman, have professed year after year after year after year that they would adore to have the opera ballet expand and flower. I don't believe them any more.

One of the Met's dancers, who has also performed for the New York City Opera, told me, "We are over-rehearsed for nothing. We're paid to turn up and just sit. The excitement is gone. I fight to keep my dance morale. With the New York City Opera the salaries were awful but we were professionals."

And this brings us to the New York City Opera, now in its new home, the State Theater, right next to the new Met at Lincoln Center. It cannot promise dance stars anything like the long-term contracts or salaries that the Met provides, but it attracts first-rate dance principals and always has (under its director of ballet, Thomas Andrew) because they get a showcase.

This season, the low-budget New York City Opera has given the Met a run for its money in the operatic department and, on several occasions, come out ahead. The same is true of the opera ballets.

Over the recent years, Mr. Andrew has obtained the services of such stunning dancers as Christine Hennessey, Rochelle Zide, Rosario Galan, Michael Maule, and they all proved to be show-stopping performers. The Met's *La Gioconda* had four weeks of rehearsal and was a near-disaster; Mr. Andrew staged his dances for *Gioconda* for the Philadelphia Opera in 24 hours, stopped the show with it and got reviews which said, "the dancers matched the brilliant appearance of a sold-out house" and "the best opera ballet seen in Philadelphia in many a moon."

Rehearsal hours don't make the ballet or the dancer. For example, Mr.

Andrew set and rehearsed his highly successful dances for the City Opera's *Merry Widow* in 12 hours (these included a cancan, a classical ballet and a folk dance); the ballet for *Fledermaus* was set in four hours and the cleanup rehearsal period took six. Incidental dances for such operas as *Don Giovanni, Marriage of Figaro* or *Tales of Hoffmann* are set in only two hours. ("Do your choreographic homework," says Mr. Andrew, "and then you don't have to waste the dancers' time.")

The ballet for the New York City Opera rehearses about two to four hours each day; there is one week rehearsal prior to the opening of the season, and seven weeks of performances with limited rehearsals. Mr. Andrew has set and rehearsed ballets for as many as ten productions a season and almost all of them have been audience favorites and successful with the critics. "Don't get too busy or complicated," he says. "Make the dancers look good." Thus, he takes a company in New York, Philadelphia or Baltimore and divides it into groups. "Some jump well. Others turn. Some girls have high extensions of the legs. Then I find some who look best just standing. I use them for what they can do."

The Metropolitan Opera, with more time and more money, could take a guideline from the successful New York City Opera's ballet enterprises. And it must. European opera houses, some in cities barely bigger than Stamford, Conn., have dance troupes which not only perform in opera ballets but which also produce independent ballet works on a large scale. Sure, they are state-subsidized, but the Met has funds too, and ballet would require a budget which would be like a speck in comparison with what the new *Antony and Cleopatra* cost.

There is, then, absolutely no excuse for the demoralized ballet activities at the Met. The potential is there and it is even conceivable that the ballet, given performing opportunities, could come close to paying its own way. Mr. Bing and Mr. Gutman have talked long enough about what they *plan* to do with ballet. The time has come to do it. And if they can't figure out the next move and if they don't know how much authority to give Dame Alicia, I suggest that they get a dance graduate from New York City's High School of Performing Arts as an advisor. He (or she) may be a teenager but at least he would be a theater professional. [*World–Journal Tribune*]

1967

SR Surveys New Stars and Astarte

Eliot Feld and Cynthia Gregory, ABT's new star choreographer and bal-
lerina • Royal Ballet's Anthony Dowell gives an interview • John Butler's
Catulli Carmina at Caramoor, N.Y. • The Santo Domingo Indians • Ballet
takes a "trip" in Robert Joffrey's Astarte • Harkness Ballet finally makes
its New York debut at the Broadway Theatre

New Stars

June 3, 1967

The most *exciting* event in ballet is the birth of a new star, a ballerina. The
most *important* event in the world of dance is the emergence of a new creative
talent, a choreographer. Both blessed events happened to the American Ballet
Theatre during its present season at Lincoln Center's New York State Theater.
Such triumphs brought back memories, at least to balletgoers. In 1942, an almost unknown soloist stood on the stage of the Metropolitan Opera House
(the old one) and received twenty-seven curtain calls. The occasion was the
world premiere, by Ballet Theatre, of Antony Tudor's *Pillar of Fire.* The
dancer who became a star overnight was Nora Kaye.

Two years and ten days later, a comparative unknown was allowed, by
Ballet Theatre, to show his feelings about choreography in a modest ballet
called *Fancy Free.* His name was Jerome Robbins. Both Robbins and Kaye
have changed the history of ballet not only for America but also for the
world.

The debuts in this spring of 1967, presided over by the American Ballet
Theatre, may not have been quite as spectacular—after all, in the 1940s, Amer-
ican ballet accomplishments were still in the area of phenomena—but they
were exciting and they were important. The choreographic debut was that of
Eliot Feld, a soloist (not a principal dancer) with the American Ballet Theatre.
His first ballet is called, with accurate augury, *Harbinger,* and it is a work

which honors the title of the company he serves—it is ballet and it is contemporary theater.

Harbinger, which finds its rhythmic springboard in Prokofiev's Piano Concerto in G major, Op. 55, is a ballet about youth. No, it has not a hint of a plot, but it does have a testament. Yes, it shows us that today's youth is uncertain, restless, reaching out, but that is a classic state—Nefertiti's children were no different. What Mr. Feld has done, however, is to show us that although youth must walk alone, cling together, snap its fingers at tradition, defy, enjoy, and shock, that it does, as in the glorious ending to the third movement of his ballet, turn its many faces toward the sun.

I guess *Harbinger* might loosely be described as a jazz ballet in American style. I suppose one could say that it shows the influence of Jerome Robbins —but how therapeutic that is in an era when almost everything in ballet is derivative of George Balanchine, for Robbins, who grew up in Weehawken, New Jersey, is as much of a dance genius as the gentleman from old St. Petersburg.

At its most obvious moments (and they are few), *Harbinger* seems to be an updating of Robbins's *Interplay,* the most popular American item on the American Ballet Theatre's repertory for foreign tours. In its peaks (and they are many) of choreographic invention, *Harbinger* mirrors the pulse of an age, an attitude toward that age, and comments both humorously and sadly on it.

There are no toe shoes in *Harbinger,* but it is a ballet, for it is filled with exuberant dancing, with formations and figurations which you have never seen before, with movement expressions of sorrow and defiance, humor and hope, with tenderness and with thrust. *Harbinger* is, I think, "ballet today." For it *is* ballet, show biz, people, lostness, discovery, uncertainty, urgency, fresh forms, and a miraculous happening which makes going to the theater of ballet not simply a pleasure but, rather, an adventure.

And now may I tell you about Cynthia Gregory? She's our ballerina. She's our star. Miss Gregory, just twenty years old and not yet ranked officially as a principal dancer, leaped onto the great stage of the State Theater in the American Ballet Theatre's fabulous new production of the four-act *Swan Lake* and made it quite clear that as Odette–Odile, she was on the threshold of entering an exclusive society which numbers among its members England's Dame Margot Fonteyn and Russia's Maya Plisetskaya.

On her entrance, it was apparent that here was a ballerina. She had, as she moved through the lyrical patterns given to Odette, the gentle Queen of the Swans, that ballet "line," that definition of the body in space, which distinguishes a ballerina from a mere dancer. No one could have taught it to her. It was instinctive, this placement of the arms, this extension of the legs, this tilt of the head.

The actual physical technique was superb, more secure than that of many of her seniors in the ballerina category. In Act III, as the harsh and evil Odile, she accomplished the exhausting and immensely difficult sequence of thirty-two whirling fouettés with stunning aplomb. With all this was the actress, for Miss Gregory made a dazzling transformation from the sad and sweet Odette to the fiery and feral Odile. But most important of all, Miss Gregory transformed the stage itself by her very presence. Only a ballerina can do that.

As the curtain fell on this historic New York debut (she had danced Odette–Odile just once before during the company's recent tour), ballet followers were asking where she came from. Her main teacher, in Hollywood, was Carmelita Maracci, who, in her dancing days, was one of the most electrifying performers of our era, and her chief professional experience was with the San Francisco Ballet. Now, through her triumph in *Swan Lake,* Miss Gregory belongs to the world of dance as its newest star.

The new has by no means replaced the cherished old during the American Ballet Theatre's memorable season at Lincoln Center. Agnes de Mille's history-making *Rodeo* was given a revival (with the best cast of dancers it has ever had) of such spanking freshness that it seemed as if de Mille were making history all over again. [*Saturday Review*]

A Newcomer Plus Two Top Stars

June 10, 1967

"I need to be driven. I need to be frightened into it. Dancing comes naturally to me, but daily discipline doesn't." Young Anthony Dowell of England's Royal Ballet, which has just concluded a triumphant stand at the Metropolitan Opera House, was speaking of both the burdens and the joys devolving upon one of the most gifted male dancers of our time. True, the luminousness of his artistry had to contend with the blaze of Rudolf Nureyev's dancing in the Royal Ballet and the golden perfection of Erik Bruhn's dancing with the American Ballet Theatre (playing next door at Lincoln Center), but even in such exalted company he made a striking impression.

That he is a natural dancer, there can be no doubt. When the Royal Ballet was last on tour of America, dance followers discovered for themselves a youngster who moved with marvelous musicality, whose lithe body appeared capable of doing whatever he demanded of it. But whether he has been driven or frightened into hard daily training in the intervening years, he has now emerged, at twenty-four, as a polished artist with a prodigious technique— projected with deceptive ease—and with a new authority as an actor–dancer (in his teens, he seemed a trifle bland).

The Dream, Sir Frederick Ashton's one-act version of Shakespeare's *A Midsummer Night's Dream,* was the first ballet created especially for Dowell (he is Oberon, the boy-king of fairyland). This was in 1964 and, he says, "It gets harder all the time. The problem is that Oberon is not a human. He's a creature, yet I must find ways of getting humor out of the character itself."

In his newest role he is also a boy—a boy-lord-of-the-jungle—in Antony Tudor's *Shadowplay,* but here he is a youth beset by fears, uncertainties, perils, and temptations not to be encountered in fairyland. In *Shadowplay,* there is a recurring stance, a semi-kneel as if the boy were sitting on an invisible throne; sometimes the face is composed, again it might be caught up in anguish, for Dowell must bring a variety of moods and responses to a powerful yet difficult role.

Variety, however, is his special gift. Not only has he mastered two aspects of youth in two different ballets, one by Ashton and one by Tudor, but he has also added to his repertory such challenging classics as *Swan Lake* and *Giselle.* He is the inexorable Messenger of Death in Kenneth MacMillan's *Song of the Earth*; he is a fine Romeo and, because of his inborn talent for pure rhythmic action, he excels in those abstract ballets which exploit the beauty and the prowess of the body.

Of his personal repertory, he says, "The classical ballets are geometric. They are firmly established in style and in step. They are familiar. If you make a mistake, it shows. In modern ballets, maybe one like *Romeo and Juliet,* you can cover a technical mistake with a dramatic movement. *The Dream*? It is so long and so difficult, I guess my main aim is to get to the end!"

Dowell's chief guide to the interpretation of a role or to the style suitable for a given ballet is the choreographer himself. Says the young star, "The choreographer is the key to it all—this is especially true of Tudor. You do exactly as he says, even when he tells you that he wants to see the sun shining out of your back. Yes, there is a little of me in *Shadowplay*, but what the audience sees is mainly what he specifies."

Whether it is "a little of me," the specifications of the choreographer, or being "driven" and "frightened" into working relentlessly at his career, or a combination of all these factors, Anthony Dowell has now become one of the top male dancers in the world. Nureyev and Bruhn may well look to their laurels.

At the instant, however, the Bruhn–Nureyev laurels are secure. Public adulation is theirs, and they accept both noisy and sighing homages with the gracious condescension of princes receiving the fealty of loyal subjects.

During the engagements now ended at Lincoln Center, Nureyev and Dame Margot Fonteyn were protected at curtain calls by phalanxes of stalwart ushers who kept the cheering fans from racing down the aisles to the stage of the Metropolitan Opera House. At the New York State Theater, Bruhn's devotees slithered through the side doors of the auditorium to stand by the orchestra pit and pelt their idol with flowers and petals. Did the two—Bruhn and Nureyev—deserve the almost hysterical ovations accorded them? Probably not. But the shrieks of the fans were directed at two of the world's great dance personalities. As two great dance artists, they earned the undivided attention and enthusiasm of the more reserved elements in their audiences.

Both, in separate theaters, gave us their Romeos. Nureyev's Shakespearean hero—which he played, oddly enough, rather like a meloncholy Dane in the Royal Ballet's evening-long *Romeo and Juliet* (choreographed by MacMillan)—was distinguished by some of the most lyrico-dramatic dancing on view this season. Bruhn, who is a Dane, played Romeo in his own pas de deux version of the great love story, with a romantic impetuosity which his Russian rival lacked. Both, of course, provided their fans with that ballet bravura which is what turns mere people into fans.

A few more words about Bruhn are in order, since I devoted more space to Nureyev in an earlier issue. It was Bruhn's superb characterization of Albrecht in *Giselle* which led to the tossing of flowers and the uncountable number of curtain calls. But his greatest performance—and it was a thing without flaw—came in that masterpiece of Danish ballet, August Bournonville's *La Sylphide,* a ballet of 1836 in a stunning and tasteful production by the American Ballet Theatre. Bruhn, trained in the Bournonville style since childhood, danced the part of the Scotsman (lured from his wedding to a mortal lass by an irresistible and elusive creature of fancy, a sylphide) with his own personal intensity coupled with a command of romantic ballet style unequaled by any other dancer.

Bruhn, of course, did not carry off *La Sylphide* by himself. He had, as his partner in the role of the sylphide, the lovely Carla Fracci, the only major Italian ballerina of the day.

Fracci, who looks as if she had stepped from the frame of a delicately tinted lithograph of the last century, is soft of movement, airy, shy, utterly feminine. She is neither a dazzling virtuosa nor even a profound actress, but she is a ballerina of great charm and sweet accomplishments. Every male in an audience would instinctively want to protect her, and so it is that she is quite captivating as the sylphide (the American Ballet Theatre's Danish-born Toni Lander is now unmatched, stylistically, in the role) and a fine Giselle, especially in the delicate and misty measures of the second act in which she is the ghost maiden whose love for Albrecht transcends deceit and death itself.

The local debut of Fracci, the eminence of Dame Margot, tended to obscure the accomplishments of other ladies of the ballet. Miss Lander not only excelled in *La Sylphide* but she also turned on her amazing flood of virtuosity in that technique showpiece, *Etudes*—choreographed by her former husband,

Harald Lander—and gave us a new view of Lander in her pure and cool dancing of the pas de deux section (with her present husband and perfect partner, Bruce Marks) of Kenneth MacMillan's fine new abstract ballet, *Concerto* (Shostakovich). And in this ballet, America's newest ballerina, Cynthia Gregory, proved that her triumph as Odette–Odile in *Swan Lake* was no fluke; she made comparable dance magic in a non-narrative ballet.

Among the Royal dancers, the blonde and coquettish Antoinette Sibley was not only the perfect Titania to Dowell's Oberon, but also a delight in music visualization ballets. A colleague, Merle Park, caught the eye in a number of vivacious assignments, but the revelation of the depth of her artistry came with her interpretation of Juliet. There, indeed, was a fourteen-year-old girl child—a shy, terrified little thing whose innocence and whose ardor were inextricably linked. Seeing Miss Park's portrait in dance of the most poignant of Shakespeare's heroines I almost forgot the Fonteyn portrayal, such was Park's freshness and force. How fortunate to have two such Juliets: Dame Margot's radiant re-creation of youth; Miss Park's bearing of the terrible vulnerability of the very young.

Finally, just as you had made up your mind quite firmly that the American Ballet Theatre's Miss Gregory did the best bourrées to be seen anywhere, a dash to the Met simply proved that Deanne Bergsma's bourrées were like a coil of flawless pearls shimmering across the stage. Or were they better? Both, in truth, represented a dance detail gloriously.

As the two overlapping ballet seasons came to a close at Lincoln Center, thousands upon thousands of balletgoers—laymen as well as aficionados—knew that they had been participants in an unprecedented ballet boom. Lucia Chase, co-director of the American Ballet Theatre, had predicted correctly. Her company and the Royal Ballet were not opposed; they were simply juxtaposed to give New York a great ballet festival with the incomparable and distinctly different artistries of Erik Bruhn and Rudolf Nureyev; with the continuing magic of Dame Margot Fonteyn; with the discovery of Carla Fracci; with the births of a new choreographer (Eliot Feld) and a new ballerina of extraordinary powers (Cynthia Gregory) by the American Ballet Theatre; by superb dancing, despite individual anonymities, of two memorable corps de ballets; and by the excitement engendered by the restless, flourishing talents of such as Anthony Dowell, who has quite a lot more than his "a little bit of me" with which to illumine the world of dance. [*Saturday Review*]

512

Erotic Dances in the Starlight

July 22, 1967

Caramoor, N.Y. John Butler creates some of the most beautiful and imaginative choreographic designs that you are likely to find in the theater of dance. The designs are almost always erotic, and they are always projected by dancing bodies of superb physical beauty. But as erotic as both the beings and the movements are, they are never offensive, for comparison, as well as passion, is to be found in Mr. Butler's choreographic explorations (and exposures) of the needs and the drives of the human, no matter what the era.

His lovely and disturbing choreographic images were on display recently in two performances for the 22nd annual festival at Caramoor, presented by the Walter and Lucie Rosen Foundation in the Venetian Pavilion of the vast Rosen estate in Katonah, New York. Eras were also on display, for the festival's dance presentations were not only all-Butler but also representative of poetic inspirations jumping from the poems of the Roman Catullus of B.C. to the lyrics of Pierre Louys, A.D. (1894).

First in dusk and then in starlight, the dancers and actors moved in and out of the columned archways of the pink-stoned pavilion. Choreography and setting were perfectly matched in these entrances and exits, for the arrivals and departures ranged from explosive thrusts forward through gentle lingerings to farewells one knew would be final.

The Louys piece, *Chansons de Bilitis* (twelve poems set to music of Debussy as completed by Pierre Boulez), had its American premiere at Caramoor in a version completely revised from that given at the Festival of Two Worlds in Spoleto, Italy. Butler's new staging—and it is so glorious that one hopes he will never alter it—has Mildred Dunnock as Bilitis, Carmen de Lavallade as Bilitis Remembered, and Veronica Mlakar as The Beloved.

Everyone knows that Miss Dunnock is one of our great actresses. But did you know that she is also a dancer? Well, she not only spoke the Louys poems (in English translation) with a rich palette of tones and dramatic intensities, but she also moved with the eloquence of a dancer. This was not simply gestural dancing—although the actress did use her hands with the artistry of an accomplished mime—for her entire body moved with the dancer's flow.

Movement flow of unequalled beauty was present in the dancing of Miss de Lavallade. Here, indeed, is a creature of incredible grace and loveliness, and so effortless is her dancing that one is never aware of the technique which underlies it. She and Miss Dunnock performed Butler's steps, gestures, and patterns with such a remarkable joint intent that one was not actually aware of parallel portrayals but, rather, of a characterization of a single person in which presence and memory were inextricably entwined.

513

Miss Mlakar was less evanescent of motion. Her role called for full-bodiedness, for urgency, and she danced it brilliantly. The three mirrored in motion the "shake thy loins" instruction of the poet or the "clambering hands" he speaks of; and who would ever forget the soft touchings, the oh-so-tender embracings of Bilitis herself and Bilitis Remembered, as the older woman caressed her own memory and, in turn, was comforted by it.

Butler's *Catulli Carmina* constituted the second half of this all-dance program at Caramoor. Eroticism of a different sort was the key as the dancers moved to the emotionally incendiary words of Catullus and to the drive, the cries, the insistently savage rhythms of Carl Orff. This stunning Butler creation has been seen only at Caramoor (where it had its premiere two years ago), but there is hope now that it will be seen soon in New York.

Julius Rudel, music director of Caramoor and the director of the New York City Opera, plans to bring *Catulli Carmina* to the New York State Theater at Lincoln Center as soon as he can find a short opera to share the bill with it. The Butler–Orff *Carmina Burana* paired with the Stravinsky *Oedipus Rex* constitutes one of the New York City Opera's most popular programs. Rudel would like to do the two *Carminas* as a full program, but he notes that, as much as he loves ballet and as much as he has fostered its expansion under his direction, "I cannot offer an all-dance evening in an opera repertory." So only an operatic companion is needed to bring *Catulli Carmina* into the repertory of the New York City Opera.

And there is every reason to urge Rudel to get the *Catulli* onto Broadway. Butler's *Carmina Burana* is the best of the several productions I have seen, and the *Catulli Carmina* is equal to it in every respect, choreographic and erotic.

At Caramoor, Miss de Lavallade was the errant Lesbia, tempting and desirable but heartless, and Miss Mlakar was the angry but sexy Ipstilla. Robert Powell, who possesses the same magic of movement that Miss de Lavallade has as her special characteristic, was the restless, ardent Catullus, attracted by both the female and the male. He, too, moves with a disarming effortlessness, as if dancing were his natural way of motion, and in his scenes with Miss de Lavallade the dancing was pure poetry—carnal perhaps, but poetic. With Buzz Miller as Caelius, Powell danced with a fierceness contained in the pounding elements of the score and in Butler's use of anticipatory silences, and the two provided the viewers with a curious combination of lustful intent and the warrior's display of prowess and muscular brutality.

Constant dancegoers can almost—but not quite—predict that a new Butler ballet will pursue a pattern of eroticism. They would seem to be right, for his next work, a ballet just now being completed to music of Lee Hoiby for the Harkness Ballet, is called *Landscape for Lovers.* But the sure predictors had better take warning, for Butler says, "The artist finds his themes in the religious or in its opposite, the sensual. It is Apollo or Dionysus, for we ourselves are both. We need both sides of the being, but the choreographer, the artist, starts with whatever happens to be uppermost at the moment."

For the moment, it would seem that John Butler finds his choreographic stimulus in the sensual rather than in the religious (although he has created dances of religious content). But no matter. As his principal teacher and long-time colleague, Martha Graham, has said about certain of her own master-pieces based upon sensual responses, "Eroticism is a lovely thing." [*Saturday Review*]

Adventure into a Celestial Sphere

September 2, 1967

Santo Domingo, N.M.   The insistent drumbeat echoes the most miraculous pulse in the world—the beat of the living heart. It is appropriate that this should provide the underlying rhythm of the ceremonial dances at the Santo Domingo pueblo, the largest pueblo (2,000 inhabitants) of the Indians of the Rio Grande, midway between Santa Fe and Albuquerque.

These Santo Domingo Indians, of Keres stock, are said to be the most conservative of all Indians. They prefer to keep away from the white man, be he Spanish or "Anglo" (as the Indian calls the non-Spanish white). Still, every year on August 4, they display their hospitality by inviting outsiders to attend a day-long celebration in honor of their patron saint, St. Dominic. A statue of the saint is brought out of the mission church before the visitors arrive and is placed in a shrine, made of green boughs, in the long plaza lined with one-story (and occasionally two-story) adobe houses. It is set between two huge *kivas*—in Santo Domingo, one is the ceremonial center for the turquoise clan and the other for the pumpkin and squash clan—and from these great, circular edifices emerge the hundreds of men and women and children who will honor their saint with a pre-Christian *Corn Dance*.

It is an unforgettable sight—I watched for ten hours—to see the long main avenue of the pueblo filled with dancing, chanting Indians dressed in gorgeous costumes ranging from somber black to vivid turquoise and fiery red and snowy white, the black to remind the living that death is ever present, but the blue of the sky, the golden glow of the sun, to symbolize the continuation of life, with white feathers serving as silent prayers.

A striking prologue to the *Corn Dance* is the appearance of the Koshare, who play a major role in the ceremony. Their bodies and costumes are

515

mostly painted white, though some use dark dye, but it is purposefully splotchy and suggests creatures from the spirit world. And that is really what the Koshare are, for they link the living with the dead. Their black loin-flaps represent the netherworld or death, and the golden tufts of dried corn husks which stand up from their white helmets symbolize the sun.

Early in the morning, before the dancing begins, the Koshare run through the streets of the pueblo clearing the town of evil spirits. "You might think of them as special police," an Indian friend told me. Although they have magical powers and serious duties to perform, the Koshare are an amiable, even mischievous lot. They run and dance where they please, and during the mass formations, they weave themselves in and out of the formal patterns made by the dancers. They do their own steps, improvise at will, even move in syncopation with the tread of the other Indians. They also pause to adjust costumes, secure slipping headdresses, and help some of the five- and six-year-olds get back into the proper patterns when they have lost their way. I asked my Indian companion if a Koshare might be described as an equivalent to the god Pan. "Partly," he replied, "but there is a great deal of Till Eulenspiegel there, too."

Once the Koshare have performed their initial duties, the dancers and singers of the two clans, one at a time (they dance together only on rare occasions), fill the plaza. The entrances and exits themselves are splendid pageantry. Adobe stairs lead to the flat peak of the tall brown *kivas*. Long ladders, which pierce the sky at one end, also descend to the sacred mysteries deep within. As the Indians mount or descend the outside staircases, they, like the thrusting tips of their ladders, are silhouetted against the blue, cloud-flecked sky. The golden corn tufts of the Koshare seem to be splinters of sunlight, and they, along with the multicolored costumes, are spectacularly defined against the vault of the firmament itself, as if we were witnesses to an adventure into a celestial sphere.

The Koshare are always men, but the two big bodies of dancers are made up of both men and women, some very old, some in their prime, some only little children. The men, bare-chested, wear white shirt-like dress, quite short, and fur-topped white moccasins. They are decorated with strings of shells (in prehistoric times, the area was a vast inland sea) worn diagonally, and with bells around the waist or below the knee. Blue, yellow, and green clusters of feathers bob from their forelocks (some wear their hair in flowing manes, while others have it bobbed or cut short). In the left hand, there is a green branch; in the right, a rattle.

The female dancers wear black dresses but they are brightly embroidered and are cinched by red belts. On their heads they carry thin boards which stand upright. These are blue and symbolize clouds and rainbows—the soft, white prayer feathers are attached. Most of the women have hair which falls below the waist, while others have the equivalent of a Dutch cut. A few wear moccasins but most are barefoot. They carry green boughs in both hands.

The large choir of men is composed mainly, but not entirely, of the seniors of the tribe. They do not wear traditional Indian dress, but they are distinctively Indian. Ordinary trousers and brightly colored shirts are augmented by bands of cloth (in every color imaginable) worn around the head or used to tie the buns of long-haired Indians; by great, turquoise-studded silver belts; necklaces and bracelets boasting the largest turquoises I have ever seen; moccasins or boots. Green branches are stuck in their belts, and their leader carries a tall pole, tipped with crimson feathers, which he waves in great arcs over singers and dancers—a blessing from the sun.

The actual steps employed in the *Corn Dance* are not many—the women frequently use a toe-touch followed by a flat-foot step while the men do little jumps kicking their heels up lightly—but there are variations on these basic steps and there is great choreographic variety. The dancers enter and depart in long-line processionals. But the lines shift swiftly and smoothly from two to four to five and, sometimes, even to eight ranks. The dancers may move up and down as in military parade or they may face each other and move back and forth, with great dexterity, through each other's ranks. They also break into blocks of dance figures and, very occasionally, into circles. Diagonal units of performers also vary the pattern, and at one point, early in the day, there was a vast ellipse which found the dancers stretched from one *kiva* to another, encompassing the shrine of the saint, nearly touching walls of homes flanking both sides of the plaza.

The singers, huddled closely to one wall of the plaza, surged slowly en masse, shifting positions as the dancers advanced and retreated. A tight semicircle was their basic formation, and their steps, a rhythmic shuffle.

As the afternoon progressed, an intensification of movement, sound, and spirit occurred. The heartbeat of the drums became swifter, the pitch of the drum itself climbed steadily to a peak at the ecstatic finale, and the dancers and singers, wholly involved in their ritual all along, seemed to find themselves in a mass, communal hypnosis. Faces were impassive, but inner dynamics, an identification with forces of mystery, could be felt by the onlooker.

As pace and pitch grew, not only did the Koshare make their choreographic infiltrations of the dance formations increasingly elaborate, but also a few of the old, old men of the pueblo, touched by the hand of unseen spirits, entered the vast dance design. They made their own way within the framework of the ceremonial; often, as they danced on old and weary legs, their veined hands were raised heavenward as they made incantational traceries in space. Each seemed to be alone, though part of many, in an awesome contact with deity. One of the gestures was an invitation for rain. It rained, lightly and briefly.

Scenes such as these can be recorded by the visitor only in the mind. The Indians of Santo Domingo permit no cameras, no drawing pads, no notebooks carried by foreigners on their huge reservation. They are even suspicious of non-Keres Indians. They hold to ancient ways, yet the new is juxtaposed to the old. On the roof of an adobe home you will see antlers, proof of a successful hunt, side by side with a television antenna. Outside the kitchen door, you will find the age-old beehive oven—and oh, how sweet the bread smells!—sharing the area with an electric washing machine.

Inside an Indian home, to which I was invited for lunch because my Indian companion (a Cherokee) knew the family well, I sat down to a delicious meal which included home-cooked bread, home-raised fruits and vegetables, and macaroni salad! A newborn baby was on a cradleboard (only his feet were showing, since his body and head were concealed beneath a tent-like structure) suspended from the ceiling as a swing. And every time Grandmother passed by, she would give the baby a push. "Sleeps better that way," she said.

In the exquisite, whitewashed mission church of Santo Domingo, one would find on one wall the Stations of the Cross, and in another very special area, murals of the squash, the corn, the maize. Behind the church, while the *Corn Dance* was being reborn in the plaza, a handful of young Indians were dancing the frug, the watusi, and variations thereof.

In the plaza, St. Dominic was greeted by prayerful visitors, by gifts of bread, by men dancers who shook their rattles in his direction, by women dancers who waved their green branches at him, by rites older than Christianity.

Which dominated? Which rhythms prevailed? As the plaza became incandescent with the patterns of ancient dance, a five-month-old baby, carried by a seven-year-old sister, waved a single green leaf, in perfect tempo, as 500 Indians of the village danced by.

Did it seem incongruous that at one point in the *Corn Dance* an old Indian should blow a trumpet, another should play a tattoo on a snare drum, and a younger man should fire a rifle? Not at all. It was a sardonic reminder that the invaders—first the Spaniards and then the "Anglos"—should also honor the saint. And that we should also. [*Saturday Review*]

Ballet Takes "The Trip"

October 7, 1967

Gods and goddesses of old, neglected and rejected, are never granted permanent burial. No one believes in any of them any more, but no one is quite ready to give them up. Choreographers are among this myth-renewal group. The latest to churn up ancient deities for the purpose of relating them to the confusions of this century is Robert Joffrey, head of the City Center Joffrey Ballet, which has just finished a four-week season at its home theater, the New York City Center of Music and Drama.

Joffrey's choreographic resurrection of a long-forgotten goddess was his *Astarte,* a psychedelic ballet. But the whole affair was not as post-garde updated to avant-garde as you might think. Decades ago, Ruth St. Denis did a ballet for the Denishawn Dancers which was called *Ishtar of the Seven Gates,* and in this ballet about a Babylonian goddess all seven gates "opened and shut on hinges," as Miss St. Denis's husband–partner, Ted Shawn, complained. And that was so avant-garde in its day that it never got out of Atlantic City until fewer hinges and gates made it suitable for touring. At this very instant, Miss St. Denis is hoping to move Ishtar from Babylon (and Atlantic City) to Las Vegas, where she might be revered in suitable fashion.

George Balanchine called up the old gods for his ballet *Electronics* just a few years ago. The revival was brief. The New York City Ballet doesn't dance it any more. Joffrey's *Astarte* has barely a nodding acquaintance with the Semitic goddess of fertility after which the ballet is named. Truth to tell, the whole affair is a very feeble pas de deux triumphantly saved from disaster by the Crome Syrcus musicians, a way-out mod group from Seattle, and a wild, wild film made by Gardner Compton. Astarte Baby needed help and she got it.

I have been told that *Astarte,* Joffrey's first creation in four years, started out as a rather lyrical pas de deux with ritual-like qualities somewhat reminiscent of his last creation, *Gamelan,* and that the psychedelic part came later. At any rate, it is the hallucinatory journey with colors, lights, films, and sounds, and not the duet, which matters here.

The "trip" for all of us in the audience begins with a light blinking brightly at us (no free LSD is given out by ushers) followed by follow-spots which travel in bright arcs across our faces. Hypnosis has begun. One of our number subsequently gets up from his seat and moves slowly, as if in a trance, down the aisle. But no, it is not really one of us, for it is a dancer, Maximiliano Zomosa (just saying that name is something of a psychedelic experience), who makes his way to the stage, drawn to it by a beautiful girl, Trinette Singleton, clad in softly hued, many-colored tights and wearing tattoo marks of stylized flowers on her brow.

Zomosa, standing before this echo of Astarte, strips in slow motion. Almost, that is, but unlike the dancers in Ann Halprin's San Francisco Dance Workshop who divested themselves of everything but their eyelashes, Zomosa chickened out at the boxer-trunks point of undress. Then, the duet on stage began. These live movements were related to the outsized, distorted, fantastic images which slid, glided, appeared, vanished, advanced, and retreated in glorious profusion on Thomas Skelton's marvelously contorted movie-screen setting. These images journeying upon the screen were Miss Singleton and Zomosa, so that there was a pair of duets going on simultaneously—one in the flesh with the limitations of actuality, the other in dreams where love's adventures are limitless.

The film, created by Compton, is fabulous, and the entire happening, brilliantly staged by Midge Mackenzie, with the perfect Skelton setting and with that superbly noisy and rhythmically hypnotic score commissioned and performed by the Crome Syrcus, makes any further stimulus to the senses unnecessary. You'll make the trip right from your seat in the theater, whenever and wherever Joffrey chooses to show it, perhaps at the Chicago Opera House January 29 through February 2 and certainly during the company's next season, February 26 through March 17, at the City Center, or wherever touring equipment permits.

At the City Center, for example, production facilities made it possible for Zomosa, who had set out from an aisle seat close to 55th Street, to end this theatrical adventure by going beyond the Skelton set, through a door which led from backstage to a back-backstage, through another door to a hallway, and on to the ordinary madness of plain old 56th Street.

The success of *Astarte*—and it is undeniably a smash hit—should not be so blinding that it makes theatergoers believe that they are seeing such psychedelic goings-on in dance for the first time. Heavens to Ishtar—Ishtar, Astarte, perhaps Esther, and certainly Betsy—adventures such as this have been going on for some time. Merce Cunningham turned the lights on us in *Winterbranch*; as far back as 1954, George Balanchine blinded us, along with stripping the skin off beings and showing the bare nervous system, in *Opus 34*; Alwin Nikolais has been our guide on many journeys involving movement, sound, shape, and color; and the avant-garde off Broadway has been as psychedelic as you can get for some seasons now. What Joffrey has done is to make the whole thing bigger and better than ever, more professional, and vastly more entertaining than small-scale studio excursions.

So now you will say, "Isn't that being derivative?" Of course. But that is not necessarily wrong, and often it works out rather well. In any event, it is something of a characteristic of the Joffrey company. Joffrey's own *Pas de Déesses* (which was adroitly juxtaposed to *Astarte,* at the latter's premiere) is a re-creation of a romantic ballet, inspired by a lithograph, in exactly the same way that Anton Dolin's *Pas de Quatre* (first re-created by Keith Lester) evoked the same era. The Joffrey evocation of an earlier ballet era is lovely and quite irresistible in its own right, but I seriously doubt that it would have materialized without the brilliant guidelines set by Dolin.

With Anna Sokolow, whose works are represented in the Joffrey repertory, you have a choreographer who drives from herself. As she moves from opus to opus, you find yourself seeing lots and lots of things (glares as well as steps) that you've seen before. As for Gerald Arpino, the City Center Joffrey Ballet's principal choreographer, he is so derivative that one of the favorite games of dancers is to look at any of his ballets and, like the late Sigmund Spaeth (known as the "Tune Detective"), who used to ferret out historic musical origins of new compositions, pinpoint where a *pas,* a passage, a lift comes from. It's a fun game, but let me make it abundantly clear that while you are spotting sizable portions of Balanchine (naturally, there is quite a bit of that), Robbins, Graham, and other major choreographers, or some dancer's highly individual warming-up exercises, Arpino's own considerable choreographic gifts shine and shimmer.

Derivativeness to the contrary, both *Astarte* and *Pas de Deesses,* though poles apart in ballet style (except that each deals with the goddess-type female), are real winners in the highly competitive field of ballet. *Astarte* speaks for the nervous adventures of our own day, for the desperate need to release our senses without inviting a holocaust. *Pas de Deesses* represents a nostalgic journey into the past where the then-current goddesses were reigning ballerinas and where refinement, even with a dash of malice, prevailed.

The Joffrey company, a handsome, lively, and versatile troupe, explores the gentle colors of old lithographs quite as well as it invades the tumbling colorations of the psychedelic. In *Pas de Deesses,* we have a dance for three of the greatest ballerinas of the 1840s—Taglioni, Cerrito, and Grahn—with St. Léon as their very busy and very attentive cavalier. Joffrey has given each of the ballerinas the movements, or movement qualities, historically associated with them (as Dolin did in *Pas de Quatre*), such as Taglioni's long line, long balances, and ethereal mien; Grahn's virtuosity; and Cerrito's effervescence. As Cerrito, Susan Magno is perfection itself as dancer and as actress, but Noel Mason is a sweet Taglioni and Lisa Bradley an irresistible Grahn.

Paul Sutherland, a superb premier danseur, is as close to faultless as a human can get as St. Léon, who plays smiling and gestural compliments to each of the ballerinas and who dances his own passages with both stylishness and brio. And if you happened to notice that Sutherland and Magno seemed to have something extra special (though subtly projected) going between them, don't read anything personal into it, for they were being purely historical— Cerrito and St. Léon were man and wife a century ago, and they felt about each other pretty much as the boy and the girl do in the new *Astarte,* which simply means that goddesses may change but that love goes on in many guises. And I guess that, too, is derivative, but divinely so. [*Saturday Review*]

521

A Very Special Jewel

November 25, 1967

All of the thousands upon thousands of balletomanes in the capital city of the dance world, New York, had been suffering for three years from a severe case of curiosity compounded with exasperation. When, oh *when*, was the newest major American dance troupe, founded in 1964, going to show itself to its well-wishers (and the usual assortment of vultures hoping for the kill) on Broadway?

If you traveled outside of New York, tantalizing glimpses were possible in, say, Cannes, France, or Dallas, Texas, or—if you received an invitation—at the White House. Words from abroad reported a group of splendid dancers, but was there a company, a distinctive style, homogeneity? In 1965 some European critics questioned this. So if the dancers were admittedly first-class, what of the repertory? Was there a point of view; was there homogeneity here? And that, too, was questioned. Over the whole enterprise was the shadow (or would it prove to be the light?) of an extremely rich woman. Would this new company be the plaything of a dilettante, or would it be a very special jewel provided by a discerning patroness of the arts?

The curiosities, the exasperations, and the queries were happily laid to rest on November 1 when the Harkness Ballet, following a glittering benefit preview the preceding night, finally made its New York debut at the Broadway Theater. The initial program and the subsequent ones made it abundantly clear that here, indeed, is a major new American company, a company with superb dancers, with homogeneity and yet variety, with a repertory boasting some of the finest creative accomplishments of our day, and with founder-patroness Rebekah Harkness, who knew exactly what she was doing all along.

The Harkness Ballet, taking its place as a *force majeure* in our world of dance, has balanced opulence of production with the lovely simplicity of perfectly trained bodies—unadorned—dancing in illuminated space. For example, you will find a brand new staging of Stravinsky's *Firebird*, choreographed by Brian Macdonald, the director of the Harkness Ballet, which is more lavish in décor and costumes than the Chagall mounting done in Balanchine choreography by the New York City Ballet. But you will also find a sweetly radiant pas de deux, *Youth*, by one of the company dancers, Richard Wagner, to music of Samuel Barber.

Not everything, of course, was perfect. So permit me to note and eliminate the imperfections first. Rouben Ter-Arutunian's scenery and costumes for *Firebird* were, at times, so gaudy that they obscured the choreography, which is possibly the best choreography that this ballet has ever had. (The usually dreary dance of the Princesses was charming, and the monsters

522

were really monsters.) But the closing wedding-scene tableau, which simply defies dancing, was saved by the designer's sumptuous setting, costumes, and masks.

I was also rather disenchanted with John Butler's *Landscape for Lovers,* set to music of Lee Hoiby, which seemed terribly superficial—you know, skin against skin but not pulses intermingling—except when headed by Lone Isaksen and Helgi Tomasson, two extraordinarily beautiful creatures who managed somehow to bring both physical perfection and the poeticisms of young love to bear on a minor work. What Butler didn't do, Norman Walker did with his *Night Song* (music of Hovhaness), a shimmering view of crepuscular sensualities.

Macdonald's *Tchaikovsky,* a sort of potpourri of Petipa–Ivanov choreographic exercises with Tchaikovsky—you could spot images from *Swan Lake, Sleeping Beauty,* and the like—turned out to be an overdressed, overstressed joke, or commentary, on earlier ballet.

Such a commentary, threaded with drama and marvelous choreographic invention, came with Agnes de Mille's triumphant new creation, *Golden Age,* in which one of the world's great dance innovators worked her very special magic in inducing laughter and tears simultaneously. *Golden Age,* with its delicious score by Genevieve Pitot (based on Rossini themes), striking décor by William and Jean Eckart, and delightfully outrageous costumes by Stanley Simmons, explores the styles, intrigues, rivalries, and multiple seductions of ballet dancers, perhaps at the Paris Opéra, a century ago.

Elizabeth Carroll, the brilliant star of *Firebird*, was bright, biting, glittering, and haughtily desperate as the aging star, and Claudia Cravey was excellent as the soft, luscious, and calculating successor, greedy but not all evil. (She, too, was shocked when the prima walked the pathway of oblivion.) I shall have more to say about this important work and the highly original art of Miss de Mille on a later occasion.

American theatergoers will be forever in the debt of the Harkness Ballet for bringing us *Monument for a Dead Boy,* choreographed by the Dutch choreographer, Rudi van Dantzig, to an electronic score by Jan Boerman, and with striking scenery and costumes by Toer Van Schayk. It is a choreographic penetration into the heart and mind of an adolescent boy who relives, through the image of his childhood, the crude, carnal capers of his parents; the love of a girl; the cruelty of bullies; the evanescent comfort of a male-with-male relationship; the terrors of shifting environments. *Monument for a Dead Boy*, cheered at every performance, is the work of one of the most powerful and fresh choreographic talents to come our way in a long, long time.

Lawrence Rhodes, a magnificent dancer and a consummate dramatic performer, played the title role in a characterization which belongs in the category of "great portrayals in the theater." Miss Isaksen, Miss Corday, and Roderick Drew as the parents, and Dennis Wayne as the tender friend, were superb.

Mr. Rhodes—yes, he is a wow in anything and everything—also shone in the title role of Mr. Butler's new conception of *Sebastian,* to the Gian-Carlo Menotti score, in which he plays the slave who gives his own body to death to spare the life of a beautiful courtesan (acted and danced to perfection by Brunilda Ruiz).

Quickly now, in capsule commentary, words of praise for Macdonald's show-stopping *Canto Indio* (Chávez), a dazzling duet for Miss Carroll and Tomasson; the same choreographer's *Zealous Variations* (Schubert), a piece which, if it seemed to change from performance to performance did so because it was split up into two separate sets of dances, and here you would have found a zealous and zestful duet by Tomasson and Finis Jhung; Stuart Hodes's masterful *Abyss* (based on a story by Andreyev and with music by Marga Richter), a tale of innocence violated by quadruple rape, the story touchingly performed by Miss Isaksen and Rhodes as the young lovers, and terrifyingly projected by Avin Harum, Robert Vickrey, and Mr. Wayne as the First Assailants. A worthy hit also was Jack Cole's *Requiem for Jimmy Dean,* an incompleted work in progress but thoroughly effective, as it now stands, as an entity. It contains practically every Cole jazz trademark I have seen, from the opening of the old Rainbow Room to now, but no one can pull off Coleisms like Cole himself. (The music is by Ronald Herder.)

But more on the Harkness Ballet anon. For the present, let it be said that the three years of pre-New York preparation have paid off handsomely. Marvelous dancers have become a wonderful company dancing a repertory which, in the words of its benefactress, "cherishes the great traditions of classical ballet . . . as it presses forward into new frontiers of dance. . . ."

[*Saturday Review*]

1968

The Spirit of Miss Ruth

*Peter Martins' dazzling debut with NYCB • An analysis of the avant
garde • The Bolshoi Ballet nearly a decade after its American debut •
Louis Falco's Huescape at Jacob's Pillow • Ruth St. Denis, High Priestess of American Dance, is gone • Caribbean dance • Dance reaches a
peak in the Children's Dance Theatre and the Repertory Dance Theatre
of Salt Lake City, Utah*

A Dazzling Dane

January 20, 1968

"I rebelled against dancing—any boy would," said the brilliant ballet newcomer who has been rousing New York audiences to cheers. "I rebelled
twice," he added. "Once when I was eleven or twelve—I had been taking daily
ballet lessons for four years and I just couldn't stand dancing any more. But
I had to stay with it. Again at sixteen, I hated dancing all over again. Now I
love it. It's my life."

The onetime rebel is tall, blond, handsome, and enormously gifted
twenty-one-year-old Peter Martins (of the Royal Danish Ballet), who has just
completed a series of guest appearances with the New York City Ballet at the
New York State Theater at Lincoln Center. Without any fanfare whatsoever,
young Mr. Martins took on the role of the Cavalier for the unusually short pas
de deux in George Balanchine's version of *The Nutcracker*. Holiday audiences
who had never heard of him applauded loud and long; one veteran balletomane who can take *Nutcrackers* or leave them alone (preferably the latter)
never missed a performance; another longtime ballet expert said, "I always
wanted to see a real Prince as the Cavalier, and now I have." Yet all young
Peter did was to partner the Sugar Plum Fairy and dance a very few measures
by himself (there is no solo variation in this staging of the old classic) in the
coda. The secret of his success was that he did both to perfection.

But will American audiences see Peter Martins again? The chances are that they will, for Peter hopes to get a series of leaves of absence from the Royal Danish Ballet in order to perform with the New York City Ballet. Its artistic director and chief choreographer, George Balanchine, "is inspiring to me," he says. "His dance style is for me. I started out as a child with Bournonville classes, as we all do at the Royal School, but although I've danced in ballets by Bournonville—*La Sylphide, Konservatoriet,* and others— I'm not really a Bournonville-style dancer. Nor am I always comfortable in modern-dance ballets. Balanchine's *Apollo,* which is both classical and modern, is my favorite ballet."

It was *Apollo* which brought Peter Martins to the attention of Balanchine. Last August, when the New York City Ballet was performing at the Edinburgh Festival, Jacques d'Amboise, perhaps the greatest interpreter of Apollo today, sustained an injury and could not dance. A call was sent for another superb Apollo, Henning Kronstam of the Royal Danish Ballet. But Kronstam, premier danseur for the Royal Danes, was already committed for performances in Copenhagen. John Taras, Balanchine's associate ballet master, then asked Vera Volkova, chief teacher of the Royal Danish Ballet, for her suggestions. Mme. Volkova said that Martins could do it.

Within twelve hours, Peter was on his way to Edinburgh. It was a Sunday. "Monday morning," he recalls, "I was called for a one-hour rehearsal, but the studio floor was so slippery none of us could dance. Mr. B. coached me by talking and through gestures. He changed some of the steps I did with the three muses but he didn't change the way I had learned my solo. We went on that night."

All five performances of *Apollo* at Edinburgh with Martins, Suzanne Farrell, Patricia Neary, and Gloria Govrin were tremendous successes. Someday he hopes to dance it in America, along with Balanchine's *Jewels* (he would like to do the third movement, "Diamonds," with Miss Farrell). Another important goal is to dance the Prince in the full-length *Swan Lake.*

As a child dancer, Peter's first part was in the opera *Figaro*; his first solo came in Hans Brenaa's *Moods*; his first leading role, at sixteen, was in Frank Schaufuss's *Garden Party*; and he danced the enormously difficult principal role in Birgit Cullberg's Lapland ballet, *Moon Reindeer*—not in Copenhagen but in San Diego—in 1965, when he came to America (for the first time) with the Royal Danish Ballet.

Oddly enough, he never danced the role of the mischievous little boy who bedevils the Nurse in *Romeo and Juliet,* Sir Frederick Ashton's famous dance version of the Shakespearean classic, created especially for the Danes. "I never did the part," he says, "because I was supposed to play 'cup and ball,' a game in which you have a ball on a string and try to catch it in a cup you hold by a handle at the bottom. I never could catch the ball, so I never got the role." (The medieval child's game of "cup and ball" might best be described as primitive yo-yo.)

A veteran of fifteen years as a professional dancer, Martins looks back on his first studies in Bournonville with Hans Brenaa and with the Danish dancer-instructor Stanley Williams, who teaches both in Denmark and for Balanchine in New York. "Stanley," he says, "was my real teacher between twelve and sixteen, the period when you're old enough to concentrate, when you're old enough to think and understand. I worked later with Volkova, and today I can't think of anyone who can teach me more than Balanchine himself."

Was he interested in choreography? "A month ago, by myself at home, I tried some. But it's not for me now. It must be satisfying to make dances. Dancers don't last, but ballets do. I feel the same about teaching—it must be wonderful to watch a pupil grow and to make something of himself. When I'm older I'll try choreography and teaching. I really want to learn to dance first, if I ever do, and then find out if I can do something more than dance."

I think it safe to predict that American dance fans will be seeing lots more of Denmark's Peter Martins in the future, but so will Denmark, for at home is his wife, the beautiful Royal dancer Lisa la Cour (they grew up together in the Royal Danish Ballet), and their year-old baby.

There are three classic "Bs" in his life as there are in music, but they are not Bach, Beethoven, and Brahms. They are: Bournonville, for it was in the virile, romantic style of the great nineteenth-century Danish ballet master and choreographer that he first learned about ballet; Erik Bruhn, the internationally famous premier danseur noble, long an inspiration to Peter; and now the great Balanchine. If there is a fourth "B" it will be "balletomane," for American ballet fans are already taking this dazzling Dane to their hearts. During the recent holiday season, the New York City Ballet racked up an astonishing 109,793 paid admissions for *Nutcracker* performances only, but what is even more important is that it racked up another dance winner in Peter Martins. [*Saturday Review*]

How Avant is the Avant-Garde?

January 27, 1968

The avant-garde! It can be as daring and dashing and defiant as the *en garde* which Escamillo, the toreador, proclaims in his great aria in *Carmen*. A minor actor-baritone portraying Escamillo can make the *en garde* seem merely pedestrian—not at all daring—and the avant-garde in dance can occasionally

527

drop its "avant" by the wayside. The question is not so much *what* is avant but *when* is it avant, for it is very often apparent that the avant-garde in dance is in a rut. A rut, I shouldn't bother to add, has been traveled before.

Musings on the avant-garde in dance came with a performance by Rudy Perez, assisted by Barbara Roan and Anthony LaGiglia, at Washington Square's Judson Church, for some seasons now a hot-bed of dance experimentation. Maybe now, however, I should say "asparagus bed," for at this performance one of the numbers was called *Bang, Bang,* and it was danced by LaGiglia to the accompaniment of a commentary by that popular television lady-of-the-recipes, Julia Child, on how to prepare asparagus. The dancer, aided by a long pole and occasionally wearing plastic gloves, moved or stood still as Miss Child noted that asparagus is "one of our most beautiful vegetables," or rambled on in her entertaining, offhand manner, which includes such casual comments as "as the saying goes, whatever it is."

You would also have seen LaGiglia and Miss Roan in *Take Your Alligator With You,* involving a dominant male and a smirking female (here, too, you would have heard a voice say, "Take your wife first class for half fare"); Mr. Perez himself in *Center Break,* in which he peels off a loose sweatsuit to disclose himself in a flesh-colored leotard while accompanying still photographs show him nude, rear view; or Perez again in the rather striking *Field-goal,* wearing a suit of many colors, reaching out a spatulate hand only to pull it back as the second hand grasps it by the wrist, or in *Countdown,* a sort of twilight study of sad reflections experienced alone and in tranquility to the accompaniment of some of the *Songs of the Auvergne* (as recorded by Madeleine Grey).

Over the entire program, except for the presumably satiric and superficial grimaces, hung the presumably avant-garde, but now repetitious, requirement that all should be done in deadpan performing. You'll find it not just with Mr. Perez but with many, many of the avant-garde. Just as contemporary dances of social comment and behavior show the individual crouching and cowering instead of marching militantly forward (as they did in the 1930s), you will also discover that any display of emotion, especially through the face, is outmoded.

But none of this is really new, even though the current avant-garde tends to view Martha Graham and her dance concept of "revealing the inner man" as old-fashioned, for Miss Graham and her dancers, in the early Thirties, used mask-like faces, and so did the performers in the Paris of the 1700s (the great Gaetano Vestris took off the traditional mask to dance in a ballet by the great Noverre), and so did the ancient Greeks, and so do tribal Congolese dancers.

Why the deadpan? Merce Cunningham used to be almost deadpan, but he also relieved it, and still does, with impish *moues,* just as Paul Taylor, who once stood immobile for an entire dance and never blinked an eye, now comments on his own air of withdrawal with near-satanic glances at us and at his fellow dancers.

Jeff Duncan, director of the lively, experimental Dance Theater Workshop, believes that some of the deadpanners are "simply trying to copy an esthetic that once existed," but that often "they don't really know what they're doing." In other words, trends are followed instead of new pathways explored. Film—movie or still—as related to live dancers is now just about as traditional as ballet's thirty-two *fouettés*; long moments of inaction in a dance piece, where the performer seems bent on outsitting and outstaring the audience, have been going on for several seasons. As for nude photographic views of Mr. Perez's gluteal areas, that is not even adventuresome when one realizes that there have been fully nude, male–female dance goings-on (not in burlesque) from here to San Francisco. It's just a hop, skip, and jump back to the turn of the century when a then-avant-garde dancer changed her name from Ruthie Dennis to Ruth St. Denis, displayed her navel in Oriental art dances, and performed barefoot.

In fact, I own a theater program which describes the spiritual content of Miss St. Denis's historic ballet-ritual, *Radha,* and winds up with "NOTE: The entire dance will be done in bare feet!" This, in 1906, was very avant-garde. Today, at ninety, the still-active "Miss Ruth" muses that as an innovator—as was her colleague, the great Isadora Duncan—her startling heresies included not only her partial nudities but also that "I wanted to dance about God in an era when dance was considered secular and trivial in America, and that I wanted to compose dances *without steps* in an age when steps *were* dancing!"

There is always, then, in any age, an avant-garde, but it is important to remember that the avant-garde is destined to become the rear guard, or forgotten, or, at best, traditional. It is also important to respect, while evaluating, the new aims of a new avant-garde. George Beiswanger, a professor of philosophy, a scholar in the arts, and an expert on the dance, once wrote in an issue of the *Journal of Aesthetics and Art Criticism*:

> While everything in choreography comes by design, everything designed comes into the choreography by chance. For the designer cannot concretely anticipate that which is to go into a dance until it confronts him in fresh immediacy . . . choreography, then, is creative activity fraught with intention and design but fertilized by the spontaneous and uncalculated.

Perhaps you will find Mr. LaGiglia's motor responses to Julia Child's recipes not your cup of tea; maybe you will not go for Rudy Perez's expressionless face; perhaps you will be outraged or bored by others of today's experiments in the avant-garde—but consider before you reject and look before you dismiss (or accept). There is fraud and there is uncertainty in too much of our avant-garde dance (there always was), but if we are to have exciting dance tomorrows, they will spring from new or renewed sources (inner or outer stimuli), from the planned and the unplanned, from design and from revelation. [*Saturday Review*]

Bolshoi on the Move

June 29, 1968

The Bolshoi Ballet from Moscow has changed noticeably since its American debut just under a decade ago. In 1959, it hit American audiences and American dancers with a terrific impact. We have not been the same, or danced the same, since. The brute strength of the Russian men dancers challenged our males. The high and daring lifts, the vaulting leaps, the perilous propulsions through space, the last-minute catchings of hurtling bodies were tested, imitated, adapted, absorbed by U.S. dancers from coast to coast. But how were we to realize that a little reciprocity was going on at the same time? The Russians were looking and learning, too.

Do you remember that the Soviet male dancer was built like a stevedore, that his provincial modesty (or rulings by the Bolshoi administration) required that his ballet tights be covered by outer Fauntleroy-like pants, and that there were a good many slam-bang attacks on movements which made for somewhat sloppy technique despite the presence of genuinely brilliant virtuosity? Much of the Bolshoi choreography seemed stilted and old-fashioned—I am not talking about the great old-classics but of newer Soviet productions. On the Russian's return, however, changes were already manifest, and, earlier this month, the influence of the West on Soviet ballet was even admitted.

The men these days are slim, sinewy, and far more elegant, yet they have lost nothing of either virility or prowess. In matters of technique, both the women and the men seem more polished. And although the repertory for this recent tour by the Stars of the Bolshoi Ballet (not the full troupe from Moscow) contained a raft of ʹaudeville-like displays of physical skill and excerpts from longer classics, an important esthetic trend was in evidence.

Nine years ago, I had written that the Bolshoi Ballet, electrifying as it was, had not yet caught up with its own famous son, Michel Fokine. Today, it can be said that it has caught up with him, or is about to. Fokine, of course, was a product of the great Maryinsky Theater in St. Petersburg and not of the Bolshoi Theater in Moscow. Western ballet, including American ballet, was far more profoundly influenced by the style of the Russian Imperial Ballet as it was evolved in Imperial Russia's capital, St. Petersburg, "Window to the West." From there came Pavlova, Karsavina, Nijinsky, Danilova, Balanchine, and many other ballet luminaries, as well as Fokine, to bring Russian ballet influences to the rest of the world. The influence of Moscow-made ballet was much, much less.

But there was more to it than a decided stylistic difference between ballet in the two great Russian cities in both Imperial and socialist days. Fokine, as all balletomanes know, was a reformer, a rebel, an innovator. In vain did he urge ballet reforms upon a conservative-minded ballet directorate. So it was that although he created *The Dying Swan* for Pavlova, *Chopiniana* (later to be renamed *Les Sylphides*), and other ballets in Russia (most of them for the Imperial Ballet and one for the Soviet State Ballet), his genius found its nurturing in Western Europe and, ultimately, in America.

For Serge Diaghileff and his Ballets Russes, he created, staged, or restaged *Chopiniana, Le Spectre de la Rose, Petrouchka, Firebird,* the dances from *Prince Igor,* and other masterworks and experiments which changed the course of ballet history. Russia itself inherited little of these dance riches, for Fokine left the Soviet Union forever in 1918.

True, *The Dying Swan* and *Chopiniana* remained in various Soviet repertories, but little else of Fokine. When I first saw the Bolshoi dance *Chopiniana,* I found it done with harshness, with a bright brittleness which works all right with much of Petipa but not with Fokine in his lyrical vein. Galina Ulanova, the great Bolshoi prima ballerina (now retired) was the exception, but Ulanova was a product of the Maryinsky (later the Kirov) and a mistress of that style which was softer, more lyrical, more aristocratic than Moscow's. Indeed, when Leningrad's Kirov first came to America, American dancers felt a closer affinity to the style in which their own *émigré* teachers had been trained than in the more circusy ways of the Bolshoi.

But ballet times, in the Soviet Union and in the world, are changing. If there has been esthetic reciprocity, there has also been a catching-up. So it was that the Bolshoi unit which has just left us gave us three works by their legendary (more legendary to them than to us, since he worked with Americans until his death in 1942) Fokine. These were *The Dying Swan*, danced by the Bolshoi's fabulous Maya Plisetskaya in, admittedly, her own unique style; *Chopiniana,* now danced with noticeably more gentleness, grace, and lyricism which we know Fokine intended; and *Le Spectre de la Rose,* which had never been in the repertory of the Bolshoi Ballet until very recently.

It was Maris Liepa, young but already a major Bolshoi artist, who introduced *Spectre* into Russian ballet repertory. He did not settle for simply learning the steps and patterns which Fokine had originated. He was out to re-create, for his own company, a dance masterpiece which would be correct in style as well as in step. The printed program note stated with no embarrassment whatsoever that "Maris Liepa consulted with a number of Western authorities to capture the proper style in the reconstruction of this ballet." When the Bolshoi Ballet company first came here, I doubt that it would have admitted that it could learn anything about ballet from the West.

Was the reconstruction successful? Most certainly. *Spectre* is a difficult work, for it is elusive in its brush with emotions; it is poetic rather than physical, in spite of the muscular virtuosity demanded of the man who dances the Spirit of the Rose, and it ends in almost immobile reverie rather than in a Bolshoi explosion. Since it has not been a part of the repertories of major companies—at least those which have toured America—for many years, it might be helpful to remind today's balletomanes that *Spectre* is an extended duet about a girl who returns from her first dance with a single rose as a memento and her own memories to record and recall this event. She falls asleep in a chair and dreams that the spirit of the rose enters her window. The rose-clad creature—for he is a creature of dreams—dances with her and for her and then leaps through an open window into the mysterious dreamworld from whence he had come. Only the girl and a single rose remain.

Liepa, in the role originated by Nijinsky, danced well indeed. The style was lyrical, the dramatic elements properly subdued, the technical requirements met with facility. I think Fokine would have approved, if not enthused. All was right and admirable and very beautiful to look at, but the element of magic, though on the threshold of his portrayal, did not quite come in the window with him. Marina Kondratieva, as the girl (the part created by Karsavina), was utterly lovely, for she *did* make gentle magic as she invited us, ever so subtly, to see and share in her dream.

But to be swept up in the sweet and dreamy music of von Weber (*Invitation to the Dance*), to look in upon a bedroom bathed in soft moonlight, and to be a participating spectator in a poetic reverie given dance embodiment, constitutes a balletic experience too long absent from our ballet repertories. And it was especially stirring to realize that the East and West in ballet were coming ever closer as two Soviet dance stars did honor to the genius of a long-dead Russian expatriate in the new halls of New York's Metropolitan Opera House in a ballet masterpiece which had heretofore belonged to the West. Russo–American reciprocity is now a working principle, at least in the world of dance. [*Saturday Review*]

Huescape—A Psychedelic Trip

July 13, 1968

Lee, Mass. The Jacob's Pillow Dance Festival, founded and directed by the veteran dance pioneer, Ted Shawn, launched its annual ten-week season on June 27 in the first theater in America to be built expressly for dance. Named, appropriately enough, the Ted Shawn Theatre, and crowning a Berkshire hill, it has housed this festival for twenty-seven years. (Before that, festival presentations were given in a barn-studio on this old New England farm.)

Mr. Shawn—trim, bronzed, and handsome in his seventy-seventh year—opened the proceedings, as he always does, with a gracious, urbane, and witty curtain talk and noted, with pride, that the Pillow, aside from playing host to great names and famous works in the dance, had always given opportunity to beginning artists and had actually presided over more than 250 world premieres.

This summer's opening bill gave accent to youth. In the ballet department were Grace Doty, until recently a principal dancer with Alan Howard's Pacific Ballet Company, and Ramon Segarra, a ballet product of our East Coast. The two were seen in two duets, the old-time Petipa showpiece, *Le Corsaire,* and in a comparatively new piece by a Uruguayan choreographer, Tito Barbon. The latter, called *Opus II,* made you grateful that you had not seen whatever might have been Opus I, for the choreography for *II* is pretty formless and the dramatics—something about two people destroying each other—are embarrassingly juvenile.

With *Le Corsaire,* the two young dancers fared much better, for here they had something of substance, albeit flashy, to work with. They displayed sturdy technique, easy command of virtuosic action, vitality, and, in the case of Miss Doty, very nice classical style—Mr. Segarra has flair but not, as yet, stylishness. I wouldn't say that they obliterated images of Bolshoi dancers in this famous "Pas de Deux," but they did very well indeed.

Modern dance was in the sure care of Louis Falco, who is, inarguably, one of the most exciting male dancers in the modern field. Just to see him move is sheer kinesthetic joy, whether he is dancing in major works by his mentor, José Limón, in whose company he has served as a featured performer, or in works of his own devising. In fact, he has barely begun his choreographic experiments, but from the first he has shown high promise.

On this program, he gave us one of his best pieces, *Argot,* set to music of Bartók, which he dances with that oh, so lovely young artist, Sally Stackhouse, also Limón-trained. Like *Opus II,* it deals with a complex relationship of a male and female, but in Falco's case, he makes some sense out of the situation and, furthermore, catches the eye with some striking designs.

Translucens, an ensemble piece to music of Messiaen, has been worked on and improved since it was first shown a few months ago, but it still has a long way to go before it is worthy of the visions evoked by its title.

The brand-new work, however, is an instant hit, the cleanest, clearest, brightest, and best-wrought choreography Falco has done to date. It is called *Huescape.* It is accompanied by a score composed of a collage of taped sounds and embellished and highlighted by a wild and wonderful backdrop and panels in red, orange, green, blue, and lavender. Here was psychedelic heaven, and its three visitors, wearing castemarks in the center of their foreheads, were Falco, Jennifer Muller, and Juan Antonio. The "trip" they took, and let us in on, was fascinating. The three were utterly composed; yet sensuality and certainly sensuousness were constants in the choreography. Nobody was frantic. There were even moments of inaction, but these were always beautifully sculpted stances energized by alertness. With action came patterns as geometric, yet as surprising, as those made by a kaleidoscope, but also as free and as instinctive in quality as the lithe, sinewy movements of an animal.

For those who would like to take a psychedelic trip but don't quite dare, I suggest they forget drugs and buy a ticket for an escape through *Huescape.* [*Saturday Review*]

The First Lady of the Dance

August 17, 1968

"Miss Ruth" is gone, and with her passing one might think that an era in dance, in the theater itself, had come to an end. I think not, for what she dreamed and what she did will influence the world of dance, the arena and the temple of theater, for untold years. Ruth St. Denis, "Pioneer and Prophet," as her husband and partner, Ted Shawn, called her in a now-historic two-volume book he wrote in 1920, died last month in Hollywood, her home for many years.

She was, by my very careful calculations, ninety-one-years old—Mr. Shawn is quite sure she was eighty-nine and others were certain she was ninety-three—and she never once faltered in a career which spanned an incredible seventy-five years as a professional dancer. Indeed, she danced for my amateur movie camera just a year ago on her patio and only five months before she died she seemed indestructible. The final heart attack (she had had some comparatively mild preliminaries) which hospitalized her had irked her (she was too busy to waste time), and the subsequent stroke which paralyzed her she never knew had happened, for it occurred in her sleep.

"Miss Ruth," as she was known to dancers of all ages from New York to New Delhi, was born or blessed with what can only be described as a divine instinct for flawless movement. But she had a brain, too.

As a child, on the New Jersey farm where she was born, she danced in the sunlight and in the rain. She also, at eleven or twelve, sat in a tree and read her three favorite books, Mary Baker Eddy's *Science and Health,* Kant's *Critique of Pure Reason,* and Dumas's *Camille.* This sounds indigestible, but, esthetically, she digested the three, and her great art, her great wit, her great wisdom partook of this wild trio of influences.

She was both reverent and irreverent—with God, the former, and with mere mortals, the latter—and she was sensuous yet spiritual (this baffled the critics in 1906). She had a self-assurance that was so great that she envied no one—she knew she was a genius and she believed it to be God-given—but she looked upon her only rival, Isadora Duncan, as her idol, and she always said that without Ted Shawn there never would have been the Denishawn schools and companies which, for nearly two decades, guided the course of dance in America.

What do I remember or know about Miss Ruth? I know that in 1938, when I was a youth, I spent my hard-earned money to travel from New England to New York City to see her dance at a big do at Rockefeller Center called Dance International. At that time, to me, she was history, she was very old, and this would probably be my last time to see her dance. For thirty years I've watched her dance, and she always laughed when I said, "Miss Ruth, I come back every year because I keep thinking it may be the last time—not for you, but for me!"

What can I tell you about Miss Ruth? In 1893, she was a skirt dancer, a high kicker, one who did splits in a variety show for which she was paid $11 a week. In 1894, she got $20—for eleven shows a day. In 1898, she danced in toe shoes for a show called *Ballet Girl,* although, in her own words, she had had "only three lessons from Mme. Bonfanti, and before I had mastered three of the possible five positions of the feet, I was asked to leave the class." Duncan had also deserted the same class at about the same time (1896).

Miss Ruth was a good hoofer, a good actress, and Belasco, the famous producer, "canonized" her from little Ruthie Dennis into Ruth St. Denis. When show business was slack, she earned money as a model and once entered a six-day bicycle race at Madison Square Garden, where she came in sixth (later she won a championship). Incidentally, the bicycle she used was a gift from an admirer, the famous architect Stanford White. Mother St. Denis would not permit her daughter to accept jewelry from a gentleman, but she approved the bicycle!

535

Although she was successful as a show business dancer and, for five years, as an actress-dancer with Belasco, she was restless and unwilling to settle for her much-admired high kicks—"I didn't really kick like chorus girls do today; I raised my leg to my ear and then let it descend very slowly. No one else could do that"—and so as far back as 1896, while attending the Packer School in Brooklyn for a brief period between shows, she experimented with a dance which has its roots in the classicism of ancient Greece. But it was ultimately the Orient which gave Miss St. Denis the inspiration for her dance rebellion, while Isadora Duncan found her sources in the Greek concept of beauty.

Today, ethnic influences and classical inspirations are everywhere in our theater, but it was not so at the turn of the century. Jack Cole, the dancer-choreographer, has seen the journals which Miss Ruth began in the 1890s, and he once told me, "We used the word 'genius' too loosely. But when you read what Miss Ruth wrote about the dance that surrounded her and what her visions were of what dance could be—and with no one to guide her or teach her or believe in her—then you know that you are in the awesome presence of genius."

Miss Ruth had, indeed, been born into a dance age which she described as "moribund." Ballet was at its lowest ebb in America—even male roles in ballets such as *Coppélia* were danced by women *en travesti*—and a dance art which could equal the best in painting, sculpture, literature, and philosophy did not exist in America. Ruth St. Denis changed all that.

Miss Ruth's particular heresy was that she made dances in which steps were less important than the movements of a breathing, sensitized body, and that she wanted to dance about God. Since America, in its churches, had long since forgotten about, if it ever knew, "David dancing before the Ark of the Lord with all his might," or Jesus's admonition, "We have piped unto you and ye have not danced," or the psalm which says, "Praise him with timbrel and dances," Ruth St. Denis turned to a culture which celebrated deity in terms of dancing: India.

But Egypt gave her the clue. While on a Belasco tour, she saw a poster advertising cigarettes. The figure on it was that of the goddess Isis. She made her roommate go back to the drugstore and get it for her. She brooded on it, she lived with it, and she said to herself, "No, I don't want to be an Egyptian dancer; I want to be Egypt herself from dawn to dusk, from life to death, the Nile, the feather of truth weighed against the human heart."

This *Egypta* was much too expensive to produce at first—it was done in 1910, though it had been conceived in 1904—so she made her historic debut as a concert dancer at the Hudson Theater in New York in 1906 in a program composed of *The Incense* (which she was to dance for the rest of her life), *The Cobras,* and the ballet *Radha,* all inspired by India. Not one was authentic in the ethnic sense, for all she knew about Oriental dancing was what she saw at Coney Island and what she found in encyclopedias. She herself was the first to say that *Radha* was about a Hindu goddess dancing a Buddhist theme in a Jain temple! Yet so perfectly and profoundly did she capture the intent of the sacred dances, the rhythmic philosophies of India, that she achieved a double triumph: for America, she re-established the right of dance to mirror the deepest feelings and highest aspirations of man himself; and for India, she was responsible, in many ways, for the renascence of ancient dance heritages in that ancient land. Indeed, on the two-year tour of the Orient which she, Ted Shawn, and their Denishawn Dancers performed in the mid-1920s, the Eastern dances which she and Shawn performed were received with unparalleled enthusiasm.

After her New York and Boston debuts in 1906, Miss Ruth toured Europe and met with her greatest success in Germany, where, if she had stayed, a theater would have been built especially for her. In 1909, she returned to her homeland in triumph and became the first dancer to appear in an engagement of dance recitals at a Broadway theater. Her personal repertory grew, expanding to countries other than India and even into dance-dramas and abstract dances without ethnic colors. Her Japanese *O-Mika,* which used dance, music, and spoken drama, heralded the great American musical theater, which was to come in such works as *The King and I,* or even *West Side Story* (although she would not approve the harshness of the theme), for she envisioned total theater.

In 1914, she met Ted Shawn, engaged him as her partner, and married him. Total theater and total dance education (ballet, Oriental, primitive, European modern dance, Delsartean principles of meaningful motion) were their special contributions to a great new age of dance, along with producing a number of towering talents, among them Martha Graham, the late Doris Humphrey, and Charles Weidman. When they separated after fifteen years of marriage (they were never divorced), each to go his own way artistically (Shawn is founder–director of the Jacob's Pillow Dance Festival), Miss Ruth turned more and more to the dance and religion.

In her years of seeking to build a liturgy of dances comparable to the vast liturgy of existing music, she was in the services of all faiths—Buddhist, Jewish, as well as her own Christian religion. She took her dance duties to religion seriously, but she was never puritanical (she disliked puritans intensely); she was always theatrical and her wit was spiced with a marvelous bawdiness.

When I visited her last summer, she said to me, "My cricket,"—she called me that because she said that the title "critic" was much too forbidding—"I really have been a faithless wench for so long that I'm trying to reform at last. I've always worshiped three gods—the God in Heaven, the god of art, and the god of physical love. Now that I'm very, very old, I know that my art and my energies must be in the service of the God in Heaven." Then she slapped me on the back and added, "As for physical love, that belongs in my past, but don't think for a moment that I don't *think* about it!"

When I talked to her by phone just a few weeks ago to ask about her health—"pretty chipper," she said—she added, "Dear cricket, do you mind if mother pontificates for a bit? I have danced for nearly all of my ninety-one years and I believe more than ever that dance is the language of man at his highest. This language can guide man to self-realization and not simply to organization—which is just a nice word for 'power.' And I would say—still pontificating, mind you—that man is an emanation of God if he is anything at all."

Those were the last words I heard her say. Shawn called me to tell me of her passing, and, though choked with grief, you could sense the understanding smile when he said, "And you know Ruth was Ruth to the last. There were four heart specialists by her hospital bed and one said, 'Miss St. Denis, would you please stick out your tongue?' and Ruth retorted as you might expect she would, 'Which of you four distinguished gentlemen should I stick my tongue out *at*?'"

I once called her "half-mystic, half-mick," and she loved it. The world of dance called her "genius." She was all three, as heady and unlikely a combination as the three books she read while perched in a tree. Behind her is a fantastic record of dance accomplishment. Ahead, is a world theater which will be forever in her debt. [*Saturday Review*]

The Conga, the Pachanga, and the Cha-Cha-Cha

September 14, 1968

The lands and islands of the Caribbean conceal untold treasures beneath the waters which wash their coasts—sunken galleons laden with gold, jewels, ancient artifacts, perhaps even one of Columbus's ships. But the Caribbean offers another treasure trove into which everyone can dip either daintily or avidly. It is the treasure of Caribbean dance, music, rhythms, songs, mystic rites, and fiesta! And you will find it everywhere.

The fabulous dances range from the kind that you and I can do to those requiring such rhythmic and muscular skills that we'd do better to watch. The ones in which the ordinary American can participate are, of course, such dances as the rumba, the mambo, the cha-cha, the merengue, the conga, la pachanga, even calypso, and—if you have a strong back, sturdy thighs, flexible knees, and good balance—that virtuosic game-dance, the limbo.

Over the years, all of these dances, and countless variations of them, have traveled to America with the speed of jets. They have long since become a part of our own social dance structure, as essential as the waltz and the fox-trot, square dancing, and all of the later twists, frugs, and their terpsichorean cousins and aunts. Indeed, when I was stationed during World War II in what is now Ghana, a very rhythmic, loose-hipped American sergeant of Italian descent taught the conga to a delighted group of field workers as they were wending a weary way homewards. Perhaps we shall never know how much of the conga ultimately crept its way into the patterns of West African dancing. As for the dances of the Caribbean, we know how much is owed to African heritage. And that, in fact, constitutes the uniqueness of Caribbean dances, with ancient roots in Africa and with the graftings of such diverse cultures as France and Spain, the aboriginal Indian, and the Indian from India!

The most enduring of Caribbean dances-for-all is, most certainly, the rumba, which had its inception probably as far back as four hundred years ago, with the first African slaves to be brought to Cuba. It was once rather like a story-ballet as danced by Afro-Cubans, but we know it as an infectious dance. The mambo is an offshoot of the rumba, and it is possible that Harlem as well as Cuba had something to do with its siring. The merengue, of course, comes from the ancient isle of Santo Domingo. One side of the island, the Dominican Republic, claims to have invented it, but Haiti's most famous dancer, Jean-Léon Destiné, says it is from his country (and when you see him dance it, you would not doubt him). Trinidad, quite firmly, claims the calypso, although you will find great calypso dances and songs in Jamaica and, indeed, throughout the Caribbean.

The Caribbean offers much more in dance than these popular social forms which have become expressions of fun and rhythmic releases for energy and high spirits in Manhattan, Chicago, and San Francisco, as well as in Kingston, Port-au-Prince, and San Juan. The Caribbean has contributed richly to the art of dance, for although it had no art dance tradition or technique, such as classical ballet, American modern dance (as developed by Martha Graham, Doris Humphrey, and others), and no complex techniques such as found in the classical dance of India, it has produced artists who have *made* a theater dance where none had existed, and it has inspired non-Caribbean choreographers, dancers, and teachers to create techniques and theater pieces rooted in the dance riches of Caribbean cultures.

The most famous creator of Caribbean theater dances is the Chicago-born Katherine Dunham. A great beauty as well as a doctor of anthropology,

Miss Dunham and her company have taken her Caribbean-rooted ballets and revues all over the world. Her unforgettable *L'Ag'ya* mirrors African memories and French colonist echoes to be found in Martinique; *Nañigo* has at its core secret African rites imported to Cuba; *Shango* is a dance of gods and sacrifices and mystic rites from Trinidad or Haiti or Cuba; *Tropics* is of the fun and romance in any Caribbean port as a boat with newcomers docks; and the great *Rites de Passage,* first done as an illustration for a lecture by Miss Dunham at Yale University (and subsequently banned in Boston), which deals with the coming of adolescence and the subsequent finding of a mate in primitive society, speaks in powerful theatrical terms not only for the mother-Africa but also for the cultures of the Caribbean.

Miss Dunham has focused more on Caribbean dances than on those evocative of Africa (although she has created African ballets and dance suites based on the Negro in the United States), while Pearl Primus, another dancer–anthropologist, though born in Trinidad, has devoted much of her career to the dances and ceremonies in the continent of her distant ancestors. Her husband, Percival Borde, from Trinidad, leans more to the dance sources of the Caribbean.

Haiti's Destiné is a brilliant example of a dance artist who transformed lore into true theater art. Destiné, an aristocrat with a fine education and equally at home in French (impeccable) and the singsong creole dialect, has made good use of French colonial dance tradition and etiquette in some of his festival dances, but on the whole, he uses a highly developed, skillfully organized movement technique derived from voodoo (or *voudoun*) rites. His countrymen were social dancers, folklore dancers, but while "possessed" in voodoo ceremonies, they accomplished virtuosic feats that transcended their conscious accomplishments. Destiné, accepted in voodoo societies, took these actions, codified them, regulated them, gave them sequence and order, and evolved for Haiti, as well as for himself, a striking theater dance technique, Haitian in flavor, African in pulse, contemporary in terms of theater.

The six-foot-six Geoffrey Holder, dancer, choreographer, singer, writer, painter, is from Trinidad, and he has created exhilarating (and sometimes humorous) dances which interrelate not only African and colonial heritages but also the contribution of East Indians who brought their neck-shifts and sinuosities of arms and hands with them to the New World. Often he choreographs for his wife, the New Orleans-born Carmen De Lavallade, one of the most beautiful women on the stage today. She is as breathtaking in lilting Caribbean dances as she is in, say, John Butler's dramatic ballets of the northland or her own Negro spirituals.

The dance climate of the Caribbean, then, has produced great dance artists for itself and, what is even better, shared them with the entire world. It has inspired non-Caribbeans of both the black and the white races to create dances and ballets, dramas and musical shows. Alvin Ailey, born on a ranch in Texas, and now one of America's major dance figures (as a choreographer and head of a superlative company), has derived as much inspiration from the West Indies as he has from spirituals, New Orleans jazz, or total Americana.

Without rhythmic stimulations from the Caribbean, we could not have had these social dances which continue to warm our own northern blood, nor could we have had such Broadway shows as *House of Flowers* and *Jamaica,* nor could we have enjoyed the very special artistries of dancers and choreographers rooted in or inspired by Caribbean lands.

In fact, Caribbean dancing is everywhere. You might even find it in very modest but delightful form in a hotel courtyard at Montego Bay, where a young boy, with bottle caps between his toes, shakes his feet as dextrously as a Jamaican Gene Kelly. If you were as fortunate as I, you might have been taken by Destiné and a voodoo priest far from tourist centers to a remote spot where a real, not staged, voodoo ceremony took place and an old man was possessed by the spirit of Yanvalou, a god of the sea. Or you might see. . . .

Once, a few years ago, when I was very tired from a long year of reviewing dance events—including five four-act *Swan Lake*s in two-and-a-half-days—I decided that much as I loved dancing, I needed a recess from both dance and dancers. Where to go? Certainly not to Jamaica or Haiti or Puerto Rico. But what island? Ah, Bermuda. No ethnic dancing there. When I boarded the plane with a murder mystery tucked under my arm, the stewardess showed me to my seat. My companion was, of all people, the great ballerina Maria Tallchief. She too was hoping to get away from dance. But did we really want to?

A day later, Miss Tallchief called me at my hotel and asked if I'd like to come over to the house she had rented and do a ballet *barre* and general dance warmup with her. I leapt at the chance. Another day passed and as I came in from the beach, the phone rang. "Walter!" Miss Tallchief shouted delightedly, "guess what, there are some gombey dancers performing tonight in a club right down the street from here. I know what we said on the plane about dancing but. . . ." I interrupted her, "What are we waiting for? C'mon, let's go!" We did. It was wonderful, but so too are the dance adventures awaiting us all the way from Bermuda southwards to the coast of South America itself. [*Saturday Review*]

541

Dance Peak in the Rockies

November 16, 1968

Salt Lake City, Utah. The $370,000 Rockefeller Foundation grant, allocated to a nonexistent enterprise in a small city of the Rocky Mountain area, is being well spent—brilliantly invested, in fact. The dance world was astonished, if not shocked, when this substantial sum was given in 1966 to establish a Repertory Dance Theatre, rooted in American modern dance, on the campus of the University of Utah. A modern dance repertory theater was much to be desired. The late Helen Tamiris attempted to organize one in New York in the 1930s with her colleagues, Martha Graham, Doris Humphrey, Charles Weidman; and it was tried again at Lincoln Center in the 1960s. But why Salt Lake City? Why a college campus?

The reasons, I think, are three: 1) we are entering an age of dance decentralization in America, a fact witnessed by the emergence of eighty or more regional ballets; 2) the newest dance trend is the drive to foster dance creativity, as distinct from standard dance education, on college campuses; and 3) the University of Utah has long been blessed with a vital modern dance department under the direction of Elizabeth Hayes, the first major collegiate ballet department under the direction of Willam Christensen (one of the famed Christensen brothers trio including Lew, the choreographer and director of the San Francisco Ballet; and Harold, director of the SF Ballet School); and that genius of dance training for children, Virginia Tanner, the Mormon teacher whose Children's Dance Theatre (sponsored by the University of Utah) attracts more than 600 students annually and whose tours, including appearances on the Jacob's Pillow Dance Festival and the American Dance Festival in New England, have had audiences cheering and weeping at choreographic expositions of dance beauty, innocence combined with vigor, remarkable discipline mated to the freest improvisation.

It was Miss Tanner, indeed, who was instrumental in getting the huge Rockefeller grant for a project in which she is involved only as an advisor. She had approached the foundation for funds for her own children's dance futures and, when asked if she had any further ideas, she said she thought a modern dance repertory company was desirable. She didn't get the grant for her children's theater—"Oh, I'll get support somewhere else," she says blithely—but her recommendation did.

The point and purpose of the new project were to build a company away from New York, but in a climate congenial to dance adventure and without the command, good or bad, of a single\individual. Most modern dance companies—though not all—are the outlets of star dancers–choreographers, such as Graham, Limón, Cunningham, Taylor, Nikolais, Lang, Walker, Sokolow,

542

Hawkins, and many more. The Repertory Dance Theatre was to have no resident choreographer, not even an artistic director. It was to be a modern dance cooperative in which junior choreographers from the Rocky Mountain areas and internationally famous modern dance creators would contribute to the building of a repertory.

All of this sounds like an invitation to chaos. True, there have been administrative changes since the project got under way, but with no director and no resident choreographer, but with Wayne Richardson (long associated with the New York City Center, Carnegie Hall, and briefly with the City Center Joffrey Ballet) as manager and a board of directors—which includes Miss Tanner, Gordon Paxman (head of the University of Utah's combined modern dance and ballet departments), and members of the Repertory Dance Theatre itself—the new company soared to unquestioned success in a series of superb performances last month in the University of Utah's big Kingsbury Hall.

The performances that I have seen here attest to the wisdom of the grant. The dancers themselves—unknown to Broadway eyes—are highly accomplished, faultlessly rehearsed (under their own direction), versatile, responsive to many approaches of choreographic style, and, in most cases, as striking as any modern dance soloists and principals you would find on Broadway or its environs. Have you found Robert Powell or Louis Falco or Michael Alum among the most exciting male dancers in New York? Well, add Albuquerque's Tim Wengerd to the roster of stellar men dancers.

Now, permit me to tell you about the new works, created by the old pros and the members of the Repertory Dance Theatre, as danced by a company which all of America should see. It is in complete tune with the youth of today—the average age is about twenty-one—yet it mirrors the silence of mountains as well as the deafening bombast of cities, and it reflects pause as well as pace, consideration as well as desperation, harmony as well as cacophony. And this is of mighty importance to American dance, for what stimuli to dance creation are engendered in the clean, open West are just as American as the inescapable violences and unrest and terror or escapism of our citadel of theater, New York.

One of the most impressive premieres was *Interim,* choreographed by the RDT's own Bill Evans to music of Henk Badings (Capriccio for Violin and Two Sound Tracks, and *Genese*). It is an abstract ballet, highly imaginative in its relating of the body (or bodies) to surrounding space, generally unhurried yet rich in controlled muscular virtuosities. In fact, Evans uses recurrent pauses—arrestings of action—rather than poses, and these permit the viewer to dwell upon a pattern and to let the eye photograph it. Wengerd, Eric Newton, and Gregg Lizenbery constituted the superb dance trio for Part I, and Kay Clark, Ruth Post, Manzell Senters, and Evans himself were the equally splendid dancers of Part II.

543

Every one in the company is required to try his hand at choreography for workshop projects and out of these certain ones are selected for inclusion in the repertory. Wengerd had three on the recent bill. One was *Night Scene* (Shostakovich, Third Movement, *Sonata for Cello and Piano*), a pas de deux performed in sort of plastique tempo and with an aura of sad sex about it. Linda Smith, onetime child dancer with Miss Tanner, and Senters danced it beautifully, but I liked Wengerd's choreography for *Chant* (Lou Harrison/ John Cage—*Double Music for Percussion Quartet*) much more. Six dancers in black leotards with almost luminescent stripes running down backs and fronts moved impeccably in shimmering, almost vibratory patterns which made the dancing figures seem almost like electronic impulses constantly being recorded on a graph.

Joan Butler's *With Gayer Sandals* (Dag Wiren's Serenade for Strings) is not only gay but also light of step and sweetly youthful; *Danse Intime* by Phill Keeler (of the University of Utah faculty) to music of Stravinsky (*Concerto for Piano and Wind Instruments*) left a good deal to be desired because of the very obscure relationships involving parents, children, and in-laws; Richard Rowsell's *The Watchers* (Bartók); Wengerd's *Encounter* (Barber); and a kind of psychedelic, hippie-type happening, *Dancing Group. Flesh. 1968.*

The guest choreographers were José Limón, represented by a new staging of his *Concerto Grosso* (Vivaldi); Anna Sokolow with her new *Steps of Silence* (Anatole Vieru); and John Butler with the premiere of his *The Initiate* (Grażyna Bacewicz's *Musica Sinfonica in Tre Movimenti,* and Zsolt Durko's *Organismi per Violino Solo e Orchestra*).

The Butler piece, and powerful it is, represents a recurrent Butler theme: youth's search for himself in a world of cruelty, uncertainty, violence. The marvelous setting (by Robert VerBerkmoes), with its rings of black, brown, and gray semicircling an off-white expanse of sky, makes it seem that the action is taking place within the crater of an extinct volcano, perhaps an ancient arena for an ageless ceremony of initiation. There is also a set piece of pipes which becomes both a cage and also a doomed device for the Initiate's reaching forth to escape. *The Initiate,* which could be said to belong to that genre which would include Stravinsky's *Sacre,* is filled with movements of shattering dynamic intensity but which also possess sculptural beauties of the highest order. Wengerd in the title part is remarkable, and the rest of the cast is worthy of his performing standard.

Miss Sokolow, always the purveyor of doom, as our choreographic Cassandra, has come up with yet another study of desperation, emptiness, aloneness, futility in her *Steps of Silence,* one of her most potent and poignant creations. The dancers, dressed at first in drab work clothes, move with deliberate, emotionless tread, or spin across the stage in uncontrolled restlessness, or with reaching, thrusting, arms and legs attempt to take flight. The curtain at the back of the theater is up, and debris rests against the wall. The dancers' costumes change to rags, and, in the final measures, the girls are stripped down to the equivalent of bikinis and the boys to their dance belts.

As the dance ends, scraps of crumpled newspaper blow across the stage, making a huge heap of trash into which the helpless humans disappear as they settle down, as human debris, to find sleep or, perhaps, death. It is not a work that will have you leaving the theater with a glad cry on your lips, but it will leave its mark on your heart.

And also conquering the heart with the handsome appearances of youth, with uncommon dance skills, with a wonderfully communicable spirit of adventure will be the Dance Repertory Theatre itself, worth every bit of $370,000. [*Saturday Review*] at the retail of the dealer to spend profit tells again this with the used, as customer charges discussed in the final measure, the cycle for slippage down to the unit count of buyers and the reversal of the real in the drive time session of estimated hamburger flow, as is the estimate cost loop in part unit which top ringdes immunication poor as that settle down, a build into forward the operating device. If it is every such that, all must be leaving the device will relatively use of tid or it will look to much on your revenue.

And the completing the team will the funds the appearance of some with the common dance seller with a reasonably reasonable sum and revenue will be the faire knowing. That of used with revenue hint of $470,000. Everything it revenue.

1969

Hail, A New Generation of Brilliance!

Harkness Ballet in its 5th year • The brilliant rise of John Cranko's Stuttgart Ballet • Robbins' masterful Dances at a Gathering danced by NYCB at Saratoga Performing Arts Center • A profile of America's Richard Cragun, star of the Stuttgart Ballet • Helgi Tomasson wins medal at Moscow Competition • Eliot Feld's American Dance Company is born

Hail, Harkness, Hail!

February 8, 1969

The Harkness Ballet, which will soon celebrate its fifth birthday, in this short span of time has become a major force in the highly competitive world of dance. As a troupe of dancers, it's dreamy; it's groovy; it's young; it's sophisticated. What a combination! Its repertory is fresh—not one old chestnut on the bill of fare—yet the technique and elegance of classical ballet at its most dazzling is given stunning representation as well as works which are pure modern dance or ethnic-flavored exotica.

Indeed, one of its dancers once joshed that the Harkness repertory was the only one in the world which could present three full programs in which every ballet would include a rape, or near-rape, scene and never once repeat itself. But this same repertory also boasts Anton Dolin's *Variations for Four Plus Four* and Benjamin Harkarvy's *Grand Pas Espagnol,* showpieces of virtuosity which would have illumined the Maryinsky in St. Petersburg in the grandest era of the Russian Imperial Ballet. The former—with a score by Margaret Keogh (on Verdi themes) and scenery and costumes by Tom Lingwood—and the latter—set to Moszkowski and with costumes by Joop Stokvis—demand nothing less than dancers of star caliber, not just athletic kids, mind you, but polished artists. Harkness has them.

Five of the troupe's six principals are in both these display pieces— Lawrence Rhodes, Lone Isaksen, Elisabeth Carroll, Helgi Tomasson, Finis

Jhung—and what they accomplish in terms of classical dancing is breathtaking. In both, you would also find your attention turning to a beautiful, assured, gifted young soloist, Marina Eglevsky, whose father, André, was one of the world's greatest *danseurs* not many years ago, and whose mother, Leda Anchutina, used to enchant an earlier ballet public with her fleetness of movement and irresistible smile.

The versatility of the principals is almost to be expected in ballet repertories as they are today, but to find the performing standards equally high in classical, dramatic, modern, and avant-garde is a special treat. Rhodes himself, of course, is nothing short of remarkable. At twenty-nine, he is the director of the company—and appears to be doing a fine job of it. If he is in the category of a d'Amboise or a Villella in matters of technical prowess, he is also an actor–dancer of superb accomplishment as attested to by his heart-tearing quietly dramatic characterizations of the tormented poet, Rimbaud, in John Butler's powerful portrait of one drawn to both homosexuality and heterosexuality, *A Season in Hell* (music of Peggy Glanville-Hicks and scenery and costumes by Rouben Ter-Arutunian); and as the embattled, tortured hero of a truly monumental *Monument for a Dead Boy,* by the Dutch choreographer, Rudi van Dantzig (to an electronic score by Jan Boerman).

Rhodes is important as director, classical dancer, actor–dancer, colleague-of-other-dancers to the Harkness Ballet; but the contributions of others—the principals I have mentioned, the soloists, the corps, the batterie of international choreographers, the support and guidance of the producer–benefactress herself, Rebekah Harkness—are the ingredients which have produced, developed, and brought the flush of triumph to the Harkness Ballet.

I've talked about the performing and choreographic skills of the Harkness Ballet in terms of classical dance and dramatic dance. But let me say that there is no lovelier pure dance work, sculptural in contour, kinetically pulsating, and muscularly lyrical, than Norman Walker's *Night Song* (Hovhaness). The entire ensemble is captivating in it, but if you have a camera in your eyes, you'll record forever the incredible air-turns to a kneeling position which Dennis Wayne dances (not just executes, but truly dances) in a diagonal across the stage. In this phrase alone, one is witness to a distillation of that purity which inhabits both the animal and the poet.

There is laughter too, and you will find this in a new production of Todd Bolender's *Souvenirs*—with Samuel Barber's music and Ter-Arutunian's delicious period (1912) décor and costumes. In this ballet about high (and decidedly low) jinks in a resort hotel, you'll love (and this is a promise) Hester Fitzgerald as a not-too-constant wife, Michael Tipton as a masher convinced of his own irresistible charm, Salvatore Aiello as a *primo gigolo assoluto* (if there is such a term), and Bonnie Mathis as a Theda Bara-type vamp, with a snarl, a hiss, and a pelvic walk which have to be seen to be believed.

There were, inevitably, some lesser moments during the first part of the three-week stand at the Music Box, one of Broadway's most delightful theaters. One, ironically, was van Dantzig's *Moments* to music of Webern (in its U.S. premiere). It had some quite brilliant and arresting designs—*die Augen blicken* kind—but the continuing choreographic patterns seemed diffuse. Harkarvy's *Madrigalesco,* despite exquisite performing, was bland, harmless, lacking the soft glow of the Vivaldi music. But then there were many exuberant pieces—among them *Canto Indio*—choreographed by Brian Macdonald (formerly director of the Harkness Ballet) to the sunny Aztec-Spanish music of Chávez, and performed like bursts of Mexican sunlight by Miss Carroll and Tomasson.

The ambitious and generally rewarding Festival of Dance 68–69, which ran for weeks at the Brooklyn Academy of Music, moved on to Broadway's Billy Rose Theater under the auspices of Richard Barr's and Edward Albee's Theater 1969. The first week was given over to Merce Cunningham and his avant-garde offerings, and the second to José Limón, who is now old-guard modern dance.

I wish I could offer an enthusiastic report about everything that these two major figures in America's modern dance offered. But I must report that the Harkness Ballet's excursions into *Augen blicken* images, and responses to electronic sounds seemed to me more avant-garde than the Cunningham efforts (and more entertaining). The ballet's investigation into the dramas of the human heart—as seen by the American Ballet Theatre or Harkness—were more modern than contemporary Limón.

Cunningham and the marvelous Carolyn Brown danced beautifully (as did his entire group), and *How to Pass, Kick, Fall, and Run,* with John Cage and David Vaughan as narrators, was great fun, as it always is, but more so audibly than visually. Limón's *The Moor's Pavane* remains his choreographic masterpiece, a remarkable movement essence of the Othello story. But his later pieces tend to run on and on, and—all too often—indulge in trite emotionalism. The disciplining, inspirational hand of his late artistic director, Doris Humphrey—herself a choreographic great—is sorely missed. But Limón does boast the dancing presence of Louis Falco—athlete, dancer, actor, artist—and the excellent Sarah Stackhouse. His own bearing, in his increasingly rare appearances, is something to cherish; for he is man himself—strong, eager, noble, with the commanding dignity of a grand old hero. But increasingly, it seems that ballet, once a stick-in-the-mud for tradition, has hoisted its sails and is catching up with modern dance, if it has not already passed it by.
[*Saturday Review*]

Steps from Stuttgart

May 31, 1969

Stuttgart.   As New York will soon discover for itself at the Metropolitan
Opera House in a season beginning on June 10, the Stuttgart Ballet has become one of the world's most important dance troupes—a real "sleeper" in
the world of dance—because of the extraordinary talents of one man, a British-
er of South African birth, John Cranko. His genius, and it is that, lies not
only in choreography but also in direction. He is something of a paradox, a
practical visionary. He came to Stuttgart ten years ago to stage a ballet; a
year later, he became the director; this year, he adds the Munich Ballet to his
realm and will direct both companies, using an exchange system in personnel
and repertory.

   Already, he is shuttling back and forth between Stuttgart and Munich in
his new Mercedes-Benz, and roars with appreciative laughter when he hears
the story that the president of Mercedes-Benz—the main factory is in Stuttgart—said that his company's only export rival in Stuttgart is the Stuttgart
Ballet.

   Why did Cranko leave Britain's Royal Ballet for Stuttgart? "They had
enviable conditions here: a beautiful theater, money, scene shops, costume
rooms, rehearsal hall, the most modern equipment imaginable, just everything
—but they simply didn't have a first-class company, and you can't have a real
company until you have a real ballet school. I don't like to teach. I don't
think I'm very good at it. Oh, I can give steps and stretches, but there is
more to teaching than that. So I have a teaching staff for the company as it
is, for the young ones just coming in, and for the children, our dancers of
tomorrow."

   This staff includes Anne Wooliams, a disciple of one of the great ballet
teachers of our age, Vera Volkova, now principal teacher of the Royal Danish
Ballet and a major training force in the careers of Dame Margot Fonteyn,
Maria Tallchief, Erik Bruhn, Henning Kronstam, and other ballet stars of both
sexes. Miss Wooliams, like Volkova and, oddly enough, like Martha Graham,
instructs in verbal images in addition to purely muscular actions. I watched
her teach both women and men, and with her stern discipline goes an almost
caressive concern for the body. She herself says, "I love each of their bodies,
but I don't always love what they do with them in class. I guess that's why
I'm here—to do something about that!"

   Alan Beale is the male side of ballet instruction at Stuttgart. He, too,
left Britain's Royal Ballet to become a part of a surging ballet movement in
Stuttgart, and he, too, credits Mme. Volkova with training his teaching eye.
He and Anne work as collaborators, not rivals. "Anne knows what the girl

dancer must do when she is dancing with a man. I know what the man must do to support the ballerina. Both are essential."

The results of this training, instituted by Cranko, are apparent in the dancing of our newest dance phenomenon, the Stuttgart Ballet. Tradition, of course, is right here in Stuttgart, as well as innovation. Ballet, in both the duchy and, as instituted by Napoleon, the kingdom of Württemberg, was a vital part of court life as it was in other royal and ducal settings. In nearby Ludwigsberg, there is a lovely court theater in the old castle, built in 1704, which is still used. The last King of Württemberg, whose reign ended fifty years ago when Germany became a republic, was a patron of ballet, and, it is said, of ballerinas too!

Cranko is responsible for most of the choreography seen here during the ballet week and for the repertory selected for New York and for the transcontinental tour in October and November. But tradition is also observed. The company has a splendid production of the old *Giselle,* with the Coralli-Perrot-Petipa choreographies staged by Peter Wright.

At the performance I saw, the Giselle was Marcia Haydée, diminutive, intense, appealing—an actress as well as a dancer. The Albrecht was that amazing Egon Madsen, who can, apparently, do anything from buffoonery through technical feats of skill in classical style to the most elegant exposition of romanticism. Jan Stripling was a rough but sympathetic Hilarion, wholly believable and not a cardboard villain—and how marvelous it was to have a senior mime (Ruth Papendick), and not a corps de ballet girl, play Giselle's mother.

On the same program you would have also seen a new Cranko ballet, but one couched in the style of the *danse d'école.* This was *Concerto for Flute and Harp* (Mozart), and it belongs to that genre of abstract ballets of movement visualizations of classical music, of which Balanchine is the indisputable master. Cranko, of course, uses this special dance idiom in his own way, so that the piece itself is fresh and new. Furthermore, instead of employing a large corps of girls, he uses twelve cavaliers for his two ballerinas, and the result is delightful.

Another program would bring, say, "Divertissements" from Tchaikovsky's *The Nutcracker,* with wholly new choreography by Cranko. In the "Pas de Huit," or in the "Dance of the Snowflakes," you would find a perfect example of his combining musicality with architectural effects; thus, canon forms and counterpoint would be inextricably related to formations not only involving divisions and subdivisions of an ensemble, but also actions and figurations taking place on different levels of height.

In contrast to this ebullient and visually regal *Nutcracker* is Cranko's *Opus One* (to Anton Webern's Passacaglia, Op. 1). It is, I think, a contemporary masterpiece. One's first thought is to categorize it as modern as distinct from classical, or avant-garde as different from something else. It is none of these. It is dance, and it speaks in its own terms, not literal but filled with passion, of youth and aloneness in the midst of many, and of that labyrinth, both inner of the heart and outer with the world, through which the individual must find his own terribly lonely way.

It was the first ballet in which Cranko created a major role especially for Richard Cragun, who shines so brilliantly in the lusty *Taming of the Shrew* and in any classical assignment. His performance, in this work of prodigious invention and profound emotional adventure, is a memorable one, physically powerful but curiously sensitive. Cragun himself says, "I have a religious feeling about *Opus One*," and it is this feeling of undefinable ecstasy of being that we, the onlookers, share with him. Ineffably lovely is Susanne Hanke as another searching being, and the ensemble is as magnificent in this as it is in its splashiest excursions into classical virtuosities.

Stravinsky's *Jeu de Cartes* has reached the stage in many guises—*Card Party* and *Poker Game* among them—but Cranko's staging, with scenery and costumes by Dorothee Zippel, is the best I've seen. And with Madsen as the irrepressible Joker, it is a special treat.

Of high quality is John Cranko's utterly beautiful production of *Romeo and Juliet*, which I have just seen with the cast that will be first in New York, Haydée and Cragun—and they must be classed with the finest to be seen in the world of dance. Miss Haydée is a Juliet so young, so vulnerable, so captured by love that you will never forget her. And Cragun is the ardent, wild, angry, fierce, and enraptured Romeo. These two artists, together, make a brand of theater magic different from but as potent as, say, that of Fonteyn and Nureyev.

Haydée and Cragun, in company with Heinz Clauss, vaulted to the other end of the theater-dance spectrum in Cranko's way-out *Présence*, a ballet with an avant-garde score (a fine one, too) by Bernd-Alois Zimmermann, crazy décor and costumes by Jürgen Schmidt-Oehm.

June 7, 1969

Stuttgart.   Bolshoi and Royal Ballets of Europe, watch to your American laurels! The Stuttgart Ballet is about to challenge your right to them. It seems incredible that a city of just slightly more than a half-million population could produce a ballet troupe to rival the great state ballets of Europe. It has. To put it succinctly: I came, I saw, and I was conquered. (New York will see the Stuttgart Ballet, under the S. Hurok banner, June 10–29 at the Metropolitan Opera House.)

Before telling you about the composition and background of this remarkable company, let me report the impact I experienced on attending my first performance in the lovely, old Württemberg State Theater. The ballet was *The Taming of the Shrew,* created by the company's director, John Cranko, an Englishman but a *Wunderkind* in any language.

Shrew is a lavishly produced full-length ballet performed to perfection by splendid artists who are not only whizzes at classical ballet, but who are also superb actor–dancers. In *Shrew,* Cranko has created a lusty, bawdy, brawling, electrifying ballet which captures, almost miraculously, the intent and content of the Shakespeare play, while at the same time giving full celebration to the prowess of the dancers.

Cranko is not afraid to use slapstick any more than Shakespeare was, nor is he skittish about the most tender expressions of romance. Sometimes, indeed, he juxtaposes the two, with only seconds separating them. I found myself roaring with laughter, sighing at moments of sweet young love, and applauding exhilarating feats of physical skill—as did my neighbors in the theater—for a work that is not only a great ballet in itself but also an unforgettable interpretation of the Shakespeare comedy. I might even add that it might possibly make you forget the ever-popular musical, *Kiss Me, Kate!,* since here in the ballet even bodies sing.

For the two principals, *Shrew* is, of course, an acting tour de force. Add dancing of high virtuosity to the basic acting assignments and you find a theater experience which will make your jaw drop. The Stuttgart Ballet has as its Katherine and its Petruchio the Brazilian Marcia Haydée and the American Richard Cragun, and they are absolutely marvelous. As they tear each other apart in fury, in amorousness, and in sheer virtuosity, they tear the house down, too.

In this role, tiny Miss Haydée is fiery, fierce, and intense, wildly comical, and yet adorable. As for Cragun, I promise that he will make you forget your favorite swashbuckler, be it Douglas Fairbanks, Sr., or Errol Flynn of earlier eras, or any of today's limited crop. In fact, Cragun is D'Artagnan, Villon, and Rupert of Hentzau rolled into one dashing hero.

The supporting cast—including Stuttgart's own Susanne Hanke (Bianca), and Denmark's Egon Madsen (hysterically funny as Gremio), and all the others—is brilliant. Among the array of scenes to roar at are those in which two blowsy ladies of easy virtue push their fading charms to the fullest, get Petruchio drunk, and strip him before our eyes; or when we are invited to attend the most raucous and chaotic wedding in history; or when we are permitted to witness the terrifying taming of Kate herself. (Miss Haydée told me that she was black-and-blue in rehearsals, but that in performance her muscles and bones are nicely numb.) Wherever you look, there are battles in ballet form, love-making in dance, antics at all times.

553

Elisabeth Dalton's sets and costumes are sumptuous, and Kurt-Heinz Stolze's score, derived from Scarlatti themes, is at one with the prankishness of the ballet all the way.

Cranko's almost uncanny skill in telling a story through dance action is revealed again in a tragedy, *Eugene Onegin.* It is not necessary to know the Pushkin novel, nor would one have to plow through program notes in order to follow the tale. It is all there on stage, as lived by flesh-and-blood characters. Each reveals the inner self—the torments, the desires, the uncertainties —through dance.

Sometimes, the secret yearnings of the heart are bared in a dreamed duet with the absent loved one; again, it is a personal drama placed in the midst of mass gaiety; or, as in the final dance of the ballet (there is no splashy finale in the usual sense), the end of the story comes with a heartbreakingly lovely dance of utter loneliness.

Here also, John Cranko displays his genuine genius in weaving the craft of storytelling-through-movement into the choreographic fabric of a dance work of art.

Miss Haydée, as Tatiana, makes clear that she is not only the irresistible comedienne of *Shrew* but also a dance tragedienne in the great tradition of Nora Kaye. Heinz Clauss, one of the company's most valuable dancers, is an excellent Onegin, and the incredibly versatile Madsen (an old fop, Mercutio, an unforgettable Albrecht in *Giselle,* the Joker in *Jeu de Cartes*) is a splendid Lenski.

The score, prepared especially for this ballet by Mr. Stolze, the conductor, is not derived from the opera but, rather, from other Tchaikovsky compositions more suitable to Cranko's choreographic needs.

And what shall I tell you of Cranko's *Romeo and Juliet* to the great Prokofiev score? Yes, Lavrovsky did one of the most famous for the Bolshoi Ballet; Ashton created a masterful one for the Royal Danish Ballet; Britain's Royal Ballet has a magnificent one (produced later than Cranko's) by Mac-Millan; and there are others. Quite simply, in my opinion, Cranko's for the Stuttgart is the finest in a galaxy of memorable *Romeos.* This does not mean the others are to be forgotten. The street dance of the mandolin players and the dance of the whores in the MacMillan version are better; Romeo's first entrance in the Ashton concept is stronger; but in its total powers, the Cranko *Romeo and Juliet* is unmatched.

The production, with settings and costumes by Jürgen Rose, is stunning, with the mobility of the scene changes being of particular value to the unbroken flow of this danced play. At the first performance that I attended, Madsen was a dazzling Mercutio; John Neumeier made Paris a being and not a shadow; Jan Stripling was the remorseless, fearless Tybalt; Hella Heim, a great old dance mime in her sixties, was the adoring, protective Nurse; and

Heinz Clauss was a Romeo you could never forget. Juliet? It was danced by Miss Hanke with a dewy beauty, inner and outer, which suffused the stage and penetrated the hearts of all of us. I think I can sum up what she, and Cranko, did: I wept unashamedly, and when the curtain fell there was a total hush in the Württemberg State Theater. Slowly, the tribute of silence ended, and the house stood and cheered.

This was ballet at its finest. This was also a man named John Cranko, a new (to many in America) and towering creative figure in the world of dance. [*Saturday Review*]

Dances at a Gathering

July 26, 1969

Saratoga Springs, N.Y. The New York City Ballet, aside from its handsome fall-winter-spring home at the New York State Theater in Lincoln Center, has a summer home with the Saratoga Performing Arts Center, where it dances at one of the most glorious outdoor amphitheaters to be found anywhere in the world.

The company, nearing the close of its festival appearances here—it will be followed by the Philadelphia Orchestra—has been performing in repertory. The program that I elected to see included Jerome Robbins's new *Dances at a Gathering,* which I had seen only once before on the closing night of the State Theater season. To put it quite simply, it is one of the most radiantly beautiful dances that I have ever experienced. "Dance," rather than "ballet," is the proper word to describe it; for although the technique of classical ballet is its base, it transcends, as does Robbins's staging of Stravinsky's *Les Noces,* any single dance method and becomes universal dance.

When I was in Stockholm recently to see the Royal Swedish Ballet's production of Robbins's *Les Noces,* Robbins told me that "making *Dances at a Gathering* was almost like it had been with *Fancy Free*—it just happened and I didn't know what was happening." *Fancy Free,* of course, was Robbins's first ballet, created for the American Ballet Theatre just twenty-five years ago.

Robbins worked on his *Dances at a Gathering*—inspired by études, mazurkas, waltzes, a scherzo, and a nocturne by Chopin—with members of the New York City Ballet (there is a cast of ten) while George Balanchine, the company's artistic director and chief choreographer, was abroad. "I kept adding to it as the pieces intrigued me, so when George got back I said to him, 'It's too long; we'll have to cut.' Well, he saw a run-through, turned to me and said, 'Add! Like eating peanuts you shouldn't stop! You should keep going.' So I kept going, and everyone seemed to like the peanuts!"

Its triumphant reception in both New York City and Saratoga Springs indicates that it was much more than being as irresistible as peanuts, yet Balanchine was quite right in his analogy, for the unaffected simplicity of the new piece is what makes it irresistible. There are dazzling, difficult movements, steps, and patterns, but they don't come off as tests of prowess.

It is a temptation to want to dissect a masterpiece to see what makes it work. Indeed, one would be unperceptive if he did not note that Miss Verdy, a true ballerina of great elegance, although she wore toe shoes, did not dance on *pointe* at all in her lovely solo; or that the booted males occasionally echo, in step or sturdy arms gestures, the Polish heritage of the composer; or if he overlooked shadings in playfulness, male bravado, girlish coquetry, reverie, celebration.

But the onlooker cannot explain *Dances at a Gathering* any more than Robbins can. It just happened; it just poured out of the consciousness and subconsciousness of a choreographic genius; it sprang, perhaps, from the pure, clean, uncalculating, ecstatic impulse to dance—like the impulse to reach for that other peanut. In *Dances at a Gathering,* the Robbins choreographic craft is there in full and awesome measure and can, therefore, be measured. But the inner magic of the Robbins art cannot be measured—it captures you in an unseen embrace and makes you an unquestioning, elated participant in *Dances at a Gathering.*

Neither can you analyze the chemistry of a great performance as distinct from a good one. At this same New York City Ballet program, Balanchine's own version of Act II of *Swan Lake* was on the bill. One of the world's major ballerinas, Melissa Hayden, was dancing Odette as she has countless times, always beautifully. At this performance, however, there was something more, something that might be described as super-Hayden. I couldn't analyze it—she is always an impeccable technician and a sensitive artist—but there was an extra about this performance. It had a hypnotic power about it, or, as the youngsters would say, it grabbed you. Later, backstage, I asked Miss Hayden if she had felt something special and if she had an explanation for it. "Yes," she said. "It did have a feeling about it. All I can say is that I just finished doing the four-act *Swan Lake* with the ballet at the Grande Théâtre du Genève, and tonight I felt impelled to distill all I had done in four acts into one—or maybe having done the four acts, the single second act took on a whole new meaning." That was Miss Hayden's analysis of what she thought about, but not even she could explain the dance miracle she had worked on stage. It just happened and it was magic. [*Saturday Review*]

556

Gypsy from Sacramento

August 2, 1969

Richard Cragun. What does that name mean to you? Well, he was one of the major reasons that the Stuttgart Ballet bowled over American balletomanes and the general public when the troupe from a small but important city in Württemburg made its U.S. debut this past June at the Metropolitan Opera House. Nobody, including the Stuttgart dancers themselves, along with their director and chief choreographer, John Cranko, could quite believe in the triumph the company enjoyed. Among the pleasantly stunned dancers was the American Cragun, who catapulted himself into that special society of male stars that includes d'Amboise, Villella (United States), Bruhn (Denmark), Nureyev (originally Soviet Union), Dowell (England), and a very few more. "It hasn't gone to my head," says Cragun of his enormous New York success. "I just think of all the talented boys in Des Moines who could have made it too if they had been willing to be gypsies. All I did was to take the chance."

Richard Cragun from Sacramento, California, took that chance. At seven, fascinated with Gene Kelly movies, he started tap dance lessons ("Tap," he says, "is one of the blessings for American dancers who go into ballet."); at eight he was performing in amateur shows; a little later, he took ballet lessons just to augment his tap technique ("Barbara Briggs was my first ballet teacher, and I owe so much to her."); through Miss Briggs he got a ballet scholarship at the Banff School of Fine Arts in Canada, where he studied with Brian Macdonald; and from Banff, he went to London, rather than to New York (because of his Canadian-English teachers), at sixteen.

He was determined to be self-supporting, so when he completed his scholarship with the Royal Ballet School in London and an Adeline Genée scholarship in Copenhagen (where he studied privately two to three hours each day with the great Vera Volkova, principal teacher of the Royal Danish Ballet), he took a corps de ballet job in Stuttgart, where, under Cranko, he performed in ballets, operas, and operettas. At eighteen, he danced his first Prince in *Swan Lake*, and at nineteen, while still in the corps, he did his first Albrecht in *Giselle* and his first Romeo. Cranko actually pushed the young dancer into roles usually performed by Ray Barra, a former director of the Stuttgart Ballet and one of its principal dancers. "Ray," says Cragun, "helped me all the way. I admired him tremendously. And to this day, when I'm doing a part, I mentally look at Ray and at Nureyev to help me develop what I should do."

Soon, Cranko began creating roles with "Rick" in mind. *Opus I* was the first ballet created for me, and I think of all the ballets in the repertory it is, in a deep sense, the most important to me. Of course I like to do Romeo—

557

every boy enjoys being romantic!—and *Taming of the Shrew,* naturally, is a very special favorite of mine. But John is wonderful. He tries to make all of us perfectly comfortable in all kinds of ballets—classical, abstract, dramatic, romantic, comic. John gives you a total idea of what he sees in a ballet or in a role, but he encourages you to develop your own ideas within his concept. If you go too far, he'll pull you back.

"Doing a great variety of roles is important. What I've done in other ballets actually prepares me for new parts. It's hard to get *into* a new role. Frankly, I come to a new part with a real hodgepodge of ideas—I find that I need to test every possible side—and then through performing, I arrive at what I really set out to do."

In *Shrew,* created for him and the company's great ballerina and his inseparable sweetheart, Marcia Haydée, he arrived at what he had set out to do. As the swashbuckling tamer, he had New York audiences cheering a star of the "matinee idol" school of two generations ago; he also won them as Romeo, and he stirred them profoundly in *Opus I.*

Although Cragun never finished formal schooling—"I hated school"—he is an articulate young man. "The family," he says, "approved of my dance career. I had no troubles there. But when I left home at sixteen, Dad, who is a professor and a Shakespeare admirer, simply said to me, 'Don't forget the books.' I never have forgotten them. That's my education."

This October, when the Stuttgart Ballet returns to America for its first transcontinental tour, a high point for Richard Cragun will occur on November 17, when he will return to Sacramento as a highly literate young man, a star dancer, and as a Shakespeare expert in the Stuttgart's *Taming of the Shrew.*

In addition to giving a great performance as Petruchio—an acting job that I think Shakespeare would have approved of—Cragun exhibits his brilliant dance technique. Among the marvels he accomplishes are triple turns in air, and they happen so swiftly, so smoothly, and so easily that you are not sure whether to trust your own eyes. His multiple pirouettes, his vaulting leaps, and those miraculous tours en l'air represent the skills of a great athlete, but Cragun is careful to point out that they must serve both the style and purpose of a given ballet. He says, "Both Romeo and Petruchio do air-turns, but Romeo does them in ecstasy and Petruchio in anger or bravado. The technical approach is the same, but the thrust of drama, the speed of the music, even the color of the movement are different because of the character you are portraying.

"In *Swan Lake* too, the Prince does big jumps in the Black Swan Pas de Deux, but it's not the same as in the classroom where all you think about is the jump and how high you can go. On stage, you need to prove the character, not yourself."

How he came to do triple air-turns was sheer fluke, for doubles are standard, although the Russians sometimes do triples. "I was taking class with Anne Woolliams, our assistant director and one of our principal teachers, when all of a sudden I lost my double air-turns. I stumbled and fumbled and couldn't do them. Anne said 'You're not snapping your neck around.' I tried some more as she called, 'Snap it! Snap it!' So I pushed and snapped and wound up with a triple and I've been able to do them ever since."

Cragun doesn't want his triples to become a trademark. "Physical tricks are not unimportant, but trademark steps are a danger. You must discriminate and use flashy technique only when it's appropriate. There is a big difference between *selling* yourself—this is what I'd call camp or what they call 'tits and teeth' approach in show biz—and in *presenting* yourself through a role."

Although he has twenty dancing years ahead of him, he is already thinking about the days when he must serve ballet in other ways. "I have no leanings toward choreography," he says. "I really don't have any talent for it. But I love teaching, especially the twelve to twenty age bracket, and I would want to be affiliated with a ballet school associated with a company, with the stage, just as we have today in Stuttgart. Then I'd have time, too, for more reading, and to bury myself in American Indian lore. I know I'm a mixture of English, Irish, Scottish, and Dutch ancestries, but the family thinks that during the westward trek in pioneer days some Indian was added. I hope so. I feel an affinity with the Indian."

For the present, the sum of all these parts is one of the most brilliant and sensitive male dancers of our day, an American who took to the gypsy trail, worked unstintingly, made a name for himself in Stuttgart (the ancient German city that, two centuries ago, gave home to one of the greatest dance pioneers of all time—Jean-Georges Noverre), and who returned to conquer the dance capital of the world, New York City. Coming up—all of America, and particularly Sacramento! [*Saturday Review*]

Contest in Moscow

August 9, 1969

"Every time you danced," said the Soviet Union's most famous ballerina, Maya Plisetskaya, "I gave you my twelve points." The Bolshoi Ballet's star was addressing the Iceland-born Helgi Tomasson, who represented the United States (as a principal dancer of the Harkness Ballet) at the First International

Ballet Competition—or, as the Russians themselves call it, "Olympics of Ballet"—this summer in Moscow. Awards—for duos, solo male, solo female—were given in gold, silver, and bronze, and Tomasson won the silver in the male soloist category.

At his own expense, he took along his wife, Marlene Rizzo (also a Harkness dancer), and had his parents babysit in Iceland (both his wife and his son are Americans, and he will be in due course). He found that he needed Marlene not just personally but professionally. "Almost every one of the eighty-nine entrants—they came from nineteen different countries—had teachers or coaches or trainers with them. I could have done the same, but I didn't understand that, so Marlene worked like mad seeing that lights and their cues were okay, that my rehearsal tapes were played at the right speed, and that everything went smoothly. (I was under terrible pressure, for I really felt that I was representing America.)

"They—the contestants—were not just first-class; they were the best that their countries—those with state theaters—could produce," he reports. "Here were the highest standards of dance I had ever seen. Unbelievable! I rehearsed every day, but I tried to see all the contestants. One fascinating dancer after another. It was nerve-wracking, but I couldn't stay away."

Tomasson arrived in Moscow with five solos. Because of a misunderstanding caused by translation of contest rules from Russian to English, he did not know that if he lasted until the final stage of the competition, he'd need a sixth. He did, of course, reach the finals and the closing gala, but what to dance? He elected to do the solo from the Black Swan Pas de Deux, a work originated in Russia and one that many of the contestants were doing. But he had no costume. He sent for one in New York, but his cable never got through. So at the last minute, with the permission of that great ballerina of just yesterday, Galina Ulanova, chairman of the board of judges, he was given access to the Bolshoi Ballet wardrobe. He was proud to dance in a costume worn by the Bolshoi's major young *danseur,* Vladimir Vasiliev. For Black Swan he had only two hours of rehearsal, yet earned a tremendous response from the public.

Black Swan was a popular vehicle for all contestants, but Tomasson recalls seeing six or seven excerpts from *Le Corsaire,* one after another, and a day that was devoted almost exclusively to *Don Quixote.*

For his own offerings in the three stages of the competition, with two solos for each stage, his dances were: (stage 1) solos from Anton Dolin's *Variations for Four* and Brian Macdonald's *Zealous Variations*; (stage 2) a solo from Jerome Robbins's *Dances at a Gathering,* in which he was rehearsed by Robbins himself, and a new solo to Berlioz's score for *Romeo and Juliet,* created especially for him by Norman Walker; (stage 3) Black Swan and a solo from Balanchine's *Sylvia* Pas de Deux. The biggest successes for him with the public that jammed the Bolshoi were the Dolin, Robbins, and Petipa solos.

He rehearsed three to four hours each day in one of twenty-six studios at the Choreographic School. Time was allotted in the Bolshoi Theater itself for rehearsals in a stage-size studio. He practiced with tapes he'd brought along, but performed with the Bolshoi Orchestra. He had ten minutes with the conductor to set tempos for each final rehearsal. "There was only one conductor," he reports, "and a wild variety of tempos for just one ballet. But he never missed; I was amazed."

For his daily ballet lesson, he worked either with a taped class made in America or took class with the Danes present. "I could have had class with the Russians," he says, "but it would have been dangerous to work, at this late stage, in a ballet style and method different from what I was used to."

The audiences, he tells, picked favorites from the start. He was one that the audiences applauded when his name was mentioned. As for the dancers present, he says, "Choreographically, with all my new pieces, I was a gold mine. The dancers from all the countries crowded the wings as I danced Robbins or Walker or the others, and they whispered *Amerikanski!* There were other whispers, too. The audiences were very knowledgeable. If anyone hopped at the end of a pirouette, you could almost hear a mass whisper, 'He missed a point.' But they were marvelous."

Except for Black Swan, Tomasson had planned a non-Russian repertory. "I felt I couldn't compete with the Russians in *their* repertory, so I brought something of an American repertory to show them *our* way of doing classical ballet." Using this approach, he won a silver medal from a board of twenty judges that included ten Russians (Mme. Ulanova, Plisetskaya, Chabukiani, Khachaturian, Sergueff among them), and Chauviré (French), Flindt (Danish), Haskell (British), de Mille (American) among the rest.

Tomasson's award was not only the silver medal but also 2,000 rubles, equal officially to $2,200. But aside from being taxed on it (300 rubles), he was not allowed to change it into other currency or take it out of the country. He had one day in which to spend it, so he and his wife settled on sable skins (on which he had to pay U.S. duty). "It's enough for part of a stole," he says.

But the rewards were in his medal, in the competition itself, and, most of all, in the prestige that the Russians bestowed upon the four-day (three days of contest and the concluding gala) affair. "They felt it was as important as the Tchaikovsky Competition," says Tomasson. "You've probably read that Londoners were incensed when the Bolshoi Ballet arrived there without the new *Swan Lake* that had been promised to them. But I can tell that to the Russians the competition was far more important than getting a new *Swan Lake* ready for export. The next competition will be held in three years, instead of four, that's how successful it was."

Competition winners were: DUOS, Nina Sorokina and Yuri Vladimirov of the Soviet Union and Francesca Zumbo and Patrice Bart of France, gold medals; SOLOISTS, Malika Sabirova, Mikhail Baryishnikov of the Soviet Union; silver medals for soloists Tomasson, U.S.A., Loipa Araujo, Cuba, and Hideo Fukagawa, Japan. (Bronze medals were won by contestants from Japan and the Soviet Union.) [*Saturday Review*]

A New Company Is Born

November 15, 1969

That lovely little law of averages was at work for Eliot Feld and his new American Dance Company during the youthful troupe's first U.S. engagement (at the Brooklyn Academy of Music). In my initial report, I noted that the young dancers were beautifully rehearsed and highly disciplined but, in several instances, still wet behind the ears with respect to performing authority; that *Cortège Burlesque,* a circus satire in pas de deux form, was amusing but needed stellar artists to carry it off; that new stagings of Donald McKayle's *Games* and Herbert Ross's *Caprichos* were excellent, with the former, because of its cast of juveniles, more successful than the latter, with its demands for mature characterizations. Feld's own *Harbinger* and *At Midnight,* which thrust him to instant fame with the American Ballet Theatre two years ago, were skillfully danced by the new company.

As the repertory continued to unfold during the rest of the two-week season, the law of averages, the pro's and con's, continued to work. There were three ballets by Feld himself: *Meadowlark* (music of Haydn arranged by Hershy Kay, décor by Robert Munford, costumes by Stanley Simmons), created last year for the Royal Winnipeg Ballet; *Intermezzo* (music of Brahms and costumes by Simmons), first presented last summer at the Festival of Two Worlds in Spoleto, Italy; and, in its world premiere, *Pagan Spring* (Bartók's *Dance Suite,* décor by Leonard Baskin).

Meadowlark is Feld's first classical ballet (his first two were closer to modern dance than to ballet) and it is a beauty. Its steps, its gestures, its choreographic figures are as gay and as sunny as its flowered *al fresco* setting and as the demeanor of eighteenth-century aristocrats playing prettily at being idealized peasants. Balletomanes might like to think of it as a *grand* (*très grand!*) *pas bucolique.*

Intermezzo is also classical and also aristocratic but it is of a different dance genre. It is pure dance, that is, a movement visualization of the sounds, phrasings, and timbres of the music. This is the genre which has already been glorified in dance history by George Balanchine's *Liebeslieder Walzer* (Brahms)

562

and Jerome Robbins's *Dances at a Gathering* (Chopin), both created for the New York City Ballet. Feld, however, speaks in his own highly original choreographic terms. Among its many charming patterns is a recurring lift (not an over-the-head Bolshoi-style lift), in which the ladies seem to be sitting in air or, perhaps, emulating Queen Elizabeth I in a lift from *lavolta*.

With *Pagan Spring,* Feld didn't make it. The genre here includes *Sacre du Printemps* or, perhaps, Robbins's *Les Noces* (both, of course, with Stravinsky's music and dramatic argument), but in this case Feld's inherent originality fails him. Here, he is self-consciously *primitif* in his overuse of flexed ankles, knees, elbows and splayed fingers. This is surface, even superficial, primitive; for anything that is primitive is "prime," that is, "first," and the compulsion to express the magic of sex, the wonder of spring, the miracle of birth and rebirth is an inner happening. Feld misses this despite some stunning ensemble designs for men and women and the chosen maiden, and the duet for himself and Elizabeth Lee, the strongest episode in the ballet.

Feld, incidentally, was not supposed to perform at all, since he had broken a bone in his foot before the opening. But he was determined, at the last minute, to dance in his *Pagan Spring,* and, with the aid of pain-killers, he did just that; and since he is a dynamic performer, he was able to contribute more as a dancer than a choreographer to his own ballet.

Two more revivals, not by Feld, again provided an average between hit and failure. The first (the failure) was *Carnaval* (1910), staged by Yurok Lazowski after the choreography by Michel Fokine to the Schumann music. It is, by today's standards, a trivial work both choreographically and dramatically, for it is one of those many "linking" ballets that served as a span from the ballets of Petipa to the new ballet of Serge Diaghilev. When Karsavina, Nijinsky, and Bolm first danced it in Western Europe (it had been seen a few months earlier in St. Petersburg), the impact was enormous. For us, the force of novelty is gone, and only the shell of a once adventuresome choreographic study remains. The Feld dancers, I must add, did nothing to restore it to life. It wasn't just dull, it was dead.

Ross's *The Maids,* based on the play by Jean Genet and set to music of Milhaud, was first seen in an American Ballet Theatre Workshop production in New York in 1957. It was a shocker then, since the two maids were danced by two boys (as Genet, according to Sartre, wished). But in this era of homosexual plays and movies, the sheer shock is gone and we can now see it for what it is, a superb dance-drama in which attraction and repulsion, desire and abnegation, physical union and individual isolation, and Genet's belief that "profound unreality" passes itself off "as reality" are projected through spare and powerful and cuttingly direct choreographic action.

Paul Olsen and Loren Hightower, who headed the first cast, restaged *The Maids* for Feld's American Ballet Company, and Bruce Marks (guest artist from the American Ballet Theatre) and John Sowinski danced the title parts with passion and a curious, tortured purity which suggested the classical catharsis of Greek drama.

All, then, was not perfect with the American Ballet Company in its first U.S. appearances, but so much was entertaining or stirring that it was inarguable that an important American dance company had come into vibrant being. [*Saturday Review*]

With Margot Fonteyn, Jacob's Pillow, 1973. Photo: Louis Martinez.

With Dame Margot Fonteyn, Louis Martinez, Peter Darrell (director, Scottish Ballet) at Jacob's Pillow, the year Walter Terry was director of the Pillow's dance festival and school, 1973. Photo: Louis Peres.

With Gabriella Taub-Darvash, Paul Russell, 1973. Photo: Frank Derbas.

With Alicia Alonso, International Ballet Competition, Varna, Bulgaria, 1974.

With Rebekah Harkness just before the opening of the Harkness Theater on Broadway, 1974. Photo: Martha Swope.

With Dame Alicia Markova, Anton Dolin, Evelyn Laye (English stage star), Lady Campbell-Ord, in Dolin's London flat, 1974. Photo: F. Randolph Swartz.

With Ivan Nagy at a lecture-demonstration in concert hall of Metropolitan Opera House, 1976.

With Cynthia Gregory at Walter Terry's 40th anniversary party, 1976.

With Hanya Holm at celebration of Walter Terry's 40th anniversary as a dance critic. Dance Collection, New York Public Library, 1976.

With Pauline Koner at Walter Terry's 40th anniversary, 1976.

With Donald Saddler and Valerie Bettis at Walter Terry's 40th anniversary party, 1976.

With Robert Joffrey, 1976.
Photo: Susan Cook.

With Harry Wilcott (Board of Directors, Boston Ballet) celebrating Walter Terry's 40th anniversary as dance critic, 1976–77.

With Martha Graham, 1973. Photo: Louis Peres.

With Ebbe Mørk, dance critic of Copenhagen's newspaper, *Politiken,* lecturing in Boston, 1975. Photo: F. Randolph Swartz.

With Paul Russell, a principal with Dance Theater of Harlem. Sculpture by Miriam Winslow, former dancer, 1978. Photo: Steven Caras.

1970

The "Baby" Turns 30

Gelsey Kirkland and John Clifford represent NYCB's accent on youth •
Sybil Shearer still something special • Daniel Nagrin gives a solo concert •
Robbins' creates In the Night for NYCB • ABT at 30 • Bella Lewitzky •
Black dance in all its phases • Feld creates Cortège Parisien, A Poem For-
gotten and The Consort for his company • Natalia Makarova defects •
Maurice Béjart's revolutionary dance in Brussels

Accent on Youth

January 31, 1970

The lovely limbs of youth were given special celebration in the program that
the New York City Ballet elected to present at the New York State Theater as
it returned to repertory following forty performances of *The Nutcracker.*
Spirits, on this occasion, seemed especially high—as were the leaps and leg extensions—because the dancers had survived the routine of all those Christmastime *Nutcrackers,* because they had broken all existing box-office records by
racking up a whopping 107,436 paid admissions in those forty performances,
and because they could now, for the rest of the engagement (through February 15), savor the joys of choreographic diversity.

Except for the closing ballet, George Balanchine's *Firebird* (created for
Maria Tallchief twenty-one years ago), headed by the company's undesignated
but very real prima ballerina, Melissa Hayden (a priceless member of the troupe
for twenty years), and Francisco Moncion (who joined the Balanchine–Lincoln
Kirstein ballet enterprises nearly a quarter of a century ago), the rest of the
program (three ballets) was centered on youth. John Clifford, Balanchine's
favored junior choreographer, was represented by two ballets, the month-old
Reveries (Tchaikovsky, first third, fourth, sixth movements of Suite No. 1)
and the older *Fantasies* (Ralph Vaughan Williams).

The third piece was Balanchine's *Valse Fantaisie* (Glinka), a suite of dances for two principals and an ensemble of four girls, not to be confused with an earlier Balanchine–Glinka ballet of the same name from the 1950s. In this, Clifford, barely into his twenties, was on hand as a dancer, and an exciting one he is. He is a virtuoso who never has to fret about multiple turns, big jumps, flying leg-beats, or, say, a batch of aerial spins ending on a knee. With this physical prowess, he also has theatrical flash, more so than the majority of the young dancers in this company, who are spirited but inclined to be a trifle *raffiné*. Clifford, the performer, youthful arrogance and all, is an asset to the New York City Ballet.

As a choreographer, he is also valuable. He hasn't turned up with a masterpiece yet, but he dares to tackle his choreographic projects with gusto; he seems unafraid of being pitted against the works of the City Ballet's chief choreographer, Balanchine, who is not only a master maker of dances but a genius in the arts of today; Clifford does not shy away from occasionally imitating (as in *Reveries*) Balanchine (which may be politic); and he is steadily displaying increased command of the craft, if not always the art, of choreography.

In *Reveries* you will experience motor echoes of, say, Balanchine's *Serenade* or other ballets in the music visualization genre, but there is a buoyancy to it, a sort of movement thrust that is Clifford's own. The very special junior dancer here was Gelsey Kirkland, just turned seventeen, who would appear to be the chief contender for the post recently vacated by the Balanchine favorite, Suzanne Farrell. Little Gelsey is as lithe, as limber, and as daring (she zooms in and out of movement difficulties with no fear at all) as Miss Farrell. Her nearest teen-age rival in this new production is her big sister (all of nineteen), Johnna Kirkland, a delightful dancer.

You would also note, in the corps, still other fetching teen-agers, among them the long-legged, coltish, and talented Colleen Neary, whose own big sister, Patricia, has already made a name for herself in Europe as well as in America. Suki Schorer, as youthful and as pert as she was just a few years back, was Clifford's co-star in *Valse Fantaisie*; and in *Fantasies* Kay Mazzo, who first impressed Jerome Robbins when she was only fifteen, once again made it abundantly clear that her shy, elfin demeanor, coupled with her stylish movement mastery, makes her an important member of the company.

Among other slightly senior dancers on this occasion were Sara Leland, who first displayed teen-age talent with the Boston Ballet; Conrad Ludlow, once the brightest teen-age principal of the San Francisco Ballet; and Anthony Blum, a product of New York City's own High School of Performing Arts. All performed well, and Blum, dancing in both of Clifford's ballets, was particularly impressive. Since his teens, he has climbed slowly and steadily to a plane of high accomplishment. The beginnings were not splashy, and I'm not at all sure that many balletomanes looked at him years ago and said, "Keep your eye on him." But Blum kept an eye on his own career, and today the fans come to see him dance, and they feel, as we all do, privileged to be exposed to his consistently growing art as a performer. Now a venerable thirty-one, Blum more than holds his own with the bright newcomers of the New York City Ballet. So, if you didn't say it before, say it now: "Keep your eye on him." [*Saturday Review*]

The Sunbeam Will Outlast Us All

February 7, 1970

Evanston, Ill.   In the days when Sybil Shearer elected to depart briefly from her beloved Middle West for rare appearances in New York City (and she gave precious little warning of an impending arrival), the dance critics would accurately report that if the roof had fallen in on whatever theater she had engaged (Carnegie, the Brooklyn Academy of Music, a Broadway house on a Sunday afternoon), there would be no American dance left the next day. For Miss Shearer, modern dance maverick, would attract a who's-who-in-American-dance audiences. "What do you suppose Sybil will do *this* time?" was heard on every lip. And at the close of the matinee, having ensorcelled everyone present, Miss Shearer would depart, leaving behind a clear statement that she was unpredictable in everything except her sweet independence, her dedication, and a vibrant, radiant, growing, living, mutating, probing, revealing dance creativity rare even in the highest echelons of art.

Miss Shearer no longer comes to us in the East; we, and the rest of the dance devotees, come to her little theater (the 800-seat Arnold) at the National College of Education, where she has been artist-in-residence since 1962. To this theater with its glorious stage for dancers (45 by 52 feet) come Shearer admirers from as far away as Los Angeles and Miami, and from countless cities in between.

It is not at all easy for Miss Shearer's legion of followers to get to see her dance. She sometimes postpones programs if she feels that not everything, including her own spirit, is in readiness; and she adds performances on short notice. She is now midway in what is expected to be a total of six appearances (one in Milwaukee), and we have slogged and mushed her way in near-blizzards, gales, and sub-zero weather.

Sybil Shearer? She's worth every inconvenience.

How to describe her? For thirty years (and she hasn't changed a bit in appearance), since she left important assignments with the Humphrey–Weidman

567

company and with Agnes de Mille in order to go her own dance way, she has defied description. She uses very little, or no, makeup; her hair is uncoifed, yet she uses costumes that range from the simplest white frock to brilliant-colored fanciful dress and headdress; there are times when she stands on one spot, perhaps on one leg, and only her arms move, accompanied by a ripple of the upper torso; and there are other occasions when she speeds across the stage, kicks high and free, or spins like a dervish.

One of her programs, some years ago, was listed simply as *Dance I, Dance II,* etc., and yet others will have dances named with poetry, with wit, with an almost childlike profundity of understanding: *The spark is the child of flame; Dead wood cannot be used for building; Stamping won't dent the world; Without wings the way is steep; All is not gold but almost;* or the concluding solo in her current *Fables and Proverbs* program for soloist (herself) and her company, *The sunbeam will outlast us all.*

She is one of the world's foremost modern dancers, yet she doesn't believe in a modern dance schooling. "It's a style of movement," she says, "not a technique." Her company has classes in ballet—the strict Cecchetti method—and she herself (Muriel Stuart of the School of American Ballet was a favorite ballet teacher) keeps her ankles strong by occasionally practicing in toe shoes.

How to explain Sybil Shearer? She met the late Ruth St. Denis when "Miss Ruth" was in her seventies. They were, superficially, separated by more than a generation, by the elaborateness of a St. Denis presentation and the almost stark simplicity of a Shearer one, by exotic ritual and Shearer's down-on-the-farm elementalism. But they found a sharing in a devotion to beauty, a detesting of inequity, and an identification with nature that has made them something more than man himself. Miss Ruth not only saw her beloved mountains, she *felt* them; and Miss Shearer not only looks at her trees, she is one with them. The total, not the selfish, pulse of life has motivated both. Perhaps this is the closest one can come to describing the Shearer message.

In *Without wings the way is steep,* your own body experiences, emphatically, the steady struggle to climb, to reach out, to get there (the where doesn't matter); and in her *All is not gold but almost,* she makes you laugh, chuckle, and roar as the fanciful, tinseled creature hops from light pool to light pool in search of an alchemy that will turn brass to gold.

The music Miss Shearer uses for herself and for her company is drawn from every possible source—Prokofiev, Poulenc, Brant, Weill, avant-garde composers, jazz, etc.—and is selected because it serves dancing. The lighting and staging are by her long-time colleague, Helen Morrison, and in both areas, Mrs. Morrison's own skills, her sensitivity to dance, and her rapport with Miss Shearer's unique art expressions represent her own claim to genius.

The Sybil Shearer Company is well disciplined, attractive, admirable; but although it is presumably of professional estate, there is the air of the amateur about it. Miss Shearer's choreography for group is well executed, but one rarely feels the sense of involvement with the subject matter that Shearer herself communicates in her solos, or even the unorthodox and disarming theatricality that the star herself projects.

Miss Shearer may be elusive as far as mere verbal descriptions are concerned—perhaps, she is rather like the title of another of her dances, *The message is in the wind,* but I promise you that she is as genuine as the wind and that her message is as varied, as real, as gentle, and as powerful as that of the unseen wind itself. Sybil Shearer will not come to you, but if the portents are right, you will find her dancing February 8 in Evanston, March 8 in Milwaukee, and, perhaps, one more time in late March or April in Evanston. [*Saturday Review*]

Lamentations and Cheers

February 14, 1970

He gives it to you right between the eyes. The bayoneted rifle is pointed at you and you and you in the audience. The man who holds it is, at first, grim-faced, but as he prepares to pull the trigger, the mask changes into an arrogant, sadistic sneer. He fires point-blank. Involuntarily, you jump. It is, of course, a fake, but the gun explodes, not with a bullet for your body but with a searing message for your mind.

The single performer in this "dance–theater collage," which runs for more than two hours, is Daniel Nagrin, a veteran (since the 1940s of the concert stage, first with his wife, the late Helen Tamiris, and subsequently as a soloist) dancer, choreographer, and Broadway musical soloist. This, his newest creation, is called *The Peloponnesian War,* and its production was made possible by grants from the National Council on the Arts and Humanities and by the New York State Council on the Arts. (The work was first done when Nagrin was artist-in-residence at the State University College in Brockport, New York, and has since been seen at the Cubiculo Theater in Manhattan, on tour, and currently on Monday evenings at the WBAI Free Music Store, 359 East 62nd Street.)

The choreography and staging are, of course, by Nagrin; the taped electronic music is by Eric Salzman, with additional music by Archie Shepp; the variety of costumes (from a near-nude dance belt to an Indo-Chinese whore done *en travesti*) are by Sally Parsons; and the contrapuntal voice heard

569

throughout the work and during intermission, as well as pre-performance, is that of Frank Langella, speaking in cultured, soothing tones about the most "perfect war" in history as accurately reported by that great historian Thucydides, who urbanely and almost gently told of killings, sinkings, a plague, defeats, honorable murders, and destruction. Nagrin points out, with ardor and considerable vehemence, that we haven't changed much since 400 B.C., except that we've learned how to kill more people faster.

The Peloponnesian War is not easy going; it has a few dull, or overextended, passages. Nagrin occasionally relies on heavy mugging, instead of dance gesture, in the mimed episodes, and at times I wondered if Nagrin hadn't said it all in a matter of minutes in an earlier solo, *Indeterminate Figure.* But there is a cumulative power about *The Peloponnesian War,* as Nagrin, playing all roles, introduces us to a villain and thoughtless hero, Hitler, an anonymous worker, a soldier and a clawing, dying victim, a tyrant and a tyro in a world of violence.

Langella's beautiful voice, telling of balances of power, declarations of war, armadas, invasions, carnage, and devastation, becomes almost hypnotic and benumbing with Thucydides's erudite description of man's continuing quest to destroy himself. But while this intentionally numbs one's thoughts, the electronic tapes jar the senses with, for example, insane mixups of "The Star-Spangled Banner," played in a jumble of rhythms and pitches and with a nightmarish variety of voices (you'll spot Kate Smith right away) or with blasts of cacophony mated to church music.

And while you sit there, numbed and silent, the terror of what is happening begins to take hold. This Everyman, this mute speaker for you and me, finally gets through to us, as he generates feelings of helplessness, outrage, anger, and rededication within us. At the very close, he departs from the "lamentations and cheers" of Thucydides, and, donning the classical robe of an ancient philosopher, he moves close to the audience, holds out his arms in love to his fellow beings, and silently mouths "Thank you, thank you."

As I say, it is not a perfect work of theater by any means. It cannot match that greatest of antiwar dances, Kurt Jooss's *The Green Table.* There are other examples of antiwar ballets—Ted Shawn included a World War I fantasia in his all-male *O Libertad,* portions of Tamiris's *Adelante* were violent protests concerning the Spanish Civil War, Agnes de Mille's superb Civil War (American) ballet in *Bloomer Girl* commented on the terrible tragedy of war, Barton Mumaw (a soldier during World War II) created a solo called *War and the Artist*—and with the Vietnam War there have been current choreographic protests, some of them (those which I happened to see) more in the nature of angry sermons than powerfully expressional dances.

Nagrin carries off his *The Peloponnesian War* successfully, if not entirely satisfactorily, for several reasons: First, he approaches his theme with intelligence and fervor, rather than anger or irritation; secondly, he mainly avoids sermonizing as he lets movement say, "This is how it is, man"; thirdly, as a good craftsman, he has constructed his evening-long dance with all kinds of contrasts in stress, rhythm, viewpoint, literalness, fantasy, humor, and madness; and finally, he has long been one of the few dancers of today who can carry off a solo recital, chiefly because of the very vigor of his stage presence, coupled with a sound modern dance technique.

Daniel Nagrin, as a program all unto himself, may not be everyone's cup of tea, but the bitter brew he offers in *The Peloponnesian War* is both cathartic, in the sense of great Greek tragedy, and therapeutic. So if you occasionally go to the theater not for diversion alone but for a challenge and to be disturbed, pay a Monday-night visit to the old church that is now WBAI's Music Store theater (it's free, although you may have to sit on the floor) and become a participant in *The Peloponnesian War*. And someday, maybe, the only soldiers left in the world will be the Radio City Music Hall Rockettes, an adorable army of thirty-six, drilling to "The Parade of the Wooden Soldiers." [*Saturday Review*]

Robbins Plus Chopin

February 21, 1970

Have you ever *seen* a nocturne? *I* have, courtesy of the choreographic magic of Jerome Robbins. *In the Night,* a continuing exploration of Chopin's music as begun by Robbins less than a year ago in *Dances at a Gathering,* is born of four nocturnes (Op. 27, No. 1; Op. 55, Nos. 1 and 2; Op. 9, No. 2) and finds its form in the dancing of three couples, each couple with their own episode, and concluding with the six in the last nocturne.

The movements that Robbins has designed for his dancers do more than give body-shape to the melodic lines, the rhythms, the textures, the sonorities, the "breathings" of the music. Relationships and incidents are indicated by the nocturnal figures as they travel their musical pathways in shadows or in shafts of moonlight, tenderly, and shyly or eagerly, reflectively or almost rhapsodically. The touchings, the pressings, the embracings of bodies are exquisitely conceived so that the whole emerges as a poem to the most natural aspects of romance.

What is especially lovely is the gallantry displayed by the gentlemen for the gentlewomen, and the etiquette that governs the enchanting patterns when the couples meet. This, by the way, is not simply of the "good manners" brand, but, rather, etiquette in its courtly mien, and that's pure choreography.

There are moments, too, when the purest dance imageries prevail, such as when Violette Verdy is held in an upside-down position by her partner (Peter Martins) and her legs, held tightly together, reach to the skies and remind one of a shaft of moonlight; slowly, a tremor comes to the legs in the most delicate *batterie,* and, as they descend slowly to the floor, one seems to see a cascade of moonbeams drifting to earth.

Two hundred years ago, Jean-Georges Noverre, choreographer, innovator, reformer, set out to restore meaningfulness, expressivity, even truth to an art that had become almost acrobatic. He wrote in his historic *Lettres sur la danse et les ballets* that "this art has remained in its infancy only because its effects have been limited, like those of fireworks designed simply to gratify the eyes.. . . No one has suspected its power of speaking to the heart." (Translation by Cyril Beaumont.)

Noverre, if he could return today, would be awed by the "fireworks" of ballet technique—he, of course, worked well before dancing sur les pointes existed—but he would also have been amazed at the emergence of a theater dance that could speak "to the heart." Perhaps Robbins's *In the Night* would have affected him most, even more than modern dance masterpieces, for he would see a vocabulary of movement rooted in his own classical traditions, and he would experience physical fireworks used to illumine the fires of the heart.

At this point in this report, it is abundantly clear, I think, that I find *In the Night* a masterwork conceived and executed on the same high plane as *Dances at a Gathering.* But may I report to you some other responses? At the performances I attended, there was a hush throughout that pays tribute to Robbins's artistry, and wild applause at the close that pays tribute to his consummate craftsmanship; a guest of mine must have searched for a special thank you card to find a lovely East Indian print that depicted "a lady going through the dark to meet her lover"; and a now-retired dancer, after seeing *In the Night,* said, "If I had seen this when I was just starting out, I would have stopped, because I could not have hoped to have reached for such perfection."

This performing perfection, which Robbins himself lauds, was provided by Kay Mazzo and Anthony Blum, Miss Verdy and Mr. Martins (the latter, appearing through the courtesy of the Royal Danish Ballet), Patricia McBride and Francisco Moncion, and Gordon Boelzner, pianist, in the New York City Ballet production at the State Theater. The superb lighting was by Thomas Skelton, and the costumes, which underwent desirable changes from performance to performance, were by Joe Eula.

Except for dance perfection as demonstrated in *Dances at a Gathering* and *In the Night,* is there a particular significance to Robbins's interest in Chopin? He told me: "I'm still fascinated by the music of Chopin. It keeps opening up further avenues for me, so there is more to come. I may do

572

another work first, but I'll be back to Chopin. There will be another Chopin ballet from me and then, I hope, a whole evening of Chopin." The reviews for such an evening cannot be prophesied, but if the full Robbins–Chopin program matches the first two creations, perhaps it will be described by the veteran dance enthusiast who said, after seeing *In the Night*: "The most refreshing and uplifting experience to be cherished in our world of today."
[*Saturday Review*]

1940–1970—An American Ballet Image

June 20, 1970

It seems like yesterday that a new American image streaked its volant way onto the international dance scene. The maker of the image was Karen Conrad, a girl from Philadelphia (the city that has provided America with major dance figures since the days of George Washington), and the occasion was the debut of a newly organized American company, Ballet Theatre. But it wasn't yesterday, it was thirty years ago that Miss Conrad, in Fokine's *Les Sylphides,* flew comet-like across the huge stage of the Center Theater (in Rockefeller Center) in what veteran balletomanes now recall as only two leaps! The audience gasped, for it sensed that something great had been launched that night, not just a dancer but a whole new era in American ballet.

To celebrate the occasion, the American Ballet Theatre (the "American" was added to the name when the company achieved international status in the 1950s) is holding an anniversary season of four weeks (June 16 to July 12) at the New York State Theater in Lincoln Center. The daring enterprise, significant then, is even more significant now, for the company itself is like no other ballet company in the world. This is not to say that it is the best—what, or who, is best?—but that it is different from our own New York City Ballet, which is the product of a single genius, George Balanchine (occasionally abetted by Jerome Robbins, Frederick Ashton, and a few more), or the Bolshoi and Kirov ballets from Russia, which focus upon tradition and upon classical ballet accomplishments.

It is different in that its repertory includes full-length productions of, say, *Swan Lake, Giselle, La Sylphide,* and *Coppélia,* which are, in many respects, superior to those of the Soviet troupes or Britain's Royal Ballet, plus choreographic creations of every possible persuasion. It was the dream and the plan of the late Richard Pleasant, its first director, to make this new ballet company of 1940 a theater company. Lucia Chase—dancer, benefactress,

573

visionary—made possible this dream. For twenty-five years now, Miss Chase and Oliver Smith have directed the company, creating the most varied and remarkable repertory in all ballet. They have cherished and renewed the old; they have honored master choreographers and have given unprecedented opportunity to newcomers.

Thirty years ago, Ballet Theatre presented in its repertory an all-Negro ballet, *Black Ritual,* choreographed by Agnes de Mille. It commissioned the first ballet to use extensive dialogue with dance, *The Great American Goof,* choreographed by Eugene Loring and with text by William Saroyan. It introduced Antony Tudor to America. It had a traditional ballet wing, a modern English ballet wing, and an Americana wing. Its prima ballerina, Nana Gollner from Texas, was the first American to become a star of a European ballet. It engaged the veteran Fokine to direct his *Les Sylphides* in a definitive version that took into account Miss Conrad's altitudinous leaps, which Fokine had *questioned* and which Fokine *accepted* when Miss Conrad explained that "sylphs from Philadelphia jump this way"—an early recognition of American ballet style as distinct from Russian (either Bolshoi or Kirov), French, English, etc.

From its corps de ballet ranks have emerged stars of the first magnitude, Nora Kaye and Alicia Alonso among them, as well as Cynthia Gregory, a young ballerina of today. The Danish Erik Bruhn grew from attractive minor soloist to superstar, for ABT has always fostered the male in dance, the durable John Kriza among many.

Choreographers? Well, I can't list all of the world-famous names represented in the choreographic credits of the company, but more than a quarter of a century ago it found that one of its best young dancers was a great choreographer, namely Jerome Robbins. Most recently it has presided over the choreographic flight of the brilliant Eliot Feld, of Michael Smuin, and of new creative forces each year.

The great theatrical manifestations of choreographic creativity range from the oldest ballet in the world, the frivolous and charming *La fille mal gardée* (1786), through a fabulous production of the first ballet of the Romantic Age, *La Sylphide* (1832—the ABT's version is the 1836 Danish staging), and a dazzling and definitive presentation of *Swan Lake,* representing the golden peak of Petipa's era of classical dance, to such great Americana as de Mille's *Rodeo,* Loring's *Billy the Kid,* Robbins's *Fancy Free,* and avant-garde ballets with roots in Tennessee Williams, García Lorca, Genet, and Strindberg. Music? From Minkus to Mahler, from Pugni to Stravinsky, from Brahms to Cole Porter and Duke Ellington. Eclectic? You bet! And it works.

The American Ballet Theatre, unlike the New York City Ballet, nurtures stars. It always has. It buys them, borrows them, but, most important, builds them. Yesterday, it gave flawless outlet to Markova and Dolin, or Alonso and

Youskevitch; today, it has the balletomanes sighing, and justifiably, over Carla Fracci and Erik Bruhn, or Toni Lander and Bruce Marks, or Lupe Serrano and Royes Fernandez, or Ivan Nagy and Cynthia Gregory, or . . . you name them. Indeed, Fracci and Bruhn are to American ballet what Dame Margot Fonteyn and Rudolf Nureyev are to European. Pelted with flowers and deafened with cheers, they are deities of the stage, popular with both balletomanes and the general public.

There is another unique aspect of the American Ballet Theatre, and that has to do with the sense of family. True, there are dancers who disagree with Miss Chase's artistic direction and who can deliver themselves, briefly, of invectives, and there are occasions when Miss Chase should fire such dissidents (she doesn't, except sometimes); but the whole, nervous, loving process works to such a degree that dancers, choreographers, former stage crew members can say, as much as twenty years later, "Oh, *we* do it this way," or "*Our* version is better," etc. They can have other jobs with other dance companies, other businesses, but it remains "we" and "our."

The current season, with Fracci and Bruhn as the special (and permanent) guest stars, is an anniversary season, but, still, a typical one. As choreographers, there will be not only Petipa, Tudor, Robbins, de Mille, Massine, and Balanchine, but Feld, Smuin, and Nahat, plus the black Keith Lee and Alvin Ailey, and the white David Blair, and the great modern dancer–choreographer, the Mexican Indian José Limón.

The anniversary season features such novelties as a recently discovered Cole Porter score composed many years ago especially for ballet and called *Cole Porter Ballet* and choreographed by Lee; *The River,* Ellington–Ailey; a revival of *Petrouchka,* staged by the late Fokine for ABT; a new production of Massine's *Gaîté Parisienne* (remember Danilova and Franklin as the lovers in the old Ballet Russe de Monte Carlo original?); Smuin's new *Soledad* (music of Rodrigo); and Limón's all-male *The Traitor* (the Jesus/Judas theme) and his *The Moor's Pavane* (the Othello motif); plus, of course, *Swan Lake, Giselle, La Sylphide,* and contemporary classics.

In America, we do not, of course, have a royal ballet, and, officially, we don't have a national ballet in the sense that France and the Soviet Union do. But, unofficially, we have the American Ballet Theatre, which must surely come closest to serving as our national ballet, and which has recently been appointed as the official ballet company of the John F. Kennedy Center for the Performing Arts. Just ten years ago, it became the first American ballet to perform in Russia. Russia, to many, was thought of as the ballet capital (no matter that little creative progress had been made there in half a century), and one critic wrote to the effect that sending ABT to the U.S.S.R. was more like sending cinders, rather than coals, to Newcastle. True, the company had had financial problems and layoffs, but it went to the bastion of ballet, and it conquered, indisputably. It proved its international stature even before it convinced the public of its national status. This year, on its thirtieth birthday, the American Ballet Theatre, because of its productions of honored masterpieces, because of its revivals of later balletic milestones, because of its continuing espousal of new choreographic and performing talent, has earned the post as "National Ballet of the United States of America." [*Saturday Review*]

Bella

September 12, 1970

Wichita, Kan. Bella Lewitzky, to those of us based on the Atlantic seaboard, is an American dance legend. I had heard of her since the days of the Federal Theater Project (Works Progress Administration) in the 1930s, read about her, and studied photographs, but because she lived and worked in California, few East Coast dance followers ever saw her. She couldn't afford to tour a modern dance company to New York, and when many of us traveled to California on business, she wasn't having a season. I saw her first this August here in Kansas, where she was teaching and dancing for the third annual American Dance Symposium, and she was a revelation. She is a major choreographer. She is a great dancer. She is a superb teacher. She is, indeed, a dance force that *must*, in the future, be experienced from coast to coast.

Historically, Miss Lewitzky does not descend from those dynastics that we think of as having established American modern dance. These post-Denishawn innovators were Martha Graham, Doris Humphrey, Charles Weidman, Helen Tamiris, and, from German origins, Hanya Holm. In California, Miss Lewitzky was first a pupil and then a colleague of the late Lester Horton, from whom stemmed such impressive contemporary dance artists as Alvin Ailey, Janet Collins, and Carmen de Lavallade. In due course, Miss Lewitzky, now in her mid-fifties, herself became the West Coast's most celebrated modern dancer.

Most dancers, especially modern dancers, are aware that they have their dance life in space, time, and energy. Bella Lewitzky, as you watch her and her dancers move, explores and caresses space. She doesn't barge, hit or miss, through the vastness of the stage space around her. In her dancing, one is aware of pockets of space just as much as of realms of space. Her concept of energy is the same; for energy, under magnificent control, may emanate from her total body or from a fingertip. With patterns of time, she may give you a long phrase, perhaps an extended pause that is as much a part of her rhythm as an explosion of action, or the snap of a turned head, completed in a trice. With herself and in her excellent company, there is a body awareness that transcends mere muscular discipline.

The Lewitzky program, presented by the Kansas Dance Council and Sacred Heart College in Wichita State University's Wilner Auditorium, was as varied as it was stirring. A high point was a Lewitzky solo, *On the Brink of Time* (music of Morton Subotnick), incredible in its display of faultlessly controlled action, hypnotic in its evocation of "brink." It opened with advances and retreats from the wings of the stage, and here came the image of one who must walk a temporal tightrope.

With the group-dance *Orrenda* (meaning oneness), with Amerindian-flavored music by Cara Rhodes, the company's fine music director, action was centered first on the dancing of men, and subsequently on women's dances, couple dances, and a "oneness" dance for all—a radiantly hopeful theme that also served the late Doris Humphrey so beautifully in her *Ritmo Jondo* (Surinach), created for the José Limón company. In contrast to this ancient heritage of human harmony was Fred Strickler's funny and biting *Bags and Things* (tape collage from noises to Johann Strauss). Everything and everybody in Uncle Sam red-white-and-blue reminded us of the gimmicks, but, more fearfully, of the non sequiturs in our lives today.

The closing work, *Kinaesonata* (music of Alberto Ginastera), might possibly be thought of as modern dance Balanchine, but only in the sense that movements and shapes were their own ends and not expressive of literal things. Unlike Balanchine, however, who is the master of the mirror-of-music method in his magnificently patterned use of human bodies, Lewitzky uses an approach more deeply rooted in the kinesthetic (as the title suggests) than in the visual. The visual elements in the Lewitzky performances, however, were handled with fine imagination in the costume and lighting departments by Darlene Neel.

Incidentally, Miss Lewitzky, at a symposium session, presented her *Trio for Saki,* one of her few creations inspired by music already composed (Dvorák), a lovely dance that fused to perfection her interrelated pathways of space, time, energy.

It must be apparent by now that I succumbed, and gratefully, to the esthetic and kinesthetic impact of Bella Lewitzky. I wish I could describe her as a person intense yet joyous—for that is who created these dances which enchanted and enlightened citizens of Wichita, along with the teachers, performers, choreographers, and students who came here (more than 100 strong) from Hawaii, Alaska, Illinois, Haiti, Lebanon, and elsewhere to attend the American Dance Symposium, directed, guided, and believed in by Alice Bauman and her twin, Elizabeth Sherbon. An anecdote about Bella Lewitzky? At a concluding panel review of the symposium, I acted as moderator. Miss Lewitzky was sitting next to me and wearing a shawl of that pink that Mexico knows as *solferino*. I mentioned that it was the color associated with the primitive-art angels in Mexican cathedrals and introduced Miss Lewitzky as the symposium's "Mexican angel." Quickly she countered, "Will you settle for a Jewish demon?" In the world of dance, focused ever so briefly in America's heartland, there was no question but that all of us would settle for the art, the teaching, the vision, and the presence of Bella Lewitzky. And happily.

(Addendum: Both Mrs. Bauman and Miss Sherbon told me that Wichita itself contributed $610 to this year's symposium. In 1969, the Wichita *Eagle* quoted the convention and tourism manager of the Wichita Area Chamber of Commerce to the effect that the symposium brought about a half-million dollars into Wichita, yet local city agencies were remiss this year in contributing—federal and state agencies gave modest amounts—enough to do any good. So there may not be a symposium in 1971. But maybe Wichita—and other cities take note!—is so affluent that it can do without dance business, dance art to one side. However, students and teachers from the United States and far-off Lebanon felt this symposium in Kansas important enough for their long, long journeys.) [*Saturday Review*]

Black Dance

September 26, 1970

Black dance and dancers, representing African, Caribbean, tap, jazz, modern dance, and balletic forms, were prominent in most of this summer's dance events. What was impressive was not only the performing and the choreographic accomplishments but also the great scope of dance styles and concepts. I cannot begin to record them all here, but let me provide a sampling.

The Dance Theatre of Harlem, founded and directed by Arthur Mitchell (a principal with the New York City Ballet) and with Karel Shook (internationally known teacher and ballet master) as associate artistic director, is the world's only black classical ballet company, just as Mr. Mitchell himself was the first of his race to become what the French would call a *premier danseur étoile* with a white classical ballet company.

It was barely two years ago that Mitchell began teaching black children classical ballet, and yet today, these very students, augmented by others discovered by Mitchell and Shook throughout the country, constitute a highly professional and engaging troupe. There have been several appearances, even

578

short tours, by the company; but its first "engagement," as Mitchell described it, was the one-week stand at the Jacob's Pillow Dance Festival in Lee, Massachusetts. And this is fitting, because ever since the Ted Shawn Theater was built nearly thirty years ago, black dancers have been participants in every Jacob's Pillow season.

(Incidentally, the concern of Ted Shawn and the late Ruth St. Denis for the black dancer goes back to Denishawn itself. At Denishawn House in New York City in the late 1920s, Edna Guy became a protégée of Miss St. Denis and founded what Shawn today recalls as the first Negro "art" dance company in America. The Negro Concert Dancers, headed by Miss Guy and her partner, Hemsley Winfield, made its debut April 29, 1931, in New York.)

The program that the Dance Theatre of Harlem presented at the Pillow was choreographed by Mitchell and ranged from the purest and most elegant examples of classical ballet to dance episodes that echoed ancient rituals. In all, the Mitchell–Shook dancers performed beautifully and gave pleasure to the seven sets of audiences who had traveled from near and far to see them. Now, how about a New York "engagement"?

The following week the festival featured one of the Pillow's most popular dance stars, Haiti's Jean-Léon Destiné and his company. M. Destiné uses neither ballet nor modern dance for his choreographic base. Indeed, he has forged his own theatrical dance technique—and a brilliant one it is—from folk materials native to Haiti, from the French-derived social dances, and especially from the intensely dynamic actions born of voudoun ceremonies.

The Destiné drummers were Alphonse Cimber and Jacques Succès, both brilliant artists. Earlier in the month, Cimber, who is a one-man Philharmonic on his drums, was out in Wichita, Kansas, as a key figure in "The Talking Drums of Africa," an informative and entertaining lecture–demonstration that Percival Borde (who comes from Trinidad and who is married to that remarkable dancer–choreographer–anthropologist, Pearl Primus) and his dancers gave at the third annual American Dance Symposium.

The New York Dance Festival, produced by Donald Saddler and presented by the New York Shakespeare Festival free to the public in the open-air Delacorte Theater in New York's Central Park, included performances by black artists, among them the integrated Donald McKayle Dance Company with a technique rooted in modern dance, and Mura Dehn's Traditional Jazz Dance Company in a program described as being "from rag to rock." The McKayle dancers gave us his long-popular *Rainbow 'Round My Shoulder*, based on chain-gang songs and chants, while Miss Dehn's performers turned on a nostalgic panorama of grand old hoofing, tapping, singing, and joking. (I shall have more to say about this important festival at the Delacorte at a later date.)

In mid-August, New Yorkers were treated to a black import, Les Ballets

579

Africains from the Republic of Guinea; the company played a week at the City Center. This panorama was a bold, bright, and brilliant dance view of West Africa, and the company itself, said to be all new in matters of personnel since its last visit here, did the fine choreographic materials full honor. Bared female bosoms caused neither a flurry nor a fuss as they had when the Africains were first here, for Broadway has since caught up with *them.* And, by the way, there was not one so-called Afro hairdo to be seen among these forty-four African dancers.

There were many other black dance artists on the American dance scene this summer, but I have simply commented on those that I saw personally in Wichita, Lee, and New York. But it would be remiss not to note that this great black dance naissance and renaissance in America could not have emerged as it has without the efforts of that super, black dance pioneer, Miss Katherine Dunham. Nearly forty years ago, she established her first school in her native Chicago, and from there she went on to capture the love and admiration of the whole world of dance. Today, she is bringing the health and the hope of dance to underprivileged children in East St. Louis, Illinois. [*Saturday Review*]

Three Hits by Feld

November 21, 1970

Eliot Feld is the whiz-kid of American ballet. In 1967, he created his first ballet, *Harbinger* (Prokofiev), for the American Ballet Theatre, in which he was serving as a splendid dancer (the title role in *Billy the Kid* among his many roles), and it was a pow! success. He followed it with *At Midnight* (Mahler's Four Rückert Songs) for the same company. In 1968, he did his first classical ballet—the first two were very modern—*Meadowlark* (Haydn) for the Royal Winnipeg Ballet, and in the same year, he left the American Ballet Theatre and founded his own company, the American Ballet Company, with a home at the Brooklyn Academy of Music. He continues to make ballets at an assembly-line pace.

This fall, in his two-week season at the Academy, Feld offered four brand-new works, three of them his own. The most substantial of his trio of new creations was *A Poem Forgotten,* set to music of Wallingford Riegger (Concerto for Piano and Wind Quintet). It is about kinetic sensations, half-remembered, recurring, on the borderline between reality and fantasy. At the beginning, a father cradles his boy-child, who contentedly sucks his thumb. Next, the mother with the baby daughter. Later, part-grown brother and

580

sister play together. An intruding girl enters the scene, and, finally, three more outsiders, all boys, become a part of the pattern. In the scenes, at all age levels, there are open-mouthed silent cries, baby cries that linger instinctively with the adult. Finally, the closing image is of the youth with his thumb still extended, as in babyhood, still ready to serve as a pacifier.

The movement language of *A Poem Forgotten* is not classical dance but, rather, dramatic action or danced acting. It is an engrossing work that has the curious power of making the onlooker search his own kinetic memories of how it all began, how patterns were formed, how a bundle of senses became an "I." Daniel Levins, a comparative newcomer of considerable talent, was excellent as the boy.

Feld's short *Cortège Parisien* (Chabrier) is all ballet froth, a sort of sip from *Gaîté Parisienne*. It boasts a generous splash of Feld's skill in devising highly original movements, including high lifts, as the boys swing the girls over their heads, which make you think this is what a gay chuckle would be if you could see, as well as hear, it.

With *The Consort,* Feld turns to period dances, to dances that evoke the Elizabethan Age. The music credits are "Dowland, Neusidler, Morley, and Anonymous Composers" in a score orchestrated by the company's musical director, Christopher Keene. *The Consort* is not as quietly historic as one might think—Feld has some surprises in store—for it begins with elegant, courtlike dances, in which dresses sweep the floor and decorum prevails, and it ends in a drunken brawl (which is just as Elizabethan). In both scenes, the ballet keeps close to the flavor of a period without pretending to be authentic, while being graced throughout with Feld movement witticisms.

Stanley Simmons's superb costumes are an essential ingredient in this ballet. The women's costumes, for example, are actually shortened on stage (by the use of tie-loops) as the dancers are transformed from well-behaved courtiers to short-skirted, bouncy, reeling peasants. Thus it is that Feld has given us yet another charming ballet—too long, admittedly—but attractive and wonderfully imaginative.

The American Ballet Company's fourth premiere was a first choreographic effort by Bruce Marks, principal dancer with the American Ballet Theatre, and I'm afraid it was just that, "an effort." Well, an essay, anyhow. It is titled *Clockwise* (with music from Jean Françaix's *L'Horloge de Flor*), and it is as thin, as sketchy, as bland as the music. It is neat, but it is not inspiring, and it is very derivative, in steps and style, of Feld in one of his ballet-jazz moods. But abstract ballets are difficult to do—they take the master's touch—and you wonder why Marks, one of the finest actor–dancers in the theater, did not test his choreographic wings with a dramatic ballet. [*Saturday Review*]

581

Russian Ballerina

December 5, 1970

The most important dance defection since Rudolf Nureyev rushed into the arms of French police at a Paris airport nearly a decade ago is that of Natalia Makarova, thirty-year-old ballerina of the Kirov Ballet, the onetime home company of Nureyev and the company that, as the Maryinsky in the imperial days of St. Petersburg, produced Pavlova, Nijinsky, Karsavina, Fokine, and other dance immortals. Makarova sought asylum in England, where the Kirov was playing, and as with her former colleague Nureyev, politics had nothing whatever to do with it. Art and artistic opportunity are what mattered.

Makarova, one of the greatest interpreters of *Giselle,* told me through an interpreter (Mme. Valentina Pereyaslavec, a principal teacher at the American Ballet Theatre School and a favorite teacher of Nureyev and Margot Fonteyn) that she was tired of doing *Giselle* and other old classics over and over again. She loved them, but she wanted new challenges. When she defected, the dance betting was that she might want to join the Royal Ballet, with which Nureyev dances, but out of many offers, she chose the American Ballet Theatre, reportedly at less money than she might have received elsewhere. But she was enthusiastic about ABT's repertory and also about English. She speaks French, but she said of English, "For me, it comes more easy to tongue."

Makarova will, of course, dance next summer in ABT's regular season at the New York State Theater, but she will also appear during the troupe's winter season (December 22 to January 10) at the New York City Center. American balletomanes will see her celebrated *Giselle*, which she will dance with Erik Bruhn, and in Fokine's *Les Sylphides,* but she will also dance her first *Coppélia* and, most important of all, her first contemporary dramatic ballet, Antony Tudor's *Lilac Garden.* Thus it is that in America we will see not only her superb Giselle but also new characterizations by one of the great artists of the dance.

Lucia Chase, co-director with Oliver Smith of ABT, put it this way: "We are delighted that she has chosen this company. We believe that she has chosen right, and we welcome her with joy. I think our repertory provides her with what she was seeking when she left her homeland. She will have the great classic ballets in which she always excels, and at the same time she will be working with more Western choreographers than any other company, I think, could offer her. This is what she has wanted—to balance the old with the new—and with ABT it is hers." [*Saturday Review*]

Béjart's 20th Century

December 19, 1970

Brussels. "He has changed the face of ballet," said the matronly chamber-maid at the handsome Hotel Amigo here. "Ballet was tutu"—and she made a gesture of a little skirt around her ample hips—"and legs." Then, with a sweep of her arms, she added, "Béjart has turned ballet into movement." As she departed, she flung back, "*I* look to the future, not to the past!"

Maurice Béjart, choreographer and innovator, settles for the present, as the name of his company, Ballet of the 20th Century (Ballet du XXe Siècle, Belgium's national dance company), indicates. The troupe will make its American debut in an engagement opening January 25 at the Brooklyn Academy of Music as part of the Academy's third Festival of Dance.

Since the founding of his company in 1959, Béjart has been both a fascinating and controversial figure. Europeans found him avant-garde; American dancers tended to describe him as old-hat modern; the young people of Europe have been so wild about him that his company has had to perform in circuses and vast arenas in order to accommodate the mobs; the mature sophisticates abroad, here at least, view him, in his appearances at the Théâtre Royal de la Monnaie (that crass "Monnaie" is there simply because the beautiful opera house was once the royal mint), as something to be treasured.

Béjart. What is he like? Where did he come from? What is he doing? Today, permit me to talk about the man, and in a subsequent report about performances—including a new *Firebird,* with a male in the title part—which I have seen here.

Maurice Béjart is short, dark, bearded, and has hypnotic sea-blue eyes. When he rehearses, although he has retired as a dancer, he illustrates what he wants with physical facility and enormous intensity. He is not modest, but neither is he arrogant. An English critic compared him with the great ballet master of the last century, Marius Petipa (*The Sleeping Beauty, La Bayadère,* half of *Swan Lake,* the concept of *The Nutcracker*), and Béjart replied smilingly (he laughs easily and makes sly quips): "Petipa and I have only one thing in common—we were both born in Marseilles."

His own training was purely classical—"I saw no modern dance, nothing of Martha Graham"—until long after he had created his first modern ballet, *Symphony for a Single Man* (1955) with an electronic score by Pierre Henri. "Maybe what I did was childish, but it was my own," he says.

Béjart's principal teachers were Mme. Rousanne (a celebrated Paris-based teacher of Armenian descent); the famous French choreographer–dancer Roland Petit; and the great Vera Volkova, leading teacher of the Royal Danish Ballet, who numbers Margot Fonteyn, Maria Tallchief, Erik Bruhn among her pupils. His first job—1949—was with Mona Inglesby's International Ballet in England; his next, in Sweden, where he did his first choreography for the Royal Opera and danced Jason (a role performed in America by Jacques d'Amboise) in Birgit Cullberg's *Medea*. Following French military service, he formed (1953) his first company, Ballet de l'Étoile (named after the theater he played in), which became, when it moved in 1956, Ballet Théâtre de Paris. The next step, of course, was the Ballet of the 20th Century, the pride of Belgium, the toast of much of Europe, and soon a contender for American recognition.

The official ballet school of the Royal Theater is now housed in recently completed studios (one with a raked, or sloped, stage like the Théâtre Royal itself, and another level) above the warehouse for opera and theater sets. Béjart calls the school Mudra, the Hindu word for gesture. A faculty of eight teaches what Béjart feels is necessary. Classical ballet of the Leningrad school (the old Maryinsky that produced Fokine, Balanchine, Nijinsky, Pavlova, Karsavina, Danilova, et al.) comes first, and two of the teachers are on loan from Cuba's Alicia Alonso, teachers who trained in Leningrad. A black American girl teaches jazz-modern. Béjart himself does not teach: "If I teach, I don't create." Someday, he may offer a course in a technique that would be a synthesis of classical ballet and his own style, which he refers to as "my private approach."

This "private approach" is apparent even in rehearsal. Béjart, as you watch him work, is not only a master of design closely related to music but, also, a creator deeply involved with the animal nature of man. I was the first, and I think the only, outsider to be permitted to see him rehearse his newest star (America's Suzanne Farrell, former Balanchine protégée who defected) in a pas de deux scheduled for Brooklyn. Here, one could see Béjart adapt the previously composed choreography to Farrell's high leg extensions and spinal flexibilities; but, more, as he guided her and her cavalier, one saw the presence of shrewdly calculated choreographic patterns (his discipline) combined with his desire to release the animal in the human (his drive). Perhaps this is the secret of the man—*discipline* and *drive*—and, in a subsequent column, let us look at how he puts these forces to use in certain of his creations, specifically, *Firebird, Les Noces,* and, of all things, Ravel's *Boléro*. [*Saturday Review*]

Béjart's 20th Century—Part II

December 26, 1970

Brussels. The dance fan usually takes off for European dance festivals in summer, since they are highly publicized, but he is likely to sit next to herds of familiar beings who seem to have been transplanted from Lincoln Center. At this time of year, there is dance in Europe, but you find yourself sitting beside Europeans and discovering what *they* think about European dance. Here in Brussels there have been few tourists, although the weather has been mild, and trips to Ghent and fabulous Bruges (an entire city that is a museum) have seen a paucity of foreigners. At the theater, Belgians have expressed, through standing ovations, what *they* think of their own ballet wunderkind, Maurice Béjart, and his Ballet of the 20th Century, which will make its American debut at the Brooklyn Academy of Music on January 25.

I first saw the Béjart troupe not at the national opera (Théâtre Royal de la Monnaie) but at the Cirque Royal (which, you'll be glad to know, in Flemish is Koninklijk Circus), where the stage is a thrust apron, and where the audience surrounds the performers on all but one side. The all-Béjart program (it is always all-Béjart) was composed of Ravel's *Boléro* (a comparatively early Béjart) for one girl and forty men; Stravinsky's *Les Noces,* totally different in concept from either the original Nijinska ballet or the recent Robbins one; and the brand-new *Firebird,* danced to the Stravinsky suite and not to the full ballet score.

None of the three was originally slated for the Brooklyn repertory engagement, but the enormous success of *Firebird* has convinced almost everyone involved with the New York season that it must be seen, perhaps at the close of the second week, or perhaps during an extension of the engagement.

This *Firebird* is truly a remarkable creation. Its principal figure is not a ballerina but a male dancer; it is not staged as a Russian ballet but, rather, as an abstract work. It is not a telling of a fairy tale but, instead, a distillation of the promise of a bright tomorrow which all fairy tales contain. For here there is a Firebird who breathes life into man's consciousness, who flashes brilliantly across the spectrum, but who must die. But as he dies, he is replaced by the phoenix—the bird reborn from ashes—and there is a hope of tomorrow.

Some Americans and some Belgians have read a political message into this *Firebird,* but Béjart says no, that his ballet is about Stravinsky's music and about the act of life. I think that what he has given us in the male figure, clad only in scarlet leotard-tights combination, is a modern-day Prometheus. I have seen two casts and both are superb. The first was headed by one of the finest men dancers in the theater today, Paolo Bortoluzzi; the second by Jorge Donn, also a brilliant dancer—they alternated in the roles of the Firebird and the Phoenix. Indeed, the male contingent of the Ballet of the 20th Century is strong and handsome and effective in a variety of assignments.

The girls of the troupe are equally distinguished. Maina Gielgud (niece of Sir John) has the actor's profile of face along with a body profile that marks an exquisite dancer. Duska Sifnios and Tania Bari are also among the

superb dancers, and fascinating ladies, of the company. Whatever New Yorkers may think of Béjart's choreography, they are certain to find exhilaration
in dancers with first-class technical prowess, personal attractiveness, and a delightful combination of sexiness and very calculated (by Béjart) theatricality.

I need not go into much detail about *Les Noces* and *Boléro*—since
America won't see them—except as they point to Béjart's highly individual
style. In *Les Noces,* for example, he has heard the Orientalisms in the score
and has thus peopled his ballet with figures that range from Russian boyars
through Kathakali figures from India to a Chinese princess-bride. Instead of
being a primitive Russian rite, this *Les Noces* is multi-racial. Furthermore, the
Bride and Bridegroom in formal dress (he Russian, she Chinese) are duplicated
in spirit by two figures in white leotards and tights, a male and a female, and
these are the visions borne by the Bride and Groom of the bliss and ecstasy to
come after the ceremonies are ended. It is an almost ghostly concept, but a
curiously powerful one.

In *Boléro,* a girl stands on a huge orange-red circular table. With the
music, she commences a movement pattern that includes a Martha Graham-like
pelvic thrust followed by a placement of the hands on the table and a simple
step in space. The forty men are dimly seen in chairs that surround three
sides of a square. Everyone is seated. The girl continues to move. One, two,
three men shift in their chairs; a pause; some rise; a pause; others move away
from their chairs; pause; some of the men come forward and begin their own
pelvic pulsations; pause: the whole arena begins to churn, and, at the end,
forty men surround the table and throw themselves at the girl as the stage
goes black.

But this is Béjart: spectacular mass patterns with a blazing spotlight
focused upon the animal in man himself. Emily Genauer, the distinguished
American art critic, told me after a performance: "Ravel's *Boléro* is not my
choice of either music or ballet fare, but I have to tell you that an elderly
Belgian gentleman sitting next to me in the box had his knee going in rhythm
against mine; so whatever Béjart has cooked up, it certainly works." Whatever
the American public's verdict may be about Maurice Béjart's artistry, there can
be no question about his theatricality. It is flamboyant, and, if you let yourself go, it will stir you from your appreciative eyes to your . . . well, what?

The Brooklyn season very probably will feature *Firebird* late in the run,
a pas de deux for America's own Suzanne Farrell, our most famous defector
from Balanchine, plus *Le Sacre du printemps, Bhakti, Nomos Alpha, Actus
Tragicus, Les Vainqueurs,* and the full-length *La Messe pour le temps présent.*
[*Saturday Review*]

586

1971

ABT: A New Star, A New Home

Makarova triumphs at ABT • Robbins' genius seen in The Goldberg Variations • Alicia Alonso returns to North American continent with her Ballet Nacional de Cuba in Montreal • ABT finds a home at Washington, D.C.'s Kennedy Center • Lar Lubovitch a new voice in the dance world

Makarova: A Marvel

January 23, 1971

The especially luminous light that shone upon the closing days of the American Ballet Theatre's thirtieth anniversary season (1940–1970) celebrated at the New York City Center (there had been a gala birthday season at the New York State Theater in the summer) was the debut of Natalia Makarova, Russian ballerina, who had defected late in the summer when her home company, Leningrad's Kirov Ballet, was playing in London. Miss Makarova made her first appearance with her new associates in the ballet in which she has been acclaimed around the world, *Giselle,* ironically enough the sort of ballet that caused her to want to escape from the continuing confinements, at the Kirov, of nineteenth-century ballets. Shortly thereafter, with ABT, she had an opportunity to dance her first major comic role in the old *Coppélia* and her first modern dramatic role in Antony Tudor's *Jardin aux Lilas.* In all, she was triumphant.

Disaster nearly struck the debut. Erik Bruhn, the world's acknowledged premier danseur noble who was to have partnered her, was taken seriously ill and hospitalized. A new Albrecht was needed for Makarova's Giselle. The ballerina asked for Ivan Nagy, an ABT star who had defected from his native Hungary in 1968 and whom she had seen with Ballet Theatre in London. The reason? "Because he is the same school." The school, of course, is the St. Petersburg-Leningrad school of ballet, which, in Imperial days, produced some of the greatest dancers of all time, and which employs the method of teaching introduced by the late Agrippina Veganova.

Since Nagy was doing guest appearances with the Boston Ballet, there was time only to rehearse the pantomime sequences and the lifts and to walk through a dress rehearsal. But it worked, and two of the world's celebrated ballet defectors from Communist countries (the third, Rudolf Nureyev, the most famous of the leapers to freedom, artistic and non-political) danced brilliantly. Nagy said later, in his heavy Magyar accent, "Was numb. Could have cut off arm—would not feel." But the audience felt the presence of two great artists who brought to the stage superb technical prowess—soaring leaps by him, floating leaps by her—and a stylishness of balletic line that simply proclaimed the elegance and the beauty of flawlessly disciplined bodies moving in space.

All balletomanes were querying each other: "How does Makarova compare with Carla Fracci?"—another superlative Giselle. Makarova does not compare with Fracci, nor Fracci with Makarova. They are both supreme interpreters of Giselle (along with Markova, Alonso, Ulanova, and, very possibly, the first Giselle, Carlotta Grisi), for watching Fracci, you think of no one else —there are no intrusions of comparisons—and watching Makarova, the same individual magic prevails.

As Swanilda in *Coppélia* (Delibes), Makarova was an enchantingly mischievous heroine—what a comedienne she is!—and in Fokine's *Les Sylphides* (Chopin), she and Nagy danced with an incandescent lyricism that one rarely sees in today's more bravura attacks on ballet phrasing. The Tudor *Jardin aux Lilas* (Chausson) found the ballerina making the leap to free-style dance movement with ease and dramatic verity. She is different from other ballerinas (including the great Nora Kaye) who have interpreted the role of a bride forced into a loveless marriage, but on her own terms she is enormously effective in combining modern dramatic gesture—clean and kinesthetic and unadorned—with old-fashioned mime and that breathtaking balletic line that is her heritage from the most royal of royal ballets. (In this performance, I was impressed with young John Prinz's portrayal of the lover, a part he had done less than adequately during the last season, and Mimi Paul's characterization of the desperate mistress of the bridegroom-to-be.)

When Bruhn had recovered, he and Miss Makarova appeared in a tastefully arranged pas de deux composed of excerpts from Act II of *Giselle*. In a word: heaven! Consummate artistry plus bouquets and wreaths and ovations and hysteria from the fans. [*Saturday Review*]

The Genius of Robbins

July 3, 1971

To the ear, J. S. Bach's "Goldberg Variations" has been a masterpiece since it was composed in 1742 as *Aria mit verschiedenen Veränderungen*; to the eye, it has now become another kind of masterpiece, a dance composition choreographed by Jerome Robbins for the New York City Ballet. I first saw it at an "open rehearsal," with the choreographer as informative host, last summer during the New York City Ballet's month-long engagement (an annual event) at the Saratoga Performing Arts Center. As a finished ballet, it had its premiere this spring with the City Ballet at the New York State Theater.

It is a ballet that belongs to that music–concert–theater genre in which Robbins has already triumphed with his *Dances at a Gathering* and *In the Night,* both to piano music (the latter, nocturnes only) of Chopin. These also are non-narrative ballets, and they are, by the nature of the music itself, more romantic in cast than the Bach. But all three are rich in incident, in suggestion. *The Goldberg Variations,* though cool, is not cold, and there is a graciousness to it, touched with shining moments of wit, that is captivating. How describe it? It is classical ballet in form and usually in step, but there is a freedom of choreographic invention that carries it beyond ballet into total dance. In a very real sense, it is a paean to dance movement, for, in stance as well as in mind, it echoes the preclassic dance forms of two hundred years ago while it progresses effortlessly and liltingly into the almost horizonless range of today's dance accomplishments.

There are endless images to savor in memory: two introductory figures in simulated court dress giving way to the spare and pure figures of multiple dancers in leotards and tights and, at the close, a full company in the elegance of court dress being given an amen by two figures in unadorned tights—a cycle of yesterday, today, tomorrow. Or, perhaps, recall Peter Martins, in a solo, standing like a hinged doll, a Petrushka-like figure, motivated by the music into the curved contours of classical ballet and, at the close, returning to the inverted figure of the puppet; or Anthony Blum ending the first section of the ballet with a grand gesture saying, "Here comes the ballerina!" and being met at the opening of Part II by an onrushing bevy of ballerinas; or the monumental circle pattern toward the end of the ballet; or . . . endless memories of dance beauty.

When *The Goldberg Variations* was done in preview at Saratoga, a harpsichord was used. At opening night in New York City, the accompaniment was piano. At a subsequent matinee, the harpsichord was tried again. In both forms of accompaniment, Gordon Boelzner was the admirable, laudable musician. Robbins himself says that he prefers the support of the piano since "I worked with the piano in rehearsal when the ballet was being created, and it is closely related to those sounds."

As for the length of the ballet—nearly an hour-and-a-half without intermission—it has disturbed a few, but Robbins carefully considered editing and then determined, "I could not violate the music. It is there, all there, and if the mind wanders, let it rest and then come back." The length, for most of us, is felt, but the ballet never bogs down, and the unhurried pace of an earlier age comes as a gratifying experience. I notice now that I have mentioned only two principal dancers, but this was done simply "for example"; all twelve featured dancers and the twenty-plus supporting artists are equally important in a superb ballet best described an an unidentified voice sitting somewhere near me on opening night: "It's perfectly simple to explain. Robbins is a genius, that's all." [*Saturday Review*]

Brava, Alicia

July 10, 1971

Montreal. Alicia Alonso is indisputably one of the great ballerinas of our era. Very probably, she is one of the great ballerinas of all time. Almost all of her ballet training took place in the United States. In 1957–58, she became the first American-sponsored ballerina to dance with Soviet companies— her trip to Russia was made possible by the good offices of the U.S. government since her own country, at that time, had no formal relations with the U.S.S.R. She is Cuban. She is no longer welcome in the United States. That is why dance lovers from all over the U.S. have traveled to Canada to see her dance with her own Ballet Nacional de Cuba. (Americans had come here during Expo to see her superlative *Giselle* with Les Grands Ballets Canadiens.)

Over the years superhuman efforts have been made to bring her back to this country for guest appearances with the American Ballet Theatre, the company that presided over her promotions from corps de ballet to demi-soloist to soloist to ballerina to prima ballerina. Lucia Chase, co-director of the American Ballet Theatre, has fought valiantly on Congressional and State Department levels to get an entry permit for Miss Alonso (the Cuban government is perfectly willing for her to return to the scenes of her greatest triumphs and to meet again with her oldest and dearest friends in dance, dating back to her career in American musicals in the late 1930s), but Miss Chase has been turned down. The reason, or excuse, was that Miss Alonso could not be protected from anti-Castroite Cubans. Canada has protected her without difficulty.

After opening night here, a very small number of us who had known Alicia since 1939 (and before) took her and her husband, Fernando Alonso, to a quiet place for supper. The group included Maria Karnilova, recently the Broadway star of *Zorba* and *Fiddler on the Roof,* and Donald Saddler, the Tony winner for his choreography for *No, No, Nanette.*

Miss Karnilova, who was in the musical *Stars in Your Eyes,* leaned across the table and asked, "Alicia, why haven't you written to me?" To which Alonso replied in a whisper: "I'm a Communist." The Karnilova retort was, "What the hell is that to me!" And Miss Alonso, who is now almost totally blind and can see only the brightest of lights, replied, "Marusia, I'm supposed to be dangerous."

We did not talk politics. It was a warm and loving and teary "Do you remember . . .?" conversation. It ranged from memories of when Karnilova did a baby-sitting job for Alicia (a mother at sixteen) and when the two got two bucks a show for jobs as supers and when a Cuban so trained in American dance had to teach Karnilova the time-step so she could land a job in a Broadway musical to wild recollections of rehearsals with the greats—Fokine, Mordkin, Balanchine, Tudor, de Mille, Robbins. Alonso, with her enormous black eyes, would look into space until she heard a voice and then turn to it. Blind and with a fractured bone in her foot, she danced divinely here in Montreal. Not only is she a great artist; she is a great woman, brave and self-disciplined to the degree that made Saddler say, "She makes us, with our petty gripes, ashamed of ourselves."

To dance when blind seems like an impossible feat. Miss Alonso will not permit it to be so. Her eyes are operable and partial vision could be restored, but it would require one year of rest. At fifty-two, Alicia Alonso cannot indulge in a year of inactivity, for she could never reschool every muscle in her body to dance again. She herself made the decision: "I must dance as long as I can—it is my life."

On stage, she has a double spotlight at the center of the footlights and two other spots, stage left and right. She sees, dimly, only brightness. On every stage new to her, she paces out each ballet. When she must make a stage exit alone, she is "talked off" by someone in the wings.

But only a few know that Alicia Alonso is blind. The vast public sees only a great artist, a remarkable virtuosa who can do multiple pirouettes or fouettés. The leg swings ear-high, the balances are what suspension is all about, in the port-de-bras you see the loveliest of arms etched in space. There are no apologies for blindness, and none are expected. Alicia Alonso is that rarest of dancing creatures, a prima ballerina assoluta.

In Montreal she danced roles that ranged from the classics to today's ballets. I saw her as Odette in Act II of *Swan Lake*—here indeed was a singing body—and in her brother-in-law's *Carmen,* created especially by Alberto

591

Alonso for the Bolshoi Ballet's Maya Plisetskaya. Alonso danced it with Azari Plisetski, Maya's brother (now a Cuban resident), and brought to it a fire that only a Latin could. Plisetskaya was a delicious hoyden; Alonso, a wanton, whose death scene tore the viewer to pieces. (Ironically, Plisetskaya can come to America, but Plisetski, from Cuba, cannot.)

For Alicia Alonso there were shouting ovations in Montreal, not only by the old-time admirers but by a new generation who had known of her only as a great legend. She transcends the pettiness of politics—she has time for nothing but the perfecting of her art—but we are supposed to think of her as dangerous! At least we are permitted to remember that as an American ballerina she brought us international luster for more than three decades. Brava, Alicia! Blind but with a vision of enduring dance beauty. [*Saturday Review*]

Ballet Theatre Finds a Home

September 25, 1971

Washington, D.C. "Advanced Arts Ballets, Inc., presents The Ballet Theatre, America's First Ballet Theatre, staged by the greatest collaboration in ballet history." The year was 1940; the place, the Center Theater (now demolished) in Rockefeller Center. The announcement was both youthfully arrogant, but not wholly inaccurate, and hopeful, and the debut (Jan. 11) was a smash. The opening program was composed of Michel Fokine's *Les Sylphides*; Mikhail Mordkin's *Voices of Spring* (Johann Strauss); and *The Great American Goof,* a theater-ballet with theme and dialogue by William Saroyan, music by Henry Brant, scenery and costumes by Boris Aronson, and choreography by a young American choreographer, Eugene Loring, who had already made his mark with *Billy the Kid,* created two years earlier for Lincoln Kirstein's Ballet Caravan.

This "greatest collaboration" included among its choreographers not only Fokine, the master (in person); Mordkin, who had been Pavlova's partner at her historic New York debut in 1910; Adolph Bolm; and Bronislava Nijinska, all products of the Russian Imperial Ballet (St. Petersburg and Moscow); but also Antony Tudor, who had stirred his native England with a new vision of ballet; Anton Dolin, a disciple of Diaghilev and a master of the old ballet classics; young Agnes de Mille, who had yet to create *Rodeo* and turn Broadway on its ear with *Oklahoma!*; Loring; plus a Spaniard, a Pole.

But even with these artists and a later roster of choreographers and dancers destined to influence profoundly the entire world of ballet and of theater, this company was doomed to be itinerant. It never found a home.

Thirty-one years later, it has found a very special base: the Kennedy Center for the Performing Arts here in the nation's capital. Lucia Chase, the company's co-director (with Oliver Smith), its indomitable commander, in blazing spirit, and, when needed, its benefactress (financially to the tune of several millions), has this to say about the event: "What it means to me most is that we have achieved national recognition at last. We've represented the United States unofficially and officially abroad as an American ballet company. Way back in 1946, we were the first major company after the war to take American ballet abroad, by playing eight-and-a-half weeks in London.

"In subsequent years, we represented the United States officially in many State Department-sponsored tours—we even changed our name, on request, from Ballet Theatre to the American Ballet Theatre. We were the first American ballet company to perform in the Soviet Union. We have danced in most of the Iron Curtain countries as well as in the democracies of our allies. We have been official abroad but not at home. Now, I am proud of our new title—'Official Company' of the John F. Kennedy Center for the Performing Arts. In our capital. It is recognition at last."

Miss Chase points out that the American Ballet Theatre will not be able to "hang" its costumes or run its essential ballet school at Kennedy Center, as the New York City Ballet does at the New York State Theater, but that "it's home when we're there; we're doing three two-week seasons for Seventy-one to Seventy-two and, most important, the Center absolutely has first call on us. This is a marvelous moment—recognition at home!"

Washington is not much of a "show town"; its affluent inhabitants are as "transient" as the American Ballet Theatre is "itinerant." Long before the city itself was built, our first President not only presided over social dance festivities but also supported ballet activities in New York, such as those featuring John Durang, the first American dancer of note. In 1834, President Andrew Jackson admired the art of the ballerina so much that he presented a Mlle. Celeste to members of the Congress—small wonder that political cartoonists referred to his "Celestial" cabinet! Six years later, President Martin Van Buren and his cabinet received the "divine" Austrian Fanny Elssler and the Congress adjourned to attend her performances. No, Washington has not been remiss about ballet or ballerinas, but it has not supported them until modern times.

The National Ballet, a professional company of high stature, directed by one of the ballet greats of this century, Frederic Franklin, makes its headquarters in Washington. Its loyal supporters were understandably miffed when it was not made the "official company" at Kennedy, although it will perform there. Mary Day's Washington Ballet, one of the best of the country's regional (non-professional) ballets, lives there. Even the American Ballet Theatre, in 1962–63, attempted residence in the capital under the auspices of the Washington Ballet Guild, but the project did not survive.

The American Ballet Theatre's battle for survival—and it has been just that, with temporary disbandings since its inception—has been fostered by grants from the federal government, as well as sponsored foreign tours, and by its own Ballet Theatre Foundation, of which Sherwin Goldman is president. At last, it has received the recognition as America's national ballet that it has sought ever since the late Richard Pleasant, its first director, conceived ballet as theater and American ballet as dedicated to international duties.

Why should the American Ballet Theatre be selected as the official company of the Kennedy Center and thereby gain national recognition in our capital? Why not the New York City Ballet, headed by that towering genius, George Balanchine? Why not the National Ballet? Or the City Center Joffrey Ballet? Or other companies? The NYC Ballet, for example, is the product of one man, Balanchine, who brilliantly dominates a repertory elevated by a handful of masterworks by Jerome Robbins and downgraded by ballets of very minor choreographers.

ABT is truly an international company with a repertory that ranges from the oldest ballet extant, *La Fille Mal Gardée*, to a contemporary ballet by Alvin Ailey and Duke Ellington, both black artists—but this is nothing new, for in 1940 it listed "A Negro Unit of 14" (and there was a Spanish unit too). It is, in fact, a treasure house of ballet, cherishing the past, fostering the present, anticipating the future.

For the official debut at Kennedy Center (September 11)—there was a subsequent performance September 15, and the full two-week repertory season runs September 21 to October 3—Miss Chase chose a program obviously planned to show off as many of her principal dancers as possible in ballets ranging from the purity and virtuosity of *ballet d'école* (with an interlude in the style of Romantic Age dancing) through danced drama to today's jazz interwoven with ballet disciplines.

Of the fourteen stars, only four were missing from the gala: Carla Fracci, Erik Bruhn, Bruce Marks, and Michael Smuin, all of whom will be on hand for the upcoming repertory season. Almost all of the seventeen soloists were present, along with the corps de ballet (numbering just under forty). Miss Chase herself, a superlative actress–dancer, will be on stage with Bruce Marks in the ABT's spectacular production of *Swan Lake* during the repertory weeks.

The attentive, applauding, and frequently cheering opening night audience saw Antony Tudor's one-act *Romeo and Juliet* (first produced by ABT in 1943) set to music of Delius and with scenery and costumes by Eugene Berman: the Ailey–Ellington *The River* (abridged); and *Etudes* by the Danish choreographer, Harald Lander, to music of the Danish Knudaage Riisager (on Czerny themes) and with scenery and costumes by Rolf Gerard.

The *Romeo*, a tragedy in theme and a somewhat static, though beautiful, ballet, seemed an odd selection for the opener. But Natalia Makarova, the great Kirov ballerina who defected and chose ABT for her artistic home, was a radiant Juliet, and our own John Prinz, coached by the first and greatest Tudor Romeo, Hugh Laing, was excellent.

Lupe Serrano, ABT's senior ballerina, was, by all odds, the star of the evening. She simply tore the place apart with her dazzling "exertions" (as they used to say about ballerina virtuosities in the 1800s) in *Etudes,* which starred yet another defector to the West, Hungary's brilliant *danseur noble,* Ivan Nagy, plus the dashing Ted Kivitt.

The River, of course, was extra, super special. It is a beautiful ballet, really beautiful, flooded with the glow of humanity, the beacon of brotherhood, carefree frolic, both reverence and irreverence, and mass moments of great architectural splendor. The audience stood and cheered it and its dancers: the black Keith Lee and Sallie Wilson, Cynthia Gregory (a true ballerina), Eleanor D'Antuono, the effervescent Dennis Nahat, Mimi Paul, Prinz, Zhandra Rodriguez, and a team of spectacular men dancers. Then the audience turned, looked to a center box, and gave a standing ovation, with cheers and tears, to Alvin Ailey, who leaned across to the next box and gave Lucia Chase a bearhug and a kiss as she presided over a new home.

There were, of course, opening night mishaps. Bad weather kept the attendance down, if not the enthusiasm; lighting cues went awry on occasion, and at one point, the weights in the hem of a curtain burst and flooded the stage with BB-shot.

And so the company that presided over the major choreographic launchings of many dance creators; that celebrated the glamorous teams of Markova and Dolin or Alonso and Youskevitch or Nora Kaye and Hugh Laing; that fostered Americana in ballet, the old and the new, modern dance and the great classics, the comfortably traditional and the disturbing avant-garde, has received the national recognition it has long sought—and richly deserves.
[*Saturday Review*]

Energetic Angels

December 11, 1971

Should dancers be pretty creatures? They *had* to be during those days at the turn of the century when dance itself had sunk to a level—in theme and in step—of mere prettiness. But as choreographic scope and thematic profundity were restored to the dance, as nixies, pixies, elves, and various assortments of *papillons* were replaced by people, prettiness became unimportant. Martha Graham was never pretty—she had (and has) great beauty—and the late Doris Humphrey, a smashing redhead, made herself repellent as the destructive Matriarch in her *With My Red Fires.* Yet dancers, no matter what roles they are playing, must remain physically attractive, for they are, to use a Graham dance title, *Acrobats of God.*

Not too many years ago, a group of dancers (who shall remain nameless) appeared in a big festival series. Most of the group's members were singularly homely, and a critic-colleague of mine felt justified in saying so. I concurred, for, at that instant, it became apparent that dance, the art of the body in rhythmic movement, had to have protagonists who were not only dedicated, technically adept, powerful in purpose, but also attractive. After all, we (audience and critics alike) had to look at them.

Today, our dance is richer and more varied than ever before. But, unfortunately, some of its representatives, especially in the modern dance area, don't seem to give a damn what they look like. *I* think they should possess attractive (not necessarily pretty) faces, slim waists, good legs, even callipygian attributes. The body is the instrument of the dancer, and it had better look good!

So it is that among our dancers you will come upon those who seem to make a cult of unattractiveness. Not so Lar Lubovitch and his company. They are attractive dancers. In their recent engagement at Stage City, I was again happily aware of this. They are young, the hair is long (or Afro where pertinent), they are experimenting. Sometimes one cannot be sure what they are dancing about, but their contours fall pleasurably upon the eye.

Lubovitch, who dances superbly, choreographs, directs, designs lighting, etc., also planned Stage City, a movie studio. The lighting is fine, of course, but what would be bleachers anywhere else are covered with foam rubber, and everyone reclines comfortably as he watches exuberant, and attractive, dancers. Irreverently, I thought of words from Beatrice Lillie's great song *Paree,* in which she referred to *les gamins, les gendarmes, les misérables . . . tout le monde les, les, les.* But on to the Lubovitch program.

He has now worked wonders with a once-sprawling dance that labors under the idiot title of *Some of the Reactions of Some of the People Some of the Time upon Hearing Reports of the Coming of the Messiah.* It is set to music of Handel, and it is, in a very real sense, a dance of jubilation, the sort of danced rite that the Prophets of old might well have used to rouse the populace to ecstasy, to involve them in a testament to faith.

Messiah still has some weaknesses—Lubovitch tends to choreograph in explosive bursts of action rather than to develop his movement statements to their fullest—but it is a paean of hope and joy danced by a most attractive group of men and women, by a delightful assembly of energetic angels.

Whirligogs (music of Luciano Berio from *Sinfonia*) forsakes the angels in the hearts of men for the demons resting there. The black-clad figures, much of the time wearing black executioner hoods, are two-faced creatures, but despite their seeming antics they are destroyers, and their final mass attack on a victim at the close of the work is what the word "predatory" is all about. The piece itself is one of Lubovitch's most popular creations; on this occasion, in the arena-like atmosphere of Stage City, it was especially effective.

The two premieres were *Social* (music from a Bach cantata) and *Clear Lake* (Mendelssohn). Neither is yet in its final form, but both have much more to offer than promise. In the former, the girls wear sleazy evening gowns and the boys ill-fitting pants as if the time were the 1930s, and all were en route to, say, Glen Island Casino to dance and listen to a name band. There is fun here, as well as comment on a period, but the humor has yet to gel.

As for *Clear Lake*, it has some absolutely beautiful moments danced by beautiful people. But they are moments. Lubovitch starts a duet and never quite resolves it; a group thrusts into space, but the journey is terminated before it really gets deep into adventure. Lubovitch, who is certainly one of the most impressive young artists of today's dance, is a restless choreographer. He is marvelously expansive of movement, but there is not always a sustained sweep to his choreographic phrasings.

Extreme members of the avant-garde in dance may find him square—he is not, of course—but when pitted against a fairly sizable array of those who represent non-dance, non-theater, non-form, non-discipline, and, heaven knows, nonattractiveness, he and his dancers come out way ahead. You probably won't like everything he choreographs—he has much to learn—but you will, I promise you, like his handsome dancers who move like dancers in celebration of both the lofty eloquence of kinetics and the lowly, but lovely, physicality of the human body. [*Saturday Review*]

597

1972

Buried (?) Treasure

Dance laughter in Robbins' The Concert at NYCB • Financial crisis may make New York Public Library's Dance Collection a buried treasure • Murray Louis teaches children in government sponsored IMPACT program in Troy, Alabama • NYCB's Stravinsky Festival • Cynthia Gregory, ballet's newest star

Dance Laughter

January 1, 1972

It is not easy to make a kinetic joke, a muscle gag. True, not all ballets are romantic, dramatic, lyric, tragic, or cryptic (avant-garde)—some are comic and satiric—but it is much easier to stir hearts or to mystify minds than it is to make people laugh. True, the two oldest ballets extant, *La Fille Mal Gardée* and the Danish *The Whims of Cupid and of the Ballet Master* (both from 1768), are comedies, but standard ballet repertory has few comedy masterpieces, perhaps one or two here and there by Tudor, Ashton, de Mille, and—Jerome Robbins.

Robbins's *The Concert* is a masterpiece of ballet comedy. It has been revived by the New York City Ballet, and you will be able to see it—you must!—when the Christmastime *Nutcracker* engagement is over and the company returns to repertory at the New York State Theater for its fifty-fifth New York engagement. *The Concert,* which Robbins subtitles "The Perils of Everybody" and describes as "A Charade in One Act," was originally created for the City Ballet just fifteen years ago and was subsequently revised (1958) and restaged for Robbins's own company, Ballets: U.S.A. At the premiere, Tanaquil LeClerq was the ballerina in the big floppy hat, and for the Ballets: U.S.A. performances in New York, after European presentations, Maria Karnilova was the star. The current revival of *The Concert* is somewhat of a

599

bravura tribute to Robbins's genius, for the City Ballet also performs his *Dances at a Gathering* and *In the Night,* beautiful and tender ballets to the music of Chopin. *The Concert,* also to Chopin, is a roaring hoot.

The idea behind the comic Chopin is that each person reacts differently while listening to music. Overtly, there are those who bend forward, close their eyes, and pinch the bridges of their noses; the ones who tap feet or fingers; the sighers and the frowners and variations thereof. Robbins has gone deeper than surfaces. What do these listeners experience inside? Do they want to dance, commit murder, pretend they are butterflies (in the *Butterfly* Etude), seek umbrellas (in the *Raindrop* Prelude), listen grimly, or swoop, sway, and swoon as the mind wanders? You'll find all these reactions in *The Concert.*

You will meet the swoopy girl who is all over the place; the grim wife who drags her husband to a concert and almost (in his mind) is stabbed by him only to have him make an error and stab himself; a swarm of angry butterflies; and all sorts of other goodies, including what Robbins himself refers to as the "mistake" ballet, a hilarious number for a group of girls in which one or more break the pattern, head in the wrong direction, louse up the port de bras, get caught in near hammer locks, and generally devastate some anonymous choreographer's intentions. We've all nervously watched "mistake" ballets in hometown dance recitals, but the Robbins work takes the nervousness out of such a situation and replaces it with humor.

At the first performance of the revival (using the Saul Steinberg décor created for Ballets: U.S.A.), Sara Leland was delightful as the swoopy lady, and Bettijane Sills and Francisco Moncion were good as the battling married couple. Jerry Zimmerman, on stage, was the imperturbable pianist. [*Saturday Review*]

Buried (?) Treasure

January 22, 1972

The Dance Collection of the New York Public Library—it now ranks as a "Division" along with the music and theater collections—is the greatest dance archives in the world. It is not old, not like the Bibliothèque in Paris, and it started very modestly in 1944 as a few folders of material in the Music Division. In 1948, Genevieve Oswald became the dance curator. In a tiny corner of the library she could—and did— literally sit on the entire dance collection. Today she presides over 28,000 books, 8,000 librettos, 80,000 manuscripts,

600

200,000 photographs, 450 original drawings and stage designs, 5,500 lithographs and engravings, 4,500 playbills and posters, 70,000 programs, more than one million feet of movie film, 450 oral history tapes, 2,000 scrapbooks, and 200,000 clippings.

The Dance Collection is housed in the Library and Museum of the Performing Arts at Lincoln Center. But unless money is raised, it will only be housed there. No visitors will be allowed. Funds have been running out for all of these research libraries. Private monies are needed, since neither the city nor the state fully supports these fabulous services. Visitors from other lands simply do not understand such governmental negligence. A writer from abroad, awed by the incredible riches of the Dance Collection, could not believe that it might have to shut down. "Surely your government would not permit that to happen. Ah, but then you don't have a king who cares, do you?"

"Who uses the Dance Collection?" you may well ask. Authors of books. I found clues to the very first dancing sur les pointes there, not in London or Paris or Copenhagen. Natalia Makarova, newly come to us from the Soviet Union, studied films of ballets unknown in Russia in order to prepare herself for a new way of dancing. Many members of Britain's Royal Ballet find in the New World treasures of ballet history that they cannot find in the Old World. There are worshipers of Fonteyn or Nureyev who come to sigh over their pictures. And there are sad, shy, even shabby beings who ask to see the great Nijinsky collection just to partake of beauty and, in passing, to find therapy.

To save this incredible Dance Collection, which contains material ranging from Ben Jonson's own copy of the very first (1581) of all ballets, *Le Ballet Comique de la Reine* (*Royne* in Old French), through the captivating lithographs of the Romantic Age of Ballet, to the weirdest of avant-garde dance records, a Gala of Galas is being held January 24 at the City Center 55th Street Theater to raise money to keep the collection available to the public. Tickets are going for $100 (and less), and stars of ballet (imported and native), of modern dance, of the avant-garde, of music and lighting and design are lending their talents to the cause. I shall not mention the names at this time, but the desire to contribute to the survival of the Dance Collection is everywhere, even among anonymous dance students in schools scattered across the United States.

How wonderful it is to visit the collection. You will see an exhibition in photos, costumes, and jewelry of Ted Shawn's fabulous sixty-year career as he looked back over eighty birthdays; lovely lithographs of Taglioni, Grisi, Grahn, Cerrito, Ellsler from the Romantic Age of the 1830s and '40s; movies of Argentinita and Pavlova and Ruth St. Denis, all dead; microfilms of data from around the world; great private collections provided by St. Denis and Shawn (600,000 items), by Walter Toscanini, by Hanya Holm and Humphrey–Weidman and La Meri, and by today's young dance creators.

Not every year can there be a gala to save the Dance Collection or other galas to keep the other great collections open. The Library and Museum of the Performing Arts at Lincoln Center is not just a musty, dusty repository of old things. It is life through the arts. It would take only a pittance of what governments spend on transitory surveys to ensure the future of these collections, which serve not just New York but the world. Perhaps we could borrow a king who cares. [*Saturday Review*]

The Impact of IMPACT

February 5, 1972

Troy, Ala. Daphne (let this serve as her name) is a little white girl who attends school in rural Alabama. When a court order required that her school in Union Springs be integrated, 250 of her schoolmates were sent by their parents to white private schools. Daphne's family was on welfare and couldn't afford private school tuition. She was offered a scholarship to a white private school, but Daphne herself turned it down because there were "better classes" in the integrated public school.

The "better classes" that Daphne wanted included the very special arts experiments provided by IMPACT, a powerful and pertinent abbreviation of the unwieldy Interdisciplinary Model Programs in the Arts for Children and Teachers, a project funded at $1-million by the Education Professions Development Act and developed jointly by—and take a deep breath!—the Arts and Humanities Program, the Bureau of Educational Personnel Development of the Office of Education, the National Art Education Association, the American Educational Theatre Association, the Music Educators National Conference, and the Dance Division of the American Association for Health, Physical Education, and Recreation. In spite of these cumbersome credits IMPACT is a direct hit.

Agencies representing national, state, and local experts in arts education cooperated in a project involving schools in Oregon, Ohio, Pennsylvania, California, and Alabama. Because of the added complication of integration in the Deep South, and in rural communities at that, Alabama interested me most. And from what I saw in Union Springs, Goshen, and elsewhere, it seemed that integration was working better here in the rural, presumably redneck counties of the South than in the presumably enlightened North.

Sara Ogletree, the bright, efficient, and highly personable principal of the Union Springs Elementary School, is quite frank about the situation. "We integrated because of a court order. Now it is up to me to make it work." With a fine staff of white and black teachers, and with guest arts instructors provided by IMPACT, such as Murray Louis in dance, Miss Ogletree has made it work. Her young charges are 500 pupils, kindergarten through third grade, drawn from the 3,000 inhabitants of Union Springs. "Thirty per cent are farm children, thirty per cent are from factory families, thirty per cent are welfare. The other ten per cent? I don't know where they come from," says Miss Ogletree. "They just come and go. They all come from families whose average income is less than one thousand dollars a year."

Miss Ogletree was enthusiastic about the success of the arts program in her newly integrated school. "The children are cleaner, neater, and more carefully dressed than ever before. A small thing, perhaps, but the parents must feel some pride in what we are doing. The most important thing of all is that each pupil's I.Q. has gone up. The dance challenges have done a lot."

Mr. Louis—the Murray Louis Dance Company and the Nikolais Dance Theater have recently concluded a joint engagement at the Brooklyn Academy of Music—sits by his drums in the cheery classroom in Union Springs. He rolls out a rhythm and props up his battered feet (most modern dancers practice and perform with bare feet and subject them to all manner of punishment). The kids are spaced out in a double classroom; they sit on the floor and stretch their lithe little bodies. They breathe in rhythm, they reach upwards and outwards, they giggle, but they are serious about what they are doing.

Now they have stand-up exercises. One little black girl stands on her head and grins upside down. Daphne tries but falls down; a black boy helps her find her balance. Now Murray moves away from exercises and gets closer to dance. There are walking, running, leaping, and turning patterns. Arm rhythms are added. "Make shapes with your bodies," says Murray. The little ones start their adventures into space: slow, fast, faster. Sometimes they copy one another, but mostly each releases the individual dance that lies within him or her.

Murray starts them counting rhythms or numbers of steps—all the arts classes are carefully related to academic studies—and then he has them make shapes, not alone but with each other, in touchings, in partnerings. White and black fingers interlock trustingly as joint shapes are evolved. A blonde Anglo-Saxon hugs a descendant of Africans as Murray praises their wildly imaginative patterns in space. There is no embarrassment at all. They are all children. There seems to be no sense of race.

Probably the last thing in the world that Union Springs wanted was integration, but when the law said they must, they did, and it has worked superbly. IMPACT, along with eager local teachers, has seen to that.

Now we rush to Goshen with no time for lunch. Murray Louis's dancers, who serve as his assistants in all the assigned schools in the Troy area, gobble some canned peaches, with lots of syrup, for quick energy. This time, the kids at Goshen Elementary, kindergarten through fourth grade, sit in the bleachers in the big gym and watch as the Louis dancers present an improvised lecture-demonstration. The first dances illustrate movements of the eyes, the mouth, the head, the legs, the toes. Murray asks the youngsters to call out what parts of the body are being used at a given moment. It's a lesson in anatomy, and they never muff a question. A bell rings and students from a nearby high school come to watch. Next, Murray has one of his dancers put all the movements—eyes, toes, legs, torso, etc.—together and the youngsters shout, "Dancing for the whole body!" If Murray makes a dance for six legs, how many of his dancers are out there? "Three!" shout the kids. How about four arms? "Two people!" Three of the dancers run to the bleachers and scoop up three black kids. Now there is a dance for what? "Twelve legs!"

Murray turns to the bleachers. "Write your names in space!" They do, and there is a great gestural dance sweeping over heads as they eagerly trace their invisible names in myriad patterns. As the hour draws to a close, six Louis dancers perform an excerpt from their avant-garde repertory. The kids don't know whether it is avant-garde or classical or what. They know it is dancing. A group of them are invited out onto the floor with the professional dancers. To the beat of Murray's drum, they choreograph not only for themselves but for the grownups, too. They imitate some of the things they've seen, but before long they make their own shapes—black shapes, white shapes, combined shapes.

The shape of things in Alabama itself is changing too, and IMPACT has helped immeasurably. A mighty chrome eagle, the school mascot, is proudly displayed on the lawn at Goshen. It was made from more than 1,000 pounds of auto bumpers bought from a junkyard. At Union Springs Elementary, there is a sculpture garden with a fountain designed by a professional sculptor, Larry Godwin, who was born in Enterprise, Alabama. But even the kids participated; each of the 500 students brought a single brick from home and laid it in the courtyard for walks, flower beds, patio designs.

For their classrooms, they have even written their own textbooks—books about their homes, their lives, their adventures, their hopes. And in their bodies breathes the ancient art of dancing. Virginia Tanner, one of the world's truly great dance leaders for children—she is almost a minister-evangelist—came from far-off Salt Lake City last year to guide the youngsters of Union Springs and, subsequently, to train their teachers in her methods of dance instruction. And this year it has been Murray Louis who has guided them in dances of fun, of discipline, of dignity, and, unquestionably, of brotherhood. IMPACT.
[*Saturday Review*]

604

Balanchine's Ballet Tribute
to Stravinsky

July 15, 1972

Onstage, in front of the great gold curtain of the New York State Theater at Lincoln Center, a slight, dapper gentleman spoke with wit and eloquence of a composer, a long-time colleague, a friend. The audience applauded warmly. At the close of the evening—June 18, 1972—the same gentleman received a tumultuous ovation. He was George Balanchine, one of the great choreographers of all time and a major architect of ballet in America.

What Balanchine has launched—with the essential aid of his own New York City Ballet, Lincoln Kirstein (the company's general director and the man who brought Balanchine to America forty years ago), Robert Irving (his superb musical director), and countless aides—was a one-week Stravinsky Festival of music (not danced) and dance, including thirty ballets, twenty of them premieres, many by Balanchine but some by others (including the great Jerome Robbins).

Backstage, on a more intimate note, the celebration, honoring the late composer's ninetieth birthday and a half-century of collaboration with Balanchine, continued. There were accolades from old friends and from critics Balanchine has known. A majority of his former wives were present, and there were affectionate expressions by beautiful girls and handsome women (a personal delight he has never concealed). The youngest of his girls had appeared onstage, but two early embraces in the wings were reserved for the beautiful Diana Adams, one of his retired ballerinas, and the dazzling Miriam Golden, an American Ballet Theatre principal in 1940.

But such warm and lovely moments were not viewed by most of the public. What happened onstage was. And Balanchine, who had seemed to be tiring and fading in certain of his ballets in recent years, was reborn in his own choreographic processes. Once again the music of Igor Stravinsky inspired him, as it had done in the 1920s. Music-movement magic surged once more.

This feast of Stravinsky and the ballet opened with an unprogramed, surprise canapé, a two-minute courtly duet with gentle pastoral airs set to an excerpt from a sonata that Stravinsky had written seventy years before, two years before Balanchine was born, although the choreographer grins and suggests it was composed in anticipation of a collaboration that would come many years later. The score had been either lost in, or was withheld by, the Soviet Union, but Mrs. André Malraux had once seen a facsimile of it, remembered the middle movement, and agreed to play it. It was charming. Charming also were the dancers, Sara Leland and John Clifford.

More substantial, in terms of full-scale ballet, were two other Balanchine–

Stravinsky premieres, *Violin Concerto* and *Symphony in Three Movements.*
Of the two, I much preferred the former. Balanchine used the same music
many years ago in a dramatic ballet he created for one of his most celebrated
student discoveries, Tamara Toumanova. It was called *Balustrade,* but its life
was short. The choreographic wedding with the *Violin Concerto* is wholly
new and lies in that genre of music visualization, or extension of sound
rhythms and timbres into body rhythms and textures. It is Balanchine at his
peak, a masterpiece worthy of joining the elite, which includes his *Concerto
Barocco* (Bach), *Serenade* (Tchaikovsky), *Symphony in C* (Bizet), and *Agon*
(Stravinsky).

Karin von Aroldingen, Kay Mazzo, Jean-Pierre Bonnefous, and Peter Martins were excellent as the soloists leading a somewhat nervous ensemble. *Symphony in Three Movements* also suffered from edgy dancers, but even Balanchine seemed a trifle nervous here. There were handsome mass patterns, but
many of the individual movement details seemed contrived rather than devised.
Indeed, there were echoes of older Balanchine works cast in somewhat experimental molds and, oddly enough, passages that reminded one of Maurice
Béjart. Miss Leland, Marnee Morris, Lynda Yourth, Helgi Tomasson, Edward
Villella, and Robert Weiss danced it beautifully (along with the insecure—rehearsals will fix that—corps de ballet).

Robbins, too, was represented by a new piece, *Scherzo Fantastique,* a
wonderfully "dancey" work that delighted the eye and lifted the heart. In
this unaffected but richly inventive pas de cinq, Gelsey Kirkland and Bart Cook
were the dancing leaders of first rank. Balanchine's fairly new version (with
an assist from Robbins) of *Firebird* closed the program. It's lavish, but it's a
bore. The earlier Balanchine *Firebird,* created for Maria Tallchief, was, to my
mind, the best of many choreographic conceptions.

Participating musicians included not only Mme. Malraux, Mr. Irving,
Joseph Silverstein (solo violinist), and Robert Craft (guest conductor), but the
New York City Ballet orchestra, the finest dance orchestra in the world. But
isn't that Stravinsky's due on a festival honoring his birthday, his memory, his
immortality? [*Saturday Review*]

Stravinsky Ballets Revisited

August 19, 1972

The New York City Ballet's Stravinsky Festival, which had New Yorkers doing
cartwheels and paying scalper prices for seven days (June 18–June 25) at the

State Theater, made the front pages as much on bravado as on artistry. At the time perspective was hardly possible, for more than thirty Stravinsky-rooted works were produced, there were twenty-plus premieres, and the ninetieth birthday tribute to the composer, who died last year at eighty-nine, spanned a prolific fifty-year music-dance association with George Balanchine, the City Ballet's artistic director.

It is now possible to separate a tour de force from actual accomplishment. Even Balanchine, whose idea it was to stage this massive ballet tribute to Stravinsky, was quick to admit that not everything that he, Jerome Robbins, Todd Bolender, John Taras, and several junior choreographers created especially for the occasion is first class. Indeed, Mr. B. gave advice to a close friend from Europe who had missed the New York City bash and who was planning to catch up with most of it at the Saratoga Festival, where the company played in July: "See Jerry's ballets," he said, "and see my *Violin Concerto*. It is very good! My other ballets?" He shrugged. "Okay, but not so good."

It was pretty good advice. In July I, too, visited Saratoga Springs, where the City Ballet is annually the resident dance company in that glorious open-air theater. In addition to standard repertory (twenty performances), there were six all-Stravinsky evenings. Nothing, perhaps, was equal to *Violin Concerto,* which I had seen at the mind-boggling opening of the festival in New York, but there were some marvelous moments—and also some very bad ones.

At Saratoga I caught up with Robbins's *Dumbarton Oaks,* a joyous, jazzy ballet filled with delicious Jerryisms—line dancing, high kicks, a tennis match (ending in love), gestural jokes. It is of the genre of Vaslav Nijinsky's *Jeux* and Bronislava Nijinska's *Les Biches* and, for me at least, it is far better than both, including later versions of *Jeux* by William Dollar and Taras. *Dumbarton Oaks* should certainly become a permanent addition to the NYCB repertory, along with Robbins's *Scherzo Fantastique,* already reviewed in this column.

Except for Robbins, Balanchine tends to surround himself with very minor choreographers, some of them comparatively young and others mature but of often debatable stature. The kindest act for several items produced by such figures would be to bury them quietly. At Saratoga there must be room for grave sites for John Clifford's *Symphony in E-Flat* (it has some nice steps but no shape), Bolender's *Serenade in A* (just dull), and some other Stravinsky tributes that fizzled.

Balanchine's *Duo Concertant* may not be a major work, but it is, unmistakably, the product of a master craftsman; it might not illumine your spirit as does *Violin Concerto,* but it will please the eye with the loveliness of its pas de deux movement fragments. Together, Balanchine and Robbins

607

manufactured (yes, I mean that word) *Pulcinella.* As an echo of *commedia dell'arte* it is nowhere near as appealing as Balanchine's own *Harlequinade,* but Eugene Berman's scenery and costumes are sheer magic, and the antics of the dancers should amuse kids from four to ten. But, please, let's not have it on-stage after 5 p.m.

It should not be presumed that all the ballets at the Stravinsky Festival were premieres or the results of forced feeding. Many were proven Balan-chine–Stravinsky masterworks—*Apollo* (from the early days), *Orpheus,* and *Agon* among them—ballets that not only celebrate for all time the linked geniuses of Balanchine and Stravinsky but that have influenced theater dance around the world. These, of course, are ballets *composed* for dancing, but Stravinsky wrote music that *invited* extension into dance. Robbins's melo-dramatic *The Cage* is a perfect example: A *Concerto in D for Strings* triggered in a choreographer's mind a violent, primal, sexual explosion.

The Stravinsky Festival at the State Theater is long over, the Saratoga Festival has given alfresco celebration to the tribute, and this fall and winter the New York City Ballet itself, back in residence at the New York State Theater, will extend its Stravinsky paean into yet another season. One hopes there will be quiet discards, for certain of the presentations did no honor to either Stravinsky or the dance, but the ballet masterpieces that came out of the most publicized ballet churning in history will serve the New York City Ballet handsomely in the years to come. [*Saturday Review*]

Ballet's Newest Star

October 7, 1972

The fans ran down the aisles and crowded close to the orchestra pit. Armfuls of curtain-call bouquets were handed to the ballerina or thrown at her feet. Blossoms were tossed across the footlights, and outsized confetti fluttered down upon her as she stood in front of the great gold curtain for a solo bow.

She was not Dame Margot Fonteyn, the world's most popular (and high-est paid) ballerina, nor was she the Royal Ballet's adored Antoinette Sibley, nor Russia's blazing Maya Plisetskaya, nor the American Ballet Theatre's de-ceptively fragile, hauntingly lovely Carla Fracci. She was Cynthia Gregory of the American Ballet Theatre—modest, retiring, and happily married. Her re-sponse to a major critic's rave review of her first full-length *Swan Lake* had been: "Heavens! Why did he have to say all that! Now people will expect something of me."

Cynthia Gregory, who has been with the American Ballet Theatre for several seasons, has risen meteorically in the last year or so from corps de ballet to demisoloist to soloist to ballerina. From the start the young, versatile Californian attracted the attention and interest of balletomanes. No technical feat that a choreographer or a teacher could dream up seemed to daunt her. Some ballerinas are famous for their turns, others for their pointe, some for extraordinary leaps, and still others for high leg extensions and spinal flexibility. Through natural facility and constant hard work Cynthia excels in *all* these departments.

The Black Swan's thirty-two spinning fouettés, which turn many other dancers grim-faced, do not faze Cynthia Gregory. "When I begin," she says, "I don't think of the thirty-two ahead of me. I do eight as nicely and neatly as I can. Then I do another eight, and pretty soon they are all done." Could she execute sixty-four? "Oh, yes." How about doing them to the left instead of to the right? "I think I could, although I'd need to practice for a half hour or so."

Cynthia Gregory is equally at ease in soft, flowing adagio movements and brisk allegro actions. Classical ballets and modern works, storyless dances and dramatic ballets, are all in her repertory. Her musicality is as sensitive as was Maria Tallchief's.

But there are flaws of sorts in this seemingly perfect dance instrument. At five feet six inches, Cynthia is tall for a ballerina. "My feet are so long that when I'm on toe I'm close to six feet!" she complains. Understandably, Bruce Marks, a six-footer and a premier danseur skilled in both classical and modern ballets, is her frequent partner. What distresses Cynthia is that her husband, Terry Orr, a splendid dancer with a brilliant technique who was just promoted from soloist to the top rank of principal, is her own height offstage, but considerably shorter when his wife is wearing toe shoes.

Cynthia's height is, of course, merely a condition that must be faced. The fact that, despite all her dazzling technical proficiency, she appears to be a cold performer is more disturbing. After her initial successes as a virtuosa she said: "I know an artist is supposed to have suffered in order to communicate something special; but I've never suffered. I had a happy childhood, and I've always loved my mother and father. Terry was my first beau. We got married, we love each other, and we're happy. There are just no hangups! I know that's what is wrong with me as a performer, so I'm trying to find tragedy and conflict through the roles I dance."

Cynthia is obviously beginning to find her way, for the dance public not only respects her skills but has warmed to her personality. During ABT's summer season at Lincoln Center's New York State Theatre she danced an incredible number of diverse roles. Her dual portrayal of Odette–Odile in *Swan Lake* won her a prodigious ovation. Her first *Giselle* in New York evoked such a demonstration that one would have thought Fonteyn, Plisetskaya, Alonso, Bruhn, Nureyev, Villella, Dowell, and Sibley had just finished dancing together. It wasn't a perfect *Giselle,* but it was clearly a performance by a genuine ballerina on her way to becoming a prima ballerina and, eventually, an American *prima ballerina assoluta.*

Giselle did not seem an ideal role for a tall and sturdy girl. "Everyone thinks of her as tiny, dark-haired, fragile," says Cynthia, "and I'm not that way at all. But Giselle is innocent, and I am too—I really have led a totally sheltered life. So in Act I I played her like myself. When my mother saw me, she said, 'It's just like you,' and I guess it was."

Martha Graham has said of dancers: "Master a craft, then cultivate a being." Cynthia Gregory is doing just that before the appreciative eyes of her huge public. [*Saturday Review*]

1973

Martha, Millie, and Mainstreet

Martha Graham and Melissa Hayden reach transitional periods in their lives and careers • Regional ballet in the U.S.A.

Transitions: Martha Graham and Melissa Hayden

July 3, 1973

Great age, behold us. Coolness of evening on the heights, breath of the open sea on every threshold, and our foreheads bared for wider spaces. . . . Great age, you lied: a road of glowing embers, not of ash. . . . Great age, behold us. Take the measure of man's heart. . . . Divine turbulence, be ours to its last eddy. . . .

These are the words of the poet St. John Perse in his *Chronique,* and in a very real sense, they are also the words of Martha Graham, now in her eightieth year, for she gives them physical substance and stage imageries in her new *Mendicants of Evening.* Martha Graham, a dancer since 1916 and a dancing star for fifty years, now speaks through her choreography, no longer through her dancing body.

When time said no to her dancing muscles four years ago, she was angry, resentful, and somewhat lost. For a period Martha Graham did something that she had never done: She retreated. She seemed to lose interest in her company and in her school. She became ill. She was hospitalized and, it was reported, near death. And then, suddenly, she re-emerged: She took full command of both company and school and, miraculously, began to create. Miss Graham has always been deeply affected by the Easter message of rebirth, and she sees in Thanksgiving both the necessity and the warm joy of gratefulness. This spring, in her company's enormously successful season at the Alvin Theater in New York, she celebrated both simultaneously.

611

Mendicants of Evening is her new paean to this newly discovered union of spring and autumn. In a curious, even hypnotic, way it seems to be answering the themes posed by such earlier Graham masterpieces as *Errand Into the Maze*; *Night Journey*; *Part-Real, Part-Dream*; or *Cave of the Heart*, while at the same time continuing her own (as well as Emily Dickinson's) *Letter to the World*. Its poetry reflects upon old age; its electronic music (David Walker) sounds the present; its actor–dancers mirror the everlasting.

There were some who professed (or confessed) they did not understand *Mendicants*. But then, forty years ago, there were those who did not understand *Frontier* (where were the cowboys and Indians?) or *Primitive Mysteries* or *Lamentation* (for whom? for what?). As for the later *Dark Meadow*—it bewildered many. Yet these great works, and the new *Mendicants,* pose no problems at all if one does not expect Miss Graham to be literal. She hasn't been literal since 1921, when she danced in Ted Shawn's Aztec ballet, *Xochitl,* in which she played a maiden fighting to uphold her virtue against the advances of the emperor. In her realistic efforts, she pummeled Shawn until he bled and she, for her efforts, got dropped on her head.

Since the *Xochitl* days, which brought her national fame, she has been more concerned with what she calls the "interior landscape"; so if you are unwilling to journey with her into that hidden world of "divine turbulence," you will miss her clear purpose. The new work is visually beautiful: in the friezes of bodies that have taken on the pulse of life, in the four ravishingly beautiful and powerful duets, and particularly in The Witness of Marian Seldes (the Tony Award-winning actress for Edward Albee's *A Delicate Balance*), who speaks with the urgency of the actor and moves with the swift directness of the dancer.

And so it was in the spring of 1973 that Martha Graham was reborn, not simply for herself, but for us. She relinquished her former roles to younger dancers and coached them brilliantly in such towering theater pieces as her evening-long *Clytemnestra.* The opening night audience gave her a standing ovation, agreeing with Perse that "time measured by the year is no measure of our days."

Another great artist who is retiring as a dancer this year is Melissa Hayden, the undisputed (if not officially recognized) prima ballerina of the New York City Ballet. Miss Hayden, now fifty, has been performing with the NYCB for twenty-three years, except for a two-year break when she returned to the American Ballet Theatre, the company that introduced her to the U.S. public in 1945. Before that, the Canadian dancer was seen (if not known) by thousands who attended stage shows at Radio City Music Hall when she was a member of the resident Corps de Ballet.

Through the years she has made for herself an unrivaled reputation in a formidable list of widely varying ballets. She is a virtuoso performer—there isn't anything she can't do in the way of difficult ballet steps—and she is a superb actress, a dancer noted for her musicality, and such a mistress of movement that she can melt your heart with the lilting flow of the body in *Swan Lake* or scare you to death with her stabbing, poisonous, insect-like gestures in *The Cage.* To every role, traditional or contemporary, she brings something that is pure Hayden. When she dances George Balanchine's *Agon,* I see Stravinsky as well as hear him. Her Profane Love in Sir Frederick Ashton's *Illuminations* is a lustful girl, the perfect definition of *wanton;* her Titania in the ballet *A Midsummer Night's Dream* is a fairy who is as willful as she is lovely; and her *Nutcracker* Sugar Plum Fairy is not only a radiant creature but, in the mimed episode with the child hero and heroine, a softly radiant mother (which she is in real life).

Indeed, "Millie," as she is known to her friends (she was born Mildred Herman in Toronto), is a star and a great artist, an impeccable technician unique in her exploration and interpretation of a fantastic gallery of roles.

To pay tribute to her during her final season at the New York State Theater and before she embarks on a teaching career in the fall at Skidmore College, Balanchine created a ballet for her, *Cortège Hongrois,* to music of Glazounov and with scenery and costumes by Rouben Ter-Arutunian. This was a magnanimous gesture on the part of a man who is known not to like ballerinas very much (although he has created many) because of their idiosyncrasies.

Balanchine's tribute to Miss Hayden, though generous, was not worthy either of her or of him. *Cortège Hongrois* is little more than a mishmash of divertissements from the old Petipa ballet *Raymonda,* from his and Alexandra Danilova's restaging of it for the Ballet Russe de Monte Carlo, from his old *Pas de Dix* and *Grand Pas-Glazounov,* etc. In fact, Miss Hayden's major solo is basically the old Petipa one. But Miss Hayden dances it, and all of her measures in *Cortège,* brilliantly.

If you can see her in your mind's eye in every role and in every performance that you have ever attended, you will have for yourself a bountiful Hayden festival. There is only one Melissa Hayden, and the world of dance is much, much richer for her dedicated and ever-dazzling service to the art she loves. [*Saturday Review*]

Dance on Mainstreet

November 20, 1973

Today Atlanta's handsome and aristocratic Dorothy Alexander has snow-white hair, but her unquenchable energy has not diminished since 1929, when, as a raven-haired young dancer, she organized the Atlanta Civic Ballet, an innovation that was to change the dance landscape of America. This year Mrs. Alexander's fifty years of service in American dance was celebrated not only by Atlanta but by the dance voice of America as well. Nancy Hanks, chairman of the National Endowment for the Arts, a federal agency, journeyed to Georgia and presented the veteran dance leader with the following citation:

> For Dorothy Alexander, who epitomizes the artist as visionary.
> Just as great architects have foreseen cities which then came to be,
> she danced and made dances. She built a company, the Atlanta
> Ballet. She built a national dream, regional ballet. Behind it all
> was the faith that someday the people of Atlanta—and Americans
> everywhere—would cherish dance as a meaningful part of their
> lives. Because of her, that day beckons.

What, one may ask, is so important about regional ballet? In European nations that are comparatively small geographically, there are opera houses in almost every city; in some instances they are only a few miles apart. Yet each has its own company, including a resident ballet troupe. But the United States, for all its size and wealth, was, until Mrs. Alexander came along, virtually a desert for dance cultivation everywhere but New York City.

And in Manhattan at the turn of the century, almost the only ballet to be seen was the resident group at the Metropolitan Opera House. Even here, professional ballet was at an ebb, with male dancers replaced occasionally by buxom ladies doing men's roles *en travesti*. Anna Pavlova came to us in 1910 and for twenty years brought the marvels of ballet to American cities—but only for brief appearances. Ruth St. Denis, Ted Shawn, and their Denishawn Dancers did the same thing for the home-grown product. But as far as American communities were concerned, dancing was occasional and fleeting, an overnight visitor.

In time, after Mrs. Alexander's pioneering efforts, ballet gained a foothold in San Francisco (first with Adolph Bolm from Russia and later with the Christensen brothers); in Chicago (with Ruth Page); in Philadelphia, the city that produced the first American dancers of note in the late 1700s and early 1800s (with the aid of the daring Catherine Littlefield). But the focus was New York, and in the late 1930s Lincoln Kirstein, now general director of the world-renowned New York City Ballet, commented rather sadly that "if you have any dance talent, you don't stay in Lynchburg."

Today you can have dance talent and earn a living in approximately 120 different communities. Doris Hering, executive director of the National Association for Regional Ballet, Inc. (funded by the National Endowment for the Arts), has written: "For the most part, New York does not really foster talent. It consumes it." And those days are also going, thanks to regional ballet.

Regional ballet is still in its teens. It started when the late Anatole Chujoy, editor and publisher of *Dance News,* attended ballet festivals in Canada and wondered out loud, in print, and to Dorothy Alexander why the United States could not institute something similar but on a yearly, country-wide, regional basis. The first festival, organized by Mrs. Alexander and held in 1955, called on the talents of five civic ballet groups. It was an instant success, and the following year the Southeastern Regional Ballet Festival Association was formed. Today there are five regional ballet associations (Southeastern, Northeast, Pacific, Southwestern, Mid-States) comprising more than 120 companies.

The regional ballet movement is not a hit-or-miss affair. It has rules. It has standards. The participating companies are non-professional, but they are on the threshold of being professional. The civic ballets that were, and are, content themselves with annual recitals in a home community. They represent the accomplishments of a local school, and the annual recital is planned to display pupil progress to interested parents, relatives, and neighbors.

Regional ballets are also rooted in local schools—all professional ballet troupes are at their best when their dancers are trained in a related school or academy—but the horizons beckon far beyond the home town. For each regional ballet hopes for, and plans for, participation in its appropriate regional festival. Technical and performing standards must not only remain high but also reach higher. Competition and local pride are involved. No regional ballet lives in splendid isolation.

A regional troupe represents its community proudly, but its dance vision is now regional rather than local. It cannot represent the culture and accomplishment of its own city unless it journeys beyond that city and invites comparison with similar enterprises in other towns throughout the region. Because standards in teaching, training, producing, choreographing, staging, and performing are rising each year, some regional ballets find it possible to take that next step and, with financial help, turn professional. The Boston Ballet was once an amateur regional group, as was the Wilkes-Barre Ballet, but under the astute leadership and careful training of its directors, E. Virginia Williams and Barbara Weisberger, respectively, and with grants from the Ford Foundation, Boston's little company became professional and the Wilkes-Barre students turned themselves into the Pennsylvania Ballet.

What is the difference between a regional ballet and a professional company? It is, of course, primarily a matter of performing standards, of that clear but difficult-to-describe line that separates the amateur from the professional. Funding is all-important. Most dancers in regional ballet are part-time dancers—they have to earn their livelihood outside dance itself. But sufficient monies enable dance directors to guarantee their dancers year-round (or almost) salaries so that dance may be not an avocation but their paying vocation.

615

Any dance company in the United States (certain border towns in Canada are also included) may apply for membership in the pertinent regional ballet association, whether it is oriented toward ballet, modern dance, or ethnic dance. Community prejudice is avoided because regional ballet associations represent many cities and several states and because there is that supergroup, the National Association for Regional Ballet, which clucks like a loving but disciplinary mother hen over its ballet brood.

A regional ballet must incorporate as a non-profit enterprise and give public performances for paying audiences. Companies and repertory are selected for regional festivals by non-related, unbiased, disinterested—but not *un*interested—adjudicators. (Regional ballet most certainly brought the word *adjudication* back into common use.) Regional associations may select their own festival adjudicators but only from a list provided by the national association. Thus, no dance figure—teacher, dancer, critic, sponsor—in a given region may adjudicate companies in that region. Dance leaders in other regions may be called on to adjudicate, since no neighborhood rivalry exists for them outside their own areas, or national dance authorities may be invited as adjudicators.

The late Mr. Chujoy was an active national adjudicator. Another is Alice Bingham, who, in a matter of weeks, visited twenty-two cities, reported on more than fifty ballet productions, and helped select the companies and the programs to be given at that particular regional festival. Miss Hering, long associated with the regional-ballet movement and a dance critic and lecturer of international stature, is also an adjudicator. Recently Miss Hering completed a tour of fifty-two regional ballet centers. (Adjudicators, incidentally, work without pay and are recompensed for expenses only by the various regions they adjudicate.)

The major virtue of the regional ballet movement is decentralization. In a country as huge as ours, this is desirable, even essential, for many reasons. New York City and, to a lesser degree, Chicago and San Francisco cannot possibly absorb all the dance talent emerging in communities from coast to coast. The communities themselves, which may have supported for many years municipal symphonies, glee clubs, and little theater groups, may now take pride in giving support to the fastest growing of the performing arts, dance. Furthermore, dancers need not necessarily desert the home front for the lights of Broadway or Hollywood TV, for stage and television opportunities at home are now open to them.

Nor can one overlook the wealth of potential choreographic material waiting to be used in every region. Naturally, regional companies will want to accept the challenges of a *Swan Lake,* or a ballet by Balanchine, or some other traditional or international classic. Indeed, they would be foolish to skirt *The Nutcracker,* the biggest money-maker and audience-getter in all ballet. But local legends and lore, folk-dance backgrounds, even geographical locations—the sea, the mountains, the plains—invite the choreographer to paint unique pictures, not with pigments or words, but with dancing bodies. Ghettos cry out for dance expression of inequities suffered, just as bayou songs long to find physical form and substance in the lilt of the human body.

Yehudi Menuhin, the great violinist, has said, "Art cannot exist only in the hands of specialists, for it will wither. It must dig into the very substance of life. It requires the help and cooperation of the whole community, and help must sometimes be given in the homes, in the schools, and in the streets."

In sixteen years the regional-ballet movement, unique to America, has presented fifty-four festivals throughout the nation in a continuing effort to raise community dance to a high theatrical level. Students, young performers, incipient choreographers, even composers and designers and librettists, are emerging.

Mrs. Alexander, justly honored by her city, by her state, and, through Miss Hanks, by the nation itself, has indeed been more than a visionary: She has transformed visions and dreams into the same reality that one of the greatest dancers of all time envisioned when she, the divine Isadora Duncan, said, "I see America dancing, beautiful, strong, with one foot poised on the highest point of the Rockies, her two hands stretched out from the Atlantic to the Pacific." [*Saturday Review*]

1974

Guides and Reflections

A guide to the international dance scene • Veteran critic Terry and friend Marusia (Maria) Karnilova, veteran dancer-turned-actress, reflect on the past and project into the future of dance

A Baedeker for Balletomanes

January 12, 1974

The so-called off-season is really the *in* season too for the theater-oriented traveler. From September until June Europe's great performing troupes are in residence in their own glorious theaters from London to Leningrad. Here they dance or sing or act for their kings and queens, presidents and prime ministers, and for the ordinary ticket holder.

There is no thrill equal to that of walking into the blue-and-silver splendor of Leningrad's Kirov Theater (formerly the fabled Maryinsky of the days of Pavlova and Nijinsky and the young George Balanchine), the red-and-gold grandeur of Moscow's Bolshoi Theater, the fairytale beauty of the ancient Royal Theater in Copenhagen, the vast opulence of Stockholm's Royal Opera, or the historic Royal Opera House in London's Covent Garden.

I have just returned from Scandinavia, where I could delight in castles and cathedrals, fjords and glaciers, smorgasbords and sweaters, and, of course, brilliant ballet productions ranging in age from 1786 to today's experiments with electronic sound and nudity. Whether you go assisted by the pampering creature comforts of SAS, by your own version of Kon-Tiki, or by other means of travel, go before the tourist crush.

Copenhagen In the daytime at the Royal Theater in Kongens Nytorv (the King's Square), the Royal Guard, with band playing, will march by the great old theater on its way to relieve the on-duty guard at the nearby residence of Queen Margrethe II. At night, for a gala performance, braziers will be aglow on the theater's roof, and, very likely, the queen herself will be present or Queen Mother Ingrid or the Queen of Greece and various princes and princesses.

Before the performance starts, note the motto, *Ei Blot Til Lyst* (*For More Than Pleasure*), on the proscenium of the century-old theater and the front curtain, with its famous painting of the Acropolis, both dating from a nearby old theater first built in 1748. Look directly above you to the Muses painted on the ceiling, then down to the names of composers and playwrights lined along the first ring, and walk along the corridors and into the grand salon, where you will find marble busts, miniature statues, paintings of performing artists.

On stage is one of the great ballet companies of the world, a company older than the legendary Russian ballets, older by far than Britain's celebrated Royal Ballet, even older than the Royal Swedish Ballet (a fact that delights the Danes, whose affection for the Swedes appears to be limited to Swedish-born Queen Ingrid, who, the Danes will tell you, "speaks Danish without a Swedish accent!"). What will you be seeing? Perhaps it will be the oldest extant ballet in the world, Vincenzo Galeotti's *The Whims of Cupid and of the Ballet Master* (1786), in which Cupid comes down from Olympus in a painted cloud, shoots his mischievous arrows, and causes a mad amorous mix-up of couples young and old, French, Greek, Danish, Quaker, and African. One of the children from the Royal Ballet School always plays Cupid. This season the role is danced by a highly gifted boy of Danish and Negro ancestry, Jacob Sparsø Nielsen.

It is likely that you will also see a new avant-garde ballet, *The Triumph of Death,* choreographed by the Royal Danish Ballet's young and enormously vital director, Flemming Flindt, to a theme by Eugene Ionesco. As marks our era, this dance–drama, in twelve scenes for thirty dancers, was created for television. It was an instant hit, and Flindt rechoreographed it for the stage, where it was a hit all over again, attracting the hip young of Europe as well as ardent balletomanes.

Dødens Triumf (in case you want to say it in Danish) deals with a variety of reactions to the coming of death. A plague has struck—or is it atomic radiation? Or creatures from outer space poisoning us? Who knows? As it sweeps inexorably through the city, we see: a proper, formal funeral procession give way to trash men shoveling bodies into rubbish trucks; trapped prisoners watching their guards die while they are unable to escape; a rich man who sprays everything (including his nude body and his food) with pesticides; women who crash through department-store windows, rip off their clothes, and try on expensive gowns and furs and jewels before they die; and two pairs of young lovers, one man fleeing his plague-stricken girl and the other male accepting his own doom and staying with his dying mate. Not pretty—but powerful.

620

The Royal Dancers will also show you their interpretations of great Russian classics such as *Swan Lake,* or French classics such as *Giselle,* or modern ballets by Fokine, Balanchine, Limón, and even the Swedish Cullberg. You are certain to see on the great stage of the Royal Theater (big enough to reproduce the Blue Grotto of Capri and a boat) ballets by the Danish master of the last century, August Bournonville. Until the 1950s nobody outside Denmark had seen his masterpieces, but now there is a Bournonville binge on, especially in America. Of course nobody can dance like the Danes themselves in Bournonville's three-act *Napoli* (the ballet with the Blue Grotto), or in his *Far From Denmark* (just revived by Flindt in a brilliant new production that preserves the unique Bournonville style of dancing), or in seven other Bournonville ballets that still exist in whole or in part.

Indeed, Bournonville, with all its century-old charm and theatrical quaintness, never grows old, never loses its Danish exuberance, never ceases to challenge the most adept dancer. This year Kirsten Ralov and Fredbjørn Bjørnsson, both trained in daily Bournonville classes since they were seven years old (which means that Miss Ralov, after forty years, is certainly the queen of Bournonville), have made a brand-new ballet out of *The Wednesday Class* (there is a Bournonville class routine for each day of the week), starting with the exactitude demanded by exercises at the ballet barre, going through the adagio passages, that require incredible balance, and closing with the bounding leaps and electrifying leg beats for which the Danes are famous. This new-old Bournonville work was an instant success, for the child dancers were adorable, the adults corps handsome, Niels Kehlet (one of the really great dancers of our day) superb, Flemming Ryberg elegant as Kehlet's alternate, and Annemarie Dybdal absolutely ravishing, a first-rank ballerina-to-be if I ever saw one.

Her Majesty's Royal Dancers will be coming to see us in 1975; meanwhile it would be fun to go to Copenhagen, where the ballet tradition goes back to the court masquerades of the 1500s, where there has been a professional Royal Theater since 1722 (Russia's ballet started in 1728), and where there has been a Royal Ballet School with an unbroken tradition since 1770 (Sweden's ballet school goes back to 1773).

Stockholm In the presence of Europe's newest and youngest monarch, King Carl XVI Gustaf, the Royal Swedish Ballet celebrated in November its two hundredth birthday at the Royal Opera with a program that spanned, in choreographic style, those two centuries. Several of these dances will be seen in our country when the Royal Swedish Ballet makes it American debut later this year, under the S. Hurok banner, with a national tour and an October–November engagement at the New York City Center.

The opening consisted of a suite of excerpts from the ballet *Cupido,* which Mary Skeaping, the English director of the Royal Swedish Ballet during the 1950s and 1960s, recreated from seventeenth-century Swedish sources for the Royal Court Theater at Drottningholm. It is the most exquisite and beautifully preserved court theater I have ever seen: The old scenic effects are still in functioning order, and one of the drops dates back to the reign of Queen Christina.

For the huge Royal Opera in Stockholm itself, the Drottningholm settings are approximated, but the costumes, including elaborate, plumed affairs for four men representing the four continents (you wouldn't believe the American Indian), are magnificent. Among the highlights here is a marvelous hornpipe accompanied by tumblers, which was danced in Drottningholm at about the same time our own John Durang danced his famous hornpipe in Philadelphia for George Washington.

It was logical that the program should move from the pre-toe-shoe era of court ballet to the beginnings of pointe in a ballet by August Bournonville, whose father, Antoine, had brought his own handsome presence, his skill as a dancer, and his choreographies from Paris to Stockholm during the very first days of the Royal Opera. The August Bournonville ballet selected for this gala was, most pertinently, *Konservatoriet* (*The Conservatory*), in which the Danish choreographer presumably put into theatrical form his memories of ballet lessons in Paris. With equal pertinence, the new Stockholm staging of *Konservatoriet* was done by Fredbjørn Bjørnsson, who, with *Wednesday Class,* did for Bournonville in 1973 what Bournonville had done for the French genius Auguste Vestris in 1849. The cast was headed by Maria Lang, who had danced the lead in *Firebird* a few nights before, a ballerina of great stylishness and sweet radiance.

The gala also paid tribute to the Fokine influence in Swedish ballet history with *The Dying Swan*; bowed to a one-time director, Antony Tudor, with a scene from his *Dark Elegies*; said thank-you to the late José Limón in an excerpt from his *There Is a Time*; celebrated two major Swedish choreographers, Birgit Cullberg and Ivo Cramér, with the former's passionate and playful *Adam and Eve* (gloriously danced by Per Arthur Segerström and Anneli Alhanko) and the latter's colorful and charming Swedish folk concept of the tale *The Prodigal Son.* The festivity ended with one of the greatest of contemporary ballets, Stravinsky's *Les Noces,* as choreographed by America's Jerome Robbins and restaged by Robbins's assistant and the present director of the Royal Swedish Ballet, the American James Moore. The Swedes, who are by all measurements the most formal of the Scandinavian peoples, have a primitive, almost fierce side lurking just beneath the surface. Thus it is that they capture the primal, almost animal force of *Les Noces* better than any other dancers do. Our American Ballet Theatre dances it superbly, but the Swedes invest it with a terrifying power.

The Swedes, who have long taken second place in Scandinavia to the

Danes in matters of ballet, are forging ahead. The Danish Erik Bruhn, the world's undisputed *premier danseur noble* until his recent retirement, during his tenure as director of the Royal Swedish Ballet, reformed, revitalized, and modernized the ballet school. The results are now showing in the splendid young dancers the school is producing. For this the Swedes should be grateful, although it is difficult for a Swede to be grateful to a Dane. When he was director, Bruhn used to say that the Swedish press was rough on him, but he'd add wryly, "The only Swede who seems to like me is Princess Christina." The Princess is known to be not only a devoted but also a highly knowledgeable balletomane.

Oslo   The youngest and smallest of the state ballets of Scandinavia is the Norwegian National Ballet, the official dance company of the Norwegian Opera. Its origins go back only as far as 1948, but its career was checkered, including a period of disbandment, until it became a part of the Norwegian Opera in 1958 and found itself a permanent home in a large, sturdy, but unglamorous building that was originally built, I was told, as a socialist meeting hall.

Although the Norwegian National Ballet, as a permanent institution, is only fifteen years old, the absence of a long ballet tradition is immediately understandable when we realize that ballet was first fostered by the crown and that for hundreds of years, beginning long before ballet was born, Norway was under the rule first of Denmark and then under the Swedish crown (with the royal court in Stockholm) until this century. In fifteen years the company has progressed admirably in its balletic efforts.

The troupe, which will make its U.S. debut this March in an east-of-the-Mississippi tour, is now under the energetic and skillful direction of its former ballerina, Anne Borg. Miss Borg, following the ancient example of Denmark and the more recent example of Sweden, has realized that a company is only as strong as its ballet school and that the school must be the chief source of supply for the company. The Norwegians have a good school—when I was visiting, Hans Meister, onetime soloist with our Metropolitan Opera Ballet and now a principal dancer with the National Ballet of Finland (which is sometimes thought of as a Scandinavian company, although it is more closely oriented to Soviet ballet), was giving excellent classes—and they have an active choreographic workshop, which is already developing some promising choreographers. An arrangement with Norwegian television is also giving a new outlet to both ballet accomplishment and experimentation.

Of the programs I saw, I was not impressed with the production of Fokine's *Petrouchka,* but the Balanchine *Apollo* was splendid as far as the three Muses were concerned (Rudolf Nureyev had danced the title role with the Norwegians not long before and had given high praise to his ballerinas),

623

and the late John Cranko's *Jeu de Cartes* (which rounded out an all-Stravinsky program) was funny in mime and first rate in movement. I was especially impressed by the dancing of Ellen Kjellberg and Terje Solberg, although other principals were fine too. Of particular interest was a strictly Norwegian ballet—it will be seen on the U.S. tour—inspired by the famous monumental sculptures in Oslo's Vigeland Park, sculptures that celebrate the ages of man: childhood, youth, maturity, and old age. This ballet, called *Forever and Ever,* choreographed for the workshop by Kari Blakstad, does not settle for duplicating Gustav Vigeland's sculptures as in a game of living statues. Rather it uses the colossal nudes as an inspiration for the thrust through time and space of an aspiring humanity. The discipline of ballet is present in the dancers' bodies, but the movements are as free as the sculptures themselves. For the American tour, projections of Vigeland will establish the visual basis of the ballet, but if you go to Oslo, the Sculpture Park is in itself an overwhelming experience.

The traveler should know that touring time for most national ballet troupes is summer, with spillovers in spring and fall. For the most part, then, the Royal Danish Ballet, the Royal Swedish Ballet, and the Norwegian National Ballet can be found in their home theaters, sharing repertories with their related opera and drama troupes from September until June. In the U.S.S.R. ballet and opera alternate in the world-famous Bolshoi Theater in Moscow and in the once-imperial Kirov (née the Maryinsky) in Leningrad. Even if it seems that Britain's Royal Ballet is straying from the Royal Opera House at Covent Garden, it is not quite so; for there is a second Royal Ballet (it hates to be called "the second company") for home audiences at Sadler's Wells, West Germany's famed Stuttgart Ballet, the two Dutch troupes (the National Ballet and the Netherlands Dance Theater) are busy at home, as are the Finnish National Ballet, Belgium's Ballet of the 20th Century (headed by Maurice Béjart), the several opera-ballet troupes of Italy and Germany, the oldest national ballet (the Paris Opera Ballet, with antecedents going back to 1661), and innumerable other state and municipal troupes.

And for those of you who are expert in the *entrechat, cabriole,* and *gargouillade,* you may submit your own prowess to a galaxy of international judges for the seventh International Ballet Competition at Varna, Bulgaria. For the loser, the consolation prize is a stay at one of Europe's most beautiful resort beaches, at Varna, on the Black Sea, where you can disport yourself without fear of being compared with Fonteyn or Nureyev.

In this hemisphere, to the north of us, three major Canadian troupes will be performing from Montreal to Vancouver. The Royal Winnipeg Ballet (the very first ballet in the British Commonwealth to be granted a Royal Charter) performs in its home city February 20–24 and April 3–7 but will also dance, from now into April, in such cities as Ottawa, Vancouver, Calgary, Saskatoon,

624

Niagara-on-the-Lake, and other Canadian centers, as well as in the United States (from Portland, Oregon, to Morgantown, West Virginia).

The National Ballet of Canada performs in its home city, Toronto, at the O'Keefe Center February 13–March 2, followed by a few days in Ottawa and a U.S. tour, which includes Boston, Chicago, San Francisco, and on April 23–May 5 engagement at New York's Metropolitan Opera House. Les Grands Ballets Canadiens, which started out as a television dance group and developed into a major Canadian ballet company, plays its home city of Montreal February 8, 9, 14–16, March 29, 30, April 4–6, and again in August, with other Canadian performances in cities across Canada and in Western Europe from May until June.

To our south is Amalia Hernandez's world-famous Ballet Folklorico de Mexico. There are two companies, one which services Mexico City and other Mexican cities the year-round and another, the global traveler, which will be in the United States through March. [*Saturday Review*]

Marusia and I: To Applaud, to Ponder the Dance

September 7, 1974

Maria Karnilova and I, earlier this year, attended—or, as the French so pertinently put it, *assisté*—a performance at the New York City Center of the exuberant, youthful, and superbly disciplined City Center Joffrey Ballet. "My God!" said the Broadway star. "In my ballet days I couldn't do all the steps that even those corps de ballet girls are doing." Later in the year she echoed the same opinion when we went to see the cool, flashing dancers of the New York City Ballet.

Her reactions were absolutely right, for the technical skills required of her and of other ballerinas of the Forties would not suffice today. But Miss Karnilova then posed a question, "Where can they go from here?" It was a casual remark, but as we talked, the implications became serious.

Where indeed with this super-physicality in dance lead us in the 50 years that lie ahead? Will ballet's triumphs of the last 50 years evaporate in the half-century ahead?

Karnilova, American-born, Russian-reared (her childhood was spent in Minsk), is known to this generation of theatergoers as a superb actress: *Fiddler on the Roof* (for which she won a Tony Award as Goldie), *Zorba*, in which she starred, and recently in *Gigi*. But exactly 35 years ago, she began

625

rehearsals as a corps dancer for the debut of the American Ballet Theatre, following stints as a child dancer at the Metropolitan Opera, a South American tour with an opera troupe at 14, and chorus jobs in musicals. With ABT, she rose to ballerina status where her versatility enabled her to excel as a brilliant comedienne in Agnes de Mille ballets, as a ravishingly beautiful, lyrical dancer in the title role of *Helen of Troy,* as a dramatic dancer and, of course, as a classical dancer.

After we had watched some of the men dancers accomplish breathtaking feats of skill, Marusia, as she is called in the world of ballet, chuckled, "Do you remember when Dolin [Anton Dolin, the great premier danseur of his day] did a double air-turn with his fingers hanging over his forehead in *Giselle*? The Met audience went wild! Just look at these kids today. They can all do doubles. And remember Alicia [Markova, the greatest Giselle of her era and, with Dolin, the Fonteyn and Nureyev of the Forties], when she would do a little jump with a little beat, everyone would scream? And look what these girls are doing today. I just can't believe it!"

We also took note of the fact that today's vast ballet public no longer applauds those examples of virtuosity which excited balletomanes two decades ago. Indeed, tours en l'air or fouettés are now standard rather than special. True, audiences yell their delight when the Stuttgart Ballet's American star, Richard Cragun, tosses off a triple tour en l'air (a feat now emulated by others). Is a quadruple possible?

Once, those 32 flashing, whipping, dizzying fouettés in Act III of *Swan Lake* made history. The Italian Pierina Legnani was the first to execute this feat in the Nineties, and when the Russian Mathilde Kschessinska succeeded in mastering them, Imperial Russia did all but call a national holiday (no wonder the czar made Kschessinska that rarest of creatures, a prima ballerina assoluta). And for years, that demanding sequence was to the ballerina what the Mad Scene in *Lucia di Lammermoor* was to the coloratura soprano. A mistress of multiple fouettés was still rare when the Ballet Russe de Monte Carlo came to America in the Thirties. The great prima ballerina Alexandra Danilova never did do them when I was looking, but the famous teenage "Baby Ballerinas"— Tamara Toumanova, Irina Baronova, Tatiana Riabouchinska—were considered phenomenal because all three could do them. Today, you'll find a whole squadron of girls awhirling on stage. And the prima? She'll be doing doubles!

Marusia and I began pondering the "what's next?" on the basis of "what was." Before Legnani, ballet had sunk to a low level in Europe, especially in Paris, the birthplace of classical ballet. Old *Giselle* was pepped up by the inclusion (and intrusion) of the all-girl military drills popular in variety shows. The public had become bored with that romantic ballet which had wildly cheering audiences in Paris, London, Vienna, Copenhagen, Milan, St. Petersburg in the 1830s and '40s. The superstars, the first ballerinas to dance sur les pointes, couldn't do much more than get onto those pointes and balance there fleetingly. There were no turns on pointe, not even a single pirouette, yet critics raved about the ballerinas "fantastic toe" and "amazing exertions." But by 1850–60, the public had become jaded and was waiting for a Legnani to emerge.

And it had happened before. The first professional ballerina, Lafontaine (1681), had worn dresses that swept the floor, wigs (with plumes and even ships on them), hoops, panniers, high heels. She could barely move, yet Paris had cheered her grace and had hailed her as "Queen of the Dance." A few years later Françoise Prévost mimed the final scene of Corneille's *Horace,* supported neither by words nor music, and caused "tears to flow." But soon Maria Camargo came along and took the heels off her shoes, cut off the bottoms of her skirts (so her legs showed), possibly invented the *entrechat* (for women, at least), and was off and going as ballet's first female virtuoso.

But what Camargo started for the ballerina and what subsequently Gaetano Vestris (who called himself the God of Dance) established in the way of prowess for the men dancers made it essential for each newcomer to top his predecessor in such matters of prowess, not simply out of vanity but because a public, given a dance that focused on physical tricks, wanted new ones.

But is physical virtuosity the essence of ballet? Jean-Georges Noverre, master choreographer, inspired reformer of the late 1700s, and author of one of the greatest books in the literature of dance, *Lettres sur la danse et les ballets,* wrote of the dancers to be seen in the "establishment" opera houses, "They apply themselves only to the material side of their art, they learn to jump more or less high, they strive mechanically to execute a number of steps. . . ." The dancer "should divide his attention between the mechanism of steps and the movements proper to express the passions."

Every now and again, a Noverre must come along to save the ballet. Karnilova and I talked about ballet cycles we have experienced, not only cycles of advanced technical skills but also the Noverre-like cycles of expressivity. Marusia spoke of Michel Fokine—an early-twentieth-century reformer who saved ballet from the mechanized offsprings of Legnani-style virtuosity and who lived long enough to influence profoundly Karnilova, Nora Kaye, and other teenagers—and of the rewards of dancing the ballets of Antony Tudor, Agnes de Mille and, later, Jerome Robbins (her contemporary) and of passionate dance-dramas, such as *Winesburg, Ohio,* choreographed by her longtime dancing colleague Donald Saddler.

Outside of the ballet orbit, modern dance came into being, almost simultaneously in America and in Europe, in a fierce protest against the mere exploitation of dance prowesses by an aesthetically weary ballet.

At the Joffrey performance, Karnilova and I noticed that there was a delightfully light-and-lively flood of applause for Gerald Arpino's *Kettentanz,*

627

with all of its fine displays of youthful skill, and a different kind of applause, just as long and somehow more resonant, for José Limón's modern-dance telling (perhaps *revelation* is a better word) of the Othello tragedy in *The Moor's Pavane.* Styles in dance gymnastics may come and go, but Noverre's "passions" are without period. The juxtaposition of *Kettentanz* and *Pavane* reminded us of Nora Kaye, as the heroine in Tudor's *Lilac Garden,* rising onto pointe not in preparation for executing an act of physical skill but rising to a plane of ecstasy, as she felt her lover's touch upon her shoulder.

Neither Karnilova nor I wish to see the end of breathtaking physical tricks in ballet, but we think it dangerous if virtuosity is simply an end in itself. An important area of ballet is the celebration of the body by the world's super-athlete, the dancer, and to see the dancer defy gravity in sustained balances or aerial excursions, to invite vertigo with vertiginous spins, and to bring elegance to circusy exploits is half the fun of ballet. But the other half of the function of ballet was well stated by Noverre in 1760 in his *Lettres* written in Stuttgart:

> If our souls determine the play and movement of our muscles and tendons, then the feet, body, features, and eyes will be stirred in the right manner, and the effects resulting from this harmony and intelligence will interest equally the heart and the mind. . . . It is shameful that dancing should renounce the empire it might assert over the mind and only endeavor to please the sight.

Noverre's warning of two centuries ago is pertinent to ballet today. In the past 50 years we have presided over a new Golden Age of Ballet. Will the next half-century bring us continuing ballet luster or will it bring a cyclic decline and fall? Marusia and I are among those who ponder as we applaud. [*Saturday Review*]

1975

From Sea to Shining Sea

An overview of American dance from sea to shining sea • ABT at 35 •
Castigating Eliot Feld • Capsule comments

American Ballet:
From Sea to Shining Sea

January 25, 1975

New York City has been called, with considerable justification, "The Dance Capital of the World." Indeed, it is possible to attend a dance event—often two or three or more—every day of the year. But it is not *the* "Dance World," any more than Washington, D.C., is *the* United States. The last 20 years, in fact, has witnessed a healthy decentralization of dance in America. The regional ballet movement, which got under way in 1956, has presided over the evolution of more than 200 ballet companies in our land, and a dozen years ago a whopping, multi-million-dollar grant from the Ford Foundation boosted ballet not only in New York (for George Balanchine's New York City Ballet and School of American Ballet) but also outside Manhattan (for Balanchine-oriented groups).

The regional ballets are non-professional, but many set for themselves high standards and display a genuine concern for the fostering of fresh choreographic talent. Among the major non-New York professional ballet companies are the Pennsylvania Ballet (which was actually brought into being by the Ford grant), the Boston Ballet Company (which Ford money elevated from regional to professional status), the San Francisco Ballet (which is the oldest non-N.Y.C. professional company—superseding the older Atlanta Ballet, which reverted from brief professional to regional status and nearly folded two months ago because of lack of funds), and the National Ballet of Washington, D.C. (which *did* fold because of insufficient funds).

Of these big four, the best—at the moment—is the Pennsylvania Ballet, founded and directed (now with Benjamin Harkarvy as a co-director) by Barbara Weisberger. In its early days the Pennsylvania Ballet had repertory troubles—it still has problems in this area—and difficulties even with performing skills, but today it stands (or, rather, dances) right up there in the top ballet echelon. It dances Balanchine ballets superbly, even better than "Mr. B.'s" own New York City Ballet, and in the case of *Serenade* (Tchaikovsky), much closer to the way it was originally danced—that is, with romantic waves hovering over it and with gestures imbued with hints of drama. Today, the New York City Ballet does it more as an exercise.

Some young observers may possibly believe that Mrs. Weisberger has tampered with *Serenade*. To the contrary, she has restored it. I once wondered whether the Pennsylvania Ballet was worth the hundreds of thousands of dollars (and even millions) lavished on it. If the 1974 performances are the gauge, Mrs. Weisberger's efforts are indeed worthy of such major support.

The Boston Ballet Company has less money and is not quite so strong in all performing areas as the Pennsylvania Ballet, but under E. Virginia Williams it has grown into a major company with a splendid repertory of classics (*Coppélia* and *Giselle* among them), Balanchine ballets, and first-rate modern works (Talley Beatty's *The Road of the Phoebe Snow* is a fine example). With young dancers, such as the fiery and muscularly resilient Tony Catanzaro and the lovely Laura Young, lyrical yet never for an instant fuzzy in movements cleanly etched, Miss Williams continues to prove her sharpness in recognizing new talent, although she has her problems finding new choreographers.

The San Francisco Ballet, founded as an opera ballet under Adolph Bolm, grew into a major American dance troupe, chiefly during the still-continuing reign of Lew Christensen (brother Willam heads Ballet West, the major ballet troupe of the Rocky Mountain states, and brother Harold long directed the San Francisco Ballet School). Last fall, with a deficit of a half-million dollars, the company was on the brink of disaster. The dancers, loyal and indomitable, took to dancing in the streets for coins. Their efforts attracted attention, and the company has been saved—for the moment.

The National Ballet (Washington, D.C.), despite the continuing generosity of its devoted patroness, Mrs. Jean Riddell, was forced to dissolve. Mrs. Riddell, an heiress, willingly sold some of her valuable possessions for further financing to keep this major company, co-directed by Frederic Franklin and Ben Stevenson, solvent; but there was insufficient outside funding to keep alive a troupe resident in the nation's capital, serving the nation through its long tours, showcasing brilliant dancers (Carmen Mathe and Kirk Peterson among them), and presenting a repertory that included the classics, new works by Mr. Stevenson (one of the few major young choreographers of our day), Balanchine ballets (including a superb *Prodigal Son*), significant revivals in new productions: Valerie Bettis's *A Streetcar Named Desire,* John Cranko's delicious *Jeu de Cartes* (Stravinsky), and *Water Study* and *The Shakers,* both masterworks by one of the greatest modern dance choreographers of the age, the late Doris Humphrey.

I find it not only unbelievable but also shocking that the nation's capital, the National Endowment for the Arts, the Ford Foundation, and the Rockefeller Foundation (which brought into being a new company, the Eliot Feld Ballet . . . but that's a story that I will review at a later date) would permit The National Ballet, a national resource, to die. Shocking indeed, is it not?

Ballet in Chicago without the internationally renowned Ruth Page is unthinkable. Miss Page, who made her Chicago debut as a child dancer in 1919, has been loyal to her city during the years through her own companies and schools and in association with others. Her newly reconstituted Chicago Ballet, with Ben Stevenson as her artistic director, has brand-new headquarters in the Ruth Page Foundation Building and a repertory that not only presents works by Miss Page herself (including the program-long *Alice in Wonderland,* based on the Lewis Carroll books), Stevenson, and Sir Frederick Ashton but also *When Summoned,* by a major young modern dance choreographer, Bill Evans, formerly of Utah's Repertory Dance Theatre and now associated with another professional modern dance group, the Fairmont Dance Theatre of Cleveland.

The Hartford Ballet Company, co-directed by Michael Uthoff and Enid Lynn, is a chamber-size troupe, but it is first-rate. I've seen it on several occasions and found myself responding with vigorous kinesthetic enthusiasm to the forceful, yet controlled, energies that the young dancers pour into modern dance pieces by José Limón or by Doris Humphrey and into Uthoff's almost savage but cleanly delineated Mayan ritual-ballet, *Cantata* (to music of Ginastera), and in modest classical pieces that neither demand too much nor challenge too little.

David McLain's Cincinnati Ballet Company I've reviewed in these columns before, noting especially that it has done great service to dance by rescuing, restoring, and producing major works by the late Lester Horton, the West Coast's modern dance pioneer.

Many of our big ballet companies have "junior" or "youth" groups, which are small enough to perform in almost any size theater, which provide experience to young professionals making the transition from classroom and studio to the parent companies, and which foster new choreographic talent. Joffrey II, described as "A New Youth Dance Ensemble" and directed by Jonathan Watts, is the handsome offspring of the City Center Joffrey Ballet, which has just returned from a triumphant tour of the Soviet Union. (The American Ballet Theatre and the New York City Ballet are among the other world-famous troupes that send out units smaller than themselves.)

I attended a performance of Joffrey II in Red Bank, N.J. The young-sters danced well in a variety of assignments, but I was especially impressed, as were the audiences and regional newspaper reporters, with a new ballet called *Rush* (to music of Poulenc) especially choreographed for the dancers by Stuart Sebastian, an immensely gifted young choreographer (just turned 24), who had previously proved his choreographic worth on the regional ballet level with Ohio's Dayton Ballet Company (his alma mater) and the Flint Ballet Theatre of Michigan. He has been re-engaged by Joffrey and newly engaged by the Hartford Ballet. Watch him. Fine performing talent is abundant; choreographic talent is rare.

And, to point to the immeasurable worth of non-New York City ballet enterprises, one may use young Sebastian as an example, for as a child and teenager he was trained in one of our finest regional ballet groups, the Dayton Ballet (directed by Josephine and Hermene Schwarz); moved on to perform with the Harkness Youth Dancers; joined The National Ballet in Washington, D.C., where he rose to the rank of principal; and now, combining university studies with teaching at Mary Day's Washington School of Ballet, he is heading for a choreographer's career in the major leagues. Other American boys and girls of special talents have, and will, come from all regions of the United States—from Main Streets and not exclusively from Broadway. [*Saturday Review*]

American Ballet Theatre: At 35, Lustier Than Ever

March 8, 1975

They came with great talent and great love, cherished memories and great expectations, to celebrate a thirty-fifth anniversary. What is so important about 35? you may well ask. Why not wait until 50? Until a golden? Because in American dance, every year of survival is cause for thanksgiving; every decade of accomplishment is reason for celebration.

Next year, the Bolshoi Ballet marks its two-hundredth anniversary; the Royal Danish Ballet is even older; and today's Paris Opéra Ballet traces its ancestry back to 1661, when Louis XIV founded the first ballet academy. But the American Ballet Theatre is so proud of reaching—against almost insurmountable financial odds—its thirty-fifth birthday that the company, the illustrious alumni, the fans around the world, and the press are as excited as if the occasion were indeed a bi- or tri-centennial.

632

A truly dazzling birthday gala was held on January 11 in New York's big, somewhat crummy, but affectionately tolerated City Center 55th St. Theater, and the street became the scene of a combination block party and riot as ticket-holders (some paid $500 a seat at this benefit) and ticket-pleaders gave mounted police a rough but cheerful time.

The audience accorded Lucia Chase and Oliver Smith, the company's co-directors for 30 years (Miss Chase was its co-founder with the late Richard Pleasant, and its patroness from the start), a standing ovation as they came down the aisle. Later, at intermission, each received New York City's highest cultural award, the Handel Medallion. The gala program itself, directed by a charter member of The Ballet Theatre (as it was originally named) and one of today's most popular Broadway choreographers, Tony Award-winner Donald Saddler, was also a winner. It was swiftly paced, not overlong, and it interwove the brilliance of ABT's current dancers with the wonderful radiance of yesterday's returning alumni.

I cannot tell you all that occurred, just some samples. The company's newest acquisitions, the dazzling Mikhail Baryshnikov and the lovely Gelsey Kirkland, were there to knock 'em in the aisles with that virtuoso blockbuster, the pas de deux from *Le Corsaire*; Natalia Makarova and Ivan Nagy stirred the nerve ends with the short and zestful *Spring Waters* and stirred the heart with the tender pas de deux from Kenneth MacMillan's *Concerto*.

The troupe's resident American prima ballerina, Cynthia Gregory, linked the past to the present by dancing the *Rose Adagio* from *The Sleeping Beauty* with four cavaliers: two greats from the past, Igor Youskevitch and André Eglevsky, Scott Douglas of the recent past, and the current Gayle Young. (Seventy-year-old Anton Dolin, one of the great premiers danseurs of yesterday, staged it.) And then Miss Gregory danced the seduction-scene duet from *Miss Julie* with the retired Erik Bruhn, except you would never have guessed that this slender, boyish man doing double airturns and high leaps has retired. (Bruhn received the ovation of the evening.)

That brilliant teenager Fernando Bujones (he can match almost any physical feat that Baryshnikov can accomplish but does not yet have the style and polish of the older lad—Baryshnikov is 26), Buddy Balough, and Terry Orr were the three sailors in an excerpt from Jerome Robbins's *Fancy Free,* and as they finished, three gentlemen in evening dress came on stage and executed a step or two—they were the original sailors: Robbins himself, John Kriza, and Harold Lang. Leonard Bernstein, who had composed it, took a bow, and Oliver Smith, who had designed this history-making ballet, was, of course, out front.

Agnes de Mille's *Three Virgins and a Devil* got under way with Miss de Mille herself (in evening gown) dancing the opening measures of the role she once played, and with old-timer Yurek Lazowsky cutting capers as the Devil.

Then there was the incredible moment when the curtain rose on the opening of Antony Tudor's first ballet made in America, *Pillar of Fire,* and there on stage was Nora Kaye, who had received 26 curtain calls at the premiere at the old Metropolitan Opera House, had become a star overnight, and was hailed as the world's first "dramatic ballerina," a rank coined to describe her powerful art.

Miss Kaye, in evening gown, danced, and her magic went undimmed. Miss Chase came on as the Eldest Sister, a role she (a superb dancer–actress) had created, Tudor himself crossed the stage in the part of the Suitor, and Hugh Laing thrust his pelvis forward with hypnotic lechery as he had three decades before. In another Tudor excerpt, Laing, in work pants and a sweat shirt, did Romeo's entrance, and the gorgeous Sono Osato made the bit part of Rosaline a miniature treasure, as she had done at the premiere. Yes, the current artists—Eleanor D'Antuono, Ted Kivitt, the upcoming Marianna Tcherkassky, the gifted Kirk Peterson, Sallie Wilson, and the other regulars I have mentioned—were all skillfully united with their dancing aunts and uncles, grandparents even.

The walk-on finale? I cannot name them all. But there one saw Karen Conrad, who had literally soared across the stage (to gasps that echo to this day) in the opening *Les Sylphides* on the initial program; the beautiful Mariam Golden; the glamorous Maria Karnilova, a starring actress on Broadway; Irina Baronova (one of the legendary "Baby Ballerinas" of the Thirties), who has not been in America for 23 years; Leon Danielian; Eugene Loring, creator of *Billy the Kid,* and—oh, I want to list them all, but I can't. Absent were Alicia Markova, recuperating from an illness in London, and another great Alicia, Alicia Alonso, unable, because of some kind of political foolishness, to come from Cuba to the company that presided over her rise to international fame. All of us, the dancers and this critic (one of my first reviews as the dance critic for the *New York Herald Tribune* was the account of the debut of The Ballet Theatre on January 11, 1940), recorded a tape with our messages of memories and love to Alonso.

And in the front row of the orchestra, as they had been 35 years earlier, were Kathleen and Leo Perper, who never missed a Ballet Theatre season, never failed to give a helping hand to Kaye, Karnilova, Saddler, Alonso, and the others when they were impoverished corps dancers and who were even known to fly in from a vacation in Bermuda or the Bahamas to attend a Ballet Theatre matinee and then fly back to the tropics for dinner!

No other American theater company, I dare say, has enjoyed such loyalty from its members past and present and from its patrons over so many years. Why?

The American Ballet Theatre possesses a very special, indeed unique, attraction for all performers. On more than one occasion, it has seemed like a mecca for defectors. Makarova chose it for her principal showcase. So did Baryshnikov. Valeri and Galina Panov have asked to dance with ABT (the offer was declined), and Rudolf Nureyev wanted to add it to his conquests (he, too, was politely refused). Several seasons ago, Nagy, who had defected from Hungary, left Washington's National Ballet and a short stint with the New York City Ballet to become a major figure with ABT.

Why? Because those leaving the U.S.S.R. and other Socialist countries could find two opportunities that no other company could offer in the same full measure: security and adventure. Security in that those trained in traditional ballets could continue to display their particular excellences in *Giselle, Swan Lake, Coppélia, La Fille Mal Gardée,* and the like, along with familiar grands pas de deux, the ballet versions of excerpted operatic arias. And adventure in mastering new techniques, new styles, new rhythms for new roles. Almost all defections were motivated not by political reasons, but by aesthetic ones. Makarova wanted to dance, say, *Pillar of Fire,* among other modern ballets, and not, as might have happened in Leningrad, *Giselle* for the rest of her life. ABT permits her to do both, and we are the richer for having her truly incandescent art in both areas.

Baryshnikov electrified us immediately in *Don Quixote* (the pas de deux), *La Bayadère,* and other classics he had long since conquered and reproduced with his great personal splendor. But he had his greatest triumph in a ballet he had never danced before, Roland Petit's *Le Jeune Homme et la Mort,* staged by the American Ballet Theatre many years ago and revived especially for Baryshnikov as the heir to its spectacular originator, Jean Babilée. ABT also engaged for him the new partner of his choice, Gelsey Kirkland, who defected from George Balanchine's New York City Ballet in order to dance with Baryshnikov and also in order to serve her own ambitions of becoming a ballerina, a rank forbidden by the NYCB chiefly because it is Balanchine's policy (and his right) to view dancers as instruments for the reproducing on stage of his choreographic images and not as highly individual personalities—with idiosyncrasies and loved by audiences—which dominate the stage.

The American Ballet Theatre is equally rewarding for homegrown talent—in all areas of dance accomplishment, modest as well as stellar. Cynthia Gregory, for example, rose from corps to ballerina rank in a year, roughly the equivalent of going from army private to general, and soon thereafter became a prima ballerina—that's a general with four stars. (The rare prima ballerina assoluta—there are two in the world today, England's Fonteyn and Russia's Plisetskaya—would rate five stars.) And look what Gregory has! *Swan Lake, Giselle, Coppélia,* those classics that are the "test" ballets that determine which girl is a ballerina and which is merely a soloist. In Tudor's *Lilac Garden* Gregory has been successful in two contrasting roles, the hard and bitter ex-mistress and the tender, vulnerable heroine. In *The River* she dances to Duke

Ellington; in José Limón's *The Moor's Pavane,* she is a Desdemona whose movements are pure modern dance, the antithesis of classical ballet; in the corny and circusy and wonderful *Grand Pas Classique,* she is a fantastic virtuosa in the straight balletic sense. My God! In what other company would a ballerina in her mid-20s find such opportunities?

Of great value also is the handsome and brilliant Michaël Denard. He is frequently a cavalier of Gregory's when he visits ABT from the Paris Opéra Ballet.

Let's take a non-star, probably someone who will never become a principal, at least not as a virtuoso. Frank Smith is a corps de ballet dancer, but he is not just a cipher. He is good in the corps, he is attractive as a demisoloist, and he's proved to be a first-rate actor as Hilarion in *Giselle,* a difficult role in which the player must be an antagonist but not a villain, and Smith is one of the best Hilarions I have seen. He's valuable to ABT, and ABT is important to his particular range of performing. And Hilda Morales, Warren Conover, Kim Highton, and Charles Ward are certainly eminently worthy of fostering.

Another example: Marianna Tcherkassky is not a ballerina yet. Will she be? She is an adept soloist and a personable performer. The ABT repertory is giving her a chance to work upward and to find her niche, and ballet-goers take pleasure not only in her performances but also in her constant progress.

Young Clark Tippet is very tall. It is a problem to get those long legs under control, but with a good teacher when he was a child and good teachers now, he is making it so well that Miss Chase is beginning to give him assignments that carefully further his career. He is just out of his teens, and his promise is very real. Bujones, the American teenager who won us a gold medal at the prestigious International Ballet Competition in Varna last summer, is already an audience favorite, as is the gifted Bonnie Mathis.

In spite of a record of fostering native talent on all fronts, the directors of the American Ballet Theatre are occasionally taken to task for engaging celebrated defectors. Miss Chase would have been a fool, as a producer, to let any other company get either Makarova or Baryshnikov, for they are not only valuable box office but also artists of world stature. Dame Ninette de Valois, when she was director of Britain's Royal Ballet, was also knuckle-rapped when she engaged Rudolf Nureyev a decade ago, but she retorted tartly that it was her job to see that the Royal had the best. The team of Fonteyn and Nureyev did, in truth, act as a depressant on other members of the Royal Ballet, but Dame Ninette, with her magical pair, presided over a magical decade in ballet history.

Nagy, though a defector, made his jump long enough ago to be one of the ABT gang today. The arrival of Baryshnikov did not edge him out. Not by a long shot. This past season, everyone awaited a Makarova–Baryshnikov

Giselle. No one was disappointed—it was a brilliant occasion. But the miracle had occurred the preceding night when Nagy had played Albrecht to Makarova's Giselle. It was one of those occasions when inexplicable sorcery was at work. The two were as one in their evocation of romantic tragedy, in their realization of dance beauty—yes, in the sublimity of their danced poetry. They knew what had happened; and when the curtain fell, they did not look at us. I am not at all certain they knew we were there. They looked deeply into each other's eyes and they kissed softly, almost reverently, as if in awe of what had transpired. We, the watchers, knew that we had been favored by that magic which is never planned, which is unpredictable, which happens.

All of these experiences—the gala, the star performances, the promise of junior artists, the opportunities of dance adventure in the world's greatest ballet repertory—are due to Richard Pleasant, who had the dream of ballet as theater, of American ballet that cherished the past and explored the present in order to assure the future, and to his partner, Miss Chase.

For many years, Lucia Chase was criticized by many who said, "What does she know about directing a company?" Whatever she does or doesn't know, she has guided the American Ballet Theatre to a peak as high as any ever reached in the ancient annals of dance. Many have given her a tough time, but as Miss de Mille said at the gala, underneath the well-bred New England exterior there is "pure granite."

Oddly enough, even after 35 years of discipline and dedication, Miss Chase is subject to far from kind remarks. Two major choreographers, a generation apart, who had their first opportunities and triumphs under her patronage still seem to resent her part in their careers and are exceedingly rude to her (but that simply represents their peculiar hangups), and others get exasperated with her casting of roles, her toughness at contract time, her occasional evasiveness. There is also, inevitably, that resentment which some hold for a wealthy person and an aristocrat—she is both. But she is also loved because she is "Lucia," not "Miss Chase," to her dancers, because on tour she stands in line on payday (she is a dancer and a union member), and because, although she is a grandmother, she goes on rigorous tours and asks for no special accommodations. She's the boss. She's the employee. She is also a servant who has been faithful in body, mind, money, talent, determination, patience, spirit, grit, and "granite" purpose, to the American Ballet Theatre for 35 years.

There are some who seem to think Oliver Smith might possibly be a figurehead co-director. Don't you believe it. Miss Chase consults him on all matters. His decisions are quick. His anger, when roused by inefficiencies, is quicker. Mistakes do not recur when he has issued orders.

Lucia and Oliver and ABT. What a triumverate! The Thirty-fifth Gala Anniversary now passed, I asked Miss Chase about the future. The next 35

637

years? Since dancers often sail into their 90s, the question was not just a casual cliché. But Lucia Chase is a planner. She knows what she has done, what she is doing, and what she hopes to do. "I promise you right here and now a fortieth anniversary. I won't look beyond that until we get there." And she'll be there, all right, along with her rare combination of granite will and a tender mother-love for the company.

In the *New York Herald Tribune* for January 12, 1940, in the days when I was referred to as "the boy critic," I started my report with "The Ballet Theatre is a new theater baby and a lusty one." We are both much older now. I won't speak for myself, but I will tell you that the American Ballet Theatre, at 35, is lustier than ever—Miss Chase did right by that very special baby. [*Saturday Review*]

Feld: La Danse, C'est Moi?

March 22, 1975

Genius. Rare talent. A gift for potential. What do we ordinary mortals owe those with these extra endowments? Richard L. Coe, the distinguished drama critic and columnist of *The Washington Post,* and I were talking recently about the scarcity of creative talent (there is an abundance of performing talent) in the theater arts, particularly in the field of choreography. "Whenever you come upon it," he said, "you must nurture it. Everyone must nurture it. All of us who work in the arts must nurture—hell! I guess I even mean 'nurse 'em'—the ones who have talent." I agree. But is there not a distinct difference between nurturing and pampering? I think so. And Eliot Feld is being pampered.

When there is lots of money floating around, no one needs to be concerned with pampering; for although too much bounty is likely to harm the pampered, it gives a nice feeling of *noblesse oblige* to the pamperers. But money is tight and getting tighter in the field of performing arts. We have lost, have nearly lost, and may well be in the process of losing dance assets of great importance to the American dance scene. The National Ballet of Washington, D.C., was permitted to go under, after 12 years of increasingly distinguished service to ballet in our capital and in our nation.

The most recent reports from the San Francisco Ballet are encouraging— if one calls assurance of survival through the next six months encouraging. The board of directors of this 30-year-old American ballet landmark were ready to throw in the towel last fall. But the dancers would not give up. As

I reported earlier, they danced in the streets. Now, Michael Smuin, the troupe's associate artistic director, tells me that the half-million-dollar deficit has almost been made up, thanks to gifts ranging from a little girl's 87 cents weekly allowance (which she donated for several weeks) to an anonymous $50,000 gift. Even people on welfare gave welcome pittances.

The Ford Foundation is cutting its performing-arts grants drastically; the Harkness Foundation is slashing back to the point of disbanding (later this year) the Harkness Ballet. And some of our most prestigious and inarguably important dance institutions, such as the Martha Graham Dance Company, the American Ballet Theatre, and the New York City Ballet, to name the three top ones, are facing financial distress and, possibly, disaster.

This, then, is a time for consolidation, not expansion. Yet the Eliot Feld Ballet, which it is now called, was given a second try (in its first guise it was named, with winning modesty, the American Ballet Company, since Feld apparently felt that George Balanchine's history-making American Ballet and the American Ballet Theatre were of little historical significance) last year with a whopping grant from the Rockefeller Foundation. The explanation offered by a Rockefeller spokesman was that the 32-year-old Feld is "a great American artist who must work in the context of his own company." Why? Because Eliot Feld wants his own company—that's why. And because someone at the Rockefeller Foundation is willing to pamper him.

So who is this Eliot Feld who, a year ago, received a $35,000 development grant and a $225,000 matching grant from the Rockefeller Foundation, a $15,000 Shubert grant, free use of a theater for two engagements a year at the Public Theater, and facilities, when available, at the Vivian Beaumont Theater, office space and the like, courtesy of Joseph Papp of the New York Shakespeare Festival?

Eliot is a brilliant product of New York City's remarkable High School of Performing Arts. He was, and is, a brilliant dancer, especially an actor-dancer. In 1967 he gave to the world a brilliant new choreographer: himself. Everyone was ecstatic over *Harbinger,* produced by the company that had nurtured him, the American Ballet Theatre. He followed this with another smash success, *At Midnight,* for the ABT. I found it a pleasure to write in *SR* (December 23, 1967) about "one of the most exciting and original choreographic talents to emerge in American ballet since Jerome Robbins made his choreographic debut."

In 1969 Feld's American Ballet Company came into being under the auspices of the Brooklyn Academy of Music, as a co-recipient with Merce Cunningham and Alvin Ailey and their companies, of Rockefeller funds, and with help from both the National Endowment for the Arts and the New York State Council on the Arts. It was easy to be direct and to say "an important American company has come into vibrant being," even while questioning the

639

advisability of forming a new company when there were already too many hard-pressed groups.

Why did Feld leave the company that had nurtured him, that had honored him both as dancer and choreographer? In *Ballet Review* (Vol. 3, No. 6, 1971), he answered this question: "Because they wouldn't make me director of the company. They wouldn't give me the whole company to do with what I liked." Feld also analyzed, in the same publication, his own importance to one of the major ballet institutions of our era, the American Ballet Theatre: "When I started choreographing for BT, they hadn't had a successful new ballet in years." He clarified this point by saying, "Ballet Theatre without its *Swan Lake* and *Giselle* and Natalia Makarova would be zero. Absolutely zero." The American Ballet Theatre repertory, it need hardly be pointed out, includes Balanchine, Robbins, Tudor, de Mille, Ashton, Bournonville, MacMillan, Massine, Fokine, Ailey, Limón . . . Need I go on? He did have a kind word for one choreographer other than himself: "I think Petipa was really quite good."

So the American Ballet Theatre, which had nurtured him but had not capitulated to him, was not right for his talent. He tried working with other companies. He made *Meadowlark,* a lovely, sunny classical ballet, for the Royal Winnipeg Ballet. But it was finished only because the Royal dancers had protested Feld's behavior vehemently and had threatened to strike. It was only then that their director told his guest choreographer to behave or leave. The trials and tribulations of the Royal Swedish Ballet with Feld's tantrums, demands, and behavior were narrated to me by that troupe's director in a list of Feld outrages that outdid Agatha Christie in matters of suspense. And so it has gone with other companies.

Is such behavior shocking? Not really. Only the most naive would think that great artists are nice people. Usually they are not. It is probably safe to say that more tears have been shed in Robbins or Tudor rehearsals than at all the viewings of the TV soap serial *As the World Turns.* So the fact that Feld has gone from an *enfant terrible* to just plain *terrible* is not of great moment. What is important is that Robbins, as difficult as he is—sometimes almost impossible—can choreograph successfully for companies other than the New York City Ballet (his home base under the Balanchine aegis), as can Tudor, and almost any other choreographer you care to name.

It is easy to say, "Well, if Martha Graham has her own company, why shouldn't Eliot?" Graham started a company of her own in the Twenties because she had invented a new way of dance, and only her own trainees could perform what she created. Dancers then, and up to recently, were likely to be specialists in some technique, style, or phase of dance. No longer. Today, we have total dancers. In almost any professional ballet company, Feld can find dancers capable of doing his bidding. Certainly he had them in the American Ballet Theatre—he even took some of them with him.

640

One major dance writer, when the Eliot Feld Ballet received its Rockefeller *largesse,* suggested that it was a calculated esthetic gamble and indicated that it would probably pay off. It had better. Feld now has everything he has asked for (well, not quite; I am sure there is more, but I dread to think what), and the masterpieces should flow. They haven't yet. *Harbinger, At Midnight, Intermezzo, Theatre* (wonderful when Feld plays Pierrot in it), and one or two more came earlier in his career. But lately there have been misses, more than would have happened if he had been disciplined by specific commissions from other companies, thus reducing demands on his choreographic output and general energy.

The newest Feld ballet, *The Real McCoy,* a tribute to Gershwin with a Cole Porter title and with two dancers and a mobile *chaise*, could have been tossed off in an afternoon by any good hack dance arranger. It was months in preparation. That costs money. *The Gods Amused*? Why not ask Balanchine for his great *Apollo* instead? Some other Feld creations have been abandoned or retired, perhaps because they did not attain a Petipa level of "quite good."

As the months roll by in 1975 and into our celebration for 1976, in dance as well as in the other arts, we shall hope that the Rockefeller gamble pays off, that it was right to dismiss Feld's nurturing by some of the great existing dance troupes of the world and to give him the pampering he demanded, the pampering due one who apparently feels he has no living (and few dead) choreographic peers. For if such American monies are wasted, then we must mourn even more deeply the passing of the National Ballet and others that may falter and fail when such monies might have saved them for longer periods of dedicated and vital service to the dance in America.

Yes, Eliot Feld will have to prove himself to be God's gift to ballet if the ballet profession is to put up with his demand for funds with which to do exactly as he pleases, with his impossible behavior when he guests with distinguished companies, with his arrogance, and with examples of rudeness that are too crude to report. If he is, in truth, a genius, none of this will matter. If he is simply a pampered pet, he may well merit the description that my drama colleague Walter Kerr once leveled at a remarkably confident person who had brought to Broadway a show which he had written, which he had directed, in which he had starred—it sticks in my mind that he had also composed music and lyrics—and which bombed. Mr. Kerr's comment, as I recall, was "I fear that this young man has delusions of adequacy." [*Saturday Review*]

641

Capsule Comments

April 19, 1975

In the City Center Joffrey Ballet's fall season, Gerald Arpino's *The Relativity of Icarus,* a duet for near-nude youths augmented by a virtuosa in orbit about them, was vulgar, pretentious claptrap redeemed only by Rouben Ter-Arutunian's brilliant setting of a spaceship on an outerspace platform. In a company that eschews stars, Rebecca Wright is emerging as a ballerina—that is, a performer with personal impact, personal style, and presence as well as technique. And Burton Taylor, beginning to shed his blandness, may well turn into a danseur. Sir Frederick Ashton's *Monotones* (Satie), newly added to the Joffrey repertory, is the epitome of what we mean by "pure" dance. The company itself? Lovely!

Mummenschanz, the Swiss Mime Theater, is not strictly dance, but its movement inventions, combined with masks and props that are surprisingly simple (you could make them yourself) but employed with brilliant ingenuity, make for entertainment that would delight anyone from the diaper generation to the dowager with her diadem.

The American Ballet Theatre's new star, Mikhail Baryshnikov, the most recent dance defector from the Soviet Union, is a remarkable artist—not only a dazzling virtuoso but also an impeccable stylist—one whose personal verve and physical prowess never coarsen the linear elegance, the aristocratic deportment, of classical ballet. Gelsey Kirkland, who defected from Balanchine's New York City Ballet in order to become Baryshnikov's favorite partner, is another major American Ballet Theatre acquisition. She has been a fascinating dancer for some seasons, but now, released from the New York City Ballet's impersonal performing requirements, she has become a stage personality—yes, a ballerina.

Rudolf Nureyev, the U.S.S.R.'s most celebrated defector, is inexhaustible or perhaps desperate to dance as much as he can while he can; so he can be found dancing almost anywhere. And whether he is dancing barefoot with Paul Taylor's modern dancers or dancing shod with the slippers of the danseur noble, he remains a titan among today's dancing gods.

Agnes de Mille's Heritage Dance Theatre is an American answer to the U.S.S.R.'s famed, folkloric Moiseyev Dance Company, and Miss de Mille's "Conversations About the Dance," a lecture-demonstration employing some members of the Heritage group, is a wonderfully theatrical answer to whatever questions we may have about our own dance heritage. "Conversations" is not simply instructional, although one learns a great deal painlessly; rather, it is a rousing and unique pas de deux, co-starring the wittiest of today's dance leaders, Miss de Mille, and the second oldest profession, the dance.

642

The José Limón Dance Company, the first modern dance troupe to survive the passing of its founder–director–choreographer–star, is very much alive under the direction of Ruth Currier. In New York and on the road, it performs with vigor and the exhilarating freshness of new performers giving new interpretations to great roles in a repertory choreographed over the years by Limón. Soon it will be adding more Doris Humphrey masterpieces to its offerings.

The Royal Swedish Ballet in its U.S. debut was thoroughly sabotaged by its sponsor, Hurok Concerts. James Moore, the American director of the Royal Swedes, told me that Hurok officers had insisted the troupe bring its full-length *Swan Lake* and divertissements from *The Sleeping Beauty*—both requiring superstars, both overdone—and the result was near disaster for a fine company that excels in its unique court ballets from Drottningholm, in a Swedish folk version of *The Prodigal Son,* in Jerome Robbins's *Les Noces,* in Léonide Massine's *Le Sacre du printemps,* and in other specialties. Hurok Concerts would not let the Swedes bring their matchless smorgasbord but insisted on imitation ballet borscht. Earlier in the year, Columbia Artists Management was equally guilty in sabotaging its presentation of the Norwegian National Ballet, for the same reasons, as well as inexcusable rehearsal skimping.

The New York City Ballet's new *Coppélia* production is a delight in those scenes that were staged by Alexandra Danilova in the tradition of this great comedy classic, in which she was once the definitive interpreter of the role of Swanilda, the mischievous heroine. The new presentation falters badly when George Balanchine attempts drastic changes in the first act's mazurka and czardas and in almost all of the third act, where his new variations miss the lilt, the bounce, the jollity, and, yes, the *schmaltz* of the old version. In fact, the new figure of Prayer looks for all the world like the head chorine at a Las Vegas nightspot. Ter-Arutunian's designs for the last act, reminiscent of the sugary *Nutcracker,* are totally inappropriate to this bright, Hungarian-spiced ballet. But elsewhere with the New York City Ballet, you'll find some Balanchine masterpieces, some fine performing, and, in young Colleen Neary, an exuberant dancer who alone is worth the price of admission.

Pilar Rioja, if listed anywhere, must be seen! Veteran Spanish-dance followers tell me there has been no one like her since La Argentina (not the later great Argentinita). She is not all gypsy—the current trend in Spanish dance—but although her flamenco and gypsy-flavored dances are brilliant, she is also a superb classicist. Her dances, spanning a glorious swath of Spanish-dance expressivity, are performed in conjunction with a challenging, stirring text (in Spanish), an essay on the mystery of *duende,* by Frederico García Lorca.

Stars of the Bolshoi Ballet brought to us Maya Plisetskaya's incomparable art—beauty of line, mesmeric presence, glorious individuality—in excerpts from

643

Swan Lake, in her unforgettable *The Dying Swan,* and in a new work created especially for her by Roland Petit, *La Rose malade,* in which, partnered by the Nordic-hero-like Aleksandr Godunov, she created an identity (not through imitation) with the ephemeral life-span of a fragrant, tremulous flower. If hopes are realized, we will see her again when the Bolshoi Ballet itself returns to the United States next summer. [*Saturday Review*]

1976

George & Martha, Rudi, Misha & Ivan . . . But Especially Walter

Nureyev in the Graham style • Danced salutes to America's Bicentennial • National vs. International at ABT • Ballet unadorned in Balanchine's splendid Chaconne • The Soviet ballet in decline • Ashton's newest masterpiece, A Month in the Country premiered by Royal Ballet at the Met • Patrick Dupond, teenage French dancer, wins gold medal at International Ballet Competition, Varna, Bulgaria • Three ballet superstars – Mikhail Baryshnikov, Rudolf Nureyev, and, especially, Ivan Nagy

Danced Salutes to the U.S.A.

January 24, 1976

Well over a year ago, as the Bicentennial of the United States of America approached, American dance companies were frantically casting about for suitably patriotic ballets. There were those who desperately wanted performing permission for George Balanchine's enormously popular *Stars and Stripes*, the Russian-born ballet master's amused and amusing glance at his adopted country's love of parades, precision drills, and field days. In lieu of the Balanchine hit, with its irresistible Sousa score (arranged and orchestrated by that musical whiz, Hershy Kay), ballet directors from coast to coast were (and are) willing to settle for "something like *Stars and Stripes*" or stepping to Sousa or Stephen Foster, Charles Ives or Scott Joplin.

But a celebration of America does not necessarily mean a red-white-and-blue ballet or one built upon American tunes or one rooted in folklore. I have seen examples of these, good and bad, and still others from different sources during the first lap of my ballet Bicentennial travels, starting last year and continuing through 1976, and of those I have seen to date the most important is a ballet based on Maxwell Anderson's great American play *Winterset*.

645

Pittsburgh, Pa. The Pittsburgh Ballet Theatre's Bicentennial productions include a revival of Ruth Page's now historic *Frankie and Johnny* (1938), Nicolas Petrov's new *Steel Symphony* (both scheduled for later this month), and Stuart Sebastian's *Winterset,* which had its immensely successful premiere (with cheering audiences and enthusiastic reviews) at the end of the year. This new creation by the 25-year-old choreographer is not only a superb ballet but also a masterwork of danced theater. In 1935, when the Anderson play, a poetic drama of the Depression, of revenge, of love, and of dying, was first done, we of the dance world were watching with eagerness the use of dance to extend the range of drama in such musicals as *Oklahoma!* with Agnes de Mille's trend-setting choreography. Today, when the ballet trend has been the evolution of abstract, non-dramatic ballets by George Balanchine and his imitators and a rash of recital-like dances to piano music, Sebastian has made a new breakthrough in giving us a ballet that extends itself in the other direction, into the actor's arena.

The setting, by Oren Parker, would do honor to a Broadway play, with its dark and forbidding street scene under a towering bridge span and with a mobile tenement unit (in one episode it moves with a melodramatic surge of choreography). The music by Heitor Villa-Lobos (*Etude in C-Sharp minor for guitar; Concerto for Guitar and Orchestra; Prelude No. 4* for guitar) provides the work sometimes with the taut and astringent base it requires and again with the haunting sweet sadness of family love and young love fated for destruction. But the key to this *Winterset* is its choreodramatic structure. Sebastian has used acting where the succinct gesture of the actor is what is needed, so phrasing it musically that it can swell into danced gesture and explode, when necessary, into stage-filling, aerial, tracing movement without a wrench, without a break.

In a prologue and three scenes, Sebastian relates the story, suggested by the Sacco–Vanzetti case of the Twenties, and reveals the emotions of the Jewish father for whom family and home are sacred, of the Italian youth whose father has been falsely accused of murdering a guard during a robbery, of the gangsters in fear of betrayal, and, especially, of the boy and the girl from opposing families who love despite. The dancing core of *Winterset* is the pas de deux for the young lovers; yet at the close, in the death scene, they are asked to be actors.

The Pittsburgh Ballet Theatre, under Sebastian's directing, turns out dancing actors. One is not surprised to see the part of Esdras, the girl's father, superlatively acted by Frederic Franklin, a great danseur of a generation ago and a masterful mime of today. But young JoAnn McCarthy as Miriamne, the daughter, and Gregory Begley, as Mio, son of the accused Romagna, have been guided into infusing the force of acting into the sweep of their dancing. Splendid also are Roger Triplett as Garth, Miriamne's weakling brother and false witness, and Peter Degnan as Trock, the murderer. The entire cast has given new stature to the Pittsburgh Ballet Theatre and done honor to Maxwell Anderson in a trend-setting choreodrama by an exceptionally gifted new choreographer.

East Haddam, Conn. *Very Good Eddie,* given its world premiere (in revival, that is) at the absolutely captivating century-old Goodspeed Opera House on the banks of the Connecticut River, is pure Americana of the show-biz variety. It is a musical comedy, just opened on Broadway, and I touch on it because its dance elements are delicious Bicentennial stuff. The period is 1913, and the characters, involved in all sorts of marital entanglements, are pretty much stock figures from the era of stock companies. The dance buff, however, will find it a real treat, for Bill Gile, the director, has staged the musical numbers with great wit in terms of gesture, stance, and tableaux, and the choreographer, Dan Siretta, has come up with some show-stopping numbers that are delicious evocations of both the social dances and the vaudeville routines of the day. "I've Got to Dance" is the high point in a batch of dance highs. For me, the show is an American answer to the English *The Boy Friend.*

New York City The City Center Joffrey Ballet's *Drums, Dreams and Banjos,* since it is set to music of Stephen Foster and is produced at Bicentennial time, presumably represents this company's major Americana offering. If, by Americana, one will accept cheap American camp as a substitute, then one must accept this as a distressing aspect of our culture. Stephen Foster is corn, but it is genuine. Agnes de Mille's classic *Rodeo* is a corn ballet, but it, too, is genuine. Both are as real and as nourishing as that indigenously American feed grain that describes them. But *Drums* is simply surface camp, rootless, unappetizing, without substance.

I must, in all honesty, report that sections of the audiences at the City Center's 55th Street Theater applauded the production enthusiastically, but I can also report that passages intended to be taken seriously were laughed at, that there were boos, and that more than one person retreated up the aisle murmuring, "I don't believe it!" But there will be later, better ballets to do choreographic honor to the beloved American composer. [*Saturday Review*]

Nureyev in the Graham Style

February 7, 1976

It was a curious twosome—a Siberian Tartar who had defected from the Soviet Union not much more than a decade ago, and the descendant of one who had reached our shores on the good ship *Mayflower*—that made Bicentennial history in Americana programs on Broadway a few weeks ago. It is hardly surprising that Martha Graham, of Miles Standish lineage, should celebrate two centuries of America's independence with her now-classic *Appalachian Spring* (the composer, Aaron Copland, conducting), with her new *The Scarlet Letter* of Nathaniel Hawthorne, and with other dance-dramas rooted in the American heritage. What is surprising, however, is that in both *Spring* and *Letter* a classically trained premier danseur, Rudolf Nureyev, should be starred. But perhaps it is not so surprising. America has had a place for immigrants since the time of . . . Miles Standish.

The question is: how did the onetime danseur of Russia's Kirov Ballet do in this totally different technique and style—a school of modern dance that Miss Graham, a half-century ago, originated in rebellion against other then-prevailing dance forms, ballet especially? Nureyev did splendidly. He was by no means perfect—not by a long shot. Ballet, to generalize, focuses upon the contours of the moving body, upon the exquisite or dazzling use of the arms and legs and head in placements or in action. Modern dance is centered in the torso, in the spine (Martha Graham refers to it as the individual's "tree of life"), and, with Graham particularly, in the viscera. Nureyev's difficulty was finding the dance within his body and bringing it forth.

But Nureyev, the most brilliant star in the ballet world, tried. He played the role of the Revivalist (not the calmer part of the Husbandman, or hero) in *Appalachian Spring,* and his own Tartar fierceness, his personal incantational forces, vulcanized the less than perfect segments of his performance. Few were bothered by his Russian looks as a Midwestern preacher, for Slavic immigrants to the Appalachians have been common rather than uncommon, and one possessed by religion is a breed apart.

Miss Graham completed choreographing *The Scarlet Letter* (with its commissioned score by Hunter Johnson) on the day of the world premiere (December 22). Thus, it is hardly surprising that the new ballet has not yet had a chance to jell, that it has not yet had time to find, through its dancers, its total dynamic thrust. Miss Graham invariably reworks her dancer after their initial performances; so at the moment it would be best to classify *The Scarlet Letter* not only as a work-in-progress but also as a work-of-promise.

In a curtain talk before the premiere, Miss Graham stated firmly that she was not treating the Hawthorne story literally, that it was the preacher Dimmesdale, not Hester Prynne, who was the sinner. It was not surprising, then, to see a scarlet *A* on the breast of the tormented (the book hints at a self-branding) Dimmesdale as the curtain rose, and to see not a narrative but those elements of lust, guilt, bigotry, envy, and torture from which the tale evolves. (Miss Graham commented that her Puritan ancestors, "wherever they are"—and she cast her eyes heavenward and downward—"probably won't approve of this.") Nureyev performed well as Dimmesdale (he'll be brilliant in the part when the ballet is finally set), and Janet Eilber was superb as Hester. Unstinted praise from the start goes to Marisol for a mood-rich setting in which a pulpit becomes a sacrificial altar and two swirling ramps suggest the pathways to hope or . . . to damnation.

Nureyev, who had bowed in the Graham style last summer in a work especially created for him by Miss Graham, *Lucifer,* at a 50th-anniversary (of the Graham company) gala, repeated that passable portrayal in a Graham work which is itself barely passable. But moving into the role of Oedipus in *Night Journey,* he acquitted himself well. There were bad insecurities, but his exit, following his self-blinding, was the essence of monumental tragedy. Rudolf Nureyev is an immigrant to the field of modern dance, but a valuable newcomer.

The total Graham season at the Mark Hellinger Theater—the longest modern-dance engagement in Broadway history—was a triumph. The 81-year-old matriarch of modern dance, celebrating the 50th birthday of her company as well as her 60th anniversary as a dancer (although she is now retired) and the completion of 152 dance works, presented a repertory including the three premieres—*The Scarlet Letter*; the rambling and over-draped, over-décored *Point of Crossing*; the delightful *Adorations,* a "staged" Graham technique class—as well as masterpieces going back to such historic Graham solos as *Lamentation* and *Frontier,* the later *Letter to the World* (a danced biography of the outer and inner lives of Emily Dickinson), and the late, great period of tragedies, comedies, myths relating the figures of the ancient Greek theater to the ageless behavior of mortals.

The Graham company is a glorious one. Takako Asakawa and Yuriko Kimura are superb in roles created by Miss Graham, and Diane Gray, who resembles Graham in appearance not at all, still moves with the same mercurial speed, the lovely lilt, as the Bride in *Appalachian Spring.* Of the men dancers— and they are handsome, virile, and virtuosic—the single most valuable is a comparative newcomer, Tim Wengerd, a master technician and a most versatile player of multiple roles. Ross Parkes, too, is an invaluable member of the troupe; and Robert Irving, moonlighting from his permanent post as musical director of the New York City Ballet, brings special distinction to Graham seasons.

Miss Graham, Rudolf Nureyev, and danced Americana are scheduled to repeat the historic collaboration with an international historic event July 19, when the Martha Graham Dance Company opens an engagement in London as the first modern-dance troupe to perform on the stage of the Royal Opera House, Covent Garden, in the 118-year history of that famous theater. Nureyev will be there too, for the gala opening—his only appearance—on the all-Americana program when the Tartar boy from Ufa, Siberia, plays an American pioneer in *Appalachian Spring.* [*Saturday Review*]

649

ABT: National vs. International

February 21, 1976

Unrest has struck the most glittering of America's ballet companies, the American Ballet Theatre. The New York press has duly reported that the troupe's American dancers have been distressed with the number of guest artists from abroad who have seemingly displaced them. And, in rebuttal, Lucia Chase and Oliver Smith, ABT's co-directors, have carefully pointed out that Richard Pleasant, the company's founder (with Miss Chase), stated in 1939, "We want this company to be American in spirit and international in scope." It has been—and is—exactly that.

The present company disenchantment with ABT's directors was brought to public attention because the troupe's American prima ballerina, Cynthia Gregory, left the company—the company in which she had been promoted from corps de ballet to stardom (by Miss Chase) with dazzling swiftness (slightly more than one year). A part of the press and a number of ballet fans chose to believe that she retired from ballet at 29 because she was not getting the roles she wanted, rather than for her stated reason of personal matters. Miss Gregory did not leave ABT; she retired, by her own explanation, from ballet itself, presumably only temporarily. ABT has mounted a three-act ballet, *Tales of Hoffman,* especially for her, and the three-act *Raymonda,* staged by Rudolf Nureyev, was produced mainly for her (with Nureyev guesting as her partner).

No, unrest is not a novelty with ABT, or, indeed, with any theatrical troupe. The first superstars of The Ballet Theatre (as it was initially named) were Britain's Alicia Markova and Anton Dolin, the Fonteyn and Nureyev of their era. There were Russians, too—Irina Baronova, the celebrated "Baby Ballerina," for one; and long before the dazzling Mikhail Baryshnikov of today there was the equally dazzling Jean Babilée (from France) of yesterday. But they and other imported stars did not snuff out the talents of Nora Kaye and Alicia Alonso (who rose from corps to ballerina status and fought over billing), John Kriza (who became the first American classical dancer of international renown), and a gifted lad named Jerome Robbins.

The 1976 ABT grumblings are little different from, say, 1946 grumblings, and it should not be overlooked that elsewhere in ballet circles, Nureyev, on his defection, did some displacing in Britain's Royal Ballet; that the great Stuttgart Ballet is headed by a Brazilian ballerina and an American premier danseur rather than by Germans.

During the American Ballet Theatre's winter run at the Uris, there were glorious opportunities for savoring the American-international flavors of this great company. Take *Giselle* to start with. It's the most celebrated example of the Romantic Age of Ballet (1832–1850), approximately), and although of French birth it belongs to the world of dance. The first cast for this season was headed by Gelsey Kirkland (American) in the title part, Baryshnikov (Russian) as Albrecht, Martine van Hamel (Dutch) as the Queen of the Wilis, and Frank Smith (American) as Hilarion. Miss Kirkland, fragile in appearance and steel-strong technically, is one of the best Giselles to be found. Baryshnikov is, in many ways (esthetically as well as in spectacular virtuosities), one of the great dance artists of the age. How marvelous!—what an honor!—to have them, to see them, to cherish their dancing together.

Frank Smith is not renowned. One might say he is unsung; yet he is the finest interpreter of the role of Hilarion—Giselle's true love, her spurned love, her devoted friend—to be seen today. This is not the part for a purveyor of balletic fireworks; it's a role for a superior actor–dancer, and Smith is that actor. ABT's long-applauded corps de ballet shimmers, in Act 2, as the ghostly wilis. Miss van Hamel, technically strong, plays the Myrtha role more like a bossy suburban women's club president than an elegantly imperious queen (Alexandra Danilova was the perfect Myrtha).

Another *Giselle* had two Italians, Carla Fracci and Paolo Bortoluzzi, as the ill-fated lovers, and they gave us different insights into *Giselle,* as do ABT's American Eleanor d'Antuono or the most passionate *Giselle* lovers to be seen, Russia's Natalia Makarova and Hungary's Ivan Nagy, the flawless partnership.

The season was given a special fillip—nothing profound, but greatly exciting—when Japan's Yoko Morishita and our own Fernando Bujones, both gold medalists of the 1974 International Ballet Competition at Varna, Bulgaria, pulled out all the stops for a bravura performance of the "Black Swan" pas de deux from *Swan Lake.* And they were topped a few nights later by Kirkland and Baryshnikov in the grand pas de deux from *Don Quixote,* in which they had their own private international competition going to see who could outdo whom.

Baryshnikov is not without fault, as masterful as he is. ABT revived Michel Fokine's *Le Spectre de la Rose* (originally created for Waslaw Nijinsky and Tamara Karsavina) for Baryshnikov, and although André Eglevsky, the restager, taught him what he remembered of the steps, he didn't direct him. The star emerged as a man in a dreadful pink costume doing gorgeous leaps. In my memory, the best recent *Spectre* was done by Niels Kehlet of the Royal Danish Ballet and Lone Isaksen (also a Dane). Kehlet not only displayed the necessary aerial prowess, but, more important, played the part as if it were not a man but a creature, and a creature that existed, evanescently, only in the girl's dreams. Miss Isaksen, with minimal dancing, communicated the magic of those dreams. Baryshnikov, however, in a masterpiece such as Antony Tudor's *Shadowplay,* has continued to grow in the role, and today his physically exhilarating prowess is equaled by his intensely moving portrayal of a boy—yes, "a creature"—who is to become lord of the jungle, the jungle of trees or the jungle of life.

And, concluding on the American-international theme of ABT, let me point out that one of the season's major premieres, *Hamlet Connotations,* though it unfortunately turned out to be choreographic claptrap, boasted an international cast of awesome prestige, breathtaking glamor, and, very possibly, unequaled talent. It was composed of Baryshnikov (Hamlet), Russian; Kirkland (Ophelia), American; Marcia Haydée (Queen Gertrude), Brazilian prima of the Stuttgart; Erik Bruhn (King Claudius), a Dane long associated with both the Royal Danish Ballet and ABT; and William Carter (Ghost of Hamlet's Father), a Cherokee.

The choreography was by John Neumeier, American director of the Hamburg Opera Ballet in Germany, and the score was made up of music composed by the American Aaron Copland (*Piano Variations; Connotations for Orchestra; Piano Fantasy*). It was lustily cheered, as well as soundly booed, at its premiere. The performers earned the cheers, but could have earned them if they had come on stage and done a ballet class. The choreography? The businessman father of an actor friend of mine, when asked for his reaction to a classical ballet performance, remarked, "Well they seem to get from one awkward position to another awkward position very gracefully." In Neumeier's *Hamlet,* and in some other things he has wrought, his policy is to get from one awkward position to another awkward position as awkwardly as possible.

Hamlet has survived disastrous performances before, and the American Ballet Theatre has also survived disastrously bad, or just dismal, ballets. It has also survived personnel unrest to become, as the late Mr. Pleasant planned and Miss Chase and Mr. Smith have since implemented, a company "American in spirit and international in scope." (Think about America's Metropolitan Opera personnel for a minute.) So "Bravo" Misha and "Bravo" Frank; and "Brava" Carla and "Brava" Gelsey. And "Bravi!" to Lucia Chase and Oliver Smith, who have been making American (and international) ballet history for more than three decades. [*Saturday Review*]

Ballet Unadorned

March 20, 1976

George Balanchine is the greatest, and most elegant, strip artist of them all. It has been his special genius, over the past decades, to rediscover and redirect the viewer's attention to the movement of ballet, movements stripped of all trappings. Perhaps his company, the New York City Ballet, has concentrated too much and too often on ballets without story, without scenery, and without elaborate costumes, but for the best of ballet that is pure and spare and unadorned, you will most often find it with the New York City Ballet, and, most certainly, in the works of Balanchine.

He began his stripping a long time ago. One of his enduring masterworks in this idiom is *Concerto Barocco* (Bach's *Concerto in D minor for Two Violins*). It isn't baroque at all, but it once was—when it was first presented, with scenery and incredibly elaborate costumes by Eugene Berman, by the American Ballet (ancestor of the NYCB) in 1941. When it was given by the Ballet Russe de Monte Carlo in 1945, Balanchine staged it with simple ballet practice clothes (black and white) only. Balanchine's *The Four Temperaments* (Hindemith), when presented by Ballet Society (the immediate forerunner of NYCB) in 1946, had elaborate surrealist costumes and scenery by Kurt Seligmann. These were discarded in 1952 in favor of standard practice clothes.

Concerto Barocco and *Four T's,* unadorned, remain flawless examples of classical ballet, and they probably always will. The former is almost totally traditional in step and stance, and the latter is an extension of ballet into newer areas of motor expression and design.

Truthfully, when new ballets of this genre keep coming from the prolific Balanchine, one can occasionally murmur, "Oh, no, not again." But then the master turns up with a masterpiece of stripping, as he did recently with *Chaconne* (to ballet music from Gluck's *Orphée et Euridice*). The ballet is derived from an opera ballet that Balanchine did for the Hamburg State Opera in 1963. Then, within the opera itself, it had elaborate costumes. For the NYCB presentation, the strip-master has peeled off everything to reveal the unencumbered movements of his dancers' bodies. The result is captivating.

Watching *Chaconne,* one has the curious feeling that he is being permitted to peek beneath the costumes of courtiers, not as a voyeur but as a connoisseur. Here are pas de deux, pas de trois, pas de cinq, and the concluding chaconne (usually the extended finale of Gluck operas) evocative of those court dances from which ballet evolved. Without hooped skirts, puffed sleeves, awesome farthingale constructions, plumes, doublets, and whatnot, we can see what actually happened underneath all the rich impedimenta. And it is all lovely.

Of course, Balanchine has not simply reproduced the steps, the gestures, the *révérences* of courtly dances—he has shown us the evolutions of those forms into ballet—but he has also retained all of the elegance, much of the form, and hints of the formalities. Louis Horst, the modern-dance composer and authority on pre-classic dance forms, once wrote of the chaconne, "When the court tired of it, it found a place on the stage." As staged by a master, the Balanchine *Chaconne* will never grow tiresome. [*Saturday Review*]

Soviet Ballet Is Down at the Heel

May 23, 1976

If you want to set the record straight about where the greatest ballet in the world is to be found, go to Russia. You *won't* find it there. It is possible—even probable—that you will find better ballet right here at home. No, I'm not being chauvinistic. Don't even take my word for it. Ask some Russians. Ask Rudolf Nureyev, Natalia Makarova, Mikhail Baryshnikov. They know where the best ballet is to be found. Not in Moscow. Not in Leningrad, which they left behind them. They were not defecting from Communism, even though many Americans would like to think they were; they were escaping a state-controlled ballet system that suffocates choreographic creativity and strangles ballet enterprise.

When the mighty Bolshoi Ballet from Moscow visited America last year, it didn't seem nearly as mighty as it had when its huge ensembles, soaring soloists and glittering stars (such as Galina Ulanova, called "The Wonder of the World," and the blazing Maya Plisetskaya) first stunned us in 1959. The reviews in 1975 were not unqualified raves. Many were tough. Audiences grumbled. Expressions of boredom greeted the huge, operatic-style *Spartacus,* so big that it had to be given in stripped-down productions in most American cities. Even Yuri Grigorovitch's more mammoth *Ivan the Terrible* didn't escape criticism. What had happened to the Bolshoi, a word which can mean big, grand or possibly great? It returned to us with only one meaning intact: "big."

It was pretty clear what had happened in the intervening decade and a half: our own dancers had mastered all of the physical and technical tricks the Bolshoi had introduced, and what had been novelty had become standard ballet fare. But since 1976 was not only the American Bicentennial but also the 200th anniversary of the founding of the Bolshoi Ballet, I headed for the Soviet Union in order to see the celebrated company on its home territory and, presumably, at its best in a gala year. I attended more than a dozen performances in both Moscow and Leningrad, and what I saw wasn't very good. Much of it was downright bad, and some of it was actually disgraceful.

The companies whose productions I saw were the Bolshoi, the Ballet of the Stanislavsky Theater (it has a longer title but this will identify it) and a youth group headed by Yuri Zhdanov (American dance fans will remember him as the Romeo to Ulanova's Juliet in 1959) in Moscow, and the Kirov Ballet (once the Imperial Maryinsky from which emerged Pavlova, Nijinsky, Karsavina and Fokine, the early defectors, as well as George Balanchine, Alexandra Danilova and the rest of the present crop of illustrious emigrés) and the Ballet of the Maly Theater in Leningrad. Of these, the best by far in both choreography and performing was the Stanislavsky Ballet. The single exception was a performance at the Bolshoi in which the always marvelous Plisetskaya, superbly supported by Alexandr Godunov (recently forbidden to tour outside the Soviet Union with Plisetskaya), took over most of the evening with two choreographically inferior vehicles, *Carmen Suite* (created for her by Cuba's Alberto Alonso) and *La Rose Malade* (by France's Roland Petit).

What is so bad about Russian ballet today? First, Soviet choreography is way behind the times; it hasn't even caught up with Michel Fokine, whose ballet innovations stem from Paris in 1909. I saw some brand new ballets, but they were so old-fashioned that, except for the dancing on pointe (unknown in ballet before 1800) and related virtuosities, they would not surprise Marie Antoinette if she were to return today. The familiar structure of the choreography includes solos and duos, ensemble dances and precision-like drills for swans or workers, warriors or courtiers. In addition, the movements used to define character or forward the plot are acted out separately from the actual dancing, quite unlike the total integration of acting and dancing found in ballets by Jerome Robbins, Antony Tudor, Agnes de Mille, John Cranko, Frederick Ashton or, in modern dance, Martha Graham.

True, today's Russian choreographers feel that they are updating old ballets and pressing forward choreographically by replacing old-time, traditional ballet mime (with its stylized sign language) with realistic acting. But the results of this so-called modernizing process have two unfortunate aspects: first, because they do not integrate the action of dance with dramatic expressivity, they are right back where they left off in esthetic dichotomy; and second, most of the Soviet dancers don't act, they emote—and one of the Random House dictionary definitions of emote is "to act a part often without talent."

Let me give you a typical example of such acting. In the Bolshoi's *The Fountain of Bakhschiserai* (a 1934 ballet), the Khan, having lost by violent deaths both his newly abducted love and his old harem favorite, goes to the side of the stage and bangs his forehead, presumably in sorrow, against a proscenium drape which isn't even a part of the set.

More worrisome is the plight of young choreographers. Konstantin Sergeyev, the veteran principal choreographer of the Kirov, told me that young choreographers must attend choreographic school for six years, following graduation from the regular state ballet school, before being permitted to even attempt workshop dances. This makes the choreographic hopefuls about 24 before they are allowed to experiment, even under strict supervision. Thus, if a young Russian has a choreographic gift, his first hope is to survive both student servitude and bureaucratic control—and his second hope, if all else fails, is to defect.

No outside influences are permitted, either. With very few exceptions, the government does not permit choreographers from non-Communist countries to come in and stage modern ballets. It is clear that the Soviet Union would not lose one dancer to the West if it offered the range of artistic opportunity the West offers.

Even worse than the choreography was the performing. Plisetskaya and her young Godunov, as I have noted, were among the exceptions. There were, of course, some individual performances of merit, of authority and occasionally of some brilliance. But in general the Bolshoi and Kirov dancers are sloppy. On stage they often loll and lounge and talk to each other when they are not actually dancing. If chewing gum were not frowned on by the state, I have no doubt that they would be happily and noisily chewing during the court dances in *Swan Lake*.

American audiences may remember some splendid corps de ballet dancing by the Bolshoi and Kirov on American tours. But what we see in the United States are carefully rehearsed companies very often composed of the best dancers from several Soviet troupes. One Soviet principal touring America told me that he had never even met some of the dancers in his troupe until they prepared for the American tour.

Even in matters of individual technique, which once awed us into inferiority complexes about American ballet, there is both carelessness and crudity of style. In 1959 and later, we gasped at Bolshoi leaps. The leaps are still high, but often at the expense of a good classical ballet bodyline, with the lead leg in a grand jeté cleanly piercing space before it while the back leg is permitted to drag along like an enlarged vestigial tail.

The final coup de grace is delivered by Soviet audiences themselves. At almost every performance I attended—in both Moscow and Leningrad—applause was so sparse (except for the Plisetskaya evening) that I found myself beating my palms wildly out of sheer embarrassment for dancers taking curtain calls to almost no response.

It is small wonder that over a period of half a century such greats as Balanchine, Danilova, Geva, Nureyev, Makarova, Baryshnikov and, from satellite Hungary, Ivan Nagy have fled their homelands. The celebrated emigrés are rarely mentioned in the Soviet Union, but one day in an airport bus a rather jolly Intourist guide shouted across the aisle: "How are our ballet defectors?" When I told her of their new accomplishments, she said, "Well, you certainly got our best." Then hurriedly she added, "But we've got lots of good ones left." How long, I wondered, would it be before they left, too? [*New York Times*]

656

A Month for All Time in Any Country

July 24, 1976

A masterpiece of art is not bounded by time; nor is it bounded by place, unless it is architecture, and there are some exceptions here (Egypt's transplanted Temple of Abu Simbel or England's transatlanticized London Bridge). A ballet masterpiece has come to America—last spring—and gone, but for those of us who saw it, its images will enrich the memory forever. For those who did not see it, I recommend a journey to wherever it can be seen—very probably London this summer-fall-winter, but worth a trip to anywhere.

This dance masterpiece is *A Month in the Country*, with choreography and book (adapted from the play of Ivan Turgenev) by Sir Frederick Ashton, music of Chopin arranged by John Lanchbery, scenery and costumes by Julia Trevelyan Oman, lighting by William Bundy. I attended every performance of it in New York at the Metropolitan Opera House and went to Washington's Kennedy Center to see it again. Dare one say that anything created by mere man is perfect? This, to me, is. All the coequal ingredients—choreography, music, book, design—of ballet in the traditional, historical sense are seamlessly woven, and the choreographed patterns are given faultless realization by a truly remarkable cast headed by Lynn Seymour, who is, very possibly, the greatest dramatic ballerina of our day, and Anthony Dowell, consummate artist.

It would seem, would it not, that such a play translated into dance would be static, that conversation could not lend itself to movement meta-morphoses. But ah! We are discussing a choreographic genius, and it is indeed within Sir Frederick's powers to make us see words and sentences, soliloquies and dialogues. There is not a static moment in *A Month in the Country*. Serenity, comtemplativeness, even stillness, yes, but a stillness charged with an emotional explosion soon to come.

In gesture, in danced acting, in lyrical dance, and in marvelous bursts of sheer physical virtuosity, Ashton defines character, situation, cumulative incidents, dramatic confrontation, the rending of emotions, resolution. Hilarity and poetry go along easily with drama and characterization, for Sir Frederick is both a master craftsman of choreography and an inspired poet of the dance.

The craftsman. He introduces his key characters with dances set to Chopin's several variations on the Mozart *Don Giovanni* aria *La ci darem là mano,* and, using the different characteristics of the variations as support, he gives each character movements that seem to paint detailed portraits before our eyes.

The poet. With the characteristics of each role clearly defined instantly, Sir Frederick moves his cast into the plot as Beliaev, a young tutor—handsome, dashing, ardent, and desirable—stirs and disturbs the emotions of the ladies of an aristocratic household, engenders angry jealousies, and leaves in order that a family may return to calm normalcy. Not much of a plot? Perhaps not, but the choreographer makes us care about the involvements, curious about the warm but different nature of the romances, concerned with the plight of the neglected suitor, delighted to know the bumbling but endearing head of the household (who loses his keys in a riotous dance sequence), captivated by the ball-bouncing, kite-flying little boy (who entertains himself in games of dazzling virtuosity as danced by Wayne Sleep).

The beautiful sunlit setting, a drawing room opening upon a garden, is both a frame for the portraits and an arena for romantic action, and the glorious costumes have the style, the elegance of the rich of the 1850s. Yes, the characters may be inconsequential and their bouts of love and jealousy not especially important. But Sir Frederick has taken us near to their outer lives and inner confessions. We find ourselves, for the duration of the ballet, engrossed in a sequence of very human experiences—experiences that jar the normal rhythms of their lives and distort, ever so briefly, the comfortable patterns they had established.

As a masterwork of the choreographer's craft and art, *A Month in the Country* represents a new and lofty peak of accomplishment for one of the great ballet-makers of this or any age. It was created this year—1976—just fifty years after Frederick Ashton had choreographed his very first ballet, *Tragedy of Fashion* (for a 1926 revue, *Riverside Nights*). In between there has been an incredible array of great ballets, creations that helped to sweep first Alicia Markova and then Margot Fonteyn to international renown, choreographies of unexcelled beauty and power in such full-length productions as *Romeo and Juliet* (made for the Royal Danish Ballet twenty-one years ago), *Ondine, Sylvia, La Fille mal gardée*, and such shorter dance miracles as the cool and shimmering *Monotones No. 1 and No. 2* or the radiant tribute to Shakespeare, *The Dream* (a danced *Midsummer Night*).

Fifty years and numberless ballets and divertissements later, Sir Frederick has given his own Royal Ballet, which he and Dame Ninette de Valois led to world renown, a new masterpiece. And the Royal dancers, led by Seymour, Dowell, Alexander Grant, Sleep, Derek Rencher, Denise Nunn, and Marguerite Porter, brought it to us. They have gone now, but if you saw them dance *A Month in the Country,* the passage of time means nothing; for the ballet will stay with you always. And if you haven't seen it, well . . . go. Place is unimportant, too . . . just see that you get there. [*Saturday Review*]

658

The Olympics of Ballet Crowns
a New Champion

August 10, 1976

Varna, Bulgaria.   The International Ballet Competition held every two years in this ancient city and modern resort on the Black Sea has been called "the Olympics of dance." This year, while the sports Olympics in Montreal had its fans glued to television sets around the world, ballet buffs converged on Varna for the eighth presentation of the most prestigious of ballet competitions.

What makes Varna so prestigious (other competitions are held in Moscow and Tokyo)? Have a look at some past winners who went on to fame: Mikhail Baryshinkov (1968 Gold Medalist); the Bolshoi's Ekaterina Maximova and Vladimir Vasiliev; Hungary's Ivan Nagy and Canada's Martine van Hamel, now principals with American Ballet Theater; and, most recently America's Fernando Bujones, who not only won a Gold Medal in 1974, but caused the international jury to invent for him a citation of unusual technical achievement. Mr. Bujones had the competition audience screaming like rock fans and returned to his dance alma mater, American Ballet Theatre, to co-star with the elite of the ballet world, including Mr. Baryshnikov, who defected from the Soviet Union at about the same time.

This year, from July 10–25, more than 100 contestants, divided into juniors (14 to 18 years old) and seniors (up to 28) came here as representatives of 27 different countries—empires, kingdoms, democracies, and socialist states. They were graded on technical skill, artistry and individuality by a panel of jurors from 20 nations and chaired by Yuri Grigorovitch, artistic director and principal choreographer of the Bolshoi Ballet, with Allan Fridericia of Denmark and Alicia Alonso of Cuba (who rose to ballet stardom in America) as his first deputies.

To select the top talent of the competition, a jury was almost unnecessary. For the moment that young (just turned 17) Patrick Dupond of France vaulted onto the stage of the beautiful, ivied, moonlit, outdoor theater and pulled off his first sheaf of impeccably accomplished, multiple pirouettes, it was apparent to audience and jury alike that here was a dazzler, a winner, the newest candidate for international fame. Only unforseen technical disaster or a blatant breach of taste could have dislodged that instant triumph. Indeed, Mr. Dupond ultimately earned the highest percentage mark of the 27 finalists on the point-by-point grading system used by the jurors. The jurors, however, had more difficult decisions to make with respect to most of the other contestants. Among the seniors there was no instantly identifiable winner, as Mr. Bujones had been last time. But unquestionably fair balloting and considered deliberation saw to it that the Gold Medal first prize for senior men went to

Rumania's Marin Boyeru, a highly gifted dancer with a fine sense of elegant style to match his technical prowess, and the Silver Medal second prize to the virtuostic, yet artistically sensitive, Mikhail Krapivin of the Soviet Union.

That the standards of the jurors were high and esthetically demanding is attested to by the fact that we felt that none of the senior women was worthy of a Gold Medal.

Second-place Silver Medals were awarded to Czechoslovakia's Hanna Vlacilova, a lovely, soubrette-style ballerina, and the technically bright but emotionally pale Larissa Vassilevskaya of the Soviet Union. Winners in the junior girls' category were headed by the Soviet Union's Alla Michaltchenko and Canada's Sylvie Chevalier. As for the Americans, Lynne Charles (a New Yorker who has danced with the Houston Ballet and West Germany's Hamburg Opera Ballet) won the third-place Bronze Medal for adults, and Pennsylvania's Ann Marie de Angelo (soloist with the City Center Joffrey Ballet) earned a citation for technical excellence. In all, approximately 20 awards, citations, or honorable mentions were given following votings which I, along with my colleagues from the West, found wholly fair.

Was there any partisanship? Of course there was. We would have been an odd lot indeed if each of us had not hoped for the best from the dancing ambassadors of our own countries. But when the chips were down, our ballots were cast not for the flags of nations but for arabesques and grands jetés, for lines of bodies etched in space, for musicality in the phrasing of movement sequences, for interpretation, for presence and, of course, for that inexplicable aura which harbors a God-given talent, a performing quality that cannot be manufactured in any dance classroom anywhere.

As important as the rivalry of this dance Olympics is that special camaraderie which, I think, exists only, or most fully, in the world of dance. The Bulgarians provided a ballet instructor to give class each day to Americans and others who wanted the daily instruction essential to all dancers of all ages. A Russian ballet mistress permitted Japanese and other nationals (Americans included) in her classes. I watched England's Anton Dolin, now 72, one of the great premiers danseurs of this century, coach Patrick Dupond in the tragipoetic final measures of a variation from *Giselle*. And I observed the internationally celebrated alumnus of Britain's Royal and Festival Ballets, John Gilpin, help Mr. Dupond in a noonday rehearsal, in the broiling sun of the outdoor theater, transform a well-executed sequence of difficult steps in Harald Lander's *Etudes* into exhilarating, stylish dancing. Russian veterans helped Americans with difficult passages, and young dancers from Eastern Europe asked Western dancers how they did this or that classical variation. Such sharing of time and talent was especially important to those contestants who, unlike contestants from state theaters, had to fund their own trips, costume and recording needs, and coaching arrangements from private resources—as all the Americans did.

Yes, it was a contest at Varna—and a fierce one—but it was held in an atmosphere of concord remarkable in the world of today. As the competition came to an end with a great dance gala, I took note of the harmony. Outside the theater stood a forest of flags of many nations, but inside, next to the burning brazier with its Olympic-like flame, flew a single standard: it was deep blue, and its design was a human figure outlined in what is certainly the most familiar and esthetically the purest movement design in all ballet—the arabesque. It is a standing position, yet it aspires upward. It is balanced, yet suspenseful. It mirrors a moment of stillness but holds the promise of flight. It is a perfect symbol for ballet, and it might not be a misleading guide for contemporary man. [*New York Times*]

Rudolf and Mikhail and Especially Ivan

August 21, 1976

It is a strange sound—squeal-gasp-gurgle—that bombards my eardrums whenever Mikhail Baryshnikov takes off on one of his aerial sorties, pauses for a moment in space so that we can comprehend lunar mini-gravity without going to the moon, and then gently descends. I don't suppose for one moment that it is the same woman who has been emitting these sounds from a seat behind me at the Metropolitan Opera House, the New York State Theater, or Kennedy Center, in Washington, whenever Baryshnikov performs, yet this inarticulate but audible tribute always sounds the same. (It is never a male sound, simply because other men cannot do what Baryshnikov does, and they are obviously mute with jealousy.)

When Rudolf Nureyev takes a curtain call, there are screams (never squeals), yells, and palm-pounding applause. It doesn't much matter what Nureyev has just danced. Maybe he hasn't even danced well (sometimes he doesn't, but he always performs brilliantly), but he stands before us as not only the superstar of the ballet world but the supreme star of the world of entertainment. We cheer and applaud him because it is his due as a modern Roi Soleil or Grand Monarque. (Yes, Louis XIV was a dancer, too.)

When Ivan Nagy, with powerful arms and gentle hands, lifts his ballerina and looks upward into her eyes, it is an act of adoration. Behind me, in the theater, I hear no squeals, no yells, only a sigh. And when, as Albrecht, he walks slowly across the stage to the tomb of his Giselle, the viewer hesitates to breathe for fear of intruding upon a sacred, private moment.

What I am endeavoring to say is that the lyrical dancer, the danseur noble, is every bit as necessary to ballet and to us, the viewers, as is the vir-

661

tuoso, and that Ivan Nagy is just as important and just as much to be cherished as Nureyev and Baryshnikov. Shakespeare's gentle "Ah, what light through yonder window breaks" has lasted quite as long as Marlowe's mighty line, "On, on, ye pampered jades of Asia."

Those who look only for the virtuosi of ballet, the superb athletes, are cheating themselves. They even cheat themselves when they attend a Baryshnikov performance in a program that does not call for physical prowess or little else. There are probably thousands of balletomanes who would sob with disappointment if they could only see Baryshnikov in the title role of Fokine's *Petrouchka.* No matter that he is one of the great interpreters of a role created by Nijinsky. No matter that his portrayal is a profound and poignant interrelating of the real and the unreal. What the mass wants of him are vaulting leaps and perilous spins in space. Perhaps the same ones would feel cheated if they saw Nureyev as the moody, musing Don Juan instead of as the exuberant master of feats of skill in *Don Quixote Pas de Deux.*

Ivan Nagy can, of course, accomplish the double air-turns, the pirouettes, the high leaps, the flashing leg beats required of the principal male dancer in a major ballet troupe. He is not the virtuoso Baryshnikov is, nor does he have the instant, stunning impact of Nureyev; nevertheless, when all three are on hand for an American Ballet Theater engagement (Nureyev is guest artist on occasion), there should be no thought on the parts of management, direction, or public than one is of greater artistic value than the other. Did you notice that I modified the word "value" with "artistic"? Good. It is absolutely true that certain stars are bigger at the box office—in opera and theater, as well as in dance—than others, but, though bills must be paid, there are values more important than a full house on a blue Monday or at a Wednesday matinee.

Distinctions in box-office draw are apparent within the dance world itself. Modern dance has never (and never will) draw as well as ballet, but that has in no way lessened the importance or value of an Isadora Duncan or a Martha Graham. And most ethnic dance arts (with the exception of Spanish dance) cannot hope to match either ballet or modern dance in popular appeal unless they are presented (à la Moiseyev) as spectacle. Thus, within the world of ballet proper, the balletomane, the choreographer, the director, the manager, are cheating themselves if they address themselves only to what is instant box office.

Ivan Nagy is a perfect example of a superb artist who does not fulfill all box-office and publicity requirements while, at the very moment, providing artistic services that have few equals in this era. He is, in my opinion, the unequaled Albrecht (in *Giselle*) of our generation. When he (not anyone else) is dancing with Natalia Makarova, the public is in the presence of a pair who make theirs *the Giselle* to see.

Nagy, in Eliot Feld's *At Midnight,* crosses over into modern dance to reveal, through slow-reaching arms, all the heart's longings. In the great Danish *La Sylphide,* he is the restless dreamer hidden in all men as they seek the desirable but unattainable; in Fokine's *Les Sylphides,* he becomes the dream itself, not the dreamer; and in the effervescent pas de deux from the nineteenth-century *Kermesse im Brugge,* his nimble legs accomplish the Bournonville beats with all the sparkle that his eyes bestow on the maid with whom he is dancing. And, yes, there is that walk of reverent mourning in *Giselle* that will haunt you, and there is also that instant of ecstatic hope when he clutches the magic scarf that will help him capture forever the elusive Sylphide while, nearby, the witch's curse promises doom.

Indeed, Mikhail Baryshnikov is not to be missed in this new Golden Age of Ballet, the first in which the male dancer has shared honors with the ballerina, and if you have not seen Rudolf Nureyev, you have not witnessed the artist-performer-personality who brought the male dancer to an unprecedented eminence. And if you have missed Ivan Nagy because you have been saving money and time for the two box-office supers, you have failed to be illuminated by a special performing radiance in today's brightly shining art of the ballet. [*Saturday Review*]

Index

665

668

C

Cage, The (Robbins), 355, 608, 613
Cage, Betty, 457
Cage, John, 172, 549
Cakewalk (Boris), 256–257
Calin, Mickey, 327
Camargo, Marie, 491, 627
Camille (Page), 421
Cantata (Uthoff), 631
Canto Indio (Macdonald), 524, 549
Cantos From a Monastery (Pomare), 403
Capriccio Espagnol (Massine), 141
Caprichos (Ross), 246–247, 562
Caldwell, Candace, 380
Carlos, Ernest, 192
Carmen (Petit), 238, 239, 291, 346–348,
    494
Carmen Suite (Alonso), 591, 655
Carmina Burana (Butler), 514
Carnaval (Fokine), 12, 55, 59, 91, 563
Carnegie Chamber Music Hall, New York,
    115, 116
Carnegie Hall, New York, 137, 138, 166,
    306, 315, 321
Caro, Rosario, 323
Carolina Playmakers, 71, 232
Caron, Leslie, 291
Carroll, Elizabeth, 523, 524, 547, 549
Carter, Carlu, 292
Carter, Elliott, 172
Carter, William, 390, 415, 416, 652
Cassandra, 217
Castor and Pollux (Lifar), 218
Catanzaro, Tony, 630
Caton, Edward, 236
Catulli Carmina (Butler), 514
Cave of the Heart (Graham), 181–183,
    186, 300, 340, 345, 612
CBS Repertoire Workshop, 465
Celeste, Mlle, 593
Center Break (Perez), 528
Center Theater, New York, 55–57, 71,
    246, 573
Cerrito, Fanny, 107, 491
Chabrier, Emmanuel, 230
Chabukiani, Vakhtan, 561
Chaconne (Balanchine), 653
Chaconne (Limón), 233
Chaffée, George, 192

Chagall, Marc, 228
Champion, Gower, 459–461
Champion, Marge, 460, 461
Channing, Carol, 459, 460
Chansons de Bilitis (Butler), 513
Chant (Wengerd), 544
Characteristic Dance Rhythms (Williams),
    24
Charade (Christensen), 40
Charles, Lynne, 660
Charisse, Cyd, 262
Charmoli, Tony, 268, 464
Chase, Lucia, 22, 23, 105, 351–352, 386,
    391, 393, 394, 448, 477, 512, 573–
    575, 582, 590, 593–595, 633, 634,
    636–638, 650, 652
Chauviré, Yvette, 217, 218, 561
Chavez, Carlos, 397
Chevalier, Sylvie, 660
Chew, King Lan, 14
Chicago Ballet, 631
Chopin Concerto (Dollar), 391, 394
Chopin, Frederic, 311
Choral (Williams), 24
Choreartium (Massine), 25
Choreographic Offering (Limón), 468–469
Choros 1 and 4 (Dunham), 307
Christensen, Harold, 542, 630
Christensen, Lew, 21, 40, 448, 452, 542,
    614, 630
Christensen, Willam, 452, 542, 614, 630
Christian, John, 302
Chujoy, Anatole, 615, 616
Cimarosiana (Massine), 25
Cincinnati Ballet, 631
Cinderella (Ashton), 466
Cirque de Deux (Boris), 204
City Center Joffrey Ballet, 498, 518–521,
    625, 631, 642, 647, 660
City Portrait (Loring), 40
City Streets (Bettis), 117
Clark, Kay, 543
Clark, Peggy, 247
Clauss, Heinz, 552, 554, 555
Clavé, Antoni, 238, 347
Clear Lake (Lubovitch), 597
Clifford, John, 565–566, 605
Clockwise (Marks), 581
Cloutier, Norman, 65
Clytemnestra (Graham), 342–346, 612

669

671

676

684

R

Rabovsky, Istvan, 290–291
Rachmaninoff, Serge, 85
Radha (St. Denis), 529, 536–537
Radio City Music Hall, New York, 60–62, 211–213, 261, 612
Rainbow Room, New York, 15, 17, 86–87, 151
Rainbow 'Round My Shoulder (McKayle), 579
Rainer, Michael, 172
Raka, Ni Gusti, 266
Rall, Tommy, 392
Ralov, Borge, 315
Ralov, Kirsten, 302, 315, 621
Ramayana (Shankar), 249
Rambert, Marie, 75, 374–376
Ramirez, Aida, 322
Randall, Carl, 112
Randazzo, Peter, 419
Rangstrom, Ture, 353
Rapp, Richard, 416, 485–486
Rasch, Albertina, 113
Rasumny, Elizabeth, 405
Ravel, Maurice, 171
Raymonda, 421, 425
Raymonda (Balanchine/Danilova), 204, 613
Raymonda (Nureyev), 650
Real McCoy, The (Feld), 641
Reed, Janet, 230, 236, 256, 286, 288, 289, 319
Reflections (Walker), 465
Reich, George, 210, 291
Reid, Albert, 403
Relativity of Icarus, The (Arpino), 641
Renard (Balanchine), 171, 180–181
Rencher, Derek, 658
Rendezvous, Le (Petit), 239
Requiem for Jimmy Dean (Cole), 524
Revel, Rudi, 172
Reveries (Clifford), 565–566
Revolutionary March (Tamiris), 498
Reyes, Goyo, 306
Reynolds, Debbie, 262
Rhodes, Lawrence, 523, 524, 547–548
Rhythm of Life (Shankar), 249
Riabouchinska, Tatiana, 26, 83–85, 91, 203, 626

Ricarda, Anna, 40
Rice, Peter, 305
Richmond, Aaron, 30, 37
Richter, Marga, 524
Riddell, Mrs. Jean, 630
Riegger, Wallingford, 580
Rikhter, Konstantin, 363
Riley, Hugh, 232
Rimbaud, Arthur, 245
Rinaldo and Armida (Ashton), 305
Rindin, Vadim, 432
Rioja, Pilar, 643
Risely, Cynthia, 198
Rite for Rejoicing (Waters), 139
Rites (Lang), 276–277
Rites de Passage (Dunham), 540
Ritman, William, 427
Ritmo Jondo (Humphrey), 277, 303
Rittman, Trude, 40, 474
Rituals (Dunham), 307
River, The (Ailey), 575, 595, 635
Rivera, Chita, 327
Rizzo, Marlene, 560
Road of the Phoebe Snow (Beatty), 379–380, 630
Roan, Barbara, 528
Robbins, Jerome, 110, 158, 174, 186, 197, 230, 243–244, 257–258, 278, 312–313, 326–327, 334, 336, 354–356, 368, 385, 393, 452, 459–461, 499–500, 507, 555–556, 566, 571–573, 574, 589–590, 599–600, 605, 606, 607, 627, 639, 640, 650
Robert Joffrey Ballet, 449, 486
Roberts, Frank (Toniea Massaquoi), 43
Robertson, Mr., 148
Robertson, Ronnie, 443
Robin Hood Dell, Philadelphia, 41
Robinson, Bill, 39, 122
Robinson, Frederick B., 36
Rockefeller Center, New York, 15
Rockefeller Foundation, 631, 639
Rockettes, The, 61–62, 571
Rodeo (de Mille), 157, 204, 297, 332, 476, 509, 574
Rodgers, Richard, 47
Rodham, Robert, 445
Rodriguez, Zhandra, 595
Rogers, Frederick Rand, 37

Rogers, Ginger, 141
Rogge, Florence, 60–62, 211–213
Rom, Meta, 40
Romanoff, Dimitri, 23, 393
Romeo and Juliet (Ashton), 314–315, 526, 554, 658
Romeo and Juliet (Cranko), 552, 554
Romeo and Juliet (Lavrovsky), 362–363, 368, 554
Romeo and Juliet (MacMillan), 482–483, 510–511, 554
Romeo and Juliet (Tudor), 296–297, 594–595
Romero, Lili, 65
Rooms (Sokolow), 298–299, 300, 468
Root of an Unfocus (Cunningham), 168
Rose des Vents, La (Petit), 347
Rose, Jürgen, 554
Rose Malade, La (Petit), 644, 655
Rosenthal, Jean, 172, 182, 219, 242, 244, 258, 261, 276, 285, 290, 318, 339, 392
Rosenthal, Laurence, 474
Ross, Bertram, 275–277, 343–344, 346, 371, 419, 480
Ross, Herbert, 246–247, 352, 361, 393, 461
Rostoff, Dmitri, 85
de Rothschild, Bethsabee, 299–300, 449
Roudenko, Lubov, 142
Rouge et Noir (Massine), 39, 46, 47, 129
Royal Academy of Dancing, London, 74–75
Royal Ballet, London, 351, 364, 367, 375, 411, 420, 437–443, 448, 458, 482–484, 489, 509, 550, 554, 573, 636, 650, 658
Royal Ballet School, Copenhagen, 497, 620–621
Royal Court Theatre, Drottningholm, Sweden, 622
Royal Danish Ballet, 297, 301–302, 313–315, 351, 367, 411, 420, 442, 448, 490, 492–494, 497, 525–527, 550, 554, 619–621, 632, 651, 658
Royal Opera House, Covent Garden, London, 649
Royal Swedish Ballet, 339, 620–623, 640, 643
Royal Theatre, Copenhagen, 492, 620–621

Royal Winnipeg Ballet, 291–293, 449, 562, 580, 624, 640
Rudel, Julius, 514
Ruins and Visions (Humphrey), 300
Ruiz, Brunilda, 524
Rumba to the Moon (Weidman), 97
Rush (Sebastian), 632
Russell, Francia, 388
Russian-American Ballet Company (Novikoff), 42
Russian Imperial Ballet, 531, 654
Russian Soldier (Fokine), 146–147
Ruth Page Chicago Opera Ballet, 419–421
Ryberg, Flemming, 621
Ryder, Mark, 183, 187

S

Sabicas, 138
Sabirova, Malika, 562
Saddler, Donald, 108, 110, 461, 462, 464, 487, 579, 591, 627, 633
Sadler's Wells Ballet, 236–238, 245, 282–283, 303–305
Sadoff, Simon, 240–242, 250, 275–276
St. Denis, Ruth, 17, 34, 37, 38, 51, 52, 96, 97, 118, 123, 136, 148, 163, 168, 234, 357–358, 451–452, 459, 519, 529, 534–538, 568, 579, 614
St. Francis (Massine), 27–28
St. James Theater, New York, 43, 54
Sala, Oskar, 405, 407
Saltonstall, Nathaniel, 36
Salzman, Eric, 569
Samokhvalova, Maya, 365
Sampih, 266
San Francisco Ballet, 286, 448, 452, 509, 542, 629, 630, 638
Sans Souci Singers, 176
Sande, Inge, 302, 315
Sanders, Dick, 347–348
Sane, Marguerite, 44
Sarabande and Passepied (Shearer), 116, 165
Saratoga (Massine), 128
Saratoga Performing Arts Center, Saratoga Springs, 555, 589
Saroyan, William, 60
Satyric Festival Song (Graham), 6

686

690